Fodor's 95 Scotland

GW00319460

Praise for Fodor's Guides

"Fodor's guides . . . are an admirable blend of the cultural and the practical."

—The Washington Post

"Researched by people chosen because they live or have lived in the country, well-written, and with good historical sections . . . Obligatory reading for millions of tourists."

—The Independent, London

"Usable, sophisticated restaurant coverage, with an emphasis on good value."

—Andy Birsh, Gourmet restaurant columnist, quoted by Gannett News Service

"Packed with dependable information."

—Atlanta Journal Constitution

"Fodor's always delivers high quality . . . thoughtfully presented . . . thorough."

—Houston Post

"Valuable because of their comprehensiveness."

—Minneapolis Star-Tribune

Fodor's Travel Publications, Inc.
New York • Toronto • London • Sydney • Auckland

Copyright © 1994
by Fodor's Travel Publications, Inc.

Fodor's Scotland

Editors: Paula Consolo, Hannah Borgeson
Area Editor: Gilbert Summers
Contributors: Robert Blake, Janet Foley, Echo Garrett, Gillian Glover, Anita Guerrini, John Hutchinson, Beth Ingpen, Bevin McLaughlin, Mary Ellen Schultz, Nancy van Itallie
Creative Director: Fabrizio La Rocca
Cartographers: David Lindroth, Mapping Specialists
Illustrator: Karl Tanner
Cover Photograph: Catherine Karnow

Design: Vignelli Associates

Special Sales

MANUFACTURED IN THE UNITED STATES OF AMERICA
10 9 8 7 6 5 4 3 2 1

Contents

Foreword *vi*

Highlights '95 *ix*

Fodor's Choice *xi*

Introduction *xx*

1 Essential Information *1*

Before You Go *2*

Government Information Offices *2*
Tours and Packages *2*
When to Go *5*
Festivals and Seasonal Events *6*
What to Pack *7*
Taking Money Abroad *8*
Getting Money from Home *9*
Scottish Currency *9*
What It Will Cost *10*
Passports and Visas *10*
Customs and Duties *10*
Traveling with Cameras, Camcorders, and Laptops *12*
Language *12*
Insurance *13*
Car Rental *14*
Rail and Bus Passes *15*
Student and Youth Travel *16*
Traveling with Children *18*
Hints for Travelers with Disabilities *19*
Hints for Older Travelers *20*
Hints for Gay and Lesbian Travelers *21*

Arriving and Departing *22*

From North America by Plane *22*
From North America by Ship *24*
From England by Plane *24*
From England by Train *24*
From England by Bus *25*

Staying in Scotland *25*

Getting Around *25*
Telephones *30*
Mail *30*
Tipping *30*
Opening and Closing Times *30*
Shopping *31*

Dining *31*
Lodging *32*
Credit Cards *33*

Great Itineraries *34*

2 Portraits of Scotland *39*

Scotland at a Glance: A Chronology *40*
"The Story of Scotland," by Gordon Donaldson *44*
"Robert Burns, Scotland's Eternal Laureate," by Holly Hughes *51*

3 Scotland: The Home of Golf *56*
Golfing throughout the Country

4 Edinburgh and the Lothians *64*

5 Glasgow *119*

6 The Borders and the Southwest *156*
Dumfries and Galloway

7 Fife and Angus *181*
St. Andrews, Dundee

8 Aberdeen and the Northeast *201*

9 The Central Highlands *233*
Stirling, Loch Lomond and the Trossachs, Perthshire

10 Argyll and the Isles *260*

11 Around the Great Glen *285*
Loch Ness, Speyside

12 The Northern Highlands *309*
Sutherland and Wester Ross, Isle of Skye, the Outer Hebrides

13 The Northern Isles *331*
Orkney and Shetland

Index *345*

Maps

Scotland *xiv–xv*
Europe *xvi–xvii*
World Time Zones *xviii–xix*
Edinburgh *74–75*
Edinburgh Dining and Lodging *94–95*
West Lothian and the Forth Valley *110*
Midlothian and East Lothian *115*
Glasgow *128–129*
Glasgow Dining and Lodging *142–143*
Glasgow Excursions: Ayrshire and the Clyde Valley *152–153*
The Borders *161*
Dumfries and Galloway *166*
Fife Area *185*
St. Andrews *186*
Angus Area *190*
Aberdeen *207*
Royal Deeside *212*
The Northeast *217*
Stirling *238*
The Central Highlands *242–243*
Argyll and the Isles *264–265*
The Great Glen Area *290–291*
The Northern Highlands and Skye *314–315*
The Outer Hebrides *321*
Shetland Islands *335*
Orkney Islands *339*

Foreword

While every care has been taken to ensure the accuracy of the information in this guide, the passage of time will always bring change, and consequently, the publisher cannot accept responsibility for errors that may occur.

All prices and opening times quoted here are based on information supplied to us at press time. Hours and admission fees may change, however, and the prudent traveler will avoid inconvenience by calling ahead.

Fodor's wants to hear about your travel experiences, both pleasant and unpleasant. When a hotel or restaurant fails to live up to its billing, let us know and we will investigate the complaint and revise our entries where the facts warrant it.

Send your letters to the editors of Fodor's Travel Publications, 201 East 50th Street, New York, NY 10022.

Highlights '95 and Fodor's Choice

Highlights '95

Transportation The police have been clamping down on speeding, making it safer than ever to rent a car in Scotland. With roadwork on the Edinburgh to Aberdeen link now completed, driving time between the two cities has been reduced to just a couple of hours. The entire road, now called the **M90/A90,** is classified as a motorway or dual carriageway.

The opening of Glasgow Airport's new international terminal confirms its claim as the premier transatlantic gateway for the northern half of the United Kingdom. Certainly, it defies logic to fly to London if intending to spend a worthwhile amount of time in Scotland.

Lodging Tourism accounts for about $2.5 billion annually in Scotland's economy, so it's no surprise that the hotel business is fiercely competitive. A recent trend is for individual hotels to group together in order to promote themselves effectively. One of the newest and most interesting groups is the **Tartan Collection.** Comprised of 20 or so hotels in the Grampian Highlands and its chief city, Aberdeen, this group includes castles, country houses, and city hotels, all of consistently high standards. And you can fly direct from a variety of European and other U.K. destinations to Aberdeen Airport or use the good rail and road connections. In fact, the area is only about two hours by road from Edinburgh thanks to the completion of the fast M90/A90 dual carriageway.

Attractions One of the most significant new visitor attractions in Scotland is, by coincidence, also in Grampian: the newly refurbished grand mansion of **Duff House** in Banff, built in 1735–41 for William Duff, Earl of Fife, by William Adam, the famous Scottish architect. Thought to be Adam's finest work, the mansion will be run by the National Gallery of Scotland as a country house gallery beginning in spring 1995.

Loch Ness, reputed home of a (mythical?) many-humped monster, now boasts a **submarine.** It takes up to six passengers per trip down into the peat-brown waters. Who knows what might be encountered? The dive site is at Drumnadrochit, south of Inverness on the west bank of the loch.

Folklore is also the subject of a new attraction at Killin, north of the Trossachs. Overlooking the picturesque Falls of Dochart, the **Breadalbane Folklore Centre** gives an insight into the folk high ground of Scotland. There are animated tales of traditional folklore, colorful clan history, and so on, all aided by hi-tech presentations. The modern gadgetry contrasts with the curious centerpiece: the healing stones of St. Fillan. These are ancient stones and pebbles of various sizes blessed by the local saint during the 7th century and still held in some reverence after 13 centuries.

Events The big memorial event in 1995 is the 50-year anniversary of World War II ending, so purely Scottish historical events are likely to be overshadowed. The Jacobites and Bonnie Prince Charlie, however, do manage a bit of flag-waving at Kelvingrove Art Gallery and Museum—1995 marks the 250th anniversary of their last uprising. Also, the British Tourist Authority has designated 1995 the **Festival of Arts and Culture,** and plans call for additional classical concerts, talks, and performances in Scotland's already-rich cultural life.

Fodor's Choice

No two people will agree on what makes a perfect vacation, but it can be fun and helpful to know what others think. We hope you'll have a chance to experience some of Fodor's Choices yourself while visiting Scotland. For detailed information on individual entries, see the relevant sections of this guidebook.

Sights to Remember

Edinburgh Castle at night, illuminated by floodlights

The view of Princes Street in Edinburgh from Calton Hill

The view of Loch Lomond from the top of Duncryne Hill, Gartocharn (Central Highlands)

The Cuillin Hills seen from Sligachan, Isle of Skye (Northern Highlands)

Scott's view of the Eildon Hills (Borders)

The Falls of Clyde at New Lanark (Glasgow)

The heather in full bloom in Glen Shee (Central Highlands) or in Deeside (Aberdeen)

Times to Remember

The train ride from Fort William to Mallaig (Argyll)

Meeting "King James IV of Scotland" in the Great Hall of Stirling Castle during the summer theater program in Stirling (Central Highlands)

Hearing the one o'clock gun on Princes Street in Edinburgh

Having an entire sandy beach to oneself on Harris in the Outer Hebrides (Northern Highlands)

Tasting Lagavulin single-malt whisky in a pub on the island of Islay (Argyll and the Isles)

Watching a herd of red deer graze by the roadside at Glen Muck, near Ballater (Aberdeen)

Buildings and Monuments

Castle Campbell, Ochil Hills, near Stirling (Central Highlands)

The facade of Marischal College, Aberdeen

The Black House at Arnol, the Isle of Lewis in the Outer Hebrides (Northern Highlands)

The Georgian House, Edinburgh

Traquair House, near Walkerburn (Borders)

The Standing Stones of Callanish, Lewis (Northern Highlands)

Torosay Castle, Isle of Mull (Argyll and the Isles)

Blair Castle (Central Highlands)

Scenic Drives

The road west of Aberdeen into Royal Deeside, on either bank of the River Dee (Aberdeen)

The east bank of Loch Ness, from Fort Augustus to Inverness via Dores (Around the Great Glen)

The route between Brig o' Turk and Aberfoyle in the Trossachs (Central Highlands)

The Drumbeg road, north of Lochinver (Northern Highlands)

Parks and Gardens

The rock garden at the Royal Botanic Gardens in Edinburgh

The rhododendron gardens at Brodick Castle, Isle of Arran (Glasgow)

The wooded vistas of Castle Kennedy Gardens (Southwest)

The Japanese pond at Kildrummy Castle Gardens (Aberdeen)

Crathes Castle Gardens, Deeside (Aberdeen)

Logan Botanic Gardens (Southwest)

Hotels

Auchterarder House, Auchterarder, Central Highlands, *$$$$*

Cameron House, Balloch, Central Highlands, *$$$–$$$$*

Channings, Edinburgh, *$$$*

Roman Camp, Callander, Central Highlands, *$$–$$$$*

Cringletie House, Peebles, Borders, *$$–$$$*

The Holly Tree, Kentallen, Argyll, *$$*

Restaurants

Auchterarder House, Auchterarder, Central Highlands, *$$$$*

The Ubiquitous Chip, Glasgow, *$$$$*

The Atrium, Edinburgh, *$$$*

The Cellar, Anstruther, Fife, *$$$*

The Old Monastery, Buckie, Aberdeen, *$$$*

Museums and Visitor Centers

Mill on the Fleet, South-West

Auchindrain Museum (Argyll)

Burrell Collection (Glasgow)

Kirkcaldy Museum and Art Gallery (Fife)

Paisley Museum and Art Gallery (Glasgow)

Scottish Fisheries Museum (Fife)

Highland Folk Museum, Kingussie, near Aviemore (Around the Great Glen)

Carnegie Birthplace Museum (Edinburgh and the Lothians)

Scotland

North Sea

ENGLAND

The Cheviot Hills

Alnwick
Hexham
Berwick
Coldstream
Kelso
Jedburgh
Carlisle
Annan
Duns
Hawick
Dunbar
North Berwick
Lockerbie
Moffat
Dalkeith
Livingston
Peebles
EDINBURGH
Dumfries
Castle Douglas
Solway Firth
Biggar
Motherwell
Hamilton
Kirkconnel
Airdrie
East Kilbride
Newton Stewart
Lucy Bay
Drummore
Falkirk
Stirling
Glasgow
Paisley
Kilmarnock
Prestwick
Irvine
Ayr
Girvan
Stranraer
Portpatrick
Greenock
Gourock
Helensburgh
Largs
Rothesay
Ardrossan
Brodick
Arran
Firth of Clyde
North Channel
Campbeltown
Kintyre
Tarbert
Jura
Islay
Port Askaig
Colonsay
Lochgilphead
Arduaine
Inveraray
Tarbet
Crianlarich
Oban
Lochaline
Firth of Lorn
Loch Linnhe
Duror
Tobermory
Coll
Tiree
Bunessan
ATLANTIC OCEAN
Pitlochry
Crieff
Blairgowrie
Perth
Kinross
Dunfermline
Kirkcaldy
Glenrothes
Cupar
St. Andrews
Firth of Forth
Firth of Tay
Dundee
Forfar
Brechin
Arbroath
Montrose

SOUTHERN UPLANDS

NORTHERN IRELAND

N

SHETLAND ISLANDS

Herma Ness
Unst
Fetlar
Yell
Baltasound
Hamnavoe
Whalsay
Ulsta
Voe
Mainland
Lerwick
Toft
Brae
Hillswick
St. Magnus Bay
Walls
Scalloway
Levenwick
Sumburgh
Sumburgh Roost

Europe

ICELAND
● Reykjavik

NORWAY
Bergen ○

SCOTLAND
● Edinburgh

North Sea

Skagerrack

NORTHERN
IRELAND

● Belfast

IRELAND   *Irish Sea*

Dublin ●

DENMARK

UNITED
KINGDOM

WALES

ENGLAND   NETHERLANDS

Cardiff ●

Hamburg ○

The Hague ● ○ Amsterdam

London ●   ○ Rotterdam

*ATLANTIC
OCEAN*

English Channel

G E R M

Bonn ○

Brussels ●

BELGIUM

Frankfurt ○

Paris ●

LUXEMBOURG

F R A N C E

Zürich ●

Bern ●

SWITZERLAND

Munich

Lyon ○

LIECHTENSTEIN

Milan ○

Venic

Monte
Carlo

Nice ○ ●
MONACO

Marseille ○

Florence ○

PORTUGAL

ANDORRA

Corsica

● Madrid

○ Barcelona

Lisbon ●

S P A I N

*Balearic
Islands*

Sardinia

Tyrrhenia

Seville ○ ○ Granada

Mediterranean Sea

○ Gibraltar

MOROCCO

ALGERIA

0 ———— 400 miles

0 ———— 600 km

TUNISIA

FINLAND

Gulf of Bothnia

Oslo ✪

SWEDEN

Helsinki ✪

Gulf of Finland

Tallinn ✪

St. Petersburg ○

Stockholm ✪

ESTONIA

Kattegat

Göteborg ○

Riga ✪

Moscow ✪

LATVIA

LITHUANIA

Copenhagen ○

Baltic Sea

Kaunas ○

RUSSIA

Vilnius ✪

RUSSIA

Kaliningrad ○

Minsk ✪

Berlin ✪

POLAND

BELARUS

ANY

Warsaw ✪

Kraków ○

Kiev ✪

Prague ✪

UKRAINE

CZECH REPUBLIC

SLOVAKIA

MOLDOVA

Vienna ✪

Bratislava ✪

○

Salzburg ✪

Budapest ✪

Chișinău ✪

AUSTRIA

HUNGARY

SLOVENIA

Zagreb ✪

ROMANIA

Ljubljana ✪

e ○

CROATIA

Novi Sad ○

BOSNIA AND HERZEGOVINA

Belgrade ✪

Bucharest ✪

Black Sea

Sarajevo ✪

SERBIA

Adriatic Sea

MONTENEGRO

Priština ✪

BULGARIA

Rome ✪

Podgorica ✪

○

Skopje ✪

Sofia ✪

ITALY

Tiranë ✪

MACEDONIA

Istanbul ○

ALBANIA

Naples ○

Ankara ✪

n Sea

GREECE

TURKEY

Aegean Sea

Ionian Sea

Athens ✪

Sicily

MALTA

Crete

CYPRUS

Mediterranean Sea

World Time Zones

Numbers below vertical bands relate each zone to Greenwich Mean Time (0 hrs.).
Local times frequently differ from these general indications,
as indicated by light-face numbers on map.

Algiers, **29**	Berlin, **34**	Delhi, **48**	Istanbul, **40**
Anchorage, **3**	Bogotá, **19**	Denver, **8**	Jerusalem, **42**
Athens, **41**	Budapest, **37**	Djakarta, **53**	Johannesburg, **44**
Auckland, **1**	Buenos Aires, **24**	Dublin, **26**	Lima, **20**
Baghdad, **46**	Caracas, **22**	Edmonton, **7**	Lisbon, **28**
Bangkok, **50**	Chicago, **9**	Hong Kong, **56**	London (Greenwich), **27**
Beijing, **54**	Copenhagen, **33**	Honolulu, **2**	Los Angeles, **6**
	Dallas, **10**		Madrid, **38**
			Manila, **57**

Mecca, **47**
Mexico City, **12**
Miami, **18**
Montréal, **15**
Moscow, **45**
Nairobi, **43**
New Orleans, **11**
New York City, **16**

Ottawa, **14**
Paris, **30**
Perth, **58**
Reykjavík, **25**
Rio de Janeiro, **23**
Rome, **39**
Saigon (Ho Chi Minh City), **51**

San Francisco, **5**
Santiago, **21**
Seoul, **59**
Shanghai, **55**
Singapore, **52**
Stockholm, **32**
Sydney, **61**
Tokyo, **60**

Toronto, **13**
Vancouver, **4**
Vienna, **35**
Warsaw, **36**
Washington, D.C., **17**
Yangon, **49**
Zürich, **31**

Introduction

On some old recordings of Scottish songs still in circulation you may run across *Roamin' in the Gloamin'* or *I Love a Lassie* or one of the other comic ditties of Harry Lauder, a star of the music halls of the 1920s. With his garish kilt, short crooked walking stick, rich rolling *R*s and *pawky* (cheerfully impudent) humor, chiefly based on the alleged meanness of the Scots, he impressed a Scottish character on the world. But his was, needless to say, a false impression and one the Scots have been trying to stamp out ever since.

How, then, do you characterize the Scots? Temperamentally, they are a mass of contradictions. They have been likened, not to a Scotch egg, but to a soft-boiled egg: a dour hard shell, a mushy middle. The Scots laugh and weep with almost Latin facility, but to strangers they are reserved, noncommittal, in no hurry to make an impression. Historically, fortitude and resilience have been their hallmarks, and there are streaks of both resignation and pitiless ferocity in their makeup, warring with sentimentality and love of family. Very Scottish was the instant reaction of an elderly woman of Edinburgh 200 years ago, when news arrived of the defeat in Mysore in India and of the Scottish soldiers being fettered in irons, two by two: "God help the puir chiel that's chained tae oor Davie."

The Scots are in general suspicious of the go-getter. "Whizz kid" is a term of contempt. But they are by no means plodders, though it is true to say that they are determined and thorough, respecting success only when it has been a few hundred years in the making. Praise of some bright ambitious youngster is quenched with the sneer: "Him? Ah kent (knew) his faither."

Yet this is the nation that built commerce throughout the British Empire, opened wild territories, and was responsible for much of mankind's scientific and technological advancement, a nation boastful about things it is not too good at and shamefacedly modest about genuine achievements. Consider the following extract from a handout about the Edinburgh School of Medicine: "If one excepts a few discoveries such as that of 'fixed air' by Black, of the diverse functions of the nerve-roots by Bell, of the anaesthetic properties of chloroform by Simpson, of the invention of certain powerful drugs by Christison and of the importance of antiseptic procedures by Lister, the influence of Edinburgh medicine has been of a steady constructive rather than a revolutionary type."

Among things that strike most newcomers to Scotland are the generosity of the Scots; their obsession with respectability; their satisfaction with themselves and their desire to stay as they are; and, above all, their passionate love of Scotland. An obstinate refusal to go along with English ideas has led to accusations that the nation has a head-in-the-sand attitude toward progress. But the Scots have their own ideas of progress, and they jealously guard the institutions that remain unique to them.

When it comes to education, Scotland has a proud record. The nation boasted four universities — St. Andrews, Aberdeen, Glasgow, and Edinburgh — when England had only two: Oxford and Cambridge. The *lad o' pairts* (man of talents) — the poor child of a feckless father and a fiercely self-sacrificing mother, sternly tutored by the village *dominie* (schoolmaster) and turned loose at the age of 13 with so firm a base of learning that he rose to the very top of his profession — this type of lad is a phenomenon of Scottish social history. The sacrifices that boys made as a matter of course to further their education are an old Scottish tradition. "Meal Monday," the long midsemester holiday at a Scottish university, is a survivor of the long weekend that once enabled students to return to their distant homes — on foot — and replenish the sack of "meal" (oatmeal) that was their only subsistence.

I t is a British cliché that an English education teaches you to think and a Scottish education stuffs your head with information. The average Scot does appear to be better informed than his English neighbor and to discuss facts rather than ideas. Scots pride themselves on their international outlook and on being better linguists than the English. The Scots get on well with foreigners, and they offer strangers a kindly welcome and a civility not often found in the modern world.

Just as the Scots have their own traditions in education, so is their legal system distinct from England's. In England the police both investigate crime and prosecute suspects. In Scotland there is a public prosecutor directly responsible to the Lord Advocate (equivalent to England's Attorney General), who is himself accountable to Parliament.

For the most part, however, you will notice few practical differences except in terminology. The barrister in England becomes an advocate in Scotland. Law-office nameplates designate their occupants "S.S.C." (Solicitor to the Supreme Court) or "W.S." (Writer to the Signet); cases for prosecution go before the "procurator fiscal" and are tried by the "sheriff" or "sheriff-substitute." The terms are different in England, and procedures are slightly different, too, for Scotland is one of the few countries that still bases its legal system on the old Roman law.

Crimes with picturesque names from ancient times remain on the statute book: *hamesucken*, for example, means assaulting a person in his home. In criminal cases Scotland adds to "Guilty" and "Not Guilty" a third verdict: "Not Proven." This, say the cynics, signifies "Don't do it again."

The Presbyterian Church of Scotland — the "Kirk" — is entirely independent of the Church of England. Until the 20th century it was a power in the land and did much to shape Scottish character. There are still those who can remember when the minister visited houses like an inquisitor and put members of the families through their catechism, punishing or reprimanding those who were not word-perfect. On Sunday morning the elders patrolled the streets, ordering people into church and rebuking those who sat at home in their gardens.

Religion in Scotland, as elsewhere, has lost much of its grip. But the Kirk remains influential in rural districts, where Kirk officials are pillars of local society. Ministers and their wives are seen in all their somber glory in Edinburgh in springtime, when the General Assembly of the Kirk takes place, and, for a week or more, Scottish newspapers devote several column-inches daily to the deliberations.

The Episcopalian Church of Scotland has bishops, as its name implies (unlike the Kirk, where the ministers are all equal), and a more colorful ritual. Considered genteel, Episcopalianism in Scotland has been described rather sourly by the Scottish novelist Lewis Grassie Gibbon as "more a matter of social status than theological conviction . . . , a grateful bourgeois acknowledgment of anglicisation."

Of the various nonconformist offshoots of the established Kirk, the Free Kirk of Scotland is the largest. It remains faithful to the monolithic unity of its forefathers, promoting the grim discipline that John Knox promoted long ago. The Free Kirk is strong in parts of the Outer Hebrides — Lewis, Harris, and North Uist. On Sunday in these areas no buses run, all the shops are shut, and there is a general atmosphere of a people cowering under the wrath of God. Among the fishing communities, especially those of the Northeast from Buckie to Peterhead, evangelical movements, such as the Close Brethren and Jehovah's Witnesses, have made impressive inroads.

Other than religion, Scotland on the whole is mercifully free of the class consciousness and social elitism that so often amuse or disgust foreign residents in England. But its turbulent history has left Scotland a legacy of sectarian bigotry comparable to that of Northern Ireland. Scotland's large minority population of Roman Catholics is still to some extent underprivileged. Catholics tend to stick together, Protestants to mix only with Protestants. Even the two most famous soccer teams in Scotland — Rangers and Celtic — are notorious for their sectarian bias.

A word, finally, is needed on the vexed subject of nomenclature. A "scotchman" is a nautical device for "scotching," or clamping, a running rope. It is not a native of Scotland. Though you may find some rather more conservative people refer to themselves as Scotchmen and consider themselves Scotch, most prefer Scot or Scotsman and call themselves Scottish or Scots.

There are exceptions to this rule. Certain internationally known Scottish products are Scotch. There is Scotch whisky, Scotch wool, Scotch tweed, Scotch mist (persistent drizzling rain). A Scotch snap is a short accented note followed by a longer one — a phrase that is characteristic of Scottish music, though certainly not unique to it. A snack food of a hard-boiled egg wrapped in sausage-meat and rolled in crumb coating, then fried, is a Scotch egg.

You may include the Scots in the broader term British, but they dislike the word *Brits*, and nothing infuriates them more than being called English. Nonetheless, there are a lot of Anglo-Scots, that is, people of Scottish birth who live in England or are the offspring of marriages between Scottish and English people. The term Anglo-Scots is not to be confused with Sassenachs, the Gaelic word for Saxon, which is applied facetiously or disdainfully to all the English. But at the same time, English people who live in Scotland remain English to their dying day, and their children after them. Similarly, the designation of North Britain for Scotland, which crept in during Victorian times, has now crept out again. It survives only in the names of a few North British hotels. Scots feel that it denies their national identity, and there are some who, on receiving a letter with "N.B." or "North Britain" in the address, will cross it out and return the envelope to the sender.

1 Essential Information

Before You Go

Government Information Offices

In the United States   **British Tourist Authority,** 551 5th Ave., Suite 701, New York, NY 10176, tel. 212/986–2200, fax 212/986–1188; 625 N. Michigan Ave., Suite 1510, Chicago, IL 60611, tel. 312/787–0490, fax 312/787–7746; World Trade Center, Suite 450, 350 S. Figueroa St., Los Angeles, CA 90071, tel. 213/628–3525; 2580 Cumberland Pkwy., Suite 470, Atlanta, GA 30339, tel. 404/432–9635, fax 404/432–9641.

U.S. Government Travel Briefings   The Department of State's **Overseas Citizens Emergency Center** (Room 4811, Washington, DC 20520; enclose S.A.S.E.) issues Consular Information Sheets, which cover crime, security, political climate, and health risks as well as embassy locations, entry requirements, currency regulations, and other routine matters. For the latest information, stop in at any passport office, consulate, or embassy; call the interactive hot line (tel. 202/647–5225, fax 202/647–3000); or, with your PC's modem, tap into the Bureau of Consular Affairs' computer bulletin board (tel. 202/647–9225).

In Canada   **British Tourist Authority,** 111 Avenue Rd., Suite 450, Toronto, Ontario M5R 35B, tel. 416/925–6326.

In the United Kingdom   **Scottish Tourist Board,** 23 Ravelston Terr., Edinburgh EH4 3EU, tel. 0131/332–2433; 19 Cockspur St., London SWIY 5BL, tel. 0171/930–8661.

Tours and Packages

Should you buy your travel arrangements to Scotland packaged or do it yourself? There are advantages either way. Buying packaged arrangements saves you money, particularly if can find a program that includes exactly the features you want. You also get a pretty good idea of what your trip will cost from the outset. Generally, you have two options: fully escorted tours and independent packages.

Escorted tours are most often via motorcoach, with a tour director in charge. They're ideal if you don't mind having limited free time and traveling with strangers. Your baggage is handled, your time rigorously scheduled, and most meals planned. Escorted tours are therefore the most hassle-free way to see a destination, as well as generally the least expensive. Independent packages allow plenty of flexibility. They generally include airline travel and hotels, with certain options available, such as sightseeing, car rental, and excursions. Independent packages are usually more expensive than escorted tours, but your time is your own.

If you want a travel agent to make all the arrangements, make sure he or she is a SCOTS—an acronym which stands for Special Counsellor on Tourism in Scotland. The North American market is important enough to the Scottish Tourist Board to run a special training program for travel agents working in the United States and Canada. Check with your travel agency to find qualified agents, who will be your best source of recommendations for both tours and packages. They will have the largest selection, and the cost to you is the same as buying direct. Whatever program you ultimately choose, be sure to find out exactly what is included: taxes, tips, transfers, meals, baggage handling, ground transportation, entertainment, excursions, sports, or recreation (and rental equipment if necessary). Ask about the level of hotel used, its location, the size of its rooms, the kind of beds, and its amenities, such as pool, room service, or programs for children, if they're important to you. Find out the operator's cancellation penalties. Nearly everyone charges them, and the only way to avoid them is to buy trip-cancellation insurance (*see* Trip Insurance, *below).* Also ask about the single supplement, a surcharge assessed to solo travelers. Some operators do not make you pay it if you agree to be matched up with a roommate of the same sex, even if one is not found by departure time. Remember that a program that has features you won't use, whether for rental sporting equipment or discounted museum admissions, may not be the most cost-wise choice for you.

Fully Escorted Tours Escorted tours are usually sold in three categories: deluxe, first-class, and tourist or budget class. The most important differences are the price, of course, and the level of accommodations. Some operators specialize in one category, while others offer a range.

Top operators include **Abercrombie & Kent** (1520 Kensington Rd., Oak Brook, IL 60521, tel. 708/954–2944 or 800/323–7308) and **Maupintour** (Box 807, Lawrence, KS 66044, tel. 913/843–1211 or 800/255–4266) in the deluxe category; **Brendan Tours** (15137 Califa St., Van Nuys, CA 91411, tel. 818/785–9696 or 800/421–8446, fax 818/902–9876), **Caravan Tours** (401 N. Michigan Ave., Suite 3325, Chicago, IL 60611, tel. 312/321–9800 or 800/227–2826), **Cavalcade Tours** (450 Harmon Meadow Blvd., Secaucus, NJ 07096, tel. 212/617–8173 or 800/346–6314), **Certified Vacations** (Box 1525, Ft. Lauderdale, FL 33302, tel. 305/522–1414 or 800/233–7260), **Collette Tours** (162 Middle St., Pawtucket, RI 02860, tel. 401/728–3805 or 800/832–4656), **Frames Tours** (c/o California Parlor Car Tours, 1101 Van Ness Ave., San Francisco, CA 94109, tel. 415/474–7500 or 800/331–9259), **Globus** (5301 S. Federal Circle, Littleton, CO 80123, tel. 303/797–2800 or 800/221–0090), **Olson-Travelworld** (Box 10066, Manhattan Beach, CA 90226, tel. 310/546–8400 or 800/421–2255), and **Trafalgar Tours** (21 E. 26th St., New York, NY 10010, tel. 212/689–8977 or 800/854–0103) in the first-class category. Globus's more budget-minded sister company, **Cosmos Tourama,** offers bargain-priced packages. **American Airlines Fly AAway Vacations** (tel. 800/321–2121), **British Airways** (tel. 800/247–9297), and **TWA Getaway Vacations** (tel. 800/438–2929) offer packages in all price categories.

Most itineraries are jam-packed with sightseeing, so you see a lot in a short amount of time (usually one place per day). To judge just how fast-paced the tour is, review the itinerary carefully. If you are in a different hotel each night, you will be getting up early each day to head out, travel to your next destination, do some sightseeing, have dinner, and go to bed, then you'll start all over again. If you want some free time, make sure it's mentioned in the tour brochure; if you want to be escorted to every meal, confirm that any tour you consider does that. Also, when comparing programs, be sure to find out if the motorcoach is air-conditioned and has a restroom on board. Make your selection based on price and stops on the itinerary.

Independent Packages Independent packages, which travel agents call FITs (for foreign independent travel), are offered by airlines, tour operators who may also do escorted programs, and any number of other companies from large, established firms to small, new entrepreneurs.

Airlines offering packages include **Aer Lingus** (tel. 800/223–6537), **American Airlines Fly AAway Vacations** and **British Airways** (*see above),* **Continental Airlines' Grand Destinations** (tel. 800/634–5555), **TWA Getaway Vacations** (*see above),* and **United Airlines Va-**

cations (tel. 800/328–6877). **CIE Tours** (108 Ridgedale Ave., Morristown, NJ 07960, tel. 201/292–3438 or 800/243–8687) and **Scots - American Travel** (26 Rugen Dr., Harrington Park, NJ 07640, tel. 201/768–5505 or 800/247–7268) also offer packages.

These programs come in a wide range of prices based on levels of luxury and options—in addition to hotel and airfare, sightseeing, car rental, transfers, admission to local attractions, and other extras. Note that when pricing different packages, it sometimes pays to purchase the same arrangements separately, as when a rock-bottom promotional airfare is being offered, for example. Again, base your choice on what's available at your budget for the destinations you want to visit.

Special- Interest Travel Special-interest programs may be fully escorted or independent. Some require a certain amount of expertise, but most are for the average traveler with an interest and are usually hosted by experts in the subject matter. When the program is escorted, it has the advantages and disadvantages of all escorted programs; because your fellow travelers are apt to be passionate or knowledgeable about the subject, they can prove as enjoyable a part of your travel experience as the destination itself. The price range is wide, but the cost is usually higher—sometimes a lot higher—than for ordinary escorted tours and packages, because of the expert guiding and special activities.

Bicycling **Classic Adventures** (Box 153–P, Hamlin, NY 14464, tel. 716/964–8488 or 800/777–8090) has seven-, eight-, and 14-day hiking and biking tours combining rolling, sheep-dotted hills and sparkling waterways with villages and towns.

Cruises **Cruise Company of Greenwich** (31 Brookside Dr., Greenwich, CT 06830, tel. 203/622–2030 or 800/824–0826) has a tour of Scotland's lochs aboard the *Hebridean Princess*. Other contacts are **Le Boat, Inc.** (Box E, Maywood, NJ 07507, tel. 201/342–1838 or 800/922–0291, fax 201/342–7498), which sails the Caledonian Canal, and **Lindblad's Special Expeditions** (720 5th Ave., New York, NY 10019, tel. 212/765–7740 or 800/762–0003), which offers a two-week exploration of the seacoasts of the British Isles in search of out-of-the-way corners.

Fishing **Fishing International** (Hilltop Estates, 4010 Montecito Ave., Santa Rosa, CA 95404, tel. 707/542–4242 or 800/950–4242) will help you find the perfect place to put on your waders and cast a few lines.

Gardens and Houses **Endless Beginnings** (9825 Dowdy Dr., Suite 105, San Diego, CA 92126, tel. 619/566–4166 or 800/822–7855, fax 619/549–9655) takes you to historic houses and glorious gardens in the lowlands, highlands, and moorlands of Scotland.

Golf Contact **Classic Golf & Leisure** (68733 Perez Rd., Cathedral City, CA 92234, tel. 619/321–2599, **Adventures In Golf** (29 Valencia Dr., Nashua, NH 03062, tel. 603/882–8367), **Celtic Golf Tours** (1062 Pennsylvania Ave., Cape May, NJ 08204, tel. 609/884–8090 or 800/535–6148), **Golfpac** (Box 94090, Maitland, FL 32794, tel. 407/660–8277 or 800/327–0878), **Golf International** (275 Madison Ave., New York, NY 10016, tel. 212/986–9176 or 800/833–1389), **Guest of Scotland Golf** (4835 N. O'Connor Rd., Suite 134–546, Irving, TX 75062, tel. 214/550–0860 or 800/344–5257), **ITC Golf Tours** (4134 Atlantic Ave., Suite 205, Long Beach, CA 90807, tel. 310/595–6905 or 800/257–4981), and **Pery Golf** (8302 Dunwoody Pl., Suite 305, Atlanta, GA 30350, tel. 404/641–9696 or 800/344–5257).

Horseback Riding **FITS Equestrian** (685 Lateen Rd., Solvang, CA 93463, tel. 805/688–9494) goes through forests, meadows, beaches, and huge private estates on its *Argyll Ride* through the romantic heart of the country. **Hoofbeats International** (162 Cambridge Ave., Englewood, NJ 07631, tel. 201/568–8371 or 800/733–2995) offers both escorted and independent countryside jaunts.

Train Tours **Abercrombie & Kent** (*see above*) offers a luxury rail journey on the *Royal Scotsman*, with gourmet meals and private cabin accommodations. **The Smithsonian Institution**'s (1100 Jefferson Dr. SW, Room 3045, Washington, DC 20560, tel. 202/357–4700) *Scotland By Train* journey crisscrosses the country, passing baronial castles, misty blue islands, and sparkling lochs.

Walking and Hiking **English Lakeland Ramblers** (18 Stuyvesant Oval, #1A, New York, NY 10009, tel. 212/505–1020) offers tours through the countryside. **Questers Worldwide Nature Tours** (275 Park Ave. S, New York, NY 10010, tel. 212/673–3120) explores the captivating Outer Hebrides, Orkney, and the Shetlands, then moves to the mountains and moors of the mainland.

When to Go

The Scottish climate has been much maligned (sometimes with justification). You can be unlucky: You may spend a summer week in Scotland and experience nothing but low clouds and drizzle. But on the other hand, you may enjoy calm Mediterranean-like weather even in early spring and late fall.

Generally speaking, Scotland is three or four degrees cooler than southern England. The east is drier and colder than the west; Edinburgh's rainfall is comparable to Rome's, while Glasgow's is more like that in Vancouver—yet the cities are only 44 miles apart.

All visitors comment on the long summer evenings, which grow longer still as you travel north. Dawn in Orkney and Shetland in June is at around 1 AM, no more than an hour or so after sunset. Winter days are very short.

Scotland has few thunderstorms and little fog, except for local mists near coasts. But there are often variable winds that reach gale force even in summer. They blow away the hordes of gnats and midges, the curse of the western Highlands.

Climate What follows are average daily maximum and minimum temperatures for major cities in Scotland.

Aberdeen	**Jan.**	43F	6C	**May**	54F	12C	**Sept.**	59F	15C
		36	2		43	6		49	9
	Feb.	43F	6C	**June**	61F	16C	**Oct.**	54F	12C
		36	2		49	9		43	6
	Mar.	47F	8C	**July**	63F	17C	**Nov.**	47F	8C
		36	2		52	11		40	4
	Apr.	49F	9C	**Aug.**	63F	17C	**Dec.**	45F	7C
		40	4		52	11		36	2

Edinburgh	Jan.	43F	6C	May	58F	14C	Sept.	61F	16C
		34	1		43	6		49	9
	Feb.	43F	6C	June	63F	17C	Oct.	54F	12C
		34	1		49	9		45	7
	Mar.	47F	8C	July	65F	18C	Nov.	49F	9C
		36	2		52	11		40	4
	Apr.	52F	11C	Aug.	65F	18C	Dec.	45F	7C
		40	4		52	11		36	2

Glasgow	Jan.	41F	5C	May	59F	15C	Sept.	61F	16C
		34	1		43	6		49	9
	Feb.	45F	7C	June	65F	18C	Oct.	56F	13C
		34	1		49	9		43	6
	Mar.	49F	9C	July	67F	19C	Nov.	49F	9C
		36	2		52	11		38	3
	Apr.	54F	12C	Aug.	67F	19C	Dec.	45F	7C
		40	4		52	11		36	2

Highlands	Jan.	43F	6C	May	58F	14C	Sept.	61F	16C
		32	0		43	6		49	9
	Feb.	45F	7C	June	63F	17C	Oct.	56F	13C
		34	1		49	9		43	6
	Mar.	49F	9C	July	65F	18C	Nov.	49F	9C
		36	2		52	11		38	3
	Apr.	52F	11C	Aug.	65F	18C	Dec.	45F	7C
		40	4		52	11		34	1

Orkney Islands	Jan.	43F	6C	May	54F	12C	Sept.	58F	14C
		36	2		43	6		49	9
	Feb.	43F	6C	June	58F	14C	Oct.	52F	11C
		36	2		47	8		45	7
	Mar.	45F	7C	July	61F	16C	Nov.	47F	8C
		38	3		50	10		41	5
	Apr.	49F	9C	Aug.	61F	16C	Dec.	45F	7C
		40	4		50	10		38	3

Information Sources For current weather conditions and forecasts for cities in the United States and abroad, plus the local time and helpful travel tips, call the **Weather Channel Connection** (tel. 900/932–8437; 95¢ per minute) from a touch-tone phone.

Festivals and Seasonal Events

Below are the main events on the Scottish calendar.

January **Burns Night dinners** and other entertainments are held on January 25 in memory of Robert Burns in Glasgow, Ayr, Dumfries, Edinburgh, and many other towns and villages.

May **Glasgow Mayfest** (Festival Dir., 18 Albion St., Glasgow G1 1LH, tel. 0141/552–8000), Glasgow's answer to the Edinburgh Festival, is a citywide international festival of theater, dance, music, and street events.
The **Perth Festival of the Arts** (tel. 01738/21031) offers orchestral and choral concerts, drama, opera, recitals, and ballet throughout Perth, Tayside, in mid-May.

July The **British Open Championship** (July 20–23, Royal and Ancient Golf Club, St. Andrews, Fife KY16 9JD, tel. 01334/72112) is played at a different course each year.

August The **Edinburgh International Festival** (21 Market St., Edinburgh EH1 1BW, tel. 0131/226–4001), which runs for three weeks from mid-August through early September, is the world's largest festival of the arts. After dark is the **Edinburgh Military Tattoo** (22 Market St., Edinburgh EH1 1DF, tel. 0131/225–1188), a display of military expertise.

September The **Braemar Royal Highland Gathering** (Princess Royal and Duke of Fife Memorial Park, Braemar, Grampian, tel. 013397/55377) hosts kilted clansmen from all over Scotland.

What to Pack

Clothing Travel light. Porters are more or less wholly extinct these days (and very expensive where you can find them).

In Scotland casual clothes are *de rigueur,* and very few hotels or restaurants insist on jackets and ties for men in the evenings. If you expect to attend some gala occasion, you may need evening wear. For summer, lightweight clothing is usually adequate, except in the evenings, when you'll need a jacket, sweater, or cardigan. A waterproof coat or parka is essential. Drip-dry and crease-resistant fabrics are a good bet, since only the most prestigious hotels have speedy laundering or dry-cleaning service.

Many visitors to Scotland appear to think it necessary to adopt a Scottish costume. It is not. Scots themselves do not wear tartan ties or Balmoral "bunnets," and only an enthusiastic minority prefer the kilt for everyday wear.

Miscellaneous Bring an extra pair of eyeglasses or contact lenses in your carry-on luggage. If you have a health problem that requires a prescription drug, pack enough to last the duration of the trip or have your doctor write a prescription using the drug's generic name, because brand names vary from country to country. Always carry prescription drugs in their original packaging to avoid problems with customs officials. Don't pack them in luggage that you plan to check in case your bags go astray. Pack a list of the offices that supply refunds for lost or stolen travelers checks.

Electricity The electrical current in Scotland is 220 volts, 50 cycles alternating current (AC); the United States runs on 110-volt, 60-cycle AC current. Unlike wall outlets in the United States, which accept plugs with two flat prongs, outlets in Scotland take plugs with three prongs.

Adapters, To use U.S.-made electric appliances abroad, you'll need an adapter
Converters, plug. Unless the appliance is dual-voltage, you'll also need a con-
Transformers verter. Hotels sometimes have 110-volt outlets for low-wattage appliances marked "For Shavers Only" near the sink; don't use them for a high-wattage appliance like a blow-dryer. If you're traveling with an older laptop computer, carry a transformer. New laptop computers are autosensing, operating equally well on 110 and 220 volts (so you need only the appropriate adapter plug). When in doubt, consult your appliance's owner's manual or the manufacturer. Or get a copy of the free brochure "Foreign Electricity is No Deep Dark Secret," published by the adapter-converter manufacturer Franzus Company (Customer Service, Dept. B50, Murtha Industrial Park, Box 142, Beacon Falls, CT 06403, tel. 203/723–6664; send a stamped, self-addressed envelope when ordering).

Luggage Free airline baggage allowances depend on the airline, the route,
Regulations and the class of your ticket; ask in advance. In general, on domestic

flights and on international flights between the United States and foreign destinations, you are entitled to check two bags—neither exceeding 62 inches, or 158 centimeters (length + width + height), or weighing more than 70 pounds (32 kilograms). A third piece may be brought aboard; its total dimensions are generally limited to less than 45 inches (114 centimeters), so it will fit easily under the seat in front of you or in the overhead compartment. In the United States the Federal Aviation Administration gives airlines broad latitude to limit carry-on allowances and tailor them to different aircraft and operational conditions. Charges for excess, oversize, or overweight pieces vary.

If you are flying between two foreign destinations, note that baggage allowances may be determined not by the piece method but by the weight method, which generally allows 88 pounds (40 kilograms) of luggage in first class, 66 pounds (30 kilograms) in business class, and 44 pounds (20 kilograms) in economy. If your flight between two cities abroad *connects* with your transatlantic or transpacific flight, the piece method still applies.

Safeguarding Your Luggage Before leaving home, itemize your bags' contents and their worth in case they go astray. To minimize that risk, tag them inside and out with your name, address, and phone number. (If you use your home address, cover it so that potential thieves can't see it.) Put a copy of your itinerary inside each bag, so that you can easily be tracked. At check-in, make sure that the tag attached by baggage handlers bears the correct three-letter code for your destination. If your bags do not arrive with you, or if you detect damage, immediately file a written report with the airline before you leave the airport.

Taking Money Abroad

Traveler's Checks Traveler's checks are preferable in metropolitan centers, although you'll need cash in rural areas and small towns. The most widely recognized are **American Express, Citicorp, Diners Club, Thomas Cook,** and **Visa,** which are sold by major commercial banks. Both American Express and Thomas Cook issue checks that can be countersigned and used by you or your traveling companion. Typically the issuing company or the bank at which you make your purchase charges 1% to 3% of the checks' face value as a fee. Some foreign banks charge as much as 20% of the face value as the fee for cashing traveler's checks in a foreign currency. Buy a few checks in small denominations to cash toward the end of your trip, so you won't be left with excess foreign currency. Record the numbers of checks as you spend them, and keep this list separate from the checks.

You should also consider buying some checks in pounds; banks will cash them with no fee, and you can use them as readily as cash in many hotels, restaurants, and shops.

Currency Exchange Banks offer the most favorable exchange rates. If you use currency-exchange booths at airports, rail and bus stations, hotels, stores, and privately run exchange firms, you'll typically get less favorable rates, but you may find the hours more convenient.

You can get good rates and avoid long lines at airport currency-exchange booths by getting a small amount of currency at **Thomas Cook Currency Services** (630 5th Ave., New York, NY 10111, tel. 212/757–6915 or 800/223–7373 for locations in major metropolitan areas throughout the United States) or **Ruesch International** (tel. 800/424–2923 for locations) before you depart.

Getting Money from Home

Cash Machines Many automated-teller machines (ATMs) are tied to international networks such as **Cirrus** and **Plus.** You can use your bank card at ATMs to withdraw money from an account and get cash advances on a credit-card account if your card has been programmed with a personal identification number, or PIN. Check in advance on limits on withdrawals and cash advances within specified periods. Ask whether your bank-card or credit-card PIN will need to be reprogrammed for use in the area you'll be visiting. Four digits are commonly used overseas. Note that Discover is accepted only in the United States. On cash advances you are charged interest from the day you receive the money from ATMs as well as from tellers. Although transaction fees for ATM withdrawals abroad may be higher than fees for withdrawals at home, Cirrus and Plus exchange rates are excellent, because they are based on wholesale rates only offered by major banks. They also may be referred to abroad as "a withdrawal from a credit account."

Plan ahead: Obtain ATM locations and the names of affiliated cash-machine networks before departure. For specific foreign Cirrus locations, call 800/4–CIRRUS; for foreign Plus locations, consult the Plus directory at your local bank.

Wiring Money You don't have to be a cardholder to send or receive a **MoneyGram from American Express** for up to $10,000. Go to a MoneyGram agent in retail and convenience stores and American Express travel offices, pay up to $1,000 with a credit card and anything over that in cash. You are allowed a free long-distance call to give the transaction code to your intended recipient, who needs only present identification and the reference number to the nearest MoneyGram agent to pick up the cash. MoneyGram agents are in more than 70 countries (call 800/926–9400 for locations). Fees range from 3% to 10%, depending on the amount and how you pay.

You can also use **Western Union.** To wire money, take either cash or a cashier's check to the nearest agent or call and use MasterCard or Visa. Money sent from the United States or Canada will be available for pickup at agent locations in 100 countries within minutes. Once the money is in the system it can be picked up at *any* one of 25,000 locations (call 800/325–6000 for the one nearest you; 800/321–2923 in Canada). Fees range from 4% to 10%, depending on the amount you send.

Scottish Currency

Britain's currency is the pound sterling, which is divided into 100 pence (100p). Notes are issued to the values of £50, £20, £10, and £5 (also £1 in Scotland). Coins are issued to the values of £1, 50p, 20p, 10p, 5p, 2p, and 1p. Scottish coins are the same as English ones, but Scottish notes are issued by three banks: the Bank of Scotland, the Royal Bank of Scotland, and the Clydesdale Bank. They have the same face values as English notes, and English notes are interchangeable with them in Scotland. Scottish £1 notes are no longer legal tender outside Scotland. English banks and post offices will exchange them for you, but fewer and fewer English shops are accepting them.

At press time, the exchange rate for the pound sterling was £.63 to the dollar.

What It Will Cost

Sample Costs A man's haircut will cost £4 and up; a woman's anywhere from £10 to £20. It costs about £1.50 to have a shirt laundered, from £4.20 to dry-clean a dress, and from £7 to dry-clean a man's suit. A local newspaper will cost you about 30p and a national daily, 40p. A pint of beer is around £1.50, and a serving of whisky, about the same. A cup of coffee will run from 50p to £1, depending on where you drink it; a ham sandwich, £2; lunch in a pub, £4 and up (plus your drink).

A theater seat will cost from £5 to £20 in Edinburgh and Glasgow, less elsewhere. Nightclubs will take all they can get from you. For dining and lodging costs, *see* each chapter under that heading.

Taxes The British sales tax, VAT (Value Added Tax), is 17.5%. The tax is almost always included in quoted prices in shops, hotels, and restaurants. Overseas visitors to Scotland can reclaim the VAT on goods by using the Foreign Exchange Tax-Free Shopping arrangements, available only in participating shops. You must complete a Tax-Free Shopping form at the shop where the goods are purchased (take your passport with you) and then present the form and the goods to HM Customs and Excise as you leave Great Britain. Full details and a list of stores offering the tax-free service are available from the British Tourist Authority, 40 West 57th Street, New York, NY 10019; and the British Travel Centre, 12 Regent Street, London SW1Y 4PQ.

Passports and Visas

If your passport is lost or stolen abroad, report the loss immediately to the nearest embassy or consulate and to the local police. If you can provide the consular officer with the information contained in the passport, he or she will usually be able to issue you a new passport promptly. For this reason, keep a photocopy of the data page of your passport separate from your money and traveler's checks. Also leave a photocopy with a relative or friend at home.

U.S. Citizens All U.S. citizens, even infants, need a valid passport to enter Scotland for stays of up to six months. You can pick up new and renewal application forms at any of the 13 U.S. Passport Agency offices and at some post offices and courthouses. Although passports are usually mailed within four weeks of your application's receipt, allow five weeks or more from April through summer. Call the Department of State Office of Passport Services' information line (tel. 202/647–0518) for fees, documentation requirements, and other details.

Canadian Citizens Canadian citizens need a valid passport to enter Scotland for stays of up to three months. Application forms are available at 23 regional passport offices as well as post offices and travel agencies. You must apply in person. Children under 16 may be included on a parent's passport but must have their own to travel alone. Passports are valid for five years and are usually mailed within two weeks of an application's receipt. For fees, documentation requirements, and other information in English or French, call the passport office (tel. 514/283–2152 or 800/567–6868).

Customs and Duties

On Arrival Entering the United Kingdom, a traveler 17 or over can take in (1) 200 cigarettes or 100 cigarillos or 50 cigars or 250 grams of tobacco; (2) one liter of alcohol over 22% volume or two liters of alcohol under

22% volume or two liters of fortified or sparkling wine; (3) two liters of still table wine; (4) 60 ml of perfume and 250 ml of toilet water; (5) other goods to a value of £136 but no more than 50 liters of beer.

Returning
Home
U.S. Customs

If you've been out of the country for at least 48 hours and haven't already used the exemption, or any part of it, in the past 30 days, you may bring home $400 worth of foreign goods duty-free. So can each member of your family, regardless of age; and your exemptions may be pooled, so one of you can bring in more if another brings in less. A flat 10% duty applies to the next $1,000 of goods; above $1,400, the rate varies with the merchandise. (If the 48-hour or 30-day limit applies, your duty-free allowance drops to $25, which may not be pooled.) Please note that these are the *general* rules, applicable to most countries, including Scotland.

Travelers 21 or older may bring back 1 liter of alcohol duty-free, provided the beverage laws of the state through which they reenter the United States allow it. In addition, 100 non-Cuban cigars and 200 cigarettes are allowed, regardless of your age. Antiques and works of art more than 100 years old are duty-free.

Gifts valued at less than $50 may be mailed to the United States duty-free, with a limit of one package per day per addressee, and do not count as part of your exemption (do not send alcohol or tobacco products or perfume valued at more than $5); mark the package "Unsolicited Gift" and write the nature of the gift and its retail value on the outside. Most reputable stores will handle the mailing for you.

For a copy of "Know Before You Go," a free brochure detailing what you may and may not bring back to the United States, rates of duty, and other pointers, contact the **U.S. Customs Service** (Box 7407, Washington, DC 20044, tel. 202/927–6724).

Canadian
Customs

Once per calendar year, when you've been out of Canada for at least seven days, you may bring in C$300 worth of goods duty-free. If you've been away less than seven days but more than 48 hours, the duty-free exemption drops to C$100 but can be claimed any number of times (as can a C$20 duty-free exemption for absences of 24 hours or more). You cannot combine the yearly and 48-hour exemptions, use the C$300 exemption only partially (to save the balance for a later trip), or pool exemptions with family members. Goods claimed under the C$300 exemption may follow you by mail; those claimed under the lesser exemptions must accompany you on your return.

Alcohol and tobacco products may be included in the yearly and 48-hour exemptions but not in the 24-hour exemption. If you meet the age requirements of the province through which you reenter Canada, you may bring in, duty-free, 1.14 liters (40 imperial ounces) of wine or liquor *or* two dozen 12-ounce cans or bottles of beer or ale. If you are 16 or older, you may bring in, duty-free, 200 cigarettes, 50 cigars or cigarillos, and 400 tobacco sticks or 400 grams of manufactured tobacco.

An unlimited number of gifts valued up to C$60 each may be mailed to Canada duty-free. These do not count as part of your exemption. Label the package "Unsolicited Gift—Value under $60." Alcohol and tobacco are excluded.

For more information, including details of duties on items that exceed your duty-free limit, ask the Revenue Canada Customs and Excise and Taxation Department (2265 St. Laurent Blvd. S, Ottawa, Ontario, K1G 4K3, tel. 613/957–0275) for a copy of the free brochure "I Declare/Je Déclare."

Traveling with Cameras, Camcorders, and Laptops

About Film
and Cameras   If your camera is new or if you haven't used it for a while, shoot and develop a few test rolls before you leave. Store film in a cool, dry place—never in the car's glove compartment or on the shelf under the rear window.

Airport security X-rays generally aren't harmful to film with ISO below 400. To protect your film, carry it with you in a clear plastic bag and ask for a hand inspection. Such requests are honored at U.S. airports, up to the inspector abroad. Don't depend on a lead-lined bag to protect film in checked luggage—the airline may increase the radiation to see what's inside. Call the Kodak Information Center (tel. 800/242–2424) for details.

About
Camcorders   Before your trip, put camcorders through their paces, invest in a skylight filter to protect the lens, and check all the batteries. Most newer camcorders are equipped with batteries that can be recharged with a universal or worldwide AC adapter charger (or multivoltage converter) usable whether the voltage is 110 or 220. All that's needed is the appropriate plug.

About
Videotape   Videotape is not damaged by X-rays, but it may be harmed by the magnetic field of a walk-through metal detector, so ask for a hand-check. Airport security personnel may ask you to turn on the camcorder to prove that it's what it appears to be, so make sure the battery is charged. Note that rather than the National Television System Committee (NTSC) video standard used in the United States and Canada, Scotland uses PAL/SECAM technology. You will not be able to view your tapes through the local TV set or view movies bought there in your home VCR. Blank tapes bought in Scotland can be used for NTSC camcorder taping, but they are pricey.

About
Laptops   Security X-rays do not harm hard-disk or floppy-disk storage, but you may request a handcheck, at which point you may be asked to turn on the computer to prove that it is what it appears to be. (Check your battery before departure.) Most airlines allow you to use your laptop aloft except during takeoff and landing (so as not to interfere with navigation equipment). For international travel, register your foreign-made laptop with U.S. Customs as you leave the country. If your laptop is U.S.-made, call the consulate of the country you'll be visiting to find out whether it should be registered with customs upon arrival. Before departure, find out about repair facilities at your destination, and don't forget any transformer or adapter plug you may need (*see* Electricity, *above*).

Language

"Much," said Doctor Johnson, "much may be made of a Scotchman *if he be caught young.*" This quote sums up—even today—the attitude of some English people to the Scots language. They simply assume that their English is superior. Since they speak the language of Parliament and much of the media, their arrogance is understandable. The Scots have long been made to feel uncomfortable about their mother tongue and have only themselves to blame, being actively encouraged—at school, for example—to ape the dialect of the Thames Valley ("Standard English") in order to "get on" in life. The Scots language (that is, Lowland Scots, not Gaelic) was a northern form of Middle English and in its day was the language used in the court and in literature. It borrowed from Scandinavian, Dutch, French, and Gaelic. After a series of historical body blows—such as the decamping of the Scottish Court to England after 1603 and the printing of the King James Bible in English, but not in Scots—it declined as a literary or official language. It survives, in various forms, virtually as an underground language spoken at home, in shops, on the playground, the farm, or quayside among ordinary folk, especially in its heartland, in northeast Scotland. (There they describe Scots who use the brayed diphthongs of the English Thames Valley as speaking with a *bool in the mou*—marble in the mouth!) Plenty of Scots speak English with only an accent and virtually all will "modulate" either unconsciously or out of politeness into understandable English when conversing with a nondialect speaker. As for Gaelic, that belongs to a different Celtic culture and, though threatened, hangs on in spite of the Highlands depopulation.

Insurance

Most tour operators, travel agents, and insurance agents sell specialized health-and-accident, flight, trip-cancellation, and luggage insurance as well as comprehensive policies with some or all of these features. Before you make any purchase, review your existing health and homeowner policies to find out whether they cover expenses incurred while travelling.

Health-and-Accident Insurance Specific policy provisions of supplemental health-and-accident insurance for travelers include reimbursement for $1,000 to $150,000 worth of medical and/or dental expenses caused by an accident or illness during a trip. The personal-accident, or death-and-dismemberment, provision pays a lump sum to your beneficiaries if you die or to you if you lose one or more limbs or your eyesight; the lump sum awarded can range from $15,000 to $500,000. The medical-assistance provision may reimburse you for the cost of referrals, evacuation, or repatriation and other services, or it may automatically enroll you as a member of a particular medical-assistance company.

Flight Insurance Often bought as a last-minute impulse at the airport, flight insurance pays a lump sum when a plane crashes, either to a beneficiary if the insured dies or sometimes to a surviving passenger who loses eyesight or a limb. Like most impulse buys, flight insurance is expensive and basically unnecessary. It supplements the airlines' coverage described in the limits-of-liability paragraphs on your ticket. Charging an airline ticket to a major credit card often automatically entitles you to coverage and may also embrace travel by bus, train, and ship.

Baggage Insurance In the event of loss, damage, or theft on international flights, airlines' liability is $20 per kilogram for checked baggage (roughly $640 per 70-pound bag) and $400 per passenger for unchecked baggage. On domestic flights, the ceiling is $1,250 per passenger. Excess-valuation insurance can be bought directly from the airline at check-in for about $10 per $1,000 worth of coverage. However, you cannot buy it at any price to cover the rather extensive list of excluded items shown on your airline ticket.

Trip Insurance **Trip-cancellation-and-interruption insurance** protects you in the event you are unable to undertake or finish your trip, especially if your airline ticket, cruise, or package tour does not allow changes or cancellations. The amount of coverage you purchase should equal the cost of your trip should you, a traveling companion, or a family member get sick, forcing you to stay home, plus the nondiscounted one-way airline ticket you would need to buy if you had to return home early. Read the fine print carefully; pay attention to sections defining "family member" and "preexisting medical conditions." **Default** or **bankruptcy insurance** protects you against a supplier's failure to deliver. Such policies often do not cover default by a travel agency, tour operator, airline, or cruise line if you bought your tour and the coverage directly from the firm in question. Tours packaged by one of the 33 members of the United States Tour Operators Association (USTOA, 211 E. 51st St., Suite 12B, New York, NY 10022; tel. 212/750–7371), which requires members to maintain $1 million each in an account to reimburse clients in case of default, are likely to present the fewest difficulties.

Comprehensive Policies Companies supplying comprehensive policies with some or all of the above features include **Access America, Inc.** (Box 90315, Richmond, VA 23230, tel. 800/284–8300); **Carefree Travel Insurance** (Box 310, 120 Mineola Blvd., Mineola, NY 11501, tel. 516/294–0220 or 800/323–3149); **Tele-Trip** (Mutual of Omaha Plaza, Box 31762, Omaha, NE 68131, tel. 800/228–9792); **The Travelers Companies** (1 Tower Sq., Hartford, CT 06183, tel. 203/277–0111 or 800/243–3174); **Travel Guard International** (1145 Clark St., Stevens Point, WI 54481, tel. 715/345–0505 or 800/826–1300); and **Wallach and Company, Inc.** (107 W. Federal St., Box 480, Middleburg, VA 22117, tel. 703/687–3166 or 800/237–6615).

Car Rental

If you're traveling to more than one country, make sure your rental contract permits you to take the car across borders and that the insurance policy covers you in every country you visit. Remember that unlike cars in the United States or the rest of Europe, British cars have the steering wheel on the right and drive on the left. Therefore, you may want to leave your rented car in Britain and pick up a left-side drive when you cross the Channel.

All major car-rental companies are represented in Scotland, including **Alamo** (tel. 800/327–9633); **Avis** (tel. 800/331–1084, 800/879–2847 in Canada); **Budget** (tel. 800/527–0700); **Hertz** (tel. 800/654–3001, 800/263–0600 in Canada); and **National** (tel. 800/227–3876), known internationally as InterRent and Europcar. In cities, unlimited-mileage rates range from $40 per day for an economy car to $150 for a large car; weekly unlimited-mileage rates for an economy car range from $170 to $230. This includes tax, which in Scotland is 17.5% on car rentals.

Requirements Your own driver's license is acceptable. An International Driver's Permit, available from the American or Canadian Automobile Association, is a good idea.

Extra Charges Picking up the car in one city and leaving it in another may entail substantial drop-off charges or one-way service fees. The cost of a collision or loss-damage waiver (*see below*) can be high, also. Some rental agencies will charge you extra if you return the car *before* the time specified on your contract. Ask before making unscheduled drop-offs. Be sure the rental agent agrees *in writing* to any changes in drop-off location or other items of your rental contract. Fill the tank when you turn in the vehicle to avoid being charged for refueling at what you'll swear is the most expensive pump in town. In Europe manual transmissions are standard and air conditioning is a rarity and often unnecessary. Asking for an automatic transmission or air-conditioning can significantly increase the cost of your rental. Find out what the standard rentals are in the country you'll be visiting and weigh that factor when making your reservation.

Cutting Costs If you're flying to Scotland and plan to spend some time first in Edinburgh, don't pick up your car until you're ready to leave the city; otherwise, arrange to pick up and return your car at the airport. And carefully weigh the convenience of renting a car from a major company with an airport branch against the savings to be had from a local company with offices in town.

Major international companies have programs that discount their standard rates by 15%–30% if you make the reservation before departure (anywhere from 24 hours to 14 days), rent for a minimum number of days (typically three or four), and prepay the rental. More economical rentals may come as part of fly/drive or other packages, even bare-bones deals that only combine the rental and an airline ticket (*see* Tours and Packages, *above*).

Several companies operate as wholesalers. They do not own their own fleets but rent in bulk from those that do and offer advantageous rates to their customers. Rentals through such companies must be arranged and paid for before you leave the United States. Among them are **Auto Europe** (Box 7006, Portland, ME 04112, tel. 207/828–2525 or 800/223–5555, 800/458–9503 in Canada), **Europe by Car** (mailing address, 1 Rockefeller Plaza, New York, NY 10020; walk-in address, 14 W. 49th St., New York, NY 10020, tel. 212/581–3040, 212/245–1713, or 800/223–1516; 9000 Sunset Blvd., Los Angeles, CA 90069, tel. 800/252–9401 or 213/272–0424 in CA), **Foremost Euro-Car** (5658 Sepulveda Blvd., Suite 201, Van Nuys, CA 91411, tel. 818/786–1960 or 800/272–3299), and **The Kemwel Group** (106 Calvert St., Harrison, NY 10528, tel. 914/835–5555 or 800/678–0678). You won't see these wholesalers' deals advertised; they're even better in summer, when business travel is down. Always ask whether the prices are guaranteed in U.S. dollars or foreign currency and if unlimited mileage is available. Find out about any required deposits, cancellation penalties, and drop-off charges, and confirm the cost of any required insurance coverage.

Insurance and Collision Damage Waiver Until recently standard rental contracts included liability coverage (for damage to public property, injury to pedestrians, and so on) and coverage for the car against fire, theft, and collision damage with a deductible. Due to law changes in some states and rising liability costs, several car-rental agencies have reduced the type of coverage they offer. Before you rent a car, find out exactly what coverage, if any, is provided by your personal auto insurer. Don't assume that you are covered. If you do want insurance from the rental company, you may only be able to get secondary coverage, which you may already have if you charge the rental to a credit card. Only Diner's Club (tel. 800/234–6377) provides primary coverage in the United States and worldwide.

In general if you have an accident, you are responsible for the automobile. Car-rental companies may offer a collision damage waiver (CDW), which ranges in cost from $4 to $14 a day. You should decline the CDW only if you are certain you are covered through your personal insurer or credit-card company.

Rail and Bus Passes

If you plan to rack up the miles, rail passes from **Britrail** (1500 Broadway, New York, NY 10036, tel. 212/575-2667 or 800/677–8585), which provide unlimited travel over the entire British train network during their period of validity, can be an excellent value. Standard passes are available for eight days ($299 in first class and $219 in second class), for 15 days ($489 and $339), and one month ($715 and

$495). **Britrail Flexipasses** allow you to travel for 4 days in an 8-day period, 8 days in a 15-day period, or 15 days of a 30 day period. You pay $249, $389, and $575 for the Flexipass in first class, $189, $269, and $395 for second class. Britrail passes must be purchased before you leave home. The **BritFrance Rail Pass** covers both France and Britain (and Hovercraft Channel crossings); cost for unlimited travel on any 5 days of a 15-day period is $359 in first class, $259 in second class; $539 and $399 for any 10 days in a 30-day period. The **Britrail Youth Pass** and **Britrail Youth Flexipass** are available for second class travel for those under 26 on their first travel day; fares for the Youth Pass are $179, $269, $339 and $395 for 8, 15, 22, and 30 days. The Youth Flexipass is $155 for 4 days of travel in an 8 day period, $219 for 8 days in a 15 day period, and $309 for 15 days in a two-month period. Or, try the **Freedom of Scotland Travel Pass,** for 8, 15, and 22 days of consecutive travel for $145, $205, and $259, respectively; or the **Freedom of Scotland Flexipass,** good for 8 days out of 15 for $185. All these passes must be purchased stateside and are sold by travel agents as well as Britrail (*see above*) or **Rail Europe** (226–230 Westchester Ave., White Plains, NY 10604, tel. 914/682–5172 or 800/438–7245 from the East, 800/848–7245 from the West). Still other passes may be purchased in Scotland. (*See also* Staying in Scotland: Getting Around by Train, *below*). EurailPasses are not valid in Great Britain.

Don't make the mistake of assuming that your rail pass guarantees you seats on the trains you want to ride. Seat reservations are required on some trains, particularly at peak travel times and on popular trains such as the London–Edinburgh route. It's a four-hour journey, and that's a long time to stand. You will also need reservations for overnight sleeping accommodations; they cost $57 in first class and $48 in second class and can be made prior to departure through your travel agent, Britrail, Rail Europe, or at any rail station in Scotland.

On bus routes, the **BritExpress Card,** available to all overseas visitors, offers savings of around 30%. It can be purchased before you leave or, as long as you have a valid air or ferry ticket, on arrival in the United Kingdom.

Student and Youth Travel

Travel Agencies **Council Travel Services (CTS),** a subsidiary of the nonprofit Council on International Educational Exchange (CIEE), specializes in low-cost travel arrangements abroad for students and is the exclusive U.S. agent for several discount cards. Also newly available from CTS are domestic air passes for bargain travel within the United States. CIEE's twice-yearly *Student Travels* magazine is available at the CTS office at CIEE headquarters (205 E. 42nd St., 16th Floor, New York, NY 10017, tel. 212/661–1450) and in Boston (tel. 617/266–1926), Miami (tel. 305/670–9261), Los Angeles (tel. 310/208–3551), and at 43 branches in college towns nationwide (free in person, $1 by mail). **Campus Connections** (1100 E. Marlton Pike, Cherry Hill, NJ 08034, tel. 800/428–3235) specializes in discounted accommodations and airline fares for students. The **Educational Travel Centre** (438 N. Frances St., Madison, WI 53703, tel. 608/256–5551) offers low-cost domestic and international airline tickets, mostly for flights departing from Chicago, and rail passes. Other travel agencies catering to students include **TMI Student Travel** (1146 Pleasant St., Watertown, MA 02172, tel. 617/661–8187 or 800/245–3672) and **Travel Cuts** (187 College St., Toronto, Ontario M5T 1P7, tel. 416/979–2406).

Discount Cards For discounts on transportation and on museum and attractions admissions, buy the **International Student Identity Card** (ISIC) if you're a bona fide student or the **International Youth Card** (IYC) if you're under 26. In the United States the ISIC and IYC cards cost $16 each and include basic travel accident and illness coverage and a toll-free travel assistance hot line. Apply to **CIEE** (*see* address *above*, tel. 212/661–1414; the application is in *Student Travels*). In Canada the cards are available for $15 each from **Travel Cuts** (*see above*). In the United Kingdom they cost £5 and £4 respectively at student unions and student travel companies, including Council Travel's London office (28A Poland St., London W1V 3DB, tel. 071/437–7767).

Hosteling A **Hostelling International** (HI) membership card is the key to more than 5,000 hostels in 70 countries; the sex-segregated, dormitory-style sleeping quarters, including some for families, go for $7 to $20 a night per person. Membership is available in the United States through **Hostelling International-American Youth Hostels** (HI-AYH, 733 15th St. NW, Suite 840, Washington, DC 20005, tel. 202/783–6161), the U.S. link in the worldwide chain, and costs $25 for adults 18 to 54, $10 for those under 18, $15 for those 55 and over, and $35 for families. Volume 1 of the *AYH Guide to Budget Accommodation* lists hostels in Europe and the Mediterranean ($13.95, including postage). HI membership is available in Canada through **Hostelling International-Canada** (205 Catherine St. Suite 400, Ottawa, Ontario K2P 1C3, tel. 613/748–5638) for $26.75, and in the United Kingdom through the **Youth Hostel Association of England and Wales** (Trevelyan House, 8 St. Stephen's Hill, St. Albans, Hertshire AL1 2DY, tel. 01727/855215) for £9.

Tour Operators **Contiki** (300 Plaza Alicante #900, Garden Grove, CA 92640, tel. 714/740–0808 or 800/266–8454) specializes in package tours for travelers 18 to 35.

University Housing Many universities and colleges throughout Britain open their halls of residence to visitors during vacation periods—that is, from mid-March to mid-April, from July to September, and during the Christmas holidays. Campus accommodations— usually single rooms with access to lounges, libraries, and sports facilities—include breakfast and generally cost about $30 per night. Locations vary from city centers to bucolic lakeside parks. For information contact the **British Universities Accommodation Consortium** (BUAC, Box 1074, University Park, Nottingham NG7 2RD, England, tel. 01602/504–571), or the **Higher Education Accommodation Consortium** (HEAC, 36 Collegiate Crescent, Sheffield S10 2BP, England, tel. 01742/683–759).

Camping Camping is another economical option for young travelers. Consult the free British Tourist Authority booklet *Camping and Caravan Parks in Britain,* or *Forestry Commission Camping and Caravan Sites* (free from the **Forestry Commission,** 231 Corstorphine Rd., Edinburgh EH12 7AT, Scotland, tel. 0131/334–0303). For help planning a bicycle camping trip, contact the **Camping and Caravanning Club** (11 Lower Grosvenor Pl., London SW1W 0EY, England).

Getting Around A **Student Coach Card** from National Express, available to full-time students aged 17 and older, provides one-third off all long-distance coach fares in Britain; contact any National Express agent in Britain. Those 16–23 are eligible for the same reduction via the National Express **Discount Coach Card.**

Traveling with Children

Publications *Family Travel Times,* published 10 times a year by **Travel With Your**
Newsletter **Children** (TWYCH, 45 W. 18th St., New York, NY 10011, tel.
212/206–0688; annual subscription $55), covers destinations, types
of vacations, and modes of travel. TWYCH also publishes *Cruising
with Children* ($22) and *Skiing with Children* ($29).

Books *Great Vacations with Your Kids,* by Dorothy Jordan and Marjorie
Cohen ($13; Penguin USA, 120 Woodbine St., Bergenfield, NJ
07621, tel. 800/253–6476) and *Traveling with Children—And Enjoying It,* by Arlene K. Butler ($11.95 plus $3 shipping per book; Globe
Pequot Press, Box 833, 6 Business Park Rd., Old Saybrook, CT
06475, tel. 800/243–0495, or 800/962–0973 in CT), both help plan your
trip with children, from toddlers to teens. *Innocents Abroad: Traveling with Kids in Europe,* by Valerie Wolf Deutsch and Laura Sutherland ($15.95 or $4.95 paperback, Penguin USA, *see above*), covers
child- and teen-friendly activities, food, and transportation.

Tour **Grandtravel** (6900 Wisconsin Ave., Suite 706, Chevy Chase, MD
Operators 20815, tel. 301/986–0790 or 800/247–7651) offers tours for people
traveling with their grandchildren. The catalogue, as charmingly
written and illustrated as a children's book, positively invites armchair traveling with lap-sitters aboard. **Families Welcome!** (21 West
Colony Pl., Suite 140, Durham, NC 27705, tel. 919/489–2555 or
800/326–0724; fax 919/490–5587) packages and sells family tours.

Getting There On international flights, the fare for infants under 2 not occupying
Air Fares a seat is generally either free or 10% of the accompanying adult's
fare; children ages 2 to 11 usually pay half to two-thirds of the adult
fare. On domestic flights, children under 2 not occupying a seat
travel free, and older children currently travel on the "lowest applicable" adult fare.

Baggage In general, infants paying 10% of the adult fare are allowed one
carry-on bag, not to exceed 70 pounds or 45 inches (length + width
+ height) and a collapsible stroller; check with the airline before
departure, because you may be allowed less if the flight is full. The
adult baggage allowance applies for children paying half or more of
the adult fare.

Safety Seats The FAA recommends the use of safety seats aloft and details approved models in the free leaflet "**Child/Infant Safety Seats Recommended for Use in Aircraft**" (available from the Federal Aviation
Administration, APA–200, 800 Independence Ave. SW, Washington,
DC 20591, tel. 202/267–3479; Information Hotline, tel. 800/322–
7873). Airline policy varies. U.S. carriers allow FAA-approved models bearing a sticker declaring their FAA approval. Because these
seats are strapped into regular passenger seats, airlines may require that a ticket be bought for an infant who would otherwise ride
free.

Facilities Some airlines provide other services for children, such as children's
Aloft meals and freestanding bassinets (only to those with seats at the
bulkhead, where there's enough legroom). Make your request when
reserving. Every other year, the February issue of *Family Travel
Times* details children's services on three dozen airlines ($12; *see
above*). "Kids and Teens in Flight" (free from the U.S. Department
of Transportation's Office of Consumer Affairs (R–25, Washington,
DC 20590, tel. 202/366–2220) offers tips for children flying alone.

Lodging Although there is no general policy regarding hotel rates for children in Scotland, **Milton Hotels** allow children under 14 to stay for

free in their parents' room. Many also have adjoining family rooms. **Embassy Hotels** allow up to two children under 16 to stay free when sharing their parents' room and offer a 25% discount for children occupying their own rooms.

Baby-Sitting Services The concierge at your hotel or guest house should be able to recommend a local baby-sitting service or agency.

Hints for Travelers with Disabilities

In Scotland, many hotels offer facilities for wheelchair users, and special carriages are beginning to appear on intercity and long-distance trains. However, since much of Scotland's beauty is found in hidden hills and corners "off the beaten track," renting a car is probably a better option.

Local Information The nonprofit **Holiday Care Service** (2 Old Bank Chambers, Station Rd., Horley, Surrey RH6 9HW, England, tel. 01293/774–535) provides a hotel reservation service, travel insurance, and free information and advice on holidays for people with special needs. **The Scottish Tourist Board** (23 Ravelston Terr., Edinburgh EH4 3EU, Scotland, tel. 0131/332–2433) has information on accommodations and transportation. Another useful source is **Disability Scotland** (Princes House, 5 Shandwick Place, Edinburgh EH2 4RG, tel. 0131/229–8632). A guidebook from the **National Trust for Scotland** (5 Charlotte Sq., Edinburgh EH2 4DU, tel. 0131/226–5922) details facilities for people with disabilities who visit its various historic houses and monuments.

Main information sources for Great Britain as a whole include the **Royal Association for Disability and Rehabilitation** (RADAR, 12 City Forum, 250 City Rd., London EC1V 8AF, tel. 0171/250–3222), which publishes travel information for people with disabilities in Britain, and **Mobility International** (228 Borough High St., London SE1 1JX, tel. 0171/403–5688), the headquarters of an international membership organization that serves as a clearinghouse of travel information for people with disabilities.

Getting Around **Hertz** (tel. 800/654–3131) can provide hand controls for individuals with lower-limb disability at its rental offices in Glasgow and Edinburgh. Upon advance notice, British Rail staff will assist passengers with disabilities; inquire at any British Rail area office.

Organizations Several organizations provide travel information for people with disabilities, usually for a membership fee, and some publish newsletters and bulletins. Among them are the **Information Center for Individuals with Disabilities** (Fort Point Pl., 27–43 Wormwood St., Boston, MA 02210, tel. 617/727–5540 or 800/462–5015 in MA between 11 AM and 4 PM, or leave message; TTY 617/345–9743); **Mobility International USA** (Box 10767, Eugene, OR 97440, tel. and TTY 503/343–1284; fax 503/343–6812), the U.S. branch of an international organization that has affiliates in 30 countries; **MossRehab Hospital Travel Information Service** (tel. 215/456–9603, TTY 215/456–9602); the **Travel Industry and Disabled Exchange** (TIDE, 5435 Donna Ave., Tarzana, CA 91356, tel. 818/344–3640, fax 818/344–0078); and **Travelin' Talk** (Box 3534, Clarksville, TN 37043, tel. 615/552–6670, fax 615/552–1182).

Travel Agencies and Tour Operators **Flying Wheels Travel** (143 W. Bridge St., Box 382, Owatonna, MN 55060, tel. 507/451–5005 or 800/535–6790) is a travel agency specializing in domestic and worldwide cruises, tours, and independent travel itineraries for people with mobility problems.

Publications Two free publications are available from the U.S. Consumer Information Center (Pueblo, CO 81009): "New Horizons for the Air Traveler with a Disability" (include Dept. 608Y in the address), a U.S. Department of Transportation booklet describing changes resulting from the 1986 Air Carrier Access Act and from the 1990 Americans with Disabilities Act, and the "Airport Operators Council's Access Travel: Airports" (Dept. 5804), which describes facilities and services for people with disabilities at more than 500 airports worldwide.

Travelin' Talk Directory (*see* Organizations, *above*) was published in 1993. This 500-page resource book ($35 check or money order with a money-back guarantee) lists names and addresses of people and organizations who offer help for travelers with disabilities. Twin Peaks Press (Box 129, Vancouver, WA 98666, tel. 206/694–2462 or 800/637–2256) publishes the *Directory of Travel Agencies for the Disabled* ($19.95), listing more than 370 agencies worldwide. Add $2 for shipping.

Hints for Older Travelers

Scotland offers a wide variety of discounts and travel bargains for men over 65 and women 60 and over. The **Senior Citizen Railcard,** available in all major British Rail stations, offers one-third off all rail fares. Travelers over 60 also get one-third off all National Express coach fares and are eligible for the **Discount Coach Card,** which provides one-third off all long-distance coach fares in Britain.

For discounted admission to hundreds of museums, historic buildings, and attractions throughout Britain, senior citizens need show only their passport as proof of age. Reduced-rate tickets to theater and ballet are also available.

Organizations The **American Association of Retired Persons** (AARP, 601 E St. NW, Washington, DC 20049, tel. 202/434–2277) provides independent travelers who are members of the AARP (open to those age 50 or older; $8 per person or couple annually) with the Purchase Privilege Program, which offers discounts on lodging, car rentals, and sightseeing, and arranges group tours, cruises, and apartment living through AARP Travel Experience from American Express (400 Pinnacle Way, Suite 450, Norcross, GA 30071, tel. 800/927–0111 or 800/745–4567).

Two other organizations offer discounts on lodgings, car rentals, and other travel products, along with such nontravel perks as magazines and newsletters: The **National Council of Senior Citizens** (1331 F St. NW, Washington, DC 20004, tel. 202/347–8800 (membership $12 annually) and **Mature Outlook** (6001 N. Clark St., Chicago, IL 60660, tel. 800/336–6330; $9.95 annually).

Note: Mention your senior-citizen identification card when booking hotel reservations for reduced rates, not when checking out. At restaurants, show your card before you're seated; discounts may be limited to certain menus, days, or hours. If you are renting a car, ask about promotional rates that might improve on your senior-citizen discount.

Educational Travel The nonprofit **Elderhostel** (75 Federal St., 3rd Floor, Boston, MA 02110, tel. 617/426–7788) has offered inexpensive study programs for people 60 and older since 1975. Held at more than 1,800 educational and cultural institutions, courses cover everything from marine science to Greek myths and cowboy poetry. Participants generally attend lectures in the morning and spend the afternoon sightseeing or on field trips; they live in dormitory-type lodgings. Fees for two- to three-week international trips—including room, board, and transportation from the United States—range from $1,800 to $4,500.

Interhostel (University of New Hampshire, 6 Garrison Ave., Durham, NH 03824, tel. 603/862–1147 or 800/733–9753) caters to a slightly younger clientele—50 and over—and runs programs in some 25 countries. The idea is similar: Lectures and field trips mix with sightseeing, and participants stay in dormitories at cooperating educational institutions or in modest hotels. Programs usually last two weeks and cost $1,500–$2,100, excluding airfare.

Tour Operators   The following tour operators specialize in older travelers: **Evergreen Travel Service** (4114 198th St. SW, Suite 3, Lynwood, WA 98036, tel. 206/776–1184 or 800/435–2288), has introduced the "Lazy Bones" tours for those who like a slower pace. If you want to take your grandchildren, look into **Grandtravel** (*see* Traveling with Children, *above*).

Publications   *The 50+ Traveler's Guidebook: Where to Go, Where to Stay, What to Do*, by Anita Williams and Merrimac Dillon ($12.95, St. Martin's Press, 175 5th Ave., New York, NY 10010), is available in bookstores and offers many useful tips. "The Mature Traveler" (Box 50820, Reno, NV 89513, tel. 702/786–7419; $29.95), a monthly newsletter, contains many travel deals.

Lodging   Many hotels advertise off-season discounts for senior citizens, and some offer year-round savings. **Scottish Highland Hotels** (tel. 0131/557–2368 in Scotland) have a special year-round "Golden Times" package offering one-third off regular rates. Budget-minded seniors may also consider overnight accommodations at a university or college residence hall (*see* **BUAC** under Student and Youth Travel, *above*).

Hints for Gay and Lesbian Travelers

Organizations   The **International Gay Travel Association** (Box 4974, Key West, FL 33041, tel. 800/448–8550), which has 700 members, will provide you with names of travel agents and tour operators who specialize in gay travel. The **Gay & Lesbian Visitors Center of New York Inc.** (135 W. 20th St., 3rd Floor, New York, NY 10011, tel. 212/463–9030 or 800/395–2315; $100 annually) mails a monthly newsletter, valuable coupons, and more to its members.

Tour Operators and Travel Agencies   The dominant travel agency in the market is **Above and Beyond** (3568 Sacramento St., San Francisco, CA 94118, tel. 415/922–2683 or 800/397–2681). Tour operator **Olympus Vacations** (8424 Santa Monica Blvd., #721, West Hollywood, CA 90069, tel. 310/657–2220) offers all-gay-and-lesbian resort holidays. **Skylink Women's Travel** (746 Ashland Ave., Santa Monica, CA 90405, tel. 310/452–0506 or 800/225–5759) handles individual travel for lesbians all over the world and conducts two international and five domestic group trips annually.

Publications   The premiere international travel magazine for gays and lesbians is *Our World* (1104 N. Nova Rd., Suite 251, Daytona Beach, FL 32117, tel. 904/441–5367; $35 for 10 issues). "Out & About" (tel. 203/789–8518 or 800/929–2268; $49 for 10 issues, full refund if you aren't satisfied) is a 16-page monthly newsletter with extensive information on resorts, hotels, and airlines that are gay-friendly.

Arriving and Departing

From North America by Plane

Flights are either nonstop, direct, or connecting. A **nonstop** flight requires no change of plane and makes no stops. A **direct** flight stops at least once and can involve a change of plane, although the flight number remains the same; if the first leg is late, the second waits. This is not the case with a **connecting** flight, which involves a different plane and a different flight number.

Airports and Airlines Airlines serving Edinburgh, Glasgow, and other major cities in Britain include **American Airlines** (tel. 800/433–7300); **British Airways** (tel. 800/247–9297); **Continental Airlines** (tel. 800/525–0280); **Northwest Airlines** (tel. 800/447–4747); **TWA** (tel. 800/892–4141); **United Airlines** (tel. 800/241–6522); **USAir** (tel. 800/622–1015); and **Virgin Atlantic** (tel. 800/862–8621).

Flying Time The flight to Glasgow is about 6½ hours from New York, 7½ hours from Chicago, and 10 hours from Los Angeles.

Cutting Costs The Sunday travel section of most newspapers is a good source of deals. When booking, particularly through an unfamiliar company, call the Better Business Bureau and your local or state Consumer Protection Bureau to find out whether any complaints have been registered against the company, pay with a credit card if you can, and consider trip-cancellation and default insurance (*see* Insurance, *above*). A helpful resource is *Airfare Secrets Exposed*, by Sharon Tyler and Matthew Wonder (Universal Information Publishing, $16.95), available in bookstores.

Promotional Airfares Less expensive fares, called promotional or discount fares, are round-trip and involve restrictions, which vary according to the route and season. You must usually buy the ticket—commonly called an APEX (advance purchase excursion) when it's for international travel—in advance (7, 14, or 21 days are usual), although some of the major airlines have added no-frills, cheap flights to compete with new bargain airlines on certain routes.

With the major airlines the cheaper fares generally require minimum and maximum stays (for instance, over a Saturday night or at least seven and no more than 30 days). Airlines generally allow some return date changes for a $25 to $50 fee, but most low-fare tickets are nonrefundable. Only a death in the family would prompt the airline to return any of your money if you cancel a nonrefundable ticket. However, you can apply an unused nonrefundable ticket toward a new ticket, again with a small fee. The lowest fare is subject to availability, and only a small percentage of the plane's total seats will be sold at that price. Contact the U.S. Department of Transportation's Office of Consumer Affairs (I–25, Washington, DC 20590, tel. 202/366–2220) for a copy of "Fly-Rights: A Guide to Air Travel in the U.S." *The Official Frequent Flyer Guidebook* (4715–C Town Center Dr., Colorado Springs, CO 80916, tel. 719/597–8899 or 800/487–8893; $14.99, + $3 shipping and handling), by Randy Petersen, yields valuable hints on getting the most for your air travel dollars. Also new and helpful is *202 Tips Even the Best Business Travelers May Not Know*, by Christopher McGinnis, president of the Travel Skills Group (Box 52927, Atlanta, GA 30355, tel. 404/659–2855; $10 in bookstores.)

Consolidators Consolidators or bulk-fare operators—"bucket shops"—buy blocks of seats on scheduled flights that airlines anticipate they won't be able to sell. They pay wholesale prices, add a markup, and resell the seats to travel agents or directly to the public at prices that still undercut the airline's promotional or discount fares (higher than a charter ticket but lower than an APEX ticket, and usually without the advance-purchase restriction). Moreover, some consolidators sometimes give you your money back. Carefully read the fine print detailing penalties for changes and cancellations. If you doubt the reliability of a company, call the airline once you've made your booking and confirm that you do, indeed, have a reservation on the flight.

The biggest U.S. consolidator, C.L. Thomson Express, sells only to travel agents. Well-established consolidators selling to the public include **UniTravel** (Box 12485, St. Louis, MO 63132, tel. 314/569–0900 or 800/325–2222); **Council Charter** (205 E. 42nd St., New York, NY 10017, tel. 212/661–0311 or 800/800–8222); and **Travac** (989 6th Ave., New York, NY 10018, tel. 212/563–3303 or 800/872–8800).

Discount Travel clubs offer their members unsold space on airplanes, cruise
Travel Clubs ships, and package tours at as much as 50% below regular prices. Membership may include a regular bulletin or access to a toll-free hot line giving details of available trips departing from three or four days to several months in the future. Most also offer 50% discounts off hotel rack rates, but double check with the hotel to make sure it isn't offering a better promotional rate independent of the club. Clubs include **Discount Travel International** (114 Forrest Ave., Suite 203, Narberth, PA 19072, tel. 215/668–7184; $45 annually, single or family), **Entertainment Travel Editions** (Box 1014 Trumbull, CT 06611, tel. 800/445–4137; price ranges $28–$48), **Great American Traveler** (Box 27965, Salt Lake City, UT 84127, tel. 800/548–2812; $29.95 annually), **Moment's Notice Discount Travel Club** (425 Madison Ave., New York, NY 10017, tel. 212/486–0503; $45 annually, single or family), **Privilege Card** (3391 Peachtree Rd. NE, Suite 110, Atlanta, GA 30326, tel. 404/262–0222 or 800/236–9732; domestic annual membership $49.95, international, $74.95), **Travelers Advantage** (CUC Travel Service, 49 Music Sq. W, Nashville, TN 37203, tel. 800/548–1116; $49 annually, single or family), and **Worldwide Discount Travel Club** (1674 Meridian Ave., Miami Beach, FL 33139, tel. 305/534–2082; $50 annually for family, $40 single).

Publications The newsletter "Travel Smart" (40 Beechdale Rd., Dobbs Ferry, NY 10522, tel. 800/327–3633; $44 a year) has a wealth of travel deals in each monthly issue. The monthly "Consumer Reports Travel Letter" (Consumers Union, 101 Truman Ave., Yonkers, NY 10703, tel. 800/234–1970) is filled with information on travel savings and indispensable consumer tips.

Enjoying the Fly at night, if you're able to sleep on a plane. Because the air aloft
Flight is dry, drink plenty of fluids while on board. Drinking alcohol contributes to jet lag, as do heavy meals. Bulkhead seats, in the front row of each cabin—usually reserved for people who have disabilities, are elderly, or are traveling with babies—offer more legroom, but trays attach awkwardly to seat armrests, and all possessions must be stowed overhead.

Smoking Since February 1990, smoking has been banned on all domestic flights of less than six hours' duration; the ban also applies to domestic segments of international flights aboard U.S. and foreign carriers. On U.S. carriers flying to Scotland and other destinations abroad, a seat in a no-smoking section must be provided for every passenger who requests one, and the section must be enlarged to accommodate such passengers if necessary as long as they have complied with the airline's deadline for check-in and seat assignment. If smoking bothers you, request a seat far from the smoking section.

Foreign airlines are exempt from these rules but do provide no-smoking sections, and some nations, including Canada, have gone as far as to ban smoking on all domestic flights; other countries may ban smoking on flights of less than a specified duration. The International Civil Aviation Organization has set July 1, 1996, as the date to ban smoking aboard airlines worldwide, but the body has no power to enforce its decisions.

From North America by Ship

Many of the transatlantic crossings are repositioning cruises for ships that cruise the Caribbean in winter and European waters in summer. Sometimes rates are reduced, and fly/cruise packages are usually available. Check with the cruise lines for the latest information.

Cunard Line (555 5th Ave., New York, NY 10017, tel. 212/880–7500 or 800/528–6273) operates the *Queen Elizabeth (QE2)* on the only regular transatlantic crossings sailing between New York City and Southampton, England, from April through December.

Other cruise lines whose ships are in Europe for the summer and the Caribbean for the winter make repositioning crossings: eastbound in spring and westbound in fall. Check the travel pages of your Sunday newspaper or contact a travel agent for lines and sailing dates.

From England by Plane

Together **British Airways** and **British Midland** operate some 17 flights to Edinburgh and 18 to Glasgow each weekday from London Heathrow. **British Midland, European, Gill Air, BusinessAir,** and **Air U.K.** also connect Scotland with English airports, including London Gatwick.

From England by Train

There are two main rail routes to Scotland from the south of England. The first, the west coast main line, runs from London Euston to Glasgow Central via Rugby, Crewe, Preston, and Carlisle; it takes just over five hours to make the 400-mile trip to central Scotland, and service is frequent and reliable, with one train every two hours on the average. Some trains have portions for Edinburgh that are detached at Carstairs. Useful for daytime travel to the Scottish Highlands, and equipped with an excellent restaurant car, the *Clansman* is the direct train to Stirling and Aviemore, terminating at Inverness. For a restful route to the Scottish Highlands, take the overnight sleeper service, with air-conditioned, soundproof sleeping carriages, which runs from London Euston, departing in late evening, to Perth, Stirling, Aviemore, and Inverness, where it arrives the following morning; family compartments are available.

The second route is the east coast main line from London King's Cross to Edinburgh via Newcastle and Durham, crossing into Scotland at Berwick-upon-Tweed; it provides the quickest trip to the Scottish capital, and between 8 AM and 6 PM there are 15 trains to Edinburgh, three of them through to Aberdeen. Limited-stop expresses like the *Flying Scotsman* make the 393-mile London to Edinburgh journey in around four hours. Connecting services to most parts of Scotland—particularly the Western Highlands—are much better from Edinburgh than from Glasgow. For travel to Glasgow Queen Street from Edinburgh there is half-hourly service, with the fast trains taking only 45 minutes.

Trains from elsewhere in England are good: There is regular service from Birmingham, Manchester, Liverpool, Bristol, Southampton, and Penzance to Glasgow and Edinburgh. From Harwich (the port of call for ships from Holland, Germany, and Denmark), you can travel to Glasgow via Manchester. But it is faster to change at Peterborough for the east coast main line to Edinburgh.

Reservations for all sleeper services are essential.

From England by Bus

Coaches (as long-distance and touring buses are usually called) provide the cheapest way to travel between England and Scotland; fares are approximately one-third of the rail fares for comparable trips. About 20 companies operate service between major cities, including **Scottish Citylink Coaches** and **National Express.** Journey time between London and Glasgow or Edinburgh is 8 to $8\frac{1}{2}$ hours, and the coaches run day and night. Most are quite comfortable; some have food service and videos on board.

The main London terminal is Victoria Coach Station, but some Scottish companies use Gloucester Road Coach Station in west London, near the Penta Hotel. Many people travel to Scotland by coach; in summer a reservation three or four days ahead is advisable. For timetables, contact Scottish Citylink Coaches (Buchanan Bus Station, Killermont St., Glasgow, G2 3NP, tel. 0141/332–9191). Travel centers and travel agents also have details, and some travel agents sell tickets.

Staying in Scotland

Getting Around

By Plane Although a small country, Scotland has a significant internal air network. Major carriers include **British Airways** and **Loganair.**

By Train Scotland has a good rail network extending all the way to Thurso and Wick, the most northerly stations in the British Isles. Lowland services, most of which originate in Glasgow or Edinburgh, are generally fast and reliable. A shuttle makes the 45-minute trip between the cities every half hour. (For information about Edinburgh's and Glasgow's train stations, *see* Chapters 4 and 5, respectively.)

Some lines in Scotland—all suburban services and lines north and west of Inverness—operate on one class only (standard). Long-distance services carry buffet and refreshment cars.

Fares Train fares vary according to class of ticket purchased and distance traveled. The fare system is complex. Before you buy your ticket, be sure to stop at the Information Office/Travel Center first and request the lowest fare to your destination and information about any special offers. Find out about *InterCity Saver* and about the *Family Railcard* if children are with you. Note that your ticket does *not* guarantee you a seat. For that you need a seat reservation, which must be made and paid for separately at a cost of £1 *per train* on your itinerary (that is, £2 if you need to book seats on two trains). You can opt to sit facing toward or away from the engine, and in a smoking or nonsmoking compartment.

Scenic Routes Although many routes in Scotland run through extremely attractive countryside, several stand out: from Glasgow to Oban via Loch Lomond; to Fort William and Mallaig via Rannoch (ferry connection to Skye); from Edinburgh to Inverness via the Forth Bridge and Perth; from Inverness to Kyle of Lochalsh and to Wick; and from Inverness to Aberdeen. One word of caution: There are very few trains in the Highlands on Sundays.

A luxury private train, the *Royal Scotsman,* does scenic tours, partly under steam power, with banquets en route. Book through Abercrombie & Kent (Sloane Square House, Holbein Pl., London SW1W 8NS, tel. 0171/730–9600; or 1420 Kensington Rd., Oak Brook, IL 60521, tel. 312/954–2944 or 800/323–7308); cost ranges from $2,490 for three days to $5,700 for six days. **British Rail** offers occasional Pullman rail cruises, partly steam-hauled, on the *Orcadian* and *West Highlander* (£250–£300 from London, depending on the season); every passenger gets a window seat, and overnights are in sleeper compartments or hotels. Details are available from the London (Euston) Travel Center; book through **InterCity Scottish Land Cruises** (Box 4472, Lichfield, Staffordshire WS13 6RU, tel. 01543/254076).

Rail Passes Many rail passes must be purchased stateside. The **Freedom of Scotland Travelpass,** sold at most stations in Scotland, some in England, and at travel agencies throughout the United States, offers unlimited travel on Scotland's rail network (with a few exceptions relating to day tours, historic steam engine excursions, and the like). With the pass you also travel free on Caledonian MacBrayne's west coast ferries, and for 33% less on many bus routes. Cost is £99 for eight days, £139 for 15 days ($145 and $205 when purchased in the United States). *See also* Rail and Bus Passes, and Hints for Older Travelers, *above.*

By Bus The country's bus network is extensive. Bus service is comprehensive in cities, less so in country districts. Express service links main cities and towns, connecting, for example, Glasgow and Edinburgh to Inverness, Aberdeen, Perth, Skye, Ayr, Dumfries, and Carlisle; or Inverness with Aberdeen, Wick, Thurso, and Fort William. These express services are very fast, and fares are quite reasonable.

For details, contact any bus station or the **Travel Center** (Buchanan Street Bus Station, Glasgow G2 3NP, tel. 0141/332–9191); **S.M.T.** (St. Andrew Bus Station, Edinburgh EH1 3DU, tel. 0131/556–8464); and **Edinburgh and Scotland Information Centre** (3 Princes St., Edinburgh EH2 2QP, tel. 0131/557–1700).

For town, suburban, or short-distance journeys, you normally buy your ticket on the bus, from a paybox or the driver. Sometimes you need exact change. For longer journeys—for example, Glasgow–Inverness—it is usual to reserve and pay at the bus station booking office.

By Ferry With so many islands, plus the great Firth of Clyde waterway, ferry services in Scotland are of paramount importance. Most of these now transport vehicles as well as foot passengers, although a number of the smaller ones are passengers only.

The main operator is **Caledonian MacBrayne Ltd.** (Ferry Terminal, Gourock PA19 1QP, tel. 01475/650100, fax 01475/637607), known generally as Calmac. Services extend from the Firth of Clyde, where there is an extremely extensive network, right up to the northwest of Scotland and all of the Hebrides. Calmac offers an **Island Rover** runabout ticket, which is ideal for touring holidays in the islands, as well as an island-hopping scheme called **Island Hopscotch.**

The Dunoon–Gourock route on the Clyde, as well as a run from Islay (Port Askaig) to Jura is served by **Western Ferries** (16 Woodside Crescent, Glasgow G3 7UT, tel. 0141/332–9766).

P & O Ferries (Jamieson's Quay, Box 5, Aberdeen AB9 8DL, tel. 01224/572615, fax 01224/574411) operates a car ferry for the Orkney Islands between Scrabster (near Thurso) and Stromness (on the main island of Orkney, called Mainland). The main ferries, the *St. Clair* and the *St. Sunniva*, have cabin accommodations and sail five times a week in each direction.

By Car
Types of Roads

A very good network of superhighways, known as motorways, and divided highways, known as dual carriageways, extends throughout Britain, though in the remoter areas of Scotland where the motorway has not penetrated, travel is noticeably slower. Motorways shown with the prefix "M" are mainly two or three lanes in each direction, without any right-hand turns. If you'll be covering longer distances, these are the roads to use, though inevitably you'll see less of the countryside. Service areas are about an hour apart or less. Dual carriageways, usually shown on a map as a thick red line (often with a black line in the center) and the prefix "A" followed by a number perhaps with a bracket "T" (for example, A304[T]), are similar to motorways, except that right turns are sometimes permitted and you'll find both traffic lights and traffic circles on them.

The vast network of other main roads, which typical maps show as either single red "A" roads, or narrower brown "B" roads, also numbered, are for the most part the old coach and turnpike roads built for horses and carriages in the last century or earlier. Travel along these roads is much slower because passing is more difficult, and your trip may take twice the time it would take along a motorway. On the other hand, you'll see much more of Scotland.

Minor roads (shown as yellow or white on most maps, unlettered and unnumbered) are the ancient lanes and byways of Britain, roads that are not only living history but a superb way of discovering the real Scotland. You have to drive along them slowly and carefully— sometimes there isn't even room for two vehicles to pass, and you must reverse into a passing place if you meet an oncoming car or tractor.

Rules of the Road

The most noticeable difference for the visitor is that when in Britain, you drive on the left. This takes a bit of getting used to, but it doesn't take very long, particularly if you're driving a British car where the steering and mirrors will be adjusted for U.K. conditions. You should be particularly careful if you have picked up your car at the airport, to give yourself time to adjust to driving on the left—especially if you have jet lag.

One of the most complicated questions facing visitors to Britain is that of speed limits. In urban areas, except for certain freeways, it is generally 30 miles per hour (mph), but it is 40 mph on some main roads, as indicated by circular red signs. In rural areas the official limit is 60 mph on ordinary roads and 70 mph on motorways—and traffic police can be hard on speeders, especially in urban areas. In other respects procedures are similar to those in the United States.

Gasoline

Though costs have been remarkably stable in recent years, you can expect to pay a good deal more for gasoline than in the United

States, about £2 a gallon (45p a liter) for 4-star—up to 10p a gallon higher in remote rural locations. Remember, too, that the British Imperial gallon is about 20% more in volume than the U.S. gallon. What you may find confusing is that although service stations advertise prices by the gallon (mainly for the benefit of the conservative British who continue to resist metrification), pumps actually measure in liters. A British gallon is approximately 4.5 liters.

Most gas stations stock 4-star (97 octane), unleaded and super unleaded, plus diesel. Service stations are located at regular intervals on motorways and are usually open 24 hours a day, though stations elsewhere usually close from 9 PM to 7 AM, and in country areas many close at 6 PM and all day on Sundays.

Auto Clubs If you belong to a motoring organization, look into reciprocal membership benefits, including breakdown assistance, available with the Automobile Association (AA) in Britain. If your auto club doesn't have such arrangements, consider taking out an associate membership in the **AA** (Fanum House, Basingstoke, Hants, RG2I 2EA, tel. 01256/20123, fax 01256/492440) or the **Royal Automobile Club** (RAC House, Bartlett St., Box 10, Croydon, Surrey CR2 6XW, tel. 0181/686–2525), available to overseas visitors. Their large touring departments offer a wealth of detailed information about motoring in Britain.

By Bicycle Because Scotland's main roads are continually being upgraded, it is easier than ever for bicyclists to access the network of quieter rural roads in such areas as Dumfries and Galloway, the Borders, and much of eastern Scotland, especially Grampian. Still, care must be taken in getting from some town centers to rural riding areas, so if in doubt, ask a local. In a few areas of the Highlands, notably in northwestern Scotland, the rugged nature of the terrain and limited population have resulted in the lack of side roads, making it more difficult—sometimes impossible—to plan a minor-road route in these areas.

The best months for cycling in Scotland are May, June, and September, when the roads are often quieter and the weather is usually better. Winds are predominantly from the southwest, so plan your route accordingly.

A variety of agencies are now promoting "safe routes" for recreational cyclists in Scotland. These routes are signposted, and the agencies have produced maps or leaflets showing where they run. Perhaps best known is the Glasgow–Lock Lomond–Killin Cycleway, which makes use of former railway track beds, forest trails, quiet rural side roads, and some main roads. The Glasgow to Irvine Cycle Route runs south and west of Glasgow and links with the Johnstone and Greenock Railway Path. In Edinburgh there is the Innocent Railway Path from Holyrood Path to St. Leonards. Contact the relevant tourist board for more information.

Cycling People in Scotland were cycling off-road long before the mountain
Off-Road bike was invented. Sometimes they cycled over rights of way in the Highlands; sometimes they biked cross-country to shorten the time taken to climb less accessible high hills. The growing popularity of mountain biking, however, has forced the Scots to focus on the suitability and availability of routes.

Scotland's legal position on off-road cycling is complex. Cycling is covered by road traffic laws because a bike is classified as a vehicle. In a strict legal sense, cycling off-road is only possible on specifically designated cycle tracks, routes that have a common-law right of way for cycles, or routes that have the consent of the landowner. Legally, cyclists are not allowed on pedestrian rights of way, but many landowners don't mind if cyclists use them. Nevertheless, it is best for off-road cyclists to seek local advice when planning routes.

Bikes on Trains The business of transporting bikes by rail has become less straightforward in the past few years, with limitations placed on both luggage and cycle space. Scotrail strongly advises making a reservation for you and your bike at least a month in advance. On several trains, reservations are compulsory. A leaflet containing the latest information is available through Scotrail and can be picked up at most manned train stations within Scotland.

Bikes on Ferries Bicycles can be taken without any restrictions on car and passenger ferries in Scotland, and it is not generally necessary to book in advance. The three main ferry service operators are **Caledonian MacBrayne** (The Pier, Gourock PA19 1QP, Renfrewshire, tel. 01475/650100) and **Western Ferries** (16 Woodside Crescent, Glasgow G3 7UT, tel. 0141/3329766), both of which carry accompanied bicycles free, and **P & O Ferries** (Orkney & Shetland Services, Jamieson's Quay, Aberdeen AB9 8DL, tel. 01224/572615 for Aberdeen-Lerwick, 01856/850655 for Scrabster-Stromness, and 01224/572615 for Aberdeen-Stromness), which charges from £6 to £10 in addition to the cost of a passenger ticket and requires cycles to be checked in early so that they can be loaded through the boat's cargo entrance.

Bikes on Buses Although some rural bus services will transport cycles if space is available, you usually can't count on getting your bike on a bus. Be sure to check well in advance with the appropriate bus company.

Useful Publications The Scottish Tourist Board's free brochure "Adventure and Special Interest Holidays," published annually, lists prepackaged vacations that may included cycling; its free "Cycling in Scotland" brochure has some suggested routes and practical advice. More detailed information on long routes, day trips, and accommodations is given in the guidebook *Cycling in Scotland*, available from Canongate Press (14 Frederick St., Edinburgh EH2 2HB) for £6.99, including postage. The Ordnance Survey Landranger series of maps, which shows gradient, is invaluable for cyclists.

Organizations **Cyclists' Touring Club** (National Headquarters, Cotterell House, 69 Medrow, Godalming, Surrey, GU7 3HS, England, tel. 01483/417217) actively campaigns for better cyclist facilities throughout the United Kingdom. It publishes a members magazine, route maps, and guides.

Sustrans LTD (53 Cochrane St., Glasgow G1 1HL, tel. 0141/552–8241) is a nonprofit organization dedicated to providing environmentally friendly routes for cyclists, notably in and around cities.

Bicycle Tours Ian Pragnell of **Bespoke Highland Tours** (The Bothy, Camusdarach, Inverness-shire PH39 4NT, tel. 016875/272) arranges treks throughout the Highlands and the islands for cyclists of all abilities. **Scottish Border Trails** (Drummore, Venlaw High Rd., Peebles EH45 87RL, tel. 01721/720336, fax 01721/723004) runs off-road mountain bike treks in the Borders and vehicle-supported road tours on which your luggage is ferried between stops. **Wildcat Mountain Bike Tours** (Foinaven, 52 Westerlee Dr., Bridge of Allan, Stirling FK9 4DQ, tel. 01786/8933447) sells guided, vehicle-supported tours throughout Scotland for novices and experts.

Telephones

The public telephone system in Britain is generally reliable, and an ongoing modernization program ensures continuing improvement. Public telephone boxes use coins or convenient phone cards, which can be purchased at post offices and at newsstands and other shops.

Long-Distance Calls The country code for Scotland is 44. Area codes in England, Northern Ireland, Scotland, and Wales were changed at press time, in order to increase the United Kingdom's telephone-system capacity. The number 1 was added after the initial 0 of all area codes. For example, Glasgow's 041 area code became 0141. To call Scotland from the United States you do not dial the initial 0, but when calling city to city within Scotland, you must dial the 0. Until April 16, 1995, both the old and new codes will work; after that date, you must use the new codes, which are listed in this book. Keep this in mind when using phone numbers from other sources, which may not reflect the change. Cellular phone numbers and the 0800 toll-free code are not affected.

To make international calls *from* Scotland, you must use the international access code, which has also changed—from 010 to 00. To call North America, dial 00–1–area code–number.

AT&T, MCI, and Sprint provide direct access to their operators through the following services: **AT&T USA Direct** (tel. 800/874–4000, 0500/890011 in Scotland), **MCI Call USA** (tel. 800/444–4444, 0800/890222 in Scotland), and **Sprint Express** (tel. 800/793–1153, 0800/890877 in Scotland). All three companies offer message delivery services to international travelers and issue telephone debit cards, which make it unnecessary to carry lots of change.

Mail

Postal Rates Airmail letters to the United States and Canada cost 41p, postcards 35p, aerograms 36p. Letters and postcards to Europe under 20 grams cost 30p (25p to other European Union member countries). Within the U.K. first-class letters cost 25p, second-class letters and postcards 19p.

Receiving Mail If you're uncertain where you'll be staying, you can arrange to have your mail sent to American Express. The service is free to cardholders; all others pay a small fee. You can also collect letters at Edinburgh's main post office; address them Poste Restante, Head Post Office, 2 Waterloo Place, Edinburgh, Scotland.

Tipping

Some restaurants and most hotels add a service charge of 10%–15% to the bill. In this case you are not expected to tip. If no service charge is indicated, add 10% to your total bill, but always check first. Taxi drivers should also get 10%, hairdressers and barbers 10%–15%. You are not expected to tip theater or movie theater ushers, elevator operators, or bartenders in pubs.

Opening and Closing Times

Banks Except on public holidays, banks are open weekdays 9:30–3:30, some days to 4:45. Some banks have extended hours on Thursday evenings, and a few are open on Saturday mornings. Some also close for an hour at lunchtime. The major airports operate 24-hour banking services seven days a week.

Shops   Usual business hours are Monday–Saturday 9–5:30. Outside the main centers, most shops observe an early closing day once a week, often Wednesday or Thursday—they close at 1 PM and do not reopen until the following morning. In small villages, many also close for lunch. Department stores in large cities stay open for late-night shopping (usually until 7:30 or 8) one day a week. Apart from some newsstands and small food stores, almost all shops are closed on Sunday.

Shopping

The best buys in Britain in general are antiques, craft items, woolen goods, china, men's shoes, books, confectionery, and toys. In Scotland, many visitors go for tweeds, designer knitwear, Shetland and Fair Isle woolens, tartan rugs and fabrics, Edinburgh crystal, Caithness glass, malt whisky, Celtic silver, and pebble jewelry. The Scottish Highlands bristle with old *bothies* (farm buildings) that have been turned into small craft workshops where visitors are welcome—but not pressured—to buy attractive handmade items of bone, silver, wood, pottery, leather, and glass. Handmade chocolates, often with whisky or Drambuie fillings, and the traditional "petticoat tail" shortbread in tin boxes are popular; so, too, at a more mundane level, are boiled sweets in jars from particular localities—Berwick cockles, Jethart snails, Edinburgh rock, and similar crunchy items. Dundee cake, a rich fruit mixture with almonds on top, and Dundee marmalades and heather honeys are among the other eatables that visitors take home from Scotland.

Dining

Scottish restaurants are noted for helpful attention and modest prices, rather than for their exotic or imaginative cuisine. In all districts you will find restaurants that have risen, or are beginning to rise, above the old dull stereotyped level—but they are still in the minority.

City Scots usually take their midday meals in a pub, wine bar, bistro, or department store restaurant (which may be nonalcoholic and nonsmoking). When traveling, the Scot generally eats inexpensively and quickly at a country pub or village tearoom. Places like Glasgow, Edinburgh, and Aberdeen, of course, offer restaurants of cosmopolitan character and various price levels; of these, the more notable tend to open only in the evening. Most smaller towns and many villages have at least one restaurant where—certainly if a local is in charge—the service is a reminder of a Highland tradition that ensured that no stranger could travel through the country without receiving a welcome.

In a country so involved in the tourism industry, "all day" meal places are becoming quite widespread. The normal lunch period, however, is 12:30–2:30. A few places offer "high tea"—one hot dish and masses of cakes, bread and butter, and jam, served with tea only, around 5:30–6:30.

To start the day with a full stomach, try a "traditional Scottish breakfast," which consists of bacon and fried eggs, served with sausage, fried mushrooms and tomatoes, and, often, fried bread or potato scones. Most places also serve kippers (smoked herring). All this is in addition to juice, porridge, cereal, toast, and other bread products. It is possible to eat a healthier breakfast—fruit, for example, is on most hotel menus—but the high-cholesterol temptations are conventional in Scotland.

You will come across restaurants that offer "A Taste of Scotland" menu, full of oddly named traditional dishes often cooked and served in traditional pots and pans. The Taste of Scotland scheme, initiated by the Scottish Tourist Board, has helped— almost by accident—to preserve some of the Scots language, especially the names for a variety of traditional dishes.

Lodging

In many small towns and villages there are inns and hotels that offer central heating, rooms with bath or shower and telephone and television, and other comforts at competitive prices. But rural Scotland is bed-and-breakfast land, and, because Scottish breakfasts are nothing if not hearty, these lodging places represent a very good value. Indeed, they can be hard to beat, especially since most offer genuinely warm hospitality, as well as home cooking and comforts. (Do note, however, that bed-and-breakfasts are generally owned and occupied by a family, which means you cannot expect the same sort of service you would receive at 5-crown hotels.) The Scottish Tourist Board's *Scotland: Hotels and Guest Houses* (£7.90 by mail) and *Scotland Bed and Breakfast* (£5.80) together give details of more than 4,000 bed-and-breakfasts.

Hotels   Hotels in the larger cities are generally also good. Glasgow and Edinburgh boast a number of very superior establishments, as well as an extensive range of good hotels in all other price categories.

If you are touring around, you are not likely to be stranded: In recent years, even in the height of the season—July and August—hotel occupancy has run at about 80%. On the other hand, if you arrive in Edinburgh at festival time or some place where a big Highland Gathering or golf tournament is in progress, your choice of accommodations will be extremely limited, and your best bet will be to try for a room in a nearby village. To secure your first choice, it's always a good idea to reserve in advance, either through a travel agent at home, directly with the lodging place, or through local Information Centres (*see* the individual city or regional chapters), making use of their "Book-a-Bed-Ahead" services. Telephone bookings made from home should be confirmed by letter, and country hotels expect you to turn up by about 6 PM.

Home Exchange   You can find a house, apartment, or other vacation property to exchange for your own by becoming a member of a home-exchange organization, which then sends you its annual directories listing available exchanges and includes your own listing in at least one of them. Arrangements for the actual exchange are made by the two parties to it, not by the organization. For more information contact the **International Home Exchange Association** (IHEA, 41 Sutter St., Suite 1090, San Francisco, CA 94104, tel. 415/673–0347 or 800/788–2489). Principal clearinghouses include: **Intervac International** (Box 590504, San Francisco, CA 94159, tel. 415/435–3497) with three annual directories; membership is $62, or $72 if you want to receive the directories but remain unlisted. **Loan-a-Home** (2 Park La., Apt. 6E, Mount Vernon, NY 10552, tel. 914/664–7640) specializes in long-term exchanges; there is no charge to list your home, but the directories cost $35 or $45 depending on the number you receive.

Apartment and Villa Rentals

If you want a home base that's roomy enough for a family and comes with cooking facilities, a furnished rental may be the solution. It's generally cost-wise, too, although not always—some rentals are luxury properties (economical only when your party is large). Home-exchange directories do list rentals—often second homes owned by prospective house swappers—and some services search for a house or apartment for you (even a castle if that's your fancy) and handle the paperwork. Some send an illustrated catalogue and others send photographs of specific properties, sometimes at a charge; up-front registration fees may apply.

Among the companies are **At Home Abroad** (405 E. 56th St., Suite 6H, New York, NY 10022, tel. 212/421–9165); **Europa-Let** (92 N. Main St., Ashland, OR 97520, tel. 503/482–5806 or 800/462–4486); **Property Rentals International** (1 Park West Circle, Suite 108, Midlothian, VA 23113, tel. 804/378–6054 or 800/220–3332); **The Invented City** (*see* IHEA, *above*); and **Vacation Home Rentals Worldwide** (235 Kensington Ave., Norwood, NJ 07648, tel. 201/767–9393 or 800/633–3284). **Hideaways International** (767 Islington St., Box 4433, Portsmouth, NH 03802, tel. 603/430–4433 or 800/843–4433) functions as a travel club. Membership ($99 yearly per person or family at the same address) includes two annual guides plus quarterly newsletters; rentals are arranged directly between members, not by the club staff.

Farmhouse and Crofting Holidays

A popular option for families with children is a farmhouse holiday, combining the freedom of bed-and-breakfast accommodations with the hospitality of Scottish family life. Information is available from the BTA, from **Scottish Farmhouse Holidays** (5 Drumtenant, Ladybank, Fife, KY7 7UG, Scotland, tel. 01337/830451), and from the **Farm Holiday Bureau** (National Agricultural Centre, Stoneleigh, Warwickshire, England CV8 2LZ, tel. 01203/696909).

Ratings

Scotland was the first part of the United Kingdom to run a national "Classification and Grading Scheme" to take some of the guesswork out of booking accommodations. Though Fodor's does not use this rating system, you will see it in Scottish publications, and when you are considering a hotel, guest house, or bed-and-breakfast, make sure that you pay close attention to its classification and its grading. The classification part is easy. The number of crowns from zero to five tells you the range of the establishment's facilities. Zero crowns (confusingly described as "Listed") is basic; five crowns luxury. The grading part is actually more important. It purports to assess the quality of the place objectively. Very roughly, the ordinary is "Approved," the good "Commended," the very good "Highly Commended," and the "De Luxe" the best of all. Thus a two-crown "Highly Commended" is probably better value all around than a four-crown "Approved." The awards are part of the accommodations listing in the *Where to Stay* guides distributed at most tourist information centers. Not all establishments participate, but the scheme is becoming popular.

Credit Cards

The following credit-card abbreviations have been used: AE, American Express; DC, Diners Club; MC, MasterCard; V, Visa. It's a good idea to call ahead to check current credit-card policies.

Great Itineraries

Scottish tourist authorities have developed numerous tourist trails that encompass everything from Scotland's brooding castles to its pungent whisky distilleries. However, you should probably avoid these thematic trails during the height of summer, when crowds and coaches tend to swarm the best-known sights. The following recommended itineraries, conceived independently of the tourist board, are offered as a guide in planning individual travel.

The Seaways of the West

From Glasgow, you and your rental car can escape into the Western Highlands in under two hours, using a short ferry crossing to save time. Then, if it isn't raining, you'll discover why the romantic landscapes of the west, with their vanished clans and tales of Bonnie Prince Charlie, continue to hold an intense fascination for visitors.

Duration Four to nine days.

The Main Route **One to two nights:** Go west from Glasgow on the A8 along the south bank of the meandering River Clyde to reach Wemyss Bay on the A78. Catch the ferry for the old-fashioned holiday resort of Rothesay on the island of Bute. Tour the hinterland and leave the island via the five-minute Rhubodach–Colintraive ferry and enjoy the typical western scenery around Cowal.

One night: Go south to Lochgilphead, take a quick peak at the Caledonian Canal, then head for Tarbert and the peninsular Mull of Kintyre. If you crave island scenery, you can hop across to the tiny island of Gigha. Otherwise, continue south toward Campbeltown.

One to three nights: Return north through Lochgilphead and head for Oban, a busy ferryport where tartan kitsch and tour buses form the backdrop. Cross from Oban to the dramatic Isle of Mull, eventually arriving at the tiny Isle of Iona, the ancient burial place of Scottish kings. Leave Iona and Mull via the Fishnish–Lochaline ferry, then loop north toward Acharacle for magnificent views of the small isles of Rhum, Eigg, and Muck.

One to three nights: If time permits continue west to Mallaig, a ferryport with connections to the rugged and wild Isle of Skye. Otherwise, head east to Fort William, taking the A82 southwards toward the famous Loch Lomond before returning to Glasgow.

Border Byways

If the bustle of Edinburgh makes you yearn for rural tranquility, discover the romance of the villages and rolling hills that perch on the English–Scottish border. In terms of scenery it's a far cry from the remote Highlands, but there's still plenty of castles and abbeys to explore.

Duration Three to five days.

The Main Route **One to two nights:** Leave Edinburgh via the A1, then abandon the A1 in favor of more scenic rural roads at the pleasant little town of Haddington. Head cross-country for Gifford, an attractive village tucked into the well-kept East Lothian countryside. Follow the B6355 through the Lammermuir Hills—peaceful, lonely hills with a strong hint of the Highland moors—before dropping into the small town of Duns.

One to two nights: From Duns you can either divert to Berwick-upon-Tweed, which is, strictly speaking, on the English side of the border; or go south to Kelso, which has a ruined abbey. Continue on the A698 to Jedburgh, an older border town with a well-preserved abbey.

One to two nights: From Jedburgh continue south on the B6375 (via Newcastleton) to Liddesdale, scene of many an ancient cross-border raid. The road eventually reaches Annan and the large, tourist-friendly town of Dumfries.

One to two nights: Take the A701 from Dumfries to Moffat, where you can pick up the A708 for St. Mary's Loch and the waterfall at Grey Mare's Tail. Souvenir hunters will want to make a brief stop in the tidy town of Peebles before returning to Edinburgh.

Anything But the Main Route

If you're on a whirlwind tour of Scotland, this driving tour offers discriminating adventurers the chance of skirting the tourist horde while still experiencing some of the country's better-known sights. A car is indispensable, as is a good road map and a love of driving. This nearly circular tour starts in Dunfermline and ends in either Perth or Edinburgh, but it could be done in either direction.

Duration Four to seven days.

The Main Route **One to two nights:** From Dunfermline, the ancient capital of Scotland and the birthplace of Andrew Carnegie, take the A823 northwest. This soon cuts through the green and rounded Ochil Hills, giving good views of the nearby Highlands. You can browse for antiques in Auchterarder before continuing to the pleasant Highland-edge town of Crieff (another good spot for bargain hunters).

One to two nights: From Crieff follow the A822 north into the Highlands through the Sma'Glen, but keep your eyes open for a sign marked GLEN QUAICH and KENMORE. This route rises through moors before zigzagging steeply down to the east end of Loch Tay. Head to Fortigall to join, a little way east, the B846. Take this high road over the hills to Tummel Bridge, then go east to join the main and busy A9 (there is no other option here). At Dalwhinnie take the A86 (via Loch Laggan) to cosmopolitan Fort William.

One night: From Fort William take the A82 north past Loch Lochy to Fort Augustus. Leave the busy A82 and keep to the scenic east bank of Loch Ness—home to the fabled and feared Loch Ness Monster (locals call her Nessie). Continue to Inverness.

One to three nights: From Inverness take the A96 and then the A939 to Cawdor Castle, the haunting ground of Shakespeare's Macbeth. Continue south on the A939 and cross the wilds of Dava Moor to reach handsome Grantown-on-Spey. Continue toward Tomintoul and the Royal Deeside region (also known as Castle Country), stopping off at one of the region's many dramatic keeps—perhaps the castles at Corgarff, Balmoral, or Braemar. You can detour along the A93 to Aberdeen, a pleasant but commercial port city. Otherwise, rejoin the A9 and head south to Pitlochry, home to the Edradour Distillery, which claims to be the smallest single-malt distillery in Scotland. Head south along the banks of the River Tummel, joining the B867 at Dunkeld. Continue south for Perth and Edinburgh.

The Highlands and Islands by Bike

Happiness is zooming down a steep coastal hill with horizon-wide views of the rugged Highlands. Biking the eastern side of Scotland, around Aberdeen, is saner since the landscape is mostly soft and gentle. But in the coastal Highlands, from Oban to the Isle of Skye to Inverness, the country turns raw and wild. Cycling in this environment requires more than a little stamina, though dining and lodging facilities are generally closely spaced. The following itinerary starts in Glasgow and ends in Inverness. Some sections take advantage of specially designated cycle routes; others follow main and secondary roads where you must be wary of vehicular traffic. No matter what time of year you visit, bring a rain suit.

Duration Eight to 14 days.

The Main Route **One night:** From Glasgow take the train to Paisley to link with the Glasgow–Irvine Pedestrian and Cycle Route (maps available from Tourist Information Centers). From Paisley via Lochwinnoch and Kilwinning, the next 30 miles lead through tame countryside to Androssan, where you can catch a summer ferry to Brodick, on Arran island.

One to two nights: From Brodick follow the A841 clockwise around the island; or, if you're short in time, turn north toward Lochranza, where there's a frequent summer-only ferry to Claonaig. Continue to the quiet town of Kenncaraig or larger Tarbert.

One to two nights: If time permits, follow the B8024 clockwise around Knapdale for outstanding views of the Hebridean islands. Otherwise, continue north from Tarbert along the western bank of Loch Gilp. Your final destination in either case is the small, very pleasant town of Lochgilphead.

One to two nights: Take the minor road (B840) northeast to Ford at the southern end of Loch Awe, Scotland's longest loch. You can make a quick detour to Carnasserie Castle, just off the A816, or continue along the loch's northwestern side to the B845 junction. Follow the B845 to Taynuilt, where there's an unlabeled backroad to Oban via Glen Lonan.

One night: North of Oban there are summer ferries to Craignure, on the Isle of Mull. On Mull, follow the A849 south past Torosay and Duart castles, then circle northward on the B8035 to reach Fishnish Pier, connected by ferry during summer with Lochaline. On the mainland, follow the A884 north to Strontian or Salen.

One night: Continue north along the coast, past Loch Ailort, to the A830 junction. Head west, either to Arisaig or Mallaig.

One to three nights: Summer ferries connect Mallaig with the rugged Isle of Skye. If you're pressed for time, head north on the A851, then east on the A850 for Kyle of Lochalsh—a five-minute ferry ride from the mainland. Otherwise, the A850 leads northwest to the lovely town of Portree and to the wild, spectacular seascapes of northern Skye. When you're ready, backtrack to the Kyle of Lochalsh ferry.

One to two nights: Continue northeast via the villages of Plockton and Stromeferry. It's a demanding uphill ride around the banks of

Loch Carron, but there's plenty of accommodation in Lochcarron, and the subsequent ride between Ardarroch and Shieldaig is spectacular. So, too, is the short ride between Shieldaig and Torridon. From Torridon, bike 20 miles to Achnasheen and continue by bike or train to Inverness.

2 Portraits of Scotland

Scotland at a Glance: A Chronology

c 3000 BC Neolithic migration from Mediterranean: "chambered cairn" people in north, "beaker people" in southeast

c 300 BC Iron Age: infusion of Celtic peoples from the south and from Ireland; "Gallic forts," "brochs" built

AD 79–89 Julius Agricola, Roman governor of Britain, invades Scotland; Scots tribes defeated at Mons Graupius (Grampians): "they make a desert and call it peace." Roman forts built at Inchtuthil and Ardoch

142 Emperor Antoninus Pius orders Antonine Wall built between the Firths of Forth and Clyde

185 Antonine Wall abandoned

367 Massive invasion of Britain by Picts, Scots, Saxons, Franks

400–1000 Era of the Four Peoples: red-haired Picts in the north, Gaelic-speaking Scots and Britons in the west and south, Germanic Angles in the east. Origins of Arthur legend (Arthur's Seat, Ben Arthur). Picts, with bloodline through mothers, eventually dominate 392 Ninian's mission to Picts: first Christian chapel at Whitehorn

563 Columba establishes monastery at Iona

780–1065 Scandinavian invasions; Hebrides remain Norse until 1263, Orkney and Shetland until 1472

1005–1034 Malcolm II unifies Scotland and (temporarily) repels the English

1040 Malcolm's heir, Duncan, is slain by his rival, Macbeth, whose wife has a claim to the throne

The House of Canmore

1057 Malcolm III, known as "Canmore" ("Big Head"), murders Macbeth and assumes the throne

1093 Death of Malcolm's queen, St. Margaret, founder of modern Edinburgh

1124–1153 David I, "soir sanct" (sore saint), builds the abbeys of Jedburgh (1118), Kelso (1128), Melrose (1136), and Dryburgh (1150) and brings Norman culture to Scotland

1290 The first of many attempts to unite Scotland peacefully with England fails when the Scots queen Margaret, "the Maid of Norway," dies on the way to her wedding to Edward, son of Edward I of England. The Scots naively ask Edward I (subsequently known as "the hammer of the Scots") to arbitrate between the remaining 13 claimants to the throne. Edward's choice, John Balliol, is known as "toom tabard" (empty coat)

1295 Under continued threat from England, Scotland signs its first treaty of the "auld alliance" with France. Wine trade flourishes

1297 Revolt. William Wallace, immortalized by Burns, leads the Scots against the English

1305 Wallace captured by the English and executed

1306–29	Reign of Robert Bruce (Robert I). Defeats Edward II at Bannock-burn, 1314; Treaty of Northampton, 1328, recognizes Scottish sovereignty
1368	Edinburgh Castle rebuilt

The House of Stewart

1371	Robert II, son of Robert Bruce's daughter Marjorie and Walter the Steward, is crowned. Struggle (dramatized in Scott's novels) between the crown and the barony ensues for the next century, punctuated by sporadic warfare with England
1411	Founding of University of St. Andrews, modeled on Paris
1451	University of Glasgow founded
1488–1515	Reign of James IV. The Renaissance reaches Scotland. The "Golden Age" of Scots poetry includes Robert Henryson, William Dunbar, Gavin Douglas, and the king himself
1495	University of Aberdeen founded
1507	Andrew Myllar and Walter Chapman set up first Scots printing press in Edinburgh
1513	At war against the English, James is slain at Flodden
1542	Henry VIII defeats James V at Solway Moss; the dying James, hearing of the birth of his daughter, Mary, declared: "It came with a lass [Marjorie Bruce] and it will pass with a lass"
1542–67	Reign of Mary Queen of Scots. Romantic, Catholic, and with an excellent claim to the English throne, Mary proved to be no match for her barons, John Knox, or her cousin Elizabeth of England
1560	Mary returns to Scotland from her childhood in France, at the same time that Catholicism is abolished in favor of Knox's Calvinism
1565	Mary marries Lord Darnley, a Catholic
1567	Darnley is murdered at Kirk o' Field; Mary marries one of the conspirators, the earl of Bothwell. Driven from Scotland, she appeals to Elizabeth, who imprisons her. Mary's son, James (1566–1625), is crowned James VI of Scotland
1582	University of Edinburgh is founded
1587	Elizabeth orders the execution of Mary
1603	Elizabeth dies without issue; James VI is crowned James I of England. Parliaments remain separate for another century
1638	National Covenant challenges Charles I's personal rule
1639–41	Crisis. The Scots and then the English Parliaments revolt against Charles I
1643	Solemn League and Covenant establishes Presbyterianism as the Church of Scotland ("the Kirk"). Civil War in England
1649	Charles I beheaded. Cromwell made Protector
1650–52	Cromwell roots out Scots royalists
1658	First Edinburgh–London coach: the journey took two weeks
1660	Restoration of Charles II. Episcopalianism reestablished in Scotland; Covenanters persecuted

1688–89 Glorious Revolution; James VII and II, a Catholic, deposed in favor of his daughter Mary and her husband, William of Orange. Supporters of James ("Jacobites") defeated at Killiecrankie. Presbyterianism reestablished

1692 Highlanders who refuse oath to William and Mary massacred at Glencoe

1698–1700 Attempted Scottish colony at Darien fails

1707 Union of English and Scots Parliaments under Queen Anne; deprived of French wine trade, Scots turn to whisky

The House of Hanover

1714 Queen Anne dies; George I of Hanover, descended from a daughter of James VI and I, crowned

1715 First Jacobite Rebellion. Earl of Mar defeated

1730–90 Scottish Enlightenment. The Edinburgh Medical School is the best in Europe; David Hume (1711–1776) and Adam Smith (1723–1790) redefine philosophy and economics. In the arts, Allan Ramsay the elder (1686–1758) and Robert Burns (1759–1796) refine Scottish poetry; Allan Ramsay the younger (1713–1784) and Henry Raeburn (1756–1823) rank among the finest painters of the era. Edinburgh's New Town, begun in the 1770s by the brothers Adam, provides a fitting setting

1745-46 Last Jacobite Rebellion. Bonnie Prince Charlie, grandson of James VII and II, is defeated at Culloden; wearing of the kilt is forbidden until 1782. James Watt (1736–1819) of Glasgow is granted a patent for his steam engine

1771 Birth of Walter Scott, Romantic novelist

1778 First cotton mill, at Rothesay

1788 Death of Bonnie Prince Charlie

1790 Forth and Clyde Canal opened

1800–1850 Highland Clearances: overpopulation, increased rents, and conversion of farms to sheep pasture led to mass migration, sometimes forced, to North America and elsewhere. Meanwhile, the lowlands industrialize; Catholic Irish immigrate to factories of southwest

1828 Execution of Burke and Hare, who sold their murder victims to an Edinburgh anatomist, a lucrative trade

1832 Parliamentary Reform Act expands the franchise, redistributes seats

1837 Victoria accedes to the British throne

1842 Edinburgh–Glasgow railroad opened

1846 Edinburgh–London railroad opened

1848 Queen Victoria buys estate at Balmoral as her Scottish residence. Andrew Carnegie emigrates from Dunfermline to Pittsburgh

1884–85 Gladstone's Reform Act establishes manhood suffrage. Office of Secretary for Scotland authorized

1886 Scottish Home Rule Association founded

1901 Death of Queen Victoria

The House of Windsor

1928 Equal Franchise Act gives the vote to women. Scottish Office established as governmental department in Edinburgh. Scottish National Party founded

1931 Depression hits industrialized Scotland severely

1945 Two Scottish Nationalists elected to Parliament

1959 Finnart Oil Terminal, Chapelcross Nuclear Power Station, and Dounreay Fast Breeder Reactor opened

1964 Forth Road Bridge opened

1970 British Petroleum strikes oil in the North Sea; revives economy of northeast

1973 Britain becomes a member of the European Economic Community ("Common Market")

1974 Eleven Scottish Nationalist MPs elected. Old counties reorganized and renamed new regions

1979 Referendum on "devolution" of a separate Scotland: 33% for, 31% against; 36% don't vote

1981 Europe's largest oil terminal opens at Sullom Voe, Shetland

1988 Revival of Scots nationalism under banner of "Scotland in Europe," anticipating 1992 economic union

1992 Increasing attention focused on Scotland's dissatisfaction with rule from London, England. Poll shows 50% of Scots want independence

The Story of Scotland

By Gordon Donaldson

Professor Gordon Donaldson of Edinburgh University was Her Majesty's Historiographer Royal in Scotland and the author of more than 30 books, mainly on Scottish history. He died in 1993.

Scotland almost defies classification. It is no longer an independent country and it has no legislative organ of its own, for the United Kingdom Parliament at Westminster legislates for it. Yet it has a distinct executive, with a Secretary of State and a number of ministers; its own legal system and its own law courts, different and separate from those of England (the British House of Lords, however, is the final court of appeal in civil cases). There is a Church of Scotland whose government is Presbyterian and totally separate from the Episcopalian Church of England. The local government system is now constructed not (as in England) of counties, but mainly of regions, each containing a number of districts, and one still finds "burghs" (not boroughs) and "provosts" (not mayors). Scottish sheriffs are salaried judges and therefore different from the sheriffs of either England or the United States. Scotland has its own banks and banknotes.

It is arguable whether there is a Scottish nation. The Scots of today are descended from Scandinavians, Irish, English, Welsh, French, and Flemings, who immigrated in earlier centuries and obliterated traces of more primitive inhabitants. The whole of Britain has a Celtic fringe, which in the south consists of Wales and Cornwall and in Scotland consists of the central and west Highlands. A new factor entered in the l9th century with a massive immigration from Ireland, which has left conspicuous features, not least a very large Roman Catholic element.

If there is no Scottish race, it is equally true that there is no Scottish language. The speech of the earliest known inhabitants has long vanished, leaving two tongues, which arrived about 500 BC. A people from Ireland calling themselves Scots settled in Argyll and brought with them the Gaelic language of Ireland, which used to be known in Scotland, quite accurately, as Irish. The fact that the name is sometimes pronounced *Gallic* must not mislead the unwary into thinking that there is anything French about it. From the European continent came the Angles or English, who settled in northeastern England and southeastern Scotland, introducing what became the speech of England and most of Scotland. The area where Irish or Gaelic was spoken shrank steadily until it was confined to the western fringe of the mainland and some of the Hebrides. The Scandinavian tongue, which was brought by immigrants from Norway—some of them Vikings—to Orkney and Shetland, has left many traces in the speech of the people there. French was spoken by the Norman immigrants of the 12th century (who introduced many familiar Scottish surnames, such as Bruce, Cumming, Fraser, Hay, Somerville, Colville, Mowat, Menzies, and Stewart), but it hardly extended much beyond the aristocracy and probably died out in the 14th century.

The Lowlands must be considered to include the Orkney and Shetland islands and to continue along a coastal plain stretching from Caithness down nearly the entire eastern seaboard, extending various distances inland, and finally crossing the country from the Firth of Forth to the River Clyde. The southern uplands, that is, the hills between the Forth–Clyde line and the Border, while not Lowland in a physical sense, are racially and linguistically part of the Lowlands. Thus the Highlands lie to the west rather than to the north of the Lowlands and include the mountainous center of Scotland and the entire west coast. There is a Highland town south of Berwick in England: Campbeltown in Kintyre.

The fertile Lowlands were suitable for arable farming, although also with good grazing on hill slopes, while the Highlands lent themselves to a mainly pastoral economy in the glens or valleys, which ran through the barren wastes of the mountains. In later times it was chiefly in the Lowlands that industries developed. The eastern Lowland areas have a fairly dry and temperate climate; in the central Highlands there are severe winters, whereas the western seaboard has in general mild conditions, usually kind to both plant and animal life, but the area is apt to be lashed by tempests of wind and rain. Few activities are more dispiriting than farming in the west Highlands, but there was little else to provide a livelihood. The Highlands could hardly ever have been economically viable without outside subsidies. For centuries these took the shape of raids by Highlanders on their Lowland neighbors, who despised and hated the westerners. It was said that after God created the first Highlander (out of a piece of horse manure),

Quoth God to the Highlander, "What will you now?"

"I will down to the Lowland, Lord, and there steal a cow."

The tourist's image of the Scot is of a bagpipe-playing figure in what is called Highland dress and sometimes miscalled Scottish national dress. In fact, if anyone arrayed in Highland dress had turned up in the Lowlands three or four hundred years ago, he would probably have been shot on sight.

The many peoples who inhabited early Scotland were gradually brought under the rule of a single king. The lands north of the Forth and Clyde were united in 844 in the kingdom of Alba—in or about 1018 the king of Alba established control over the country between those rivers and the present border. In 1266 the western isles were ceded by Norway, and in 1468–69 Orkney and Shetland, too, came under Scottish rule.

The geography of the country presented so many obstacles to communications that, until a relatively late date, order could not be maintained everywhere, especially in the Highlands and the Borders. It is noticeable that the cathedrals for the dioceses that covered the Highlands were in towns situated in or near the Lowlands—Dunblane, Dunkeld, Elgin, Dornoch, and Fortrose. Similarly, the sheriffs who were supposed to administer justice in the Highlands sat in Dingwall, Inverness, Banff, and Perth.

They were safer there! Highland chiefs often allied with the English against their own kings. It was not until after James VI became king of England in 1603 that joint Anglo-Scottish action could be taken against disorderly Borderers who sought refuge across the frontier and against disorderly Highlanders who sought refuge in Ireland.

There were strong local loyalties, arising partly from the fact that even in the Lowlands one fertile and populous area was often separated from another. Thus the Tweed valley was cut off by bleak hills from Edinburgh and its hinterland, while Angus and Kincardinshire were isolated from Aberdeenshire by mountains thrusting eastward to the sea near Stonehaven. Then there were elements in Scottish society that made the task of government difficult. The head of a great family was acknowledged as the leader of his own blood relations, of collateral branches of the family descended from a common ancestor, of tenants and vassals whose links with him sprang from land tenure and not from blood, of men who contracted to serve him, and of men who simply happened to share his surname. Very much the same kind of social organization existed throughout the whole country in the Middle Ages.

In the Highlands, the practice of accepting the leadership of a chief persisted until well into the 18th century. The "clan" has somehow captured the imagination of those who have no idea what a clan was. The historic Highland clan did not consist of people with the same surname, and indeed until the 18th century few Highlanders had surnames at all. The Highland clan comprised people associated for much the same reasons as the Lowland groupings just described. The modern clan, composed on the basis of surnames, has little historical foundation. It may be added that nearly all the clan tartans were devised by manufacturers in the 19th or 20th century and are simply big business.

While the government of Scotland involved many internal problems, the country was fortunate to escape the kind of competition for the throne that led to the Wars of the Roses in England: The succession in the house of Stuart proved so stable that for three centuries (1371–1649) the crown passed from father to child without deviation. This did mean, however, that at a time when almost everything depended on the ability of the monarch in person, the throne was frequently occupied by minors and government was weak.

The great external problem was relations with England. In the 12th and 13th centuries the ruling families of the two countries frequently intermarried and peace generally prevailed, but at the end of the 13th century there was a disputed succession in Scotland that gave Edward I of England an opportunity to attempt conquest. The Scots resisted, at first unsuccessfully under William Wallace (who was victorious at Stirling in 1297, but defeated at Falkirk in 1298) and then successfully under Robert the Bruce (who defeated the English at Bannockburn in 1314). In 1320 the Scottish nobles put their seals to a Declaration of Independence, dated at Arbroath, in which they declared: "As long as a hundred of us remain alive, we will never be subject to the English king; because it is not for riches, or honors, or glory that we fight, but for liberty alone, which no worthy man loses save with his life." But war went on intermittently for more than another two centuries, with many Scottish defeats like Flodden (1513) and Pinkie (1547). Yet the Scots succeeded in preserving their independence against their mighty neighbor.

As a result of the marriage in 1503 of James IV, king of Scots, to Margaret Tudor, daughter of Henry VII of England, their great-grandson, James VI, became king James I of England in 1603 on the death of Elizabeth, the last of the Tudors. Scotland and England were still distinct kingdoms, each with its own parliament and its own administration. Such an arrangement could work only if there were no conflicts of interest or if the Crown was more powerful than the parliaments. In the middle of the century, as a result of the civil war occasioned by the unpopular policies of Charles I, the union broke down, for after the execution of the king, the English declared a republic while the Scots proclaimed their allegiance to Charles II; the result was the conquest of Scotland by the armies of Oliver Cromwell. In 1660, when the monarchy was restored, there were again two kingdoms, separate but under the same king.

The next crisis arose in the 1690s, after James VII (of Scotland) and II (of England) had been deposed in favor of William of Orange. This revolution increased the powers of the two parliaments and made friction more likely. The Scottish parliament adopted independent economic policies that threatened to lead to separate foreign policies. It became clear that either the existing union might have to be dissolved (which would probably have led to war) or the countries would have to be more closely united. It was the latter course that prevailed, when the two parliaments agreed on May 1, 1707, that the kingdom of Scotland and the kingdom of England alike should come to an end and be replaced by a United Kingdom of Great Britain, with one parliament.

William of Orange was followed by Anne and then by the house of Hanover, beginning with George I (1714), but James (VII and II) left a son, "the Old Pretender," and had two grandsons, the elder of them Charles Edward, "Bonnie Prince Charlie," and the claims of this line were supported by the Jacobites, who raised two serious rebellions, in 1715 and 1745. The "Fifteen" was a dull affair led by dull men and ended in an indecisive battle at Sheriffmuir. But the "Forty-Five" was a dashing affair led by the glamorous Prince Charlie and supported mainly by gallant Highlanders. They gained a brilliant victory at Prestonpans and made a spectacular dash into the heart of England before suffering a disastrous defeat at Culloden (1746).

The union preserved Scots law and the existing Scottish church system, which had characteristics rooted in a long history. In simple terms, whereas in England the more extreme reformers, the Puritans, failed, in Scotland they succeeded. In the course of opposition to Charles I, the Scots adopted a manifesto called the National Covenant (1638), from which developed the concept of a "covenanted nation," or Chosen People, comparable to the Jews. After parliament finally decided in 1690 that the Church was to be Presbyterian, there were many divisions within it, especially the Disruption of 1843, which founded the Free Church, and although there have been many reunions, some small dissenting Presbyterian churches still exist, especially in the west Highlands.

Perhaps the ecclesiastical disputes were related to the fact that the Scots were not only argumentative, but sufficiently well educated to grasp the finer points that were at issue. From its earliest days the reformed church had stressed the need for education, and already in the 17th century it was normal for a parish in Lowland Scotland to have a school, although the Highlands were not adequately served until later. One looks in vain in Scottish literature for the "ignorant yokel" so familiar in English literature, and for generations Scotland was far ahead of England in its educational standards. Scots like to boast that they had five universities when England had only two, and it was claimed that higher education and a successful career were always open to a "lad o' pairts" (a boy with the ability to make his way in the world).

In the Middle Ages Scotland was not alone in being constantly under threat from England. France also faced English aggression, and it was natural that France and Scotland should form The Auld Alliance, first formulated in 1295 and continuing to the reformation and even after it. In the 16th century it was agreed that the two peoples should have joint nationality. There was thus a strong Continental influence on Scottish law, universities, and architecture, and French words found their way into Scottish speech. Scotland, although more physically remote, was a less insular, more Continental country than England, where the law in particular followed its own unique development. Apart from the French connection, Scotland had close ties with the Low Countries, Denmark, and the Baltic, so that she was not isolated in a distant northern backwater but drew cultural inspiration from the mainstream of European civilization.

Partly because resources at home were limited and the ambitious saw better prospects abroad, already in the Middle Ages Scots were to be found all over Europe as merchants, soldiers, and scholars. With the development of colonization, new fields opened up, and Scots peopled lands overseas in numbers far out of proportion to the population of their own country. There are some common misconceptions about the causes. Many inhabitants of the American continent are convinced that their ancestors were Jacobites who had to flee after Culloden. It is true that a small number of rebels were deported to America as their punishment, but there is little evidence of involuntary flight. Others see the Highland Clearances as a main reason for emigration; in the Highlands, as elsewhere, the population had so increased as to outstrip subsistence by about 1800, and people were trying to live on tiny holdings, precariously dependent on the potato crop, which sometimes failed. Some landlords decided to turn their estates over to sheep farming and to develop fishing, which meant displacing tenants. However, few of those tenants went overseas immediately, and the population of the Highlands actually increased during that period. Curiously, it was only after tenants gained protection against arbitrary eviction in 1886 that the Highland population fell disastrously.

Whatever the causes, there was not a part of the world in which Scots were not to be found, and they gained a reputation for success. An observer in 1888 remarked that "from Canada to Ceylon, from Dunedin to Bombay, for every Englishman that you meet who has worked himself up to wealth from small beginnings without external aid, you find ten Scotchmen. . . . Wherever abroad you come across a Scotchman, you invariably find him prosperous and respected." It was put more briefly: "You never find a foolish Scot abroad; all the fools stay at home."

Thomas Edison; Samuel Morse; Edgar Allan Poe; Washington Irving; Robert E. Lee; Presidents Jefferson, Monroe, Jackson, Grant, and Polk; Patrick Henry; and James McNeil Whistler all claimed Scottish ancestry. Allan Pinkerton of the detective agency was born in Glasgow; John Paul Jones, founder of the U.S. Navy, came from the Solway shore. Samuel Wilson, whose parents sailed to America from Greenock on the Clyde, has been officially recognized as the original Uncle Sam.

The Scottish John Macdonald and Alexander Mackenzie were Canada's first and second prime ministers. That country's Fraser and Mackenzie rivers are named for Scottish pioneers, as is her leading university, McGill.

Some pioneers carried royal blood to the New World, if the genealogists are to be believed. Jimmy Carter, through his alleged descent from King Henry III, must be linked with the Stuarts; the Irish Kennedys' Scottish cousins went back to Robert the Bruce, as did those of Thomas Jefferson, James Monroe, and James Buchanan; Ulysses S. Grant claimed descent from an earlier king, David I; and Theodore Roosevelt boasted three clan chieftains—a Stuart, a Drummond, and a Douglas—in his ancestry.

Perhaps the most famous American Scot was Andrew Carnegie, steel baron and multimillionaire, who started work as a bobbin boy in a Pittsburgh mill. When he was a baby in Dunfermline (Fife), his parents sold everything they had to raise the fare for the passage to New York.

While it was often the enterprising rather than the economically depressed who emigrated, periods of slump usually saw heavy emigration: During the 1920s, when Scotland's heavy industries felt the full blast of depression, nearly 400,000 people left the country, and its population fell for the first time.

Although the Union of 1707 gave Scotland and England a single parliament, there was at first little to stimulate the Scots to an interest in British politics. The Liberal party had a majority of Scottish seats at almost every election between 1832 and 1914, and sometimes the Scottish Liberal vote ensured a Liberal government in London for which the majority of the English had not voted. In the past few decades the Labour party began to take the place of the Liberals in Scottish attachment, with the result that, in a reversal of the earlier situation, the Scots have had Conservative governments sitting in Westminster for which they did not vote. (On the other hand, it should be remembered that out of nine successive prime ministers between 1892 and 1924, six were Scots.)

For over a century now there have been intermittent demands for legislative devolution, and Home Rule was proposed several times before 1914. In recent years anxiety over the poor state of the Scottish economy has led to renewed agitation for Home Rule, though its cause usually makes a poor showing at general elections, and in a referendum on the subject in 1979, Home Rule did not raise the required 40% of the votes needed. However, an election in Govan, a Glasgow constituency, was won overwhelmingly by a Scottish Nationalist candidate at the end of 1988; since then the cause of Scotland for the Scots has been firmly back on the agenda.

Robert Burns, Scotland's Eternal Laureate

By Holly Hughes

Holly Hughes has written books on Dickens and Eliot and is a contributing editor to Literary Cavalcade *magazine.*

Before I ever visited Scotland, I had only a foggy sort of notion of who Robert Burns was. Then I traveled to Edinburgh one summer for the arts festival and discovered Burns everywhere. His rakish dark eyes and bold features peered skeptically from portraits and monuments and even biscuit tins; phrases from his poems popped up in advertising jingles and newspaper headlines and in the names of tea shops and bed-and-breakfasts.

On subsequent trips, I discovered that Scotland's map is covered with places that claim an association with Burns—not just his own homes (and there are plenty, for he was constantly on the move, leaving behind him a trail of debts and lovelorn lasses), but pubs where he drank, landscapes he praised, cemeteries where his lovers and enemies were buried—it's almost like the proliferation of historic homes in the eastern United States that claim "Washington slept here."

Ayrshire is officially Burns country, beginning with the thatched cottage in Alloway, near Ayr, where Burns was born in 1759, and ending with Dumfries, where Burns was buried in St. Michael's churchyard in 1796 (the very same day his youngest son, Maxwell, was born). Tarbolton was the village where young Burns enjoyed many a late evening drinking with the Bachelor's Club and where he fell in love with Mary Campbell, the subject of some of his finest love lyrics ("Ye banks and braes and streams around/ The castle o' Montgomery!/ Green be your woods, and fair your flowers,/ Your waters never drumlie./ There Simmer first unfald her robes,/ And there the langest tarry;/ For there I took the last fareweel/ O' my sweet Highland Mary"). At the Burns farm in Mossgiel, visitors can see the field where he ploughed up the "Wee, sleekit, cowrin, tim'rous beastie" eulogized in "To A Mouse." Kilmarnock, with its Burns monument and museum, was where his first book of poetry, *Poems Chiefly in the Scottish Dialect*, was printed in 1786. Mauchline was where Burns and his wife, Jean Armour, married and had their first home together, and its churchyard's graves are covered with names familiar from his poems. Moffat, Lochlea, Kirkoswald, and many other Ayrshire towns all boast some kind of Burns connection, often of a purely imaginative provenance: Grey Mare's Tail, near Moffat in Galloway, is simply a magnificent cascade that has been named after the tail of Tam O'Shanter's horse, Meg, who was pursued by a horde of witches in one of Burns's most famous comic ballads.

Even the Highlands boasts Burns associations, quoting his song "My heart's in the Highlands" ("Wherever I wander, wherever I rove/ The hills of the Highlands forever I love"). Burns traveled there in 1787, following what was probably a fairly typical tourist's itinerary. He began in Stirling, where he visited the battlefield of Bannockburn, then up the north road to Inverness, with side trips to Culloden Moor and to Cawdor, with its Macbeth associations. From there he went east along the Moray Firth, down to Peterhead, and along the coast to Aberdeen, Dundee, and Perth, where there were side trips to Scone Palace and to Ossian's grave at Crieff.

Wherever you go throughout Scotland, it's easy to believe that Robert Burns must be as important a poet as Shakespeare or Milton or Keats or any of those English scribblers. Burns didn't just spring out of nowhere, of course. He was one of the many fruits of the Scottish Enlightenment, that glorious era of the 18th century when Scotland, seeking its own identity after being swallowed up in a political union with England, suddenly produced an astonishing crop of scientists, philosophers, and writers. Scotland's literary history up to that point could boast only of the 15th century's so-called Scottish Chaucerians, William Dunbar and Robert Henryson, and Gavin Douglas, who translated the *Aeneid* into Scots in 1513. The earliest lights of the 18th-century Scottish literary renaissance had to prove themselves by writing in English and hobnobbing in London, as did Edinburgh-born James Thomson, who published the first book of the immensely popular poem *The Seasons* in 1726, and James Boswell, whose *Journal of a Tour of the Hebrides*, documenting his travels with the sage Samuel Johnson, appeared in 1785. In midcentury, two somewhat more homegrown talents, Allan Ramsay and Robert Fergusson, brought forth some rather good poetry written in a literary mixture of Scots (the dialect of the Lowlands) and English, and Invernesshire's James Macpherson published several volumes of Gaelic epic poems supposedly written by Ossian, the son of the ancient Scottish hero Fingal, which Macpherson said he had simply translated into modern English. This turned into a scandal, however, when Macpherson, encouraged by his success, kept "discovering" more lost poems to translate and couldn't even produce authentic manuscripts for them.

Although this hoax tarnished Scotland's reputation in London, Edinburgh was still a flourishing cultural capital in 1786 when the first edition of Robert Burns's poetry appeared. Intellectuals and wealthy patrons of the arts in Edinburgh were quick to seize upon this Ayrshire farmer's son, praising his portraits of rural Scotland and extolling the vigor and grace of his use of Scots dialect, much the same way as music critics in the early 1960s rushed to praise the Beatles as natural untutored geniuses. And like the Beatles, Burns came equipped with dashing good looks, a way with the ladies, dangerously radical political views, and a taste for hard liquor. Though not conventionally handsome, with his stocky build, thick features, and thin dark hair, he managed to cut quite a figure at fashionable Edinburgh soirees during the year and a half, from 1786 through 1788, after the phenomenal success of his first volume. Perhaps it helped that everyone, expecting to meet a clownish Ayrshire farmer with clods of mud still sticking to his boots, found instead a literate, intelligent fellow in a genteel dark jacket, light-colored waistcoat, and modestly ruffled linen shirt.

Yet while Edinburgh's elite pursued this new prodigy, Burns himself seemed uncomfortable with all this lionizing, asserting himself with a forthright honesty that all too often bordered on rudeness. He became increasingly restless as his stay in the capital dragged on (and his debts piled up and his love affairs grew more entangled), and one senses in his letters a note of relief once he cut himself free and returned to Ayrshire and to the uncertain prospect of life as a farmer and, after the failure of his crops, as an excise collector. Centuries later, this is the image of Burns his fans treasure most: riding about the countryside, singing to himself as he molded random bits of song into polished poems, or hunkering down with a congenial group of local wits at a country pub.

Neither of Scotland's other two great literary figures, Sir Walter Scott (1771–1832) and Robert Louis Stevenson (1850–94), have remained as firmly lodged in the hearts of their countrymen as Burns has. Scott, who celebrated Scotland in both poetry (*The Lay of the Last Minstrel, Marmion,* and *The Lady of the Lake*) and novels (*Ivanhoe, The Heart of Midlothian,* and *Waverly*) was enormously popular throughout the 19th century, and his career was longer and his output greater than Burns's. Stevenson, although born in Edinburgh, was never associated as closely with Scotland as Burns and Scott were, since frail health, poverty, and a roaming spirit conspired to make him live abroad from the age of 23 on. Except for a handful of Scottish historical novels—*The Master of Ballantrae, Kidnapped, David Balfour,* and *Weir of Hermiston*—Stevenson's best-known works (*Dr. Jekyll and Mr. Hyde, Treasure Island*) are not even set in Scotland.

As an English major whose professors never bothered to teach me about Burns, after my travels I became curious to reread his poetry, and I discovered that it really is wonderful. And looking back at my old school anthologies, I see that, with the exception of "To A Mouse," almost every one had a different selection of Burns's poems to include, which is a clue to just how many good things he really wrote. Of course, Robert Burns has never really faded from the general public's literary consciousness. For instance, just about every song that we associate with Scotland turns out to have lyrics by Burns: "My Love Is Like a Red, Red Rose," "Auld Lang Syne," "Flow Gently, Sweet Afton," "Green Grow the Rushes," "My Heart's in the Highlands," "The Banks O' Doon." *Bartlett's Quotations* devotes several pages to Burns, listing such well-known phrases as "the best-laid schemes of mice and men," "man's inhumanity to man," "to see ourselves as others see us," "death's untimely frost," "a man's a man for all that," "nursing her wrath to keep it warm," and "nae man can tether time or tide."

I suppose the main barrier for modern readers is the unfamiliar Scots dialect that peppers Burns's poems, but it is nowhere near as incomprehensible as, say, Chaucer's Middle English. And if you read the verses out loud—the best way to enjoy those lilting stanzas anyway—many of the oddly spelled Scots words are perfectly easy to understand. After all, Burns was not writing in some kind of primitive, substandard rural slang. He was following a very specific literary style, following the precedent of Allan Ramsay and Robert Fergusson. Despite his rural upbringing, Burns had enough education to write perfectly standard English English, as shown by all his personal correspondence and a good number of his poems (though, tellingly, these are usually not his most successful verses). Burns himself, teetering precariously between social classes, probably shifted in conversation from correct English—which he would have spoken at dinner parties thrown by his wealthy Edinburgh patrons—to broad Scots dialect, which would have been useful when he took his farm produce to market or set about wooing local peasant girls. (Scots was the everyday speech of Lowland Scotland, as opposed to the Highlands' Gaelic dialect, and therefore it is also sometimes called Lowlands, or Lallans.) In his poems, he inserted dialect where any good poet uses his or her most unusual vocabulary—as intensifying adjectives, line endings, and rhymes. The result is an extraordinarily effective poetic language, with a wide range of emotion and humor.

There are other reasons, though, apart from the quality of his verse, why Robert Burns has become enshrined as Scotland's national bard and why his birthday, January 25, is still celebrated with formal dinners (called Burns Suppers) around the globe. Burns's personality somehow speaks to us across the ages, corny as that may sound. People who knew him wrote invariably of his personal magnetism—his dark, flashing eyes; his lively wit; his zest for living—and what has survived of his correspondence suggests that he must have been one of those people you can't help being fond of. He also embodies something that is very near and dear to the Scottish national character: He had a wonderful common touch. He felt at home with ordinary village life; loved bawdiness and roistering; and was deeply suspicious of authority, especially as it was vested in the Scottish kirk, with all its dour piety. Instinctively he was a hardy partisan of individual liberty, though his political convictions were inconsistent—he also nursed a sentimental fondness for Scottish royalty, especially the romantic figure of Mary Queen of Scots. Sentimentality, indeed, was curiously mixed with cynicism in his emotional makeup. Burns was capable of writing both achingly romantic love poetry and bawdy verses about lust; while poems such as "The Cotter's Saturday Night" mawkishly extol the virtues of humble poverty, in other poems Burns is just as likely to lament how hard it is to eke out a living, as in the poignant last stanza of "To A Mouse": "Still thou are blest, compar'd wi' me;/ The present only toucheth thee,/ But och! I backward cast my e'e,/ On prospects drear!/ An' forward, tho' I canna see,/ I guess an' fear!"

Burns's myth, in truth, has been distorted a bit to make him even more glamorous to 20th-century fans. For example, popular imagination wants to believe that Burns drank himself to death.

There's no question that Burns enjoyed a good carouse as well as the next Scotsman—after all, this is the man who wrote, in "Scotch Drink," "O whisky! soul o' plays and pranks!/ Accept a bardie's gratefu' thanks!/ When wanting thee, what tuneless cranks/ Are my poor verses!" Contemporary accounts, however, confirm that he was only a social drinker. His death was most probably a result of bacterial endocarditis, brought on by rheumatic fever, although he didn't help matters any by going out one night to a local tavern, getting roaring drunk, and passing out in the January cold on his way home. Never really robust, he had been subject to periods of weakness and depression ever since he was a teenager working long, hard days on his father's Ayrshire farm.

Another indelible part of the Burns myth is the image of him as a great womanizer, seducing well-born ladies, making peasant girls swoon wherever he went, and scattering bastard bairns around the countryside. It's true that his first children with Jean Armour were born out of wedlock, and one of his finest poems is written to the illegitimate child he fathered on Elizabeth Paton ("Welcome! my bonie, sweet, wee dochter,/ Tho' ye come here a wee unsought for,/ And tho' your comin' I hae fought for,/ Baith kirk and queir;/ Yet, by my faith, ye're no unwrought for,/ Thast I shall swear!"). But Burns was no mere rake—he was usually romantically in love with whatever girl he was chasing, and when it came down to it, he was a loyal (if not entirely faithful) husband to Jean. She herself seemed calmly resigned to his ardent nature, saying philosophically, "Our Robbie should ha' had twa wives."

3 Scotland: The Home of Golf

Golfing throughout the Country

By John Hutchinson

John Hutchinson worked for many years with the Scottish Tourist Board and is an expert on the history and lore of sport in Scotland.

There are more than 400 golf courses in Scotland and only 5 million local residents, so the country has probably the highest concentration of courses to people anywhere in the world. Some of these courses are world famous as venues for major championships, and any golfer coming to Scotland will probably want to play the "famous names" sometime in his career. Telling your friends in the clubhouse back home that you got a birdie at the Road Hole on the Old Course in St. Andrews, where Lyle, Faldo, and Jacklin have played, somehow carries more weight in terms of prestige than an excellent round at an obscure but delightful little course that no one has ever heard of.

So, by all means, play the championship courses and get your prestige, but remember they are championship courses and, therefore, they are difficult; you may enjoy the actual game itself much more at an easier, if less well-known, location. Remember, too, that everyone else wants to play them, so booking can be more of a problem, particularly on peak days during the summer. Do book early, or, if you are staying in a hotel attached to a course, get them to book for you.

There has always been considerable debate as to who invented golf, but there is no doubt that its development into one of the most popular games in the world stems from Scotland. Like many other games that involve hitting a ball with a stick, golf evolved during the Middle Ages and gradually took on its present form.

The first written reference to golf, variously spelled as "gowf" or "goff," was as long ago as 1457, when James II of Scotland declared that both golf and football should be "utterly cryit doune and nocht usit" because they were distracting his subjects from their archery practice. Mary Queen of Scots, it seems, was fond of golf. When in Edinburgh, she played on Leith Links and on Bruntsfield Links, perhaps the oldest course in the world where the game is still played. When in Fife, she played at Falkland near the palace and St. Andrews itself.

Golf must surely rank as one of Scotland's earliest cultural exports. In 1603, when James VI of Scotland also became James I of England, he moved his court to London. With him went his golf-loving friends, and they set up a course on Blackheath Common, then on the outskirts of London.

Golf clubs as we know them today first began in the middle of the 18th century. The earliest written evidence of the existence of a club is of the Honourable Company of Edinburgh Golfers, now residing at Muirfield, in 1744, and of the Royal and Ancient at St. Andrews in 1754. From then on, clubs sprang up all over Scotland: Royal Aberdeen (1780), Crail Golfing Society (1786), Dunbar (1794), and the Royal Perth Golfing Society (1824).

By the early years of the 19th century, golf clubs had been set up in England, and the game had begun to be carried all over the world by enthusiastic Scots. With them, these Scottish golf missionaries took their knowledge not only of golf, but of golf courses. Scotland is fortunate in that large parts of its coastline are natural golf courses, and the origins of bunkers and the word *links* are to be found in the sand dunes of the Scottish shore. But other countries were not so fortunate. The natural terrain did not exist, and courses had to be designed and created. Willie Park of Musselburgh (who laid out Sunningdale), James Braid, and C. K. Hutchison (whose crowning glory is at Gleneagles Hotel) are some of the best known of Scotland's golf architects.

Golf has always had a peculiar classlessness in Scotland. It is a game for everyone, and for centuries towns and cities in Scotland have had their own golf courses for the enjoyment of the citizens. The snobbishness and exclusivity of golf clubs in some parts of the world have few echoes here.

Many of the important changes in the design and construction of balls and clubs were pioneered by the professional players who lived and worked around these town courses and who made the balls and clubs themselves. The original balls, called "featheries," were leather bags stuffed with boiled feathers. When, in 1848, the gutta percha ball, called a *guttie*, was introduced, there was considerable friction, particularly in St. Andrews, between the makers of the two rival types of ball. The gutta percha proved superior and was in general use until the invention of the rubber-core ball in 1901.

Clubs were traditionally made of wood: shafts of ash, later hickory, and heads of thorn or some other hardwood like apple or pear. Heads were spliced then bound to the shaft with twine. Players generally managed with far fewer clubs than today. About 1628 the marquis of Montrose, a great golf enthusiast, had a set of clubs made for him in St. Andrews that illustrate the range of clubs used in Stuart times: "Bonker clubis, a irone club, and twa play clubs."

Caddies—the word comes from the French *cadet*, a young boy, and was used, particularly in Edinburgh, for anyone who ran messages—carried the players' clubs around, usually under the arm. Golf carts did not come into fashion in Britain until the 1950s.

The technology of golf may change, but its addictive qualities are timeless. Toward the end of the 18th century, an Edinburgh golfer called Alexander McKellar regularly played golf all day and refused to stop even when it grew dark. One night his wife carried his dinner and nightcap on Bruntsfield Links where he was playing in an attempt to shame him into changing his ways. She failed.

And the addiction continues.

Where to Play

Scotland's courses are well spread throughout the country in all areas but the far northern Highlands and some of the islands. So finding a holiday golf course is never a problem. The country's main golfing areas are outlined below. Some suggestions are also given for the things nongolfers could do in an area. For more information region by region, *see* Sports and Fitness in Chapters 4 through 13.

The Stewartry Starting at the very southern border, the first of these areas is a delightful part of Scotland set in the rich farmlands around Dumfries, a golfing holiday area since Victorian times.

Powfoot and Southerness are excellent links courses with magnificent views over the Solway Firth, while inland, Dumfries and Moffat have long-established courses that provide excellent golf in a clean invigorating environment. There are also several fine 9-hole courses in the area.

Ayrshire and the Clyde Coast Lying just an hour to the south of Glasgow either by car or by train, Ayrshire and the Clyde Coast has been a holiday area for Glaswegians for generations. Few people need an introduction to the famous names of Turnberry, Royal Troon, Prestwick, or Western Gailes, all excellent links courses along this coast. In addition, there are at least 20 courses in the area within an hour's drive. Remember, too, that at major locations, such as Turnberry, Troon, and Ayr, there are several different courses to play from the same base.

East Lothian The sand dunes that stretch eastward from Edinburgh along the southern shore of the Firth of Forth made an ideal location for some of the earliest golf courses in the world. Muirfield is perhaps the most famous course in the area, but around it are over a dozen more, at Gullane, North Berwick, Dunbar, and Aberlady and, nearer Edinburgh, at Longniddry, Prestonpans, and Musselburgh. All are links courses, many with views to the island of the Firth of Forth and northward to Fife, and if you weary of the East Lothian courses, just 20 or so miles away there are nearly 30 more within the city of Edinburgh.

Fife Few would dispute the claim of St. Andrews to be the Home of Golf, holding as it does the Royal and Ancient, the organization that governs the sport worldwide. Golf has been played in the area since the very beginning, and to play in Fife is for most golfers a cherished ambition. St. Andrews itself has a wide range of full 18-hole courses in addition to the famous Old Course, and along the shores of the Firth of Forth is a string of ancient villages, each with its harbor, ancient red-roofed buildings, and golf course. In all, there are about 30 in the area.

Perthshire The first inland golfing area to be considered, Perthshire has a variety of really excellent courses developed specifically for holiday golf and for visitors, rather than for large numbers of local club members. Gleneagles Hotel is, of course, the most famous of these golf resort hotels. Its facilities are considered outstanding when compared with anywhere in the world. But other courses in the area, set on the edges of beautiful Highland scenery, will delight any golfer. Crieff, Taymouth, and other courses are in the mountains; Blairgowrie and Perth are set amid the rich farmlands nearer the sea.

Angus East of Perthshire, north of the city of Dundee, is a string of excellent courses along the shores of the North Sea and inland into the foothills of the Grampian Mountains. The most famous course in Angus is probably Carnoustie, one of several British Open Championship venues in Scotland, but there are many more along the same stretch of coast from Dundee northward as far as Stonehaven. Golfers who excel in windy conditions will particularly enjoy the breezes blowing eastward from the sea. Inland Edzell, Forfar, Brechin, and Kirriemuir all have courses nestling in the farmlands of Strathmore.

Aberdeenshire The city of Aberdeen, Scotland's third largest, is particularly known for its sparkling granite buildings and the amazing displays of roses each summer. It also offers a good range of courses for the golfer. Aberdeen itself has four major courses, and to the north, as far as Fraserburgh and Peterhead, there are five others, including the popular Cruden Bay. Royal Deeside has three, and in the rich farmlands to the north are three more with at least six 9-hole courses as well.

Speyside Set on the main A9 road an hour south of Inverness amid the Cairngorm Mountains, the valley of the River Spey is one of Scotland's most attractive all-year sports centers, with winter skiing and in summer, sailing and canoeing, pony-trekking, fishing, and some excellent golf. The main courses in the area are Newtonmore, Grantown on Spey, and Boat of Garten, all fine inland courses with wonderful views of the surrounding mountains and challenging golf provided by the springy turf and the heather. For a change of pace, the Moray Firth courses, with their seaside attractions, are only an hour's drive away.

Moray Coast No one can say that the Lowlands of Scotland have a monopoly of Scotland's fine seaside golf courses. The Moray Coast, stretching eastward from Inverness, has some spectacular sand dunes, and these have been adapted to create stimulating and exciting links courses.

The two courses at Nairn have long been known to golfers famous and unknown. Charlie Chaplin regularly played here. But in addition there are a dozen courses looking out over the sea from Inverness as far along as Banff and Macduff and several inland amid the fertile Moray farmland.

Dornoch North of Inverness, the east coast is deeply indented with firths
Firth along whose shores are to be found some excellent and relatively unknown golf courses. Royal Dornoch has recently been "discovered" by international golf writers, but knowledgeable golfers have been making the northern pilgrimage for well over a hundred years. There are half a dozen excellent links courses around Dornoch and inland, another Victorian golfing holiday center, Strathpeffer, preserves much of the atmosphere these gentlemen of a past age set out to achieve.

Courses Around the Country

Most courses welcome visitors with the minimum of formalities and often at surprisingly low cost. (Out of season, a few clubs still use the "honest box," in which you drop your fees!) Admittedly, there are at least a few clubs that have always been noted for their exclusive air, and there are newer golf courses emerging as part of exclusive leisure complexes. These are exceptions to the long tradition of recreation for all. Golf in Scotland is usually a very democratic game, played by ordinary folk as well as the rich and leisured. Here is a selection of clubs that welcome visitors. Just three short pieces of advice (particularly for North Americans): 1) in Scotland the game is usually played fairly quickly, so please don't hang about if others are waiting, 2) caddy carts are hand-pulled carts for your clubs, not the electric golf carts that are more familiar to U.S. golfers and rarely available in Scotland, and 3) when they say "rough" they really mean "rough."

Balgownie, Royal Aberdeen Golf Club. This old, established club (1780) is the archetypal Scottish links course: long and testing over uneven ground with the frequently added hazard of a sea breeze. Prickly gorse is inclined to close in and form an additional hurdle. The course is tucked behind the rough, grassy sand dunes, and there are surprisingly few views of the sea. One historical note: In 1783, this club originated the five-minute-search rule for a lost ball. *Tel. 0224/702221. 18 holes. Yardage: 6,372. Par 70. Fees: £35/round, £45 daily. Weekend restrictions, letter of introduction required. Advance reservations. Facilities: practice area, catering.*

Ballater. This club has a holiday atmosphere and a course laid out along the river flats of the River Dee. Originally opened in 1906, the club makes maximum use of the fine setting between river and woods and is ideal for a relaxing round of vacation golf. The variety of shops and pleasant walks in nearby Ballater make this a good place for nongolfing partners. *Tel. 013397/55567 or 013397/55658. 18 holes. Yardage: 5,638. Par 67. Fees: On application. Visitors welcome* *daily. Advance reservations. Facilities: practice area, caddy carts, catering.*

Banff, Duff House Royal Gold Golf Club. Although it is within moments of the sea, this club is a curious blend of a coastal course with a parkland setting. The course, which is only minutes from Banff center, lies within the parkland grounds of Duff House, an Adam mansion that was donated to the town. The club has inherited the ancient traditions of seaside play (golf records here go back to the 17th century). Mature trees and gentle slopes create a pleasant playing atmosphere. *Tel. 01261/812062. 18 holes. Yardage: 6,161. Par 69. Fees: weekdays, £12/round, £16 daily; weekends, £18/round, £24 daily. Advance reservations. Facilities: practice area, caddy carts, catering.*

Boat of Garten. Possibly one of the greatest "undiscovered" courses in Scotland, Boat of Garten was designed by famous golf architect James Braid. Each of the 18 holes is individual: Some cut through birchwood and heathery rough, most have long views to the Cairngorms and a strong Highland ambience. An unusual feature is the preserved steam railway that runs along part of the course. The occasional puffing locomotive can hardly be considered a hazard. *Tel. 01479/831282. 18 holes. Yardage: 5,837. Par 69. Fees: weekdays, £14/round; weekends, £18/round; £70 weekly. Starting sheet used on weekends. Advance reservations. Facilities: caddies, caddy carts, catering.*

Callander. Another course well worth seeking out, Callander was designed by Tom Morris and has a scenic upland feel. Pine and birchwoods and hilly fairways offer fine views, and the tricky moorland layout demands accurate hitting off the tee. *Tel. 01877/330090. 18 holes. Yardage: 5,125. Par 66. Fees: weekdays, £13/round, £18 daily; weekends, £17/round, £22 daily; £69 weekly. Facilities: practice area, caddies, caddy carts, catering.*

Carnoustie. Home in former days of the British Open Championship, the extensive coastal links around Carnoustie have been played for generations. Carnoustie was also once a training ground for golf coaches, many of whom went to the United States. The choice municipal course here is therefore full of historical snippets and local color, as well as being tough and full of interest. *Tel. 01241/53789. 18 holes. Yardage 6,936. Par 74. Fees: £36/round, £108 3 days, £144 5 days. Visitors welcome except Sat. morning, Sun. before 11:30 AM. Advance reservations. Facilities: caddies, caddy carts (May–Oct.), catering.*

Cruden Bay. Another east-coast Lowland course sheltered behind the extensive sand hills, this one offers a typical Scottish golf experience. Runnels and valleys, among other hazards, on the challenging fairways ensure plenty of excitement, and some of the holes are rated among the finest anywhere in Scotland. Like Gleneagles and Turnberry, this course owes its origins to an association with the grand railway hotels that were built in the heyday of steam. Unlike the other two, however, Cruden Bay's railway hotel and the railway itself have gone, though the course has only gotten better. *Tel. 01779/812285. 18 holes. Yardage: 6,370. Par 71. Fees: weekdays, £20 daily; weekends, £28 daily; £85 weekly; £140 for 2 weeks. Visitors welcome weekdays, restricted weekends. Advance reservations. Facilities: practice area, caddy carts, catering.*

Dornoch. This course, which was laid out by Tom Morris in 1886 on a sort of coastal shelf behind the shore, has matured to become one of the world's finest. Its location in the north of Scotland, though less than an hour's drive from Inverness Airport, means that it is far from overrun even in peak season. It may not have the fame of a Gleneagles or a St. Andrews, but if time permits, Dornoch is a memorable golfing experience. The little town of Dornoch, behind the course, is both sleepy and charming. *Tel. 01862/810219. 18 holes. Yardage 6,581. Par 70. Fees: on application. Advance reservations. Max handicap: men 24, women 35. Facilities: practice area, caddies, caddy carts, catering.*

Dunbar. This ancient golfing site by the sea even has a lighthouse at the 9th hole. It's a good choice for a typical east-coast Lowland course within easy reach of Edinburgh. *Tel. 01368/862317. 18 holes. Yardage: 6,426. Par 71. Fees: weekdays, £25 daily; weekends, £40 daily. Visitors welcome after 9:30 AM except Thurs. Advance reservations. Facilities: practice area, caddies (by reservation), catering.*

Fraserburgh. A northeast town with extensive links and dunes that seem to have grown up around the course rather than the other way around. Be prepared for a hill climb and a tough finish. *Tel. 01346/518287. 18 holes (4 additional for warm-up). Yardage: 6,279. Par 70. Fees: weekdays, £12 daily; weekends, £16 daily; £40 weekly. Facilities: practice area, catering.*

Girvan. An old established course with play along a narrow coastal strip and a more lush inland section beside the Water of Girvan—the neighborhood river that constitutes a particular hazard at the 15th, unless you are a big hitter. This is quite a scenic course, with good views of the Clyde estuary. *Tel. 01465/4272. 18 holes. Yardage: 5,078. Par 65. Fees: weekdays, £10/round, £18 daily. Visitors welcome daily. Facilities: caddy carts, catering.*

Killin. A splendidly scenic course, typically Highland, with a roaring river, woodland bird song, and backdrop of high green hills. There are a few surprises, including two blind shots to reach the green at the 4th. The village of Killin is very attractive, almost alpine in feel, especially in spring when the hilltops may still be white. *Tel. 01567/820312. 9 holes. Yardage: 2,410. Par 65. Fees: weekdays, £10/round; weekends, £12/round. Facilities: caddy carts, catering.*

Ladybank. Fife is famous for its choice of coastal courses, but this one offers an interesting contrast: Though Ladybank is laid out on fairly level ground, the firwoods, birches, and heathery rough give it a Highland flavor among the gentle Lowland fields. Qualifying rounds of the British Open are played here when the main championship is played at St. Andrews. *Tel. 01337/830814. 18 holes. Yardage: 6,641. Par 71. Fees: Nov.–Apr., weekdays, £16/round, £23 daily; weekends, £19/round, £27 daily. May–Sept., weekdays, £25/round, £34 daily; weekends, £27/round, £37 daily. Oct., weekdays, £19/round, £27 daily; weekends, £22/round, £30 daily. Visitors welcome daily. Advance reservations essential. Facilities: practice area, caddy carts, catering.*

Leven. Another fine Fife course used as a British Open qualifier, this one also feels like the more famous St. Andrews, with hummocky terrain and a tang of salt in the air. The 1st and 18th share the same fairway. *Tel. 01333/428859. 18 holes. Yardage: 6,436. Par 71. Fees: weekdays, £18/round, £26 daily; weekends, £24/round, £36 daily. Visitors welcome except Sat. Advance reservations. Facilities: catering.*

Lossiemouth, Moray Golf Club. Discover the mild airs of the "Moray Riviera," as Tom Morris did in 1889 when he was inspired by the lie of the natural links. There are two courses plus a 6-hole minicourse. There is lots of atmosphere here, with golfing memorabilia in the clubhouse, as well as the tale of the British prime minister, Lord

Asquith, who took a holiday in this out-of-the-way spot, yet still managed to be attacked by a crowd of militant suffragettes at the 17th. All other hazards on these testing courses are entirely natural. *Tel. 01343/812018. 18 holes each (6 separate). Yardage: 6,643, 6,005. Par 71, 69. Fees: Old Course, weekdays, £21/round, £26 daily; weekends, £15/round, £20 daily. New Course, weekdays, £30/round, £35 daily; weekends, £20/round, £25 daily. Facilities: practice area, caddy carts, catering.*

Machrihanish, by Campbeltown. This is a western course that many enthusiasts discuss in hushed tones—a kind of out-of-the-way golfers' Shangri-La. It was laid out in 1876 by Tom Morris on the links around the sandy Machrihanish Bay. The drive of the first tee is across the beach to reach the green—an intimidating start to a memorable series of very individual holes. If you are short on time, consider flying from Glasgow to nearby Campbeltown, the last town on the long peninsula of Kintyre. *Tel. 0158681/277. 18 holes. Yardage: 6,228. Par 70. Fees: weekdays, £16 daily; weekends, £22 daily; £90 weekly. Advance reservations. Facilities: practice area, caddy carts, catering.*

Nairn. Widely regarded in golfing circles as a truly great course, Nairn dates from 1887 and is the regular home of Scotland's Northern Open. Huge greens, aggressive gorse, a beach hazard for five of the holes, a steady prevailing wind, and distracting views across the Moray Firth to the northern hills make play here a memorable experience. *Tel. 01667/453208. 18 holes. Yardage: 6,722. Par 72. Fees: weekdays, £26/round, £37 daily; weekends, £32/round, £42 daily. Advance reservations. Facilities: practice area, caddy, caddy carts, catering.*

Rosemount, Blairgowrie Golf Club. Well known to native golfers looking for an exciting challenge, Rosemount's 18 are laid out in the firwoods, which certainly bring a wild air to the scene. You may encounter a browsing roe deer if you stray too far. There are also, however, wide fairways and at least some large greens. *Tel. 01250/872622. 18 holes. Yardage: 6,556. Par 72. Fees: on application. Visitors welcome Mon., Tues., Thurs. Facilities: practice area, caddies, caddy carts, catering.*

4 Edinburgh and the Lothians

By Gilbert Summers

Gilbert Summers, author of most of this book, is a native Scot who writes frequently about Scotland, tourism, and leisure activities.

The first-time visitor to Scotland may be surprised that the country still has a capital city at all, thinking perhaps that the seat of government was drained of all its resources and power after the union with England in 1707. Far from it. The Union of Parliaments brought with it a set of political partnerships—such as separate legal, ecclesiastical, and educational systems—that Edinburgh, as former seat of the Scottish parliament, assimilated and integrated with its own surviving institutions. In the trying decades after the union, many influential Scots, both in Edinburgh and beyond, went through an identity crisis, but out of the 18th-century difficulties grew the Scottish Enlightenment, during which great strides were made by educated Scots in medicine, economics, and science.

By the mid-18th century, it had become the custom for wealthy Scottish landowners to spend the winter in town houses in the Old Town of Edinburgh, huddled between the high castle rock and the Royal Palace below. In the tall crowded buildings—called, in Scots, *tenements*—of old Edinburgh, the well-to-do tended to have their rooms on the middle floors, while the "lower orders" occupied dwellings on the top and ground floors. Such an overcrowded arrangement bred plenty of unsavory and odorous hazards (more on this later), but it also bred ideas. Uniquely cross-fertilized in the coffeehouses and taverns, intellectual notions flourished among a people determined to remain Scottish yet deprived of their identity in a political sense. One result was a campaign to expand and beautify the city, to give it a look worthy of its nickname, Athens of the North. Thus was the New Town of Edinburgh built, with broad streets and gracious buildings creating a harmony that even today's throbbing traffic cannot obscure.

Edinburgh today is the second-most-important financial center in the United Kingdom. Its residents come from all over Britain—not least of all because the city regularly ranks near the top of surveys that measure "quality of life"—and New Town apartments in fashionable streets sell for considerable amounts of money. In some senses the city is showy and materialistic, but the legacy of Thatcherism appears to be at odds with older intellectual values. Edinburgh still supports several learned societies, many of which have their roots in the Scottish Enlightenment: The Royal Society of Edinburgh, for example, established in 1783 "for the advancement of learning and useful knowledge," is still an important forum for interdisciplinary activities, both in Edinburgh and in Scotland as a whole, publishing scientific papers, holding academic symposia and meetings, and administering research fellowships in many Scottish universities. Hand in hand with the city's academic and scientific life is a rich cultural life, with the Edinburgh International Festival attracting lovers of all the arts. Running for three weeks from late August into September, this is simply one of the top cultural and artistic festivals in the world. It attracts performers from all parts of the globe: top orchestras and conductors, international dance troupes and ballet companies, and leading opera and theater performers.

Thousands of years ago, an eastward-grinding glacier encountered the tough basalt plug or core of an ancient volcano. It swept around the core, scouring steep cliffs and leaving a trail of material like the tail of a comet. This material formed a ramp, gently leading down from the rocky summit. On this "crag and tail" would grow the city of Edinburgh. The lands that rolled down to the sea were for centuries open country, between Castle Rock and the tiny community clustered by the shore that grew into Leith, Edinburgh's seaport.

By the 12th century Edinburgh had become a walled town, still perched on the hill. Its shape was becoming clearer: like a fish with its head at the castle, backbone running down the ridge, with "ribs" leading briefly off on either side. The backbone gradually became the continuous thoroughfare now known as the Royal Mile, and the ribs became the "closes" (alleyways), some still surviving, which were the scene of many historic incidents. By the early 15th century Edinburgh had become the undisputed capital of Scotland. The bitter defeat of Scotland at Flodden in 1513 (when Scotland aligned itself with France against England) caused a new defensive wall to be built there, and, though the castle escaped, the city was burned by the English earl of Hertford under the orders of King Henry VIII of England. By the time that Mary, Queen of Scots, returned already widowed from France, in 1561, the guest house of the Abbey of Holyrood had grown to become the Palace of Holyroodhouse. Mary's legacy to the city included the destruction of most of Edinburgh Castle, held by her supporters after she was forced to flee her homeland.

By the end of the 18th century the grand New Town was taking shape, though it never was taken as far as the sea at Leith, which had been the original intention. Victorian suburbs added to the gradual sprawl. Despite the expansion, the guardian castle remained the focal point. Princes Street—a master stroke in city planning—was built up only on one side, allowing magnificent views of the great rock on which the fortress stands. The result for today's visitor is a skyline of sheer drama and an aura of grandeur. Edinburgh Castle watches over the city, frowning down on Princes Street, now the main downtown shopping area, as if disapproving its modern razzmatazz. Its ramparts still echo with gunfire each day when the traditional one o'clock gun booms out over the city, startling unwary shoppers. To the east, the top of New Town's Calton Hill is cluttered with sturdy, neoclassical structures, somewhat like an abandoned set for a Greek tragedy.

These theatrical elements give a unique identity to downtown, but turn a corner, say, off George Street, and you will see, not an endless cityscape, but blue sea and a patchwork of fields. This is the county of Fife, beyond the inlet of the North Sea called the Firth of Forth—a reminder, like the Highlands to the northwest glimpsed from Edinburgh's highest points, that the rest of Scotland lies within easy reach.

Essential Information

Important Addresses and Numbers

Tourist Information   Visitors arriving in Edinburgh can get expert advice on what to see and do, where to go, and what's going on throughout Scotland at the **Edinburgh and Scotland Information Centre,** adjacent to Waverley Station. Follow the TIC signs in the station and throughout the city. In addition to free information and literature, its comprehensive range of services also includes an accommodations service (Book-A-Bed-Ahead), coach tour tickets, theater reservations, route planning, a Scottish bookshop, and currency exchange. Visitors can also buy National Trust, Historic Scotland, and Great British Heritage passes here. For 24-hour recorded information call 01891/775770; the charge is 48p per minute. *3 Princes St., tel. 0131/557–1700. Open May, June, Sept., Mon.–Sat. 9–7, Sun. 11–7; July, Aug., Mon.–Sat.*

9–8, Sun. 11–8; Nov.–Mar., Mon.–Sat. 9–6, closed Sun.; Oct. and Apr., Mon.–Sat. 9–6, Sun. 11–6.

Complete information is also available at the tourist-information desk at **Edinburgh Airport.** *Tel. 0131/333–1000. Open Apr.–Oct., Mon.–Sat. 8:30 AM–9:30 PM, Sun. 9:30–9:30; Nov.–Mar., weekdays 9–6, weekends 9–5.*

The List, a publication available from city-center bookshops and newsagents, and ***What's On in Edinburgh,*** from the Edinburgh and Scotland Information Centre, both list information about all types of events, from movies and theater to sports. ***The Scotsman,*** a national newspaper published in Edinburgh, is good for both national and international news coverage, as well as for reviews and notices of upcoming events in Edinburgh and elsewhere in Scotland.

Consulate **American Consulate General** (3 Regent Terr., tel. 0131/556–8315).

Emergencies For **police, ambulance,** or **fire,** dial 999. No coins are needed for emergency calls made from pay phones.

Hospital **Edinburgh Royal Infirmary** (51 Lauriston Pl., tel. 0131/229–2477) is south of the city center—down George IV Bridge and then to the right.

Where to Change Money Most city-center banks have a **bureau de change** (usual banking hours are weekdays 9:30–4:45). The bureau de change at the Tourist Centre, Waverley Market is open on Sunday from May to September. There are also bureaux de change at **Waverley Rail Station, Edinburgh Airport,** and **Frasers** department store (west end of Princes Street).

Late-Night Pharmacies You can find out which pharmacy is open late on a given night by looking at the notice posted on every pharmacy-shop door. A pharmacy—or "dispensing chemist"—is easily identified by its sign, showing a green cross on a white background.

Boots (48 Shandwick Pl., west end of Princes St., tel. 0131/225–6757) is open weekdays 8:30–9, Saturday 8:45–9, Sunday 10–5.

Travel Agencies **American Express** (139 Princes St., tel. 0131/225–7881) is near Frasers department store, at the west end of Princes Street. **Thomas Cook** (79a Princes St., tel. 0131/220–4039) is near Littlewoods department store, in the middle of Princes Street.

Lost and Found To retrieve lost property, try the **Lothian and Borders Police Headquarters** (Fettes Ave., tel. 0131/311–3131).

Post Offices The **Head Post Office** is at 2 Waterloo Place, at the east end of Princes Street (tel. 0131/550–8232; open weekdays 9–5:30, Sat. 9 AM–12:30 PM). Main post offices in the city center are at 40 Frederick Street, 33 Forrest Road, and 7 Hope Street. Many newsagents also sell stamps.

Arriving and Departing by Plane

Airports and Airlines Edinburgh is in the embarrassing position of being a capital city without its own international airport. **Glasgow Airport** (tel. 0141/887–1111, ext. 4552), 50 miles west of Edinburgh, is now the major point of entry into Edinburgh for transatlantic flights (*see* Arriving and Departing in Chapter 5). **Edinburgh Airport** (tel. 0131/333–1000), 7 miles west of the city, has airlinks throughout the United Kingdom—London Heathrow/Gatwick/Stansted/London City, Birmingham, Aberdeen, Bristol, Kirkwall (Orkney), Shetland, Manchester, Leeds/Bradford, Norwich, Southampton, East Midlands, Humberside, and Belfast in Northern Ireland—as well as with a number of European cities, including Amsterdam, Dublin, and Brussels. There are flights to Edinburgh Airport virtually every hour from London's Gatwick and Heathrow airports; it's usually faster and less complicated to fly through Gatwick, which has excellent rail service from London's Victoria Station. Airlines serving Edinburgh include **British Airways, British Midland, Air UK, Enterprise, BusinessAir, Servisair, Sabena, Aer Lingus,** and **Air France.**

Between Edinburgh Airport and City Center   There are no rail links to center city, despite the fact that the airport sits between two main lines. By bus or car you can usually make it to Edinburgh in a comfortable half hour, unless you hit the morning or evening rush hours (7:30–9 AM and 4–6 PM).

By Bus   Two companies, **Lothian Regional Transport** (tel. 0131/220–4111) and **Guide Friday** (tel. 0131/556–2244), run buses between Edinburgh Airport's main terminal building and Waverley Bridge, in center city and within easy reach of several hotels. The buses run every 30 minutes on weekdays (9–5) and less frequently (roughly every hour) during off-peak hours and on weekends. The trip takes about 30 minutes (about 45 minutes during rush hour). Single fare for Lothian Regional Transport is £2.80, for Guide Friday, £3.

By Taxi   These are readily available outside the terminal. The trip takes 20–30 minutes to center city, 15 minutes longer during morning and evening rush hours. The fare is roughly £12. Note that because of a local regulation, airport taxis picking up fares from the terminal are any color, not the typical black cabs, although these do take fares going to the airport.

By Rental Car   There is a good choice of car rental companies operating from the terminal building. The cost is from £40 a day, depending on the firm. If you choose to plunge yourself into Edinburgh's traffic system, take care on the first couple of traffic circles (called roundabouts) you encounter on the way into town from the airport—even the most experienced drivers find them challenging. By car the airport is about 7 miles west of Princes Street downtown and is clearly marked from A8. The usual route to downtown is via the suburb of Corstorphine. The following rental firms have booths at the airport: **Avis** (tel. 0131/333–1866), **Alamo** (tel. 0131/344–3250), **Europcar** (tel. 0131/344–3114), and **Hertz** (tel. 0131/344–3260).

By Limousine   The following Edinburgh firms provide chauffeur-driven limousines to meet flights at Edinburgh Airport: **David Grieve Chauffeur Drive** (8 Merchiston Mews, tel. 0131/229–8666; cost, about £30), **Scothire Chauffeur Drive** (46 Ladywell Ave., tel. 0131/334–9017; cost, £25), and **Sleigh Ltd.** (6 Devon Pl., tel. 0131/337–3171; cost, about £40).

Between Glasgow Airport and Edinburgh *By Bus and Train*   **Scottish Citylink Coaches** (tel. 0141/332–9191) buses leave Glasgow Airport every hour at five minutes to the hour for Buchanan Bus Station in downtown Glasgow (a 20-minute trip) and then continue to St. Andrew Bus Station in downtown Edinburgh. The trip takes one hour and 40 minutes, including the stop in Glasgow, and costs about £6. A somewhat more pleasant option is to take a cab from Glasgow Airport to Glasgow's Queen Street Train Station (15 minutes, £11) and then take the train to Waverley Station in Edinburgh. Trains leave about every 30 minutes; the trip takes 50 minutes and costs £6. Another, less expensive alternative—best for those with little luggage—is the bus from Glasgow Airport to Glasgow's Buchanan Bus Station, walk five minutes to the Queen Street train station, and take the train to Edinburgh.

By Taxi   Taxis to downtown Edinburgh take about 70 minutes and cost around £70.

Arriving and Departing by Car, Train, and Bus

By Car   Downtown Edinburgh centers on Princes Street, which runs east–west. Drivers from the east coast will come in on A1, Meadowbank Stadium serving as a landmark. The highway bypasses the suburbs of Musselburgh and Tranent; therefore, any bottlenecks will occur close to downtown. From the Borders the approach to Princes Street is by A7/A68 through Newington, an area offering a wide choice of accommodations. From Newington the east end of Princes Street is reached by North Bridge and South Bridge. Approaching from the southwest, drivers will join the west end of Princes Street (Lothian Rd.), via A701 and A702, and those coming west from Glasgow or Stirling will meet Princes Street from M8 or M9, respectively. A slightly more complicated approach is via M90—from Forth Road Bridge/Perth/east coast; the key road for getting downtown is Queensferry Road, which joins Charlotte Square close to the west end of Princes Street.

By Train   Edinburgh's main train station, **Waverley,** is downtown, below Waverley Bridge and around the corner from the unmistakable spire of the Scott Monument. Recorded information on services to King's Cross Station in London is available over the telephone for weekday service (tel. 0131/557–3000), Saturday service (tel. 0131/557–2737), and Sunday service (tel. 0131/557–1616). For information on all other destinations or for other inquiries, call 0131/556–2451. King's Cross Station can be reached by dialing 0171/278–2477. Travel time from Edinburgh to London by train is as little as four hours for the fastest services.

Edinburgh's other main station is **Haymarket,** about four minutes (by rail) west of Waverley. All Glasgow and other western and northern services stop here. Haymarket can be slightly more convenient for visitors staying in hotels beyond the west end of Princes Street.

By Bus   **Scottish Citylink Coaches** (Bus Station, St. Andrew Sq., tel. 0131/556–8464; recorded timetable, tel. 0131/556–8414) and **NationalExpress** (Walnut Grove, Perth, tel. 01738/33481) provide bus service to and from London. The main terminal, St. Andrew Square Station, is only a couple of minutes (on foot) north of Waverley rail station, immediately east of St. Andrew Square. Long-distance coaches must be booked in advance from the booking office in the terminal. Edinburgh is approximately eight hours by bus from London.

Getting Around

By Car   Driving in Edinburgh has its quirks and pitfalls, but competent drivers should not be intimidated. Metered parking in center city is scarce and expensive, and the local traffic wardens are alert. When parking, note that illegally parked cars are now routinely wheel-clamped and towed away. Getting your car back will be expensive. After 6 PM, however, the parking situation improves considerably, and you may manage to find a space quite near your hotel, even downtown. But if you park on a yellow line or in a resident's parking bay, be prepared to move your car by 8 AM the following morning, when the rush hour gets under way.

Princes Street is usually considered the city center. The street runs east–west; motorists using the A1 east-coast road enter the city from the east end of Princes Street. Using the bypass, it is possible to reach key points to the west, such as the airport or the Forth Road Bridge (gateway to the north), from many parts of the outskirts and from East Lothian without getting tangled up in downtown traffic.

By Train Edinburgh has no urban or suburban rail system.

By Bus **Lothian Regional Transport,** operating dark-red-and-white buses, is the main operator within Edinburgh. The **Edinburgh Freedom Ticket** (£2), allowing unlimited one-day travel on the city's buses, can be purchased in advance. More expensive is the **Tourist Card** (£4.80 for 2 days, £1.40 each additional day), available in units of 2 to 13 days, which gives unlimited access to buses (except Airlink) and includes vouchers for savings on tours and entrance fees. *Waverley Bridge, tel. 0131/220–4111. Open Mar.–Oct., Mon.–Sat. 8 AM–7 PM, Sun. 9–4:15; Nov.–Feb., Mon.–Sat. 8–6, closed Sun. Also 27 Hanover St., tel. 0131/554–4494. Open Mon.–Sat. 8:30–6.*

S.M.T. (St. Andrew Sq., tel. 0131/556–8464), operating green buses, provides much of the service into Edinburgh and offers day tours around and beyond the city. You will also see other bus companies, including **Lowland Scottish** and **Fife Scottish,** which generally operate routes into and out of Edinburgh to other parts of Scotland.

By Taxi Taxi stands can be found throughout the downtown area; the following locations are the most convenient: the west end of Princes Street, South St. David Street and North St. Andrew Street (both just off St. Andrew Sq.), Waverley Market, Waterloo Place, and Lauriston Place. Alternatively, hail any taxi displaying an illuminated "For Hire" sign.

Maps Several excellent city maps are available at bookshops. The *Bartholomew Edinburgh Plan,* with a scale of approximately 4 inches to 1 mile, by the once-independent and long-established Edinburgh cartographic company John Bartholomew and Sons Ltd., is particularly recommended.

Guided Tours

Orientation **Scottish Tourist Guides** (contact Bob Motion, 14 East Court, Thistle Foundation, Niddrie Mains Rd., Edinburgh EHI6 4ED, tel. and fax 0131/661–7977), endorsed by the Scottish Tourist Board, offers knowledgeable guides appropriate for an individual or a group. The tours are wide ranging and flexible.

Lothian Regional Transport's Edinburgh Classic Tour provides a worthwhile introduction to the Old Town and the New Town. The tour doesn't offer the most in-depth commentary, but it is useful for orienting new visitors to the city. The ticket is quite a bargain because it is valid on any other Lothian bus (except Airlink and night buses) for the remainder of the day. There are frequent departures from Waverley Bridge (outside the rail station) and other points around the city. Open-top buses operate in suitable weather. This is a flexible, show-up-and-hop-on service, meaning that you can get off the bus at any attractions you may want to see more closely. Allow an hour for the complete tour. You can buy tickets from the Lothian Regional Transport office on Waverley Bridge (*see* Getting Around, *above),* or you can buy them from the driver. *Cost: £4.50 adults, £1 children.*

Scotline Tours' City Tour offers a comprehensive introduction to the city, as well as visits to Edinburgh Castle, the High Kirk of St. Giles, and the Palace of Holyroodhouse. (Note that the fees quoted below include admission to the castle and palace.) Allow at least four hours for the entire tour. Scotline also offers a range of day tours to points beyond the city. *87 High St., tel. 0131/557–0162. Call 8 AM–11 PM for reservations. Cost: £16.50 adults, £9.50 children.*

Guide Friday, Ltd., also offers an orientation tour. It runs less frequently than Lothian Regional Transport's equivalent, but you may enjoy riding through the streets of Edinburgh on one of Guide Friday's cheerful open-top, double-decker buses. The commentaries provided tend to be more colorful than accurate. The minimum tour time is one hour. *Reception Centre, Waverley Station, tel. 0131/556–2244. Cost: £5.50 adults, £1.50 children 5–12, £4 senior citizens.*

The Cadies and Witchery Tours, fully qualified members of the Scottish Tourist Guides Association, have since 1983 steadily built a reputation for combining entertainment and historical accuracy in their lively, enthusiastic, and varied walking tours through the Old Town. *Tel. 0131/225–6745. Cost: £5.*

Special-Interest **Scottish Tourist Guides** (*see* Orientation Tours, *above*) will design tours tailored to your interests; it also offers a special Nightlife Tour. **The Cadies and Witchery Tours** (*see above*) operates a Ghosts and Ghouls tour through the narrow Old Town alleyways and closes with costumed guides and other theatrical characters showing up en route.

Robin's Edinburgh Tours, run by an Edinburgh native, offers a number of tours built around specific themes, such as Georgian Edinburgh, Robert Burns in Edinburgh, and Holyrood Royal Park, as well as a range of talks and slide shows. *66 Willowbrae Rd., tel. 0131/661–0125. Cost: £4.*

Tours from Edinburgh Both **Lothian Regional Transport** and **Scotline Tours** (*see* Orientation Tours, *above*) offer day trips to destinations such as St. Andrews and Fife or the Trossachs and Loch Lomond.

Personal Guides **Scottish Tourist Guides** (tel. 0131/661–7977) can supply guides (in 19 languages) who are fully qualified and will meet clients at any point of entry into the United Kingdom or Scotland.

Exploring Edinburgh

Orientation

The Old Town, which bears a great measure of symbolic weight as the "heart of Scotland's capital," is for lovers of atmosphere and history. The New Town, by contrast, is for those visitors who appreciate the unique architectural heritage of Edinburgh's Enlightenment. If you belong in both categories, don't worry—the Old and the New Towns are only yards apart. For visitors with more time, a wider Edinburgh lies beyond (*see* Off the Beaten Track and Shopping, *below*). Remember that Edinburgh, as cities go, is compact, and much of the interesting city-center environment can be covered on foot.

Time and progress (of a sort) have swept away some of the narrow "closes" (alleyways) and tall tenements of the Old Town, but enough remain for the visitor to imagine the original shape of Scotland's capital. The Old and the New are the essence of Edinburgh, even if, away from this central core, Victorian expansion and urban sprawl have greatly increased the city's dimensions. The following tours bring out the contrasts between the two facets of the city. The first samples the flavor of the Old Town, with a leisurely stroll down the Royal Mile; the second takes in the best of New Town architecture.

Highlights for First-Time Visitors

Edinburgh Castle (*see* Tour 1)
Forth Road and Rail Bridges (*see* Tour 3 in Excursions from Edinburgh)
Georgian House (*see* Tour 2)
National Gallery of Scotland (*see* Tour 2)
Palace of Holyroodhouse (*see* Tour 1)
Princes Street (*see* Tour 2)
Rosslyn Chapel (*see* Tour 4 in Excursions from Edinburgh)
Royal Mile (*see* Tour 1)
Scottish National Portrait Gallery (*see* Tour 2)

Tour 1: The Old Town

Numbers in the margin correspond to points of interest on the Edinburgh map.

❶ Probably every visitor to the city tours **Edinburgh Castle,** which is more than can be said for many of the city's residents. Its popularity as an attraction is due not only to the castle's historic and symbolic value, but to the outstanding views offered from its battlements.

Recent archaeological investigations have established that the rock was inhabited as far back as AD 1000, in the latter part of the Bronze Age. There have been fortifications here since the mysterious people called the Picts first used it as a stronghold in the 3rd and 4th centuries BC. The Picts were dislodged by Saxon invaders from northern England in 452 BC, and for the next 1,300 years the site saw countless battles and skirmishes.

The castle has been held by Scots and Englishmen, Catholics and Protestants, soldiers and royalty; during the Napoleonic Wars it even contained French prisoners of war, whose carvings can still be seen on the vaults under the great hall. In the 16th century, Mary, Queen of Scots, gave birth in the castle to the future James VI of Scotland, who was also to rule England, as James I. In 1573 the castle defended Mary as rightful Catholic queen of Scotland; it was her last stronghold and was virtually destroyed by English artillery.

The oldest surviving building in the complex—in fact, in the entire city—is the tiny 11th-century **St. Margaret's Chapel,** named in honor of Saxon Queen Margaret, who had persuaded her husband, King Malcolm, to move his court from Dunfermline to Edinburgh because the latter's environs—the Lothians—were occupied by Saxon settlers with whom she felt more at home, or so the story goes. (Dunfermline was surrounded by Celts.) The chapel was the only building spared when the castle was razed in 1313 by the Scots, having won it back from their English foes. Also worth seeing are the **crown room,** which contains the **regalia of Scotland**—the crown, scepter, and sword that once graced the Scottish monarch; the **old parliament hall**; and **Queen Mary's apartments,** where she gave birth to James. The **great hall** features an extensive collection of arms and armor and has an impressive vaulted, beamed ceiling.

There are several military features of interest, including the **Scottish National War Memorial,** the **Scottish United Services Museum,** and the famous 15th-century Belgian-made cannon *Mons Meg.* This enormous piece of artillery has been silent since 1682, when it exploded while firing a salute for the duke of York; it now stands in an ancient hall behind the Half-Moon Battery, the curving ramparts that give Edinburgh Castle its distinctive appearance from miles away. Contrary to what you may hear from locals, it is not *Mons Meg* but the battery's time gun that goes off with a bang every weekday at 1, frightening visitors and reminding Edinburghers to check their watches.

The **Esplanade,** the huge forecourt of the castle, was built in the 18th century as a parade ground, using earth from the foundation of the Royal Exchange to widen and level the area. Although it now serves as the castle parking lot, it comes alive with color each year during the festival, when it is used for the Tattoo, a magnificent military display and pageant. *Edinburgh Castle, tel. 0131/244–3101. Admission: £5 adults, £1 children, £3 senior citizens. Open Apr.–Sept., daily 9:30–5:15; Oct.–Mar., daily 9:30–4:15.*

Time Out	At the castle, **Mills Mount Restaurant** offers coffee, light lunches, and afternoon teas in a bright premise with panoramic views over the city.

❷ The **Royal Mile** starts immediately below the Esplanade. It runs roughly west to east, from the castle to the Palace of Holyroodhouse (*see below*), and changes its name as it progresses, from Castlehill to Lawnmarket, High Street, and Canongate. On your stroll downhill from the castle, note on Castlehill the bronze plaque recalling the burning of witches here in the late 16th century. Notice also the cannonball imbedded in the west gable of **Cannonball House.** Legend says it was fired from the castle during the Jacobite rebellion in 1745 led by Bonnie Prince Charlie, the most romantic of the Stuart pretenders to the British throne. Most authorities agree on a more prosaic explanation, however, saying it was a height marker for Edinburgh's first piped water-supply system, installed in 1681.

❸ On the left of Castlehill the **Camera Obscura** in **Outlook Tower** offers armchair views of the city. This 17th-century building was significantly altered in the 1840s and 1850s with the installation of the present system of lenses, which, on a clear day, project an image of the city onto a white, concave table. *Castlehill, tel. 0131/226–3709. Admission: £2.90 adults, £1.50 children, £2.30 student, £1.85 senior citizens, £7.90 family ticket. Open Apr.–Oct., weekdays 9:30–6, weekends 10–6; Nov.–Mar., weekdays 10–5, weekends 10–3:30 (shop open until 5 PM).*

❹ Opposite, the **Scotch Whisky Heritage Centre** reveals the mysterious process that turns malted barley and spring water into one of Scotland's most important exports. Although the process of making whisky is not in itself packed with drama, the center manages an imaginative presentation using models and tableaux viewed while riding in low-speed barrel-cars. At one point visitors find themselves inside a huge vat surrounded by bubbling sounds and malty smells. A gift shop offers a variety of malt whiskies. *358 Castlehill, tel. 0131/220–0441. Admission: £3.80 adults, £2 children, £2.30 senior citizens, £3.20 students, £10.60 family ticket. Open daily 10–5 (extended hours in summer).*

❺ Farther down on the left the Gothic **Tolbooth Kirk,** built in 1842–44 for the General Assembly of the Church of Scotland (*kirk* means *church*), boasts the tallest spire in the city—240 feet.

Continuing down to the intersection at the end of Castlehill, look for ❻ the **Upper Bow** on the right, immediately east of where Johnston

Edinburgh

Acheson House, **24**
Arthur's Seat, **26**
Calton Hill, **32**
Camera Obscura/
Outlook Tower, **3**
Canongate Kirk, **23**
Canongate
Tolbooth, **21**
Charlotte Square, **34**
City Chambers, **17**
Edinburgh Castle, **1**

Georgian House, **35**
Gladstone's Land, **7**
Grassmarket, **10**
High Kirk of St.
Giles, **15**
Huntly House, **22**
John Knox House, **20**
Kirk of the
Greyfriars, **12**
Mercat Cross, **16**
Moray Place, **37**

The Mound, **27**
Museum of
Childhood, **19**
National Gallery of
Scotland, **28**
National Library of
Scotland, **11**
Palace of
Holyroodhouse, **25**
Parliament House, **14**
Register House, **31**

Royal Botanic
Garden, **39**
Royal Mile, **2**
Royal Museum of
Scotland, **13**
Royal Scottish
Academy, **29**
St. Andrew Square, **33**
Scotch Whisky
Heritage Centre, **4**
Scott Monument, **30**

Scottish National
Gallery of Modern
Art, **40**

Scottish National
Portrait Gallery/
Museum of
Antiquities, **38**

Tolbooth Kirk, **5**

Tron Kirk, **18**

Upper Bow, **6**

The Writers'
Museum, **8**

Victoria Street, **9**

West Register
House, **36**

Terrace joins the Lawnmarket. This was once the main route westward from town and castle. Before Victoria Street was built, in the late 19th century, Upper Bow led down into a narrow dark thoroughfare canyoned with tenements. All traffic struggled up and down this steep slope from the Grassmarket, which joins the now-truncated West Bow at its lower end.

From **Lawnmarket** you can start your discovery of the **Old Town closes,** alleyways that are like ribs leading off the Royal Mile backbone.

Time Out   There are a number of atmospheric pubs and restaurants in this section of the Royal Mile. Try the **Jolly Judge** (James Ct.), a friendly pub where bright firelight cheers the gloom of dark-wood beams.

---

❼   The narrow six-story tenement known as **Gladstone's Land,** just beside the Assembly Hall on the left, is a survivor from the 17th century, demonstrating typical architectural features, including an arcaded ground floor and an entrance at second-floor level (livestock sometimes inhabited the ground floor). It is furnished in the style of a 17th-century merchant's house. *Lawnmarket, tel. 0131/226–5856. Admission: £2.50 adults, £1.30 children, students, and senior citizens. Open Apr.–Oct., Mon.–Sat. 10–5, Sun. 2–5. Last admission 4:30 PM.*

❽   Close by Gladstone's Land, down yet another close, is **The Writers' Museum,** housed in a building known as Lady Stair's House, a good example of 17th-century urban architecture. Built in 1622, it evokes Scotland's literary past with exhibits on Sir Walter Scott, Robert Louis Stevenson, and Robert Burns. *Off Lawnmarket, tel. 0131/225–2424, ext. 4901. Admission free. Open June–Sept., Mon.–Sat. 10–6, Sun. during festival 2–5; Oct.–May, Mon.–Sat. 10–5.*

For a worthwhile shopping diversion, turn right down George IV
❾   Bridge, then down **Victoria Street** to the right, a 19th-century improvement—or intrusion—on the shape of the Old Town. Its shops offer antiques, new designer clothing, and high-quality giftware.
❿   Down in the **Grassmarket,** which for centuries was, as its name suggests, an agricultural market, the shopping continues, though here the expensive designer wares seem a little out of place, especially when viewed alongside the panhandlers who often gather here in argumentative huddles.

Sections of the Old Town wall can be approximately traced on the north (castle) side by a series of steps that runs steeply up from Grassmarket to Johnston Terrace above. By far the best-preserved section of the wall, however, is to be found by crossing to the south side and climbing the steps of the lane called **The Vennel.** Here you can see a section of the 16th-century **Flodden Wall,** which comes in from the east and turns southward at Telfer's Wall, a 17th-century extension. From here there are outstanding views northward to the castle.

On your way back across Grassmarket to the Royal Mile, note the cobbled cross set in the ground and railed off. This is the site of the town gallows. Among those hanged here were many 17th-century Covenanters (*see below*). Judges were known to issue the death sentence for these religious reformers with the words, "Let them glorify God in the Grassmarket."

Walk from the Grassmarket back along Victoria Street to George
⓫   IV Bridge, where you'll see the **National Library of Scotland**

straight ahead. *Tel. 0131/226–4531. Admission to exhibitions free. Open Mon., Tues., Thurs., Fri. 9:30–8:30, Wed. 10–8:30, Sat. 9:30–1.*

Turn right, walk over the bridge, and a little farther down, on the right, is the **Kirk of the Greyfriars,** built on the site of a medieval monastery. Here, in 1638, the National Covenant was signed, declaring the independence of the Presbyterian Church in Scotland from government control. The covenant plunged Scotland into decades of civil war. *Greyfriars Pl., tel. 0131/225–1900. Admission free. Open Easter–Sept., weekdays 10:30–4:30, Sat. 10:30–2; Oct.–Easter, Thurs. 1:30–3:30 only.*

At the corner of George IV Bridge and Candlemaker Row, near the Greyfriars church, stands one of the most-photographed sculptures in Scotland, *Greyfriars Bobby.* This famous West Highland terrier kept vigil beside his master's grave in the churchyard for 14 years, leaving only for a short time each day to be fed at a nearby pub after the one-o'clock salute from the castle.

Before returning to Lawnmarket, you might detour down Chambers Street, which leads off from George IV Bridge. Here, in a lavish Victorian building, the **Royal Museum of Scotland** displays a broad collection drawn from natural history, archaeology, and scientific and industrial history. The great Main Hall, with its soaring roof, is architecturally interesting in its own right. *Chambers St., tel. 0131/225–7534. Admission free. Open Mon.–Sat. 10–5, Sun. 12–5.*

Return to High Street via George IV Bridge, and, near Parliament Square, look on the right for a heart set in cobbles. This marks the site of the vanished **Tolbooth,** the center of city life from the 15th century until the building's demolition in 1817. This ancient civic edifice, formerly housing the Scottish parliament and used as a prison from 1640 onward, inspired Scott's novel *The Heart of Midlothian.* Nearly every city and town in Scotland once had a tolbooth. Originally a customs house where tolls were gathered, the name came to mean "town hall" and later "prison" because detention cells were located in the basement.

Parliament House—the seat of Scottish government until 1707, when the crowns of Scotland and England were united—is partially hidden by the bulk of St. Giles's. It's now the home of the Supreme Law Courts of Scotland. Parliament Hall inside is remarkable for its hammer beam roof and its display of portraits by major Scottish artists. *Parliament Sq., tel. 0131/225–2595. Admission free. Open weekdays 9:30–4:30.*

The **High Kirk of St. Giles,** originally the city's parish church, became a cathedral in 1633 and is now often called **St. Giles's Cathedral.** There has been a church on the site since AD 854, although most of the present structure dates from 1829. The spire, however, was completed in 1495. The **Chapel of the Order of the Thistle,** bearing the belligerent national motto NEMO ME IMPUNE LACESSIT ("No one provokes me with impunity"), was added in 1911. *High St., tel. 0131/225–4363. Kirk admission free. Thistle Chapel admission: 50p. Open Mon.–Sat. 9–5 (until 7 in summer), Sun. 2–5 (services 8 AM, 10 AM, 11:30 AM, 8 PM).*

Another landmark in Old Town life can be seen just outside Parliament House. The **Mercat Cross** (*mercat* means *market*), a focus of public attention for centuries, is still the site of royal proclamations. The cross itself is modern, but part of its shaft is as old as the city.

Time Out   **Le Sept,** a popular bistro-style restaurant, does a brisk business at lunchtime. Noteworthy are the crepes, omelettes, and the salmon with strawberry cassis. *7 Old Fishmarket Close. Open daily noon–2:15 and 6–10:30.*

⑰ Across High Street from St. Giles's are the **City Chambers,** now the seat of local authority. Designed by John Adam in 1753, the building brings a flavor of the New Town's neoclassicism to the Old Town's severity. The chambers were originally known as the Royal Exchange and intended to be a place where merchants and lawyers could conduct business. Note that the building drops 12 stories to Cockburn Street on its north side.

⑱ Farther down on the right is the **Tron Kirk.** A "tron" is a weigh beam used in public weigh houses, and the church was named after a salt tron that used to stand nearby. The kirk itself was built after 1635, when St. Giles's became an Episcopal cathedral for a brief time. In this church in 1693 a minister offered an often-quoted prayer for the local government: "Lord, hae mercy on aa [every] fool and idiot, and particularly on the Magistrates of Edinburgh."

⑲ On the right, two blocks past the North Bridge–South Bridge junction, is the not-to-be-missed **Museum of Childhood,** a celebration of toys that even adults will enjoy. *42 High St., tel. 0131/225–2424. Admission free. Open June–Sept., Mon.–Sat. 10–6, Sun. during festival 2–5; Oct.–May, Mon.–Sat. 10–5.*

⑳ Opposite is **John Knox House.** It is not certain that Scotland's severe religious reformer (1514–72) lived here, but mementos of his life are on view inside. This distinctive dwelling offers a glimpse of what Old Town life was like in the 16th century. The projecting upper stories were once commonplace along the Royal Mile, darkening and further closing in the already narrow passage. Look for the initials of former owner James Mossman and his wife, carved into the stonework on the "marriage lintel." Mossman was goldsmith to Mary, Queen of Scots, and was hanged in 1573 for his allegiance to her. *45 High St., tel. 0131/556–2647. Admission: £1.25 adults, 75p children, £1 senior citizens. Open Mon.–Sat. 10–4:30.*

Beyond this point you would once have passed out of the safety of the town walls. A plaque outside the **Netherbow Arts Centre** depicts the **Netherbow Port,** a gate that once stood on the site. Look for the brass studs in the street cobbles that mark its location.

Below is the **Canongate,** named for the canons who once ran the abbey at Holyrood, now the site of Holyrood Palace. In Scots, "gate" means "street." Canongate itself was originally an independent "burgh," another Scottish term used to refer to a community with trading rights granted by the monarch. This explains the presence **㉑** of the handsome **Canongate Tolbooth,** on the left, where the town council once met. Now the tolbooth houses a museum called The People's Story, which focuses on the lives of "ordinary" people from the 18th century to today; special displays include a reconstruction of a cooper's workshop and a 1940s kitchen. *Canongate Tolbooth, tel. 0131/225–2424, ext. 4057. Admission free. Open June–Sept., Mon.–Sat. 10–6, Sun. during festival 2–5; Oct.–May, Mon.–Sat. 10–5.*

㉒ Opposite the tolbooth is gable-fronted **Huntly House** (1570), now a museum of local history. The exhibits include collections of Scottish pottery and Edinburgh silver and glass. *142 Canongate, tel. 0131/225–2424, ext. 4143. Admission free. Open June–Sept., Mon.–Sat. 10–6, Sun. during festival 2–5; Oct.–May, Mon.–Sat. 10–5.*

㉓ In the graveyard of **Canongate Kirk** are buried some notable Scots, including Adam Smith, author of *The Wealth of Nations* (1776), who once lived in 17th-century Panmure House nearby. Here you can also visit the grave of the undervalued Scots poet Robert Fergusson. The fact that Fergusson's grave is even marked is due to the efforts of the much more famous Robert Burns. On a visit to the city Burns was dismayed to find the grave had no headstone, so he commissioned an architect—by the name of Robert Burn—to design one. (Burn reportedly took two years to complete the commission, so Burns, in turn, took two years to pay.) Burn also designed the Nelson Monument, the tall column on Calton Hill to the north, which you can see from the churchyard.

Before you leave the cemetery, look for the monument to Robert Burns himself, also on Calton Hill and visible from the churchyard; it is the circular temple below Regent Road (*see* Tour 2: The New Town, *below*). Devotees of Burns will want to visit one other grave. Against the eastern wall of the churchyard is a bronze sculpture of the head of Mrs. Agnes McLehose, "Clarinda" of the copious correspondence Burns engaged in while confined to his lodgings with an injured leg in 1788. Burns and Mrs. McLehose—an attractive and talented woman who had been abandoned by her husband—exchanged passionate letters for some six weeks that year, Burns signing his name "Sylvander"; Mrs. McLehose, "Clarinda." The missives were dispatched across town by a postal service that delivered them for a penny an hour. The curiously literary affair ended when Burns left Edinburgh to take up a farm tenancy and marry Jean Armour.

㉔ Opposite the churchyard is **Acheson House** (c. 1633), once a fine town mansion, which, like so much of the property in the Canongate, fell on hard times. It has now been restored, as has Moray House, which dates from 1628, a little farther up the street.

Time Out — You can get a good cup of tea and a sticky cake (a quintessentially Scottish indulgence) from **Clarinda's** (69 Canongate) or the **Abbey Strand Tearoom** (The Sanctuary, Abbey Strand), near the palace gates.

Facing you at the end of Canongate are the elaborate wrought-iron
㉕ gates of the **Palace of Holyroodhouse,** official residence of the queen when she is in Scotland.

The palace came into existence originally as a guest house for the Abbey of Holyrood, which was founded in 1128 by Scottish king David I. Before you enter the gates, look for the brass letters "SSS" set into the road at the beginning of Abbey Strand (the continuation of the Royal Mile beyond the traffic circle). The letters stand for "sanctuary" and recall the days when the former abbey served as a retreat for debtors (until 1880, when the government stopped imprisoning people for debt). Curiously, the area of sanctuary extended across the former royal hunting forest, now Holyrood Park, so debtors could get some fresh air without fear of being caught by their creditors. Oddest of all, however, was the agreement that after debtors checked in at Holyrood they were able to go anywhere in the city on Sunday. This made for great entertainment on Sunday evening as midnight approached: the debtors raced back to Holyrood before the stroke of 12, often hotly pursued by their creditors. The poet Thomas de Quincey and the comte d'Artois, brother of the deposed King Louis XVIII of France, were only two of the more exotic of Holyrood's denizens.

After the Union of the Crowns in 1603, when the Scottish Royal Court packed its bags and decamped for England, the building fell into decline. Oliver Cromwell, the Protestant Lord Protector of England, who had conquered Scotland, ordered the palace rebuilt after a fire in 1650, but the work was poorly carried out and lasted only until the restoration of the monarchy, after Cromwell's death. When Charles II ascended the British throne in 1660, he ordered Holyrood rebuilt in the architectural style of the French "Sun King," Louis XIV, and that is the palace that visitors see today.

In 1688 an anti-Catholic faction ran riot within the palace, and in 1745 the palace was occupied by Prince Charles Edward Stuart, during the last Jacobite campaign. After the 1822 visit of King George IV, in more peaceable times, the palace sank into decline once again. However, Queen Victoria and her grandson King George V renewed interest in the palace, and the buildings were once more refurbished and made suitable for royal residence.

When the royal family is not in residence, you can go inside for a conducted tour. The highlights include the **King James Tower,** the oldest surviving section, which contains the rooms of Mary, Queen of Scots, on the second floor, and Lord Darnley's rooms below. Though much has been altered, there are fine fireplaces, paneling, plasterwork, tapestries, and 18th-century furniture throughout the structure. Along the front of the palace, between the two main towers, are the duchess of Hamilton's room and the Adam-style dining room.

Along the southern side of the palace are the **Throne Room** and other drawing rooms now used mainly for social and ceremonial occasions. Among the rooms at the back of the palace is the **King's Bedchamber.** Another notable attraction is the **Picture Gallery,** which has a huge collection of portraits of Scottish monarchs (some of the royal figures honored here are actually purely fictional, and the likenesses of others are purely imaginary). All the portraits were painted by a Dutch artist, Jacob De Witt, who, in 1684, signed a contract with the Queen's Cashkeeper Hugh Wallace that bound De Witt to deliver 110 pictures within two years, for which he received an annual stipend of £120. Surely one of the most desperate scenes in the palace's history is that of the Dutch artist feverishly turning out potboiler portraits at the rate of one a week for two years. *Tel. 0131/556–7371. Recorded information tel. 0131/556–1096. Admission: £3.50 adults, £3 senior citizens, £1.80 children, £9 family ticket. Open Apr.–Oct., Mon.–Sat. 9:30–5:15, Sun. 10:30–4:30; Nov.–Mar., Mon.–Sat. 9:30–3:45; closed during royal and state visits.*

26 Behind the palace lie the open grounds and looming crags of Holyrood Park, which enclose Edinburgh's minimountain, **Arthur's Seat** (822 ft.). The park was the hunting ground of early Scottish kings. The views of the city and the surrounding area from the top of Arthur's Seat are breathtaking.

Tour 2: The New Town

At the dawn of the so-called Scottish Enlightenment, in the 18th century, the city fathers busied themselves with various schemes to improve the capital. By that time Edinburgh's unsanitary ambience—created primarily by the crowded conditions in which most people lived—was becoming notorious. The well-known Scots fiddle tune "The Flooers (flowers) of Edinburgh" was only one of many ironic references to the capital's unpleasant atmosphere, which greatly embarrassed the Scot James Boswell, biographer and companion of the English lexicographer Dr. Samuel Johnson. In his *Journal of a Tour of the Hebrides,* Boswell recalled that on retrieving the newly arrived Johnson from his grubby inn in the Canongate, "I could not prevent his being assailed by the evening effluvia of Edinburgh. . . . Walking the streets at night was pretty perilous and a good deal odoriferous. . . ."

To help remedy this sorry state of affairs, in 1767 the city's Lord Provost (Scots for mayor), James Drummond, urged the town council to hold a civic competition to design a new district for Edinburgh. The winner was an unknown young architect named James Craig. His plan was for a grid of three main east–west streets, balanced at either end by two grand squares. These streets survive today, though some of the buildings that line them were altered by later development. Princes Street is the southernmost, with Queen Street to the north and George Street as the axis, punctuated by St. Andrew and Charlotte squares. A look at the map will show you the district's symmetry, unusual in Britain.

㉗ Start your walk on **The Mound,** the sloping street that joins the Old and New towns. The Mound originated in the need for a dry-shod crossing of the muddy quagmire that was left behind when Nor' Loch, the body of water below the castle, was drained (the railway now cuts through this area). The work is said to have been started by a local tailor, George Boyd, who tired of struggling through the mud en route from his New Town house to his Old Town shop. The building of a ramp was under way by 1781, and by the time of its completion, in 1830, "Geordie Boyd's mud brig" (bridge), as the street was first known, had been built up with an estimated 2 million cartloads of earth dug from the foundations of the New Town.

Two galleries immediately east of this great linking ramp are the work of W. H. Playfair (1789–1857), an architect whose neoclassical buildings contributed greatly to Edinburgh's title, the Athens of the **㉘** North. The **National Gallery of Scotland,** immediately east of The Mound, has a wide selection of paintings, from the Renaissance to the Post-Impressionist period, with works by Velázquez, El Greco, Rembrandt, Turner, Degas, Monet, and Van Gogh, among others, as well as a fine collection of Scottish art. The rooms of the gallery are attractively decorated, and it is a pleasure to browse. *The Mound, tel. 0131/556–8921. Admission free. Open Mon.–Sat. 10–5 (extended during festival), Sun. 2–5. Print Room, weekdays 10–noon and 2–4, by arrangement.*

㉙ The other gallery, the **Royal Scottish Academy,** its imposing, columned facade overlooking Princes Street, holds an annual exhibition of students' work. *Princes St., tel. 0131/225–6671. Admission charges vary depending on exhibition. Open late-Apr.–July, Mon.–Sat. 10–5, Sun. 2–5.*

The north side of **Princes Street** is now one long sequence of chain stores whose unappealing modern fronts can be seen in almost any large British town. Luckily the other side of the street is occupied by well-kept gardens, which act as a wide green moat to the castle on its rock. Walk east until you reach the unmistakable 200-foot-high **㉚** Gothic spire of the **Scott Monument,** built in 1844 in honor of Scotland's most famous author, Sir Walter Scott (1771–1832), author of *Ivanhoe, Waverley,* and many other novels and poems. (Note the marble statue of Scott and his favorite dog.) On the death of Sir Walter Scott, public sentiment demanded a grand acknowledgment of the work of the then wildly popular writer. After much delay the committee supervising the construction of a suitable memorial an-

nounced a competition for its design. (If in doubt about how to pro-
ceed with any civic development, the burghers of Edinburgh usually
hold a competition.) After the Gothic skyrocket that you now see
was chosen, the committee was somewhat dismayed to learn that
the design, submitted under a pseudonym, turned out to be not the
work of a prestigious architect, but rather that of a carpenter and
self-taught draughtsman, George Meikle Kemp. A well-traveled
man, Kemp incorporated elements of France's Rheims Cathedral
into his design for the Scott Monument. *Princes St., tel. 0131/225–
2424. Admission: £1. Open Apr.–Sept., Mon.–Sat. 9–6 (last admission
5:45); Oct.–Mar., Mon.–Sat. 9–3.*

Just opposite is **Jenners**—Edinburgh's equivalent of London's Har-
rod's department store. Jenners is noteworthy not only for its high-
quality wares and good restaurants, but also because of the
building's interesting architectural detail—baroque on the outside,
with a mock-Jacobean central well inside. By way of a contrast, Edinburgh's high-tech shopping district is just beyond, on the other
side of the road in the **Waverley Market.** Apart from a selection of
Scottish woolens and tweeds, nothing differentiates this shopping
development from any other modern shopping mall of the indoor-
plant, tinkling-waterfall variety. There is another mall—the **St.
James Centre**—farther on, beyond Register House.

🗅 **Register House,** opposite the main post office, marks the end of
Princes Street. This was Scotland's first custom-built archives de-
pository and was partly funded by the sale of estates forfeited by
Jacobite landowners, following their last rebellion in Britain (1745–
46). Work on the building, designed by Robert Adam, Scotland's
most famous neoclassical architect, started in 1774. The statue in
front is of the Duke of Wellington. *Princes St., tel. 0131/556–6585.
Admission free. Open weekdays, legal collection 9:30–4:30, historical
collection 9–4:30.*

Time Out | Immediately west of Register House is the **Café Royal** (17 W. Reg-
ister St.), one of the city's most interesting pubs. It has good beer
and lots of character, with ornate tiles and stained glass contributing
to the atmosphere.

🗅 The monuments on **Calton Hill,** growing ever more noticeable ahead
as you walk east along Princes Street, can be reached by first continuing along Waterloo Place, the eastern extension of Princes
Street. There is some fine neoclassically inspired architecture on
this street, all designed as a piece by Archibald Elliott. The Regent
Bridge or, more precisely, the **Regent Arch**—a simple, triumphal,
Corinthian-column conceit on top of the bridge, was intended as a
war memorial. The road then continues in a single sweep through
the **Calton Burial Ground** to the screen walling at the base of Calton
Hill. On the left you'll see steps that lead to the hilltop. Drivers—or
walkers who don't feel up to the steep climb—can take the road
farther on to the left, which loops up the hill at a more leisurely pace.
This was Robert Louis Stevenson's favorite view of his beloved city.

The architectural styles represented on Calton Hill include the
Gothic—the Old Observatory, for example—and the neoclassical.
Under the latter heading fall William Playfair's monument to his
talented uncle, the philosopher and mathematician John Playfair, as
well as his cruciform **New Observatory.** The piece that commands
the most attention, however, is the so-called **National Monument,**
often referred to as "Edinburgh's [or Scotland's] Disgrace." Intended to copy Athens's Parthenon, this monument for the dead of

the Napoleonic Wars was started in 1822 to the specifications of a design by the ubiquitous Playfair. In 1830, however, only 12 columns later, money ran out, and the columned facade became a monument to high aspirations and poor fund-raising. The tallest monument on Calton Hill is the 100-foot-high **Nelson Monument,** completed in 1814 in honor of Britain's naval hero. *Tel. 0131/556–2716. Admission Nelson Monument: £1. Open Apr.–Sept., Mon. 1–6, Tues.–Sat. 10–6; Oct.–Mar., Mon.–Sat. 10–3.*

After leaving Calton Hill you may wish to continue east along Regent Road, perhaps as far as the **Robert Burns Monument,** to admire the views westward of the castle and of the facade of the former Royal High School (directly above you). Then retrace your steps to the Waterloo Place traffic lights and make your way to **St. Andrew Square** by cutting through the St. James Centre shopping mall, across Leith Street, and then through the Bus Station.

➌➌ On St. Andrew Square, immediately south of the bus station, is the headquarters of the **Royal Bank of Scotland**; take a look inside at the lavish decor of the central banking hall. In the distance, at the other end of George Street, on Charlotte Square, you can see the copper dome of the former St. George's Church. In Craig's symmetrical plan for the New Town, a matching church was intended for the bank's site, but Sir Lawrence Dundas, a wealthy and influential baronet, somehow managed to acquire the space for his town house. The grand mansion was later converted into the bank. The church originally intended for the site, St. Andrew's, is a little farther down George Street on the right.

Walk west along George Street, with its variety of shops, noting on the way the statue of King George IV, at the intersection of George and Hanover streets. George IV visited Scotland in 1822; he was the first British monarch to do so since King Charles II, in the 17th century. By the 19th century Scotland was perceived at Westminster, distant English seat of Parliament, as being almost civilized enough for a monarch to visit in safety.

Time Out   Hanover Street, the first cross-street west of St. David Street, offers a choice of good eating places. Try **La Lanterna** (83 Hanover St.), situated in a wood-panel basement, for value, cheerful service, and no-nonsense Italian home cooking.

The ubiquitous Sir Walter Scott turns up farther down the street. It was at a grand dinner in the Assembly Rooms (between Hanover and Frederick streets on the left) that Scott acknowledged having written the *Waverley* novels (the name of the author had hitherto been a secret.) You'll meet Scott once again, in the form of a plaque just downhill to your right, at 39 Castle Street, where he lived from 1797 until his death.

➌➍ The essence of the New Town spirit survives in **Charlotte Square,** at the western end of George Street. Note the palatial facade of the square's north side, designed by Robert Adam—it is considered one of Europe's finest pieces of civic architecture. Here you will find the ➌➎ **Georgian House,** which the National Trust for Scotland has furnished in period style to show the elegant domestic arrangements of an affluent family of the late 18th century. The hallway was designed to accommodate sedan chairs, in which 18th-century grandees were carried through the streets. *7 Charlotte Sq., tel. 0131/225– 2160. Admission: £3 adults, £1.50 senior citizens and children. Open Apr.–Oct., Mon.–Sat. 10–5, Sun. 2–5 (last admission 4:30).*

Also in the square, the former St. George's Church, mentioned above as part of the New Town Plan, now fulfills a different role, as
36 **West Register House,** an extension of the original Register House. *Charlotte Sq. Admission free. Open weekdays, exhibitions 10–4, research room 9–4:45.*

Time Out	Try **Bianco's** (9–11 Hope St.), close to the Georgian House, for coffee and croissants. You never have to wait in line; the atmosphere is relaxed; the seats are comfortable; and the coffee, by Edinburgh standards, is very good.

To explore further in the New Town, choose your own route north-
37 ward, down to the wide and elegant streets centering on **Moray Place,** a fine example of an 1820s development, with imposing porticoes and a central, secluded garden (for residents only).

38 A neo-Gothic building on Queen Street houses the **Scottish National Portrait Gallery** and the **Museum of Antiquities.** The gallery contains a magnificent Gainsborough and portraits by the Scottish artists Ramsay and Raeburn. In the museum, don't miss the 16th-century Celtic harps and the Lewis chessmen—mysterious, grim-face chess pieces carved from walrus ivory in the Middle Ages. *Gallery and museum, Queen St., tel. 0131/225–7534. Admission free. Open Mon.–Sat. 10–5, Sun. 2–5.*

39 Another attraction within reach of the New Town is the **Royal Botanic Garden.** Walk down Dundas Street, the continuation of Hanover Street, and turn left across the bridge over the Water of Leith, Edinburgh's small-scale river. These 70-acre gardens offer the largest rhododendron and azalea collection in Britain. There is also a convenient cafeteria and a shop on the premises. *Inverleith Row, tel. 0131/552–7171, fax 0131/552–0382. Admission free (voluntary donation for greenhouses). Open Mar., Apr., Sept., and Oct., daily 10–6; May–Aug., daily 10–8; Nov.–Feb., daily 10–4. Shop, café, and exhibition areas, Mar.–Oct., daily 10–5, Nov.–Feb., daily 10–3:30, closed Christmas and New Year's Day.*

40 The **Scottish National Gallery of Modern Art,** also close to the New Town, occupies a former school building on Belford Road and features paintings and sculpture, including works by Picasso, Braque, Matisse, and Derain. *Belford Rd., tel. 0131/556–8921. Admission free. Open Mon.–Sat. 10–5, Sun. 2–5 (extended during the festival).*

Edinburgh for Free

Festival Fringe street events (during the three-week-long Edinburgh Festival)
Huntly House (*see* Tour 1)
Museum of Childhood (*see* Tour 1)
New Town Conservation Centre displays a continuing program of exhibitions on architectural restoration and conservation in the New Town. *13a Dundas St., tel. 0131/557–5222. Open weekdays 9–1 and 2–5.*
Princes Street Gardens (*see* Tour 2)
Royal Botanic Garden (*see* Tour 2)
Royal Museum of Scotland (*see* Tour 1)
Scottish National Gallery of Modern Art (*see* Tour 2)
Scottish National Portrait Gallery (*see* Tour 2)
Scottish Record Office. On display in Register House is an exhibition on 800 years of Scottish history (*see* Tour 2).
The Writers' Museum (*see* Tour 1)

What to See and Do with Children

Edinburgh emphasizes its history and architecture to such a great degree that children's facilities have to be hunted down. The Tourist Centre above Waverley Market offers up-to-date listings of facilities and activities for children.

Leisure Centers and Activities The **Brass Rubbing Centre,** near John Knox House on the Royal Mile, provides all the materials children (and adults) need to create do-it-yourself replicas from original Pictish stones and markers, rare Scottish brasses, and medieval church brasses. No experience is needed for this pastime, which children find quite absorbing. *Trinity Apse, Chalmers Close, tel. 0131/225–2424, ext. 4143. Admission free but a charge (40p–£10.50) is made for every rubbing. Open June–Sept., Mon.–Sat. 10–6 (Sun. during festival 2–5); Oct.–May, Mon.–Sat. 10–5.*

Dalkeith Park is the nearest boisterous woodland-adventure playground (offering some cause for anxiety for the nervous parent). The more sedate will enjoy the woodland walks and 18th-century bridge. It is not suitable for toddlers. *Dalkeith Park, east end of Dalkeith High St., Dalkeith (10 mi south of Edinburgh; regular bus service from St. Andrew Sq. Bus Station), tel. 0131/663–5684. Admission: £1.50 for adult-and-child ticket. Open Easter–Oct., daily 10–6.*

Hillend Ski Centre operates a ski school throughout the year that offers group and individual tuition on an artificial surface. All equipment can be rented, although there is nothing available for children under six years. *Biggar Rd. (south of the city), tel. 0131/445–4433. Charge for chair lift: £1.45 adults, 95p children and senior citizens. Open July–Aug., weekdays 9:30–6, weekends 10:30–7; Sept.–June, weekdays 9:30–9, weekends 9:30–7.*

Little Marco's Leisure Centre is an indoor play area with slides, mazes, crawling tunnels, bouncy castles, and other paraphernalia for energetic toddlers. *51–59 Grove St., tel. 0131/228–2341. Admission for 1½ hrs of supervised play: £1.50 children 4–10, £3 children under 4. Open weekdays 9:30–7, weekends 9:30–8.*

Museums The **Museum of Childhood** (*see* Tour 1, *above*) appeals to both adults and children. The museum offers a collection of childhood memorabilia, vintage toys, and dolls, as well as a reconstructed schoolroom, street scene, fancy-dress party, and nursery. This often (cheerfully) noisy museum was the first in the world to be devoted solely to the history of childhood.

Zoos **Deep Sea World.** This aquarium on the Firth of Forth offers a fascinating view of underwater life. Go down an acrylic see-through tunnel for a diver's eye look at over 5,000 fish, and visit the exhibition hall with displays and an audiovisual presentation on local marine life. Ichthyophobes will feel more at ease in the adjacent café and gift shop. *North Queensferry, tel. 01383/411411. Admission: £4.50 adults, £3 children (and senior citizens on weekdays only), £13.50 family ticket. Open Apr.–Oct., daily 9–6; Nov.–Mar., weekdays 10–4, weekends and holidays 10–6, closed Christmas and New Year's Day.*

Edinburgh Butterfly and Insect World is a breath of the tropics—a sticky and humid, indoor, walk-through, junglelike experience filled with brightly colored butterflies and other creepy-crawlies. *Melville Nurseries, near Dalkeith, tel. 0131/663–4932. Admission: £3.25 adults, £1.90 children, £2.55 senior citizens and students, £9.30 family ticket. Open Mar.–Dec., daily 10–5 (last entry 4:30).*

Edinburgh Zoo offers traditional zoo delights plus animal contact and handling sessions in the main season, as well as its ever-popular Penguin Parade (held daily in summer). *Corstorphine Rd., beside Post House Hotel (4 mi west of city), tel. 0131/334–9171. Admission: £4.80 adults, £3 senior citizens, £2.50 children, £13 family ticket. Open Apr.–Sept., Mon.–Sat. 9–6, Sun. 9:30–6; Mar. and Oct., Mon.–Sat. 9–5, Sun. 9:30–5; Nov.–Feb., Mon.–Sat. 9–4:30, Sun. 9:30–4:30.*

Off the Beaten Track

Duddingston. Tucked behind Arthur's Seat—about an hour's walk from Princes Street via Holyrood Park—this little community (formerly of brewers and weavers) has an interesting church with a Norman doorway and a watchtower that was built to keep body snatchers out of the graveyard. The church overlooks Duddingston Loch, popular with birdwatchers, and moments away is an old-style pub called the Sheep's Heid Inn, which offers a variety of beers and the oldest skittle-alley in Scotland. *LRT Bus 42 or 46.*

Cramond. This compact settlement on the coast west of the city is the place to watch summer sunsets over the Firth of Forth, with the Cramond Inn nearby offering refreshment. The River Almond joins the main estuary here. Its banks, once the site of mills and works, now offer pleasant leafy walks and plenty to interest the industrial archaeologist. *LRT Bus 40 or 41 (41A in evening and on Sun.).*

Swanston. In the shadow of the Pentland Hills, this conservation village is in sight of, but a world apart from, the southern suburbs and bypass road. There are picturesque white-washed cottages and walks into the hills. Information boards explain the Robert Louis Stevenson connection—his family had a summer cottage here. *LRT Buses 4, 32, or 52 to Fairmilehead, then walk along the footpath leading west along the edge of the golf course. Also LRT Buses 11 and 15 to Comiston. Ask the conductor where to get off for Swanston.*

Leith. Edinburgh's ancient seaport has been revitalized in recent years, with the restoration of those fine commercial buildings that survived an earlier, and insensitive, redevelopment phase. It is worth exploring the lowest reaches of the Water of Leith, an area where pubs and restaurants now proliferate. *LRT Buses 7, 10, 14, 16, 17, 22, 25, 32, 34, 35, 52, or 87, or circle route 2/12.*

Colinton. Here you can sample the flavor of a leafy Edinburgh suburb on the banks of the Water of Leith. Tall trees shelter a riverside walkway that leads to (and beyond) Colinton's Parish Church, another site associated with Robert Louis Stevenson (his grandfather was the local minister). *LRT Buses 32, 45, 47, or 52, then look for signs to Colinton Dell.*

The Pentlands. This unmistakable range of hills immediately south of the city has the longest artificial ski slope in Britain, at Hillend, and an all-year chair lift offering magnificent views (even to nonskiers). There are several other access points along the A702 running parallel to the hills—the best is Flotterstone (where there is a parking lot; pub; and easy, quiet road-walking). *LRT Bus 4 or Edinburgh Transport 315 to Hillend, or 101/102 to Flotterstone (SMT service).*

Shopping

To make the most of shopping in Edinburgh you will need at least two days, in part because the town's most interesting shops are distributed among several districts. In Edinburgh's downtown are the High Street–type chain stores, lined up shoulder to shoulder and offering identical goods. But within a few yards, down some of the side streets, you'll find shops offering more exclusive wares, such as designer clothing; unique craft items; 18th-century silverware; and wild-caught, smoked Scottish salmon.

As the capital city and an important tourist center, Edinburgh features a cross section of Scottish specialties, such as tartans and tweeds, rather than products peculiar to the Edinburgh area. Once you venture into Edinburgh's "villages"—perhaps Stockbridge, Bruntsfield, Morningside, or even the Old Town itself—you will find many unusual stores specializing in single items, such as brushes, antique clocks, and designer knitwear using the finest Scottish wool and cashmere. In many cases the goods sold in these stores are unavailable elsewhere in Scotland.

If you are interested in antiques, Edinburgh should be a productive hunting ground. Scotland has a strong tradition of distinctive furniture makers, silversmiths, and artists, and top-quality examples of their work can still be found, at a price. Most reputable dealers are able to arrange transport abroad for your purchases if you buy something too bulky to fit into your luggage. Antiques dealers tend to cluster together, so it may be easier to concentrate on one area— St. Stephen Street, Bruntsfield Place, Causewayside, or Dundas Street, for example—if you are short of time. Suggestions for particular shops are made below.

In most shops the prices quoted include the 17½% value-added tax (VAT), if applicable. For certain goods the VAT is not included in the price but will be added to the bill. In any case VAT may be reclaimed once you're home, and most shops that are accustomed to handling foreign customers will supply the necessary forms. Keep your receipt as proof of purchase—refunds will be refused without it.

Shopping hours are generally 9 to 5 or 5:30; many shops stay open until 7 or 8 on Thursday evening. Some of the more specialized shops, such as antiques dealers, may have shorter opening hours. Laws passed in Scotland (not in England) several years ago allow stores to open their doors on Sunday; though this practice has by no means been universally embraced by Scottish shopkeepers, you will find shops with Sunday hours, especially in the main tourist season.

Shopping Districts

Princes Street Although it is world renowned as a shopping street, Princes Street in the New Town may disappoint many visitors because of its plethora of anonymous modern architecture, chain stores, and fast-food outlets. It is, however, one of the best spots to shop for tartans, tweeds, and knitwear—especially if your time is limited—and the view upward toward the castle is still magnificent.

Holding their ground amid the general banality at ground level are a few gems, the most noteworthy being **Jenners,** Edinburgh's last surviving independent department store (4 Princes St., opposite the Scott Monument). Claiming to be the world's oldest department store (established in 1838), Jenners is housed in a handsome Victorian (and later) building, graced outside with caryatids, which emphasize the importance of women to the business. Although you can buy almost anything here, the store does specialize in china and glassware and in upmarket tweeds and tartans. Its Food Hall features Scottish products—shortbreads and Dundee cakes, honeys and marmalades, many available in attractive gift packs—as well as a range of high-quality groceries. **The Scotch House** (39–41 Princes St.) is popular with overseas visitors for its top-quality (if top-price) clothing and accessories.

Rose Street, one block north of Princes Street, has many smaller specialty shops; part of the street is a traffic-free pedestrian zone, so it's a pleasant place to browse. **Alistir Tait** (116a Rose St.) offers a collection of high-quality antique and fine jewelry, silver, clocks, and crystal. If you plan on doing a lot of hiking or camping in the Highlands or the Islands once you leave Edinburgh, you may want to look over the selection of outdoor clothing, boots, jackets, and heavy- and lightweight gear at **Tiso** (121 Rose St.).

George Street The shops here tend to be fairly upscale. London names, such as **Laura Ashley, Liberty,** and **Waterstones** bookshop, are prominent, though some of the older independent stores continue to hold their own. Try **Waterstons** (35 George St., not to be confused with the above bookshop) not only for stationery but for an excellent selection of small gift items. **Grays** (89 George St.) is a long-established ironmonger and hardware store that believes in old-fashioned service. The jeweler **Hamilton and Inches** (87 George St.), established in 1866, is a silver- and goldsmith, worth visiting not only for its modern and antique gift possibilities, but also for its late-Georgian interior, designed by David Bryce in 1834—all gilded columns and elaborate plasterwork.

The streets crossing George Street—Hanover, Frederick, and Castle—are also worth exploring. **Dundas Street,** the northern extension of Hanover Street, beyond Queen Street Gardens, features several antiques shops. **Howe Street** (beyond Frederick St.) has **Touch Wood** (No. 19) for hand-crafted pine; **Linens Fine** (No. 22) for a wonderful selection of embroidered and embellished bed linen, tablecloths, cushion covers, and such; and **In House** (No. 30) for designer furnishings and collectibles at the forefront of modern design. At the foot of the street, **Rowland's** delicatessen will tempt you with excellent cheeses (try the Lanark Blue—a local specialty). **Thistle Street,** originally George Street's "back lane," or service area, has several boutiques and more antiques shops, including **Joseph Bonnar,** a specialist in antique jewelry. **South St. Andrew Street,** at the east end of George Street, is home to the oldest hatters in Scotland, **Cunningham and Co.,** founded in 1817; this is the place to go for a genuine Scottish tammie or a length of tweed or cashmere.

The Royal Mile As may be expected, many of the shops along the Royal Mile in the Old Town sell what may be politely or euphemistically described as tourist-ware. Careful exploration, however, will reveal some worthwhile establishments. For example, **Aika** (60 High St.) specializes in hand-knit garments in natural fibers—wool, cotton, angora, alpaca, mohair, silk, and linen. **Geoffrey (Tailor) Highland Crafts** (57–59 High St.) can clothe you in full Highland dress, with kilts made in its own workshops.

In addition to offering a good selection of whiskies, tartans, and tweeds, shops on the Royal Mile cater to some highly specialized interests and hobbies. For example, one store offers a large selection of playing cards, and another is devoted to doll houses and doll furniture.

Victoria Street/ West Bow/ Grassmarket Close to the castle end of the Royal Mile, just off George IV Bridge, the specialty shops of Victoria Street are contained within a small area. If you aren't overwhelmed by the choices here, follow the tiny West Bow to Grassmarket for more of the same. The interior design shop **Ampersand** (18 Victoria St.) stocks a large selection of sundry collectibles, mostly jugs, plates, lamps, and vases, as well as unusual fabric by the meter. **Robert Cresser's** brush shop (40 Victoria St.) features brushes of all kinds, every one handmade. On the topic of unusual presents and souvenirs, **Mr. Wood's Fossils** (in the Grassmarket) can provide you with a small prehistoric (and Scottish) shark encased in rock. This shop offers fossils to suit every budget. Diagonally opposite is **Bill Baber** (66 Grassmarket), one of the most imaginative of the many Scottish knitwear designers, and a long way from the conservative pastel "woollies" stocked by some of the large mill shops. Back up Victoria Street again, try **Byzantium** (9A Victoria St., tel. 0131/225–1768) for an eclectic mix of antiques, crafts, clothes—and an excellent coffee shop on the top level.

Stockbridge North of Princes Street, on the way to the Botanic Gardens, this is an oddball shopping area of some charm, particularly on St. Stephen Street. Look for **Hand in Hand** (3 North West Circus Pl.) for beautiful antique textiles; there are also several antique furniture shops. To get to Stockbridge, walk down Frederick Street and Howe Street north away from Princes Street, then turn left onto North West Circus Place.

Stafford Street/ William Street This is a small, upscale shopping area in a Georgian setting. **Studio One** (10–16 Stafford St., tel. 0131/226–5812) has a well-established and comprehensive inventory of kitchen goods and gift articles. **Something Simple** (10 William St.) and **The Extra Inch** (16 William St.) both stock clothes for all occasions, including some designer names. The latter also stocks a full selection of clothes European size 38 and over. To get to this neighborhood, walk to the west end of Princes Street and along its continuation, Shandwick Place, then turn into Stafford Street. William Street crosses Stafford halfway down.

Department Stores In contrast to other major cities, Edinburgh has few true department stores. However, in the city center you will find not only **Jenners** (*see* Princes Street, *above*) but also **Frasers,** at the other (west) end of Princes Street, and the ubiquitous **John Lewis,** in the St. James Centre. Unlike Jenners, the two latter stores are not local, independently owned firms, and the goods are similar to those stocked in other, United Kingdom–wide branches. The High Street multiples, **Marks and Spencer, Littlewoods, British Home Stores,** and so on, are also represented on Princes Street. However, even given the competition, if you plan a morning or a whole day wandering from department to department, trying on beautiful clothes, buying crystal or china, or stocking up on Scottish food specialties, with a break for lunch at an in-store restaurant, then Jenners is the store to choose.

Arcades and Shopping Centers

Like most large towns Edinburgh has succumbed to the fashion for "under one roof" shopping. If you dislike a breath of fresh air (or a wonderful view) between shops—or if it's raining—try **Waverley Market** (east end of Princes St.), which offers three floors of shops and a fast-food area. The **St. James Centre,** at the same end of Princes Street, has just undergone extensive refurbishment. **Cameron Toll** shopping center, on the south side of the city, likewise caters to local residents, with food stores and High Street brand names. The newest shopping center is at **South Gyle,** on the outskirts of the city near the airport, where you will find the High Street brand names again, including a huge **Marks and Spencer.**

Clothing Boutiques

Edinburgh is home to several top-quality designers (although, it must be said, probably not as many as are found in Glasgow, the country's fashion center), some of whom make a point of using Scottish materials in their creations, such as **Bill Baber** and **Aika** (mentioned above). Well-heeled Edinburgh also has a branch of **Droopy and Brown** (37–39 Frederick St.), whose distinctive clothing—from silk ball gowns and wedding dresses to flowing cord skirts and matching jackets, and pretty cotton print summer dresses—is guaranteed to make the wearer stand out from the crowd. Equally unusual items can be found at **Judith Glue** (64 High St.), which stocks brilliantly patterned Orkney knitwear, as well as crafts, cards, and candles.

If you are shopping for children, especially those who fit the tousled-tomboy mold, try **Baggins** (12 Deanhaugh St., Stockbridge, tel. 0131/315–2011) for practical, reasonably priced clothes made from natural fibers. All the clothes here are made to the owner's design in the store-cum-workshop. **Sprogs** (45 William St., tel. 0131/220–0320) is a children's boutique offering end-of-season lines at 50%–70% off normal prices; designs tend to be modern.

Scottish Specialties

If you want to identify a particular tartan, several of the shops in Princes Street will be pleased to assist. The **Clan Tartan Centre** (70–74 Bangor Rd., Leith, tel. 0131/553–5100) has extensive displays of various aspects of tartanry. For craftware, use as your quality guide the **Royal Mile Living Craft Centre** (12 High St.). Here, crafts are made on the premises, and you can talk to the craftspeople as they work. The range of items available includes hand-woven tartan, kilts, bagpipes, silver, pottery, and Aran knitwear; there is also the Taste of Scotland coffee shop. **Edinburgh Crystal** makes fine glassware that is stocked by many large stores and gift shops in the city center, but you can also visit its premises (visitor center, restaurant, and shop) at Penicuik, just south of the city (Eastfield, Penicuik, tel. 01968/675128). The complex is open Monday through Saturday from 9 to 5 and Sunday from 11 to 5. Tours are given weekdays 9:15–3:30. Admission runs £2 for adults, 50p for children, and £1 for senior citizens.

Bookstores

As a university city and cultural center, Edinburgh is well endowed with excellent bookshops, some of the most central being **James Thin, The Edinburgh Bookshop** (57 George St., tel. 0131/225–4495; and 53 South Bridge, tel. 0131/556–6743), and **Waterstones** (83 George St., tel. 0131/225–3436, and 13/14 Princes St., tel. 0131/556–3034). All stock a wide range of guides and books giving information about every aspect of Edinburgh life, and all have extended opening hours (until 10 PM on certain nights), including Sunday.

Sports and Fitness

Edinburgh has shared in the fitness boom of the past decade, as can be noted in **Holyrood Park,** where at almost any time of day or night joggers run the circuit around Arthur's Seat. The **Royal Commonwealth Pool** (nearby on Dalkeith Rd., tel. 0131/667–7211), the largest swimming pool in the city, is part of a complex that includes a fitness center and a cafeteria. **Meadowbank Stadium** (northeast of the city center, tel. 0131/661–5351) has facilities for more than 30 different track and indoor sports.

Some of the larger Edinburgh hotels have their own fitness centers. Examples include the **Calton Highland** (North Bridge; swimming pool, snooker, squash, gymnasium, massage), **Capital** (Clermiston Rd.; pool, gymnasium), **Edinburgh Sheraton** (Lothian Rd.; pool, gymnasium), **Swallow Royal Scot** (Glasgow Rd.; pool, gymnasium), **Forth Bridges Moat House** (South Queensferry; pool, gymnasium, snooker, squash). Most facilities are free to guests, although there may be a charge for snooker and squash. The facilities are generally open to nonguests only through private membership.

Bicycling Edinburgh is a fairly compact, if hilly, city, and **bicycling** is a good way of getting around, though careful route planning may be needed to avoid traffic. The East Lothian countryside, with its miles of twisting roads and light traffic, is within cycling distance of the city. Cycles may be hired from **Sandy Gilchrist Cycles** (1 Cadzow Pl., tel. 0131/652–1760), **Secondhand Bike Shop** (31–33 Iona St., Leith, tel. 0131/553–1130), and **Central Cycle Hire** (13 Lochrin Pl., tel. 0131/228–6333). Rates in summer are about £35 per week for a 3-speed, £50 for a 10-speed, and £50–£60 for a mountain bike. The Secondhand Bike Shop runs a sell-and-buy-back scheme for longer periods (say, more than two weeks), which can save you money.

Golf Golf courses abound—there are about 20 courses within or close to the city (not including the easily accessible East Lothian courses), many of which welcome visitors. The Tourist Centre will provide local details, and the Scottish Tourist Board offers a free leaflet on golf in Scotland, available from the Edinburgh and Scotland Information Centre (*see* Important Addresses and Numbers in Essential Information, *above*).

The following courses are open to visitors:

Braids (3 mi south of Edinburgh, tel. 0131/447–6666). Course 1: 18 holes, 5,731 yards, SSS 68. Course 2: 18 holes, 4,832 yards, SSS 63.

Carrick Knowe (5 mi west of Edinburgh, tel. 0131/337–1096). 18 holes, 6,229 yards, SSS 70.

Craigentinny (3 mi east of Edinburgh, tel. 0131/554–7501). 18 holes, 5,418 yards, SSS 68.

Liberton (Kingston Grange, 297 Gilmerton Rd., tel. 0131/664–8580). 18 holes, 5,229 yards, SSS 66.

Lothianburn (Biggar Rd., tel. 0131/445–2206). 18 holes, 5,750 yards, SSS 69.

Portobello (Stanley St., tel. 0131/669–4361). 9 holes, 2,410 yards, SSS 32.

Silverknowes (Silverknowes Pkwy., tel. 0131/336–3843). 18 holes, 6,210 yards, SSS 70.

Swanston (Swanston Rd., tel. 0131/445–2239). 18 holes, 4,825 yards, SSS 64.

Torphin Hill (Torphin Rd., tel. 0131/441–1100). 18 holes, 5,025 yards, SSS 66.

For information on golfing throughout Scotland, *see* Chapter 3.

Skiing At Hillend on the southern edge of the city is the longest artificial ski slope in the United Kingdom—go either to ski (equipment can be hired on the spot) or to ride the chair lift for fine city views. *Biggar Rd., tel. 0131/445–4433. Charge for chair lift: £1.45 adults, 95p children and senior citizens. Open Apr.–June, Mon. and Fri. 9:30–6; Tues., Wed., and Thurs., 9:30–9, weekends 10:30–7; July and Aug., weekdays 9:30–6, weekends 10:30–7; Sept.–Mar., Mon.–Sat. 9:30–9, Sun. 9:30–7.*

Soccer and Rugby The **Heart of Midlothian Football Club** (soccer) is based at Tynecastle (tel. 0131/337–6132) and its rival club **Hibernian** at Easter Road (tel. 0131/337–2346). Murrayfield Stadium is the venue for international rugby matches. Crowds of good-humored rugby fans from Ireland and Wales add greatly to the atmosphere in the streets of Edinburgh during the early spring, when Scotland plays its international matches at Murrayfield.

Dining

Edinburgh is a sophisticated city, and its restaurants offer an interesting, diverse mix of traditional and exotic cuisines, from Scottish to Mexican, Thai, Chinese, Greek, and Russian.

Be sure, particularly at festival time, to make reservations well in advance. Also, be warned that there is an element of "it'd be fun to open a restaurant" about Edinburgh's eating scene; restaurants can open and close with the passing of a season.

Also note that it is possible to eat well in Edinburgh without spending a fortune. Even those restaurants that are ranked in the $$$$ category could be squeezed into the top of the $$$ range, depending on how one picks and chooses from the menu. A service charge of 10% may be added to your bill, though this practice is not adhered to uniformly. If no charge has been added and you are satisfied with the service, a 10% tip is appropriate.

Dining hours in Edinburgh are much the same as in the rest of Great Britain, with the main rush at lunchtime, from 1 to 2, and at dinner, from 8 to 9.

Highly recommended restaurants are indicated by a star ★.

Category	Cost*
$$$$	over £30
$$$	£20–£30
$$	£15–£20
$	under £15

*per person for a three-course meal, excluding VAT, tax, service, and drinks

$$$$ **The Grill Room.** Set in the Edwardian splendor of the Balmoral Hotel, the Grill Room has established itself at the top end of Edinburgh's dining scene. The room has a luxurious ambience created by a green marble floor, Chinese lacquer wall panels, an abundance of silver and crystal, and an Oriental theme. The seating is particularly comfortable, and the tables are widely spaced, which makes it a great place for a private conversation or romantic dinner. The service is formal but relaxed, with no pressure to finish up. As its name suggests, the restaurant specializes in grills, which you can see being cooked on the open grill, but there is also an extensive à la carte menu. *Princes St., tel. 0131/557–6727. Reservations required. Jacket and tie required. AE, DC, MC, V.*

$$$$ **L'Auberge.** A number of Edinburgh restaurants take the best Scottish food and prepare it French style, but L'Auberge is French through and through. A large number of tables are set for two—the French are so romantic here in the heart of reserved Edinburgh. The menu is all in French with only a cursory translation; owner-manager Monsieur Daniel wants to have the pleasure of explaining the recipes to you in detail, so you must ask. The menu changes frequently, but you may be able to choose, for example, the terrine of seafood, the guinea fowl with mushrooms and claret sauce, or venison with Armagnac. The impressive wine list is French (unsurprisingly) and includes—unusual in Edinburgh—excellent dessert wines. *58 St. Mary St., tel. 0131/556–5888. Reservations advised. Jacket and tie advised. AE, DC, MC, V. Closed Christmas Day, Dec. 26, New Year's Day.*

$$$$ **Pompadour.** Insulated by arched windows and lilac drapes from the
★ bustle of west-end Princes Street, the Pompadour aims to impress. The decor, with its subtle plasterwork and rich murals, is inspired by the court of Louis XV, as may be expected in a restaurant named after the king's mistress, Madame de Pompadour. The cuisine is also classic French, with top-quality Scottish produce completing the happiest of alliances. The extensive well-chosen wine list complements such dishes as sea bass with crispy leeks and caviar butter sauce, whole lobster with mustard and cheese, or loin of venison with potato pancakes. This is the place to go if you want a festive night out. It's more relaxed and informal at lunchtime. *Caledonian Hotel, Princes St., tel. 0131/225–2433. Reservations advised. Jacket and tie required. AE, DC, MC, V. No weekend lunch.*

$$$ **The Atrium.** With its cream-color tented fabric ceiling, smart cream cotton chair covers, and wrought-iron candlesticks and candelabra of most unusual design, the Atrium is a distinctive setting for pre- or post-theater dinner (the Traverse Theatre is right next door). The chef-proprietor Andrew Radford uses typical Scottish ingredients in very untypical combinations: Curly kale, once the staple of every Scottish rural home, may be married with beef, bacon, and shallots, and salmon might be presented with zucchini, red pepper, and Parmesan. The menu changes daily, but there is always a vegetarian option. *10 Cambridge St. (beneath Saltire Ct.), tel. 0131/228–8882. Reservations advised. Jacket and tie preferred. AE, MC, V.*

$$$ **Beehive Inn.** One of the oldest pubs in the city, the Beehive snuggles in the Grassmarket, under the majestic shadow of the castle. Some 400 years ago the Beehive was a coaching inn, and outside the pub's doors once stood the main set of city gallows, where over the centuries numerous executions were held. The upstairs **Rafters** restaurant lies hidden in an attractive and spacious attic room, crammed with weird and wonderful junk. The menu features mostly steaks and fish: try the charcoal-grilled trout with Drambuie and oregano

Edinburgh Dining and Lodging

Dining
The Atrium, **8**
Beehive Inn, **31**
Buntoms Thai
Restaurant, **23**
The Doric Tavern, **36**
The Grill Room, **29**
Hendersons, **27**
Howie's, **57**
Jackson's, **37**

Kalpna, **49**
Kelly's, **48**
Kweilin, **21**
La Lanterna, **26**
Lancers, **15**
L'Auberge, **47**
Loon Fung, **4**
Martins, **17**
Merchants, **35**
Old Orleans, **5**

Peter's Cellars, **11**
Pierre Victoire, **32,
34, 41, 42**
Pompadour, **28**
Spices, **33**
Vito, **18**
Waterfront Wine
Bar and Bistro, **43**
The Witchery by
the Castle, **30**
Xian City Chinese
Restaurant, **38**

Lodging
Albany, **44**
Ashdene House, **50**
Balmoral Hotel, **29**
Caledonian, **9**
Channings, **12**
Classic Guest
House, **51**
Crannoch
But & Ben, **13**

Drummond House, **24**	Mrs. Coleman, **52**	Silverburn Steading, **1**
Edinburgh Grand Sheraton, **6**	Mrs. Graham, **53**	Stakis Grosvenor Hotel, **7**
Ellesmere Guest House, **2**	Mrs. Valerie Livingstone, **46**	Stuart House, **40**
George Intercontinental, **25**	Norton House, **3**	Teviotdale House, **56**
Howard Hotel, **22**	Roselea House, **54**	Thrums Private Hotel, **55**
Lodge Hotel, **10**	Roxburghe, **14**	Turret Guest House, **58**
Mount Royal Hotel, **16**	Royal Terrace, **45**	28 Northumberland Street, **20**
	Scandic Crown, **39**	
	Sibbet House, **19**	

sauce, or veal panfried with thyme and mushrooms. *18/20 Grassmarket, tel. 0131/225-7171. Reservations advised on weekends. Dress: casual. AE, MC, DC, V.*

$$$ **Kelly's.** This Scottish restaurant with a French influence is slightly off the beaten track on the south side of the city but still only a short taxi ride or 20-minute walk from the center. The entrance to this former bakery, difficult to spot in a line of residential properties, leads into a pine-furnished, peach-tinted dining room with only 9 or 10 tables. The ambience is intimate, ideal for a quiet discussion over an unhurried meal. Among the fine choices here are smoked Scottish salmon with mushrooms in Pernod sauce and Border lamb cutlets with a Grand-Marnier-and-rosemary glaze. *46 W. Richmond St., tel. 0131/668-3847. Reservations advised. Dress: casual but smart. AE, MC, V. Lunch during festival only. Closed Sun., Mon.*

$$$ **Martins.** Don't be put off by the look of this restaurant from the
★ outside. It's tucked away in a little back alley between Frederick and Castle streets and has a typically forbidding northern facade. All's well inside, though, and the food is tops. Organically grown local products, both animal and vegetable, are prominent on the menu, which has a strong hint of Scotland yet could not be further from a haggis-and-whisky theme. The best Scottish salmon, venison, fish, and west-coast shellfish appear in various forms—poached, baked, roasted, and in casseroles—usually with inventive sauces. Starters may include rabbit liver and mushrooms with wild-mushroom sauce or terrine of rabbit and chicory with orange. There's also a far-famed cheese board. This is the place for serious eating in an unstuffy atmosphere, and lunches are an excellent value. The wine list is serious but affordable and includes an excellent choice of half-bottles. Smoking is not permitted. *70 Rose St. North La., tel. 0131/225-3106. Reservations required. Jacket and tie preferred. AE, DC, MC, V. No Sat. lunch. Closed Sun., Mon.*

$$$ **Merchants.** On a street running below George IV Bridge and only moments from the Grassmarket and looming Edinburgh Castle, Merchants is competent and reliable. The decor is gently understated, with pinewood flooring, crisp white tablecloths, cane chairs, and exposed beams. The light jazz music playing in the background is definitely not intrusive. A sophisticated fixed-price menu (lunch £8.50–10.50, dinner £16.50–£18.50) in French and English, has such adventurous moments as veal in dill and coriander; lamb chops with raspberry-and-mint sauce; and herb roulade filled with prawns and avocado mousse, with orange-and-tarragon vinaigrette. *17 Merchant St., tel. 0131/225-4009. Reservations required. Dress: casual but neat. AE, DC, MC, V. Closed Sun.*

$$$ **Spices.** As its name implies, this restaurant specializes in spicy foods drawn from places like India, Persia, Zanzibar, and Goa. Try the Murgh Reshmee Kebab (barbecue chicken breast), the Lamb Pukhraj with pistachios, or the Jhinga Imlidhar (king prawns with tamarind and spices). Don't be afraid to experiment with Spice's phenomenal menu—all dishes have individually chosen and freshly ground spices, a world away from the usual restaurant "curry." The stylish russet decor with black chairs is complimented with carved wooden screens and attentive service. Health-conscious people will appreciate Spice's no-smoking dining area. *110 West Bow, tel. 0131/225-5028. Reservations advised. Dress: casual but smart. MC, V. Closed Sun.*

$$$ **Vito.** Like La Lanterna (*see below*), this is a basement restaurant, but here you'll find a whitewashed wine cellar with vaulted ceiling, arches, and nooks and crannies for intimate meals. The vaguely rustic Italian decor complements the genuinely Italian cuisine (there's a southern Italian owner and northern Italian chef, so all regions are featured on the menu). Dishes include king prawns in a sauce of tomato, cream, and brandy and veal stuffed with cheese and ham. The separate bar area is a good place for a quiet drink before dinner. *53A Frederick St., tel. 0131/225–5052. Reservations advised. Dress: casual but smart. AE, DC, MC, V.*

$$$ **The Witchery by the Castle.** As the name indicates, a somewhat eerie ambience—complete with flickering candlelight—reigns here. There are, in fact, supposed to be three ghosts in the place, one of whom haunts the refrigerator! The lugubrious, cavernous interior is festooned with cauldrons and broomsticks and decorated with cabalistic insignia. The inspiration for this spooky haunt derives from the fact that some 300 years ago hundreds of witches were executed on the Castlehill, barely a few dozen yards from where you will be seated. There's nothing spooky about the food, however, with fine venison, duck, lamb, salmon, and fillet steak among the specialties. *352 Castlehill, Royal Mile, tel. 0131/225–5613. Reservations required. Dress: casual. AE, DC, MC, V.*

$$ **Buntoms Thai Restaurant.** A room in the Linden Hotel was recently converted into this authentic-looking Thai restaurant by the addition of genuine Thai wall coverings and antiques. You can leave Georgian New Town at the door and be transported halfway around the world with such savory delights as hot-and-sour squid and mushroom salad, seafood cooked with broccoli in oyster sauce, or spiced chicken fried with cashew nuts and onions (one of this restaurant's best offerings). Don't come here if you're on a tight schedule—each dish is prepared fresh, but it's definitely worth the wait, and you'll want to savor each bite. *Linden Hotel, 9–13 Nelson St., tel. 0131/557–4344. Reservations required. Dress: casual. AE, DC, MC, V. Closed Sun. lunch.*

$$ **Jackson's.** Intimate and candlelit in a historic Old Town close, Jackson's offers good Scots fare, including excellent Aberdeen Angus steaks and Border lamb. Seafood and vegetarian specialties are always on the menu. The decor is rustic, with lots of greenery, stone walls, pine farmhouse-style tables and chairs, and fresh flowers. The wine list includes 60 malt whiskies and some Scottish country wines to complete the Scottish experience. *2 Jackson Close, 209–213 High St., Royal Mile, tel. 0131/225–1793. Reservations advised. AE, MC, V. Closed for lunch Sat. and Sun.*

$$ **Kweilin.** This pleasant family-run restaurant in Edinburgh's sedate New Town is popular with the city's Chinese community, as well as with tourists. The decor is traditional Chinese, with several large paintings depicting scenes from the Kwangsi province, of which Kweilin is the capital. There are always several suggested menus for two, three, or four diners, which are recommended; but you can, of course, select your own combinations of dishes. The fixed-menu offerings are a good value, starting at £13.50 per person and going up to £21.50 a head for the Executive Choice menu. *19–21 Dundas St., tel. 0131/557–1875. Reservations advised. Dress: casual. MC, V.*

$$ **La Lanterna.** This inconspicuous basement-level trattoria serves
★ wholesome and straightforward pastas—among them tagliatelle carbonara and spaghetti mare—and other Italian dishes, all in the best of humor. The family who runs the business can afford to be cheerful—their straightforward approach is popular and packs in the customers. The decor is pine-walled and postcard-pinned. Seats

are comfortable, though tables are set close. The restaurant is well located in center city, two minutes from Princes Street. *83 Hanover St., tel. 0131/226–3090. Reservations advised. Dress: casual. AE, MC, V. Closed Sun.*

$$ **Lancers.** This intimate Indian restaurant, decorated with rosewood tables and chairs, is located in the Stockbridge area of Edinburgh, just a short taxi ride from city center. It's on a fairly busy road, but external distractions are blocked out by window blinds, which add to the sense of intimacy. The feel of this place is a little like that of an officers' mess in Bengal, which is entirely appropriate, since it was named after the famed Bengal Lancers, who fought with such distinction alongside the British army in every quarter of the globe. As a simple introduction to Bengali cuisine, you could try the vegetarian (or nonvegetarian) *thali* (a sampler tray including rice, lentils, curries, and more.); those already initiated to the delights of this cuisine can pick and choose among varieties of *pasandas, kurmas, tikkas,* and *bhundas. 5 Hamilton Pl., tel. 0131/332–3444 or 0131/332–9559. Reservations advised. Dress: casual but neat. AE, MC, V.*

$$ **Old Orleans.** A first in Edinburgh: Cajun cooking, served with real Southern panache, plus Mexican and American dishes that include red snapper and alligator. Choose the spareribs and you are thoughtfully provided with a large bib and finger bowl of hot water. Decor is typical New Orleans: trellis and metalwork, brass instruments, and travel-related items; the music is blues and jazz. There is also a large, mirrored, American-style bar. *30 Grindlay St., tel. 0131/229–1511. Reservations advised. Dress: casual. AE, MC, V.*

$–$$ **The Doric Tavern.** Do not be put off by the rather tatty entrance staircase plastered with posters and playbills: Inside this café/bistro bar, the stripped wood floor, dark wood tables, and navy velvet curtains create a superbly subdued, languid atmosphere. The menu always features a daily special—like roast pigeon salad with raspberry vinegar dressing—and a selection of fresh fish poached with basil and cream. Lunch can be anything from a large salad, perhaps with strips of venison, to chicken with tarragon or a wild mushroom stir-fry. If you still can't decide, try the fixed-price lunch (£10.50) or dinner (£15.50), both excellent values. *15/16 Market St., tel. 0131/225–1084. Reservations advised Fri. and Sat. nights. Dress: casual. AE, MC, V. Closed Sun. Restaurant closes 11 PM (last orders 10:30), wine bar open until 1 AM weekdays, 2 AM weekends.*

$–$$ **Hendersons.** This was Edinburgh's original vegetarian restaurant, long before it was fashionable to offer wholesome, meatless creations. If you haven't summoned the courage to try an authentic haggis while in Scotland, come here to sample a vegetarian version. *94 Hanover St., tel. 0131/225–2131. Reservations not required. Dress: casual. AE, DC, MC, V. Closed Sun. except during festival.*

$–$$ **Howie's.** This simple neighborhood bistro doesn't have a liquor license, but you can bring your own bottle. The steaks are tender Aberdeen beef, the Loch Fyne herring are sweet-cured to Howie's own recipe, and the clientele is lively. *75 St. Leonard's St., tel. 0131/668–2917 (also at 63 Dalry Rd., tel. 0131/313–3334). Reservations advised. Dress: casual. MC, V. Open lunch Tues.–Sun., dinner daily.*

$–$$ **Kalpna.** This vegetarian Indian restaurant is on the city's south side,
★ close to the university. Don't be put off by the unremarkable facade among an ordinary row of shops, or by the low-key decor enlivened by Indian prints and fabric pictures: The food is unlike anything you are likely to encounter elsewhere in the city. If you can't decide what

you want to eat, order an Anapurna Thali, a sampler tray that generally comes with curried vegetables or meats complimented with coconut, peas, melt-in-the-mouth halva, fresh coriander, and a touch of garlic. Kalpna tends to fill up as the evening progresses, so book ahead if you want to eat after 8. At lunchtime and in the early evening (except perhaps at festival time) you can usually just drop in. *2/3 St. Patricks Sq., tel. 0131/667–9890. Reservations advised for dinner. Dress: casual. MC, V. Closed Sun., Christmas Day, Dec. 26, New Year's Day.*

$–$$ **Loon Fung.** Seafood is the specialty of this Cantonese restaurant. Delicious dishes include jumbo king prawns with garlic sauce and black pepper, fresh mussels with ginger and black bean sauce, and fried oysters with ginger and spring onions. The Loon Fung is small, friendly, and candlelit, with rapid service. The green and pink decor is relaxing, although tables are quite closely spaced. For two or more people, the set menu banquets are a good value. A take-out menu is available. *32 Grindlay St., tel. 0131/229–5757. Reservations advised. Dress: casual but smart. AE, MC, V.*

$–$$ **Peter's Cellars.** With a traditional "country cottage" look, complete with wooden booths, flowered curtains, and well-spaced tables, this cellar wine-bar-cum-restaurant is a relaxing venue where you are not expected to dress up. The food, though not elaborate, is carefully cooked with some imaginative touches. Try the seafood ragout, pork kebabs with plum sauce, or supreme of chicken stuffed with pineapple and cream cheese. The fixed-price lunch (£7) and dinner (£15) are a good deal. *11–13 William St., tel. 0131/226–3161. Reservations advised. Dress: casual. AE, MC, V.*

$–$$ **Pierre Victoire.** Edinburgh has four branches of this very popular bistro chain. All are fairly chaotic, enjoyable eateries serving healthy portions of French country cooking at low prices. The fish is fresh and especially good. Try the baked oysters with bacon and hollandaise. *38 Grassmarket, tel. 0131/226–2442 (open daily); 10 Victoria St., tel. 0131/225–1721 (closed Sun.); 8 Union St., tel. 0131/557–8451 (closed Mon.); and 5 Dock Pl., Leith, tel. 0131/556–6178 (closed Sun.). Reservations advised. Dress: casual but smart. MC, V.*

$–$$ **Waterfront Wine Bar and Bistro.** In the heart of Leith, Edinburgh's port, and one of the city's longest-established wine bars, the Waterfront is always busy with a local crowd in their twenties and thirties: Don't come here if you want a quiet meal *à deux*. Blackboards listing wines and daily specials hang on the stone walls, surrounded by shipping memorabilia. Grilled sardines with rosemary butter, wild mushrooms (in season), pan-fried pigeon breasts with strawberry and orange sauce, and fillets of sea bass in white wine and cream sauce are examples of the food on offer. *1a Dock Pl., Leith, tel. 0131/554–7427. Reservations advised (essential on weekends). Dress: casual but smart. MC, V.*

$–$$ **Xian City Chinese Restaurant.** Named after the fabled home of Chinese warriors, the Xian City specializes in Cantonese fare and provides a wealth of choices: The menu runs to five pages, offering a selection of duck, chicken, beef, pork, and vegetarian creations, in addition to the seafood dishes that head the list. The walls are adorned with back-lit Chinese scenes, and a large fish tank stands proudly in the middle of the restaurant, dividing it into two pleasant, comfortably sized dining rooms. Fixed-menu dinners are priced at around £15 per person for five courses. *217 High St., Royal Mile, tel. 0131/225–2999. Reservations advised. Dress: casual. AE, MC, V.*

Lodging

Edinburgh offers a variety of accommodations, many in traditional Georgian properties, some even in the New Town, only a few minutes from downtown. There are also a number of upscale hotels in the downtown area, each with an international flavor. If you are planning to stay in the area during the festival, be sure to reserve several months in advance. Also note that weekend rates in the larger hotels are always much cheaper than midweek rates, so if you want to stay in a plush hotel, come on the weekend.

Highly recommended lodgings are indicated by a star ★.

Category	Cost*
$$$$	over £120
$$$	£100–£120
$$	£80–£100
$	under £80

All prices are for a standard double room, including service, breakfast, and VAT.

$$$$ **Balmoral Hotel.** The attention to detail in the elegant rooms and
★ the sheer élan that has re-created the Edwardian heyday of this former grand railroad hotel all contribute to the Balmoral's growing popularity. Staying here, below the impressive clocktower marking the east end of Princes Street, gives a strong sense of being at the center of Edinburgh life. The hotel's main restaurant is the plush and stylish Grill Room (*see* Dining, *above*). *Princes St., EH2 2EQ, tel. 0131/556–2414, fax 0131/ 557–8740. 167 bedrooms, 22 suites. Facilities: 2 restaurants, bar, wine bar, patisserie, health club. AE, DC, MC, V.*

$$$$ **Caledonian.** A conspicuous block of red sandstone beyond the west
★ end of Princes Street Gardens, "the Caley" was built as the flagship hotel of the Caledonian Railway, and its imposing Victorian decor has been faithfully preserved. The public areas feature marbled green columns and an ornate stairwell with a burnished-metalwork balustrade. Rooms are exceptionally large and well appointed, and the generous width of the corridors reminds guests that this establishment was designed in a more sumptuous age. *Princes St., EH1 2AB, tel. 0131/225–2433, fax 0131/225–6632. 239 rooms with bath. Facilities: 2 restaurants, in-house movies. AE, DC, MC, V.*

$$$$ **Edinburgh Grand Sheraton.** Built in 1985, this property underwent a major refurbishment in 1992/3, when two new restaurants were added: the brasserie-style **Terrace,** overlooking Edinburgh Castle and Festival Square, and the intimate **Grill Room,** featuring fine fish, game, and Scottish beef. Bedrooms are well above average size, and many of them are decorated in traditional style with tartan furnishings and prints of old Edinburgh. The grandest rooms face the castle. You can enjoy piano music in the bar and lounge area, and there's a shopping gallery to browse in. A ground floor reception area features a sweeping grand staircase. The hotel's popularity with locals, especially after work and in the evening before and after concerts at Usher Hall, across the street, testifies to its continuing part in Edinburgh's social life. *1 Festival Sq., EH3 9SR, tel. 0131/229–*

9131, fax 0131/228–4510. 261 rooms with bath. Facilities: 2 restaurants, bar; in-house movies, health club, pool, sauna. AE, DC, MC, V.

$$$$ **Royal Terrace.** Over 150 years ago, the renowned Edinburgh archi-
★ tect Playfair designed the street called Royal Terrace as a tribute
to King George IV. Most of the impressive Georgian homes on this
block were owned by merchants, and the upper floors command a
view across the Firth of Forth to Fife. The present hotel consists of
a half dozen of these original merchant houses, combined to create
one of the most luxurious lodgings in the city. The exterior is unas-
suming, giving no hint of the sybaritic interior. That this is a hotel
devoted to comfort, however, becomes immediately apparent as one
enters the reception area, which is deeply carpeted and adorned
with a massive pair of chandeliers and an eclectic collection of objets
d'art. All rooms are furnished to an equally high standard and even
include telephones in the marble bathrooms. The best rooms— commanding the view across the city to the Forth—are on the top floors
at the front. *18 Royal Terr., EH7 5AQ, tel. 0131/557–3222, fax
0131/557–5334. 97 rooms with bath. Facilities: restaurant; bar; health
club with whirlpool, pool, steam room, and sauna; in-house movies;
patio; gardens. AE, DC, MC, V.*

$$$ **Channings.** Five Edwardian terraced houses make up this elegant
★ hotel in an upscale neighborhood just minutes from the west end of
Princes Street. Quiet rooms with restrained colors such as beige,
cream, and gray, antiques, and great views of Fife (from those facing
north) set an elegant and refined tone. The **Brasserie** restaurant
offers excellent value, especially at lunchtime. Try the crab cakes
with crayfish bisque. *South Learmonth Gardens, EH4 1EZ, tel.
0131/315–2226, fax 0131/332–9631. 48 rooms with bath. Facilities: res-
taurant. AE, DC, MC, V.*

$$$ **George Intercontinental.** Part of this hotel served as an insurance-
★ company office during the 19th century, and the splendidly ornate
business hall remains intact as the Carvery Restaurant, the less
expensive of the two dining rooms. The hotel's modern extension,
added in 1972, is carefully blended with the original structure (1881),
and the George retains a more intimate feeling than you'd expect
from a rather large hotel. Guest rooms are light, airy, and immaculate, with reproduction-antique furnishings; sizes range from adequate to spacious, and the desks are unusually large. The best rooms
are at the back of the hotel, high up and looking north over the New
Town roofs to the Firth of Forth and to Fife beyond. However, even
rooms overlooking George Street southward are quiet, and they
have bird's-eye views of the 18th-century surroundings. The central
location, only yards from the financial center of St. Andrew Square,
has only one disadvantage: difficult parking. The pricey French-
style Le Chambertin restaurant has excellent food, and its somme-
lier is one of only two members of the Guild of Master Sommeliers
in Scotland. *19–21 George St., EH2 2PB, tel. 0131/225–1251, fax
0131/226–5644. 195 rooms with bath. Facilities: 2 restaurants, bar;
minibars and tea- and coffee-making facilities in rooms. AE, DC,
MC, V.*

$$$ **Howard Hotel.** The Howard, close to Drummond Place, is a good
example of a New Town building, elegant and superbly propor-
tioned. It is also small enough to offer personal attention. All bed-
rooms are spacious and well equipped—you'll find trouser presses,
hairdryers, and tea- and coffee-making equipment, for example—
and some overlook the garden. *32 Great King St., EH3 6QH, tel.
0131/557–3500, fax 0131/557–6515. 16 rooms with bath. Facilities: res-
taurant, garden. AE, DC, MC, V.*

$$$ **Mount Royal Hotel.** Perched above the ground-floor shops on Princes Street and overlooking Edinburgh Castle and the Princes Street Gardens, the entrance to the Mount Royal is almost hidden between two of the city's major stores (Jenners and Marks & Spencer) and could easily be overlooked at first. Bedrooms have wood furnishings and pastel color schemes; the best views are from the rooms at the front of the hotel. *52 Princes St., EH2 2DQ, tel. 0131/225–7161, fax 0131/220–4671. 159 rooms with bath. Facilities: restaurant. AE, DC, MC, V.*

$$$ **Norton House.** This magnificent 1861 manor house was once the home of the Usher brewing family and still has the feeling of a private country home. Situated on idyllic grounds on the outskirts of Edinburgh, the Norton House provides a lovely alternative to downtown lodgings, yet is easily accessible from center city. The elegant reception area is graced by marble pillars, and there is a striking wooden staircase leading to the upper floors. The airy guest rooms are decorated with modern furniture and delicate pastel shades. Guests can choose between two restaurants—the elegant main dining room inside, which offers decent Continental food, or the Conservatory, with its fine views of the gardens. *Ingliston, EH28 8LX, tel. 0131/333–1275; fax 0131/333–5305. 47 rooms with bath. Facilities: 2 restaurants, bar; tea- and coffee-making facilities in rooms; parking, courtesy bus to airport and train stations. AE, DC, MC, V.*

$$$ **Scandic Crown.** Although it was built late in the 1980s, this modern hotel blends into its surroundings among the ancient buildings on the Royal Mile. Its location is the main reason to stay here. Bedrooms are roomy, but the decor is bland beiges and woods and the atmosphere lacking. The restaurant serves some Scandinavian dishes, including a smorgasbord. *80 High St., Royal Mile, EH1 1TH, tel. 0131/557–9797, fax 0131/557–9789. 238 rooms with bath. Facilities: restaurants, leisure center, conference facilities. AE, DC, MC, V.*

$$$ **Stakis Grosvenor Hotel.** This attractive, comfortable hotel in the West End comprises several converted terrace houses and is distinguished by an elegant Victorian facade. Guests are pampered as soon as they enter the large reception area, which is furnished with ample Chesterfield armchairs. The single rooms are fairly small, and the doubles are just adequate. All are brightly decorated with peach curtains and floral bedspreads; the furniture is made of dark wood. First- and second-floor bedrooms have high ceilings with attractive plaster cornices. Just a short walk from the West End's shopping district, the hotel is convenient to the Haymarket railway station. *Grosvenor St., EH12 5EA, tel. 0131/226–6001, fax 0131/220–2387. 136 rooms with bath. Facilities: restaurant, 2 bars. AE, DC, MC, V.*

$$ **Albany.** Three fine Georgian houses with many original features have been carefully converted into this comfortable city-center hotel. Rooms have high ceilings, neutral color schemes, and plain brown furnishings. Multicolored bedspreads match the curtains, a pleasant compliment to the furniture. There's a good restaurant in the basement and a bar with piano. *39 Albany St., EH1 3Q4, tel. 0131/556–0397, fax 0131/557–6633. 20 rooms with bath. Facilities: restaurant, bar. MC, V.*

$$ **Roxburghe.** As you sit in a deep leather armchair, the ticking of an antique clock in the background, and look out over the trees of Charlotte Square, it is easy to forget you are half a minute from Princes Street and in the heart of Edinburgh's financial center. The furniture, which includes many antique pieces, has the sheen of genera-

tions of polish. In the rooms, Adam fireplaces and ornate plaster-work complement the hotel's harmonious Georgian architecture. This country-house-come-to-town moves nearer modern times with its busy bar and informal ground-floor restaurant, **The Melrose Room,** but becomes positively overdone in its excessively draped, main dining room downstairs. (The food, unlike the decor, is forgettable.) Not as expensive as the Sheraton or the Caledonian, the Roxburghe is hard to beat for a convenient location, though it can be a little noisy. *38 Charlotte Sq., EH2 4HG, tel. 0131/225–3921, fax 0131/220–2518. 75 rooms with bath. Facilities: restaurant, bar, coffee shop, tea- and coffee-making facilities in rooms. AE, DC, MC, V.*

$ **Ashdene House.** On a quiet residential street on the south side of Edinburgh, yet only 10 minutes from the city center by bus, this Edwardian house is a first-class bed-and-breakfast where smoking is not permitted. Bedrooms are decorated without frills or flounces, just modern furnishings and floral fabrics, but in the downstairs public areas, deep, rich color schemes complement the age of the house. The owners are particularly helpful in arranging tours and evening theater entertainment, and they will recommend local restaurants. There is ample parking on the street and in a lot. *23 Fountainhall Rd., EH9 2LN, tel. 0131/667–6026. 5 rooms with shower. No credit cards.*

$ **Classic Guest House.** It is easy to find this Victorian terraced house, on a main route from the south into Edinburgh. The decor is modern classic: stripped pine floors throughout, elegant chinoiserie in the dining room, and pastel florals in the warm bedrooms. Smoking is not permitted. *50 Mayfield Rd., EH9 2NH, tel. 0131/667–5847. 4 rooms, 3 with en suite shower, 1 with private bath (not en suite). MC, V.*

$ **Crannoch But & Ben.** This is a top-of-the-range bed-and-breakfast offering private facilities, a comfortable residents' lounge, and excellent fried breakfasts. Located only 3 miles from the city and on a good bus route, it's also particularly convenient for the airport. *467 Queensferry Rd., EH4 7ND, tel. 0131/336–5688. 2 rooms with bath. No credit cards.*

$ ★ **Drummond House.** Many hotels would be put to shame by the accommodations at this top-of-the-range guest house in the heart of the New Town, within walking distance of the city center. The Georgian terraced house has spacious rooms, sumptuously decorated and furnished with swagged curtains, canopied beds, and antique furniture—all in elegant taste to suit the age of the house. Dinner (for guests only) is of Cordon Bleu standard. Smoking is not permitted inside Drummond House, but guests can smoke while strolling through the several acres of private gardens open only to Drummond Place residents and guests. *17 Drummond Pl, EH3 6PL, tel. and fax 0131/557–9189. 4 rooms, 2 with bath, 2 with shower. Facilities: dining room. MC, V.*

$ **Ellesmere Guest House.** Yet another Victorian terraced house, this bed-and-breakfast is close to the King's Theatre and several good restaurants. Its first-class rooms have modern furniture with pleasant pastel floral bedspreads and curtains; one room has a four-poster bed. Guests can relax in the comfortable sitting room, but the owners prefer that they not smoke. Ellesmere is stocked with brochures covering things to do in Edinburgh. *11 Glengyle Terr., EH3 9LN, tel. 0131/229–4823, fax 0131/229–5285. 6 rooms, 2 with bath, 2 with shower. No credit cards.*

$ Lodge Hotel. This stone detached Georgian house is easy to find on
★ the main A8 Edinburgh–Glasgow road, a 15-minute walk from
Princes Street. It is furnished in period style, with swagged curtains
and canopied beds. The spacious bedrooms are stocked with fresh
flowers and fruit as well as a decanter of sherry. Downstairs, there
is a cocktail bar and peaceful pink-and-gray sitting room. The dining
room has well-spaced tables covered with crisp white cloths and a
menu that features fresh Scottish produce, along with the standard
beef, game, salmon, and seafood. *6 Hampton Terr., West Coates
EH12 5JD, tel. 0131/337–3682, fax 0131/313–1700. 12 rooms with bath
or shower (most rooms are reserved for nonsmokers). MC. V.*

$ Mrs. Coleman. This bed-and-breakfast is an elegant Victorian de-
tached house, which still has many period trimmings, such as the
original plaster cornices in many of the spacious rooms. The decor
is marked by cheerful colors and floral fabrics, and the furnishings
are modern. The owners are particularly friendly and helpful. *54
Craigmillar Park, EHI6 5PS, tel. 0131/668–3408. 3 rooms with
shower. No credit cards.*

$ Mrs. Graham. It may be difficult to find a parking space on the quiet
★ back street where this Victorian terraced house is situated, but it's
easy enough to take Bus 3, 31, 69, 80, or 81 here, south from the city
center. The spotlessly clean bed-and-breakfast has antique furniture complemented by beautiful kilim rugs and wall hangings. *18
Moston Terr., EH9 2DE, tel. 0131/667–3466. 2 rooms, share 1 bathroom. No credit cards. Open May–Oct.*

$ Mrs. Valerie Livingstone. This is a modern terraced villa close to
Arthur's Seat, with fine views over the Firth of Forth. Smoking is
not permitted, and Mrs. Livingstone maintains a high standard of
accommodation and meals. *50 Paisley Crescent, EH8 7JQ, tel.
0131/661-6337. 2 rooms. No credit cards. Open Apr.–Oct.*

$ Roselea House. Another south-side bed-and-breakfast guest house,
on the main route from the south, the Roselea is easy to find. The
Victorian house is decorated in pink-and-blue floral swags and wallpaper, and there is a sitting room for guests. *11 Mayfield Rd., EH9
2NG, tel. 0131/667–6155, fax 0131/667–3556. 7 rooms, 2 with bath, 5
with shower. AE, MC, V.*

$ Sibbet House. The late-18th-century Georgian elegance of this small
★ terraced town house in Edinburgh's New Town has been enhanced
by careful attention to drapery, decor, and period antique furniture.
Prices are reasonable, and breakfasts are traditionally Scottish and
sustaining, to say the least. You must eat out in the evenings, but all
kinds of restaurants are only a few minutes' stroll away. This establishment also offers a facility that few others can match—the host
plays the bagpipes (but only on request). *26 Northumberland St.,
EH3 6LS, tel. 0131/556–1078, fax 0131/557–9445. 4 rooms, 3 with
shower, 1 with bath. MC, V.*

$ Silverburn Steading. Just outside Edinburgh in a rural setting at
the foot of the Pentland Hills, this bed-and-breakfast makes a relaxing base to return to after a day sightseeing in the city center,
only 20 minutes away by car. Ask for a room at the back if traffic
noise bothers you. *Silverburn, Penicuik, Midlothian EH26 9LJ, tel.
01968/78420. 3 rooms, 2 with bath. No credit cards.*

$ Stuart House. Within 15 minutes' walk of the city center, this bed-
★ and-breakfast is in a Victorian terraced house with some fine plasterwork. The decor suits the structure: Bold colors, floral fabrics,
and generously curtained windows combine with antique and tradi-

tional-style furniture and chandeliers to create an opulent ambience. A light supper can be served in guests' rooms in the evening, if required. Smoking is not permitted. *12 E. Claremont St., EH7 4JP, tel. 0131/557–9030. 7 rooms with bath or shower. No credit cards.*

$ **Teviotdale House.** This is a small, family-run and owned hotel in Edinburgh's genteel south side. The hosts, the Covilles, are friendly, and the house is a warm retreat on a tree-lined street away from but within reach of center-city bustle (a 30-minute walk from Charlotte Sq.). Individually decorated rooms and innovative, appetizing home cooking make this a pleasant, reasonable budget alternative to center-city hotels. The establishment is entirely nonsmoking. *53 Grange Loan, EH9 2ER, tel. and fax 0131/667–4376. 7 rooms, 5 with en suite bath, 2 with bath (not en suite). Facilities: dining room. AE, MC, V.*

$ **Thrums Private Hotel.** There is a pleasing mix of the modern and traditional in this detached Victorian house. It is small, cozy, and quiet, yet surprisingly close to downtown Edinburgh. *14 Minto St., EH9 1RQ, tel. 0131/667–5545. 14 rooms, 12 with bath. Facilities: restaurant, bar, garden. MC, V. Closed Christmas Day, New Year's Day, and 1 week Jan.*

$ **Turret Guest House.** On a quiet residential street on the south side, this bed-and-breakfast is close to bus routes as well as the Commonwealth Pool and Holyrood Park. Cheerful and cozy, it has modern furnishings, but many of the building's Victorian cornices, paneled doors, and high ceilings remain. *8 Kilmaurs Terr., EH16 5DR, tel. 0131/667–6704. 6 rooms, 3 with shower. No credit cards.*

$ **28 Northumberland Street.** An exceptional standard is set at this
★ bed-and-breakfast in the center of the New Town. The Georgian terraced house has shuttered windows and antique furniture and rugs (some used as wall hangings). One single bedroom has been transformed into an Indian-style tent with fabric-covered walls and ceiling. The host, a keen golfer, and the hostess, a lawyer, both enjoy meeting guests and are very helpful. *28 Northumberland St., EH3 6LS, tel. 0131/557–8036, fax 0131/558–3453. 3 rooms with bath or shower. Facilities: dining room. DC, MC, V.*

The Arts and Nightlife

The Arts

Edinburgh is world renowned for its flagship arts event, the **Edinburgh International Festival,** and there is no escaping a sense of theater if you visit the city from August to early September. The annual festival has attracted all sorts of international performers since its inception in 1947. Even more obvious to the casual stroller during this time is the refreshingly irreverent Edinburgh Festival Fringe, unruly child of the official festival, which spills out of halls and theaters and onto the streets all over town. At other times throughout the year professional and amateur groups alike offer a range of cultural options appropriate to a capital city, even if the publicity that emanates from Edinburgh's rival, Glasgow, would want you to believe otherwise.

The List, available from newsagents throughout the city, and *What's On in Edinburgh,* available from the Information Centre (*see* Important Addresses and Numbers in Essential Information, *above*) carry the most up-to-date details about cultural events. *The Scots-*

man, an Edinburgh daily, also carries reviews on its arts pages on Monday and Wednesday. Tickets are generally available from the relevant box office in advance; in some cases, from certain designated travel agents; or at the door, although concerts by national orchestras often sell out long before the day of the performance.

The **Edinburgh International Festival** (1995: Aug. 13–Sept. 2), the premier arts event of the year, has for nearly 50 years attracted performing artists of international caliber to a celebration of music, dance, and drama. *Advance information, programs, tickets, and reservations available from the Edinburgh Festival Office, 21 Market St., Edinburgh EH1 1BW, tel. 0131/226–4001.*

The **Edinburgh Festival Fringe** offers many theatrical and musical events, some by amateur groups (you have been warned) and is more of a grab bag than the official festival. During festival time it's possible to arrange your own entertainment program from morning to midnight and beyond, if you do not feel overwhelmed by the variety available. *Information, programs, and tickets available from Edinburgh Festival Fringe, 180 High St., Edinburgh EH1 1QS, tel. 0131/226–5257 or 0131/226–5259.*

The **Edinburgh Film Festival** (1995: August 12–27) is yet another aspect of this busy summer festival logjam. *Advance information and programs available from the Edinburgh Film Festival, at the Filmhouse, 88 Lothian Rd., Edinburgh EH3 9BZ, tel. 0131/228–4051. Box office, tel. 0131/228–2688.*

The **Edinburgh Military Tattoo** (1995: Aug. 4–26) may not be art, but it is certainly entertainment. It is sometimes confused with the festival itself, partly because the dates overlap. This celebration of martial music and skills is set on the castle esplanade, and the dramatic backdrop augments the spectacle. Dress warmly for late-evening performances. Even if it rains the show most definitely goes on. *Tickets and information available from Edinburgh Military Tattoo, 22 Market St., Edinburgh, EH1 1QB, tel. 0131/225–1188.*

Away from the August-to-September festival overkill, the **Edinburgh Folk Festival** (Box 528, Edinburgh, EH10 4DU, tel. 0131/556–3181) usually takes place around Easter each year. This 10-day event blends performances by Scottish and international folk artists of the highest caliber.

Traditional Theater Edinburgh's three main theaters are the **Royal Lyceum** (Grindlay St., tel. 0131/229–9697) and the **King's** (Leven St., tel. 0131/229–1201), both of which offer contemporary and traditional dramatic works, and **Edinburgh Festival Theatre,** (Nicolson St., tel. 0131/529–6000), which hosts a variety of theatrical and musical entertainment.

The Playhouse (Greenside Pl., tel. 0131/557–2692) hosts mostly popular artists and has a Christmas pantomime. At Musselburgh, on the eastern outskirts of Edinburgh, the **Brunton Theatre** (Brunton Hall, High St., Musselburgh, tel. 0131/665–2240) offers a regular program of performances. At the **Church Hill Theatre** (Morningside Rd., tel. 0131/447–7597), local dramatic societies mount productions of a high standard.

Modern Theater The **Traverse Theatre** (Cambridge St., tel. 0131/228–1404) has developed a solid reputation as a venue for stimulating new work—though it has toned down its previously avant-garde approach a little in an effort to secure sponsorship.

The **Netherbow Arts Centre** (43 High St., tel. 0131/556–9579) includes modern plays in its program of music, drama, and cabaret, as does the **Theatre Workshop** (34 Hamilton Pl., tel. 0131/225–7942), which hosts fringe events during the Edinburgh Festival and modern, community-based theater all year.

Music   The **Usher Hall** (Lothian Rd., tel. 0131/228–1155) is Edinburgh's grandest concert hall, venue for the Scottish National Orchestra during its winter season. More intimate in scale and used generally for smaller recitals and chamber music is the **Queen's Hall** (Nicolson St., tel. 0131/668–3456). You can find popular artists at the **Playhouse** (*see above*).

For jazz enthusiasts the main focus of entertainment is the **International Jazz Festival** (116 The Canongate, Edinburgh, EH8 8DD, tel. 0131/557–1642), held in August each year, but throughout the year live jazz can also be found in the city. Consult *The List* for information.

Dance   Edinburgh has no ballet or modern-dance companies of its own, but visiting companies perform from time to time at the King's Theatre or Royal Lyceum (*see above*).

Film   Apart from cinema chains, Edinburgh has the excellent **Filmhouse** (88 Lothian Rd., tel. 0131/228–6382; box office, 0131/228–2688), which is the best venue for modern, foreign-language, offbeat, or simply less-commercial films. A copy of its diverse monthly program is available from the box office and at a variety of other locations throughout the city (at the Tourist Centre, for example, or in theater foyers).

Of the other cinemas, the family-owned and run **Dominion** (Newbattle Terrace, tel. 0131/447–2660) is by far the most pleasant to visit—it is small and friendly and has a bar and restaurant offering light meals. The choice of films is as good as that of the larger movie houses.

Nightlife

Edinburgh's nightlife is quite varied and includes discos, Scottish musical evenings, and *ceilidhs* (pronounced *kay-lees*). The Edinburgh and Scotland Information Centre above Waverley Market (*see* Important Addresses and Numbers in Essential Information, *above*) can supply information on various categories of nightlife, especially on spots offering dinner-dances. Jazz and folk music in general are wide ranging, though pub and hotel venues change. *The List* gives much information on the music scene. In quiet-living Edinburgh, there are no nightclubs of the cabaret-and-striptease variety.

Casinos   **Berkeley Casino Club** (2 Rutland Pl., tel. 0131/228–4446) is a private club that offers free membership on 48 hours' notice, as do **Casino Martell** (7 Newington Rd., tel. 0131/667–7763), the **Stanley** (5b York Pl., tel. 0131/556–1055), and **Stakis Regency Casino** (14 Picardy Pl., tel. 0131/557–3585), whose restaurant is highly rated.

Pubs/Bars   **Abbotsford** (3 Rose St., tel. 0131/225–1894) offers five real ales (changing all the time), bar lunches, and lots of Victorian atmosphere.

Drum and Monkey (80 Queen St., tel. 0131/538–8111), with cozy dark wood booths and a maroon color scheme, is just the place for soup and sandwich lunches with a pint of Old Wallop beer.

Milne's Bar (21–25 Rose St., tel. 0131/225–6738) is known as the poets' pub because of its popularity with the Edinburgh literati. Pies and baked potatoes go well with seven real ales and varying guest beers. The place was recently redecorated and made to look old with Victorian advertisements and photos of old Edinburgh.

Tiles (1 St. Andrew Sq., tel. 0131/558–1507), a converted banking hall, gets its name from the wealth of tiles covering the walls. The ceiling is elaborate plasterwork. The 10 to 15 real ales are complemented by an à la carte bistro menu.

Discos/ Nightclubs Many Edinburgh discos offer reduced admission and/or less expensive drinks for early revelers.

Buster Browns (25–27 Market St., tel. 0131/226–4224) offers mainstream chart sounds Friday–Sunday 10:30 PM–2 AM.

The Lanes (S. Charlotte La., tel. 0131/226–6828), a basement bar with a dance floor, is popular with the twenties and thirties crowd. It's open Monday–Thursday 9 PM–3 AM, Friday 5 PM–3 AM, Saturday and Sunday 7 PM–3 AM.

Minus One (Carlton Highland Hotel, North Bridge, tel. 0131/556–7277) has live music and a DJ on Friday and Saturday and a DJ only on Thursday. The sounds here are mainstream, not for teenyboppers or old fogies. It's open Thursday–Saturday 10 PM–3 AM.

The **Cavendish** (West Tollcross, tel. 0131/228–3252) is a venue used by different groups and offering a variety of music. Open Thursday–Saturday 9 PM–3 AM.

Red Hot Pepper Club (3 Semple St., tel. 0131/229–7733) features mainstream music Friday and Saturday 10 PM–4 AM.

Folk Clubs There are always folk performers in various pubs throughout the city. **Edinburgh Folk Club** (Cafe Royal, 17 W. Register St., tel. 0131/339–4083) features folk music every Wednesday at 8 PM.

Scottish Evenings and Ceilidhs Several hotels feature traditional Scottish-music evenings in the summer season, including the **Carlton Highland Hotel** (North Bridge, tel. 0131/556–7277) and **George Hotel** (George St., tel. 0131/225–1251). Contact the individual hotels for information.

Other well-established Scottish entertainments include **Jamie's Scottish Evening** (King James Hotel, Leith St., tel. 0131/556–0111) and **The Scottish Experience** (12 High St., tel. 0131/557–9350).

Cocktail Bars **Harry's Bar** (7b Randolph Pl., tel. 0131/539–8100) is in a basement and decorated with Americana. Despite the disco music, it is hugely popular with locals. Harry's is open daily noon–1 AM.

L'Attache (beneath the Rutland Hotel, 1 Rutland Pl., tel. 0131/229–3402), another basement bar, has live folk and rock music Sunday–Thursday 8 PM–1:30 AM, Friday and Saturday 8 PM–2 AM.

Madogs (38A George St., tel. 0131/225–4308) was one of Edinburgh's first all-American cocktail bar-restaurants. It's popular with professionals after work and has live music most weeknights. It's open Sunday 6:30 PM–2 AM, Monday–Wednesday noon–2 AM, Thursday–Saturday noon–3 AM. No sneakers.

Excursions from Edinburgh

Tour 3: West Lothian and the Forth Valley

Numbers in the margin correspond to points of interest on the West Lothian and the Forth Valley map.

The Lothians is the collective name given to the swath of country-side surrounding Edinburgh. This driving tour of West Lothian explores the Forth Valley west of Edinburgh, as well as some of the territory north of the River Forth. In a round-trip of about 70 miles, it is possible to see plenty of the central belt of Scotland and to skirt the edge of the Central Highlands. The river Forth snakes across a widening floodplain on its descent from the Highlands, and by the time it reaches the western extremities of Edinburgh, it has already passed below the mighty Forth bridges and become a broad estuary.

This is the route to take if your interests incline toward castles and stately homes because they sprout thickly on both sides of the Forth. Note that it is possible to visit some of the places included in this excursion by train: Dalmeny, Linlithgow, and Dunfermline all have rail stations. Bus services link most areas as well, but working out a detailed itinerary by bus would be best left to your travel agent or guide.

Leave Edinburgh by Queensferry Road—the A90—and follow signs for the Forth Bridge. Beyond the city boundary at **Cramond** (*see* Off the Beaten Track, *above*) take the slip road, B924, for South
❶ Queensferry, watching for signs to **Dalmeny House,** the first of the stately homes clustered on the western edge of Edinburgh. Home of the Earl and Countess of Rosebery, this 1815 Tudor Gothic pile displays among its sumptuous contents the best of the family's famous collection of 18th-century French furniture. (Much of this collection was formerly displayed at Mentmore, the country seat 40 miles north of London, which belonged to the present earl's grandfather, Baron Mayer de Rothschild.) Highlights include the library; the drawing room, with its tapestries and highly wrought French furniture; the Napoleon Room; and the Vincennes and Sevres porcelain collections. *B924, by South Queensferry (7 mi west of Edinburgh), tel. 0131/331–1888. Admission: £3.40 adults, £1.80 children, £2.70 students. Open May–Sept., Mon. and Tues. noon–5:30, Sun. 1–5:30. Last admission 4:45.*

Follow the B924 for the descent to South Queensferry and views of
❷ the **Forth bridges.** The **Forth Rail Bridge,** which looms over the former Forth ferry port, was opened in 1890 and is 2,765 yards long, except on a hot summer's day when it expands by about another yard! Its neighbor is the 1,993-yard-long **Forth Road Bridge,** opened in 1964.

The B924 continues westward under the approaches to the suspension bridge and then meets the A904. On turning right, onto A904,
❸ you'll see signs for **Hopetoun House.** These palatial premises, home of the marquesses of Linlithgow, are considered to be among the Adam family's finest designs. The pile was started in 1699 to the original plans of Sir William Bruce, then enlarged between 1721 and 1754 by William Adam and his son Robert. There is a notable painting collection, and the house has decorative work of the highest order, plus all the paraphernalia to amuse visitors: nature trail, restaurant, stables, museum, garden center. Much of the wealth that created this sumptuous building came from the family's mining in-

West Lothian and the Forth Valley

KEY

— Rail Lines

Edinburgh

Leith

Lauriston Castle

Dalmeny House **1**

Cramond

Dalmeny

Forth bridges **2**

Queensferry

Firth of Forth

Inverkeithing

Hopetoun House **3**

Rosyth

Blackness **5** **4** House of the Binns

6 Linlithgow Palace

Linlithgow

Union Canal

Dunfermline Abbey and Palace **10**

Andrew Carnegie Birthplace Museum **9**

Dunfermline

Culross **8**

Bo'Ness

Grangemouth

Falkirk

Larbert

Denny

Stirling

Alloa

Clackmannan

Dunmore

Airth

Carron

River Carron

River Forth

Kincardine

Saline

BLAIRADAM FOREST

Kelty

Cowdenbeath

Lochgelly

Ballingry

Scotlandwell

Loch Leven

Glenrothes

Thornton

Kirkcaldy

Kinghorn

Burntisland

Auchtertool

River Devon

Dollar

Castle Campbell **7**

Rumbling Bridge

Powmill

Tillicoultry

Alva

Fallin

N

6 miles

9 km

A915

A955

A92

A921

A911

B921

A910

A907

A909

A925

A921

A909

A823

B914

B996

M90

A985

A994

A904

A985

A903

A904

A801

A706

M9

B924

A90

M9

A803

M9

A876

A977

A985

A91

B908

A908

B913

B9037

A977

B996

M876

A872

M80

M9

A9

A823

A907

terests. *West of South Queensferry, tel. 0131/331–2451. Admission: £3.80 adults, £1.90 children, £3.10 students and senior citizens, £10.50 family ticket. Open Apr.–Sept., daily 10–5:30 (last admission 4:45).*

❹ On this Forth Valley castle trail you can also visit the **House of the Binns,** signed from the A904. Here the 17th-century General Tam Dalyell transformed a fortified stronghold into a gracious mansion. The present exterior dates from around 1810 and shows a remodeling into a kind of mock fort with crenellated battlements and turrets. Inside there are magnificent plaster ceilings in Elizabethan style. *Off A904, 4 mi east of Linlithgow, tel. 0131/226–5922. Admission: £3 adults, £1.50 children, students, and senior citizens. Open June–Sept., Sat.–Thurs. 1:30–5:30 (last tour 5 PM).*

For a look at a more austere fortress, follow signs off the A904 to ❺ **Blackness.** The castle here stands like a grounded gray hulk on the very edge of the Forth. A curious 15th-century structure, it has had a varied career as a strategic fortress, state prison, powder magazine, and youth hostel. The countryside is gently green and cultivated, and open views extend across the blue Forth to the distant ramparts of the Ochil Hills (seen in close-up later on the route). *B903, 4 mi northeast of Linlithgow, tel. 0131/244–3101. Admission: £1.50 adults, £1 senior citizens, 75p children. Open Apr.–Sept., Mon.–Sat. 9:30–6, Sun. 2–6; Oct.–Mar., Mon.–Wed. and Sat. 9:30–4, Thurs. 9:30–noon, Sun. 2–4.*

From Blackness, take the B903 to its junction with the A904. Turn left for Linlithgow on the A803.

Time Out The **Four Marys** (67 High St., Linlithgow) specializes in uncomplicated but wholesome pub lunches.

❻ On the edge of Linlithgow Loch stands the splendid ruin of **Linlithgow Palace,** birthplace of Mary, Queen of Scots (1542). Burned, perhaps by accident, by Hanoverian troops during the last Jacobite rebellion in 1746, this impressive shell stands on a site of great antiquity, though nothing for certain survived an earlier fire in 1424. The palace gatehouse is from the early 16th century, and the central courtyard's elaborate fountain dates from around 1535, but the halls and great rooms are cold stone echoing husks. *South shore of Linlithgow Loch, tel. 0131/244–3101. Admission: £2 adults, £1.25 senior citizens, 75p children. Open Apr.–Sept., Mon.–Sat. 9:30–6, Sun. 2–6; Oct.–Mar., Mon.–Sat. 9:30–4, Sun. 2–4.*

At this point it's best to join the M9, which will speed you westward. From the M9 you will begin to gain tempting glimpses of the Highland hills to the northwest and the long humped wall of the Ochil Hills, across the river-plain to the north. The **River Carron,** which flows under the M9, gave its name to the *carronade,* a kind of cannon manufactured in Falkirk, a few minutes to the southwest. On your right you'll notice the apocalyptic complex of Grangemouth Refinery (impressive by night), which you may also smell if the wind is right (or wrong!). The refinery processes North Sea crude, but was originally sited here because of the now extinct oil-shale extraction industry of West Lothian, pioneered by a Scot, James "Paraffin" Young. This short section may not be the most scenic in Scotland, but it has certainly played its role in the nation's industrial history.

Follow Kincardine Bridge signs off the motorway, cross the Forth and take the A977 north from Kincardine, formerly a trading port and distillery center. Take the A985 to Alloa, get on the A908 (signed Tillicoultry) for a short stretch, and then pick up the B908 (signed

Alva). At this point you'll be leaving the industrial northern shore of the Forth behind.

The scarp face of the **Ochil Hills** looms unmistakably ahead, an old fault line, bearing up the harder volcanic rocks in contrast to the softer coal measures through which you have just traveled. The steep Ochils provided grazing land and water power for Scotland's second-largest textile area. Some mills still survive in the so-called Hillfoots towns on the scarp edge east of Stirling. You can explore this region by following the A91 eastward at **Alva.** Several walkers' routes run into the narrow chinks of glens here. Behind Alva is **Alva Glen** (park near the converted Strude Mill, at the top and eastern end of the little town). A little farther east is the **Ochil Hills Woodland Park,** which provides access to Silver Glen. The **Mill Glen,** behind Tillicoultry (pronounced *tilly-COOT-ree*), and its giant quarry, fine waterfalls, and interesting plants is another option for energetic explorers. The tourist information center at Tillicoultry can provide further information, as well as a *Mill Trail* brochure, which can lead you to a variety of mill shops offering bargain woolen and tweed goods.

The main road, squeezed between the gentle River Devon and the steep slopes above, continues to **Dollar.** This *douce* (Scots for *well - mannered* and *gentle*) and tidy town below the slopes lies at the mouth of Dollar Glen. At first sight, the tilting slopes seem an unlikely terrain for wheeled vehicles. By following signs for **Castle Campbell,** however, you will find a road that angles sharply up the east side of the wooded defile. The narrow road ends in a parking lot from which it's only a short walk to Castle Campbell, high on a great sloping mound in the center of the glen. With the green woods below, bracken hills above, and a view that on a clear day stretches right across the Forth Valley to the tip of Tinto Hill near Lanark, this is certainly the most atmospheric fortress within easy reach of Edinburgh. Formerly known as Castle Gloom, Castle Campbell stands out among Scottish castles for the sheer drama of its setting. The sturdy square of the tower house survives from the 15th century, when this site was first fortified by the Earl of Argyll. Other buildings and enclosures were subsequently added, but the sheer lack of space on this rocky eminence ensured that there were never any drastic changes. The castle is associated with the earls of Argyll, as well as with John Knox, the fiery religious reformer, who preached here. It also played a role in the religious wars of the 17th century, having been captured by Oliver Cromwell in 1654 and garrisoned with English troops. *Dollar Glen, 1 mi north of Dollar; tel. 0131/244–3101. Admission: £2 adults, £1.25 senior citizens, 75p children. Open Apr.–Sept., Mon.–Sat. 9:30–6, Sun. 2–6; Oct.–Mar., Mon.–Wed. and Sat. 9:30–4, Thurs. 9:30–noon, Sun. 2–4.*

From the castle, retrace your route to A91 and turn left. Just a few minutes outside Dollar, turn right onto a minor road (signed Rumbling Bridge). Then turn right onto the A823. Follow A823 through Powmill (signs for Dunfermline); turn right off of A823, following the signs for Saline (a pleasant if undistinguished village), and take an unclassified road due south to join the A907. Turn right, and then within a mile go left on the B9037, which leads down to **Culross.** On the muddy shores of the Forth, this is one of the most remarkable little towns in all Scotland. It once had a thriving industry and export trade in coal and salt (the coal was used in the salt-panning process). It also had, curiously, a trade monopoly in the manufacture of baking *girdles* (griddles). But as local coal became exhausted, the impetus of the Industrial Revolution passed it by and other parts of the Forth Valley prospered. Culross became a backwater town, and the merchants' houses of the 17th and 18th centuries were never replaced by Victorian developments or modern architecture. In the 1930s, the very new and then very poor National Trust for Scotland started to buy up the decaying properties. With the help of a variety of other agencies, these buildings were conserved and brought to life, and Culross is now a vigorous community, even if it has the air of a film set. With its mercat cross, cobbled streets, tolbooth, and narrow wynds, Culross is a living museum of a 17th-century town. *7¹/₂ mi west of Dunfermline, tel. 0131/226–5922. Admission to Palace, Study, and Town House £3.50 adults, £1.80 children. Open Easter and May–Sept. daily, Study and Town House 11–5:30 (Oct. 1–5:30); Palace 1:30–5:30.*

Take the B9037 east to join the A994, which leads to **Dunfermline,** once the world center for the production of damask linen; the **Dunfermline District Museum** on Viewfield Terrace, tel. 01383/721–814, tells the full story. Today the town is better known as the birthplace of millionaire philanthropist Andrew Carnegie. Undoubtedly Dunfermline's most famous son, Carnegie endowed the town with a library, health and fitness center, spacious park, and, naturally, a Carnegie Hall, still the focus of culture and entertainment. The 1835 weaver's cottage in which Carnegie was born is now the **Andrew Carnegie Birthplace Museum.** Don't be misled by the cottage's exterior. Inside it opens into a larger hall, where documents, photographs, and artifacts tell Carnegie's fascinating life story. You will learn such obscure details as the fact that Carnegie was only the third man in the United States to be able to translate Morse code by ear as it came down the wire! *Moodie St., tel. 01383/724–302. Admission £1.50 adults, 75p senior citizens, children under 15 free. Open Apr.–Oct., Mon.–Sat. 11–5, Sun. 2–5; Nov.–Mar., daily 2–4.*

Also of note in the town are the **Dunfermline Abbey and Palace** complex. The abbey was founded by Queen Margaret, the English wife of the Scots King Malcolm Canmore (1057–93). Some Norman work can be seen in the present church, where Robert the Bruce lies buried. The palace grew from the abbey guest house and was the birthplace of Charles I. Dunfermline was the seat of the Royal Court of Scotland until the end of the 11th century, and its central role in Scottish affairs is explored by means of display panels dotted around the drafty but hallowed buildings. *Monastery St., tel. 0131/244–3101. Admission: £1.50 adults, £1 senior citizens, 75p children. Open Apr.–Sept., Mon.–Sat. 9:30–6, Sun. 2–6; Oct.–Mar., Mon.–Wed., Fri., and Sat. 9:30–4, Thurs. 9:30–noon, Sun. 2–4.*

From Dunfermline, follow Edinburgh signs to the A823 and return via the Forth Road Bridge (toll: 40p).

Tour 4: Midlothian and East Lothian

Numbers in the margin correspond to points of interest on the Midlothian and East Lothian map.

In spite of the finest stone carving in Scotland (at Rosslyn Chapel), associations with Sir Walter Scott, outstanding castles, and miles of varied rolling countryside, for years Midlothian, the area south of Edinburgh, remained off the beaten tourist path. Perhaps a little in awe of sophisticated Edinburgh to the north and the well-manicured charm of the stockbroker belt of nearby upmarket East Lothian, Midlothian remained quietly preoccupied with its own workaday little towns and dormitory suburbs. Now Midlothian has decided it is at least as interesting as several other parts of Scotland that are fervently marketing themselves as tourism destinations. Judge for yourself in this tour.

As for East Lothian, it started with the advantage of golf courses of world-rank, most notably Muirfield, plus a scattering of stately homes and interesting hotels. Red pantiled and decidedly middle class, East Lothian is an area of glowing grainfields in summer and quite a few discreetly polite, "strictly private" signs at the end of driveways. It nevertheless has plenty of interest for the visitor, including photogenic villages, active fishing harbors, and vistas of pastoral Lowland Scotland, a world away (but much less than an hour by car) from bustling Edinburgh.

The tour described here can certainly be driven in one day, although it could be split into two separate excursions if you want to budget more time for some individual sights. Public transport is available to many of the venues described. Inquire at the St. Andrew Square bus station for bus services.

Leave Edinburgh via the A701 (Liberton Rd.). At the not-very-picturesque community of Bilston, look for signs left for **Rosslyn Chapel** (signed Roslin B7006). Conceived by Sir William Sinclair and dedicated to St. Matthew in 1450, the chapel is famous for the quality and variety of the stone carving inside. Human figures, animals, and plants are all included, covering almost every square inch of stonework. The chapel was actually never finished. The original design called for a cruciform structure, but only the choir and parts of the east transept walls were completed. *Roslin, off A703, 7½ mi south of Edinburgh, tel. 0131/440–2159. Admission: £2 adults, £1.50 senior citizens, 75p children. Open Apr.–Oct., Mon.–Sat. 10–5, Sun. noon–4:45.*

From Roslin return to the A703 for **Penicuik.** There are fine views of the Pentland Hills beyond the town, but its chief attraction for the tourist is the **Edinburgh Crystal Visitor Centre.** You may have seen this distinctive style of glassware in Edinburgh's upscale shops. Guided tours reveal the stages involved in the manufacture of cut crystal. In addition, groups of 6–12 people can pre-book a VIP tour (adults over 18 only). This includes the chance to blow a glass bubble and also to cut your own piece of glass, which will then be polished and given to you as a keepsake. Advance booking is essential for this tour. The Visitor Centre itself has crystal pieces on display, as well as an audiovisual exhibition on the production of crystal. *Eastfield, Penicuik, 10 mi south of Edinburgh, tel. 01968/675128. Admission to center free. Cost of tours: £2 adults, £1 senior citizens, 50p children. VIP tour: £20. Center, restaurant, and shop open Mon.–Sat. 9–5, Sun. 11–5. Tours weekdays 9:15–3:30.*

Time Out   The **Old Bakehouse** (tel. 01968/660830) at West Linton, southwest of Penicuik on the A702, serves home-cooked fare in quaint, wood-beamed rooms. Danish open sandwiches are the specialty, but home-made soups and a hot main course are also included on the menu. Tuesday through Sunday, lunch is served noon–2:30, dinner 6–9. On weekends between 3 and 4:30 you can also take afternoon tea.

After pausing to admire the Pentland Hills arching along the skyline to the southwest, from West Linton follow the B7059 and the A701 to Leadburn and then Howgate. Get onto the A6094 for a few minutes, then turn right onto the B6372 and continue past Temple, an attractive village on the edge of the Moorfoot Hills, toward Gorebridge.

Midlothian and East Lothian

North Sea

Firth of Forth

LAMMERMUIR HILLS

Belhaven Bay
Gullane Bay
Aberlady Bay
Gosford Bay

Thorntonloch
Dunbar **7**
Spott
Stenton
East Linton
John Muir Country Park **8**
Tantallon Castle **10**
Whitekirk **9**
North Berwick **11**
Dirleton Castle **12**
Drem
Aberlady
Athelstaneford
Luggate Burn
Garvald
Gifford
Lennoxlove House **14**
Haddington **13**
Tyne R.
Whiteadder Reservoir

Soutra Mains **6**
Humbie
Tynehead
Crichton Castle **5**
Gorebridge
Borthwick Castle **4**
Middleton
Pencaitland
Tranent
Port Seton
Prestonpans
Musselburgh
Dalkeith
Newtongrange
Scottish Mining Museum **3**
Carrington
Rosslyn Chapel **1**
Loanhead
Roslin
Penicuik
Temple
Howgate
West Linton
Edinburgh Crystal Visitor Centre **2**
Edinburgh
Portobello
Leith
Cramond
Burntisland
Spott

KEY
— Rail Lines

N

6 miles
9 km

A1087
A1
B6355
B6370
B6355
B6369
B1377
B1343
A6137
A198
A6093
A68
B6367
B6372
A7
A68
A6106
A702
A703
A720
A701
A702
B7026
B7059
A199
A902

At the junction of B6372 with A7, just before Gorebridge, you have a choice. If your interests tend toward social history, turn left and ❸ drive 2 miles to reach the **Scottish Mining Museum** at **Newtongrange.** Here, in the buildings of a now-closed colliery, you can learn something about the history of Scotland's coal miners. You can visit various buildings in the complex and view the giant winding engine, as well as the ranks of rusty, coal-dusty boilers that supplied the steam to turn it. The mine's former offices now relate, by means of realistic tableaux, the power that the mining company had over the lives of the individual workers in a frighteningly autocratic system that survived well into the 1930s. The mining company owned the houses, shops, and even the pub. Newtongrange was in fact the largest planned mining village in Scotland. The scenery is no more attractive than you would expect around a former mining community, though the green Pentland Hills are still in view in the distance. *Tel. 0131/663–7519. Admission: £1.95 adults, £1 children. Open Apr.–Sept., daily 10–4.*

If you instead turn right at the Gorebridge junction (A7/B6372), a few moments' travel takes you a world away from gloomy thoughts of worker exploitation by the mine-owning aristocracy. Follow the A7 south to a sign for **Borthwick.** Take a left onto an unclassified road off A7, and a few minutes later, in green countryside with scat- ❹ tered woods and lush hedgerows, you can see **Borthwick Castle.** Dating from the 15th century and still occupied (it is now a hotel), this stark, tall twin-towered fortress is associated with Mary, Queen of Scots. She came here on a kind of honeymoon with her ill-starred third husband, the Earl of Bothwell. Their already dubious bliss was interrupted by Mary's political opponents, often referred to as the Lords of the Congregation, a confederacy of powerful nobles who were against the queen's latest liaison and who instead favored the crowning of her young son James. Rather insensitively, they laid siege to the castle while the newlyweds were there. The history books relate that Mary subsequently escaped "disguised as a man." She was not free for long, however. It was only a short time before she was defeated in battle and imprisoned. She languished in prison for 21 years before Queen Elizabeth of England signed her death warrant (1587). Bothwell's fate was equally gloomy: He died insane in a Danish prison.

❺ From Borthwick, you can reach the next destination—**Crichton Castle**—by taking a peaceful walk through the woods (there are signposts along the way) or by doubling back by car to the B6372 and turning right onto the A68. Crichton Castle is just beyond the village of Pathhead (you'll see signs on A68). This was a Bothwell family castle. Queen Mary attended the wedding here of Bothwell's sister, Lady Janet Hepburn, to Mary's natural brother, Lord John Stewart. Of particular interest in the extensive ruin is the curious arcaded range with its diamond faceted stonework. This particular geometric pattern cut into the stone is unique in Scotland and is thought to have been inspired by Renaissance styles on the Continent, particularly Italy. The oldest part of the work is the 14th-century keep (square tower). Like Borthwick Castle, Crichton is set in attractive, rolling Lowland scenery, interrupted here and there with patches of woodland. *B6367, 7 mi southeast of Dalkeith, tel. 0131/244– 3101. Admission: £1.20 adults, 75p children. Open Apr.–Sept., Mon.– Sat. 9:30–6, Sun. 2–6.*

If the attractive setting of Crichton has beguiled you, you may want to end this section of the tour to explore the countryside and then return to Edinburgh via the A68 and Dalkeith. To continue the tour

into East Lothian, follow the A68 south, away from Edinburgh, to the very edge of the Lammermuir Hills. Just beyond the junction
6 with the A6137 you'll come to a spot called **Soutra Mains.** There's a small parking lot here, from which you can enjoy glorious unobstructed views extending northward over the whole of the Lothian plain.

Make your way back to the A6137 and turn right onto it; turn right again onto the B6355, and head east for the junction with the B6370, which leads to Dunbar.

Time Out The **Goblin Ha' Hotel** (tel. 0162081/244) in Gifford, a peaceful backwater town on the B6355, offers a wholesome afternoon tea that is very popular with day-trippers from Edinburgh. Gifford itself, with its 18th-century kirk and mercat cross, is a good example of a tweedily respectable, well-scrubbed, red-pantile-roofed East Lothian village.

In the days before tour companies started offering package deals
7 to the Mediterranean, **Dunbar** was a popular holiday resort. Now a bit faded, the town is of interest primarily because of a number of spacious Georgian-style properties, characterized by the astragals, or fan-shaped windows, above the doors; the symmetry of the house fronts; and the parapeted roof lines. Though not the popular seaside playground it once was, Dunbar does still have an attractive beach and a picturesque harbor, as well as opportunities for golf and sailing.

West of Dunbar, on the way back to Edinburgh, the A1087 leads to the sandy reaches of **Belhaven Bay,** signposted from the main road,
8 and to the **John Muir Country Park,** which takes in the estuary of the River Tyne winding down from the Moorfoot Hills. The country park offers varied coastal scenery: rocky shoreline, golden sands, and the mixed woodlands of Tyninghame, teeming with wildlife. Dunbar-born John Muir (whose family emigrated to the United States when he was a child) founded the U.S. National Park system. Only recently has the work of this early conservationist been acknowledged in his native Scotland.

From the park, drive north on the A198 (a right turn off the A1), to
9 reach **Whitekirk.** The unmistakable red sandstone church, with Norman tower, stands on a site occupied since the 6th century. It was a place of pilgrimage in medieval times because of its healing well. Behind the kirk, in a field, stands a tithe barn. Tithe barns originated in the practice of giving to the church a proportion of local produce, which then required storage space. At one end of the structure is a 16th-century tower house, which at one point in its history accommodated visiting pilgrims. The large three-story barn was added to the tower house in the 17th century. *St. Mary's Parish Church, A198. Admission free. Open early morning to late evening.*

10 Only minutes farther on, grim and battered **Tantallon Castle** rises on a cliff beyond the flat fields. This substantial ruin defends a headland with the sea on three sides. The red sandstone is pitted and eaten by time and sea-spray, with the earliest surviving stonework dating from the late-14th century. The fortress was besieged in 1529 by the cannons of King James V. (Rather inconveniently, the besieging forces ran out of gunpowder.) Cannons were used again, to deadlier effect, in a later siege during the Civil War in 1651. Twelve days of battering with the heavy guns of Cromwell's General Monk greatly damaged the flanking towers. However, much of the curtain wall of this former Douglas stronghold survives. *A198, 3 mi east of North Berwick, tel. 0131/244–3101. Admission: £2 adults, £1.25 senior citizens, 75p children. Open Apr.–Sept., Mon.–Sat. 9:30–6, Sun. 2–6; Oct.–Mar., Mon.–Wed. and Sat. 9:30–4, Thurs. noon–4, Sun. 2–4.*

⓫ The seaside resort of **North Berwick,** a few minutes west on the A198, is a pleasant little place that manages to retain a small-town personality even when it's thronged with city visitors on warm summer Sunday afternoons. Munching on ice cream, the city folk stroll on the beach and in the narrow streets or gape at the sailing craft in the small harbor.

⓬ **Dirleton Castle** is a 12th-century castle surrounded by a high outer wall. Within the wall you'll find a 17th-century bowling green, set in the shade of yew trees and surrounded by a herbaceous flower border that comes ablaze with color in high summer. Dirleton Castle was once occupied by King Edward I of England, in 1298, as part of his campaign for the continued subjugation of the unruly Scots. *A198, 8 mi west of North Berwick, tel. 0131/244–3101. Admission: £2 adults, £1.25 senior citizens, 75p children. Open Apr.–Sept., Mon.–Sat. 9:30–6, Sun. 2–6; Oct.–Mar., Mon.–Sat. 9:30–4, Sun. 2–4.*

Very noticeable along this coastline are the golf courses of East Lothian on every available links space. Next to Dirleton is **Gullane,** which is respectable and clad mostly in expensive golfing sweaters. **Muirfield,** venue for the Open Championship, is nearby, as is **Greywalls,** now a hotel, but originally a private house designed by Sir Edwin Lutyens. Away from the golf, Gullane's beach, well within driving distance of the city, offers opportunities for restful summer evening strolls.

⓭ A198 eventually leads to Aberlady, from which you take the A6137 south to the former county town of **Haddington,** one of the best-preserved medieval street plans in the country. Among the many buildings of architectural or historical interest is the Town House, which was designed by William Adam in 1748 and enlarged in 1830. A wall plaque at the Sidegate recalls the great heights of floods from the River Tyne. Beyond is the medieval Nungate footbridge, with the Church of St. Mary a little way upstream.

⓮ Just to the south of Haddington, by way of the B6369, is **Lennoxlove House,** which displays items associated with Mary, Queen of Scots. A turreted country house, part of it dating from the 15th century, Lennoxlove is a cheerful mix of family life and Scottish history. Housed in the beautifully decorated rooms are collections of portraits, furniture, and porcelain. *B6369, 1 mi south of Haddington, tel. 0162/082–3720. Admission: £3 adults, £1.50 children. Open May–Sept., Wed., Sat., and Sun. 2–5.*

Return to the A1 at Haddington and head west back to Edinburgh. From Haddington it's about 15 miles back to center city.

5 Glasgow

By John
Hutchinson

Updated by
Gillian Glover

In the days when Britain still had an empire, Glasgow pronounced itself the Second City of the Empire. The people of Glasgow were justifiably proud of their city, since it was there that Britain's great steamships (including the 80,000-ton *Queen Elizabeth*) were built. The term *Clydebuilt* (from Glasgow's River Clyde) became synonymous with good workmanship and lasting quality. It was also the Glaswegians who built the railway engines that opened up the Canadian prairies, the South African veldt, the Australian plains, and the Indian subcontinent. Scots engineers were to be found wherever there were engines (and so it was perhaps no coincidence that even Captain Kirk on the Starship *Enterprise* had to say, "Beam me up, Scottie" to his engineer).

Scholars have argued for years about what the name Glasgow means (pronounce it to rhyme with *toe* and put the stress on the first syllable), but, generally, "dear green place" is the interpretation that finds most favor today. Most suitable it is, too, for a town that, despite industrialization, has more city parks than anywhere else in Britain, and even the famous River Clyde is now clean enough for trout and salmon.

Glasgow first came into prominence in Scottish history somewhere around 1,400 years ago, and typically for this rambunctious city it was all to do with an argument between a husband and his wife. One of the local chieftains suspected, with some justification, that his wife had been having an affair, so he crept up on the suspect, one of his knights, and took from him a ring that she had rather foolishly given her lover—foolishly, because it had originally been given to her by her husband. The furious husband flung the ring into the River Clyde, then told his wife the next day that he wanted her to wear it that evening. The lady was distraught and called on the local holy man, Mungo, to help. Clearly a useful man to have in a tricky situation, Mungo sent a monk out fishing, and the first bite the monk had was a salmon with the ring in its mouth. Whether the lady learned her lesson or called on Mungo's services regularly after that, history does not relate.

Mungo features in two other legends: one of a pet bird that he nursed back to life and another, of a bush or tree, the branches of which he used to relight a fire. Tree, bird, and the salmon with a ring in its mouth are all to be found on the city of Glasgow's coat of arms, together with a bell that Mungo brought from Rome. Mungo is now the city's patron saint. His tomb is to be found in the mighty medieval cathedral that bears his name.

Glasgow led a fairly quiet existence in the Middle Ages. Its cathedral was the center of religious life, and although the city was made a Royal Burgh in 1175 by King William the Lion, its population was never more than a few thousand. What changed Glasgow irrevocably and laid the foundations for its immense prosperity was the Treaty of Union between Scotland and England in 1707. This allowed Scotland to trade with the essentially English colonies in America, and with their expansion Glasgow prospered. In came cotton, tobacco, and rum; out went various Scottish manufactured goods and clothing. The key to it all in the early days was tobacco, and the prosperous merchants were known as the Tobacco Lords. It was they who ran the city, and their wealth laid the foundation stone for the manufacturing industries of the 19th century.

As Glasgow prospered, so her population grew. The "dear green place" became built over. The original medieval city around the cathedral and the High Street expanded westward. The 18th-century

Merchant City, today the subject of a great deal of refurbishment, lies just to the south and west of George Square, and the houses of the merchants are even farther westward, along the gridiron pattern of Glasgow's streets up the hill toward Blytheswood Square.

But the city is not known as an 18th-century city; that honor is left to Edinburgh, in the east. Rather, Glasgow is known as the greatest Victorian city in Europe. The population grew from 80,000 in 1801 to over 700,000 in 1901, and with this enormous growth there developed also a sense of exuberance and confidence, which is reflected in its public buildings. The City Chambers, built in 1888, are an extravaganza of marble and red sandstone, a clear symbol of the Victorian merchants' hopes for the future.

Yet, always at the forefront of change, Glasgow boasts, side by side with the overtly Victorian, an architectural vision of the future in the work of Charles Rennie Mackintosh. The Glasgow School of Art, the Willow tearoom, and the churches and school buildings he designed point clearly to the clarity and simplicity of 20th-century lines.

Today, Glasgow has taken the best of the past and adapted it for the needs of the present day. The "dear green places" still remain in the city-center parks, to be enjoyed by citizens and visitors alike; the medieval cathedral stands proud, as it has done for 800 years; the Merchant City is revived and thriving; the Victorian splendor has been cleaned of its grime and will look good for many years to come; and the cultural legacy of museums and performing arts lives on stronger than ever (Glasgow was crowned European City of Culture in 1990). To cap it all, its superb location also makes it an ideal base from which to enjoy day tours of the Scottish countryside. Burns Country, the gardens of Galloway, the islands of the Clyde, Loch Lomond, the Trossachs, and Argyll are only about an hour or so from the city center, as is Edinburgh.

Essential Information

Important Addresses and Numbers

Tourist Information The **Greater Glasgow Tourist Board** (tel. 0141/204–4400) offers an excellent all-around tourist-information service from its headquarters at 35 St. Vincent Place, which is just around the corner from George Square and Queen Street Station. At this location there is also an accommodations-booking service; bureau de change; and ticket office for the theater, city bus tours, guided walks, boat trips, and extended coach tours around Scotland. Books, maps, and souvenirs are sold. The office is open Monday–Saturday 9 AM–6 PM and, in summer, Monday–Saturday 9AM–8 PM and Sunday 10 AM–6 PM. The tourist board's branch office at the airport is open daily 8–6.

Information about goings-on around town can be found in the Greater Glasgow Tourist Board's own publications, as well as in *The List* and the *Glasgow Herald* and *Evening Times* newspapers.

Emergencies For fire, police, or ambulance, dial 999 from any telephone. No coins are needed for emergency calls from public phone booths.

Hospitals Twenty-four-hour accident and emergency services are provided at **Glasgow Royal Infirmary** (Castle St., tel. 0141/552–3535). The hospital is by the cathedral. Facilities are also available at **Glasgow Western Infirmary** (Dumbarton Rd., tel. 0141/339–8822), near the university.

Dentists Most dentists will treat visitors by appointment. A full list can be found in the Yellow Pages telephone directory. Emergency dental treatment can be obtained from the **Glasgow Dental Hospital** (378 Sauchiehall St., tel. 0141/332–7020).

Late-Night Pharmacies Pharmacies in Glasgow operate on a rotating basis for late-night opening (hours are posted in storefront windows), but **R. H. Brown** (693 Great Western Rd., tel. 0141/339–0012) is open daily 9–9.

Post Office The **head post office** is at 1–5 George Sq. (tel. 0141/248–2882); there are many smaller post offices around the city.

Arriving and Departing by Plane

Airports and Airlines **Glasgow Airport**, about 7 miles west of the city center on the M8 to Greenock, offers internal Scottish and British services, European and transatlantic scheduled services, and vacation-charter traffic. Most major European carriers fly into Glasgow, offering frequent and convenient connections to Amsterdam, Berlin, Brussels, Copenhagen, Dusseldorf, Frankfurt, Hanover, Munich, Paris, and Stavanger. There are frequent shuttle services from London, as well as regular flights from Birmingham, Bristol, East Midlands, Leeds/Bradford, and Manchester. There are also flights from Wales (Cardiff) and Ireland (Belfast, Carrickfinn, Dublin, and Londonderry).

Local Scottish connections can be made to Aberdeen, Barra, Benbecula, Campbeltown, Edinburgh, Inverness, Islay, Kirkwall, Shetland, Stornoway, and Tiree. There is an airport information desk (tel. 0141/887–1111) and a tourist information desk and accommodations-booking service (tel. 0141/848–4440).

Airlines operating through Glasgow Airport to Europe and the rest of the United Kingdom include **British Airways** (tel. 01345/222–111), **British Midland** (tel. 0141/204–2436), **Air UK** (tel. 01345/666777), **Loganair** (tel. 0141/889–3181), **Manx** (tel. 0141/221–0162), **Aer Lingus** (tel. 0141/248–4121), **Air France** (tel. 01345/581393), **Icelandair** (tel. 0181/388–5599), **Lufthansa** (tel. 0141/221–7132), **Sabena** (tel. 01345/056341), and **SAS** (tel. 01345/090900).

Scheduled services to and from North America are provided by **American Airlines** (tel. 0800/0101–51), **Air Canada** (tel. 0800/181–313), **British Airways** (tel. 0141/226–4175), **Northwest Airlines** (tel. 0141/848–4794), and **United** (tel. 0800/888–555).

Between the Airport and Center City Though there is a railway station (Paisley Gilmour St.) about 2 miles from Glasgow airport, most people travel the short distance to the city center by bus or taxi. Journey time is about 20 minutes except at rush hour.

By Bus Express buses run from Glasgow Airport to the Central railway station (tel. 0141/204–2844) and to the Anderston Cross and Buchanan Street bus stations (tel. 0141/248–7432, 0141/332–7133, or 0141/332–9191). There is service every 30 minutes throughout the day. The fare is about £2.

By Taxi Metered taxis are available at the terminal building. The fare should be about £12.

By Rental Car All the usual rental companies, including **Avis** (tel. 0141/221–2827), **Hertz** (tel. 0141/887–2451), **Budget** (tel. 0141/887–0501), **Europcar** (tel. 0141/423–5661, and **Eurodollar** (tel. 0141/887–7915), have offices within the terminal building. Costs vary according to the size of the cars, but average about £20–£30 per day.

The drive from Glasgow Airport into the city center is normally quite easy even for visitors who are used to driving on the right. The M8 motorway runs beside the airport (junction 29) and takes you straight into Glasgow city center (and offers excellent views of the city and the River Clyde). Thereafter Glasgow's streets follow a grid pattern, at least in the city center, but a map is useful and can be supplied by the rental company.

By Limousine   Most of the companies that provide chauffeur-driven cars and tours will also do limousine airport transfers. Companies that are currently members of the Greater Glasgow Tourist Board are **Broom** (tel. 0141/638–6588), **Charter** (tel. 0141/942–4228), **Kingston** (tel. 0141/554–6066), **Little's** (tel. 0141/883–2111), **Rowan** (tel. 0141/332–0000), and **Windsor** (tel. 01505/31777 or 01836/766085).

Arriving and Departing by Car, Train, and Bus

By Car   Visitors who come to Glasgow from England and the south of Scotland will probably approach the city from the M6, M74, and A74. The city center is clearly marked from these roads. From Edinburgh the M8 leads straight to the city center and is the motorway that cuts straight across the city center and into which all other roads feed. From the north either the A82 from Fort William or the A/M80 from Stirling also feed into the M8 in Glasgow city center. From then on, you only have to know your exit. Exit 16 serves the north of the city center; Exit 17/18 leads to the northwest and Great Western Road; Exit 18/19 for the hotels of Sauchiehall Street, the Scottish Exhibition Centre, and the Anderston Centre.

By Train   Glasgow has two main rail stations: **Central** and **Queen Street.** Central is the arrival and departure point for trains from London Euston (journey time is approximately 5 hours), which come via Birmingham, Crewe, and Carlisle in England, as well as via Edinburgh from Kings Cross. It also serves other cities in the northwest of England and towns and ports in the southwest of Scotland. These include Kilmarnock, Dumfries, Ardrossan (for the island of Arran), Gourock (for Dunoon), Wemyss Bay (for the island of Rothesay), and Stranraer (for Ireland). Queen Street Station has connections to Edinburgh (journey time 45 minutes) and onward on the east coast route to Aberdeen or south via Edinburgh to Newcastle, York, and London Kings Cross. Other services from Queen Street go to Stirling, Perth, and Dundee; northward to Inverness, Kyle of Lochalsh, Wick, and Thurso; along the Clyde to Dumbarton and Balloch (for Loch Lomond); and on the scenic West Highland line to Oban, Fort William, and Mallaig. Oban and Mallaig have island ferry connections. The passenger-information line (tel. 0141/204–2844) for both Central and Queen Street stations operates 24 hours.

A regular bus service links Queen Street and Central stations. Both of these are close to stations on the Glasgow Underground (subway). At Queen Street go to Buchanan Street, and at Central go to St. Enoch. Black city taxis are available at both stations.

By Bus   Glasgow also has two bus stations: **Buchanan Street** (tel. 0141/332–7133 or 0141/332–9191), which serves a wide variety of towns and cities in Scotland, Wales, and England, including London (journey time from London is approximately 8 hours); and **Anderston Cross** (tel. 0141/248–7432), which also serves Scottish destinations. Both bus stations have services to Glasgow Airport and Edinburgh. Buchanan Street is close to the underground station of the same name and to Queen Street station. Anderston Cross is close to many of the new hotels in the southwestern part of the city center north of the River Clyde.

Getting Around

Glasgow city center—the area defined by the M8 motorway to the north and west, the River Clyde to the south, and Glasgow Cathedral to the east—is relatively compact, and visitors who are staying in this area should make some of their excursions on foot. Glaswegians themselves walk a good deal and the streets are designed for pedestrians (some are for pedestrians only). The streets are relatively safe even at night (but you should be sensible), and good street maps are available from bookstores and the excellent tourist-information center (*see* Important Addresses and Numbers, *above*). Most of the streets follow a grid plan; if you get lost, though, just ask a local—they are famous for being friendly.

To go farther afield, to the West End (the university, the Transport Museum, Kelvingrove Museum and Art Gallery, or the Hunterian Museum) or to the south (for example, the Burrell Collection), some form of transportation is required.

By Subway As befits the Second City of the Empire, Glasgow is the only city in the United Kingdom besides London that has a subway, or underground, as it's called here. It was built at the end of the last century and takes the simple form of two circular routes, one going clockwise and the other counterclockwise. All trains will eventually bring you back to where you started, and the complete circle takes 24 minutes. This extremely simple and effective system operated relatively unchanged in ancient carriages (cars) until the 1970s when it was entirely modernized. The tunnels are relatively small, so the trains themselves are tiny (by London standards) and this, together with the affection in which the system is held and the bright orange paintwork of the trains, gives it the nickname the Clockwork Orange.

Flat fares (50p) and day tickets (£2.50) are available. Trains run regularly Monday to Saturday, with a limited Sunday service, and connect the city center with the West End (for the university) and the city south of the River Clyde. Look for the orange "U" signs marking the 15 stations. Further information is available from the Strathclyde Passenger Transport Executive Travel Centre, St. Enoch Square (tel. 0141/226–4826).

By Car A car is not necessary in the city center. Though most of the newer hotels have their own parking lots, parking in the city center can be very trying. More convenient are the park-and-ride schemes at underground stations (Kelvinbridge, Bridge St., and Shields Rd.) that will bring you into the city center in a few minutes. The West End museums and galleries have their own parking lots, as does the Burrell, so there are no problems there. Remember, parking wardens are constantly on patrol, and you will be fined if you park illegally. Multistory parking garages are open 24 hours a day at the following locations: Anderston Centre, George Street, Waterloo Place, Mitchell Street, Cambridge Street, and Buchanan Street. Rates at the individual garages vary between £1 and £2 per hour.

By Train In addition to the underground, the Glasgow area has an extensive network of suburban railway services. They are still called the Blue Trains by local people, even though most of them are now orange. Look for signs to LOW LEVEL TRAINS at Queen Street and Central stations. For further information and a free map, call Strathclyde

PTE (tel. 0141/226–4826) or Scotrail (tel. 0141/204–2844). Details are also available from the tourist board.

By Bus The many different bus companies cooperate with the underground and Scotrail to produce the Family Day Tripper Ticket (from £13.50), which is an excellent way to get around the whole area from Loch Lomond to Ayrshire. Tickets are a good value and are available from the PTE and at main railway and bus stations and post offices.

By Taxi Metered taxis (usually black and of the London type) can be found at taxi ranks all over the city center. Most are radio controlled, so they can be called very easily. Some have also been specially adapted to take wheelchairs. In the street, a taxi can be hailed if it is displaying its illuminated FOR HIRE sign. Taxi firms also arrange tours of the city. They vary from one to three hours, usually at a fixed price. They can be booked in advance, and you can be picked up and dropped off where you like. Contact the **Taxi Owners Association** (tel. 0141/332–7070) or the **Taxi Cab Association** (tel. 0141/332–6666).

By Limousine Several chauffeur-driven limousine companies (*see* Between the Airport and City Center, *above*) also provide tours of the city center and beyond.

Guided Tours

Orientation **Discovering Glasgow** bus tours leave daily from the west side of George Square. The Greater Glasgow Tourist Board (*see* Important Addresses and Numbers, *above*) can give further information and arrange reservations. **Strathclyde** buses (the orange ones) also follow a similar route from George Square. (Tickets may be purchased on the bus, or call 0141/226–4826 for information.) Details of longer tours northward to the Highlands and Islands can be obtained from the tourist board.

Special-Interest **The Scottish Tourist Guides Association** (tel. 0141/776–1052) can tailor a tour to suit you. Standard fixed fees apply. **Classique Sun Saloon Luxury Coaches** (tel. 0141/889–4050) operates restored buses from the '50s, '60s, and '70s on tours to the north and west.

Boat Tours There are cruises on the Clyde, starting from the Broomielaw, the traditional departure pier for over 100 years for vacationers on the river. Services are operated by the *Waverley* (tel. 0141/221–8152, prices £9.95–£19.95), the world's last oceangoing paddle steamer, which sails down the Clyde to Largs, Dunoon, Rothesay, and elsewhere during the day and evening in summer. You can make reservations through the tourist board or call direct. Cruises are also available on Loch Lomond and to the islands in the Firth of Clyde; details are available from the tourist board.

Helicopter Tours **Clyde Helicopters** (tel. 0141/226–4261) swoop over downtown Glasgow and the immediate environs, taking off from the helipad at the Scottish Exhibition Centre. Trips normally last 10 to 30 minutes and cost between £30 and £70.

Personal Guides and Walking Tours In each case your first contact should be the tourist board, where you can find out about special walks on a given day. The **Scottish Tourist Guides Association** (tel. 0141/776–1052) also offers an all-around service.

Exploring Glasgow

Orientation

The first walking tour is relatively flat and almost entirely on city streets; it includes the ancient cathedral, the oldest house in Glasgow, the High Street, and the center of medieval activity, the Merchant City, which developed as Glasgow prospered. Included, too, is the River Clyde, on which Glasgow's trade across the Atlantic developed. The river is always at the center of the city, cutting it in half and offering often surprising views across to the buildings on the other side. In this central part of the city are some of the best examples of the confidence and exuberance in architecture that so characterized the Glasgow of 100 years ago and that today are experiencing a renaissance and a newfound appreciation.

The second tour goes westward and encompasses the university and that other "forgotten" side of Glasgow, unjustly perceived as a grimy center of heavy industry. Glasgow has had a university since 1451, making it the third-oldest in Scotland after St. Andrews and Aberdeen, and at least 130 years ahead of the University of Edinburgh. It has thrived as a center of educational excellence, particularly in the sciences. The university buildings are set in parkland, reminding the visitor that Glasgow is a city with more green space per citizen than any other in Europe. It is also a city of museums and art galleries, having benefited from the generosity of industrial and commercial philanthropists and from the deep-seated desire of the city fathers to place Glasgow at the forefront of British cities. The second walk is quieter and less bustling, though there are some gentle slopes to walk up.

Highlights for First-Time Visitors

Burrell Collection and Pollok House (*see* Off the Beaten Track)
City Chambers (*see* Tour 1)
Glasgow Cathedral (*see* Tour 1)
Glasgow School of Art (*see* Tour 2)
Hunterian Art Gallery (*see* Tour 2)
Kelvingrove Museum and Art Gallery (*see* Tour 2)
Merchant City (*see* Tour 1)
Museum of Transport (*see* Tour 2)
People's Palace (*see* Tour 1)
Tenement House (*see* Tour 2)

Tour 1: Medieval Glasgow and the Merchant City

Numbers in the margin correspond to points of interest on the Glasgow map.

❶ **George Square,** the focal point of Glasgow's business district, is the natural starting point for any walking tour. It's in the very heart of Glasgow and convenient to the Buchanan Street bus and underground stations and parking lot, as well as to the Queen Street railway station. The tourist information center of the Greater Glasgow Tourist Board is also close by on St. Vincent Place. The square itself is lined with an impressive array of statues of worthies from days gone by: Queen Victoria; Scotland's national poet Robert Burns; the inventor and developer of the steam engine, James Watt; Prime Minister William Gladstone; and towering above them all, Scotland's foremost writer, Sir Walter Scott. The column was intended for George III, after whom the square is named, but his statue was not erected after he was found to be insane toward the end of his reign. A statue of Sir Walter Scott stands in its place.

② The magnificent Italian Renaissance-style **City Chambers** on the east side of the square was opened by Queen Victoria in 1888. Among the outstanding features of the interior are the vaulted ceiling of the entrance hall, marble and alabaster staircases, and the banqueting hall, as well as a number of the smaller suites, each furnished in different woods. *George Sq., tel. 0141/227–4017. Free guided tours weekdays except Thurs. at 10:30 and 2:30.*

Leave George Square by the northeast corner and head eastward through a not particularly pretty part of the city along George Street, past the University of Strathclyde. Turn left at High Street,
③ then go up the hill to **Glasgow Cathedral,** an unusual double church, one above the other. Dedicated to St. Mungo, Glasgow's patron saint, the cathedral was begun in the 12th century and completed about 300 years later. It was spared the ravages of the Reformation, which destroyed so many of Scotland's medieval churches, because the trade guilds of Glasgow regarded it as their own church and defended it. In the lower church is the splendid crypt of St. Mungo, who is sometimes also called St. Kentigern. (*Kentigern* means "chief word," while *Mungo* is perhaps a nickname meaning "dear name.") The site of the tomb has been revered since the 6th century, when St. Mungo founded a church here. *Cathedral St., tel. 0131/244–3101. Admission free. Open Apr.–Sept., Mon.–Sat. 9:30–6, Sun. 2–5; Oct.– Mar., Mon.–Sat. 9:30–4, Sun. 2–4.*

Take time to visit the St. Mungo Museum and Cathedral Visitor Center, opened in 1993. On display is material covering the many religious groups who've settled throughout the centuries in Glasgow and the west of Scotland. The centerpiece is Salvador Dali's magnificent painting, *Christ on the Cross.* Inside there's a gift shop, toilets, and a café. *Cathedral Square. Open Mon.–Sat. 10–5, Sun. 11–5.*

One fascinating if macabre place just off Cathedral Square is the
④ **Necropolis,** a burying ground since the beginning of recorded history, with some extraordinarily elaborate Victorian graves, watched over by a statue of John Knox. It includes the tomb of 19th-century Glasgow merchant William Miller, author of the "Wee Willie Winkie" nursery rhyme. *Behind Glasgow Cathedral, tel. 0141/333– 0800.*

⑤ Opposite the cathedral, across Castle Street, is **Provand's Lordship,** Glasgow's oldest house. It was built in 1471 by Bishop Andrew Muirhead as the manse of the Hospital of St. Nicholas. Mary, Queen of Scots, is said to have stayed here. After her day, however, the house fell into decline and was used alternately as a sweet shop, a soft-drink factory, the home of the city hangman, and a junk shop. It was eventually rescued by the city and turned into a museum. Exhibits show the house as it might have looked in its heyday. *Castle St., tel. 0141/552–8819. Admission free. Open Mon.–Sat. 10–5, Sun. noon–6.*

Retrace your steps down Castle Street and High Street. Look for the Greek goddess Pallas on top of the imposing gray sandstone building on the right, the former Bank of Scotland building, before
⑥ reaching the Tolbooth Steeple at **Glasgow Cross.** This was the very center of the medieval city. The mercat cross, topped by a unicorn, marked the spot where merchants met, where the market was held, and where criminals were executed. Here, too, was the *tron,* or weigh beam, used to check merchants' weights, installed in 1491.

Glasgow

KEY

Pedestrian Zone

Rail Lines

ⓤ Metro Stop

AE American Express Office

i Tourist Information

The Barras, **7**
Botanic Gardens, **18**
City Chambers, **2**
George Square, **1**
Glasgow Cathedral, **3**
Glasgow Cross, **6**
Glasgow Green, **8**
Glasgow School of
Art, **22**
Hunterian Art
Gallery, **17**

Hunterian
Museum, **16**
Hutcheson's Hall, **10**
Kelvingrove, **14**
Mitchell Library, **19**
Museum of
Transport, **15**
Necropolis, **4**
People's Palace, **9**
Provand's Lordship, **5**

Regimental Museum of
the Royal Highland
Fusiliers, **20**
Royal Exchange, **12**
Scottish Stock Exchange, **13**
Tenement House, **21**
Virginia Court, **11**

Dobbie's Loan

M8

Dobbie's Loan

Cowcaddens Rd.

Buchanan Bus Station

North Hanover St.

St. James Rd.

Castle St.

Sauchiehall St.

Bath St.

Queen St. Station

Cathedral St.

Strathclyde University

⊔

③

④

⑤

John Knox St.

St. Vincent St.

George St.

⑬ Nelson Mandela Pl.

① George St.

② Cochrane St.

Cathedral Square

Central Station

Gordon St.

Hope St.

Buchanan St.

St. Vincent Pl.

ℹ

⑫

Queen St.

Ingram St.

⑩

Duke St.

Union St.

Argyle St.

Princes Sq.

Argyll Arcade

⑪ Virginia St.

Glassford St.

Hutcheson St.

Wilson

Merchant City

Albion St.

High St.

Jamaica St.

Oswald St.

⊔

St. Enoch Shopping Centre

Trongate

Tolboth Steeple ■

Howard St.

Stockwell St.

Osborne St.

⑥

Clyde St.

Bridgegate

Saltmarket

London Rd.

Gallowgate

⑦

R. Clyde

St. Andrews Sq.

⑧ ⑨

Greendyke St.

The Tolbooth Steeple itself dates from 1626 and served as the civic center and place where travelers entering the city paid tolls.

❼ Continue east along London Road (under the bridge) about a quarter of a mile and you'll come to **The Barras** ("barrows", or pushcarts), Scotland's largest indoor market, a mecca for those addicted to searching through piles of junk for bargains. Open only on weekends, this is probably the nearest Scotland gets to a flea market. The atmosphere is always good humored, and you can find just about anything here, in any condition, from old model railroads to cheese rolls. *Tel. 0141/552–7258. Admission free. Open weekends 9–5.*

❽ Turn down Greendyke Street from London Road to reach **Glasgow Green** by the River Clyde. Glasgow's oldest park has a long history as a favorite spot for public recreation and political demonstrations. Note the Nelson Column, erected long before London's; the Arch, now the finish line for the thousands of runners of the Glasgow Half Marathon; and the Templeton Business Centre, designed late the last century in the style of the Doge's Palace in Venice. The most **❾** significant building in the park is the **People's Palace**, an impressive Victorian red sandstone building that houses an intriguing museum dedicated to the city's social history; included among the exhibits is one devoted to the ordinary folk of Glasgow, called "The People's Story." Also on show are the writing desk of John McLean, the "Red Clydeside" political activist who came to Lenin's notice, and the famous "banana boots" worn on stage by Billy Connolly. Behind the museum are the well-restored Winter Gardens, a relatively sheltered spot favored by visitors who want to escape the often-chilly winds whistling across the green. A wide variety of tropical plants and rare birds are found here. *Tel. 0141/554–0223. Admission free. Open Mon.–Sat. 10–5, Sun. 11–5.*

Go back to Greendykes Street, past the new St. Andrew's Square development—with the magnificent St. Andrew's Church (1750) as its centerpiece—then via Saltmarket northwards to Tolbooth Steeple. Continue westward along Trongate. This is where the powerful "tobacco barons" who traded with the Americas presided. On the right, down Albion Street, are the offices of Glasgow's daily papers, the *Glasgow Herald* and the *Evening Times*. On the left, jutting out into Trongate, is the Tron Steeple, all that remains of a church burned down in 1793 when a joke by the local chapter of the Hell-Fire Club (young aristocratic troublemakers) got a little out of hand. The rebuilt church has now been converted into the Tron Theatre.

Continue down the Trongate then turn right into Hutcheson Street. This is Glasgow's **Merchant City**, a once run-down area but now renovated. Among the preserved Georgian and Victorian buildings are elegant designer boutiques. The City and County Buildings, on your right, were built in 1842 to house civil servants; note the impressive arrangement of bays and Corinthian columns. At the end **❿** of the street, just south of George Square, look for **Hutcheson's Hall,** a visitor center, shop, and regional office for the National Trust for Scotland. This elegant, neoclassical building was designed by David Hamilton in 1802. The hall was originally a hospice founded by two brothers, George and Thomas Hutcheson; you can see their statues in niches in the facade. *158 Ingram St., tel. 0141/552–8391. Admission free. Open weekdays 9–5, Sat. 10–4. Shop open Mon.–Sat. 10–4.*

Turn west onto Ingram Street and left down Glassford Street to see the **Trades House** on the right, which has a facade built in 1791 to designs by Robert Adam. Turn right along Wilson Street to reach Virginia Street, another favorite haunt of Glasgow's tobacco merchants. At No. 33, a former tobacco exchange survives, now an indoor shopping center. Nearby, **Virginia Court,** somewhat faded now, also echoes those far-off days. Peer through the bars of the gates and note the wagon-wheel ruts still visible in the roadway. Nearby is a good range of antiques shops, notably the Virginia Galleries with its pleasant indoor café.

Walk northward up Virginia Street back to Ingram Street. To the left you'll have a good view down to the elegant Royal Exchange Square and the **Royal Exchange** itself. Designed by David Hamilton and finished in 1829, the Exchange was a meeting place for merchants and traders but was transformed in the 1950s into **Stirling's Library.** It incorporates the mansion built in 1780 by William Cunninghame, one of the wealthiest of the tobacco lords. Royal Exchange Square leads, for pedestrians, westward to the pedestrian-zone shopping area of Buchanan Street. The Princes Square shopping area on the east side has a particularly good selection of specialty shops.

Make your way down to Argyle Street. Looking to the west, you'll see the large railway bridge supporting the tracks going into **Central Station.** The depot is known as Heilanman's Umbrella, because it was the point of meeting and shelter for so many Highlanders who had moved to Glasgow in search of better economic opportunities in the last century. Pause to look at the lovely iron arcading of **Gardner's Warehouse** at 36 Jamaica Street. Head north up Union Street and note the extraordinary architecture of Nos. 84–100, the so-called **Egyptian Halls,** designed and built in 1871 by Alexander "Greek" Thomson.

From here continue north to St. Vincent Street and turn right to reach Nelson Mandela Place, also called St. George's Place. If you want to see today's commercial life, visit the **Scottish Stock Exchange** on Buchanan Street, worthwhile for the exterior alone: It was built in 1877 in an ornate "French Venetian" style. *7 Nelson Mandela Pl., tel. 0141/221–7060, ext. 25424/25434. Admission free. Visitors gallery open weekdays 9–6:30.*

Pause briefly at the handsome **Merchants' House** on the corner of West George Street and George Square (now the home of Glasgow's Chamber of Commerce) to look at the golden sailing ship against the sky, a reminder of the importance of trade to Glasgow's prosperity. *West side of George Sq., tel. 0141/221–8272. Admission free. Hall and anterooms may be seen by arrangement. Open May–Sept., weekdays 2–4.*

Tour 2: The West End

You can use the suggested route here to acquaint yourself with the rich legacy of education, culture, art, and parkland that is to be found in Glasgow's West End. Included are a number of museums and galleries, each of which could take up an enjoyable day in itself, so you could think of this as the basis of several walks.

A good place to start is at the city's main art gallery and museum, **Kelvingrove**—looking like a combination of cathedral and castle—in Kelvingrove Park, west of the M8 beltway, at the junction of Sauchiehall and Argyle streets (note that Sauchiehall is pronounced *socky-hall*). There are parking facilities, and plenty of buses go there from downtown. The building is a magnificently ornamented red sandstone edifice dating from the early part of this century. There has always been debate as to which facade is the front and which is the back. However you enter, Kelvingrove houses what is claimed to be Britain's finest civic collection of British and Continental paintings, with 17th-century Dutch art, a selection from the French Barbizon school, French Impressionism, Scottish art from the 17th century to the present, silver, ceramics, European armor, even Egyptian archaeological finds. *Tel. 0141/357–3929. Admission free. Open weekdays 10–5, Sat. 10–10, Sun. 11–5.*

Across Argyle Street in the Old Kelvin Hall exhibition center is the **⑮ Museum of Transport.** Here Glasgow's history of locomotive building is dramatically displayed with full-size exhibits. The collection of Clyde-built ship models is world famous. Anyone who remembers Britain in the 1950s will be able to wallow in nostalgia at the re-created street scene from that era. *Kelvin Hall, 1 Bunhouse Rd., tel. 0141/357–3929. Admission free. Open Mon.–Sat. 10–5, Sun. noon–6.*

Kelvingrove Park takes its name from the River Kelvin, which flows through it. Lord Kelvin, the scientist who pioneered a great deal of work in electricity, is remembered by a statue in the park. The city purchased the land for the park in 1852, and, apart from the abundance of statues of prominent Glaswegians, the park is graced by a massive fountain commemorating a Lord Provost of Glasgow from the 1850s, a duck pond, a play area, a small open-air theater, and lots of exotic trees. It can be a charming retreat from the noise and bustle of the city.

As you walk up Kelvin Way through the trees, the skyline to your left is dominated by the Gilbert Scott building, the University of Glasgow's main edifice. Built just over a century ago, the building is a good example of the Gothic Revival style. The **University of Glasgow Visitor Centre** has exhibits on the university, a coffee bar, and a gift shop, and is the starting point for walking tours of the campus. *University Ave., tel. 0141/330–5511. Admission free. Open Mon.–Fri. 9:30–5, Sat. 9:30–1.*

Turn left up University Avenue, past the Memorial Gates, which were erected in 1951 to celebrate the university's 500th birthday. On either side of the road here are two important galleries, both maintained by the university. They house the collections of William Hunter, an 18th-century Glasgow doctor who assembled a staggering quantity of extremely valuable material. On the south side of University Avenue, in the Victorian part of the university, is the **⑯ Hunterian Museum,** the city's oldest (1807), which displays Hunter's hoards of coins, manuscripts, scientific instruments, and archaeological artifacts in a striking Victorian building. *Glasgow University, tel. 0141/330–4221. Admission free. Open weekdays 9:30–5, Sat. 9:30–1.*

⑰ Even more interesting is the **Hunterian Art Gallery,** in an unremarkable building from the 1970s across the road. The gallery houses the doctor's collection of paintings, together with prints and drawings by Reynolds, Rodin, Rembrandt, and Tintoretto, as well as a major collection of paintings by James McNeill Whistler, who had a great affection for the city that bought one of his earliest paintings. Also in the gallery is a replica of Charles Rennie Mackintosh's town house, which used to stand nearby. The rooms are all furnished with Mackintosh's distinctive Art Nouveau chairs, tables, beds, and cupboards, and the walls are decorated in the equally distinctive style devised by him and his wife, Margaret. *Glasgow University, Hillhead St., tel. 0141/330–5431. Admission to gallery free; Mackintosh House 50p weekdays and Sat. morning. Open weekdays 9:30–5, Sat. 9:30–1. Mackintosh House closed weekdays 12:30–1:30.*

At this point you can either make a small detour to the Botanic Gardens and return along the banks of the River Kelvin to Kelvingrove Park or go directly through some of Glasgow's elegant 19th-century districts to the extreme northwest of the downtown area, where the rest of the tour resumes.

🔞 The walk from the university to the **Botanic Gardens** is unfortunately not very exciting, but it's worth the effort. Continue along University Avenue and turn right at Byres Road, going as far as Great Western Road and the Grosvenor Hotel. The 40 acres of gardens are across the busy Great Western Road. Begun by the Royal Botanical Institute of Glasgow in 1842, the displays here include an herb garden, a wide range of tropical plants, and a world-famous collection of orchids. The most spectacular building in the complex is the **Kibble Palace,** built in 1873; it was originally the conservatory of a Victorian eccentric named John Kibble. Its domed, interlinked, almost spaceshiplike greenhouses have a unique collection of tree ferns, palm trees, and plants from temperate climates, together with appropriately exotic Victorian statues. Elsewhere on the grounds are more conventional greenhouses, as well as well-maintained lawns and colorful flower beds. *Great Western Rd., tel. 0141/334–2422. Admission free. Gardens open daily 7–dusk; Kibble Palace open daily, 10–4:45.*

After leaving the Botanic Gardens, cross the River Kelvin on St. Margaret Drive just past the BBC Scotland building. Turn right, then right again down the steps to the Kelvin Walkway on the north bank of the river. (Farther upstream the Kelvin Walkway connects with the West Highland Way, an official long-distance footpath leading to Fort William, approximately 100 miles away.) The walkway headed downstream back toward the city center first crosses a footbridge, then passes old mill buildings and goes under Belmont Street and the Great Western Road at Kelvinbridge before passing Kelvinbridge underground station and going under the Gibson Street bridge and back into Kelvingrove Park.

At this point, you can choose to take one of the paths up the hill and explore the stately Victorian crescents and streets of the park area or you can take the lower road past the fountain and head directly back to Sauchiehall Street. Whichever way you choose, you should end up, having walked eastward, at the point where Sauchiehall Street crosses the M8 motorway. Down North Street to your right
🔞 (southward) you'll see the front of **Mitchell Library,** the largest public reference library in Europe; it houses over a million volumes, including what is claimed to be the largest collection on Robert Burns in the world. The library's founder, Stephen Mitchell, who died in 1874 (the same year the library was founded), is commemorated by a bust in the entrance hall. Minerva, goddess of wisdom, looks down from the library's dome, encouraging the library's users and frowning at the drivers thundering along the motorway just in front of her. The western facade (at the back) is particularly beautiful. *North St., tel. 0141/221–7030. Admission free. Open weekdays 9:30–9, Sat. 9:30–5.*

🔞 Cross the M8 motorway, and continue down Sauchiehall Street to the **Regimental Museum of the Royal Highland Fusiliers,** which displays the history of this famous regiment and the men who served in it. Exhibits include medals, badges, and uniforms. *518 Sauchiehall St., tel. 0141/332–0961. Admission free. Open Mon.–Thurs. 9–4:30, Fri. 9–4.*

㉑ Turn up Garnet Street and go to the top, then right on Buccleuch (pronounced *buck-LOO*) Street. On the left is the **Tenement House,** a very special find tucked away from normal tourist routes. This is an ordinary, simple city-center apartment that was occupied from 1911 to 1965 by the same lady, Miss Agnes Toward, who never seemed to throw anything away. What is left is a fascinating time capsule, painstakingly preserved with her everyday furniture and belongings. The red sandstone tenement building itself dates from 1892. *145 Buccleuch St., tel. 0141/333–0183. Admission: £1.20 adults, 60p children. Open early Jan.–Mar. and early Nov.–mid-Dec., weekends 2–4. Apr.–Oct., daily noon–5.*

Coming out of the Tenement House, turn east on Buccleuch Street to Scott Street. Turn south on Scott Street, noticing the mural that reflects the name of the area, Garnethill, then turn left onto Renfrew **㉒** Street to reach Charles Rennie Mackintosh's masterpiece, the **Glasgow School of Art.** The building—exterior and interior, structure, furnishings, and decoration—forms a unified whole, reflecting the inventive genius of this man, who was only 28 years old when he won the competition for the design of the building. Architects and designers from all over the world come to admire it, but because it is a working school of art, general visitor access is sometimes limited. Conducted tours are available, and there is always the chance that you can have a quick look inside. It's best to call ahead for more information. *167 Renfrew St., tel. 0141/332–9797.*

Time Out   The **Willow Tearoom** (above a jeweler's shop at 217 Sauchiehall St.) is restored to its original archetypal Art Nouveau design by Charles Rennie Mackintosh, right down to the decorated tables and chairs. The building was designed by Mackintosh in 1903 for Miss Kate Cranston, who ran a chain of tearooms. The tree motifs are echoed in the street address, since *sauchie* is an old Scots word for *willow.*

To return to the city center you can either continue down Sauchiehall Street or turn south down Blythswood Street, noting the elegant Blythswood Square (1823–29).

Glasgow for Free

Most of Glasgow's museums, churches, galleries, and all the parks are free. Street entertainment and free open-air concerts are not very common, but during the specific festivals, such as Mayfest (May), the city streets take on a livelier appearance and become free attractions for visitors. Major shopping areas, such as Princes Square and the St. Enoch Centre, also have entertainments, as do some of the art galleries, cafés, and restaurants.

What to See and Do with Children

Many of Glasgow's attractions are also suitable for children, in small doses. The tourist board (*see* Important Addresses and Numbers in Essential Information, *above*) can provide detailed information and can tell you about swimming pools and sports centers. Most of Glasgow's parks have tennis, lawn-bowling, and putting facilities. In addition, the following attractions are available at individual parks: boating, dry ski slope, windsurfing, croquet, trampolines, and table tennis. Check with the Parks Department (tel. 0141/227–5064 or 0141/227–5066) for details.

Eastwood Butterfly Kingdom, set in lovely Rouken Glen Park not far from the city center, offers a touch of the exotic, with free-flying butterflies and moths in a tropical setting. There is also a tearoom and gift shop. *Rouken Glen Park, tel. 0141/620–2084.*

Glasgow Zoo, situated on a wooded hillside above the North Calder Water, is a modern open-plan collection with a fine tiger house and a large number of deer, camels, rhinos, and other exotic animals. Inside, the zoo specializes in pythons, boas, and other reptiles; the reptile breeding house is a particularly popular attraction. The zoo is at Calder Park in Uddingston, 6 miles from Glasgow city center, at the end of London Road and near the M74. There is ample parking. *Tel. 0141/771–1185. Admission: £2 adults, £1 children. Open Sept.–June, daily 10-5; July–Aug., daily 10–6.*

Haggs Castle, an ancient house of the Maxwell family, has been given over entirely to children. Adults are tolerated if they behave themselves. Many of the rooms are designed to illustrate what life was like for children in days gone by; during school holidays the museum runs an extensive interactive program aimed at helping children experience history firsthand. *100 St. Andrews Dr., tel. 0141/427–2725. Admission free. Open Mon.–Sat. 10–5, Sun. 11–5.*

The **Museum of Education** is of great interest to children (even though some profess to hate it). Located in Scotland Street School, one of Charles Rennie Mackintosh's elegant buildings (1906), the museum's classrooms are fitted out in the styles of different historical periods, and the staff is dressed in appropriate costume. *225 Scotland St., tel. 0141/429–1202. Admission free. Open Mon.–Sat. 10–5, Sun 2–5.*

People's Palace (*see* Tour 1)

Tenement House (*see* Tour 2)

Victoria Park has a pleasant boating lake and an arboretum, as well as a remarkable Fossil Grove, where the fossilized stumps of trees said to be over 330 million years old have been preserved. (Glasgow has obviously been laying out excellent parks for a long time.) *Victoria Park Dr. N, off Airthrey Ave., tel. 0141/959–2128. Admission free. Open Mon.–Sat. 8– dusk, Sun. 10–dusk; Fossil Grove open by appointment.*

Off the Beaten Track

Pollok Country Park **Pollok Country Park** provides a peaceful green oasis off Paisley Road, just 3 miles southwest of the city center. (You can get there by taxi or car, by city bus, or by a train from Glasgow Central Station to Pollokshaws West Station.) The key attraction here is the **Burrell Collection,** Scotland's finest art collection. A custom-built, ultramodern yet elegant building houses 8,000 exhibits of all descriptions, from ancient Egyptian, Greek, and Roman artifacts to Chinese ceramics, bronzes, and jade to medieval tapestries, stained glass, Rodin sculptures, and exquisite French Impressionist paintings—all from the magpie collection of an eccentric millionaire, Sir William Burrell, who donated his treasures to the city in 1944. The building was designed with large glass walls so that the items on display could relate to their surroundings: art and nature, supposedly, in perfect harmony. It does, however, seem an incongruous setting for Chinese porcelain and the reconstruction of medieval castle rooms. *Tel. 0141/649–7151. Admission free. Open Mon.–Sat. 10–5, Sun. 2–5.*

Also located in Pollok Country Park is **Pollok House,** which dates from the mid-1700s and contains the Stirling Maxwell Collection of paintings, including works by El Greco, Murillo, Goya, Signorelli, and William Blake. Fine 18th- and early 19th-century furniture, silver, glass, and porcelain are also on display. The house has fine gardens and looks over the White Cart River and Pollok Park, where, amid mature trees and abundant wildlife, the City of Glasgow's own highland cattle peacefully graze. *Tel. 0141/632–0274. Admission free. Open Mon.–Sat. 10–5, Sun. 2–5.*

Paisley   Once a distinct burgh in its own right, Paisley is now part of the Greater Glasgow suburban area. If your taste runs toward the urban rather than the rural, this town offers plenty of gritty character, largely because of vestiges of its industrial heritage. Paisley can be easily reached by taxi, car, or bus. Trains also run regularly from Glasgow Central to Paisley Gilmour Street Station. Town trail leaflets are available from the tourist information center.

Paisley's industrial prosperity came from textiles and, in particular, from the woolen Paisley shawl. The internationally recognized Paisley pattern is based on the shape of a palm shoot, an ancient Babylonian fertility symbol brought to Britain by way of Kashmir. The full story of the pattern and of the innovative weaving techniques introduced in Paisley is told in the **Paisley Museum and Art Gallery,** which has a world-famous shawl collection. *High St., tel. 0141/889–3151. Admission free. Open Mon.–Sat. 10–5; closed public holidays.*

The life of the workers in the textile industry is brought to life in **Sma' Shot Cottages,** re-creations of mill workers' houses. *11/17 George Pl., tel. 0141/814–2513. Admission free. Open May–Sept., Wed. and Sat. 1–5 or by appointment.*

Paisley's 12th-century Cluniac **Abbey** dominates the town center. Almost completely destroyed in 1307 and then rebuilt after the Battle of Bannockburn, the abbey is traditionally associated with Walter Fitzallan, the High Steward of Scotland, who gave his name to the Stewart monarchs of Scotland. Outstanding features include the fine stone-vaulted roof and stained glass of the choir. Paisley Abbey is today a busy parish church. *Tel. 0141/889–7654. Admission free; group visits by arrangement. Open Mon.–Sat. 10–12:30 and 1:30–3:30.*

Shopping

The old image of industrial Glasgow has changed considerably in recent times as the city has strenuously shrugged off its poorcousin-to-Edinburgh label. This is evidenced by the many stores, individual shops, and malls that have enhanced Glasgow's style without sacrificing its undoubted character.

Department Stores

The three main department stores are **Lewis's, Debenham's,** and **Frasers;** other High Street names—**Littlewoods, British Home Stores, C&A,** and **Marks and Spencer**—are also represented. Frasers is the store most worth visiting, not only for its exceptional interior and display (*see* Buchanan Street, *below*), but also for its variety of designer names and helpful, friendly staff.

Shopping Districts

Argyle Street/ St. Enoch Square
Start at St. Enoch Square (which is also the main underground station); it houses the St. Enoch Shopping Centre. Walk east toward the main pedestrian area of Argyle Street and you will find all the usual High Street chain stores. The recently much-improved **Debenham's** department store may be of particular interest (it can also be entered from the St. Enoch Centre). The pedestrian zone on Argyle Street is invariably overcrowded, especially on Saturday, and is certainly not for the impatient shopper. An interesting diversion off Argyle Street is the **Argyll Arcade,** which is the largest collection of jewelers under one roof in Scotland. This L-shape arcade, built in 1904, houses several locally based jewelers and a few shops specializing in antique jewelry. To be recommended are **Bercotts** (56 Argyll Arcade) and the arcade branch of **Laing the Jeweller** (48 Argyll Arcade) for handmade and contemporary designs, while **Mr. Harold** (33 Argyll Arcade) and **Michael James** (4 Argyll Arcade) have good collections of antique and reproduction designs. Because these shops are privately owned, it is not unheard of to get a cash discount (try asking, you may be lucky). The other end of the Argyll Arcade leads to Buchanan Street.

St. Enoch Square/Argyle Street can be reached on the underground system and directly by the internal rail system. Many buses run along either part of Argyle Street or streets nearby.

Buchanan Street
This is probably Glasgow's premier shopping street and is almost totally pedestrianized. Immediately opposite the exit of the Argyll Arcade is **Frasers** (45 Buchanan St.), Glasgow's largest and most interesting department store. Frasers is a Glasgow institution, and its wares reflect much of Glasgow's new and traditional images, leading European designer clothes and fabrics combining with home-produced articles, such as tweeds, tartans, glass, and ceramics. The magnificent interior is itself worth a visit, set off by the grand staircase rising to various floors and balconies.

Other shops to look out for in Buchanan Street include **R. G. Lawrie Ltd** (110 Buchanan St.), which specializes in highland outfitting, Scottish gifts, woolens, and cashmere, and **Henry Burton** (corner of Gordon St.), a traditional gentleman's outfitter. You will find excellent outerwear at **Graham Tiso** (129 Buchanan St.). Household names like Laura Ashley, Burberry's, Liberty, Jaeger, and Roland Cartier are found here as well. Buchanan Street also sports the entrances to the excellent **Princes Square** development. Elegant and stylish, this houses many of the finest specialty stores.

Running perpendicular to Buchanan Street, about halfway along to the left, is Gordon Street. Along this street, toward Central Station, you will find **Waterstones** bookstore and one or two other smaller shops of interest, including **Catherine Shaw** (24 Gordon St.), where there is an excellent range of specially designed and unique Charles Rennie Mackintosh–style clocks and jewelry.

For another shop worthy of mention, follow Buchanan Street to St. Vincent Street, turn to your left, and you will find **Graham's** tobacconist (71 St. Vincent St.). This shop has a tremendous variety of tobaccos and pipes. Much of Glasgow's wealth was generated by the Tobacco Lords during the 17th and 18th centuries; at Graham's you will experience a little of that colorful history.

Buchanan Street runs perpendicular to Argyle Street. At one end are Buchanan Street underground and Scotrail Queen Street stations.

Merchant City This area on the edge of the city center is a recent upscale development consisting of some new buildings and old warehouses converted into living space. It is home to many of Glasgow's young and upwardly mobile. Shopping here is expensive, but the area is certainly worth visiting for those who are seeking the young Glasgow style.

Visit **The Warehouse** (61–65 Glassford St.) or **Blondes** (18 Wilson St.) if you are looking for something exclusive to wear. Top off the outfit with a creation from **The Hat Shop** (Wilson St.), where there are some really unusual concoctions. Also worth a visit are **In House** (24–26 Wilson St.) and **Casa Fina** (2 Wilson St.), for stylish and modern furniture and giftware. Wander around **Stockwell China Bazaar** (67–77 Glassford St.) for a huge array of fine china and earthenware, glass, and ornaments. While in this area you will also find the **National Trust for Scotland**'s shop (Hutcheson's Hall, 158 Ingram St.). Many items for sale are designed exclusively for National Trust properties and are generally handmade.

The Merchant City is close to ScotRail's High Street station or can be easily reached by walking eastward from ScotRail's Argyle Street station.

The Barras This is Glasgow's famous weekend street market and should certainly not be missed during your visit. Apart from the excellent opportunity to pick up a bargain while you browse among the stalls, you will enjoy the lively and colorful surroundings. Stalls sell antique (and not-so-antique) furniture, bric-a-brac, student-designed jewelry and textiles—you name it, it's here. The Barras is approximately 80 years old and is made up of nine markets—the largest indoor market in Europe. It prides itself on selling everything "from a needle to an anchor."

You can reach the Barras by walking from Scotrail's Argyle Street station, or take any of the various buses to Glasgow Cross at the foot of the Gallowgate.

West Regent Street/ Blythswood Square For antiques connoisseurs and art lovers, a walk along West Regent Street is highly recommended. Your first stop should be the **Victorian Village** (57 West Regent St.), a complex of small antiques shops. Of particular interest among the jewelry, coins, and bric-a-brac are stores specializing in antiquarian books, army memorabilia, clothing, and sporting items. Farther along West Regent Street are various galleries and antiques shops, some specializing in Scottish antiques and paintings. **Cyril Gerber** (148 West Regent St.), specialists in 20th-century British paintings, will export, as will most galleries. The **Compass Gallery** usually has interesting exhibitions on view.

In this area you are not far from **Glasgow School of Art** (167 Renfrew St.), and apart from the famous Charles Rennie Mackintosh building itself, there is a shop selling various books, cards, jewelry, and ceramics. There are also guided tours during the summer months. Students often sell their work, if you are lucky enough to be visiting during the degree shows in June.

West Regent Street can be reached by walking from Renfield Street (parallel to Buchanan St.); most buses from the West End coming into town travel along this street or one running parallel to it. Renfrew Street can be reached by walking to the right along Pitt Street at the end of West Regent Street.

The West End/ Byres Road This part of the city is dominated by the university, and the shops cater to local and student needs. One place of interest is **De Courcey's** antiques and crafts arcade (5–21 Cresswell La.). There are quite a few shops to visit, and a variety of goods, including paintings and jewelry, are regularly auctioned here. De Courcey's is in one of the cobblestone lanes to the rear of Byres Road.

Byres Road is reached on the underground system: Get off at Hillhead station. By bus from the city center, numbers 44 and 59 pass by the university and cross over Byres Road (get off at the first stop on Highburgh Rd. and walk back).

Arcades and Shopping Centers

As in many other major cities and towns, various centers can be found in and around the city. **St. Enoch's Shopping Centre** is relatively new and is Europe's largest glass-roof shopping center (eye-catching if not especially pleasing). It houses various stores, but most could be found elsewhere. There is, however, an indoor ice-skating rink where equipment can be rented, an interesting diversion during a day's shopping. Other centers include Sauchiehall Street Centre and The Forge Shopping Centre at Parkhead, which both offer a variety of shopping. By far the best complex, however, is **Princes Square** (48 Buchanan St.), high-quality shops in an art-nouveau setting, with cafés and restaurants. Look particularly for the **Scottish Craft Centre,** which has an outstanding collection of work created by some of the best craftspeople in Scotland.

Specialty Stores

Clothing Glasgow has a very fashion-conscious image in Scotland, and a variety of both local and international fashion houses can be visited. The Merchant City area, with the stores already mentioned in that section, is popular with young people. At Princes Square there are famous design names like **Katherine Hamnett** and **Ted Baker.** The West End has a number of shops where you may find items of local design. Worth a special mention is **Strawberry Fields** (517 Great Western Rd.), housing a colorful array of children's wear. At **Riah Harvey** (Sheddens Rd., Clarkston), on the south side of the city, there is a good selection of fashion for women 5′2″ and under. **Romika** (14 Royal Exchange Sq.), back in the city center, offers shoes, umbrellas, and some unusual accessories.

Gifts All the usual Scottish-theme gifts can be found in various locations in Glasgow. Gift items here tend to be a little more interesting and of a higher quality than those found in other, more tourist-oriented areas of the country.

MacDonald MacKay Ltd (105 Hope St.) makes and sells Highland dress and accessories, ladies' kilts, and skirts made to measure and offers an export service. **W M Houston** (216 Argyle St.), featuring Scottish gifts and clan memorabilia, is worth a visit; it specializes in large sizes for men.

Glasgow has a definite place in the history of art and design, being most famous for its association with Charles Rennie Mackintosh. For high-quality giftware in his style, **Catherine Shaw** (24 Gordon St. and in the Argyll Arcade) offers a unique selection.

Glasgow Environs

Both Ayr and Troon can be reached easily from Glasgow by train from Central Station; trains run every half hour during the week.

Ayr   Ayr has a good mixture of traditional and new shops. Queen's Court, Sandgate, combines small crafts and gift shops. The **Diamond Factory** (27 Queen's Ct.) is a jewelry workshop where visitors are invited to view craftsmen at work. All jewelry is designed and made on the premises. Ask about rings that can be engraved with a family crest and about seal engraving. The store will export your purchases if you do not have time to wait for completion of the work. At **New Courtyard Craft Supplies** you'll find various crafts materials, mainly wools and silks. The **Mill Shop, Begg of Ayr** (Viewfield Rd.) has a good selection of scarves, stoles, plaids, and travel rugs that are handmade on the premises. **Acanthus** (11–15 Old Bridge St.), specialists in china and crystal, will export any purchase worldwide.

Troon   This small coastal town north of Ayr is famous for its international golf course, Royal Troon. Many Glaswegians frequent **Regalia** (44–48 Church St.) for its unusual collection of designer outfits. **Vallance** (39 Ayr St.) is a traditional confectionery; try the specially boxed handmade fudge and shortbread.

Sports and Fitness

Bicycling and Jogging   The tourist board (*see* Important Addresses and Numbers in Essential Information, *above*) can provide a list of cycle paths and of the many parks and gardens in Glasgow with facilities for these sports; many of the parks also have tennis courts and/or bowling greens.

Fishing   With loch, river, and sea fishing available, the area is a mecca for fishermen. Details of fishing permits and locations are available from the tourist board.

Golf   Seven courses are operated within Glasgow proper by the local authorities. Bookings are relatively inexpensive and can be made with ease, especially during the week. A comprehensive list of contacts, facilities, and charges of the 30 or so other courses nearby the city is available from the Greater Glasgow Tourist Board.

Alexandra Park (Alexandra Parade, tel. 0141/556–3991). 9 holes, 2,281 yards.
King's Park (Croftfoot, tel. 0141/637–1066). 9 holes, 2,103 yards, SSS 32.
Knightswood (Lincoln Ave., tel. 0141/959–2131). 9 holes, 2,717 yards, SSS 33.
Lethamhill (Cumbernauld Rd., tel. 0141/770–6220). 18 holes, 6,081 yards, SSS 69.
Linn Park (Simshill Rd., tel. 0141/637–5871). 18 holes, 4,814 yards, SSS 64.
Littlehill (Auchinairn Rd., tel. 0141/772–1916). 18 holes, 6,199 yards, SSS 69.
Ruchill (Brassey St., tel. 0141/946–9728). 9 holes, 2,208 yards, SSS 32.

Health and Fitness Clubs   There are some 40 clubs throughout the city. Most include a swimming pool and gymnasium, and some have squash, karate, horseback riding, shooting, badminton, or sailing facilities. See the brochure available from the tourist board for details. The larger hotels in the city also offer a variety of sports and leisure facilities, usually free of charge, to their guests. Currently, the following hotels have at least a pool and gym: **Central** (tel. 0141/221–9680), **Moat House** (tel. 0141/204–0733), **Marriott** (tel. 0141/226–5577), **Jury's Pond** (tel. 0141/334–8161), **Hilton** (tel. 0141/204–5555), and **Swallow** (tel. 0141/427–3146).

Sailing and Water Sports The Firth of Clyde and Loch Lomond both offer water-sports facilities with full equipment rental. Details are available from the tourist board.

Soccer The city has been sports-mad, especially for football (soccer), for over 100 years, and the rivalry between its two main clubs, Rangers and Celtic, is legendary. Rangers wear blue, are predominantly Protestant, and play at Ibrox (pronounced *EYE-brox*) to the west of the city; the Celtics wear green, are predominantly Roman Catholic, and play in the east. Matches are played usually on a Saturday in winter, and Glasgow has in total nine different teams playing in the Scottish Leagues. Admission prices start at about £5. Do not go looking for the family-day-out atmosphere of many American football games; soccer remains a man's game played in relatively primitive surroundings, though Ibrox is an exception to this.

Dining

The restaurants of Glasgow have diversified over the past several years; as a result, this is one of the cities in Scotland where you'll find Chinese, Italian, and Indian food in addition to the usual French and Scottish offerings. Some of the shopping-arcade cafés provide acceptable alternatives for lunch and afternoon tea. Pubs are also good bets for cheap bar lunches.

Highly recommended restaurants are indicated by a star ★.

Category	Cost*
$$$$	over £25
$$$	£15–£25
$$	£10–£15
$	under £10

per person for a three-course meal, including VAT

★ **Rogano.** This restaurant's art deco interior, modeled after the style of the *Queen Mary* liner—bird's eye maple paneling, chrome trim, and dramatic ocean murals—is enough to recommend it; the excellent food in the sumptuous main restaurant, the lively downstairs diner, and the oyster bar near the entrance is a bonus. Portions are generous in the main restaurant, where specialties include venison liver pâté and classic seafood dishes that are impeccably prepared though predictable. The vegetables can be disappointing. Downstairs, where the menu changes monthly, the brasserie-style food is more modern and imaginative; the menu might list clam chowder or Mediterranean grilled swordfish. The theater menu provides early-evening and late-night bargains, and the fixed-price lunch menu is popular upstairs. Rogano is patronized by the Glasgow establishment and visiting glitterati, who appreciate, as you will, the extremely good service. *11 Exchange Sq., tel. 0141/248–4055. Reservations required. Jacket and tie required. AE, DC, MC, V. Closed Sun. and bank holidays. $$$$*

Glasgow Dining and Lodging

KEY
- Pedestrian Zone
- Rail Lines
- (U) Metro Stop
- AE American Express Office
- i Tourist Information

Dining

Ashoka West End, **4**
Buttery, **15**
Café Gandolfi, **22**
The Ho Wong, **18**
La Parmigiana, **9**
Loon Fung, **13**
Rogano, **20**
Two Fat Ladies, **5**
The Ubiquitous Chip, **2**

Lodging

Angus, **10**
Babbity Bowster's, **21**
The Carrick, **16**
Central Hotel, **19**
Forte Crest, **14**
Kirklee Hotel, **7**
Marie Stuart, **23**
One Devonshire Gardens, **1**

Queen's Park Hotel, **25**
The Sandyford, **12**
Sherbrooke Castle Hotel, **17**
Smith's Hotel, **11**
The Stakis Grosvenor, **6**
Tinto Firs, **24**
The White House, **8**
Wickets, **3**

The Ubiquitous Chip. Set in a courtyard inside a Victorian mews (once used for stables) with a fountain and lots of plants, this is one of the most interesting locales in which to relax over a meal. The menu changes daily but usually includes seafood from the West Coast, roe-deer steaks, and lamb. For traditionalists there is braised venison and silverside, and for the more adventurous, pigeon with wild mushroom sauce or turbot with a crust of pine kernels. The cellar here is the best in the city, with a comprehensive wine list and a huge selection of single malts. Lunches are informal; a large variety of salads and one or two hot dishes are served. The clientele is steady—executives from the nearby BBC headquarters and academics from Glasgow University. *12 Ashton La., tel. 0141/334–5007. Reservations advised. Dress: casual. AE, DC, MC, V. $$$$*

★ **Buttery.** Trying to locate the Buttery, which is in a former Masonic temple, is the biggest challenge. Get a cab to navigate confusing Argyle Street and leave you at this spot behind a wall of council flats and close to the ring road expressway tangle. Inside, the Victorian decor, dark and domineering, eases you back to another century. The food is now significantly lighter than it was just several years ago: Heavily sauced classics have been replaced by such dishes as grilled fillet of brill on a sharp peppercorn butter and steamed mussels with a scampi-and-prawn velouté. Vegetarians should not pass up the chesnut-and-spinach ravioli. Downstairs, the Belfry serves inexpensive bistro food, from healthy vegetarian options to such robust favorites as kidneys turbigo. There's a better selection of good desserts and Scottish cheeses than upstairs, and the service is friendly and the ambience more relaxed. There is also a good selection of teas and tisanes. *652 Argyle St., tel. 0141/221–8188. Reservations required. Dress: casual. AE, DC, MC, V. Closed Sat. lunch, Sun., and bank holidays. $$$ (Belfry: $)*

The Ho Wong. Genuine Chinese watercolors adorn the wood-panel walls of this peaceful restaurant. This isn't the place to go if you want fast food: The seating is comfortable and patrons are encourged to relax and enjoy the experience. The menu offers a selection of Cantonese- and Peking-style food. For the really adventurous there are such specialties as the Imperial State Banquet. *82 York St., tel. 0141/221–3550. Reservations advised. Dress: casual. AE, MC, V. Closed Sun. $$$*

Ashoka West End. This Punjabi restaurant consistently outperforms its many competitors in quality, range, and taste. Its extensive menu is split into popular and gourmet sections, but all portions are large enough to please the ravenous. There is nothing heavy-handed about the cooking here: Vegetable samosas are crisp and light; the spicing for the lamb, chicken, and prawn dishes is fresh and fragrant; and the milder kormas are pleasantly creamy. The selection of breads is superb. The eclectic Eastern decor, involving a bizarre mixture of garish pictures, rugs, and brass lamps, and inappropriate Western music simply emphasize the Ashoka's idiosyncracy. *1284 Argyle St., tel. 0194/339–0936. AE, DC, MC, V. Open 5:30–12:30 (Fri. till 1 AM). Closed lunch. $$*

Café Gandolfi. Once a Victorian pub, this café's location and decor reflect its trend-setting aspirations. On the edge of the Merchant City, it is now a haven for the design-conscious under-thirty crowd. Wooden tables and chairs carved by Scottish artist Tim Stead are so fluidly shaped it is hard to believe they're inanimate. The café opens early for breakfast, serving croissants, eggs en cocotte, and espresso. The rest of the day is filled with interesting soups, salads, local specialties, and Mediterranean favorites. Don't miss the smoked venison or the finnan haddie. Homemade ice cream and good pastries ensure busy afternoons, and evenings are livened up with good beers but less compelling wines. *64 Albion St., tel. 0141/552–6813. Dress: casual. No credit cards. Closed Sun. and bank holidays. $$*

La Parmigiana. Like most successful Italian restaurants in Scotland, La Parmigiana has allowed Scottish tastes to influence the menu, and it uses the wealth of local ingredients with flair. The inexpensive three-course lunch may include the predictable bean and tuna salad, lasagna, and grilled sole, but the restaurant also cooks up *vitello tonnato* (veal in tuna and anchovy sauce), char-grilled quail, and unusual pastas such as paporadelle and orecciette. Although small—it seats just 30 customers—it has a relaxed atmosphere and efficient, cheerful service. The tile floor, green blinds, and white walls look nice enough, but the chairs are uncomfortable. The wine list is rather limited. *447 Great Western Rd., tel. 0141/334–0686. Reservations advised. AE, DC, MC, V. Closed bank holidays lunch and Sun. $$*

Loon Fung. There is plenty of space in this popular Cantonese restaurant, which was once a cinema and now seats 200. The pleasant and efficient staff guides you enthusiastically through the house specialties, including the famed dim sum. If you like seafood, try the deep-fried won ton with prawns, crispy stuffed crab claws, or lobster in garlic and cheese sauce. The business lunch and fixed-price dinner are reasonably priced. *417 Sauchiehall St., tel. 0141/332–1240. AE, DC, MC, V. Closed three days of Chinese New Year. $$*

Two Fat Ladies. It's easy to mistake this restaurant for an all-night grocery because the kitchen is seen through the window. Inside there is no ornamentation of any sort, just Formica tables, nicotine-yellow walls, and a vinyl floor. The cooking, however, compensates for the austere, institutional decor. Fish predominates: fresh and prepared with imagination and skill. Squad lobster, turbot, John Dory, and monkfish are a typical selection. Portions are generous; the salads, colossal. Desserts are less interesting—tiramisù, apple tart, and chocolate mousse—and the wine list is like the decor, minimalist. Unforgettable, nevertheless. *88 Dumbarton Rd., tel. 0141/339–1944. DC, MC, V. Open 6:30 PM–10:30 PM. Closed Sun., Mon., and 2 weeks at Christmas. $$*

Lodging

Glasgow is now better equipped with hotels of all categories than it has ever been. The city has become a major business destination in the past several years, with the Scottish Conference and Exhibition Centre serving as the focal point. There are now some big city-center hotels (including the Hilton and Marriott) of both expensive and moderate character, and some good and reasonable small hotels and guest houses in the suburbs (in most cases, transportation into town is quick and dependable). All the larger hotels have restaurants open to nonguests.

Highly recommended lodgings are indicated by a star ★.

Category	Cost*
$$$$	over £120
$$$	£100–£120

$$	£80–£100
$	under £80

All prices are for a standard double room, including service, breakfast, and VAT.

★ **One Devonshire Gardens.** This hotel is comprised of a group of Victorian houses on a sloping tree-lined street to the west of the city, only 10 minutes from the center. It was voted British Hotel of the Year in 1993, and such celebrities as Luciano Pavarotti and Elizabeth Taylor name it as their favorite. The sophisticated ivory-walled drawing room has comfortable navy sofas. Each individually decorated bedroom has rich wallpaper, heavy drapes, and French mahogany furniture; three rooms have four-poster beds. The restaurant is equally stylish with a menu that changes daily and specialties including salmon with orange and ginger sauce, chicken livers with almonds, and magnificent tournedos of Scotch beef fillet steaks. The staff, appropriately garbed in long white aprons, provides impeccable service. The wine list is commanding, as are the prices. *1 Devonshire Gardens, G12 0UX, tel. 0141/339–2001, fax 0141/337–1663. 27 rooms with bath/shower. Facilities: restaurant. AE, DC, MC, V. $$$$*

Forte Crest. Well positioned in the center of the city, the Forte Crest, formerly the Albany, is generally rated as one of the best of Glasgow's hotels. Rooms are tastefully decorated in pale colors and unmemorable pictures. The bar area has a set of the world's ugliest high-backed purple chairs as a "tribute" to Charles Rennie Mackintosh. With 251 rooms it's hardly intimate, but the service is very professional and friendly. *Bothwell St., G2 7EN, tel. 0141/248–2656, fax 0141/221–8986. 251 rooms with bath. Facilities: restaurant, lounge, bar. AE, DC, MC, V. $$$*

The Stakis Grosvenor. Set away from downtown, the Stakis Grosvenor is convenient for the Botanic Gardens and the bohemian atmosphere of Byres Road with its remarkable concentration of pubs. Its Victorian facade, cunningly reconstructed of fiberglass after a fire, is best seen at night, when it is spectacularly floodlit. Behind this magnificent facade is a disappointingly routine business hotel. Room decor is pink-and-beige with gentle floral fabrics; public areas are more stylish with deep sofas and big lamps. There are two restaurants, the Terrace and the Steakhouse, as well as several bars and a coffee shop. *Grosvenor Terr., Great Western Rd., G12 0TA, tel. 0141/339–8811, fax 0141/334–0710. 95 rooms with bath. Facilities: 2 restaurants, bars, coffee shop. AE, DC, V. $$$*

The White House. This is an unusual Glasgow hotel insofar as it has no dining room. All accommodations at the White House are in self-contained suites, and guests can either cook their own food in the fully appointed kitchen or have food delivered to their suites. The larger suites comprise several linked rooms, and the less expensive have a kitchen area in the sitting room. Stays can be as short as one night or as long as one year. *11–13 Clevedon Crescent, G12 0PA, tel. 0141/339–9375, fax 0141/337–1430. 31 suites. AE, DC, MC, V. $$$*

The Carrick. Although it has an unappealing modern exterior and is located in a rather seedy part of town overlooking the river, this hotel offers one of the best values in the city. It is also convenient to all city-center shopping. Its rooms are bright and modern, and its restaurant serves better than average Scottish food. Take a cab at night. *377 Argyle St., G2 8LL, tel. 0141/248–2355, fax 0141/221–1014. 121 rooms with bath or shower. Facilities: restaurant, bar, free parking. AE, DC, MC, V. $$*

★ **Central Hotel.** At this typical Victorian railroad hotel, there are thick carpets, mobcapped chambermaids, and ample rooms from another era. Public areas feature brass chandeliers and plenty of greenery. The **Entresol** restaurant serves breakfast, lunch, and dinner. *Gordon St., G1 3SF, tel. 0141/221–9680, fax 0141/226–3948. 221 rooms, most with bath/shower. AE, DC, MC, V. $$*

Sherbrooke Castle Hotel. Come to the Sherbrooke for a flight of Gothic fantasy. Its cavernous rooms hark back to grander times when the south side of Glasgow was home to the immensely wealthy tobacco barons, whose homes were built with turrets and towers. The spacious grounds are far from the noise and bustle of the city, yet only 10 minutes' drive from the city center. Like the tobacco barons, the hotel's proprietor insists on tasteful decor and good traditional cooking. The busy bar is well patronized by locals. *11 Sherbrook Ave., Pollokshields, G41 4PG, tel. 0141/427–4227, fax 0141/427–5685. 25 rooms with bath/shower. Facilities: AE, DC, MC, V. $$*

Tinto Firs. This modern hotel on the parklike south side of Glasgow is more country-house than city style. The lounge/cocktail bar has dark wood paneling and rattan chairs; the bedrooms have stunning wall coverings and matching fabric furnishings. *470 Kilmarnock Rd., G43 2BB, tel. 0141/637–2353, fax 0141/633–1340. 27 rooms with bath/shower. AE, DC, MC, V. $$*

Angus. Another privately run city-center hotel on Sauchiehall Street, the Angus is intimate yet spacious. Its biggest plusses are the friendly staff and their eye for detail. All rooms have been tastefully decorated creating a Victorian ambience. *966 Sauchiehall St., G3 7TQ, tel. 0141/357–5155, fax 0141/357–5155. 17 rooms with bath/shower. AE, DC, MC, V. $*

Babbity Bowster's. There's a lively atmosphere at this small, intimate hotel in a restored 18th-century town house designed by Robert Adam. In addition to a gallery on the first floor that features many works by Glaswegian artists, the hotel offers a bar, restaurant, and café. *16–18 Blackfriars St., G1 1PE, tel. 0141/552–5055. 6 rooms with shower. Facilities: restaurant, bar, café. AE, DC. V. $*

★ **Kirklee Hotel.** Located in a quiet district of Glasgow near the university, this hotel is small and cozy. Its owners take pride in being friendly and helpful and in keeping the hotel spotless and comfortable. *11 Kensington Gate, G12 9LG, tel. 0141/334–5555, fax 0141/339–3828. 9 rooms with bath. No credit cards. $*

Marie Stuart. Well-equipped rooms and excellent service highlight this hotel. The bar is lively and popular, and the staff is friendly. *46 Queen Mary Ave., G42 8DT, tel. 0141/424–3939, fax 0141/423—9070. 28 rooms, 18 with bath/shower. Facilities: bar. No credit cards. $*

Queen's Park Hotel. There's a good all-around standard of comfort and service here. Meal hours are flexible, a plus for late-nighters or late sleepers. *10 Balvicar Dr., G42 8QT, tel. 0141/423–1123, fax 0141/423–4917. 35 rooms, 30 with bath/shower. No credit cards. $*

The Sandyford. With a fine Victorian exterior, this hotel reopened in November 1993 after extensive renovations and refurbishment. On the west end of famous Sauchiehall Street, it is convenient to all city-center facilities, including the Scottish Exhibition Centre and many art galleries. The Sandyford is more an upscale bed-and-breakfast than a hotel, although its rooms are somewhat spartan, with stark white interiors and pine furniture. *904 Sauchiehall St., G3 7TF, tel. 0141/334–0000, fax 0141/337–1812. 26 rooms with bath/shower. AE, DC, MC, V. $*

Smith's Hotel. The carpeting may be mismatched and the wood paneling cheap, but the rock-bottom price of Smith's Hotel is a wonder.

With a white facade and net curtains, it lacks pretension as well as glamour. The wisecracking staff is lots of fun, and the breakfast is splendid. *963 Sauchiehall St., G3 7TQ, tel. 0141/339–6363 or 0141/339–7674. 33 rooms, none with bath. No credit cards. $*

Wickets. In the heart of Billy Connolly's neighborhood, Partick, this hotel dominates one of the area's few green spaces—the West of Scotland cricket ground. It is a handsome white mansion house with an airy, continental feel. Its glass-fronted restaurant looking onto an extensive garden is a rare pleasure in the city. The bar areas are split between the traditional and the artfully Parisienne. Since cricket is not Glasgow's premier sport, Wickets enjoys a tranquil, leafy setting. The rooms are furnished with a cheerful bravado. *52 Fortrose St., G11 5LP, tel. and fax 0141/334–9334. 10 rooms with bath or shower. AE, DC, MC, V. $*

The Arts and Nightlife

Glasgow was the 1990 European City of Culture, the first British city to be so designated. Given that the previous European Cities of Culture were Athens, Florence, Amsterdam, Berlin, and Paris, it's clear just how strong Glasgow's international reputation is when it comes to cultural events. That reputation has grown from the strong base developed by the city authorities in the 19th century and has continued in the remarkable renaissance the city has enjoyed in the past 10 years.

The Arts

Theater Glasgow offers a plethora of live theater. One of the most exciting is the internationally renowned **Citizen's Theatre** (119 Gorbals St., tel. 0141/429–0022), where productions, and their sets, are often of hair-raising originality. The **King's Theatre** (Bath St., tel. 0141/227–5511) stages drama, light entertainment, variety shows, musicals, and amateur productions. The **Mitchell** (Mitchell Library, North St., tel. 0141/227–5511) mostly accommodates amateur productions, but also hosts lectures and meetings. The **Pavilion** (Renfield St., tel. 0141/332–1846) offers family variety entertainment along with rock and pop concerts. The **Royal Scottish Academy of Music and Drama** (100 Renfrew St., tel. 0141/332–5057) stages a variety of international and student performances. The **Tramway** (25 Albert Dr., tel. 0141/227–5511), the city's old museum of transport, is now an exciting venue for opera, drama, and dance. The **Tron** (63 Trongate, tel. 0141/552–4267) houses Scottish and international theater. The **Arches** (Midland St., tel. 0141/221–9736) stages serious and controversial drama from around the world. **Theatre Royal** (Hope St., tel. 0141/332–9000) also has performances of major drama, including an occasional season of plays by international touring companies.

Tickets for performances can be purchased at theater box offices or at the **Ticket Center** (Candleriggs, tel. 0141/227–5511).

Concerts Glasgow's **Royal Concert Hall** (2 Sauchiehall St., tel. 0141/227–5511) was opened for the City of Culture celebrations in 1990. It has 2,500 seats and is the permanent home of the Royal Scottish Orchestra, which performs a winter series of concerts and a summer proms series. Other concert halls include **City Halls** (Candleriggs, tel. 0141/227–5511); the **Henry Wood Hall** (Claremont St., tel. 0141/332–3868), a former church now used for classical concerts; and the **Scottish Exhibition and Conference Centre** (Finnieston, tel. 0141/248–3000), which is a regular venue for pop concerts.

Film   The **Glasgow Film Theatre** (Rose St., tel. 0141/332–6535) is an independent public cinema screening the best nonmainstream films from all over the world. The **MGM Film Centre** (Sauchiehall St., tel. 0141/332–9513) and the **Odeon Film Centre** (Renfield St., tel. 0141/332–8701) both show all the latest releases. For details of programs, consult the daily newspapers.

Opera and   Glasgow is home to the Scottish Opera and Scottish Ballet, both of
Ballet   which perform at the **Theatre Royal** (Hope St., tel. 0141/332–9000). Visiting dance companies from many countries perform here also.

Nightlife

Glasgow's pubs were once famous for hard drinkers who demanded few comforts. Times have changed and many pubs have been turned into smart wine bars. For a taste of an authentic Glasgow pub with some traditional folk music occasionally thrown in, go to the Stockwell Street area and search out **Scotia Bar, The Victoria Bar,** or **Clutha Vaults.** If you visit only one pub in Glasgow, make it the **Horseshoe Bar** (17–21 Drury St., tel. 0141/221–3051), which offers a sepia-tinted sentimental glimpse of all the friendlier Glasgow myths, and serves that cheerful distillation over what is purported to be the world's longest bar. Refurbishment would be a curse on its original tiling, stained glass, and deeply polished woodwork. Almost as intriguing as the decor is the clientele—a complete cross section of the city's populace. The upstairs lounge serves the steak pie Britain became famous for, and the waitress will ask some pretty stiff questions if you don't finish. In the center of town try the **Drum and Monkey** (93 St. Vincent St.), a trendy pub with a classic Victorian look and live music during the week. **Nico's** (375 Sauchiehall St.), designed along the lines of a Paris café, is a favorite with the nearby art school students and young Glaswegian professionals. The best Gaelic pub is **Uisge Beatha** (232–246 Woodlands Rd., tel. 0141/332–0473), pronounced *oos-ka-va-hah* and meaning the "water of life," a euphemism for scotch. The pub rambles over three rooms containing a wide assortment of furniture and antiques and the bartenders wear kilts. There is good live music in the **Halt** (106 Woodlands Rd.), which has a mixed-age clientele. Farther afield, the **Riverside Club** (Fox St., off Clyde St.) features traditional ceilidh bands on the weekend.

Any tourist office (*see* Important Addresses and Numbers in Essential Information, *above*) provides up-to-date listings, as does the fortnightly magazine, *The List.*

Among the city's large number of dancing hot spots are **Volcano** (Benalder St., off corner of Dumbarton and Byres Rds.; open 11 PM–2:30 AM; admission £4), dark and spartan, with a different mood and music nightly; **Cleopatra's** (508 Great Western Rd., tel. 0141/332–0712; open 11 PM–1 or 3 AM; admission £5), favored by Glasgow University students as well as trendy young professionals; and **The Tunnel** (84 Mitchell St., tel. 0141/204–1000; open 11 PM–3 AM; admission £5–£7), unpredictable yet fashionable.

Short Excursions from Glasgow

Glasgow is well placed as a touring base for excursions northward to the Highlands or south to the fertile farmlands of Ayrshire and the Clyde Valley. Here are two one-day itineraries you could do by car or, in a modified form, by public transportation. You will find details of places to visit in the north covered in the Central Highlands section of this book.

Tour 1: Ayrshire and the Clyde Coast

Numbers in the margin correspond to points of interest on the Glasgow Excursions: Ayrshire and the Clyde Valley map.

Robert Burns is Scotland's national and well-loved poet. His birthday is celebrated with speeches and dinners, drinking and dancing (Burns Suppers) on January 25, in a way in which few other countries celebrate a poet. He was born in Alloway, just an hour or so to the south of Glasgow, and the towns and villages where he lived and loved make an interesting day out from the city.

Ideally, you need a car, but if not, you can go by bus or train (*see* Getting Around in Essential Information, *above,* for excursion-ticket details) Take the bus or train to Largs for Cumbrae; Ardrossan for Arran; Ayr and Kilmarnock for the Burns Heritage Trail; and Troon, Prestwick, and Ayr to play golf. Bus companies also operate one-day guided excursions to this area. The Scottish Tourist Guides Association provides guides.

If you travel by car, begin your trip from Glasgow city center westbound on the M8, signposted for Glasgow Airport and Greenock.
❶ You will pass the Erskine Bridge and look across to **Dumbarton** and its Rock, a nostalgic farewell point for emigrants leaving Glasgow. Note, too, how narrow the river is here and remember that the *Queen Elizabeth 2* and the other *Queens* and great ocean liners sailed these waters from the place of their birth.

Join the A78 and follow it from Greenock to Gourock and around the coast past the Cloch lighthouse. The views north and west to Loch Long, the Holy Loch, and the Argyll Forest Park are outstanding on a clear day—and may make you want to abandon your plans and take the ferry across the estuary to Dunoon. Head south, having
❷ resisted the temptation, to the old Victorian village of **Wemyss Bay,** where the station and especially the covered walkway between platform and steamer pier, with its exuberant wrought-ironwork, are a reminder of the grandeur and style of the Victorian era and the generations of visitors who used trains and ferries for their summer holidays. From here there is a ferry service to the Isle of Bute, a favorite holiday spot for Glaswegians earlier this century. South of Wemyss Bay, the island of Arran, another Victorian holiday favorite, comes into view and then the island of Great Cumbrae (a weighty name for a tiny island) and its ferryport, Largs.

❸ South of Largs is **Kelburn Castle and Country Park,** the historic estate of the Earl of Glasgow. There are walks and trails through the mature woodlands, showing off the trees and shrubs from all over the world. The visitor center explains it all, and the adventure center and commando-assault course will wear out overexcited children. (They tell a tale here of rescuing an elderly lady from halfway around the assault course, who commented "Well, I did think it was rather a *hard* nature trail." Make sure you read the signposts.) *Fairlie, Ayrshire KA2Q ORE, tel. 01475/568685. Admission: £3 adults, £1.50 children. Open Easter–Sept., daily 10–6; grounds only, Oct.– Easter, daily 11–5.*

Follow the A78 ever southward through Ardrossan to Irvine (pronounced not like the place in California, but as *Irvin*), where the Magnum Leisure Centre, Sea World Exhibition, and Scottish Maritime Museum are all of interest. Robert Burns puts in an appearance at Irvine. He came here to learn to dress flax (the raw material for linen), and the heckling (flax-dressing) shed where he worked and the house where he lived are museums. The Irvine Burns Club is possibly the oldest in the world.

Continue on A78 past Troon and Prestwick, two holy places for golfers, particularly since the first British Open was played at Prestwick. You can easily see why golf is so popular here. The whole Ayrshire coast, 60 miles long, seems one endless golf course. Go past

4 Prestwick airport to reach **Ayr,** a peaceful and elegant town with an air of prosperity and some good shops. Burns was baptized in the Auld Kirk (Old Church) in the town and wrote a humorous poem about the Twa Brigs (two bridges) that cross the river nearby. He described Ayr as a town unsurpassed "for honest men and bonny lasses." The Tam o' Shanter Museum has plenty of Burns relics and reminders of one of his most famous poems, "Tam o' Shanter."

5 The poet was born at **Alloway** on the B7024 about 2 miles south of town. The thatched whitewashed cottage (and adjacent museum), which his father built, is a shrine to Burns's memory. Just to the south is a whole cluster of places associated with Burns: the Old Kirk of Alloway (where the witches were holding their meeting in "Tam o' Shanter"); the Brig o' Doon (to where the disturbed witches chased Tam in the same poem); the Burns Memorial and Gardens, which overlook it; and, around the corner, the Land o' Burns Centre, which tells the story of Burns's life.

Time Out   Ayr has a number of attractive cafés and hotels. Try the **Tudor Restaurant** (tel. 01292/261404) or the **Honey Pot** (tel. 01292/611953), both in Burns Statue Square. The **Land o' Burns Centre** in Alloway (Mill Rd., tel. 01292/443700) also serves food and drinks in an attractive setting. In Ayr, **Fausto's** (16 Cathcart St., tel. 01292/268204) offers superb but reasonably priced Italian food and **Fouter's Bistro** (2A Academy St., tel. 01292/261391) serves French fare.

6 If you have time, continue south from Ayr and Alloway to **Culzean Castle and Country Park.** This magnificent mansion was built by Robert Adam on a dramatic clifftop setting. It stands just off the A719, and you could easily spend a whole day here walking around the classically elegant rooms, the gardens, and the estate. The people of Scotland made a gift of a flat in the castle to President Eisenhower. Also inside is the Eisenhower Presentation, an exhibition of memorabilia. *Tel. 016556/2293. Admission: county park, £5 car; £3 adults, £1.50 children. Park open year-round. Castle open Apr.–Oct., daily 10:30–5:30.*

You'll return to Ayr, then turn eastward on the A758, the Mauchline

7 Road, but before you get there, turn left on a little road to **Tarbolton,** where you will find the **Bachelors' Club,** a 17th-century house where Burns learned to dance, founded a debating and literary society, and

became a Freemason. *Admission: £1 adults. Open summer daily in afternoon.*

8 **Mauchline** also has strong connections with the poet. There is a Burns House here; four of his daughters are buried in the churchyard; and Poosie Nansie's pub, where he used to drink, is still in use today. The village is also famous for making curling stones.

Head north on A76 to Kilmarnock, an industrial town, home of Johnny Walker whiskey, where again Burns enthusiasts will enjoy the Burns Museum and the Dick Institute. If you are looking for **9** something different by now, go to **Dean Castle and Country Park** off Glasgow Road to enjoy a 14th-century castle with a wonderful collection of medieval arms and armor. Burns also inevitably gets a mention. Glasgow is only half an hour away on the fast A77.

Tour 2: The Clyde Valley

The River Clyde is (or certainly was) famous for its shipbuilding and heavy industries, yet its upper reaches flow through some of Scotland's most fertile farmlands, which concentrate on growing tomatoes. It is an interesting area, with ancient castles as well as industrial and social museums that tell the story of manufacturing and mining prosperity.

Take A724 out of Glasgow south of the river through Rutherglen toward Hamilton. It is not a very good road, but in Blantyre look **10** for signs to the **David Livingstone Centre,** a park area around the tiny (tenement) apartment where the great explorer of Africa was born in 1813. Displays tell of his journeys, of his meeting with Stanley ("Doctor Livingstone, I presume"), of Africa, and of the industrial heritage of the area. *Tel. 01698/823140. Admission: £1.70 adults, £1 senior citizens, 85p children. Open all year Mon.–Sat. 10–6, Sun. 1–6.*

Close by in Uddingston is **Bothwell Castle,** dating from the 13th century. Its walls are well preserved and stand above the River Clyde.

The Hamilton Mausoleum, in Strathclyde Country Park near the industrial town of Hamilton, was built in the 1840s as an extraordinary monument to the lavish eccentricities of the dukes of Hamilton **11** (who had more money than sense). Also nearby is **Chatelherault** (pronounced *SHAT-lerro*), a unique one-room-deep facade, part shooting lodge, part glorified dog kennel, designed in elegant Georgian style by William Adam, also for the dukes of Hamilton. Within Chatelherault is an exhibition describing life on the estate in all its former glory. *Tel. 01698/426213. Admission: free to grounds, small fee for Visitor Centre. Open Apr.–Sept., daily 10:30–5:30; Oct.–Mar., daily 10:30–4:30. House occasionally closed for functions.*

Time Out For a cup of tea and some homemade baked goods, stop at the **Hamilton Old Parish Church,** built by William Adam, Robert's father, in 1734. The church is open in the morning and contains an ancient cross, a Covenanters Memorial, and fine embroideries.

From Hamilton, take the A72 toward **Lanark,** a pleasant agricultural town. You pass the ruins of medieval Craignethan Castle, lots of greenhouses for tomatoes, plant nurseries, and gnarled old orchards running down to the Clyde. Before reaching Lanark, follow **12** the signs down a long winding hill, to **New Lanark,** one of the world's most important industrial heritage sites—though in this wooded river valley, the ambience is hardly industrial. Here in 1785 a "model" village was set up to house the workers employed in cotton mills, which were powered by the fast-flowing waters of the Clyde. After many changes of fortune the mills eventually closed, but the site has been saved and has a new lease on life with renovated housing. The refurbishment was excellent, and the arty-types who bought the houses seem to lead normal lives despite having tourists peering in all day. One of the mills has been converted into an interpretation center, which tells the story of this brave social experiment. Upstream, the Clyde flows through some of the very finest river scenery anywhere in Lowland Scotland, with woods and spectacular waterfalls. *Tel. 01555/665876. Admission: £2.60 adults, £1.60 children. Open daily 11–5.*

⑬ A72 continues south of Lanark to join A702 near Biggar. The **Biggar Street Museum** offers a fascinating portrayal of life in the town; the old gasworks—which is actually much more interesting than it sounds—is preserved and there is a puppet theater. *Gladstone Ct., Biggar, tel. 01899/21050. Open Apr.–Oct., Mon.–Sat. 10:30–12:30 and 2–5, Sun. 2–5.*

By the time you get to Biggar, you are near the headwaters of the Clyde, on the moors in the center of southern Scotland. The Clyde flows west toward Glasgow and the Atlantic Ocean, while the Tweed, only a few miles away, flows eastward toward the North Sea. There are fine views around Biggar: to Culter Fell and to the Border Hills in the south.

Time Out   In Biggar High Street, try the **Elphinstone Hotel** (tel. 01899/20044) or one of the several excellent cafés nearby. Outside Biggar, the **Shieldhill House Hotel** (tel. 01899/20035), near the curiously named village of Quothquan, is excellent, as is Symington's **Tinto Hotel** (tel. 018993/454). In Lanark, try the **Cartland Bridge Hotel** (tel. 01555/664426), on the Carluke–Hamilton road, or the **Clydesdale Hotel** (tel. 01555/663455) in Bloomgate.

At the end of a full day of touring you can return to Glasgow the quick way by joining the M74 from the A744 west of Lanark (the Strathaven road). Or take a more scenic route through Strathaven (pronounced *STRA-ven*) itself, A726 to East Kilbride, and enter Glasgow from south of the river.

6 The Borders and the Southwest

Dumfries and Galloway

By Gilbert
Summers

If you are coming to Scotland from any point south of the border in England, then the Borders is the first region of Scotland you will encounter. Let it be said straightaway that although the border has no checkpoints or customs outposts, the Scottish tourist authorities firmly promulgate the message that it is indeed Scottish land you are on once you cross the border. All the idiosyncracies that distinguish Scotland—from the myriad names for beer, to the seemingly unpredictable Monday local holidays—start as soon as one reaches the first Scottish signs by the main roads north.

Although most visitors inevitably pass this way, the Borders and especially Galloway to the west are unfortunately overlooked. So strong is the tartan-ribboned call of the Highlands that many visitors rush past, pause for breath at Edinburgh, then plunge northward, thus missing a scenic portion of upland Scotland. This area never possessed the high romance of the Gaelic-speaking clans in the Highlands to the north, but it did have (and still has) powerful Border families, whose ancestry is soaked in the bloodshed that occurred along this once very real frontier between Scotland and her more opportunist neighbor to the south.

The Borders folk take great pride in the region's heritage as Scotland's main woolen-goods manufacturing area. And to this day the residents possess a marked determination to defend their towns and communities. The changing times, however, have thankfully allowed them to reposition their priorities: Instead of guarding against southern raiders, they now concentrate on maintaining a fiercely competitive rugby team for the popular intertown rugby matches. The Borders are a stronghold of this European counterpart to American football.

Border communities are also reestablishing their identities through the curious affairs known as the Common Ridings. Long ago it was essential that each town be able to defend its area, and over the centuries this need has become formalized in mounted gatherings to "ride the boundaries." The observance of the tradition lapsed in certain places but has been revived. Leaders and attendants are solemnly elected each year, and Borderers who now live away from home make a point of attending their own event. (You can watch and are welcome to enjoy the excitement of clattering hooves and banners proudly displayed, but this is essentially a time for the native Borderers.) The Common Ridings possess as much, if not more, authenticity and historic significance as the concocted Highland Games, so often taken to be the essence of Scotland. The little town of Selkirk, in fact, claims its Common Riding to be the largest mounted gathering anywhere in Europe.

Both the Borders and the Dumfries and Galloway regions feature as broad a selection of stately homes and fortified castles as you will encounter in Scotland (with the possible exception of Grampian). Galloway, the area west of Dumfries, has the advantage of a coastline facing south, made even more appealing by the North Atlantic Drift (Scotland's part of the Gulf Stream), which bathes the coastal lands with warmer water. With its coastal farmlands giving way to woodlands, high moors, and some craggy hills, Galloway may not be the Highlands, but it gives a convincing impression to those seeking the authentic Scotland.

Essential Information

Important Addresses and Numbers

Tourist Information The main tourist-information centers in the area are open all year. They are the **Dumfries and Galloway Tourist Board Information Centre** (Whitesands, Dumfries, tel. 01387/53862), **Gretna Gateway** (M74 northbound at Gretna, tel. 01461/338500), **Scottish Borders Tourist Board Administration Centre** (70 High St., Selkirk, tel. 01750/20555), and the **Scottish Borders Tourist Board Tourist Information Centre** (Murray's Green, Jedburgh, tel. 01835/863435). Seasonal information centers are located at Castle Douglas, Coldstream, Dalbeattie, Eyemouth, Galashiels, Gatehouse-of-Fleet, Gretna, Hawick, Kelso, Kirkcudbright, Langholm, Melrose, Moffat, Newton Stewart, Peebles, Sanquhar, Selkirk, and Stranraer.

Emergencies For **police, fire,** or **ambulance,** dial 999 from any telephone. No coins are needed for emergency calls from public telephone booths.

Late-Night Pharmacies All towns in the region have at least one pharmacy. Pharmacies are not found in rural areas, where general practitioners often dispense medicines. The police will provide assistance in locating a pharmacist in an emergency.

Arriving and Departing by Plane

Airports and Airlines The nearest Scottish airports are at **Edinburgh** and **Glasgow.** *See* Chapters 4 and 5 for details.

Arriving and Departing by Car, Train, and Bus

By Car Route A68, in the east, makes an attractive border crossing from England into Scotland. (The A1 along the east coast is not recommended north of the border because of the high volume of traffic.) However, the main route into both the Borders and Galloway from the south is the M6, which deteriorates into the less well-maintained A74 north of the Border (it is currently being upgraded). The A7 through Hawick makes an attractive although slow alternative to the A74.

By Train Visitors can use the Intercity services from **London Euston,** in England, to **Glasgow;** these trains stop at **Carlisle,** just south of the border, and some stop at **Lockerbie.** There are also direct trains from Carlisle to **Dumfries,** stopping at **Gretna Green.** On the east coast some Intercity services stop at **Berwick-Upon-Tweed,** just south of the border. The Borders are not well served by rail. For more information, call Glasgow's Central Station (tel. 0141/204–2844).

By Bus From the south the main bus services use the M6 or A1, with appropriate feeder services into the hinterland; contact **Citylink** (tel. 0141/332–9191). There are also bus links from Edinburgh and Glasgow. Contact **Lowland Omnibuses** (tel. 01896/2237) or **Western Scottish** (tel. 01563/25192, 01387/53496, or 01776/704484).

By Ferry There are no ferry services into Edinburgh or other east coast ports in this area. However, it is possible to travel from Northern Ireland to Scotland: **P&O European Ferries** runs a service from **Larne** to **Cairnryan** several times daily, with a crossing time of 2 hours, 15 minutes. Details are available from P&O at Cairnryan, Stranraer, Wigtownshire DG9 8RF, tel. 01581/200276.

Getting Around

By Car A solid network of rural roads allows you to avoid the A1 in the eastern borders, as well as the A75, which runs along the Solway coast east to west, linking **Dumfries** and **Stranraer.** Both roads carry heavy traffic, partly because of the poor rail connections.

By Train Train travel is not very practical in the Borders. In fact the **Scottish Borders Rail Link** is nothing of the kind: it's actually a bus service linking **Hawick, Selkirk,** and **Galashiels** with Intercity rail services at **Carlisle.** In Galloway there are connecting trains from Carlisle to **Stranraer,** which also has a direct link to Ayr and Glasgow. There is also a direct service twice daily between **Dumfries** and Stranraer. (Both the Borders and Galloway suffered badly in the shortsighted contraction of Britain's rail network in the 1960s.) Contact **British Rail** (tel. 01228/44711) for further details.

By Bus Bus service in the area includes **Citylink** (tel. 0141/332–9191) long-distance coaches that call at main towns along the A75, including **Annan, Dumfries, Castle Douglas, Kirkcudbright, Twynholm, Gate-house-of-Fleet, Creetown, Newton Stewart,** and **Glenluce. Western Scottish** (tel. 01776/704484) serves towns and villages in Dumfries and Calloway, while **Lowland Omnibuses** (tel. 01896/2237) offers Reiver Rover and Waverley Wanderer flexible tickets, which provide considerable savings for travel in the Borders.

Guided Tours

Orientation The bus companies mentioned above also run a variety of orientation tours in the area. In addition, tours are run by **Galloway Heritage Tours** (Rosemount Guest House, Kippford, tel. 01556/620214) and **Nelson's Coaches** (107 S. Drumlanrig St., Thornhill, tel. 01848/330376).

Special- The area is primarily covered through Edinburgh- or Glasgow-
Interest based companies (*see* Chapters 4 and 5 for details). The following local companies offer chauffeur-driven tours tailored to customers' requirements: **Ramtrad Holidays** (54 Edinburgh Rd., Peebles, tel. 01721/720845) and **Jas French** (Coldingham, tel. 018907/71283).

Exploring the Borders and the Southwest

Orientation

If you are coming by car from the south, you can choose from a number of routes into Scotland. Starting from the east, the A1 brings you from the English city of **Newcastle** to the border in about an hour. The A1 has the added attraction of Berwick-Upon-Tweed, on the English side of the border. Moving west, the A697, which leaves the A1 beside **Alnwick** (in England) and crosses the border at **Coldstream,** is a leisurely back-road option with an attractive view of the countryside. The A68 offers probably the most scenic route to Scotland: after climbing to **Carter Bar,** it reveals a view of the rolling blue Border hills and windy skies before dropping into the ancient town of **Jedburgh,** with its ruined abbey.

The fast M6 becomes the A74 (currently being upgraded) as soon as it arrives in Scotland. The M6 gives car-borne visitors the choice of the leisurely A7 northeastward toward Edinburgh or the A75 and other parallel routes westward into Galloway and to the ferry ports of **Stranraer** and **Cairnryan.** If you choose to get off one of these main arteries and explore some back roads on your way west, you may occasionally be delayed by a herd of cows on their way to the milking parlor, but this is often far more pleasant than tussling with heavy-goods vehicles rushing to make the Irish ferries.

Highlights for First-Time Visitors

Abbotsford (*see* Tour 1)
Caerlaverock Castle (*see* Tour 2)
Castle Kennedy Gardens (*see* Tour 2)
Dryburgh Abbey (*see* Tour 1)
Floors Castle (*see* Tour 1)
Glen Trool (*see* Tour 2)
Jedburgh Abbey (*see* Tour 1)
Logan Botanic Gardens (*see* Tour 2)
Scott's View (*see* Tour 1)
Smailholm Tower (*see* Tour 1)
Threave Gardens (*see* Tour 2)

Tour 1: The Borders—Towns, Towers, and Countryside

Numbers in the margin correspond to points of interest on the Borders map.

❶ The town of **Jedburgh** (-*burgh* is always pronounced *burra* in Scots) on the A68 makes a good starting point for a circle through the best sights of the Borders—a route that also encompasses all four of the great ruined abbeys. The monks in these long-abandoned religious foundations were the first to work the fleeces of their sheep flocks, hence laying the foundation for what is still the area's main industry. It should be noted that this route will certainly take more than one day. To travel it in a leisurely way and spend time at some of the grand mansions noted, one could easily allow three days, although the total driving distance is not great. In the Borders there are several points of interest located quite close to one another.

Jedburgh was for centuries the first major Scottish target of invading English armies. In more peaceful times it developed textile mills, most of which have since perished. The large landscaped area around the town's tourist-information center was once a mill but now provides an encampment for the modern armies of tourists. The past still clings to this little town, however. The ruined abbey dominates the skyline and is compulsory visiting for anyone interested in acquiring a feeling of the former role of the border abbeys.

Still impressive, though it is now only a roofless shell, **Jedburgh Abbey** was destroyed by the English earl of Hertford's forces in 1544–45, during the destructive time known as "the Rough Wooing." This was the English King Henry VIII's armed attempt to persuade the Scots that it was a good idea to unite the kingdoms by the marriage of his young son to the infant Mary, Queen of Scots. (The Scots disagreed and sent Mary to France instead.) The full story is explained in vivid detail at the Jedburgh Abbey Visitor Centre, which provides information on interpreting the ruins. Only ground patterns and foundations remain of the once-powerful religious complex. *High St., tel. 0131/244–3101. Admission: £2.50 adults, £1.50 senior citizens, £1 children. Open Apr.–Sept., Mon.–Sat. 9:30–6, Sun. 2–6; Oct.–Mar., Mon.–Sat. 9:30–4, Sun. 2–4.*

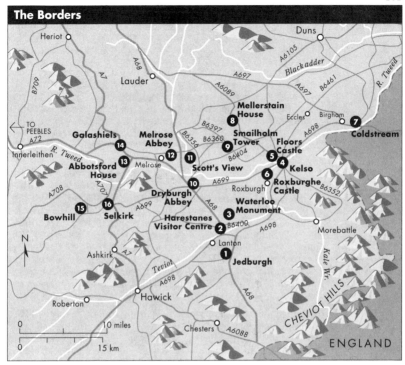

The Borders

There is much else to see in Jedburgh, including the **Mary, Queen of Scots House.** This *bastel* (from the French *bastille*) was the fortified town house in which, some say, Mary stayed before embarking on her famous 20-mile ride to visit her wounded lover, the earl of Bothwell, at **Hermitage Castle** (*see* Off the Beaten Track, *below*). An interpretive center in the building relates the tale. *Queen St., tel. 01835/863331. Admission: £1.20 adults; 60p children, students, and senior citizens. Open Easter–mid-Nov., Mon.–Sat. 10–5, Sun. 2–5.*

Just a few miles to the north along the A68 you'll encounter signs for the **Harestanes Visitor Centre,** where you can learn about the role that the Borders estates—major landholdings with woodland and tenanted farms—played in shaping the Borders landscapes. The center is on the estate of the marquis of Lothian and conveys life in the Borders through a custom-built interpretative center which contains audiovisuals and displays on the themes of the countryside and wildlife. *Monteviot, at the junction of A68 and B6400, tel. 01835/830306. Admission free. Open Apr.–Oct., daily 10–5.*

You can then navigate eastward on the A698, keeping the **Waterloo Monument** on your left. This pencil-thin tower is another reminder of the whims and power of the landowning gentry: An earlier marquis of Lothian built the monument in 1815, with the help of his tenants, in celebration of the victory of Wellington at Waterloo. If you have time, you can walk to the tower from the Woodland Centre. *Off B6400, 5 mi north of Jedburgh.*

Kelso, about 5 miles to the northeast, is one of the most attractive Borders burghs. Often described as having a Continental flavor—some visitors think it resembles a Belgian market town—the town has a broad, paved square and accurate examples of Scots town architecture. **Kelso Abbey** is the least intact ruin of the four great Border abbeys—just a gaunt fragment of what was once the largest of the group. Tall and slim with little rounded turrets, it must have looked reassuringly fortresslike when the Benedictines from Picardy moved in, in 1128. The River Tweed crossing at Kelso was important to both sides in the Border wars, however, and the abbey was much knocked about by armies advancing to or retreating from each other's countries. The last monks (and the townsfolk who had taken refuge with them) died leaping from the turrets onto English spikes and spears in 1545, after which the structure was reduced to its present fragmentary—but highly atmospheric—state. *Bridge St., tel. 0131/244–3101. Admission free. Open Apr.–Sept., Mon.–Sat. 9:30–6, Sun. 2–6; Oct.–Mar., Mon.–Sat. 9:30–4, Sun. 2–4.*

5 Just 2 miles northwest of Kelso, on the bank of the River Tweed, stands the palatial mansion of **Floors Castle.** Ancestral home of the duke of Roxburghe, the castle was built by William Adam in 1721 and modified with mock-Tudor touches by William Playfair in the 1840s. A holly tree in the deer park marks the place where King James II was killed in 1460 by cannon-shot. *A6089, tel. 01573/223333. Admission: £3.40 adults, £2.60 senior citizens, £1.70 children, £8.50 family ticket, grounds £1.50. Open Easter and May–Sept., Sun.–Thurs. 10:30–5:30; Oct., Sun. and Wed. 10:30–4. Check locally for variations.*

6 Do not confuse the comparatively youthful Floors Castle with **Roxburghe Castle,** nearby, off the A699. Only traces of rubble and earthworks remain of this ancient pile. The modern-day village of **Roxburgh** is young. The original Roxburgh, one of the oldest burghs in Scotland, has virtually disappeared, though its name lives on not only in the duke's title, but in the name of the old county of Roxburghshire.

7 Follow the A698 eastward about 5 miles along the north bank of the Tweed to **Coldstream,** perched on the English border. This stretch of the Tweed is lined with dignified houses and gardens, the best known of which is **The Hirsel,** the estate of former British prime minister Sir Alec Douglas Home (Lord Home of The Hirsel). A complex of farmyard buildings now serves as a craft center and museum, and there are interesting walks in the extensive grounds. It's a favorite spot for bird-watchers, and superb rhododendrons bloom here in late spring. The house itself is not open to the public. *A697, immediately west of Coldstream, tel. 01890/882834. Admission free. Open daily during daylight hrs.*

Three miles above Coldstream the England-Scotland border extends down from the hills and runs beside the Tweed for the rest of its journey to the sea. Coldstream itself, like Gretna, was once a marriage place for runaway couples from the south (a plaque on the former bridge tollhouse recalls this fact). It is also celebrated in military history: In 1659, General Monck raised a regiment of foot guards here on behalf of his exiled monarch Charles II. Known as the Coldstream Guards, the successors to this regiment have become an elite corps in the British army. The **Coldstream Museum,** situated in the guards' former headquarters, investigates the themes of "continuity and change": the history of the community of Coldstream past and present. A special exhibition recalls the history of the Coldstream Guards. *Market Sq., Coldstream, tel. 01890/882630. Small admission charge. Open Easter–Oct., Mon.–Sat. 10–1 and 2–5, Sun. 2–5.*

If you are spending a lot of time in the area, you could tour even farther east, certainly as far as **Berwick-Upon-Tweed** and **Manderston House** (*see* Off the Beaten Track, *below*). Otherwise circle westward on any of a number of minor routes west of the A697 to reach

⑧ **Mellerstain House,** 7 miles northwest of Kelso. Devotees of ornate country houses are well served in the Borders. Begun in the 1720s, Mellerstain was finished in the 1770s by Robert Adam and is considered to be one of his finest creations. Sumptuous plasterwork covers almost all interior surfaces, and there are outstanding examples of 18th-century furnishings. The beautiful terraced gardens are as renowned as the house. *Off A6089, tel. 01573/410225. Admission: £3.50 adults, £3 senior citizens, £1.50 children. Open Easter and May–Sept., Sun.–Fri. 12:30–5.*

West of Mellerstain is the B6397, and a short way west of that sits a characteristic Borders structure that certainly contrasts with the

⑨ luxury of Mellerstain House. **Smailholm Tower** stands gaunt and uncompromising on top of a barren, rocky ridge. Built solely for defense, this 16th-century Border *peel* (small fortified towers common to this region) offers memorable views. If you let your imagination wander in this windy spot, you can almost see the flapping pennants and rising dust of an advancing raiding party and hear the anxious securing of doors and bolts. Sir Walter Scott found this an inspiring spot. His grandfather lived at nearby Sandyknowe Farm (not open to the public), and the young Scott visited the tower often during his childhood. *Off B6404. Admission: £1.50 adults, £1 senior citizens, 75p children. Open Apr.–Sept., Mon.–Sat. 9:30–6, Sun. 2–6.*

⑩ Sir Walter's final resting place, **Dryburgh Abbey,** is another 5 miles to the southwest. Situated on gentle parkland in a loop of the Tweed, Dryburgh is certainly the most peaceful and secluded of the abbeys on this excursion. The abbey suffered from English raids until, like Melrose, it was abandoned in 1544. The style is Transitional, a mingling of rounded Romanesque and pointed Early English. The side chapel, where the Haig and Scott families lie buried, is lofty and pillared, detached from the main buildings. *Off A68. Admission: £2 adults, £1.25 senior citizens, 75p children. Open Apr.–Sept., Mon.–Sat. 9:30–6, Sun. 2–6; Oct.–Mar., Mon.–Sat. 9:30–4, Sun. 2–4.*

⑪ There is no escaping Sir Walter in this part of the country: Four miles from Dryburgh is **Scott's View,** possibly the most photographed rural view in the south of Scotland. (Perhaps the only view that is more often used to summon a particular interpretation of Scotland is Eilean Donan Castle, far to the north.) You arrive at this peerless vista by taking the B6356 north from Dryburgh. A poignant tale is told of the horses of Scott's funeral cortege: On their way to Dryburgh Abbey they stopped here out of habit as they had so often in the past. The sinuous curve of the River Tweed, the gentle landscape unfolding to the triple peaks of the **Eildons,** then rolling out into shadows beyond, is certainly worth seeking—and costs nothing to enjoy.

⑫ Next cross the main A68 to reach Melrose, another 5 miles to the west. **Melrose Abbey,** last of the four Borders abbeys in the tour, is in the center of this handsome community. "If thou would'st view fair Melrose aright, go visit it in the pale moonlight," wrote Scott in *The Lay of the Last Minstrel,* and so many of his fans took the advice literally that a sleepless custodian begged him to rewrite the lines. Today the abbey is still impressive: a red sandstone shell with slender windows in the Perpendicular style and some delicate tracery and carved capitals, carefully maintained. Among the carvings high on the roof is one of a bagpipe-playing pig, a figure you are not likely to encounter elsewhere in your travels. *Main Sq., Melrose, tel. 0131/244–3101. Admission: £2.50 adults, £1.50 senior citizens, £1 children. Open Apr.–Sept., Mon.–Sat. 9:30–6, Sun. 2–6; Oct.–Mar., Mon.–Sat. 9:30–4, Sun. 2–4.*

Next to the abbey is the National Trust for Scotland's **Priorwood Gardens,** which specializes in flowers for drying. There is also an orchard adjacent to the gardens with a variety of old apple species. *Admission: £1. Open Apr.–Dec. 24, Mon.–Sat. 10–5:30, Sun. 1:30–5:30.*

Also in the main square—which is really a triangle—is the renovated **Melrose Station,** the only surviving station of the old **Waverley Route,** which until 1969 ran between Edinburgh and Carlisle. (The first main line in Britain to be abandoned, the Waverley Route was discontinued amid much public protest.) Built in Jacobean style and long considered one of the most handsome small-town stations in Scotland, the Melrose Station was saved and its exterior restored. It is now used as offices, with a restaurant on the ground floor.

Time Out   The **Melrose Station Restaurant** (tel. 0189/682–2546) offers morning coffee and light lunches as well as complete evening meals.

Also in the center of Melrose at the Ormiston Institute is the **Trimontium Exhibition,** which reveals the fact that the largest Roman settlement in Scotland was at Newstead nearby and displays artifacts discovered there. Tools and weapons, a blacksmith's shop, pottery and scale models of the fort are included in the display. *Admission: £1 adults, 50p children. Open Easter.–Oct., daily 10:30–4:30.*

Two miles west of Melrose stands one of the Borders' most visited attractions, **Abbotsford House,** home of Sir Walter Scott. In 1811, already an established writer, Scott bought a farm on this site named Cartleyhole, which was a euphemism for the real name, Clartyhole (*clarty* means muddy or sticky in Scots). The name was surely not romantic enough for Scott, who renamed the property and eventually had it entirely rebuilt in the Romantic style, emulating several other Scottish properties. The resulting pseudo-monastic, pseudo-baronial mansion became the repository for the writer's collection of Scottish memorabilia and historic artifacts. The library holds some 9,000 volumes. Scott died here in 1832. Today the house is owned by his descendants. *B6360, tel. 01896/2043. Admission: £2.60 adults, £1.30 children. Open late Mar.–Oct., Mon.–Sat. 10–5, Sun. 2–5.*

14 **Galashiels,** a gray and busy Borders town a few miles farther northwest, is still active with textile mills and knitwear shops. At the **Peter Anderson Woollen Mill** is a museum of the town's history and industry; visitors can go on a mill tour and learn about the manufacture of tartans and tweeds. *Nether Mill, Galashiels, tel. 01896/2091. Admission: £1 adults, 50p children. Open year-round, Mon.–Sat. 9–5; June–Sept., also Sun. 10–5. Guided tours Mon.–Thurs. 10:30, 11:30, 1:30, 2:30, Fri. 10:30 and 11:30.*

If time permits, head west on A72 to Innerleithen, then south on B709 to reach **Traquair House,** said to be the oldest continually occupied house in Scotland; ale is still brewed in the 18th-century brewhouse here, and is recommended! *Near Innerleithen, tel. 01896/830323. Admission: £3.50 adults, £3 senior citizens, £1.50 children, £8 family ticket. Open Easter, May, June, and Sept., daily 1:30–5:30; July and Aug., daily 10:30–5:30 (last admission 5 PM).*

From Traquair, head south to join A707 and travel east to reach ⑮ **Bowhill.** Another of the stately homes in the Borders, this 19th-century building houses an outstanding collection of works by Gainsborough, Van Dyck, Canaletto, Reynolds, and Raeburn, as well as porcelain and period furniture. *Off A708, 3 mi west of Selkirk, tel. 01750/20732. Admission to house: £3 adults, £2 senior citizens, £1 children; admission to grounds: £1 adults, children free. House open July, daily 1–4:30; grounds and playground open May–Aug., Sat.– Thurs. noon–5:30 (open Fri. in July).*

⑯ **Selkirk** itself is a hilly outpost with a smattering of antiques shops and an assortment of bakers selling the Selkirk Bannock and other cakes—evidence of Scotland's incurable sweet tooth. The local museum, **Halliwell's House,** contains a reconstructed old-style ironmonger's shop. *Off main square, tel. 01750/20096. Admission free. Open Apr.–June and Sept.–Oct., Mon.–Sat. 10–4, Sun. 2–4 (July and Aug., daily 10–6); Nov.–mid-Dec. daily 2–4.*

The main A7 then switchbacks gently southward to **Hawick,** the largest of the Borders towns but not necessarily the most interesting. The town does have a good leisure center, as well as a number of shops on its bustling main street. There are also mill tours: try **Wrights of Trowmill** (tel. 01450/72555). Hawick also has an attractive recreational area, **Wilton Lodge Park,** which encompasses the **Hawick Museum,** featuring, inevitably, plenty of material on textile heritage, as well as other aspects of Borders life, notably rugby football. *Wilton Lodge Park, western outskirts of Hawick, tel. 01450/73457. Admission: 80p adults, 40p children. Open Apr.–Sept., Mon.–Sat. 10–noon and 1–5, Sun. 2–5; Oct.–Mar., weekdays 1–4, Sun. 2–4.*

From Hawick it's just a short drive back to Jedburgh.

Tour 2: The Galloway Highlands

Numbers in the margin correspond to points of interest on the Dumfries and Galloway map.

Galloway is the name given to the southwest portion of Scotland, west of the main town of Dumfries. This tour takes in a number of the area's diverse scenic options—from its gentle coastline and breezy uplands to places that are gradually disappearing below blankets of conifers. Use caution when negotiating the various side roads off the A75 that are mentioned in this tour: Although the main trunk road has been improved in recent years, dawdling visitors are liable to find aggressive trucks tailgating them as these commercial vehicles race for the Irish ferries at Stranraer and Cairnryan. (Anything as environmentally sensible as a direct east–west railway link was closed years ago.) Trucks notwithstanding, Galloway offers some of the most pleasant touring roads in Scotland. The local folk are also quite friendly; the area has not yet been overrun by tourists.

⑰ The M6 deteriorates into the A74 before reaching **Gretna** (though it is currently being upgraded). Gretna and **Gretna Green** are, quite simply, an embarrassment to native Scots. What else can you say about a place that advertises "amusing joke weddings," as does one of the visitor centers here? The reason for all these strange goings-on is tied to the reputation the community received as a refuge for runaway couples from England, who once came north to take advantage of Scotland's less strict marriage laws. At one time anyone could perform a legal marriage in Scotland. Often the village black-

Dumfries and Galloway

KEY

Rail Lines

Ferry

20 miles
30 km

ENGLAND

Carlisle

North Channel

TO BELFAST, LARNE

TO ISLE OF MAN

Solway Firth

Langholm

Greina **17**

M6

Davington

Eskdalemuir

A7

B723

Moffat

Newton Wamphray

Boreland

Lockerbie

Annan

A74

A75

Comlongon

Ruthwell Parish Church

18

19

20

21

Caerlaverock National Nature Reserve

B724

B725

Lochmaben

R. Nith

22 Dumfries

Caerlaverock Castle

23

New Abbey

Sweetheart Abbey

24 Arbigland Gardens

A710

Southerness

Sandyhills

Rockcliffe

FOREST OF AE

Duisdeer

Thornhill

A76

Colt Hill

DALMACALLAN FOREST

Crocketford

A75

Dalbeattie **25**

Threave Gardens

26

27 Kirkcudbright

Abbey Head

CARSPHAIRN FOREST

A713

Carsphairn

Bogue

New Galloway

Edward

Castle Douglas

A711

Water of Fleet

A75

A755

Cardoness Castle **28**

Dee

A711

Crosshill

Barr

A714

Pinwherry

GALLOWAY FOREST PARK

The Moors

R. Cree

Glen Trool **31**

B7027

Cairnsmore of Fleet

29

30 Newton Stewart

Creetown

B712

Wigtown

The Machars

A746

A747

Whithorn

Isle of Whithorn

Eggerness Point

Wigtown Bay

Port William

Maybole

Dailly

Girvan

Lendalfoot

Ballantrae

Crammag Head

Stranraer **32**

Castle Kennedy Gardens

Glenluce

New Luce

A75

A77

Cairnryan

Loch Ryan

33

Sandhead

Ardwell

A718

Drummore

B7065

B7041

Luce Bay

Mull of Galloway

Logan Botanic Gardens **35**

Portpatrick **34**

Rhins of Galloway

B7042

A716

B7064

Kirkcolm

N

smith did the honors, presumably because he was conveniently situated near the main road.

The landscape is not very impressive around the flat fields of the **Upper Solway Firth.** You'll find more of interest as you continue west beyond the town of Annan. Inside **Ruthwell Parish Church,** 4 miles west of Annan, is the 8th-century **Ruthwell Cross,** an Anglican Christian sculpture admired for the quality of its carving. Considered an idolatrous monument, it was destroyed by the Scottish authorities in 1640 but was later reassembled. Nearby is the **Savings Bank Museum,** which tells the story of the savings-bank movement, founded by the Reverend Doctor Henry Duncan in 1810. *Ruthwell, 6¹/₂ mi west of Annan, tel. 0138/787–640. Admission free. Open daily 10–1 and 2–5; closed Sun. and Mon. Oct.–Mar.*

Less obscure perhaps is what may be the first Scottish castle you'll see, **Comlongon,** on the B724. A more recent mansion house adjoins this well-preserved 15th-century border keep. Visitors can also enjoy the accommodations of a bed-and-breakfast at the castle. *B724, midway between Dumfries and Annan, tel. 0138/787–283, fax 0138/787266. Admission: £2 adults, £1 children. Open Mar.–Nov., Sun. 10–6.*

Farther along, on a coastal loop of the B725, is **Caerlaverock Castle,** moated and built in a triangular design unique in Britain. This 13th-century fortress has solid-sandstone masonry and an imposing double-tower gatehouse. King Edward of England besieged the castle in 1300, when his forces occupied much of Scotland as the Wars of Independence commenced. The castle suffered many times in Anglo-Scottish skirmishes. *Off B725, 9 mi south of Dumfries, tel. 0131/244–3101. Admission: £2 adults, £1.25 senior citizens, 75p children. Open Apr.–Sept., Mon.–Sat. 9:30–6, Sun. 2–6; Oct.–Mar., Mon.–Sat. 9:30–4, Sun. 2–4.*

Also on the B725 is the **Caerlaverock National Nature Reserve,** a treat for bird-watchers, who can observe wintering wildfowl from blinds and a visitor center. *B725, by Caerlaverock Castle, tel. 0138/777–275. Admission free. Open year-round.*

The nearby town of **Dumfries,** where Robert Burns spent the last years of his short life, is a no-nonsense, red-sandstone community. The **River Nith** meanders through Dumfries, and the pedestrian-only town center makes shopping a pleasure (the A75 now bypasses the town). The town also contains Robert Burns's favorite pub (the Globe Inn), the house he lived in, and his mausoleum.

Not surprisingly, in view of its close association to the poet, Dumfries has a **Robert Burns Centre,** housed in a sturdy former mill overlooking the river. The center has an audiovisual program and an extensive exhibit on the life of the poet. *Mill Rd., tel. 01387/64808. Admission free (small charge for audiovisual show). Open Apr.– Sept., Mon.–Sat. 10–8, Sun. 2–5; Oct.–Mar., Tues.–Sat. 10–1 and 2–5.*

As you travel westward again, the real Galloway begins. Cross the River Nith and head out of town by the A710, another coastal loop. Within a few minutes you reach the village of **New Abbey. Sweetheart Abbey,** which provides a mellowed red and roofless backdrop to the village, was founded in 1273 by Devorgilla Balliol, in memory of her husband, John. The couple's son, also named John, was the puppet king installed in Scotland by Edward of England, when the latter claimed sovereignty over Scotland. After John's appointment the Scots gave him a scathing nickname that would stay with him for the rest of his life: *Toom Tabard,* meaning "Empty Shirt." *A710 at*

New Abbey, tel. 0131/244–3101. Admission: £1 adults, 50p children. Open Apr.–Sept., Mon.–Sat. 9:30–6, Sun. 2–6; Oct.–Mar., Mon.–Wed. and Sat. 9:30–4, Thurs. 9:30–noon, Sun. 2–4.

Continue south through bright-green landscape along the A710 to ㉔ the sign for **Arbigland Gardens.** Here pops up another of Galloway's curious tales: The son of the former gardener of Arbigland, whose name was John Paul, left Scotland and became the founder of the U.S. Navy. This seafaring son, John Paul Jones, returned to his native coast in a series of daring raids in 1778. The gardens tended by Jones's father are typical of the area: lush and sheltered, with blue water visible through the protecting trees. You are only moments from the coast. *Off A710, by Kirkbean, tel. 0138/788–283. Admission: £2 adults, £1.50 senior citizens, 50p children. Open May–Sept., Tues.– Sun. and bank holidays.*

The road to **Southerness** (A710) ends in a welter of caravan holiday homes in the shadow of one of Scotland's earliest lighthouses, built in 1749 by the port authorities of Dumfries, anxious to make the treacherous River Nith approaches safer.

The road then turns west and becomes faintly Riviera-like. You can take a brisk walk from **Rockcliffe** to **Sandyhills,** two of the sleepy coastal communities overlooking the creeping tides and endless shallows of the **Solway coast.** Eventually the road turns north to ㉕ **Dalbeattie.** Like the much larger Aberdeen far to the northeast, Dalbeattie's buildings were built with local granite from the town's quarry. Granite has a well-scrubbed gray glitter, but Dalbeattie is not typical of Galloway towns, whose house fronts are predominantly painted in pastels.

Castle Douglas lies just a few minutes west, away from the coast. Although it is a pleasant town with a long main street where the home bakeries vie for business, Castle Douglas's main attraction is ㉖ its proximity to **Threave Gardens.** As Scotland's best-known charitable conservation agency, the National Trust for Scotland cares for several garden properties. This horticultural undertaking demands the employment of many gardeners—and it is at Threave that the gardeners train, thus ensuring there is always some fresh development or experimental planting here. This gives lots of vigor and interest to the sloping parkland around the mansion house of Threave. There is a good visitor center as well. *South of A75, 1 mi west of Castle Douglas, tel. 01556/502575. Admission: £3 adults, £1.50 senior citizens and children. Gardens open daily 9:30–sunset; walled garden and greenhouses open daily 9:30–5. Visitor Centre and shop open Apr.–Oct., daily 9:30–5:30.*

Threave Castle (not to be confused with the mansion house in Threave Gardens) is a few minutes away by car and is signposted from the main road. To get there you must leave your car in a farmyard (trying to pretend you don't have the feeling you're intruding) and walk the rest of the way. Reassured by the Historic Scotland signs (because Threave is being cared for by the national government), you make your way down to the reeds by the river on an occasionally muddy path. At the edge of the river you can then ring a bell, and, rather romantically, a boatman will come to ferry you across to the great, gaunt tower looming from a marshy island in the river. Threave was an early home of the Black Douglases, the earls of Nithsdale, and lords of Galloway. The castle was dismantled in the religious wars of the mid-17th century, though enough of it remains to have housed prisoners from the Napoleonic Wars of the 19th century. *North of A75, 3 mi west of Castle Douglas, tel. 0131/244–*

So, you're getting away from it all.

Just make sure you can get back.

AT&T Access Numbers
Dial the number of the country you're in to reach AT&T.

Country	Number	Country	Number	Country	Number
*AUSTRIA††	022-903-011	*GREECE	00-800-1311	NORWAY	800-190-11
*BELGIUM	078-11-0010	*HUNGARY	00◇-800-01111	POLAND†♦²	0◇010-480-0111
BULGARIA	00-1800-0010	*ICELAND	999-001	PORTUGAL†	05017-1-288
CANADA	1-800-575-2222	IRELAND	1-800-550-000	ROMANIA	01-800-4288
CROATIA†♦	99-38-0011	ISRAEL	177-100-2727	*RUSSIA† (MOSCOW)	155-5042
*CYPRUS	080-90010	*ITALY	172-1011	SLOVAKIA	00-420-00101
CZECH REPUBLIC	00-420-00101	KENYA†	0800-10	S. AFRICA	0-800-99-0123
*DENMARK	8001-0010	*LIECHTENSTEIN	155-00-11	SPAIN•	900-99-00-11
*EGYPT† (CAIRO)	510-0200	LITHUANIA♦	8◇196	*SWEDEN	020-795-611
*FINLAND	9800-100-10	LUXEMBOURG	0-800-0111	*SWITZERLAND	155-00-11
FRANCE	19◇-0011	F.Y.R. MACEDONIA	99-800-4288	*TURKEY	00-800-12277
*GAMBIA	00111	*MALTA	0800-890-110	UKRAINE†	8◇100-11
GERMANY	0130-0010	*NETHERLANDS	06-022-9111	UK	0500-89-0011

Countries in bold face permit country-to-country calling in addition to calls to the U.S. **World Connect**℠ prices consist of **USADirect**® rates plus an additional charge based on the country you are calling. Collect calling available to the U.S. only. *Public phones require deposit of coin or phone card. ◇Await second dial tone. †May not be available from every phone. ††Public phones require local coin payment through the call duration. ♦Not available from public phones. • Calling available to most European countries. ¹Dial "02" first, outside Cairo. ²Dial 010-480-0111 from major Warsaw hotels. ©1994 AT&T.

Here's a travel tip that will make it easy to call back to the States. Dial the access number for the country you're visiting and connect right to AT&T. It's the quick way to get English-speaking AT&T operators and can minimize hotel telephone surcharges.

If all the countries you're visiting aren't listed above, call **1 800 241-5555** for a free wallet card with all AT&T access numbers. Easy international calling from AT&T. **TrueWorld Connections.**

AT&T

American Express offers Travelers Cheques built for two.

Cheques *for Two*℠ from American Express are the Travelers Cheques that allow either of you to use them because both of you have signed them. And only one of you needs to be present to purchase them.

Cheques *for Two* are accepted anywhere regular American Express Travelers Cheques are, which is just about everywhere. So stop by your bank, AAA* or any American Express Travel Service Office and ask for Cheques *for Two*.

Travelers Cheques

3101. Admission: £1.50 adults, £1 senior citizens, 75p children (includes ferry). Open Apr.–Sept., Mon.–Sat. 9:30–6, Sun. 2–6.

From Threave you can make your way from **Castle Douglas** southwest to **Kirkcudbright,** an 18th-century town of unpretentious houses, some of them color washed in pastel shades and roofed with the blue slates of the district. For much of this century it has been known as an artists' town, and its L-shaped main street is full of crafts and antiques shops. Conspicuous in the town center is **Maclellan's Castle,** the shell of a once-elaborate castellated mansion dating from the early 16th century. *Off High St., tel. 0131/244–3101. Admission: £1.20 adults, 75p children. Open Apr.–Sept., Mon.–Sat. 9:30–6, Sun. 2–6; Oct.–Mar., Sat. 9:30–4, Sun. 2–4.*

The delightfully old-fashioned **Stewartry Museum,** stuffed with all manner of local paraphernalia, allows you to putter and absorb as much or as little as takes your interest in the mahogany display cases. *St. Mary St., tel. 01557/331643. Admission: £1.50 adults, 75p senior citizens and students, children free if accompanied. Open Mar., Apr., and Oct., Mon.–Sat. 11–4; May, Mon.–Sat. 11–5; June and Sept., Mon.–Sat. 11–5, Sun. 2–5; July and Aug., Mon.–Sat. 10–6, Sun. 2–5; Nov.–Feb., Sat. 11–4.*

The **Tolbooth Arts Centre,** in the old tolbooth, gives a history of the town's artists' colony and its leaders E.A. Hornell, Jessie King, and Charles Oppenheimer and displays some of their paintings as well as work by modern artists and craftspeople. *High St., opening times as for Stewartry Museum, above.*

You can twist your way westward by the A755, across the bridge to reach **Gatehouse of Fleet,** a peaceful, pleasant backwoods sort of place, with a castle guarding its southern approach from the A75. **Cardoness Castle** is a typical Scottish tower house, severe and uncompromising. The 15th-century structure once was the home of the McCullochs of Galloway, then later the Gordons. *A75, 1 mi southwest of Gatehouse of Fleet, tel. 0131/244–3101. Admission: £1.20 adults, 75p children. Open Apr.–Sept., Mon.–Sat. 9:30–6, Sun. 2–6; Oct.–Mar., Sat. 9:30–4, Sun. 2–4.*

If you single-mindedly pursue the suggested policy of avoiding the A75, then your route will loop to the northwest. Take a right by the Anwoth Hotel in Gatehouse of Fleet, where the signpost points to Gatehouse Station. This route will provide you with a taste of the Galloway hinterland. Beyond the wooded valley where the **Water of Fleet** runs (local rivers are often referred to as "Water of . . ."), dark hills and conifer plantings lend a brooding, empty air to this lonely stretch. Soon the road circles left, returning to the low-ground community of **Creetown,** noted for its **Gem Rock Museum.** The museum has an eclectic mineral collection and is the perfect place to pick up a pair of earrings or another rocky trinket. *A75, tel. 01671–820357. Admission: £2.25 adults, £1.75 senior citizens, £1.25 children, £5.75 family ticket. Open Mar.–Oct., daily 9:30–6; Nov.–Christmas, Sat.–Wed. 10–4; Mid-Jan.–Feb., weekends 10–4, and by appointment.*

The solid and bustling little town of **Newton Stewart** makes a good touring base with the far western region of Galloway (*see* The Machars in Off the Beaten Track, *below*). One possible excursion to the north from Newton Stewart takes you to the **Galloway Forest Park** (open at all times, admission free). Take the A714 north from town along the wooded valley of the **River Cree** (there is a nature reserve, the Wood of Cree, on the far bank). After about 10 miles turn right at the signpost for **Glen Trool.** This road leads you toward the hills that have thus far been the backdrop for the woodlands.

Watch for another sign for Glen Trool. Follow this little road through increasingly wild woodland scenery to its terminus at a car park. Only after you have left the car and climbed for a few minutes onto a heathery knoll does the full, rugged panorama become apparent. With high, purple-and-green hilltops shorn rock-bare by glaciers, a dark, winding loch, and thickets of birch trees sounding with bird-calls, the setting almost looks more highland than the real Highlands to the north. Glen Trool is one of Scotland's best-kept secrets. Note **Bruce's Stone,** just above the car park, marking the site where Scotland's champion Robert the Bruce (King Robert I) won his first victory, in 1307, in the Scottish Wars of Independence.

If this excursion has whetted your appetite for the wilder side of Galloway, retrace your route to the A714, then cross over to the B7027 farther westward, taking a road west at **Glassoch Bridge** (on the B7027). Once you escape the thick conifers, this passage leads high into the moorland. If in doubt, follow signs for the moor community of **New Luce.** You can drop down to the green valleys of the

32 Lowlands from there to visit **Castle Kennedy Gardens,** a high point of the area. The original Castle Kennedy is the gaunt shell seen on the grounds. It was burned out in 1716. The present property owners, the Earl and Countess of Stair, live on the grounds, at **Lochinch Castle,** built in 1864. Pleasure grounds dispersed throughout the property were built by the second earl of Stair in 1733. The Earl was a field marshal and used his soldiers to help with the heavy work of constructing banks, ponds, and other major landscape features. When the rhododendrons are in bloom, the effect is kaleidoscopic. *North of A75, 3 mi east of Stranraer, tel. 01776/702024. Admission: £2 adults, £1.50 senior citizens, £1 children. Open Easter–Sept., daily 10–5.*

Time Out   There is a pleasant **tearoom** at the Castle Kennedy Gardens, but if a more substantial meal is required, try the **Eynhallow Hotel** nearby, for its homecooked bar food (tel. 01581/400256).

The green and rolling countryside of the western end of Galloway
33 affords dairy herds plenty of pasture. **Stranraer** is the main ferry port (if you happen to make a purchase in one of its shops, you may wind up with some Irish coins in your change). More scenic, perhaps,
34 is the holiday town of **Portpatrick,** a few miles west on the A77, across the Rhinns of Galloway. Once an Irish ferry port, Portpatrick's exposed harbor eventually proved too risky for larger vessels. Today the village is the starting point for Scotland's longest official long-distance footpath, the **Southern Upland Way,** which runs a switchback course for 212 miles to **Cockburnspath,** on the eastern side of the Borders. Just south of Portpatrick are the lichen-yellow ruins of 16th-century **Dunskey Castle,** accessible by a cliff-top path. Within the village is **Little Wheels Museum,** which displays model cars and railways and toys. *Tel. 01776/810536. Open July–Aug. (telephone to confirm times and admission charges).*

Portpatrick is halfway down the **Rhinns of Galloway,** and this area's southern portion has a number of interesting places to visit. Take the B7042/A716 to **Ardwell House Gardens,** a pleasant garden on a domestic scale. *Ardwell, 11 mi southeast of Stranraer. Tel. 01776/860227. Admission: £1 adults, 50p senior citizens and children. Open Mar.–Oct., daily 10–6.*

35 More spectacular for garden lovers are the **Logan Botanic Gardens,** an outstation of Edinburgh's **Royal Botanic Garden.** The Logan Gardens feature plants that enjoy the prevailing mild climate: especially tree ferns, cabbage palms, and other southern-hemisphere exotica. *Off B7065, 14 mi south of Stranraer. Tel. 01776/860231, fax 01776/860333. Admission: £1.50 adults, £1 senior citizens, 50p children. Open Mar. 15–Oct., daily 10–6.*

If you wish to continue to the southern tip of the Rhinns, to the **Mull of Galloway,** follow the B7065/B7041 until you run out of land. The cliffs and seascapes here are rugged, and there is a lighthouse and a bird reserve.

The Borders and the Southwest for Free

Glen Trool (*see* Tour 2)
Scott's View (*see* Tour 1)
View from Smailholm Tower (*see* Tour 1)
Walks on the Southern Upland Way (*see* Tour 2)

What to See and Do with Children

Biggar Puppet Theatre regularly presents performances by Purves Puppets. The theater also has games and a picnic area. *B7016, east of Biggar, tel. 01899/20631. Admission: £4 adults, £3 children. Open all year, Mon., Tues., and Thurs.–Sat 10–5; also Easter–Sept., Sun. 2–5. (Telephone for additional opening times).*

Castle Douglas's **Blowplain Open Farm** provides guided tours showing the area's daily life on a small hill farm. *Balmaclellan, Castle Douglas, tel. 016442/206. Admission: £1.50 adults, 75p children. Open Easter–Oct., Mon.–Fri. and Sun., tour at 2 PM (lasts 2 hrs).*

Bowhill Adventure Playground, Bowhill (*see* Tour 1). *Off A708, 3 mi west of Selkirk, tel. 0750/20732. Admission to grounds and playground: £1 adults, children free. Open May–Aug., Sat.–Thurs. noon–5:30 (also Fri. noon–5:30 in July).*

Drumlanrig Castle adventure playground (*see* Off the Beaten Track, below)

Little Wheels Museum, Portpatrick (*see* Tour 2)

Robert Smail's Printing Works, a fully operational restored print shop with reconstructed waterwheel, will fascinate older children, who can try their hand at typesetting. *7/9 High St., Innerleithen, tel. 01896/830206. Admission: £2 adults, £1 children. Open Apr.–Oct., Mon.–Sat. 10–1 and 2–5, Sun. 2–5.*

Teviotdale Leisure Centre, one of the best-equipped centers in the area, has all manner of recreational facilities, including a swimming pool, squash courts, indoor bowls hall and Turkish steam room. *Mansfield Rd., Hawick, tel. 01450/74440. Open Sat.–Mon., Wed., Thurs. 10–9, Tues., Fri. noon–9.*

Tweedhope Sheepdogs (*see* Off the Beaten Track, *below*)

At the children's nursery in **Thirlestane Castle,** children are allowed to play with Victorian-style toys and masks and to dress up in costumes. The nursery is one of myriad rooms in the 17th-century castle. *Lauder, 28 mi south of Edinburgh, tel. 01578/722430. Admission: £3.50 adults, £9 family ticket; grounds only, £1. Open Easter week, May, June, and Sept., Mon., Wed., Thurs., and Sun. 2–5; July–Aug., Sun.–Fri. 2–5 (grounds open 2–6). Last admission to house and grounds 4:30.*

Off the Beaten Track

Drumlanrig Castle is an ornate red-sandstone structure built on the site of an earlier Douglas stronghold about 15 miles northwest of Dumfries in Nithsdale. The 17th-century castle contains Louis XIV furniture and a valuable collection of paintings by Leonardo da Vinci, Holbein, Rembrandt, and others. There's also a bird of prey center with falconry displays, a crafts shop, and visitor center on the grounds. *Off A76, tel. 01848/330248. Admission: £4 adults, £2.50 senior citizens, £2 children, £10 family ticket; park only £2. Castle open May–Aug., Mon.–Wed., Fri., and Sat. 11–5, Sun. 1–5, last entry 4. Grounds open May–Aug., daily.*

Grey Mare's Tail waterfall, on the wild road to Selkirk (A708), makes a dramatic 220-foot plunge as it drops down a cataract from Loch Skene. The short path to the cascade is treacherous in wet weather, but after heavy rain a close-up view is impressive. (Heed the warnings at the information kiosk on the site.) The area around the falls is noted for its wildflowers. *Off A708, 10 mi north of Moffat, tel. 0141/552–8391 (the National Trust for Scotland).*

Hermitage Castle is the most complete remaining example of the gaunt and grim medieval border castles. Restored in the early 19th century, it was built in the 14th century (replacing an earlier structure) to guard what was at the time one of the important routes from England into Scotland. The original owner, Lord Soulis, notorious for diabolical excess, was captured by the local populace, who wrapped him in lead and boiled him in a cauldron, or so the tale goes. The castle lies on an unclassified road between the A7 and B6399, about 10 miles south of Hawick. *Liddesdale, tel. 0131/244–3101. Admission: £1.20 adults, 75p children. Open Apr.–Sept., Mon.–Sat. 9:30–6, Sun. 2–6; Oct.–Mar., Sat. 9:30–4, Sun. 2–4.*

Manderston House is a good example of the grand, no-expense-spared Edwardian country house. The family who built it made its fortune selling herring to Russia. An original 1790s Georgian house on the site was completely rebuilt to the specifications of John Kinross. The staircase is silver plated (thought to be unique) and was modeled after the Petit Trianon at Versailles. There is also much to see downstairs in the kitchens, and outdoors, among a cluster of other buildings, is the one-of-a-kind marble dairy. *Off A6105, 2 mi east of Duns, tel. 01361/83450. Telephone for admission charges. Open mid-May–Sept., Thurs. and Sun. 2–5:30.*

The **Museum of Scottish Lead Mining,** which can be reached from the A76 (the main Dumfries–Kilmarnock road) by taking the Mennock Pass through rounded moorland hills, tells the story of one of Scotland's lesser-known industries. There are underground trips for the stout-hearted. The museum is at Wanlockhead, a fairly bleak spot and Scotland's highest elevated village. *B797, tel. 0165974/387. Admission: £2.99 adults, £2.50 senior citizens and students, £1.25 children, £7.50 family tickets. Open Apr.–Oct., daily 11–4:30 (last guided tour at 4). Open in winter by appointment only.*

Tweedhope Sheepdogs demonstrate their skills twice a day; the sheepdog is an essential aid to the Scottish hillfarmer as he manages his flock over difficult terrain. There is also a craft shop and, adjacent, a fishery and fish smoker which welcomes visitors. The fishery also has a pleasant tearoom. *Moffat Fisheries, Hammerlands, tel. 01683/21471. Admission: £2 adults, £1 children. Open Easter–Oct., Mon.–Fri. 10:30–4:30. Sheepdog demonstrations at 11 AM and 3 PM.*

The Machars **The Machars** is the name given to the triangular promontory south
of the main east–west route (A75) in western Galloway, roughly 10
miles from the Rhinns of Galloway (*see* Tour 2). This is an area of
gently rolling farmlands, yellow gorse hedgerows, rich grazings for
dairy cattle, and a number of stony prehistoric sites. Most of the
glossy, green expanse is used for dairy farming. Fields are bordered
by dry stane dykes (dry walling) of sharp-edge stones; and small
hills and hummocks give the area its characteristic frozen-wave
look, a reminder of the glacial activity that shaped the landscape.

Places of interest in the Machars include the sleepy hamlet of **Wigtown,** which has a broad main street and colorful housefronts. Down
by the muddy shores of Wigtown Bay there's a monument to the
Wigtown Martyrs, two women who were tied to a stake and left to
drown in the incoming tide during the anti-Covenant witch-hunts of
1685. Much of Galloway's history is linked with Border feuds, but
even more with the ferocity of the so-called Killing Times, when the
Covenanters were persecuted for their belief that the king should
be second to the church, and not vice versa. Wigtown, like several
other places in the region, is dominated by a hilltop Covenanters'
Monument, a reminder of the old persecutions.

The Machars are well known for their early Christian sites. The
A746 was a pilgrim's way and a royal route. It ends at **Isle of
Whithorn** (which is not in fact quite an island), a place that early
Scottish kings and barons sought to visit at least once in their lives.
The pilgrimage was often prescribed as a penance, but these pleasant shores impose no penance today. The goal was St. Ninian's
chapel, the 4th-century cell of Scotland's premier saint. Some pilgrims made for Whithorn village and others for the sandspit "isle."
Both places claimed to be the site of the original "Candida Casa" of
the saint. As you approach Whithorn's 12th-century priory, observe
the royal arms of pre-1707 Scotland (that is, Scotland before the
Union with England) carved and painted above the arch of the Pend
(covered way). The **Whithorn Dig and Visitor Centre** explains the
significance of what is claimed to be the site of the earliest Christian
community in Scotland. *45–47 George St., Whithorn, tel. 01988/
500508. Admission: £2.70 adults, £1.50 senior citizens and children,
£7.50 family ticket. Open Easter–Oct., daily 10:30–5 (last tour 4:30).*

Near the visitor center stands the **Whithorn Museum,** which includes a collection of early-Christian crosses and the shell of a 12th-
century priory. *Main St., Whithorn, tel. 0131/244–3101. Admission:
£1.20 adults, 75p children. Open Apr.–Sept., Mon.–Sat. 9:30–6, Sun.
2–6; Oct.–Mar., Sat. 9:30–4, Sun. 2–4.*

Shopping

As with other, more rural areas of Scotland away from the Central
Belt, shopping in the Borders and Galloway area centers on the
larger towns; stores in the smaller towns and villages usually fulfill
only day-to-day requirements. The Borders in particular has a fairly
affluent population, which is reflected in the variety of upscale shops
in Peebles, for example, where there are more deluxe stores than
might be expected. If you want to spend a morning shopping,
Peebles is the place to do it. Below are a few of the interesting shops
to be discovered on your travels.

The Borders As the center of Scotland's woolen-goods industry, this area
provides the country's widest choice of ready-made items. Try **Peter
Anderson Woollen Mill** in Galashiels (Nether Mill, tel. 01896/2091);

Hawick's cashmere and lambswool specialist, **Tom Scott Knitwear Shop** (Kirkside, Denholm, tel. 0145087/283); or the **Scottish Museum of Woollen Textiles** (Walkerburn, tel. 0189/687–281), where a large mill shop offers a wealth of styles.

Throughout the Borders region look for the specialty sweets indigenous to the area—Jethart Snails, Hawick Balls, Berwick Cockles, and Soor Plums—which, with tablet (a solid caramellike candy) and fudge, are available from most local confectioners.

Peebles You can easily spend a day browsing on Peebles High Street and in the courts and side streets leading off it, where you will find temptation at every turn. Do not miss **Scott's Hardware Store** (50 High St.), which modern merchandising methods have thankfully not yet penetrated. Every kind of tool, implement, fixture, fitting, and garden requirement (and mousetraps) is spread in glorious array over floors and walls—and even hang from the ceiling. Not far away is **Jumpers** (38 High St.), which sells its namesakes, as well as cardigans in a variety of colors and designs in cotton or wool. **Head to Toe** (43 High St.) stocks natural beauty products of all descriptions; dried flowers and porcelain display dishes are also available. Craftspeople and jewelers are also well represented on the street: Gold- and silversmith **Keith Walter** (28 High St.) makes items on the premises and stocks jewelry made by other local designers. Visitors to **The Country Shop** (56 High St.) will have a hard time leaving this upscale gift store without purchasing something. If you need a rest after all that shopping, The Country Shop has a coffee shop upstairs, with views over the town and bustling High Street.

Dumfries and Galloway In the western half of the area covered in this chapter, **Dumfries** is the main shopping center, with all the big-name chain stores. Here there are also specialty shops, such as the **Bryden Gallery** (11 Galloway St.), which offers an assortment of artists' work—mainly paintings but also ceramics and porcelain. You can even commission a painting, perhaps a portrait or a favorite landscape, and it will be ready in two weeks. **Greyfriars Crafts** (56 Buccleuch St.) has mainly Scottish goods, including Edinburgh Crystal, Caithness Glass, and Ettrick Valley textiles. For a souvenir that's easier to pack, try **David Hastings** (Marying, Shieldhill, Amisfield, Dumfries, tel. 01387/710451; visitors by appointment; approval service offered), which has more than 80,000 old postcards.

If you are visiting Drumlanrig Castle (*see* Off the Beaten Track, *above*), north of Dumfries at **Thornhill,** do not miss the crafts center (tel. 01848/31555) in the stable block, chock full of all types of crafts work, including stainless steel jewelry and cutlery, leathercraft, blown-glass pieces and designer knitwear, among others. To the northeast, at **Moffat, The Corner Gallery** (Churchgate, tel. 01683/21010) stocks Scottish designer knitwear from the smaller producers; here you are likely to see a more original selection of goods than in the larger knitwear outlets. Farther west, at Castle Douglas, **The Posthorn** (26–30 St. Andrew St., tel. 01556/502531) consists of two shops specializing in gift items, including the figurines made by Border Fine Art; export facilities are provided. **Galloway Gems** (King St.) not only has gold and silver jewelry, but also stocks mineral specimens and polished stone slices. At **Gatehouse of Fleet,** there is a well-stocked gift and crafts shop (and a tearoom with delicious home-baked goods) at the **Mill on the Fleet** heritage center (High St., tel. 01557/814099). Also in the town is **Galloway Lodge Preserves** (24–28 High St., tel. 01557/814357), whose Marmalade, Mustard, and Merchandise Shop stocks the complete line of the company's locally made produce, plus Scottish pottery.

At **Kirkcudbright,** the **Harbour Cottage Art Gallery** may be just the place to find a painting of the part of Scotland that is dearest to you; prices vary, depending on the artist exhibiting. Pictures of a different sort can be found at **Benny Gillies Books, Maps and Prints** (31 Victoria St., Kirkpatrick Durham), which stocks an outstanding selection of hand-colored antique maps and prints featuring areas throughout Scotland.

Finally the **Creetown Gem Rock Museum** (Creetown, tel. 01671/820357; *see also* Tour 2 in Exploring the Borders and the Southwest, *above*) sells extraordinary mineral and gemstone crystals in its gift shop—both loose and in settings.

Sports and Fitness

Bicycling This is an essentially farming, rural area with some upland stretches but with a wide choice of quiet side roads to avoid the heavy traffic on "A" routes. The Craik Forest is typical of Forestry Commission properties with mountain bike routes and trails in the network of forestry access roads.

Bicycles may be rented in the Borders from **Hawick Cycle Centre** (45 N. Bridge St., Hawick, tel. 01450/73352), **Glentress Bike Centre** (Glentress, Peebles, tel. 01721/722934), and **Scottish Border Trails** (Bowhill, Selkirk, tel. 01750/22515). In Dumfries and Galloway, you can rent from **Ace Cycles** (11 Church St., Castle Douglas, tel. 01556/504542), **KLR Cycles** (High St., Gatehouse of Fleet, tel. 01557/814392), **Greirson and Graham** (Academy St., Dumfries, tel. 01387/53405), **GM Group Mountain Bike Hire** (near Dumfries, tel. 01387/59303), and **Nithsdale Cycle Centre** (Rosefield Mills, Dumfries, tel. 01387/54870).

Fishing The **Solway Firth** is noted for sea angling, notably at **Isle of Whithorn, Port William, Portpatrick, Stranraer,** and **Loch Ryan.** Game fishing far exceeds the reputation (and the expensive salmon beats) of the River Tweed, sometimes called the Queen of Scottish Rivers. A comprehensive guide, *Angling in the Scottish Borders,* is the only way to find your way around the many Borders waterways. The *Castabout Anglers Guide to Dumfries and Galloway* covers the southwest. The tourist boards for Galloway and the Borders (*see* Important Addresses and Numbers in Essential Information, *above*) carry these and other publications (including a comprehensive information pack). In short, finding suitable water in this area is quite easy.

Golf There are 23 courses in Galloway and 17 in the Borders. Both tourist boards (*see* Important Address and Numbers in Essential Information, *above*) supply comprehensive leaflets.

Health and Fitness Clubs The **Teviotdale Leisure Centre** (Mansfield Rd., Hawick, tel. 01450/74440), one of the best-equipped centers in the area, has a swimming pool, squash courts, indoor bowls hall, Turkish steam room, and locker-room facilities. *Open 10–9.*

Horseback Riding The Borders and Galloway have a strong tradition of horseback riding, sustained partly through the Common Ridings, a popular annual rite. There are many riding and trekking centers, including **Pony Trekking Centre** (Brighouse Bay Holiday Park, Borgue, Kirkcudbright, tel. 015577/267), **Barend Properties Riding School and Trekking Centre** (Sandyhills, by Dalbeattie, Kirkcudbright, tel. 0138778/663), **Westertoun Riding Centre** (Westruther, Gordon, Berwickshire, tel. 01578/740270), and **Hazeldean Holiday and Riding Centre** (Hassendean Burn, Hawick, tel. 01450/870373).

Water Sports   The **Galloway Sailing Centre** (Loch Ken, tel. 016442/626) rents dinghies, windsurfing equipment, and canoes.

Dining and Lodging

The Borders region is reasonably well served by hotels ranging from the budget to the luxury categories. Being slightly off the beaten tourist track, Dumfries and Galloway offer a good selection of relatively inexpensive options for accommodations and food.

Dining

Category	Cost*
$$$$	over £40
$$$	£30–£40
$$	£15–£30
$	under £15

per person for a three-course meal, including VAT

Lodging

Category	Cost*
$$$$	over £120
$$$	£100–£120
$$	£80–£100
$	under £80

All prices are for a standard double room, including service, breakfast, and VAT.

Highly recommended restaurants and hotels are indicated by a star ★.

Boreland   **Nether Boreland.** A member of the Farm Holiday Bureau, Nether
Lodging   Boreland offers an insight into Scottish farming, combined with spacious accommodations and fresh local produce at meals. Golf, fishing, and pony trekking are close by. *Boreland, Lockerbie, Dumfriesshire, tel. 015766/248. 3 rooms with bath. No credit cards. Closed Nov.–Feb. $*

Dalbeattie   **Auchenskeoch Lodge.** This quaint and informal Victorian shooting
Lodging   lodge, now a country-house hotel, has five bedrooms and delicious
★   food (for residents only). Guests are urged to help themselves to each of the delectable puddings on offer. Many of the vegetables and herbs are home grown on the 20 acres of gardens and woodland surrounding the house. The furnishings have a comfortable, faded, chintzy elegance; there is a full-size billiards table in the game room. The sitting room offers crammed bookshelves and an open fire. A private loch, turf and gravel maze, and croquet lawn provide outdoor entertainment. *Auchenskeoch, by Dalbeattie, tel. 0138778/277. 5 rooms; 4 with bath, 1 with shower. MC, V. Closed Nov.–Easter. $*

Galashiels
Dining and Lodging

Woodlands House Hotel. This hotel has stunning views over Tweeddale. The main restaurant specializes in fresh seafood and hearty Scottish cuisine, while Sanderson's Steakhouse is named after a former owner of the house whose portrait gazes down on diners. *Windyknowe Rd., TD1 1RG, tel. and fax 01896/754722. 9 rooms with bath. Facilities: 2 restaurants, garden, golf, fishing, horseback riding. MC, V. $$*

Gatehouse-of-Fleet
Dining and Lodging

Cally Palace. This hotel was once a private mansion (built in 1759), and many of the public rooms in the Georgian building retain their original grandeur, which includes elaborate plaster ceilings and marble fireplaces. The house is surrounded by 150 acres of gardens, loch, and parkland, including an 18-hole golf course, and has an indoor leisure center with pool, solarium, and sauna. Scottish produce features in the French-influenced restaurant in such dishes as poached salmon with hollandaise sauce, and the bedrooms are individually decorated and well equipped. The staff is exceptionally friendly and prepared to spoil you. *Gatehouse-of-Fleet, Galloway, tel. 01557/814341, fax 01557/814552. 56 rooms with bath. Facilities: restaurant, bar, pool, sauna, extensive leisure facilities. MC, V. Closed Jan. and Feb. $–$$*

High Auchenlarie Farmhouse. This working beef farm, set high on a hillside overlooking Wigtown Bay, offers bed-and-breakfast and, for a small additional charge, evening meals. It's an excellent place to come to enjoy the throaty call of moo-cows. *Gatehouse of Fleet, DG7 2DW, tel. 01557/841231. 3 rooms. No credit cards. Open Mar.–Oct. $*

Jedburgh
Lodging
★

Spinney Guest House. Made up of unpretentiously converted and modernized farm cottages, this is a bed-and-breakfast offering the highest standards for the price. *Langlee, TD8 6PB, tel. and fax 01835/863525. 3 rooms; 1 with bath, 2 with shower. No credit cards. Closed Nov.–Feb. $*

Kelso
Dining and Lodging
★

Sunlaws House. Situated a few miles from Floors Castle, home of the duke of Roxburghe, this magnificent country house is also owned by him and is reputed to have accommodated Prince Charles Edward Stuart in 1745. More than 200 acres of secluded woodlands surround the hotel, and croquet, game shooting, tennis, and fishing are available along private stretches of the Tweed and Teviot rivers. Public rooms are comfortably furnished with relaxing lighting and plenty of plants. The bedrooms, decorated in keeping with the style of this country-gentleman's retreat, are well equipped; bedrooms are also available in the stable courtyard for avid sports enthusiasts who are likely to want to come and go at odd hours. Decor depends on the room you're in, but you'll likely see antique furniture and ornaments and pastel floral curtains. Fresh local produce cooked in hearty but contemporary style with a Scottish/French flavor (salmon with Dublin Bay prawns, for example) satisfies the largest appetites, and packed lunches are prepared on request. *Heiton, by Kelso, TD5 8JZ, tel. 015735/450331, fax 01573/450611. Restaurant reservations required. Jacket and tie advised. 22 rooms with bath. Facilities: restaurant, bar, fishing, tennis, helipad, trapshooting school. AE, DC, MC, V. $$$$*

Ednam House Hotel. This large, attractive hotel is on the banks of the River Tweed, close to Kelso's grand abbey and the many fine Georgian and early Victorian buildings in the old Market Square. Ninety percent of the guests are return visitors, and the open fire in the hall, sporting paintings, and cozy armchairs give the place a homey feeling. *Bridge St., TD5 7HT, tel. 01573/224168, fax 01573/226319. 32 rooms with bath or shower. Facilities: restaurant,* garden, fishing, horseback riding. MC, V. Closed Christmas–early Jan. $$–$$$

Melrose
Dining
★

Marmion's Brasserie. This cozy restaurant features outstanding country-style cuisine. It is a great place to stop for lunch after a visit to nearby Abbotsford or Dryburgh Abbey. Try the honey-and-orange lamb, or the Stilton-stuffed mushrooms. *Buccleuch St., tel. 0189/682–2245. Reservations advised. Dress: casual. MC, V. Closed Sun.* $

Dining and
Lodging

Burts Hotel. Built in 1772, this quiet hotel in the center of Melrose retains a considerable amount of its period style, updated with modern conveniences. It has a particularly welcoming bar, with a cheerful open fire and a wide selection of fine malt whiskies, that is ideal for a quiet dram before or after a meal in the elegant dining room, which has dark-green striped wallpaper, high-back upholstered chairs, and white linen tablecloths. Saddle of venison and roast duck terrine are typical entrées. The bedrooms and public areas are individually decorated with reproduction antiques and floral pastels. *Market Sq., Melrose, TD6 9PN, tel. 0189/682–2285, fax 0189/682–2870. Restaurant reservations advised. Dress: casual but neat. 21 rooms; 14 with bath, 7 with shower. AE, DC, MC, V.* $$

Moffat
Lodging

Wellview. Set in beautiful gardens and overlooking both the town and the nearby hills, this Victorian house offers the highest standard of accommodation, Taste of Scotland cuisine, and a wide-ranging wine list. *Ballplay Rd., Moffat DGIO 9JU, tel. 01683/20184. 6 rooms with bath. MC, V.* $

Peebles
Dining and
Lodging
★

Cringletie House. Surrounded by grounds that include an old-fashioned walled garden whose produce is used in the hotel, this privately owned property, personally supervised by the owners and their family, is well worth seeking out. There are turrets and crow-step gables in traditional Scottish baronial style, and the spacious first-floor drawing room has an elaborate ceiling and pretty views of the valley. The simple yet comfortably furnished bedrooms are a prelude to the hotel's major achievement: its food. The restaurant is popular with locals (especially for Sunday lunch) for its straightforward, delicious home-cooked meals, such as roast duckling with red currant-and-Cassis sauce, a welcome contrast to the oversauced and overdecorated food served in many country-house hotels. *Eddleston, by Peebles, EH45 8PL tel. 01721/730233, fax 01721/730244. Restaurant reservations required. Dress: casual but neat. 13 rooms with bath. MC, V.* $$–$$$

★

Peebles Hydro. This is one of those rare places that not only has something for everyone, but has it in abundance: Archery, snooker, pony trekking, squash, a whirlpool, and a sauna are just a few of the diversions the hotel offers. The elegant Edwardian building, reminiscent of a French château, is set on 30 acres. Bedrooms are comfortably furnished, though inevitably in a hotel of this size, room sizes and decorative standards can vary. In the public areas the high ceilings emanate an airy, spacious ambience. The restaurant features a Scottish menu, with local salmon, lamb, and beef. *Peebles, tel. 01721/720602, fax 01721/722999. Restaurant reservations essential. Jacket and tie required. 137 rooms with bath. AE, DC, MC, V.* $$–$$$

Park Hotel. This hotel, on the banks of the River Tweed at the northern tip of the Ettrick Forest, offers comfort and tranquility. The restaurant serves superior Scottish cuisine, many of the dishes based on local salmon, trout, and seafood. *Innerleithen Rd., EH45 8BA, tel. 01721/720451, fax 01721/723510. Restaurant reservations* advised. Dress: casual. 24 rooms with bath. Facilities: restaurant. AE, DC, MC, V. $–$$

Lodging **Drummore.** This hillside bed-and-breakfast, set in an acre of wild garden full of bird life, is well-positioned both for touring the Borders and for visiting Edinburgh. The house is modern and clean, and the guest lounge has a vast picture window which overlooks the River Tweed. *Venlaw High Rd., EH45 8RL, tel. 01721/720336, fax 01721/723004. 2 rooms. No credit cards. Open Apr.–Oct. $*

Port William **Corsemalzie House.** This attractive 19th-century mansion is set on
Dining and 40 acres of peaceful grounds behind the fishing village of Port Wil-
Lodging liam. Sporting pursuits are the hotel's main attraction, with shooting, sea and game fishing, and golf on tap. The restaurant features a "Taste of Scotland" menu, and the public rooms and bedrooms are in keeping with the country-house style of the hotel. *Corsemalzie, Port William, Newton Stewart, Wigtownshire, tel. 01988/860254, fax 01988/860213. 15 rooms with bath. MC, V. Closed late-Jan.–Feb. $–$$*

Quothquan **Shieldhill.** This foursquare Norman manor has stood on this spot
Dining and since 1199 (though it was greatly enlarged in 1560). It is in an ideal
Lodging location for touring the Borders—just 27 miles from Edinburgh and 31 from Glasgow. The rooms are named after great Scottish battles—Culloden, Glencoe, Bannockburn—and are furnished with great comfort (miles of Laura Ashley fabrics and wallpaper). *Quothquan, near Biggar, ML12 6NA, tel. 01899/20035, fax 01899/21092. 11 rooms with bath. Facilities: restaurant, garden. AE, DC, MC, V. $$$–$$$$*

St. Boswells **Dryburgh Abbey Hotel.** Right next to the abbey ruins, this civilized
Dining and hotel is surrounded by beautiful scenery and features a restaurant
Lodging specializing in traditional Scottish fare. The restaurant is nonsmoking only. Bar snacks are also available. *St. Boswells TD6 0RQ, tel. 01835/22261, fax 01835/23945. Restaurant reservations advised. Jacket and tie required. 26 rooms with bath. Facilities: restaurant, golf. MC, V. $$*

Selkirk **Philipburn House.** An 18th-century house set on 4 acres of gardens,
Dining and Philipburn is an ideal place for families. The property has deluxe
Lodging accommodations furnished in traditional style. The house has recently been extended and the bedrooms updated; these rooms and the dining room have a Scandinavian feeling, all pine and floral prints. A bit of advice: The hotel is renowned for its food, so work up a good appetite in the heated swimming pool and do not gorge yourself on the superb home-baked afternoon teas. Venison, Borders lamb, and, of course, salmon and trout from the nearby River Tweed are featured on Philipburn's imaginative menu. *Linglie Rd., Selkirk, TD7 5LS, tel. 01750/20747, fax 01750/21690. 16 rooms with bath or shower. DC, MC, V. $$$*

Swinton **Four Seasons Restaurant.** This eatery is part of the Wheatsheaf
Dining Hotel, a country inn on the main street, which also offers good bar lunches. However, if you are not in a hurry, lunch or dine in this little restaurant for a real taste of the chef's skills. The sheer class of the cuisine, whether the meal is beef, salmon, or venison, has won widespread praise, yet neither the food nor the small but carefully chosen wine list is overpriced. *Wheatsheaf Hotel, Swinton, tel. 01890/860257. Reservations required. Jacket and tie advised. $$–$$$*

The Arts and Nightlife

The Arts

Some of the Borders area approaches the sphere of Edinburgh and its artistic life. Farther afield, **Gracefield Arts Centre** (Edinburgh Rd., Dumfries, tel. 01387/62084) has public art galleries and studios with a constantly changing exhibition program. **The Dumfries and Galloway Arts Festival** is usually held at the end of May, at several venues throughout the region.

Some of the major towns have movie houses showing films on general release. Note also the **Robert Burns Centre Film Theatre** (Mill Rd., Dumfries, tel. 01387/64808), which features special-interest, foreign, and other films that are not widely released.

Nightlife

Small towns in a rural hinterland generally do not offer a wild, urban-style nightlife. Overall, there is a wide choice of hotel bars and pubs.

7 Fife and Angus

St. Andrews, Dundee

By Gilbert Summers

The regions of Fife and Angus sandwich Scotland's fourth-largest—and often overlooked—city, Dundee. This is typical eastern-seaboard country: open beaches, fishing villages, and breezy cliff-top walkways. Scotland's east coast has only light rainfall throughout the year; northeastern Fife, in particular, may claim the record for the most sunshine and the least rainfall in all Scotland. Though the hills that attract so many visitors to Scotland may seem a long way west when you're touring the East Neuk of Fife (*neuk*, pronounced *nyook*, is Scots for *corner*), the particular charm of Angus is its variety: In addition to its seacoast and pleasant Lowland market centers, there's also a hinterland of lonely rounded hills with long glens running into the typical Grampian Highland scenery beyond.

Fife stretches far up the Forth Valley (which is west and a little north of Edinburgh). In these western parts the region still bears the scars of heavy industry, especially coal mining. Yet these signs are less evident as you move farther east: Northeastern Fife, around the university-and-golf town of St. Andrews, seems to have played no part in the industrial revolution; the residents instead earned a livelihood from the grain fields or from the sea. Fishing has been a major industry, and in the past a string of Fife ports traded across the North Sea. Today the legacy of Dutch-influenced architecture—crow-step gables and distinctive town houses, for example—is still plain to see and gives these East Neuk villages a distinctive charm.

St. Andrews is unlike any other Scottish town. Once Scotland's most powerful ecclesiastical center, seat also of the country's oldest university, and then, much later, the very symbol and spiritual home of golf, the town has a comfortable, well-groomed air, sitting almost smugly apart from the rest of Scotland.

Angus—Dundee's hinterland—provides considerable attractions and diversions, though they're often overlooked by travelers who are driving between Fife or Perth and the Grampian countryside to the north. One of Angus's interesting features, which it shares with the eastern Lowland edge of Perthshire, is its fruit-growing industry. Seen from roadside or railway, what at first sight appear to be sturdy vineyards on field-length wires, turn out to be soft-fruit plants, mainly raspberries. The chief fruit-growing area is Strathmore, the broad vale between the northwesterly Grampian mountains and the small coastal hills of the Sidlaws behind Dundee. Striking out from this valley—the heart of the Angus region—visitors can make a number of day trips to uplands or seacoast.

Essential Information

Important Addresses and Numbers

Tourist Information

Information is available from the **St. Andrews and North East Fife Tourist Board** (Information Centre, 70 Market St., St. Andrews, tel. 01334/472021, fax 01334/478422), **City of Dundee Tourist Board** (4 City Sq., Dundee, tel. 01382/27723, fax 01382/26353), **Angus Tourist Board** (Information Centre, Market Pl., Arbroath, tel. 01241/77883, fax 01241/78550). Smaller tourist-information centers operate seasonally in the following towns: Anstruther, Brechin, Carnoustie, Crail, Cupar, Forfar, Kirriemuir, and Montrose.

Emergencies

For police, fire, or ambulance, dial 999 from any telephone. No coins are needed for emergency calls made from public telephone booths.

Doctors and Dentists Consult your hotel, a tourist-information center, or the yellow pages of the telephone directory for listings of local doctors and dentists.

Late-Night Pharmacies Late-night pharmacies are not found outside the larger cities. In St. Andrews, Dundee, and other larger centers, pharmacies use a rotating system for off-hours and Sunday prescription service. Consult the listings displayed on pharmacy doors for the names and addresses of pharmacies that provide service outside regular hours. In an emergency the police can help you contact a pharmacist. Note that in rural areas general practitioners may also dispense medicines.

Arriving and Departing by Plane

Glasgow Airport (tel. 0141/887–1111, ext. 4552), 50 miles west of Edinburgh, is now a major point of entry for international flights. Passengers landing in Glasgow have easy access to Edinburgh and Fife and Angus. **Edinburgh Airport** (tel. 0131/333–1000), 7 miles west of downtown Edinburgh, has airlinks throughout the United Kingdom, as well as with a number of cities on the Continent.

Arriving and Departing by Car, Train, and Bus

By Car The M90 motorway from Edinburgh takes visitors to within a half hour of St. Andrews and Dundee. Travelers coming from Fife can use Route A914 or A92, then cross the Tay Bridge to reach Dundee, though the quickest way is to use the M90 and the A85. Travel time from Edinburgh to Dundee is about 1 hour, from Edinburgh to St. Andrews, 1½ hours.

By Train **Scotrail** (tel. 0131/556–2451) stops at Leuchars (for St. Andrews), Dundee, Arbroath, and Montrose.

By Bus Two companies, **Lothian Regional Transport** (tel. 0131/220–4111) and **Guide Friday** (tel. 0131/556–2244), run buses between Edinburgh Airport's main terminal building and Waverley Bridge in downtown Edinburgh. The buses run every 30 minutes during the day (9–5) and less frequently (roughly every hour) during off-peak hours and on weekends. The trip from the airport takes about 30 minutes (about 45 minutes during rush hour). From Edinburgh's St. Andrew Square Bus Station, **Fife Scottish** (tel. 0131/556–8464) buses run to various points throughout Fife and Angus.

Getting Around

By Car Fife is an easy area to get around and presents no major obstacles to the traveler. Most of the roads are quiet and uncongested. The most interesting sights are in the east, which is served by a network of cross-country roads. Angus is likewise an easy region to explore, being serviced by a main fast road—the A94—which travels through the middle of the Strathmore valley and then on to Aberdeen; another, gentler road—the A92—that runs to the east near the coast; and a network of rural roads between the Grampians and Route A94.

By Train The stations listed in Arriving and Departing, above, are the area's only stations.

By Bus A local network provides service from St. Andrews and Dundee to many of the smaller towns throughout Fife and Dundee. The fare for the Kirkaldy–St. Andrews run is £2.60; St. Andrews–Dundee, £1.55; Perth–Montrose, £5.50. For information about routes and fares call **Fife Scottish** (tel. 01592/642394) or **Strathtay Scottish** (tel. 01382/28054).

Guided Tours

Orientation **Tayside Transport** (tel. 01382/201121) in late July–early August offers a variety of general orientation tours of the main cities and the region.

Special-Interest The following operators offer tours tailored to individual requirements: **Colzie Hill Recreation** (Auchtermuchty, Fife, tel. 01337/827075, fax 01337/827077), and **Links Golf Tours** (7 Pilmour Links, St. Andrews, tel. 01334/478639).

Exploring Fife and Angus

Highlights for First-Time Visitors

Angus Folk Museum (*see* Tour 2)
Crail Harbour (*see* Tour 1)
Edzell Castle (*see* Tour 2)
Falkland Palace (*see* Tour 1)
Glamis Castle (*see* Tour 2)
House of Dun (*see* Tour 2)
Scottish Fisheries Museum (*see* Tour 1)

Tour 1: Around Fife

Numbers in the margin correspond to points of interest on the Fife Area and St. Andrews maps.

❶ This tour starts in **St. Andrews,** Scotland's golf mecca and possibly the most visited town in the country after Edinburgh. The center of this compact city retains its original medieval street plan of three roughly parallel streets—North Street, Market Street, and South Street—leading away from the city's earliest religious site, near the cathedral. The local legend regarding the founding of St. Andrews has it that a certain St. Regulus, or Rule, acting under divine guidance, carried relics of St. Andrew by sea from Patras in Greece. He was shipwrecked on this Fife headland and founded a church. The

❷ holy man's name survives in the square-shaped **St. Rule's Tower,** consecrated in 1126 and the oldest surviving building in St. An-

❸ drews. Nearby is the city **cathedral,** today only a ruined, poignant fragment of what was formerly the largest and most magnificent church in Scotland. Work on it began in 1160, and consecration was finally celebrated in 1318, after several setbacks. The cathedral was subsequently damaged by fire and repaired, but finally fell into decay during the Reformation, in the 16th century. Only ruined gables, parts of the nave south wall, and other fragments survive, although you can still enjoy dizzying views of town from St. Rule's Tower, accessed via a steep set of stairs. The on-site museum helps visitors interpret the remains and gives a sense of what the cathedral must once have been like. *Museum and St. Rule's Tower, tel. 0131/244–3101. Admission: £1.50 adults, £1 senior citizens, 75p children. Open Apr.–Sept., Mon.–Sat. 9:30–6, Sun. 2–6; Oct.–Mar., Mon.–Sat. 9:30–4, Sun. 2–4.*

❹ Directly north of the cathedral on the shore stands **St. Andrews Castle,** which was started at the end of the 13th century. Although now a ruin, the remains include a rare example of a bottle dungeon, cold

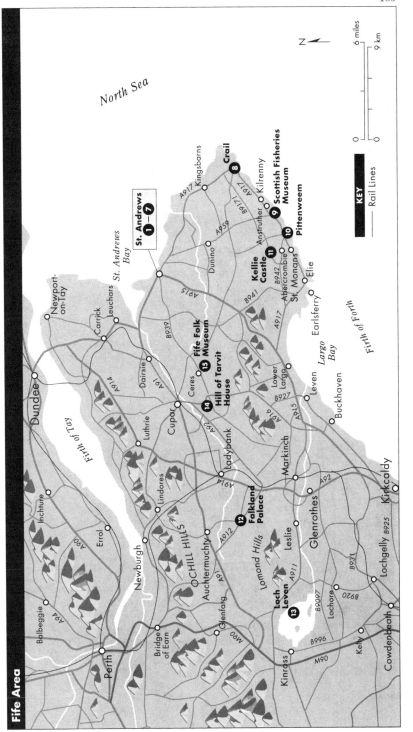

Fife Area

North Sea

Firth of Tay

St. Andrews Bay

St. Andrews 1–7

Crail **8**

Scottish Fisheries Museum **9**

Pittenweem **10**

Kellie Castle **11**

Fife Folk Museum **13**

Hill of Tarvit House **14**

Falkland Palace **12**

Loch Leven **13**

Largo Bay

Firth of Forth

Kingsbarns
Kilrenny
Anstruther
St. Monans
Elie
Earlsferry
Leven
Lower Largo
Buckhaven
Dunino
Leuchars
Carrick
Newport-on-Tay
Dundee
Dairsie
Luthrie
Lindores
Ceres
Cupar
Ladybank
Markinch
Glenrothes
Kirkcaldy
Lochgelly
Cowdenbeath
Kelty
Lochore
Kinross
Leslie
Auchtermuchty
Glenfarg
Bridge of Earn
Newburgh
Errol
Inchture
Balbeggie
Perth

OCHIL HILLS
Lomond Hills

A917 A959 B9171 B9131 A915 B939 B941 A917 B942 B927 A916 A915 A92 A912 A911 A91 A914 A90 A94 A913 M90 B996 B920 B925 B931 B9007

KEY

— Rail Lines

N

0   6 miles
0   9 km

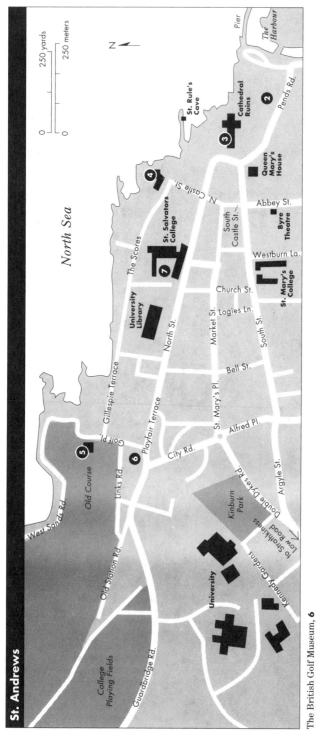

St. Andrews

North Sea

The British Golf Museum, **6**
Cathedral, **3**
Royal & Ancient Golf
Club of St. Andrews, **5**
St. Andrews Castle, **4**
St. Andrew's
University, **7**
St. Rule's Tower, **2**

and gruesome, in which many prisoners spent their last hours. Even more atmospheric is the castle's mine and countermine. The former was a tunnel dug by besieging forces in the 16th century; the latter, a tunnel dug by castle defenders in order to meet and wage battle below ground. You can stoop and crawl into this narrow passage—way—an eerie experience, despite the addition of electric light. The Visitor Centre has a good audiovisual presentation on the castle's history. *Tel. 0131/244–3101. Admission: £2 adults, £1.25 senior citizens, 75p children. Joint ticket to cathedral and castle: £3 adults, £1.75 senior citizens, £1 children. Open Apr.–Sept., Mon.–Sat. 9:30–6, Sun. 2–6; Oct.–Mar., Mon.–Sat. 9:30–4, Sun. 2–4.*

After visiting the castle, you can walk west along the street called
❺ The Scores to reach the **Royal & Ancient Golf Club of St. Andrews**. This is the ruling house of golf worldwide, and the spiritual home of all who play or follow the game. Its clubhouse on the dunes—a building of some dignity, more like a town hall than a clubhouse and open to club members only—is adjacent to St. Andrew's famous **Old Course.** The town of St. Andrews prospers on golf, golf schools, and golf equipment (the manufacture of golf balls has been a local industry for more than 100 years), and the Old Course is associated with the greatest players of the game.

❻ Just opposite the Royal & Ancient Golf Club is **The British Golf Museum,** which explores the centuries-old relationship between St. Andrews and golf, and displays a variety of golf memorabilia. *Golf Pl., tel. 01334/478880. Admission: £3.50 adults, £2.50 senior citizens and students, £1.50 children, £9 family ticket. Open Mar. and Apr., Thurs.–Tues. 10–5; May–Oct., daily 10–5:30; Nov.–Feb., Thurs.–Mon. 11–3.*

St. Andrews is also the home of Scotland's oldest university.
❼ Founded in 1411, **St. Andrew's University** now consists of two stately old colleges in the middle of town and some attractive modern buildings on the outskirts. A third weather-worn college, originally built in 1512, has become a fashionable girls' school. The handsome university buildings can be explored on guided walks, sometimes led by students in scarlet gowns. *Tel. 01334/476161, ext. 258/488.*

Having sampled the religious, academic, and sporting ambience of St. Andrews, leave town by Route A917, which leads to the east and then south past the numerous East Neuk fishing communities along
❽ the Fife coast. Stop in the town of **Crail** to see its picturesque Dutch-influenced Town House, or Tolbooth, which contains the oldest bell in Fife, cast in Holland in 1520. Full details on the heritage and former trading links of this tiny port can be found in the **Crail Museum and Heritage Center.** *62 Marketgate, Crail, tel. 01333/450869. Admission free. Open Easter week and June–early-Sept. 10–12:30 and 2:30–5; Apr., May, and late Sept., weekends 2:30–5.*

A few minutes farther along A917 to the southwest is **Anstruther,** which boasts an attractive waterfront (larger than Crail's) with a few shops brightly festooned with children's buckets and spades as
❾ a gesture to seaside vacationers. Facing the harbor is the **Scottish Fisheries Museum,** housed in a colorful cluster of buildings, the earliest of which dates from the 16th century. This museum illustrates the difficult life of Scottish fishermen, past and present, through documents, artifacts, paintings, and tableaux. (These displays, complete with the reek of tarred rope and net, have been known to induce nostalgic tears in not a few old deckhands.) There are also floating exhibits at the quayside. *Anstruther harbor, tel. 01333/310628. Admission: £2.20 adults, £1.20 senior citizens and chil-*

dren. Open Apr.–Oct., daily 10–5:30, Sun. 11–5; Nov.–Mar., daily 10–4:30, Sun. 2–4:30.

⑩ About 1¹/₂ miles farther down the road is **Pittenweem,** a working harbor with many examples of East Neuk architecture. Look for the crow-step gables (the stepped effect on the ends of the roofs), the white *harling* (Scots for *rough-casting,* the rough mortar finish on walls), and the red pantiles (S-shaped in profile). The "weem" part of the town's name comes from the Gaelic *uaime,* or *cave.* This town's particular cave is at Cove Wynd up a close (alleyway) behind the waterfront. It contains the shrine of St. Fillan, a 6th-century hermit who lived therein. *Cove Wynd, near harbor, tel. 01333/311495 (St. John's Episcopal Church). Admission: 40p adults, children free. Open Tues.–Sat. 10–5, Sun. noon–5.*

For a break from this nautical atmosphere follow B942 inland to ⑪ **Kellie Castle.** Dating from the 16th and 17th centuries and restored in Victorian times, the castle stands among the grain fields and woodlands of northeastern Fife. The castle is surrounded by 4 acres of attractive gardens. *B9171 (3 mi northwest of Pittenweem), tel. 01333/720271. Admission: castle and gardens, £3.80 adults, £1.50 children; gardens only, £1 adults, 50p children. Castle open Easter weekend and May–mid-Oct., daily 1:30–5:30 (last admission 4:45); also weekends only in Apr., 1:30–5:30. Garden and grounds open all year, 9:30–sunset.*

You could continue along the coast to take in **St. Monans,** with its working harbor and ancient church by the sea, as well as the twin communities of Elie and Earlsferry, whose sheltered waters are appreciated by sailboard enthusiasts. Alternatively, rejoin the A917 and pass through **Lower Largo,** birthplace of Alexander Selkirk, the Scottish sailor who was the prototype for Daniel Defoe's Robinson Crusoe. Follow signs for **Glenrothes,** a modern town with a selection of sporting facilities that is also notable for its public murals and sculptures.

From Glenrothes take the A92 north then the A912 northwest to reach **Falkland,** one of the most attractive communities in all Fife. A royal burgh of twisting streets and crooked stone houses, the town ⑫ is dominated by **Falkland Palace,** a former hunting lodge of the Stuart monarchs and one of the earliest examples in Britain of the French Renaissance style. Overlooking the main street is the palace's most attractive feature—the south range of walls and chambers, rich with Renaissance buttresses and stone medallions, built for James V in the 1530s by French masons. James V died here in 1542, and the palace was a favorite resort of his daughter, Mary, Queen of Scots. Behind the palace are gardens that contain a most unusual survivor: a "royal" tennis court (not at all like its modern counterpart) built in 1539 and still in use. *A912 (11 mi north of Kirkcaldy, tel. 01337/857397. Admission: £4 adults, £2 children and senior citizens; gardens only, £2 adults, £1 senior citizens and children. Open Apr.–mid-Oct., Mon.–Sat. 11–5:30, Sun. 1:30–5:30 (last admission to palace 4:30, to garden 5).*

Farther to the west as you follow A911 is Scotland's largest Lowland ⑬ loch, **Loch Leven,** famed for its fighting trout. The area is also noted for its birdlife, particularly its wintering wildfowl. You can find out more about the ecology of the loch at the **Vane Farm Nature Reserve,** a well-equipped visitor center run by the Royal Society for the Protection of Birds, on the southern shore overlooking the loch. *Vane Farm, Rte. B9097, just off M90 and B996, tel. 01577/862355. Admis-*

sion: £2 adults, £1 senior citizens, 50p children. Open Apr.–Dec. 20, daily 10–5; Jan.–Mar., daily 10–4.

Your next destination is **Cupar,** a busy market town with a variety of shops. On rising ground south of town (take Route A916) is the **⓮** National Trust for Scotland's **Hill of Tarvit House.** A 17th-century mansion, the house was later altered in the high-Edwardian style at the turn of the 20th century by the Scottish architect Sir Robert Lorimer. Inside the house are fine collections of antique furniture, Chinese porcelain, bronzes, tapestries, and Dutch paintings. *A916 (2 mi south of Cupar), tel. 01334/653127. Admission: £3 adults, £1.50 children, students, and senior citizens; gardens only, £1 adult, 50p children. Open Easter and May–Oct., daily 1:30–5:30 (last admission 4:45); Apr., Sat. and Sun. 1:30–5:30.*

Time Out In summer the National Trust operates a **tearoom** inside Hill of Tarvit House, which is always stocked with tasty homemade Scottish baked goods.

Before making your way back to St. Andrews, you can learn more **⓯** about the history and culture of rural Fife by visiting the **Fife Folk Museum** at Ceres, reached by going south on A916 and east on B939. The life of local rural communities is reflected in artifacts and documents, all housed in suitably authentic buildings that include a former weigh house and adjoining weavers' cottages. *Tel. 01334/828250. Admission: £1.50 adults, £1.20 senior citizens, 50p children. Open Easter and May–Oct., Sat.–Thurs. 2–5.*

Tour 2: Dundee and Angus

Numbers in the margin correspond to points of interest on the Angus Area map.

⓰ This tour starts with a walk through **Dundee** and continues with a drive up the coast as far as Montrose. The return loop leads you along peaceful back roads as far as Kirriemuir. Most of the roads in this area are uncluttered, with the exception of the main road from Perth/Dundee to Aberdeen—the A94—on which special care is needed.

Dundee's urban-renewal program—its determination to shake off its grimy industrial past—was motivated in part by the arrival of the **RRS (Royal Research Ship)** *Discovery,* the vessel used by Captain Robert Scott on his polar explorations. The steamer was originally built and launched in Dundee; now it's a permanent tourist exhibit. A new Visitor Centre and on-board exhibition allows visitors to sample life as it was aboard the intrepid *Discovery. Discovery Point, Discovery Quay, Dundee, tel. 01382/201245. Admission: £4 adults, £2.90 senior citizens, children, and students, £11–£13 family ticket. Open Mon.–Sat 10–5, Sun. 11–5; daily until 4 in winter.*

At nearby Victoria Dock is another historic vessel, the frigate *Unicorn,* a 46-gun wooden warship. The *Unicorn* has the distinction of being the oldest British-built warship afloat (the fourth-oldest in the world), having been launched at Chatham, England, in 1824. Onboard models and displays offer a glimpse into the history of the Royal Navy. *Victoria Dock (just east of Tay Rd. Bridge), tel. 01382/200900. Admission: £3 adults, £2 children, students, and senior citizens. Open daily 10–5.*

Dundee's principal museum and art gallery is **The McManus Galleries,** which offers displays—many of them new—on a range of sub-

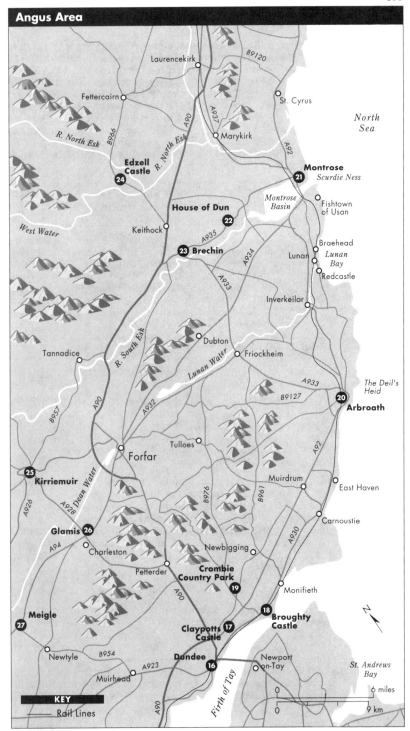

190

Angus Area

Laurencekirk

B9120

Fettercairn

St. Cyrus

R. North Esk

B966

North Sea

A937

Marykirk

Edzell Castle
24

R. North Esk

Montrose
21
Scurdie Ness

A92

Montrose Basin

Fishtown of Usan

Keithock

A935

House of Dun
22

Braehead

23 **Brechin**

A934

Lunan

Lunan Bay

West Water

A933

Redcastle

Inverkeilor

Tannadice

R. South Esk

Dubton

Friockheim

The Deil's Heid

A933

Lunan Water

A932

B9127

B957

A90

20
Arbroath

Tulloes

Forfar

Dean Water

A926

25 **Kirriemuir**

A928

Muirdrum

B976

B961

A92

East Haven

Carnoustie

Glamis 26

Charleston

A94

Newbigging

A830

Petterden

Crombie Country Park
19

Monifieth

Meigle
27

A90

18
Broughty Castle

Claypotts Castle 17

Newtyle

B954

A923

Dundee
16

Newport on-Tay

St. Andrews Bay

Muirhead

Firth of Tay

N

KEY
— Rail Lines

0   6 miles
0   9 km

jects, including local history, trade, and industry. *Albert Sq., tel. 01382/23141. Admission free. Open Mon.–Sat. 10–5.*

The **Barrack Street Museum** specializes in natural history, offering exhibitions on the wildlife and geology of Angus and the Highlands. The museum also displays the skeleton of the famous Tay Whale, immortalized by Scotland's worst poet, William MacGonagall, born in Dundee in 1830. His consistently dire poems caused him to be lionized by Edinburgh's legal and student fraternity. The stranding of a whale locally was one of many incidents that moved him to verse. *Barrack St. and Meadowside, tel. 01382/23141, ext. 65152. Admission free. Open Mon.–Sat. 10–5.*

The **University Botanic Gardens** are a well-landscaped collection of native and exotic plants. Also on the premises are tropical and temperate greenhouses and a visitor center. *Riverside Dr., tel. 01382/66939. Admission: £1 adults, 50p senior citizens and children. Open Mar.–Oct., Mon.–Sat. 10–4:30, Sun. 11–4; Nov.–Feb., Mon.–Sat. 10–3, Sun. 11–3.*

⑰ In the eastern suburbs of Dundee, away from the surviving Victorian architecture of the city center, are two castles of interest. **Claypotts Castle** is a well-preserved 16th-century tower house laid out on a Z-plan. *South of A92 (3 mi east of city center), tel. 0131/244–3101. Admission: £1.20 adults, 75p children. Open Apr.–Oct. Mon.–Sat., 9:30–6, Sun. 2–6.*

⑱ Approximately 1 mile farther east is **Broughty Castle.** This former fortress guarding the Tay estuary is now a museum with displays on fishing, ferries, and the history of the town's whaling industry. There is also a display of arms and armor. *Broughty Ferry (4 mi east of city center), tel. 01382/76121. Admission free. Open Oct.–June, Mon.–Thurs., Sat. 10–1 and 2–5; July–Sept., Mon.–Thurs., Sat. 10–1 and 2–5, Sun. 2–5.*

⑲ Dundee is ringed by country parks that offer ample sports and leisure activities. **Crombie Country Park** features a reservoir with extensive woodlands in 250 acres, as well as wildlife blinds, nature trails, a children's play park, picnic areas, and a display-and-interpretation center staffed by a ranger. *Off Rte. B961 (7 mi from Newbigging), tel. 01241/860360. Admission free. Open daily 10–dusk.*

⑳ Leave Dundee by the A92 coast road, which leads to **Arbroath** (15 mi north of Dundee), a holiday resort and fishing town where traditional boat-building can still be seen. Arbroath has several small curers and processors, with shops offering the town's most famous delicacy, "Arbroath smokie"—whole haddock gutted and lightly smoked.

Arbroath Abbey, founded in 1178, in the center of town, is unmistakable and seems to straddle whole streets, as if the town was simply ignoring the redstone ruin in its midst. Surviving today are remains of the church, as well as one of the most complete examples in existence of an abbot's residence. From here in 1320, a passionate plea was sent by King Robert the Bruce and the Scottish church to Pope John XXII in far-off Rome. The pope had until then sided with the English kings, who adamantly refused to acknowledge Scottish independence. The Declaration of Arbroath stated firmly, "For as long as but a hundred of us remain alive, never will we on any conditions be brought under English rule. It is in truth not for glory, nor riches, nor honours that we are fighting, but for freedom—for that alone, which no honest man gives up but with life itself." Some historians describe this plea (originally drafted in Latin) as the single most important document in Scottish history. The pope advised English King Edward to make peace, but warfare was to break out along the border from time to time for the next 200 years. *Arbroath town center, tel. 0131/244–3101. Admission: £1.20 adults, 75p children. Open Apr.–Sept., Mon.–Sat. 9:30–6, Sun. 2–6; Mar.–Oct., Mon.–Sat. 9:30–4, Sun. 2–4.*

Also notable in the town is the **Signal Tower Museum.** Arbroath was the shore base for the construction of the Bell Rock lighthouse, on a treacherous, barely exposed offshore rock in the early 19th century. This signal tower was built to facilitate communication between the mainland and the builders working offshore. The museum in the tower now tells the story of the lighthouse, built by Robert Stevenson in 1811. (The name Stevenson is strongly associated with the building of lighthouses throughout Scotland, though the most famous son of that family is remembered for another talent. In fact, Robert Louis Stevenson gravely disappointed his family by choosing to become a writer instead of an engineer.) The museum also houses a collection of items related to the history of the town, its folk life, and the local fishing industry. *Ladyloan (west of harbor), tel. 01674/673232. Admission free. Open Mon.–Sat. 10–5.*

A 15- to 20-minute drive to the north, along the coast via the A92, is **Montrose,** a handsome, unpretentious town with a museum and a selection of shops. The town is also noted for its attractive beach. Behind Montrose the River Esk forms a wide estuary known as the Montrose basin. The Scottish Wildlife Trust operates a nature reserve here, with a good number of geese, ducks, and swans.

From Montrose head west on the A935. Signs will direct you to the National Trust for Scotland's leading attraction in this area, the **House of Dun,** overlooking the Montrose Basin. This 1730s mansion, built by architect William Adam, is particularly noted for its ornate plasterwork. *A935 (4 mi west of Montrose), tel. 01674/810264. Admission: £3.50 adults, £1.80 children. Open Easter and May–Sept., daily 11–5:30; Oct., Sat. and Sun. 11–5:30 (last admission 5). Garden and grounds, daily 9:30–sunset.*

Farther west is **Brechin,** a small market town in Strathmore. Its cathedral was founded in about 1200 and contains an interesting selection of antiquities. Also nearby is the 10th-century **Round Tower,** one of only two on mainland Scotland (they are more frequently found in Ireland). It was originally built for the local Culdee monks.

Make your way due north by the B966, north of Edzell (which most Scots now associate with the U.S.-run military listening post nearby). **Edzell Castle,** an impressive ruin from the 16th century, is nestled among the Grampian foothills. This structure was originally a typical Scottish fortified tower, but was later transformed into a house that gave some degree of domestic comfort as well as protection from the elements. The simple "L" shape of the original building was extended, and a pleasance, or walled garden, was added in 1604. This formal garden, along with unique heraldic and symbolic sculptures, survives today. *Off B966 (6 mi north of Brechin), tel. 0131/244–3101. Admission: £2 adults, £1.25 senior citizens, 75p children. Open Apr.–Sept., Mon.–Sat. 9:30–6, Sun. 2–6; Oct.–Mar., Mon.–Wed. and Sat. 9:30–4, Thurs. 9:30–noon, Sun. 2–4.*

You can rejoin the hurly-burly of the A90 for the journey back to Dundee, though the more pleasant route leads southwestward using minor roads (there are several options) along the face of the Grampians, following the fault line that separates highland and lowland at this point.

㉕ At the intersection of Routes B957 and A926 is **Kirriemuir,** heart of Angus's red sandstone countryside and birthplace of the writer and dramatist Sir James Barrie (1860–1937), most well known abroad as the author of *Peter Pan.* Barrie's house, now in the care of the National Trust for Scotland, has upper floors furnished as they might have been in Barrie's time, with manuscripts and personal mementoes displayed. The outside washhouse is said to have been Barrie's first theater. Next door, at 11 Brechin Road, is an exhibition on "The Genius of J. M. Barrie" giving literary and theatrical background. *9 Brechin Rd., Kirriemuir, tel. 01575/72646 or 01575/72353. Admission: £1.80 adults, 90p children. Open Easter weekend; May–Sept., Mon.–Sat. 11–5:30, Sun. 1:30–5:30; Oct., Sat. 11:30–5:30, Sun. 1:30–5:30 (last admission 5).*

About 6 miles due south on the A928, across pleasantly rolling coun-

㉖ tryside, is the village of **Glamis,** site of the **Angus Folk Museum.** This museum village is made up of a row of 19th-century cottages with unusual stone-slab roofs; exhibits focus on the crafts and tools of domestic and agricultural life in the region over the past 200 years. *Off A94 (5 mi southwest of Forfar), tel. 01307/84288. Admission: £2 adults, £1 children. Open Easter and May–Sept., daily 11–5:30; Oct., Sat. and Sun. 11–5:30 (last admission 5).*

Approximately another mile to the southwest is **Glamis Castle,** one of Scotland's best-known castles because of its association with the present Royal Family. This was the childhood home of the current Queen Mother and the birthplace of Princess Margaret. The property of the earls of Strathmore and Kinghorne since 1372, the castle was largely reconstructed in the late-17th century; the original keep, which is much older, is still intact. One of the most famous rooms in the castle is Duncan's Hall, the legendary setting for Shakespeare's *Macbeth.* Guided tours offer visitors a look at fine collections of china, tapestries, and furniture. Other visitor facilities include shops, a produce stall, and tearoom. *A94 (6 mi southwest of Forfar), tel. 01307/840242. Admission: £4.20 adults, £3.30 senior citizens and students, £2.30 children, £12.50 family ticket. Open Easter–mid-Oct, daily 10:30–5:30 (last tour at 4:45).*

㉗ The local museum at **Meigle,** on the A94 in the wide swathe of Strathmore, has a magnificent collection of some 25 sculptured monuments from the Celtic Christian period (8th to 10th centuries), nearly all of which were found in or around the local churchyard. This is one of the most notable collections of medieval work in Western Europe. *A94 in Meigle (12 mi west/southwest of Forfar), tel. 0131/244–3101. Admission: £1.20 adults, 75p children. Open Apr.–Sept., Mon.–Sat. 9:30–6, Sun. 2–6.*

From Meigle you can take Route B954 back to Dundee, just 15 miles east.

Fife and Angus for Free

Arbroath Cliffs Nature Trail stretches for 3 miles along sandstone cliffs that are home to varied birdlife. The trail starts at the north end of the Arbroath Promenade.
Claypotts Castle (*see* Tour 2)
Mills Observatory. This public observatory has an astronomer in residence. Here you'll find telescopes, displays on astronomy and space exploration, a planetarium, and an audiovisual program.

Viewing of the skies is subject to weather conditions. *Balgay Hill, Dundee, tel. 01382/67138. Admission free. Open Apr.–Sept., weekdays 10–5, Sat. 2–5; Oct.–Mar., weekdays 3–10, Sat. 2–5.*

Red Castle, Lunan Bay. This 15th-century sandstone tower house overlooks a sandy beach. *Off A92 (7 mi south of Montrose).*

St. Andrews Cathedral (*see* Tour 1)

White and Brown Caterthun Hill Forts (*see* Off the Beaten Track, *below*)

What to See and Do with Children

Craigtoun Country Park. Here children can choose from among a miniature railway, a re-created Dutch village, boating, bowling, putting, trampolines, adventure play area, bouncy castles, and guided country walks. *Off A915 (2¹/₂ mi southwest of St. Andrews), tel. 01334/473666. Admission: £2 adults, £1 children under 5, senior citizens, and students. Open Easter–early Oct., daily 10:30–6:30 (last admission 5:30).*

Kerr's Miniature Railway. Established in 1935 and hauled by steam and diesel engines, this railway has a real old-time feel to it. Tunnel, footbridge, turntable, and locomotive shed are all in scale. *Sea front, Arbroath, tel. 01241/79249. Admission: £1 adults, 60p children. Open Apr.–June and late Aug.–Sept., Sat. and Sun. 2–5; July and early Aug., daily 2–5.*

Scottish Deer Centre. Here children can see red deer at close quarters on ranger-guided tours. There are also nature trails, a winery, falconry displays, an adventure playground, a shop, and a restaurant. *A91, near Rankelour Farm (3 mi west of Cupar), tel. 01337/810391. Admission £4 adults, £3 senior citizens and students, £2.50 children, £11 family ticket. Open Apr.–Oct., daily 10–5.*

Sea Life Centre. Sea lions, penguins, and many other forms of marine life are displayed here in settings designed to simulate their natural environment. The exhibits include numerous aquariums and pool gardens. *The Scores, West Sands, St. Andrews, tel. 01334/474786. Admission: £3.95 adults, £3.45 senior citizens and students, £2.95 children 4–14. Open daily 10–6 (until 9 in July and Aug.).*

Off the Beaten Track

Fife   Two points of interest are often overlooked by motorists touring rural Fife. Only minutes from the famous Old Course of St. Andrews, on Route A191 at **Leuchars,** is a 12th-century church with some of the finest Norman architectural features to be seen anywhere in Scotland. Note in particular the blind arcading (arch shapes on the wall) and the beautifully decorated chancel and apse.

A few minutes west of St. Andrews on the B939, an unclassified road goes through Strathkinness and about 3 miles later runs by the River Eden. The nearest community is at Dairsie (back on the A91). Stop for a moment at **Dairsie Bridge** over the river. It is 450 years old and has three arches. Above the trees rises the spire of **Dairsie Church,** dating from the 17th century, and the stark ruin of **Dairsie Castle,** often overlooked, stands gloomily over the river nearby. With wild-rose hedges, grazing cattle, and pheasants calling from the woody thickets, this is the very essence of rural, Lowland Fife, yet it's only about 15 minutes from the Old Course.

Angus   The **White and Brown Caterthuns** are the remains of Iron Age hill forts that crown two rounded hills to the west and south of Edzell

Castle. Lovers of wild places will enjoy the drive to the Caterthuns from Edzell (if in doubt at junctions, turn left), especially the climb up the narrow road (from Balrownie to Pitmudie) that passes between the two hills; along the way there are magnificent views southward to the patterned fields of Strathmore. Marked paths run up to each fort (both are now officially protected sites) from the main road. The White Caterthun, so called because of the pale quartzite rock that was used to build its now-tumbled ramparts, is the better preserved of the two. After you've explored the Caterthuns, drop southward to rejoin main routes running along Strathmore. *Tel. 0131/244–3101. Admission free.*

The **Glens of Angus** extend north from various points on Route A94. Known individually as the glens of Isla, Prosen, Clova, and Esk, these long valleys run into the high hills of the Grampians and offer a choice of clearly marked walking routes (those in Glen Clova are especially appealing).

Shopping

Shopping in this mainly rural region is inevitably concentrated in the larger towns. St. Andrews, with its university and its world-renowned golfing facilities, attracts enough affluent people to sustain some interesting smaller specialty shops. Dundee, as Scotland's fourth-largest city, is an important retail shopping center for the northern part of Angus, but the choices for shoppers here are similar to those found in most large towns (department stores, such as Marks and Spencer, predominate).

Fife If you're approaching the shopping mecca at St. Andrews from the south and are interested in women's fashion, it's worth stopping in **Cupar** to visit **Margaret Urquhart** (13–17 Lady Wynd, tel. 01334/52205), a boutique that attracts customers from as far away as Edinburgh and Glasgow and stocks a wide range of British and international designer names. Among the worthwhile specialty shops you'll find in **St. Andrews** are **Graeme Renton** (72 South St., tel. 01334/476334), the best place in the region, if not in all Scotland, for Oriental rugs and carpets of all colors, patterns, and sizes—many of them antiques; **Church Square Ceramics and Workshops** (Church Sq., between South St. and Market St., tel. 01334/477744), which offers decorative and domestic stoneware, ceramic, and enameled jewelry; **Bonkers** (80 Market St., tel. 01334/473919), with a huge selection of clothing, clocks, books, cards, pottery, and gift items; and **St. Andrews Fine Art** (84 Market St., tel. 01334/474080), the place to go for Scottish paintings from 1800 to the present (oils, watercolors, drawings, and prints are available).

In the west of Fife, **Glenrothes, Dunfermline,** and **Kirkcaldy** are the main shopping towns for day-to-day needs. The **Balbirnie Craft Centre** (tel. 01592/758759), however, in an 18th-century stable mews near Balbirnie House, Glenrothes, is a peaceful setting in which to buy items made by craftspeople who live on the premises: their work includes pottery, fashion design, furniture, silver, jewelry, and leather goods.

Dundee The modern covered shopping mall in **Dundee**—the Wellgate Shopping Centre, off Panmure Street—is the place to visit if you're looking for the major retail chains. If you search around a little, however, you'll find a scattering of smaller shops that have more character and unusual selections. The **Compleat Cookshop** (27 Wellgate Centre, tel. 01382/21256), for example, stocks an enormous variety of cooking equipment and other kitchenware. A treat for overseas visitors whose own home grocers may only stock tea bags and packaged coffee is **J. Allan Braithwaite** (6 Castle St., tel. 01382/22693), where you can select from over 30 blended teas (including mango and apricot) and 13 freshly roasted coffees (remember that such specialty teas can usually be taken home without import restriction if you purchase them as gifts). There are also several good jewelers in Dundee; try **Rattrays** (32 Nethergate, tel. 01382/27258), which has been in business for over 140 years, or **Stephen Henderson the Jeweller** (1 Union St., tel. 01382/21339) for a good selection in silver and pewter Ortak jewelry from Orkney, *skean dhus* (ornamental Highlander daggers), and *quaichs,* a small dish traditionally used for whisky tasting.

Sports and Fitness

Bicycling The back roads of Fife make pleasant bicycling terrain, as does the long valley of Strathmore (except for the A94), where some roads run deep into the Angus Glens. The following firms rent bicycles: **Rocky's Mountain Bike Hire** (The Harbour, St. Andrews, tel. 01333/730010, evenings), **East Neuk Outdoors** (Cellardyke Park, Anstruther, tel. 01333/311929), **Nicholson's Cycle Centre** (2 Forfar Rd., Dundee, tel. 01382/461212), and **Gordon Christie Cycle and Toy Shop** (86 Market St., St. Andrews, Fife, tel. 01334/72122).

Fishing As in most of the rest of Scotland, there is a wide choice of fishing in sea, loch, and river. Leaflets giving detailed information are available at tourist-information centers (*see* Important Addresses and Numbers in Essential Information, *above*).

Golf Every golfer's ambition is to play at St. Andrews, and once you are in Fife the ambition is easily realized. The following five St. Andrews courses are open to visitors (all are part of the St. Andrews Club). For details of availability—there is sometimes a waiting list—call the course number listed below or contact the secretary, Links Management Committee, Golf Place, St. Andrews (tel. 01334/475757).

Old Course (15th century). Tel. 01334/473393. 18 holes, 6,578 yards, SSS 72, handicap certificate required.

New Course (1894). Tel. 01334/473938. 18 holes, 6,604 yards, SSS 72.

Jubilee Course (1899). Tel. 01334/473938. 18 holes, 6,284 yards, SSS 72.

Eden Course (1913). Tel. 01334/474296. 18 holes, 5,971 yards, SSS 69.

Strathyrum Course (1993). Tel. 01334/475757. 18 holes, 5,195 yards, SSS 69.

There are more than 40 other courses in the region. Most have refreshment facilities and offer golf to the visitor by the round or the day. Details about locations and opening hours are available from tourist-information centers (*see* Important Addresses and Numbers in Essential Information, *above*). Many of the area's hotels offer golfing packages or will arrange a day's golf.

Health and Fitness Clubs **Arbroath Sports Centre** (Keptie Rd., Arbroath, tel. 01241/72999) offers a swimming pool, squash courts, games hall, and a gymnasium.

The **Saltire Centre** (Montrose Rd., Arbroath, tel. 01241/431060) has fitness rooms, sauna, and exercise equipment.

Cupar Sports Centre (Main St., Cupar, tel. 01334/654793) has a swimming pool, sports hall, fitness rooms, squash, steam bath, and sunbeds.

Dundee Olympia Leisure Centre (Earl Grey Pl., Dundee, tel. 01382/23141, ext. 4187) has four swimming pools, a diving pool, sauna, water slides, exercise equipment, and a restaurant.

Montrose Sports Centre (Marine Ave., Montrose, tel. 01674/676211) is an indoor sports center with a gymnasium.

Dining and Lodging

Dining

In St. Andrews and in some of the West Fife towns, such as Kirkcaldy and Dunfermline, you will find restaurants serving traditional Scottish fare, as well as ethnic food (Italian and Chinese are popular), in addition to numerous small cafés of all kinds. Bar lunches are becoming the rule in large and small hotels throughout the region, and in seaside places the "carry oot" (to go) meal is an old tradition.

Category	Cost*
$$$$	over £30
$$$	£20–£30
$$	£10–£20
$	under £10

per person for a three-course meal, excluding VAT, tax, service, and drinks

Lodging

If you're staying in Fife, the obvious base is St. Andrews, where you will find ample accommodations of all kinds. Other towns also offer a reasonable selection, and you will find good hotels and guest houses at Dunfermline and Kirkcaldy. Along the coastal strip and in the Howe of Fife between Strathmiglo and Cupar there are some superior country-house hotels, many with their own restaurants.

Category	Cost*
$$$$	over £120
$$$	£100–£120
$$	£80–£100
$	under £80

All prices are for a standard double room, including service, breakfast, and VAT.

Highly recommended restaurants and hotels are indicated by a star ★.

Aberdour
Lodging

Hawkcraig House. This old ferryman's house offers an interesting accommodation option not only for Fife and Angus, but also for Edinburgh, only 30 minutes away by road or rail. The historic house is set on the waterfront with lovely views of a serene stretch of coast— an ideal place to escape the noisy bustle of cities. Accommodation is bed-and-breakfast with the option for evening meals (the hostess offers a Taste of Scotland menu). *Hawkcraig Point, Fife KY3 OTZ, tel. 01383/860335. 2 rooms, 1 with bath, 1 with shower. No credit cards. Open Feb.–Nov.* $

Anstruther   **The Cellar.** Specializing in fish, but offering a selection of Scottish
Dining   beef and lamb as well, the Cellar is devoted to serving top-quality
★   ingredients cooked simply to preserve all the natural flavor. The crayfish-and-mussel bisque is famous, and the wine list reflects high standards. Entered through a small courtyard, the restaurant is charmingly furnished in an unpretentious, old-fashioned style. It is popular with the locals, and its fame is spreading quickly. Reservations are essential, but you still stand a better chance of getting a table here more quickly than at the Peat Inn (*see below*). *24 E. Green St., Anstruther, Fife, tel. 01333/310378. Reservations required. Dress: casual. AE, MC, V.* $$

Ceres   **The Peat Inn.** This popular inn and eatery is best known for its out-
Dining and   standing restaurant, generally considered one of the finest in Scot-
Lodging   land. Mouth-watering entrées like pigeon in pastry with wild
★   mushrooms justify the high prices charged for dinner; lunch is slightly cheaper, but for either you may have to book well in advance. In a detached building there are eight comfortable double suites, making the inn into a French-style restaurant with rooms. *Junction of B940 and B941, 5 mi southwest of St. Andrews, tel. 01334/840206, fax 01334/840530. 8 rooms with bath. Facilities: restaurant (reservations required), bar. AE, MC, V. Closed Mon. and Sun. and 2 wks in Jan.* $$$$

Dundee   **Angus Thistle Hotel.** In the center of Dundee, this hotel offers pleas-
Dining and   ant views extending in all directions, especially from rooms on the
Lodging   higher floors. Some suites have four-poster beds, whirlpool baths, and private sitting rooms. The decor is modern throughout. The hotel's restaurant serves adequate meals, drawn mostly from the beef and fish categories. *101 Marketgait, Dundee DD1 1QT, tel. 01382/26874, fax 01382/22564. 58 rooms with bath. Facilities: restaurant, bar. AE, DC, MC, V.* $–$$

Forfar   **Forester's Seat.** On a hillside just outside Forfar, Forester's is an airy,
Dining   oak-furnished conservatory-style restaurant serving a hearty Scottish menu—steaks, lamb, and salmon appear in various guises, with plentiful supplies of vegetables and salad. It's not haute cuisine, but the food is appetizing and the welcome friendly. Do not be alarmed by the many birds of prey and other wildlife gazing down at you from the rafters: They are all stuffed! Afterwards, there is a garden center, craft shop, and winery to explore. *Forester's Centre, Arbroath Rd., Forfar, tel. 01307/818786. Reservations advised. Dress: casual. MC, V.* $–$$

★   **The Drovers Inn.** Set in the heart of the Angus farmlands, the Drovers is a rare find in Scotland, having more of the feeling of an English country pub. Plain but friendly surroundings, decorated with old farm implements and historic photographs, are the setting for simple bar food, homemade pies, and nourishing soups. It's a popular place with locals; on weekends it's best to make reservations, even for bar meals. *Memus, near Forfar, tel. 01307/860322. Reservations advised. Dress: casual. MC, V. Closed Wed. dinner in winter.* $

Dining and Lodging **Redroofs.** Once a cottage hospital, Redroofs is now a spacious and immaculately kept bed-and-breakfast establishment set among the green fields of Angus just a few minutes' drive from Forfar. The freshly decorated rooms are enlivened with curios from all over the world, collected by the owners on their travels. *Balgavies, by Forfar, tel. 01307/830303. 3 rooms, 1 with shower. No credit cards.* $

Royal Hotel. In the center of Forfar, this former coaching inn has been fully modernized and has a leisure complex with swimming pool, gymnasium, and roof garden. The bedrooms are well equipped, though some in the most modern part of the hotel are rather small. All have dark wood, Victorian reproduction furniture and striped burgundy-and-gold easy chairs set off by pink and floral fabrics. The public rooms have retained their 19th-century charm. This hotel provides an attractive base for exploring or golfing. *Castle St., Forfar, Angus DD8 3AE, tel. and fax 01307/462691. 19 rooms with bath. Facilities: 2 restaurants, leisure complex. AE, DC, MC, V.* $

St. Andrews Dining and Lodging **Rufflets Country House Hotel.** This ivy-bedecked country house just outside St. Andrews is surrounded by 10 acres of formal and informal gardens. All the rooms are attractively decorated and comfortable, with all the amenities one would expect of a top-class hotel, but at a moderate price. Dinner is served in the roomy Garden Restaurant, famous for its use of local produce to create memorable Scottish dishes. Recommended are the Tay salmon and fillet of Aberdeen Angus beef. *Strathkinness Low Rd., St. Andrews, Fife KY16 9TX, tel. 01334/472594, fax 01334/478703. 26 rooms with bath. Facilities: restaurant, bar. AE, DC, MC, V.* $$–$$$$

The Grange Inn. On a breezy hilltop overlooking St. Andrews, the Grange Inn offers an attractive blend of old-fashioned charm with polished brass, low lights, and open fires. The commendable restaurant draws on seasonal local produce—haddock, salmon from the River Tay, venison from Perthshire—for its creative weekly menus. Try the gravadlax with sweet dill mustard. Two guest rooms are plain and on the small side, but they're reasonably comfortable (and within stumbling distance of the inn's cozy pub). *Grange Rd., St. Andrews, Fife KY16 8LJ, tel. 01334/472670. 2 rooms with bath. Reservations advised. Dress: smart but casual. AE, DC, MC, V.* $–$$

University of St. Andrews. For accommodation within walking distance of all the town's attractions, it's hard to better the university for value and convenience. Room sizes—mainly singles—vary from adequate in the new building to happily spacious in the old building. The newer rooms have private bathrooms (all rooms come equipped with sinks), and all have access to a restaurant, bar, lounge, TV room, and laundry facilities. *79 North St., tel. 01334/477641, fax 01334/477922. 350 rooms, 150 with shower. MC, V. Open late June–late Sept.* $

The Arts and Nightlife

The Arts

Theater **Byre Theatre** (Abbey St., St. Andrews, tel. 01334/476288) has a resident repertory company that performs during the summer months.

Dundee Repertory Theatre (Tay Sq., Dundee, tel. 01382/23530). This award-winning complex, which includes an exhibition gallery, is home to a resident theater group, as well as a dance company. Both offer diverse programs.

Little Theatre (Victoria Rd., Dundee, tel. 01382/25835) presents a wide variety of performances, especially modern theatrical works by local and visiting groups.

Whitehall Theatre (Wellfield St., Dundee, tel. 01382/23141) offers a variety of choices, including Scottish shows, light opera, and variety and musical entertainments.

Music **Bonar Hall** (Park Pl., Dundee, tel. 01382/29450).

Caird Hall (City Sq., Dundee, tel. 01382/23141, ext. 4288) is one of Scotland's finest concert halls.

Film **Cannon Film Centre** (Seagate, Dundee, tel. 01382/25247).

Odeon Film Centre (Stacks Leisure Park, Dundee, tel. 01382/ 400855).

Steps Film Theatre (Wellgate Centre, Dundee, tel. 01382/24938).

Nightlife

Discos Dundee has about 10 discos in and around the city, including **De Sthils** (S. Ward Rd., Dundee, tel. 01382/200066), **Fat Sam's Disco** (31 S. Ward Rd., Dundee, tel. 01382/26836), and **The Venue** (Stacks Leisure Park, Dundee, tel. 01382/400515). Brechin offers **Flicks** (High St., tel. 01356/24313), while Arbroath dances at **Club Metro** (Queen's Dr., tel. 01241/72338).

Folk Music The following establishments occasionally offer ceilidhs and/or evening performances of traditional folk music: **Royal Jubilee Arms Hotel** (Dykehead, Cortachy, Angus, tel. 015754/381) has a regular Thursday folk night, while **West Port Bar** (Henderson's Wynd, Dundee, tel. 01382/200993) offers folk music on most Mondays—phone to confirm.

Pubs In St. Andrews, **Bert's Bar** (South St.) is a spartan, no-nonsense drinking den where leathery old men like to swill pints and swap stories. The crowd is quite friendly, and the decor—even down to the black-and-white television and pickled eggs—is decidedly Scottish. **Chariots** (The Scores), located inside the Scores Hotel, is popular with an older but no less lively crowd of locals. With open fires and dark wood paneling, the **Grange Inn** (*see* St. Andrews Dining and Lodging, *above*) has a pleasant old-style, traditional feel, not to mention an excellent food menu. In Anstruther, the **Dreel Tavern** (High St.) is a 16th-century coaching inn famous for its hand-drawn ales (no gas-powered autopumps here). In Arbroath, seek out the **Foundry Inn** (E. Mary St.), another spartan bar frequented by locals, which is enlivened by impromptu music sessions: Customers bring along their fiddles and accordians and all join in.

8 Aberdeen and the Northeast

By Gilbert Summers

Because of its geographic isolation, Aberdeen has, throughout its history, been a fairly autonomous place. Even now, it is still perceived by many inhabitants of the United Kingdom as lying almost out of reach in the north. In reality, this northeastern locale is only 90 minutes flying time from London or—thanks to recent road improvements—a little more than two hours by car from Edinburgh.

In the 18th century, local granite quarrying produced a durable silver stone that would be used to build the Aberdonian structures of the Victorian era. Thus granite was used boldly—in glittering blocks, spires, columns, and parapets—to build Aberdeen. Downtown Aberdeen remains one of the United Kingdom's most distinctive urban environments, although some would say it depends on the weather and the brightness of the day. The mica chips embedded in the rock are a million mirrors in sunshine. In rain and heavy clouds, however, their sparkle is snuffed out.

The North Sea has always been an important feature of Aberdeen: In the 1850s, the city was famed for its fast clippers, sleek sailing ships that raced to India for cargoes of tea. In the late-1960s, the course of Aberdeen's history was unequivocally altered when oil and gas were discovered in the North Sea. Aberdeen at first seemed destined to become an oil-rich boomtown, and throughout the 1970s the city was overcome by new shops, new office blocks, new hotels, new industries, and new attitudes. Fortunately, some innate local caution has helped the city to retain a sense of perspective and prevented it from selling out entirely.

Yet even if Aberdeen, the country's third-largest city after Glasgow and Edinburgh, vanished from the map of Scotland, an extensive portion of the Northeast would still be worth exploring. Aberdeen's hinterland is now called, for administrative purposes, Grampian, which encompasses the old counties of Aberdeenshire, Kincardineshire to the south, and, hanging from the Moray Firth coast to the north, Banffshire and Morayshire.

Grampian's chief scenic attraction lies in the gradual transition from high mountain plateau—by a series of gentle steps through hill, forest, and farmland—to a coastline where the word *unadulterated* truly applies. The Grampian coastline includes some of the United Kingdom's most perfect wild shorelines, both sandy and high cliff. The Grampian Mountains to the west contain some of the highest ground in the United Kingdom, in the area of the Cairngorms. But the Grampian hills have also shaped the character of the folk who live in the Northeast. In earlier times, the massif made communication with the south somewhat difficult. As a result, native Northeasterners still speak the richest Lowland Scottish (*not* Gaelic, which is an entirely different language).

Essential Information

Important Addresses and Numbers

Tourist Information

The **City of Aberdeen Tourist Board** (St. Nicholas House, Broad St., Aberdeen, tel. 01224/632727, fax 01224/620415) provides information on rental cars, tour tickets, and Rail Rovers and sells maps, souvenirs, and tour publications. In fact, this tourist information center supplies information on all Scotland's Northeast. The Aberdeen Tourist Board also has a currency exchange.

The other area tourist boards covering the region include: **Banff and Buchan Tourist Board** (Collie Lodge, Banff, tel. 01261/812419, fax 01261/815807), **Gordon District Tourist Board** (St. Nicholas House, Broad St., Aberdeen, tel. 01224/632727, fax. 01224/620415), and **Kincardine and Deeside Tourist Board** (Bridge St., Banchory, tel. 01330/822066, fax. 01330/825126). Other tourist board information centers in the region include **Aboyne–Kincardine and Deeside** (information caravan, Ballater Rd. Car Park, tel. 013398/86060), **Alford–Gordon District** (information center, Railway Museum, Station Yard, tel. 019755/62052), **Ballater** (information center, Station Sq., tel. 013397/55306), **Ellon** (information caravan, Market St. Car Park, tel. 01358/720730), **Huntly** (information center, 7a The Square, tel. 01466/792255), **Inverurie** (information center, Town Hall, Market Place, tel. 01467/620600), and **Banff–Banff and Buchan** (Collie Lodge, Banff, tel. 01261/812419, fax 01261/815807).

In **Elgin** contact the **Moray Tourist Board** (Information Center, 17 High St., tel. 01343/543388, fax 01343/552982). In the Moray District, seasonal offices open generally from Easter through the end of September are found in Buckie, Cullen, Dufftown, Forres, Keith, Lossiemouth, and Tomintoul.

Emergencies For fire, police, or ambulance, dial 999 from any telephone. No coins are needed for emergency calls made from public telephone booths.

Grampian Police (Force Headquarters, Queen St., Aberdeen, tel. 01224/639111). There is a lost property office here.
Aberdeen Royal Infirmary (Accident and Emergency Department, Foresterhill, Aberdeen, tel. 01224/681818).
Dr. Gray's Hospital, Elgin (Accident and Emergency Department, at end of High St. on A96, tel. 01343/543131, ext. 77310.

Doctors and Dentists The **Grampian Health Board** (Primary Care Department, Woolmanhill, tel. 01224/681818, ext. 55537) can help you find a doctor or dentist.

Late-Night Pharmacies The following Aberdeen pharmacies keep longer hours than most:

Anderson Pharmacy (4 Union Grove, tel. 01224/587148) and **Boots the Chemists Ltd.** (Bon Accord Centre, George St., tel. 01224/626080). There also is an in-store pharmacist at **Safeway Food Store** (215 King St., tel. 01224/624398).
Notices on pharmacy doors will guide you to the nearest open pharmacy at any given time. The police can provide assistance in an emergency.

Arriving and Departing by Plane

Airport and Airlines Aberdeen's airport—serving both international and domestic flights—is in Dyce, 7 miles west of the city center on the A96 (Inverness). The terminal building is modern (expanded in recent years because of Dyce's prominent role in North Sea oil-rig communications) and generally uncrowded.

Airlines linking Aberdeen with Europe include **Air U.K.,** with flights to Amsterdam (the Netherlands), Paris (France), and Bergen and Stavanger (Norway); **SAS (Scandinavian Airlines),** serving Copenhagen (Denmark) and Stavanger; and **Business Air,** with flights to Esbjerg (Denmark). An extensive network of domestic flights linking Aberdeen with most major U.K. airports is operated by **Air U.K., British Airways, Business Air,** and **Gill Air.** Consult the individual airlines or your travel agent for arrival and departure times (airport information desk, tel. 01224/722331). Also worth noting is the direct

Amsterdam–Aberdeen link enabling transatlantic passengers to visit Scotland's northeast by first flying from the United States to Amsterdam and then flying on to Aberdeen with Air U.K.; this can actually be faster than traveling to Aberdeen from other parts of Scotland or England.

Between the Airport and City Center
By Bus

Grampian Transport's number 27 bus operates between the airport terminal and Union Street in the center of Aberdeen. Buses (exact fare £1.25) run every 40 minutes, and the journey time is approximately 40 minutes.

By Train

For those interested in train service to the airport, Dyce is on **Scotrail's** Inverness–Aberdeen route. The rail station is a short taxi ride from the terminal building. The ride by rail into Aberdeen from the airport takes 12 minutes. Trains run approximately every 90 minutes (more frequently at peak times, less frequently in the middle of the day). If you are intending to visit the western part of the area first, it is possible to travel northwest, away from Aberdeen, by rail direct to Elgin via Inverurie, Insch, Huntly, and Keith.

By Rental Car

The following car rental firms have desks at Aberdeen Airport: **Avis** (tel. 01224/722282), **Europcar** (tel. 01224/770770), and **Hertz** (tel. 01224/722373). The drive to the center of Aberdeen is very easy via the A96 (which can be busy in the rush hour).

Arriving and Departing by Car, Train, and Bus

By Car

It is now possible to travel from Glasgow and Edinburgh to Aberdeen on a continuous stretch of the A90/M90, a fairly scenic route that runs up Strathmore, with a fine hill view to the west. The coastal route, the A92, is a more leisurely alternative, with its interesting coastal resorts and fishing villages. The most scenic route, however, is probably the A93 from Perth, north to Blairgowrie and into Glen Shee. The A93 then goes over the Cairnwell Pass, the highest main road in the United Kingdom. (This route is not recommended in the winter months when snow can make driving over high ground difficult.)

By Train

Travelers can reach Aberdeen directly from Edinburgh (2½ hours), Glasgow (3 hours), and Inverness (2½ hours). See ScotRail timetable for full details. There are also London–Aberdeen routes that go through Edinburgh and the east-coast main line. Both Motorail and sleeper service are available.

By Bus

Long-distance coach service operates to and from most parts of Scotland, England, and Wales. Main operators include **Scottish Citylink** (Aberdeen bus station, tel. 01224/212307) and **National Express** (tel. 01738/33481).

By Ferry

There is a ferry service between Aberdeen, Lerwick (Shetland), and Bergen (Norway), which means that it is possible to travel from Norway to Aberdeen by boat. It is operated by Smyril Line P&O Ferries (contact via Box 5, Jamieson's Quay, Aberdeen, tel. 01224/572615, fax 01224/574411) and is subject to annual review; if you plan to use this route, check carefully that the service will be running.

Getting Around

Aberdeen is not a large city, and its center is Union Street, the main throughfare running east–west. Anderson Drive is an efficient ring road on the western side of the city; inexperienced drivers should be extra careful on its many traffic circles. In general, road signs are clear and legible, and parking near the center of Aberdeen is no worse than in any other U.K. city.

By Car Car rental firms in Aberdeen include **Arnold Clark** (tel. 01224/ 248842), **Budget Rent a Car** (tel. 01224/488770), **Europcar** (tel. 01224/631199), **Alamo** (tel. 01224/770955), **Mitchell Self-Drive** (tel. 01224/642642), **Watson's Self-Drive** (tel. 01224/625625), and **Kenning** (tel. 01224/571445). Street maps are available from the tourist-information center or from newsagents and booksellers.

By Bus **Grampian Transport** operates services throughout the city. There is an inquiry kiosk on St. Nicholas Street, outside Marks and Spencers department store, and timetables are available at the kiosk or from the tourist information center at St. Nicholas House nearby.

By Taxi Taxi stands can be found throughout the center of Aberdeen: along Union Street, at the railway station at Guild Street, at Back Wynd, and at Regent Quay. Taxis are mostly black, though variations in beige, maroon, or white exist.

Guided Tours

Orientation City tours are available on most days between June and mid-September. Contact **Grampian Transport** (tel. 01224/637047). **Grampian Coaches** (operated by Grampian Transport), **Bluebird Northern** (tel. 01224/212266), and **McIntyre Coaches** (tel. 01224/493112) all operate tours encompassing the Northeast coastline and countryside. Some of the tours are of general interest, others are based on one of the area's various trails: Malt Whisky, Coastal, Castle, or Royal.

Personal The **Scottish Tourist Guides Association** (contact Mrs. Anne Sin-
Guides clair, 32 Henderson Dr., Skene, Aberdeen AB32 6RA, tel. 01224/741314, fax 01224/644822) can supply experienced personal guides, including foreign-language-speaking guides if necessary.

The following firms offer chauffeur-driven limousines to take clients on tailor-made tours: **Guy Salmon Chauffeur Drive** (tel. 01764/663556) and **Scotland Scene Ltd.** (tel. 01343/541468).

Walking Tours The **Scottish Tourist Guides Association** (*see above*) organizes an "Old Aberdeen" walk during the summer months. **Hiking and Biking Scotland** (tel. 01467/643441 or in the United States 800/548–6375) organizes walking and cycling tours to various parts of Scotland's Northeast, including Royal Deeside, Castle Country, and the coastline.

Exploring Aberdeen and the Northeast

A major attraction in the Northeast is its wealth of castles. There are so many that one part of the area, Gordon District, has assembled them into a Castle Trail, leading you to fortresses like the ruined medieval Kildrummy Castle, which once controlled the strategic routes through the valley of the River Don. Later work, such as Craigievar, a narrow-turreted castle resembling an illustration from a fairy-tale book, reflects the changing times of the 17th century, when defense became less of a priority. Later still, grand mansions, such as Haddo House, with its symmetrical facade and elegant interiors, surrender any defensive need entirely and instead make statements about their owner's status and power. Nowhere else in Scotland offers such an eclectic selection of castles. The Northeast offers visitors an opportunity to touch the fabric of Scotland's story, with the added advantage that the area is slightly off the beaten path.

As a visitor to Scotland, you can be sure of one thing: No matter where you are, a whisky distillery can't be far off, an assessment that would undoubtedly hold true in Morayshire. In this part of Scotland the distilling is centered in the valley of the River Spey and its tributaries. Just as the Loire in France has famous vineyards clustered around it, the Spey has famous single-malt distilleries. Instead of Muscadet, Chinon, Vouvray or Pouilly-sur-Loire, there's Glenfiddich, Glen Grant, Tamdhu, or Tamnavulin. As well as being sweeter and less peaty than some of the island malts, eastern or Speyside malts have the further advantage of having generally easier-to-pronounce brand names.

Orientation

Union Street is the center of Aberdeen, and through traffic from the north and northwest is signposted through Aberdeen beyond its east end and to the harbor. Through traffic from the south is signposted around Anderson Drive, from where all the main routes into the Grampian hinterland are also signposted: for example, the Deeside and Donside routes, the main Inverness A96, as well as coastal routes to the north. Outside Aberdeen, the Castle and Whisky trails are generally well marked.

Highlights for First-Time Visitors

Craigievar Castle (*see* Tour 3)
Cullen (*see* Tour 4)
Duthie Park (*see* What to See and Do with Children)
Elgin Cathedral (*see* Tour 4)
Glen Muick (*see* Tour 3)
Glenfiddich Distillery (*see* Tour 4)
Haddo House (*see* Off the Beaten Track)
Kildrummy Castle and Gardens (*see* Tour 3)
King's College Chapel (*see* Tour 2)
Marischal College (facade) (*see* Tour 1)
Maritime Museum (*see* Tour 1)
Upper Deeside, beyond Braemar (*see* Tour 3)

Tour 1: Aberdeen—The Silver City Center

Numbers in the margin correspond to points of interest on the Aberdeen and Royal Deeside maps.

❶ What Princes Street is to Edinburgh, Union Street is to **Aberdeen:** the central pivot of the city plan and the product of a wave of enthusiasm to rebuild the city in a contemporary style. This tour encompasses some of Aberdeen's best early-19th-century buildings. Some hints of an older Aberdeen have survived and can be noticed while touring. Conversely, this tour will also show you how today's plans are changing the face of Aberdeen, a city of handsome granite buildings that give it a silvery complexion.

Start outside the tourist information center on Broad Street. Im-
❷ mediately opposite is **Marischal College,** founded in 1593 by the earl of Marischal as a Protestant alternative to the Catholic King's College in Old Aberdeen (*see* Tour 2: A Short Excursion in Old Aber-

Aberdeen Art
Gallery, **5**
Commercial Union
Assurance building, **8**
His Majesty's
Theatre, **6**
King's College, **13**
Marischal College, **2**
Mercat Cross, **10**
Provost Ross's
House, **12**
Provost Skene's
House, **3**
Robert Burns
statue, **7**
Robert Gordon's
University, **4**
St. Machar's
Cathedral, **15**
St. Nicholas Kirk, **9**
Seaton Park, **16**
Tolbooth, **11**
Town House, **14**

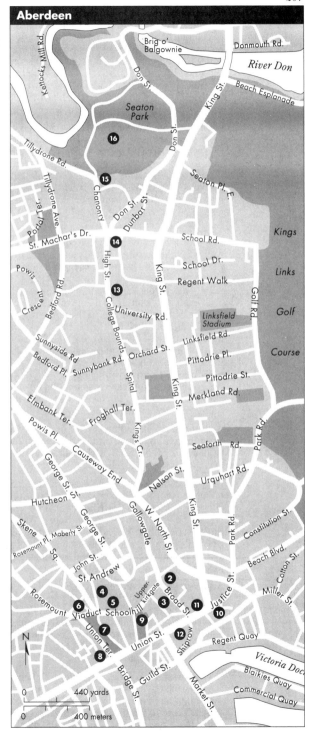

Aberdeen

deen, *below*), though the two combined to form Aberdeen University in 1860. (The earls of Marischal held the hereditary office as keepers of the king's mares.) The original university buildings on this site have undergone extensive renovations. What you see in front of you is a facade built in 1891. The spectacularly ornate work is set off by the gilded flags, and this turn-of-the-century creation is still the second-largest granite building in the world. Only the Escorial in Madrid is larger. *Broad St., tel. 01224/632727. Admission free. Museum open weekdays 10–5, Sun. 2–5.*

To find a survivor from an earlier Aberdeen, go underneath the concrete supports of St. Nicholas House (of which the tourist-information **❸** tion center is a part) to find **Provost Skene's House** (*provost* is Scottish for mayor). Formerly one of a closely packed area of town houses, Provost Skene's House, steeply gabled and rubble-built, survives in part from 1545. It was originally a domestic dwelling house and is now a museum portraying civic life, with restored furnished period rooms and a painted chapel. *Guestrow, off Broad St., tel. 01224/641086. Admission free. Open Mon.–Sat. 10–5.*

The tour then takes on a more contemporary twist, away from the well-wrought granite and the portion of a 16th-century townscape. Provost Skene's House is close to a 1960s shopping development, the St. Nicholas Centre. Go down Upperkirkgate to the lowest point, where you will see shopping malls—the **St. Nicholas Centre** on the left, the **Bon-Accord Centre** on the right. Until recent years, George Street, at the foot of the hill here, was a bustling shopping street running at right angles. But not even Aberdeen—in its far northern perch—has exempted itself from the British trend toward chain-store anonymity, and it has thus demolished traditional stonework to accommodate the chains. If you do enter the portals of the Bon-Accord Centre, you will eventually emerge at the truncated George Street. Note the spacious John Lewis Store, built in a design closely resembling a double-decker sandwich, with an illuminated filling and the crusts left on.

Although shopping is hard to resist here, try to do so for the moment and continue up Schoolhill, with its range of smaller speciality shops. Opposite is St. Nicholas Kirk, which you can examine on your way back, along Union Street.

On your right, as the slope eases off, is a complex of silver-toned buildings, in front of which stands a statue of General Charles Gordon, the military hero of Khartoum (1885). Interestingly, he is not, **❹** however, the Gordon recalled in **Robert Gordon's University** behind the statue. Built in 1731, the structure was originally called Robert Gordon's Hospital and it was used to educate poor boys. It became an independent school later and then an institute of technology, before gaining university status in 1992.

❺ Adjacent is the **Aberdeen Art Gallery,** which plays an active role in Aberdeen's cultural life and is a popular rendezvous for locals. It houses a wide-ranging collection—from the 18th century to contemporary work. The sculpture court is certainly worth seeing, with its gallery supported by columns of polished granite, each showing a different shade. *Schoolhill, tel. 01224/646333. Admission free. Open Mon.–Sat. 10–5, Thurs. 10–8, Sun. 2–5.*

Cross the street to get a better view of a library, church, and nearby theater, collectively known by all Aberdonians as Education, Salvation, and Damnation. Silvery and handsome, the **Central Library** and **St. Mark's Church** date from the last decade of the 19th century, **❻** while **His Majesty's Theatre** (1904–08) has been restored inside to its full Edwardian splendor. If you carry a camera, you can choose an angle that includes the statue of Scotland's first freedom fighter, Sir William Wallace, in the foreground, pointing majestically to Damnation. *Rosemount Viaduct in city center, box office tel. 01224/641122.*

Turning left onto Union Terrace, you will see another statue, this **❼** one of **Robert Burns** addressing a daisy. Behind Burns are the **Union Terrace Gardens,** faintly echoing Edinburgh's Princes Street Gardens in that they separate the older part of the city to the east, from the 19th-century development of Union Terrace and points westward (as well as Union Street itself). Most of the buildings on Union Terrace around the grand-looking Caledonian Hotel are late-Victorian, when exuberance and confidence in style was at its height. The results are impressive. Note for example, at the corner of Union **❽** Street, the wonderfully elaborate **Commercial Union Assurance building** (1885). Its Doric portico (plain-column extension) has been a landmark and meeting place for generations of locals. They call it the "monkey house," though few can tell you why. Perhaps the close columns resemble the bars of a cage.

Turn left onto Union Street (though there is plenty of this main street to explore should you wish to turn right). Note the smug cats seated primly on the parapet of **Union Bridge.** The bridge was built in the early years of the 19th century, as was much of Union Street. The bridge has a gentle rise—or descent, if you are traveling east— and the street is carried on a series of blind arches. The north side of Union Bridge is the most obvious reminder of the grand thoroughfare's artificial levels. Much of the original work remains.

As you make your way through the main-street crowds, you will also pass, on your left, the colonnaded facade of 1829 that screens the **❾** churchyard of **St. Nicholas Kirk** from the shopping hustle and bustle. Behind the facade is the church itself, already seen from Schoolhill. This is the Mither Kirk, the original burgh church, yet curiously it is not within the bounds of the early settlement that was located to the east, near the end of present-day Union Street. During the 12th century, the port of Aberdeen flourished and room could not be found for the church within the settlement. Its earliest features are the pillars—supporting a tower built much later—and its clerestory windows: Both date from the original 12th-century structure. St. Nicholas was divided into east and west kirks at the Reformation, followed by a substantial amount of renovation from 1741 on. Some early memorials and other works have survived. *Union St. Open weekdays 10–1.*

Arriving at the east end of Union Street you are not only within a few moments of your starting point at the tourist-information center, but also within the original old town. This is the **Castlegate.** The actual castle once stood somewhere behind the Salvation Army Citadel of 1896, an imposing baronial granite tower whose design was inspired by Balmoral Castle. Just beyond King Street is the **❿** impressive **Mercat Cross** (built in 1686 and restored in 1820), always the symbolic center of a Scottish medieval burgh. Note that along its parapet, among its 12 panels are the portraits of the Stewart **⓫** monarchs. Opposite is the handsome tower of the **Tolbooth,** dating from the 17th century. Also in sight here is the stylishly colonnaded facade of the Atheneum, built as a library, but now serving mainly as offices and eating places.

As the final reminder of this older part of Aberdeen, turn away from the Town House and head down to the left to Shiprow, once the main

⑫ road into town in bygone days. Much has been swept away and redeveloped, but one building has survived since 1593: **Provost Ross's House,** which now houses **Aberdeen's Maritime Museum,** telling the story of the city's involvement with the sea, from early inshore fisheries by way of tea clippers to the North Sea oil boom (*see* What to See and Do with Children, *below*).

Below is the harbor, which contains some fine architecture from the 18th and 19th centuries. Explore it only if time permits and you don't mind the background traffic.

Tour 2: A Short Excursion in Old Aberdeen

Old Aberdeen was once an independent burgh and lies to the north of the city, near the River Don. Although swallowed up by the expanding main city before the end of the 19th century, Old Aberdeen, which lies between **King's College** and **St. Machar's Cathedral,** still retains a certain degree of character and integrity. Reach it by taking a No. 20 bus north from a stop near Marischal College or a No. 1, 2, or 3 up King Street, off the Castlegate.

⑬ Visitors should alight in **College Bounds,** with its handsome 18th- and 19th-century houses, cobbled streets, and paved sidewalks. **King's College,** founded in 1494, can be seen, the flying (or crown) spire of its Chapel unmistakable. The structure was built around 1500, and the fact that it has survived at all was due to the zeal of the principal, who managed to defend his church against the destructive fanaticism that swept through Scotland during the Reformation, when the building was less than a century old. Today's visitor will find a renovated structure with the chapel playing an important role in university life. The tall oak screen that separates nave from choir, along with the ribbed wooden ceiling and stalls, constitutes the finest medieval wood carving to be found anywhere in Scotland.

⑭ Continuing up what is now the High Street of Old Aberdeen, you will see some restored Georgian houses, including the **Town House,** straight ahead. This Georgian work, plain and handsome, uses parts of an earlier building from 1720. Behind the Town House the modern intrusion of St. Machar's Drive destroys some of the old-town ambience, but the atmosphere is restored by a stroll down the **Chanonry,** past the elegant houses once lived in by the officials connected with the cathedral nearby. Today, they house mainly university staff. *High St. Visitor Centre (with shop and cafeteria) open Mon.–Sat. 10–5; summer, Mon.–Sat. 10–5, Sun. noon–5.*

⑮ It is said that St. Machar was sent by St. Columba to build a church on a grassy platform near the sea, where a river flowed in the shape of a shepherd's crook. This spot fitted the bill, and **St. Machar's Cathedral** was built in AD 580. However, nothing remains of the original foundation. Much of the existing building dates from the 15th and 16th centuries. The central tower collapsed in 1688, reducing the building to half its original length. The twin octagonal spires on the western towers date from the first half of the 16th century. The nave is thought to have been rebuilt in red sandstone in 1370, but the final renovation was completed in granite by the middle of the 15th century. Along with the nave ceiling, the twin spires were finished in time to take a battering in the Reformation, when the barons of the Mearns stripped the lead off the roof of St. Machar's and stole the bells. The cathedral suffered further mistreatment—including the removal of stone by Oliver Cromwell's English garrison in the 1650s—until a 19th-century restoration program restored the church to its former grandeur. *Chanonry, tel. 01224/485988. Open daily 9–5.*

⑯ Beyond St. Machar's Cathedral lies **Seaton Park,** with its spring daffodils, tall trees, and herbaceous borders boldly colored. Until 1827, the only way out of Aberdeen to the north was over the River Don on the Brig o' Balgownie, a single-arch bridge found at the far end of Seaton Park—a 15-minute walk. It dates from 1314 and is thought to have been built by Richard Cementarius, Aberdeen's first provost. After enjoying the scenery of Seaton Park, which today has restored houses at either end, you can return to the city center.

Tour 3: Royal Deeside and Castle Country

Numbers in the margin correspond to points of interest on the Royal Deeside map.

Although basically a car tour, much of this area is accessible either by public transportation or on tours from Aberdeen. Deeside, the valley running west from Aberdeen down which the River Dee flows, earned its "Royal" appellation when discovered by Queen Victoria. To this day, where royalty goes, lesser aristocracy and fast-buck millionaires from across the globe follow. In fact, it is still the aspiration of many to own a grand shooting estate on Deeside. In a sense, this yearning is understandable, since piney hill slope, purple moor, and blue river intermingle most tastefully here, as you will see from the main road. Royal Deeside's gradual scenic change adds a growing sense of excitement as the road runs deeper and deeper into the Grampians.

There are castles along the Dee and to the north. This tour rises out of the river valley to find them, returning to Aberdeen by a route illustrating this gradual geological change: uplands lapped by a tide of farms.

The first 15 miles toward Banchory by either north or south Deeside roads (leaving the city by the Bridge of Dee) have only a subtle **⑰** scenic flair. Castle hoppers can explore **Drum Castle,** an ancient foursquare tower dating from the 13th century, with later additions. Note the rounded corners of the tower, said to make battering-ram attacks more difficult. Nearby, fragments of the ancient Forest of Drum still stand, dating from the early days when Scotland was covered by great woodlands of oak and pine. *Off the A93, 10 mi west of Aberdeen, tel. 01330/811204. Admission to castle and garden: £3.50 adults, £1.80 senior citizens and children; to grounds and garden only: £1.50 adults, 80p children. Open daily, May–June 1:30–5:30, July–Aug. 11–5:30, Sept. 1:30–5:30; early Oct., weekends 1:30–5:30 (last admission 4:45). Garden of historic roses open May–early Oct., daily 10–6. Grounds open all year, 9:30–sunset.*

⑱ Perhaps of greater interest is **Crathes Castle,** roughly 4 miles west on the A93. The Burnett family had been keepers of the Forest of Drum for generations but acquired lands here by marriage and later built a new castle, completed in 1596. Crathes is in the care of the National Trust for Scotland; the trust also looks after the grand gardens, with their calculated symmetry and clipped yew hedges. Be careful not to confuse Crathes Castle, near Aberdeen, with Crathie Kirk, near Balmoral, where folk go to gaze at royalty. *Off the A93, 3¹/₂ mi east of Banchory, tel. 01330/844525. Admission: grounds only £1.80 adults, 90p senior citizens and children; castle, garden, and grounds £4 adults, £2 senior citizens and children. Castle open*

Royal Deeside

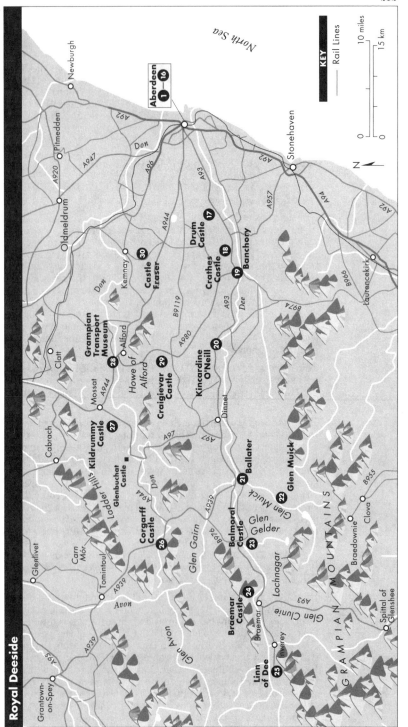

North Sea

Aberdeen
1 – 16

Newburgh

Pitmedden

Oldmeldrum

Clatt

Cabrach

Glenlivet

Grantown-on-Spey

Tomintoul

Mossat

Kemnay

Alford

30
Castle Fraser

Grampian Transport Museum
28

29
Craigievar Castle

Kildrummy Castle
27

Ladder Hills

Glenbuchat Castle

Corgarff Castle
26

Carn Mór

Braemar Castle
24

Linn of Dee
25

Inverey

Braemar

Balmoral Castle
23

Glen Gelder

Lochnagar

Glen Muick
22

Ballater
21

Dinnet

Kincardine O'Neill
20

Crathes Castle
19
Banchory

Drum Castle
18

17

Stonehaven

Laurencekirk

Spittal of Glenshee

Glen Clunie

Braedownie

Clova

GRAMPIAN MOUNTAINS

Don

Avon

Glen Avon

Glen Gairn

Glen Muick

Dee

Howe of Alford

Don

KEY

Rail Lines

10 miles

15 km

N

Easter–Oct., daily 11–5:30 (last admission 4:45). Garden and grounds open all year, 9:30–sunset.

Time Out   Sample the excellent National Trust of Scotland's home baking in Crathes Castle's **tearoom** (tel. 01330/844525).

---

⑲ **Banchory,** a few minutes west on the A93, is an immaculate place with a pinkish tinge to its granite. It is usually bustling with ice cream–eating city strollers, out on a day trip from Aberdeen. If you visit in autumn and have time to spare, drive out to the **Brig o'Feuch** ("Bridge of," then pronounce it "Fyooch" with "ch" as in loch). Here, salmon leap in season, and the fall colors and foaming waters make for an attractive scene.

If you are pressed for time, continue west on the A93, through a landscape where the mixed farmlands are confined to the valley floor, sheltered by birch thickets and blankets of dark woods. Note, ⑳ as you pass through, the ruined kirk in **Kincardine O'Neill.** Built in 1233, it was once a shelter for travelers, the last hospice before the Mounth, the name given to the massif that shuts off the south side of the Dee Valley. Beyond Banchory (and the B974), no motor roads run south until you reach Braemar, though the Mounth is crossed by a network of tracks used in former times by Scottish soldiers, invading armies (including the Romans), and cattle drovers.

There are many other intricate features to examine in the area, especially if you have the time. There's the picture-postcard bridge at **Potarch** and the **Braeloine Interpretative Centre** in Glen Tanar beyond Aboyne, which has a display on natural history, a picnic area, and walks. *Glen Tanar, tel. 013398/86072. Open daily 10–5.*

Back on the main road, look for a large granite boulder on which is carved, YOU ARE NOW ENTERING THE HIGHLANDS. You may find this piece of information superfluous, given the quality of the scenery. ㉑ Drive another 5 miles west on the A93 and you will reach **Ballater.** This quaint holiday resort, once noted for the curative properties of its local well, has profited from the proximity of the royals, nearby at Balmoral. Visitors are amused by the array of BY ROYAL APPOINT-MENT signs proudly hanging from many of its various shops (even monarchs need bakers and butchers). If you get a chance, take time to stroll around this neat community—well laid out in silver-gray masses. Note that the railway station now houses the tourist information center and a display on the former glories of this Great North of Scotland branch line, closed in the 1960s along with so many others in this country.

Ballater makes a good pausing place, and, if you can afford it, Craigendarroch is an excellent base (*see* Dining and Lodging, *below*). Nearby, visitors have the opportunity to capture the feel of the eastern Highlands—as long as they have their own transporta- ㉒ tion. Start your expedition into **Glen Muick** (pronounced "mick," Gaelic for pig) by crossing the River Dee and turning upriver on the south side, shortly after the road forks into this fine Highland glen. The native red deer are quite common throughout the Scottish Highlands, but Glen Muick is one of the very best places to see them in abundance, with herds grazing the flat valley floor. Beyond the lower glen, the prospect opens to reveal not only grazing herds, but also fine views of the battlement of cliffs edging the mountain called Lochnagar.

However, there is no public transportation into this cul-de-sac glen, and your tour or local coach service will instead take you west again,

on the A93. The enormous car park roughly 7 miles ahead is indica-
㉓ tive of the popularity of **Balmoral Castle,** the rebuilt castle modified
by Prince Albert in 1855 for his queen. Balmoral's visiting hours
depend on whether the royals are in residence. In truth, there are
more interesting and historic buildings to explore, as the only part
of the castle on view is the ballroom, with an exhibition of Royal
artifacts. *On the A93, tel. 013397/42334. Admission: £2 adults, £1.50
senior citizens, children free. Open May–July, Mon.–Sat. 10–5.*

Continuing west into Highland scenery, you can get further pine-
framed glimpses of the "steep frowning glories of dark Lochnagar,"
as it was described by the poet Byron. About 8 miles farther on the
㉔ A93 sits **Braemar Castle,** dating from the 17th century, with defensive walls later built in the plan of a pointed star. At Braemar (the
braes or slopes of the district of Mar), the standard or rebel flag was
first raised at the start of the spectacularly unsuccessful Jacobite
rebellion of 1715. Thirty years later, during the last rebellion, Braemar Castle was strengthened and garrisoned by Hanoverian (government) troops. *On the A93, at Braemar, tel. 013397/41219,
off-season tel. 013397/41224. Admission: £1.70 adults, £1.30 senior
citizens, 90p children. Open Apr.–Oct., Sat.–Thurs. 10–6.*

The village of Braemar is associated with the Braemar Highland
Gathering held every September. Although it's one of many such
events celebrated throughout Scotland, Braemar's gathering is distinguished by the presence of the royal family. Braemar also has a
tricky golf course laden with foaming waters. Erratic duffers take
note: The compassionate course managers have installed, near the
water, poles with little nets on the end for those occasional shots that
may go awry.

Although the main A93 slinks off to the south from Braemar, a little
unmarked road will take you farther west into the hilly heartlands.
In fact, even if you do not have your own car, you can still explore
the area by catching the post bus that leaves from Braemar Post
Office once a day. The road offers you delectable views over the
winding river Dee and the blue hills before passing through the tiny
㉕ hamlet of Inverey and crossing a bridge at the **Linn of Dee.** *Linn* is
a Scots word meaning rocky narrows, and the river's rocky gash
here is deep and roaring. Park beyond the bridge and walk back to
admire the sylvan setting of the river and woodland, replete with
bending larch bows and deep, tranquil pools with salmon glinting in
them.

Now return to Braemar, retracing the route as far as Balmoral.
From Balmoral, there is an interesting way out of Royal Deeside by
car. Look for a narrow road going north, signposted B976. Be careful
on the first twisting mile through the trees. Soon you will emerge
from scattered pines into the open moor in upland Aberdeenshire.
Behind is the massif of Lochnagar again, and to the west are snow-
tipped domes of the big Cairngorms. Roll down to a bridge and go
left on the A939, which comes in from Ballater. Another high moor
section follows: As the road leaves the scattered buildings by the
bridge, see if you can spot the roadside inscription to the company
of soldiers who built the A939 in the 18th century.

The soldiers paved their military highway roughly 12 miles north
㉖ to **Corgarff Castle,** a lonely tower house with another star-shaped
defensive wall—a curious replica of Braemar Castle. To get there,
you will find it signposted left at the next junction. Corgarff was
built as a hunting seat for the earls of Mar in the 16th century. After
an eventful history that included the wife of a later laird being

burned alive in a family dispute, the castle ended its career as a garrison for Hanoverian troops. The troops also had the responsibility of trying to prevent illegal whisky distilling, at one time a popular hobby in these parts. *Off A939, tel. 0131/244–3101. Admission: £2 adults, £1.25 senior citizens, 75p children. Open Apr.–Sept., Mon.–Sat. 9:30–6, Sun. 2–6.*

If you return south to the A939/A944 junction and then make a left onto the A944, the excellent castle signposting will tell you that you are on **Gordon District's Castle Trail.** The A944 meanders along the River Don to the village of Strathdon, where a great mound by the roadside—on the left—turns out to be a *motte,* or the base of a wooden castle, built in the late 12th century. Surviving mottes are significant in terms of confirming the history of Scottish castles, but it is difficult for visitors to become enthusiastic about a great grassed-over heap, no matter what its historic content.

From here, a sign points to **Glenbuchat Castle,** a plain Z-plan tower house; about 12 miles to the northeast you will encounter the more ❷⓻ interesting **Kildrummy Castle.** Visitors can enjoy the ruins of the castle itself, the gardens behind it, and the country house–style Kildrummy Castle Hotel. Kildrummy is significant because of its age (13th century) and because it has ties to the mainstream medieval traditions of European castle building. It shares features with Harlech and Caernarvon in Wales, as well as with continental sites, such as Château de Coucy near Laon, France. Kildrummy had undergone several expansions at the hands of English King Edward I when, in 1306, back in Scottish hands, the castle was besieged by King Edward I's son. The defenders were betrayed by a certain Osbarn the Smith, who had been promised a large amount of gold by the English besieging forces. They gave it to him after the castle fell, pouring it molten down his throat, or so the ghoulish story goes. Kildrummy's prominence came to an end after the collapse of the 1715 Jacobite uprising. It had been the rebel headquarters and was consequently dismantled. *Tel. 0131/244–3101. Admission: £1.50 adults, £1 senior citizens, 75p children. Open Apr.–Sept., Mon.–Sat. 9:30–6, Sun. 2–6; Oct.–Mar., Sat. 9:30–4, Sun. 2–4.*

The **garden** behind the castle—with a separate entrance from the main road—is built in what was the original quarry for the castle. This sheltered bowl within the woodlands has a broad range of shrubs and alpine plants and a notable water garden. If the weather is pleasant, it makes for a nice place to pause and plan the next stage of your journey. *A97, off the A944, Aberdeenshire, tel. 019755/71264 or 019755/71277. Admission: £1.70 adults, 50p children. Open Apr.–Oct., daily 10–5 (telephone to confirm opening times late in the season).*

Time Out The **Mossat Shop,** 4 miles past Kildrummy, at the junction of the A97 and the A944, is another possible pit stop for tea or some light shopping. If you have more time, however, then the **village hall** in the tiny rural community of **Clatt,** 7 miles northeast just off the A97, has a savory reputation for its home baking. Local ladies bake the delicious breads and cakes at this cooperatively run establishment (weekends only). People come from miles around to sample the results. There is also a produce and crafts shop.

If you wish to forego Clatt and its cream cakes, make a right onto the A944 for Alford (pronounced *Ah*-furd) at the A97/A944 junction. Alford, a plain and sturdy settlement in the Howe (Hollow) of Alford, gives those visitors who have grown somewhat weary from

28 castle hopping a break: It has a museum instead. The **Grampian Transport Museum** specializes in road-based means of locomotion. One of its more unusual exhibits is the *Craigievar Express,* a steam-driven creation invented by the local postman to deliver mail more efficiently. *Alford, tel. 019755/62292. Admission: £2.50 adults, £1.80 senior citizens, 80p children, £5.50 family ticket. Open Apr.–Oct., daily 10–5.*

29 Your return to Aberdeen leads you to two of the finest castles on the trail. The first is **Craigievar.** Located about 5 miles to the south on the A980, this historic structure represents one of the finest traditions of local castle building. It also has the advantage of having survived intact, much as the stonemasons left it in 1626, with its pepper-pot turrets and towers, the whole slender shape covered in a pink-cream pastel. It was built in relatively peaceful times by William Forbes, a successful merchant in trade with the Baltic Sea ports (hence he was also known as Danzig Willie). Centuries of care and wise stewardship have ensured that the experience proffered today's visitor is as authentic as possible. *On the A980, tel. 013398/83635. Admission: £5 adults, £2.50 senior citizens and children. Open May–Sept., daily 1:30–5:30 (last admission 4:45). Grounds open all year 9:30–sunset.*

30 Your return to Aberdeen could be by way of **Castle Fraser,** a massive structure—in fact, it is the largest of the castles of Mar. While this building shows a variety of styles reflecting the taste of previous owners from the 15th to the 19th centuries, its design is typical of the cavalcade of castles that exist here in the Northeast. It has the further advantages of a walled garden, a picnic area, and a tearoom. *3 mi south of Kemnay off the A944, tel. 01330/833463. Admission: £3.50 adults, £1.80 senior citizens and children. Open May, June, and Sept., daily 1:30–5:30; July and Aug., daily 11–5:30; early Oct., weekends 1:30–5:30 (last admission 5). Gardens and grounds open all year 9:30–6 (or sunset if earlier).*

From Castle Fraser, your quickest route back to the city is to turn south to join the A944 or north to the A96.

Tour 4: The Northeast

Numbers in the margin correspond to points of interest on the Northeast map.

Tour 3 covered the immediate hinterland of Aberdeen. This tour ranges more widely to sample the seaboard, including some of the best-preserved coastal scenery in Scotland. The tour also meanders inland, to revisit briefly the malt-whisky theme. Speyside—the valley or strath of the River Spey—is famed for its whisky distilleries, which it promotes in yet another signposted trail. Whisky distilling is not an intrinsically spectacular process. It involves pure water, malted barley, and sometimes peat smoke, then a lot of bubbling and fermentation, all of which causes a range of extremely odd smells. The end result is a prestigious product with a fascinating range of flavors that you either enjoy immensely or not at all.

On this tour, instead of assiduously following the whisky trail, we will dip into it and blend it with some other aspects of the lower end of Speyside—the old county of Moray, now part of Grampian. Whisky notwithstanding, Moray's scenic qualities, low rainfall, and other reassuring weather statistics are worth remembering when you plan your route.

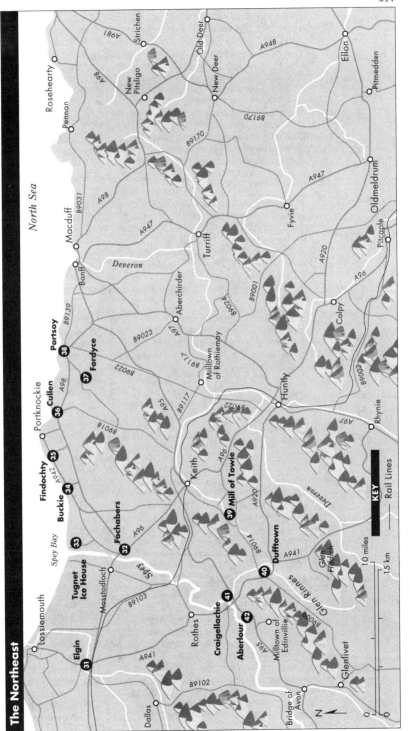

Because of its convenient transport links to both the coast and the countryside, this tour starts from **Elgin.** As the center of the fertile Laigh (low-lying lands) of Moray, it has been of local importance for centuries. Like Aberdeen, it is self-supporting and previously remote, sheltered by great hills to the south and lying between two major rivers, the Spey and the Findhorn. Beginning in the 13th century, Elgin became an important religious center, a cathedral city with a walled town growing up around the cathedral and adjacent to the original settlement. Left in peace for at least some of its history, Elgin prospered and became, by the early 18th century, a mini-Edinburgh of the north and a place where country gentlemen came to spend the winter. It even echoed Edinburgh in the widescale reconstruction of the early 19th century: Much of the old town was swept away in a wave of rebuilding, giving Elgin the fine neoclassical buildings that survive today.

The old shape of the town survived almost intact until this century, when it succumbed to the modern madness of demolishing great swaths of buildings for the sake of better traffic flow. It suffered from its position on the Aberdeen–Inverness main road. However, the central main street plan and some of the older little streets and wynds (alleyways) remain. Visitors can also recall Elgin's past by observing the arcaded shop fronts—some of which date from the late-17th century—that give the main shopping street its gruffy, aged appeal.

At the center of town, the most conspicuous, positively unavoidable building is **St. Giles Church,** which divides High Street. The grand foursquare building built in 1828 exhibits the style known as Greek Revival: Note the columns; the pilasters (half-columns attached to the walls); and the top of the spire, surmounted by a representation of the Lysicrates Monument. Farther east, past the arcaded shops, you can see the **Little Cross** (17th century), which marked the boundary between the town and the cathedral grounds.

Cooper Park, located a short distance to the southeast across the modern bypass road, is home to a magnificent ruin, the cathedral consecrated in 1224. The cathedral's eventful story included devastation by fire: a 1390 act of retaliation by Alexander Stewart, the Wolf of Badenoch. The illegitimate son-turned-bandit of King David II had sought revenge for his being excommunicated by the bishop of Moray. The cathedral was rebuilt but finally fell into disuse after the Reformation in 1560. By 1567, the highest authority in the land at the time, the regent earl of Moray, had stripped the lead from the roof to pay for his army. Thus ended the career of the religious seat known as the Lamp of the North. Some traces of the cathedral settlement survive, although they have been drastically altered: the gateway Pann's Port and the Bishop's Palace.

Take the A96 east to **Fochabers.** Just before reaching it, you will see the works of a major local employer, Baxters of Fochabers, a family-run firm with an international reputation for fine foods. From Tokyo to New York, upmarket stores stock their soups, jams, chutneys, and other gourmet products—all of which are made here, close to the River Spey. Factory tours yield glimpses of impeccably attired staff stirring great vats of boiling marmalade and other concoctions. The **Baxters Visitors Centre** also offers a video presentation, a re-creation of the Baxters' first grocery shop, as well as a real shop and a restaurant offering an assortment of delectables. *1 mi west of Fochabers on the A96, tel. 01343/820–393. Admission free. Open weekdays 9:30–5, weekends 10–5. Guided tours on* *weekdays only, Mon.–Thurs. 10–4, Fri. 10–2; no tours during factory holiday weeks in April (1 wk), June (2 wks), and Aug. (1 wk).*

After traversing the Spey bridge and entering Fochabers, visitors will find this community has the symmetrical village green typical of the planned village. Perhaps this pleasing, mellow ambience attracts the extraordinary range of antiques dealers in Fochabers, with shops' wares ranging from near-junk to designer pieces. Through one of these shops you can enter the **Fochabers Folk Museum,** which offers an excellent display of rural items in a converted church, ranging from carts and carriages to interesting farm implements. *Tel. 01343/820362. Admission: 60p adults, 40p senior citizens and children, £1.50 family ticket. Open winter, daily 9:30–1 and 2–5; summer, daily 9:30–1 and 2–6.*

If you have your own car, you may care to divert up the road that runs south directly opposite the museum. Leaving the houses behind for well-hedged country lanes, you will discover a Forestry Commission sign to the **Earth Pillars.** These curious eroded sandstone pillars are framed by tall-trunked pines and overlook a wide prospect of the lower Spey Valley. Another option for motorists is to take the B9108 from Fochabers down to the mouth of the River Spey. Here, by a storm beach with a high stone swell of smooth-washed pebbles, the river enters the sea. Nearby is the **Tugnet Ice House,** once the centerpiece of the local salmon fishing industry. Before the days of mechanical refrigeration, the salmon were stored in icy chambers. The ice was gathered in the winter and lasted in its insulated cellars throughout the fishing season. Now a museum housed in the Ice House tells the story. *Spey Bay, 5 mi west of Buckie, tel. 01309/673701. Admission free. Open May–Sept., daily 10–4.*

③③

From Fochabers, take the A98 east for about 3 miles before making a left on the A942, which runs closer to the coast through the fishing port of **Buckie** and its satellite villages. This outpost is gray and workaday, with plenty of Victorian architecture. But don't miss its latest acquisition: the **Buckie Drifter** maritime museum. Housed in specially designed new premises that look like an old drifter, this is a hands-on visitor center that tells the story of the herring industry and Buckie's development as a herring port. Upstairs, you enter a 1920s quayside scene, with a replica steam drifter that you can board, barrels you can pack with herring, and a cooper at work. *Freuchny Rd., off Commercial Rd., tel. 01542/834646. Admission: £2.50 adults, £1.60 senior citizens and children, £7 family ticket. Open Apr.–Oct., Mon.–Sat. 10–6, Sun. 11–5 (shop and restaurant open until 7 daily).* The **Peter Anson Gallery** shows a selection of watercolor works also related to the development of the fishing industry. *Cluny Pl., tel. 01309/673701. Admission free. Open weekdays 10–8, Sat. 10–12.*

③④

Visitors will find a string of other fishing communities down by the shore, running east. These salty little villages paint a colorful scene with their gable-ended houses and fishing nets set out to dry amid the rocky shoreline.

③⑤ The residents of **Findochty**—located about 2 miles east of Buckie on the A942—are known for their fastidiousness and creativity in painting their fisher-houses, taking the fine art of housepainting to a new level. Some residents even paint the mortar between the stonework a different color. The small town also has a harbor with a faint echo of the Mediterranean about it.

③⑥ You will see some wonderfully painted homes again at **Cullen,** a few miles from Findochty on the A98, in the old fishermen's town below the railway viaduct. But the real attractions of this little resort are its white-sand beach and the fine view west toward the Bowfiddle Rock. A stroll along the beach reveals the shape of the fishing settlement below and planned town above. Cullen and its little shops are far enough away from major town superstores to survive on local, intermittent trade; most unusual for a town of its size, Cullen has a full range of speciality shops—ironmongers, butchers, a baker, a haberdasher, and a locally famous ice-cream shop among them.

Time Out   **The Seafield Arms,** built as a coaching inn for the new town, serves a friendly pub lunch.

If Cullen represents a neat and planned town, contrast it with the much more ancient layout of **Portsoy,** about 6 miles east along the coast. But travelers with their own means of transportation can make another discovery before they even reach Portsoy. Midway between Cullen and Portsoy, make a right turn, heading south in the direction of the conservation village of **Fordyce,** which lies among the barley fields of Banffshire like a small slice of rural England gone far adrift. You can stroll by the churchyard; picnic on the old bleaching green (an explanatory notice board tells you all about it); or buy stamps from the local post office, where the lady behind the counter still weighs the letters using old-style brass weights. There is also a restored 19th-century carpenter's workshop to visit.

Public transportation will take you straight from Cullen to **Portsoy.** This substantial village boasts the oldest harbor on the Moray Firth, built in the 17th century. Once a North Sea trading port and later participating in the 19th-century fishing boom, the community thereafter fell into a decline. But thoughtful conservation programs have revitalized much of Portsoy's old fabric.

Although there's a lot more of the coast to explore (*see* Off the Beaten Track, *below*), there are a number of inland routes that lead to the **Mill of Towie,** a fully restored oatmeal mill, dating from a time when the meal mill played a vital role in the local economy. Mill tours are available. *Drummuir, Keith, Banffshire, tel. 01542/810307. Admission: £1.50 adults, 75p children. Mill open daily 8–5; craft shop (tel. 01542/810355) open Easter and May–Oct., daily 10:30–4:30.*

Time Out   The Mill of Towie's former grain store is now a **restaurant** (tel. 01542/810328) serving morning coffee, lunches, and teas.

Dufftown, on one of the Spey tributaries, farther south on the B9014, is a town planned in 1817 by the Earl of Fife. One of the most famous malt whiskies of all, the market leader **Glenfiddich** is distilled here. The independent company of William Grant and Sons Limited was the first distillery to realize the tourist potential of the distilling process. It subsequently built an entertaining visitor center in addition to offering tours. In short, if you do intend to visit a distillery, it may as well be Glenfiddich, especially because it probably offers the most complete range of on-site activities, from floor malting to bottling. In fact, it is the only Speyside distiller that bottles on the premises. The audiovisual show and displays in the visitor center are also worthwhile, and the traditional stone-walled premises with the typical pagoda-roofed malting buildings have a pleasant period ambience. Not all visitors have to like whisky to come away feeling they've learned something about a leading Scottish export. *North of Dufftown on the A941, tel. 01340/820373. Admission* *free. Open weekdays 9:30–4:30, except Christmas and New Year's; Easter–mid-Oct., Sat. 9:30–4:30, Sun. noon–4:30.*

On a mound just above the distillery is a grim, gray, and squat curtain-walled castle, **Balvenie.** This fortress, dating from the 13th century, once commanded the glens and passes toward Speyside and Elgin. Back in the center of Dufftown, the conspicuous battlemented clock tower—the centerpiece of the planned town and a former jail—houses a local museum open in summer. *Dufftown, A941, tel. 0131/244–3101. Admission: £1.20 adults, 75p children. Open Apr.–Sept., Mon.–Sat. 9:30–6, Sun. 2–6.*

Down the hill (east), look for a sign to Mortlach Church. Set in a hollow by the Dullan Water, this church is thought to be one of the oldest Christian sites in Scotland, perhaps founded by St. Moluag, a contemporary of St. Columba, as early as AD 566. Note the weathered Pictish cross in the churchyard and the even older stone under cover in the vestibule, with a strange Pictish elephantlike beast carved on it. Though much of the church was rebuilt after 1876, some early work survives, including three lancet windows from the 13th century and a leper's squint (a hole extended to the outside of the church so that lepers could hear the service but be kept away from the rest of the congregation).

41 From Dufftown take the A941 about 4 miles northwest to **Craigellachie,** renowned as an angling resort on the Spey. Like so many Speyside settlements, Craigellachie is sometimes enveloped in the malty reek of the local industry. As you arrive in the village, you will notice the huge cooperage, the place where barrels are made and repaired. The Spey itself is crossed by a handsome suspension bridge, designed by Thomas Telford in 1814 and now bypassed by **42** the modern road. Go left and upstream by the A95 to **Aberlour** (often marked as Charlestown of Aberlour on maps). This is another handsome little burgh, essentially Victorian in style, though actually founded in 1812 by the local landowner. While Glenfarclas, Cragganmore, and Aberlour itself are names of noted local whiskies, for a nonalcoholic change of pace, take a look at the Village Store. After the owners died the shop was locked away intact, complete with stock. In the late 1980s, new owners discovered they had bought a time capsule—a range of products dating from the early decades of the present century—as well as all the paraphernalia, books and ledgers, accounts, and notes of a country business.

Time Out In Aberlour, **The Old Pantry** (The Square, tel. 01340/871617) serves everything from a cup of coffee to a four-course spread.

At this point, you are only about 15 miles south of Elgin, the starting point of this tour.

Aberdeen for Free

The **Aberdeen Art Gallery** (*see* Tour 1) hosts a varied entertainment program.

Aberdeen Maritime Museum (*see* What to See and Do with Children)

The Crombie Woollen Mill, where Crombie cloth was made until recently, houses a museum and has an audiovisual program describing the history of the company. *Grandholm Mill, Woodside. Open Mon.–Sat. 9–4:30, Sun. 12–4:30.*

The **Marischal Museum** houses artifacts from around the world and exhibitions on world history from prehistoric times, with a special emphasis on Scotland. *Broad St., tel. 01224/273131, open weekdays 10–5, Sun. 2–5.*

Provost Skene's House (*see* Tour 1)

What to See and Do with Children

Amusement Centers The **Adventure Playground** has a fishing-village theme, including model houses, fishing nets, and a paddling pool. *Beach Esplanade.*

Codona's Amusement Park, like Adventure Playground, is also located on the shore. *Beach Blvd. Open Easter school holidays and June–July, daily; May–Sept., holiday Mon.*

Museums The **Aberdeen Maritime Museum** is a fascinating place for grade-schoolers, with its ship models, paintings, and equipment associated with the fishing, local shipbuilding, and North Sea oil and gas industries. *Provost Ross's House, Ship Row, tel. 01224/585788. Admission free. Open Mon.–Sat. 10–5.*

Satrosphere is a hands-on exhibition of science and technology that makes science come alive. Children (and adults) of even the most unscientific bent will love it. *19 Justice Mill La., tel. 01224/213232. Admission: £3 adults, £1.50 children and senior citizens. Open daily, Mon.–Sat. 10–5, Sun. 1:30–5 (closed Tues. during the school year).*

The **Rosemount Celebration Centre** has an activities-based heritage museum and learning center called Jonah's Journey, based on life in a 2,000-year-old Israelite village. The center offers costumes, spinning and weaving, mosaic making, puppet plays, and jigsaw puzzles. *Rosemount Pl., tel. 01224/647614. Admission: £1 adults, £2 children. Open weekdays 9–3:30 (closed Tues. PM and 3 weeks at Christmas/New Year).*

Zoos and Parks All the city's parks have free entry, including the very popular **Winter Gardens** in **Duthie Park.**

Doonies Farm, run by Aberdeen's Department of Leisure and Recreation, is a model farm with Clydesdale horses, ponies, cattle, sheep, and small animals, some of which children may handle. *Off A956 from Aberdeen. Open daily dawn–dusk.*

Duthie Park and Winter Gardens. In addition to being a great place to feed the ducks, Duthie Park has a boating pond and trampolines, carved wooden animals, and playgrounds. In the Winter Gardens children can see fish in ponds, free-flying birds, turtles, and terrapins. *Polmuir Rd., Riverside Dr. Admission free. Park and gardens open all year; entertainment in summer only. Gardens open daily 10–dusk.*

Hazlehead Park and Zoo has a potpourri of domestic animals and birds, a free-flight aviary, and an aquarium house. A maze (very uncommon in Scotland), electric cars, putting, and trampolines are also available during the summer. *Groats Rd., Hazlehead Ave. Admission free. Zoo open all year, daily 10–dusk; maze open July–Sept., daily 10–dusk, also weekends in early summer.*

Storybook Glen displays a fairy-tale theme in a 20-acre parkland/garden setting: the Jolly Miller, Old MacDonald's Farm, and the Old Woman Who Lived in a Shoe are some of the characters featured in large-scale models. Take care with small children: some of the models are rather decrepit. *Off S. Deeside Rd., B9077, about 4 mi from Aberdeen, tel. 01224/732941. Admission: £3 adults, £2 sen-*

ior citizens, £1.50 children. Open Mar.–Oct., daily 10–6, Nov.–Feb., weekends 11–4.

Off the Beaten Track

A unique re-creation by the National Trust for Scotland of a 17th-century garden, **Pitmedden Garden,** is best visited in high summer, from July onward, when annual bedding plants form intricate formal patterns of the garden plots. The 100-acre estate also has a variety of woodland and farmland walks, as well as the Museum of Farming Life. *Tel. 01651/842352. Admission £3 adults, £1.50 senior citizens and children. Open May–Sept., daily 10–5:30 (last admission 5).*

Created as the home of the earls and marquesses of Aberdeen, **Haddo House**—designed by William Adam—is now cared for by the National Trust for Scotland. Built in 1723, the elegant mansion has a light and graceful design, with curving wings on either side of a harmonious facade. It is promoted within Gordon District's Castle Trail, but its potential as a defensive fortress was minimal. Much of the interior is circa 1880, at a time when Adam features, such as ornate plasterwork, were revived. The house, which also has a tearoom, is set in sprawling parkland, popular with the locals for country walks and picnics. *Off B99, northwest of Ellon. Admission: £3.50 adults, £1.80 senior citizens and children. House open Easter and May, June, and Sept., daily 1:30–5:30; July, Aug., daily 11–5:30; early Oct., weekends 1:30–5:30 (last admission 4:45). Garden and country park, all year daily 9:30–sunset.*

The Bullers of Buchan, located off the A975 south of Peterhead, is worth seeing for those explorers who like their sites austere and elemental. On a stretch of windy cliff and cove coastline—once used by smugglers—the sea has cut through a cave, collapsing its roof and forming a great rocky cauldron, fearsome in bad weather. This natural phenomenon has been a tourist spectacle since the English man of letters Dr. Samuel Johnson came this way in 1773 with his Scottish biographer, James Boswell. The two men dined at nearby Slains Castle to the south, now in ruins. A later visitor was Bram Stoker, and the castle's setting is said to have inspired him to create Dracula. The Bullers of Buchan is an impressive site, but not for the vertigo prone. Approach the cliff edge with great care.

A major element in Aden Country Park, the **Northeast Scotland Agricultural Heritage Centre,** tells the moving story through videos of life on the land and the hard toil of the farming folk. Implements, tableaux, models, and displays create a vivid impression. Aden Country Park is also an important recreational resource for the locals, with countryside trails that meander throughout the park's 230 acres. *Off A92, just west of Mintlaw, tel. 01771/622857. Admission to Heritage Centre: £1 adults, children free. Open May–Sept., daily 11–5; Apr. and Oct., weekends noon–5 (last admission 4:30).*

A huddle of houses tucked below a crescent of grassy cliffs, **Pennan** shot to minor fame as the setting for some of the filming of *Local Hero,* which starred Burt Lancaster. The phone box and the hotel featured in the film are still there. Pennan is set in a remote cliff coastline about as far from the tourist trail as is possible. *Off B9031 between Fraserburgh and Macduff.*

In an area rife with castles, many are distinguished within their own categories: Craigievar for untouched perfection, Corgarff for sheer loneliness, Haddo House for elegance. Perhaps **Fyvie** stands out in its own category: most complex. Five great towers built by five successive powerful families turned a 13th-century foursquare castle into an opulent Edwardian (early 20th century) statement of wealth. There's an array of superb paintings on view, including 12 Raeburns, as well as myriad sumptuous interiors and walks on the castle grounds. Fyvie is praised for its sheer impact, if you like your castles oppressive and gloomy. *Off A947 between Oldmeldrum and Turriff, tel. 0165/16–266. Admission: £3.50 adults, £1.80 senior citizens and children. Castle open Easter, May, June, and Sept., daily 1:30–5:30; July, Aug., daily 11–5:30; early Oct., weekends 1:30–5:30 (last admission 4:45). Grounds open all year daily, 9:30–sunset.*

Given the general destruction caused by the 16th-century religious upheaval of the Reformation, abbeys in Scotland tend to be ruinous and deserted sites, but at **Pluscarden Abbey** the way of life of the monks continues. Originally a 13th-century foundation, the religious community abandoned their abbey after the Reformation. The third Marquis of Bute bought the remains in 1897 and initiated a repair and restoration program that continues to this day. Monks from an abbey near Gloucester, England, returned here in 1948, and today the abbey is an active religious community. *Off B9010 from Elgin. Admission free. Open daily 5 AM–8:30 PM.*

Shopping

Aberdeen serves a large and fairly prosperous hinterland. Elgin is a smaller center. The shopping pattern fits accordingly: Aberdeen with the widest choice, Elgin with a few shops of interest. However, because of the fishing and farming prosperity, plus new money from oil and even newer money from people moving from the south, there are a few shopping surprises in some of the smaller towns.

Aberdeen Aberdeen's shopping scene is in the throes of change. For generations, folk from round about would come into Aberdeen for the day—the city is a kind of large-scale market town—and their chief delight would be to stroll the length of Union Street and perhaps take in George Street as well. Now this pattern is changing, thanks mainly to the modern and faceless shopping developments (pleasant enough in an anonymous way), the St. Nicholas and Bon-Accord centers (George St.), which have taken the emphasis away from Union Street.

However, smaller specialty shops are still to be found, particularly in the Chapel Street/Thistle Street area at the west end of Union Street and on the latter's north side, which has a series of interesting little businesses well worth discovering. These include **Nova** (20 Chapel St., tel. 01224/641270), where the locals go for gifts. Nova stocks major U.K. brand names, such as Liberty of London, Dartington Glass, and Crabtree and Evelyn, as well as a wide range of Scottish silver jewelry. **Colin Wood** (25 Rose St., tel. 01224/643019) is the place to go for antiques and prints. **Harlequin** (65 Thistle St., tel. 01224/635716) stocks a large selection of embroidery and tapestry kits, designer yarns, and colorful expensive knitwear. Antiques collectors will also enjoy a browse in **Elizabeth Watt's** little shop (69 Thistle St., tel. 01224/647232).

Elsewhere in town, **Helen Hunter** (100 Rosemount Pl., tel. 01224/630967) is where discriminating, slightly older women go to be looked after and advised in matters of smart dressing. Visitors looking for bargains can try the **Crombie Woollen Mill** on the edge of town (Grandholm Mills, Woodside, off the A96, tel. 01224/483201);

a particularly good value are the men's overcoats bearing the Crombie name (known for high quality).

At the **Aberdeen Family History Shop** (164 King St., tel. 01224/646323) you can browse through a huge range of publications related to local history and genealogical research. For the payment of a small membership fee (to the Aberdeen & North East Family History Society), they will undertake some research on your behalf.

Aberdeen shops catering to children include **The Toy Bazaar** (45 Schoolhill, tel. 01224/640021), which stocks a range of toys for children preschool age and up. **Craftplay** (282 Holburn St., tel. 01224/584784) stocks toys and crafts materials. **The Early Learning Centre** (Bon-Accord Centre, George St., tel. 01224/624188) specializes in toys with educational value.

Deeside Farther afield from Aberdeen, the opportunities for shopping are certainly more scattered. The **McEwan Gallery** (on A939, 1 mi west of Ballater, tel. 013397/55429) displays a good range of fine paintings, watercolors, prints, and books (many with a Scottish theme) in an unusual house built by the Swiss artist Rudolphe Christen in 1902. For a low-cost gift you could always see what is being boiled up at **Dee Valley Confectioners** (Station Sq., tel. 013397/55499), sweets makers in **Ballater.**

Also in Ballater (where the royals seem to do much of their Scottish shopping, as evidenced by the many BY APPOINTMENT TO signs), you can buy Scottish designer knitwear at **Goodbrand Knitwear** (1 Braemar Rd., tel. 013397/55947). **Jane Knitwear** (18 Bridge St., tel. 01339/755920) has a wide range of Scottish designer knits; there are styles to suit all tastes and color preferences. At either of **Countrywear's** two shops (15 and 35 Bridge St., tel. 013397/55453) you'll find everything you need for Scottish country living, including fishing tackle, shooting accessories, cashmere, tweeds, and that flexible garment popular in Scotland between seasons: the bodywarmer.

Elsewhere in To the north of the region is **Fochabers,** the place for antiques hunt-
the Northeast ers, with nearly a dozen antiques shops. Try **Sylvan Antiques** for pottery and bric-a-brac; **Granny's Kist** for kitchenware and furniture; and **L'Antiquitée's** for small furniture, pottery, glassware, and jewelry. All the shops are within a few yards of each other on the main street. Another interesting shop is **Balance,** which stocks homeopathic remedies, potpourris, and the like. Finish your visit at **The Gallery,** a good place to sit with a cup of tea and a home-baked snack.

In **Portsoy, Portsoy Marble** (at the old harbor, tel. 01261/842404) stocks not only marble items—eggs, platters, etc.—but also local pottery, books, cards, knitwear, and ornaments. (The greenish or reddish Portsoy marble even found its way to the Palace of Versailles in France.)

Elgin has, in addition to the usual range of High Street stores, **Gordon and MacPhail** (South St., tel. 01343/545111), an outstanding delicatessen and wine merchant that, in addition to wine, stocks a breathtaking range of otherwise scarce malt whiskies. This is a good place to shop for gifts for those foodies among your friends. **J. D. Yeadon** (32 Commerce St., tel. 01343/542411) is a dependable bookshop. **Johnstons of Elgin** (Newmill, tel. 01343/547821) has a worldwide reputation for its luxury fabrics, including cashmere. The color range is particularly noteworthy because it breaks away from the otherwise slightly predictable pastel blue, pink, yellow, and green of most mill shops.

Sports and Fitness

Bicycling Northeast Scotland is excellent biking country, with networks of minor roads and farm roads crisscrossing rolling fields. Tourist-information centers can provide lists of suggested cycle tours. Rates for bicycle rentals vary, depending on the type of bike. An average rate for a three-speed bike is £3 a day.

You can rent bicycles at **Aberdeen Cycle Centre** (188 King St., Aberdeen, tel. 01224/644542), **Alpine Bikes** (70 Holburn St., Aberdeen, tel. 01224/211455), or **Outdoor Gear** (88 Fonthill Rd., Aberdeen, tel. 01224/573952).

Camping Most of the population centers in the area have campsites. It is possible to camp on private land, but you must obtain the permission of the landowner first. Except for the more remote upland areas, "wild land" camping is better pursued farther west.

Canoeing For information on canoeing in the area, contact **Aberdeen University Canoe Club** (Secretary, AA Office, Butchart Recreation Centre, Aberdeen, tel. 01224/272311), **Aberdeen Kayak Club** (tel. 01358/43846), **Inverurie Surf Kayak Club** (contact R. Flemming, tel. 01224/572809), **Donside Canoe Club,** (contact J. Gilbert, tel. 019755/81369), or **Ellon Centre Canoe Club** (contact K. Cameron, tel. 01358/722810).

Fishing With major rivers, such as the Dee, Don, Deveron, and Ythan, as well as popular smaller rivers, such as the Ugie, plus loch and estuary fishing, this is one of Scotland's leading game-fishing areas. Details of beats, boats, and permit prices can be obtained from local tourist-information centers. Some local hotels offer fishing packages or, at least, can organize permits. Prices vary widely, depending on the fish and individual river beat.

Golf The Northeast has over 50 golf clubs, some of which have championship courses. All towns and many villages have their nine- and 18-hole municipal links, at which you pay £3–£5 per round. The more prestigious clubs charge up to £40 a day and expect you to book by letter or to bring a letter of recommendation from a member. The following courses in and around Aberdeen are open to visitors.

Balnagask (St. Fitticks Rd., tel. 01224/876407). 18 holes, 5,986 yards, SSS 69.
Hazlehead (tel. 01224/321830). Course 1: 18 holes, 6,204 yards, SSS 70. Course 2: 18 holes, 5,801 yards, SSS 68.
Murcar (Bridge of Don, tel. 01224/704354). 18 holes, 6,240 yards, SSS 70.
Westhills (tel. 01224/740159). 18 holes, 5,921 yards, SSS 68.

Health and Fitness Clubs The major clubs in the area are **Bon-Accord Swimming and Leisure Centre** (Justice Mill La., Aberdeen, tel. 01224/587920), **Kincorth Sports Centre** (Corthan Dr., Aberdeen, tel. 01224/879759), **Sheddocksley Sports Centre** (Springhill Rd., Aberdeen, tel. 01224/692534), **Balmedie Leisure Centre** (Eigie Rd., Balmedie, tel. 01358/743725), **Fitness n' Fun** (130 High St., Elgin, tel. 01343/549307), and **Westerdyke Leisure Centre** (4 Elrick Way, Skene, tel. 01224/743098).

Skiing The area's main skiing development is at **Glenshee,** just south of Braemar, though the season can be brief here. Visitors accustomed to long alpine runs and extensive choice will find the runs here short, unlike the lift lines. The **Lecht** lies at even lower altitude, also within easy reach of the area, and is mainly suitable for beginners. The development at **Cairngorm** by Aviemore is also within easy reach (*see* Chapter 11). There is a dry ski slope at **Alford** (tel. 019755/62380).

Dining and Lodging

Dining

Partly in response to the demands of spendthrift oilmen, the number of restaurants in Aberdeen has grown over the past several years, and the quality of the food has improved. Elsewhere in the region you will never be far from a good pub lunch or a hotel high tea or dinner.

Highly recommended restaurants are indicated by a star ★.

Category	Cost*
$$$$	over £40
$$$	£30–£40
$$	£15–£30
$	under £15

per person for a three-course meal, including VAT

Lodging

The Northeast has some splendid country hotels with log fires and rich furnishings, where you can also be sure of eating well if you have time for a leisurely meal.

Highly recommended hotels are indicated by a star ★.

Category	Cost*
$$$$	over £120
$$$	£100–£120
$$	£80–£100
$	under £80

All prices are for a standard double room, including breakfast and tax.

Aberdeen
Dining
★

The Silver Darling. Situated right on the quayside, the Silver Darling is one of Aberdeen's most acclaimed restaurants. It specializes, as its name suggests, in fish. The style is French provincial, with an indoor barbecue guaranteeing flavorful grilled fish and shellfish. *Pocra Quay, Footdee, AB2 1DQ, tel. 01224/576229. Reservations advised (essential on weekends). Dress: casual but neat. AE, DC, MC, V. Closed weekend lunch, Sun. evening, and 2 weeks at Christmas/New Year. $$$*

Dining and
Lodging
★

Ardoe House Hotel. A magnificent, Baronial-style country house situated on expansive grounds by the River Dee, the Ardoe House is full of charm and character. Although a huge extension has been added, try for a room in the older, original part of the building. *Banchory Devenick, Aberdeenshire AB1 5YP (a few mi from the city* *center), tel. 01224/867355, fax 01224/861283. 71 rooms with bath. Facilities: restaurant, 2 bars. AE, DC, MC, V. $$$*

The Marcliffe at Pitfodels. New on the Aberdeen hotel scene, the Marcliffe at Pitfodels shows the skills and experience of leading Scottish hotelier Stewart Spence. This spacious building, in the upmarket "west end" of the city, surrounds an old country house. The combination of old and new is impressive, and the air one of confidence—an establishment that will meet your every need. *N. Deeside Rd., Pitfodels, Aberdeen AB1 9PN, tel. 01224/861000, fax 01224/868860. 45 rooms with bath. AE, DC, MC, V. $$$*

Caledonian Thistle Hotel. Well situated and offering pleasant views over tidy gardens, the Caledonian, one of the larger hotels in the Granite City, is generally considered to be one of the best hotels in the city. Despite its size, the service here is very friendly. *Union Terr., AB9 1HE, tel. 01224/640233, fax 01224/641627. 80 rooms with bath. Facilities: restaurant, wine bar, coffee shop. AE, DC, MC, V. $$–$$$*

Lodging **Atholl Hotel.** One of Aberdeen's many splendid silver granite properties, turreted and gabled and set within a leafy residential area to the west of the city, the Atholl Hotel has recently had major refurbishment to a very high standard. The best views are from the top floor; the larger rooms are on the first floor. *54 Kings Gate, Aberdeen AB9 2YN, tel. 01224/323505, fax 01224/321555. 35 rooms with bath/shower. MC, V. $–$$*

Auchterless **Towie Tavern.** On the main Aberdeen–Turriff road, the Towie Tav-
Dining ern, a friendly and informal traditional-style eating place, is a good place to recharge your batteries while on an excursion to Fyvie Castle. The menu emphasizes hearty local fare—check the blackboard carefully for the "Towie Treats," which change daily and often feature excellent fresh seafood specials. The puddings, on the other hand, are not of great interest. The good-natured staff and the tavern's cozy atmosphere add to the experience and make it well worth seeking out. *Near Turriff, AB5 8EP, tel. 018884/201. Reservations advised. Dress: casual. MC, V. $$*

Ballater **Craigendarroch.** This magnificent country house hotel, located just
Dining and outside Ballater on a hillside overlooking the River Dee, really does
Lodging manage to keep everyone happy. Hotel guests are cosseted in luxurious surroundings and can use the nearby leisure facilities—pool, squash courts, and beauty salon, to name just a few. An even better value are the pine lodges set among the trees around the hotel. These self-catering cottages are geared for families and fitted with every kind of labor-saving appliance. There is also a solid choice of on-site restaurants, including the top-rate **Oaks** for à la carte dinners. *Ballater, AB35 5XA, tel. 013397/55858, fax 013397/55447. 50 rooms with bath. Facilities: swimming pools, tennis and squash courts. AE, DC, MC, V. $$$–$$$$*

Darroch Learg Hotel. Amid tall trees on a hillside, the Darroch Learg is everything a Scottish country-house hotel should be, with the added bonus that the charming town of Ballater is moments away. Built in the 1880s as a country residence, the hotel exudes relaxing charm. Most bedrooms enjoy a stunning panoramic view south across Royal Deeside. Food in the conservatory restaurant is sophisticated—delicately flavored terrines and soups—but also substantial, with the rich flavors of local beef and fish produce. *Braemar Rd., Ballater, Aberdeenshire AB35 5UX, tel. and fax 013397/55443. 20 rooms with bath. Facilities: restaurant. DC, MC, V. $–$$*

Banchory
Dining and Lodging

Banchory Lodge. With the River Dee running past just a few yards away at the bottom of the garden, the Banchory Lodge, a fine example of a Georgian country house, is an ideal resting place for anglers. The lodge has retained its period charm and is well maintained inside and out. Tranquillity is the keynote here. *Kincardineshire AB3 3HS, tel. 01330/822625, fax 01330/825019. 22 rooms with bath. Facilities: restaurant, fishing. AE, DC, MC, V. $$–$$$*

Raemoir Hotel. The core of this large mansion dates from the 18th century, though a number of additions have been built over the years. Central heating has been added as well, so there is no need to fear chilly, windy rooms. All the guest rooms are comfortable and well appointed; many are hung with beautiful tapestries. The hotel is set on spacious grounds and overshadowed by the 1,500-foot-high Hill of Fare. Adjoining the hotel's property are 3,500 acres of land on which fishing, stalking, and shooting can be arranged. Guests who don't want to venture too far away from the hotel can make use of the minigolf course and tennis court. *Raemoir, Kincardineshire AB3 4ED, tel. 01330/824884, fax 01330/822171. 28 rooms with bath. Facilities: restaurant, baby-sitting service, golf, tennis, fishing, helipad. AE, DC, MC, V. $$*

Banff
Lodging

Eden House. This Georgian mansion house, set high above the River Deveron and with magnificent views, makes a comfortably elegant base from which to explore the Northeast. The rooms are all individually decorated and furnished with antique pieces complementing the age of the house. The sitting room retains its original early 19th-century hand-painted wallpaper. Tennis, billiards, fishing, and shooting can all be arranged, while numerous golf courses are within easy reach. Dinner in the river-view dining room might include local seafood, Deveron salmon, game, or Scottish beef. *Banffshire, AB45 3NT, tel. 012616/282. 5 rooms; 2 with bath, 1 with shower. Reservations essential. No credit cards. Closed Christmas and New Year. $–$$*

Braemar
Dining and Lodging

Invercauld Arms. A Scottish Baronial hotel in the grand manner, the Invercauld Arms underwent major refurbishment recently and has completely thrown off its previously rather drafty and decayed atmosphere. Now its welcoming entrance, with plush sofas and elegant velvet chairs, leads to beautifully restored public rooms with attractive plasterwork and to comfortable bedrooms with floral drapes and reproduction antique furniture. Overlooking the site where the standard was raised for the 1715 Jacobite uprising, the hotel also makes an ideal base for exploring the other historic sites on Royal Deeside. End the day looking out to Braemar Castle from the restaurant's bay windows while enjoying such dishes as Aberdeen Angus steak with tomato and wild mushroom sauce or chicken with bean sprouts and water chestnuts with oyster sauce. *Braemar AB35 5YR, tel. 01339/741605, fax 01339/741428. 68 rooms with bath or shower. Restaurant reservations advised. Jacket and tie preferred. AE, DC, MC, V. $–$$*

Drybridge
Dining
★

The Old Monastery. Standing on a broad, wooded slope set back from the coast near Buckie, with westward views as far as the hills of Wester Ross, the Old Monastery was once a Victorian religious establishment. This theme has been preserved and carries through to the restrained decor of the Cloisters Bar and the Chapel Restaurant, with its hand stenciling. The local specialties—the freshest fish from sea and river and Aberdeen Angus beef—make up the major part of the menu, all cooked in traditional style with flashes of adventure. Chicken breast coated in oatmeal and pan-fried, served with a lemon, mustard, and cream sauce, is typical of other options. Homemade soups and delicious puddings are bonuses, as is the no-smoking dining room. This is quite simply the best for miles around. *Buckie, Banffshire AB5 2JB, tel 01542/32660. Reservations advised. Jacket and tie advised. Closed Sun., Mon., 3 weeks in Jan. and 2 weeks in Nov. AE, DC, MC, V. $$$*

Fordyce — *Lodging* **Academy House.** This top-of-the-range bed-and-breakfast offers accommodation in what was once the headmaster's house for the local secondary school, now closed. Traditional decor and some well-chosen antique furniture decorate the spacious, well-proportioned rooms. *School Rd., AB45 2SJ, tel. 01261/842743. 3 rooms (no private facilities). No credit cards. Evening meal if desired. $*

Glenlivet — *Dining and Lodging* **Minmore House.** Former home of George Smith, founder of the Glenlivet Distillery, Minmore is now a family-run hotel that retains a strong private-house feel. Faded chintz in the drawing room and a paneled library (which now houses the bar) are complemented by very comfortable bedrooms (one, allegedly, with a ghost) and exceptionally well-cooked food. *Glenlivet, Ballindalloch, Banffshire, tel. 01807/590378, fax 01771/22320. 9 rooms with bath. Facilities: restaurant, walking (on the Speyside Way), bird-watching. MC, V. $*

Old Deer — *Dining* **Saplinbrae House.** The restaurant in this country-house hotel is very popular with the locals. As elsewhere in this farming region, with its bounteous salmon rivers, local produce is the basis of the menu. Game pie, roast duck, and hefty steamed puddings require forward planning to ensure that you have the capacity to stay the course (try a healthy breakfast followed by a day's hill walking before booking a meal here). *Near Mintlaw, Aberdeenshire AB4 8PL, tel. 01771/23515. Reservations advised. Dress: smart but casual. AE, DC, MC, V. $$*

Sandend — *Lodging* **Broom Farm.** Set on a hilltop overlooking Sandend Bay, with its beautiful, deserted sandy beach, seals basking on the rocks, and dolphins cruising the Moray Firth, this working farm offers bed-and-breakfast accommodations in a private wing of the main house. Guests have their own newly refitted bathroom, a bunkroom for children, bedroom, and dressing room, all with traditional pine furniture and pastel color schemes. There is also a large sitting room downstairs for guest use. The owners take great care to ensure that visitors get the most out of their stay in this still undiscovered corner of Scotland. *Broom Farm, Sandend, Portsoy Banffshire AB45 2UD, tel. 01542/840401. 1 suite for couple or family. No credit cards. $*

Udny Station Village — *Dining* **Muffin and Crumpet Bistro.** Do not be put off by the rather unprepossessing exterior of this restaurant: Inside you will find excellent food served amid an eclectic array of ornaments ranging from dolls' prams to china jugs arranged on shelves around the walls. The cook is Marilyn Rattray, well-known throughout Scotland for her Taste of Scotland menus that feature fresh local beef, chicken, pork, fish, and game, with a wealth of vegetables to choose from. There is a separate cozy bar with comfortable sofas where you can have a drink before or coffee after your meal. *Udny Station Village, near Aberdeen, tel. 01651/842210. Reservations advised. Dress: casual. MC, V. $-$$*

The Arts and Nightlife

The Arts

As you would expect, Aberdeen is the main cultural center of the region. The main Aberdeen newspapers—the *Press and Journal* and the *Evening Express*—and *Aberdeen Leopard* magazine can fill you in with what's going on anywhere in the Northeast. Outside Aberdeen a number of small-town local papers list events under the "What's On" heading. Tourist information centers usually print their own listings of events. Aberdeen's tourist-information center has a monthly "What's On" with a full calendar, as well as contact telephone numbers.

Theater **His Majesty's Theatre** (Rosemount Viaduct, Aberdeen, tel. 01224/641122) is one of the most beautiful theaters in Britain. Live shows are presented throughout the year, many of them in advance of their official opening in London's West End.

Concerts **The Music Hall** (Union St., Aberdeen, tel. 01224/632080) presents seasonal programs of concerts by the Scottish National Orchestra, the Scottish Chamber Orchestra, and other major orchestras and musicians. Its wide-ranging program of events also includes folk concerts, crafts fairs, and exhibitions.

Aberdeen Arts Centre (King St., tel. 01224/635208) is a theater and concert venue where experimental theater, poetry readings, exhibitions by local and Scottish artists, and many other arts-based presentations can be enjoyed.

The **Aberdeen International Youth Festival** in August has worldwide recognition and attracts youth orchestras, choirs, dance, and theater companies from many countries. During the festival, many of the companies that appear also take their productions to other venues in the Northeast. For details, contact AIYF Box Office (Music Hall, Union St., Aberdeen, tel. 01224/641122).

Another arts base in the area is **Haddo House,** 20 miles north of Aberdeen (off B9005 near Methlick, tel. 01651/851770), where the Haddo House Hall Arts Trust runs a wide-ranging program of events.

Dance **His Majesty's Theatre** and **Aberdeen Arts Centre** (*see above*) are regular venues for dance companies. Contact the box offices for details of current productions.

Film Major theaters in the area include the **Cannon** (Union St., Aberdeen, tel. 01224/591477), **Capitol** (Union St., Aberdeen, tel. 01224/583141), **Odeon** (Justice Mill La., Aberdeen, tel. 01224/587160), **Moray Playhouse** (High St., Elgin, tel. 01343/542680), **Victoria** (W. High St., Inverurie, tel. 01467/621436), and the **Playhouse** (Queen St., Peterhead, tel. 01779/471052).

Opera Both **His Majesty's Theatre** in Aberdeen and **Haddo House** (*see above*), near Methlick, present operatic performances at certain times throughout the year; telephone for details or inquire at the tourist-information center in Aberdeen's St. Nicholas House.

Nightlife

In part because of the oil-industry boom, Aberdeen has a fairly lively nightlife scene, though much of it revolves around pubs and hotels.

Visitors interested in trying their luck at the gaming tables can place their bets at the **Stakis Regency Casino** (61 Summer St., tel. 01224/645273). Several of the larger hotels in the area run dinner dances in the summer season; check with the local tourist information centers for details.

Discos   Two notes of warning about discos in Aberdeen: Most of these establishments do not allow jeans or athletic shoes, and it's advisable to check beforehand that a particular disco is not closed because of a private function. Below is a list of the city's most popular discos.

Bonkers (Bridge Pl., Aberdeen, tel. 01224/581135).
Cotton Club (491 Union St., Aberdeen, tel. 01224/581858).
Eagles (120 Union St., Aberdeen, tel. 01224/640641).
Hotel Metro (17 Market St., Aberdeen, tel. 01224/583275).
The Ministry (Dee St., Aberdeen, tel. 01224/211661).
Mr G's (70–78 Chapel St., Aberdeen, tel. 01224/642112).
The Soda Fountain (492–494 Union St., Aberdeen, tel. 01224/636331).
Zig-Zag (2 Diamond St., Aberdeen, tel. 01224/641580).

Jazz Clubs   There is jazz on Saturday night at the **Masada Continental Lounge** (Rosemount Viaduct, Aberdeen, tel. 01224/641587). The **Lemon Tree** (5 W. North St., tel. 01224/642230) stages frequent jazz events in its wide-ranging music program.

Rock Club   **Ibis Productions** (10 Belmont St., Aberdeen, tel. 01224/621188, fax 01224/621218) can give details on rock artists appearing locally.

By Gilbert
Summers

The Central Highlands consist of what were once the counties of Perthshire and Stirlingshire. Today the county seats of Perth and Stirling, respectively, still play important roles as the primary administrative centers in the region. Both municipalities lie on the edge of a Highland area that offers reliable road and rail connections to the central belt of Scotland. Just how near the area is to the well-populated Midland Valley can be judged by the visitor who looks out from the ramparts of Edinburgh Castle: The Highland hills—which meander around the Trossachs and above Callander—are clearly visible. Similarly, the high-tower blocks of some of Glasgow's peripheral housing developments are noticeable from many of the higher peaks, notably Ben Lomond.

In fact, the Lowland/Highland contrast is quite pronounced in this region. Geologists have designated a prominent boundary between the two distinct landscapes as the Highland Boundary Fault. This geological barrier, however, also marked the differences between Scotland's two languages and cultures, Gaelic and Scots, with the Gaels ensconced within a mountain barrier. In the Central Highlands the fault line runs through Loch Lomond, close to Callander, to the northeast above Perth, and into the old county of Angus.

As early as 1794 the local minister in Callander, on the very edge of the Highlands, wrote: "The Trossachs are often visited by persons of taste, who are desirous of seeing nature in her rudest and unpolished state." What these early visitors came to see was a series of lochs and hills, whose crags and slopes were hung harmoniously with shaggy birch, oak, and pinewoods. The tops of the hills are high but not too wild (real wilderness would have been too much for these fledgling nature lovers). The Romantic poets, especially William Wordsworth, sang the praises of such locales. Though Wordsworth is most closely associated with the Lake District in England, his travels through Scotland and the Trossachs inspired several poems. But it was Sir Walter Scott who definitively put this Highland-edge area on the tourist map by setting his dramatic verse narrative *The Lady of the Lake*, written in 1810, firmly in the physical landscape of the Trossachs. Scott's verse was an immediate and huge success, and visitors flooded in to trace the events of the poem across the region. Today visitors continue to flock here, though few can quote a line of his poem.

If the Trossachs have long attracted those with discriminating tastes, then much of the same sentimental aura has attached itself to Loch Lomond. This is Scotland's largest loch in terms of surface area. By looking at the map, you will see that the loch is narrow to the north and broad in the south. The hard rocks to the north confine it to a long thin ribbon, and the more yielding Lowland structures allow it to spread out and assume a softer, wider form. Thus Lowland fields and lush hedgerows quickly give way to dark woods and crags (all this just a half hour's drive from the center of Glasgow). The song "The Banks of Loch Lomond," said to have been written by a Jacobite prisoner incarcerated in Carlisle, England, seems to capture a particular style of Scottish sentimentality, resulting in the notoriety of the "bonnie, bonnie banks" around the world, wherever exiled Scots are to be found.

The main towns of Perth and Stirling serve as roadway hubs for the area, but there are also a number of options in many of the area's smaller towns, places like Callander, Crieff, Pitlochry, Dunkeld, and Aberfeldy. There is also a string of small but embracing villages: Killin, Crianlarich, Lochearnhead, Kenmore, and Kinlochrannoch, minor route centers tucked into the hills and covered in the tours described below.

Finally, remember that even though the Central Highlands are easily accessible, there is still much high, wild country in the region. Ben Lawers, near Killin, is the ninth-highest peak in Scotland, and the moor of Rannoch is as bleak and empty a stretch as can be seen anywhere in the northlands. But if the glens and lochs prove to be too lonely or intimidating, it's a short journey to the softer and less harsh Lowlands.

Essential Information

Important Addresses and Numbers

Tourist Information The **Loch Lomond, Stirling, and Trossachs Tourist Board** (41 Dumbarton Rd., Stirling FK8 2QQ, tel. 01786/475019, fax 0786/471301) and the **Perthshire Tourist Board** (45 High St., Perth PH1 5TJ, tel. 01738/38353, fax 0738/30416) can provide information on the region. Local tourist-information centers can be found throughout the region and are open during the peak season (generally Apr.–Oct.) in the following towns: Aberfeldy, Aberfoyle, Auchterarder, Balloch, Blairgowrie, Callander, Crieff, Dunblane, Dunkeld, Helensburgh, Inveralmond, Killin, Milton, Pirnhall, Pitlochry, Tarbet, Tillicoultry, and Tyndrum. All are clearly marked with the standard ı sign in white on a blue background.

Emergencies For police, fire, or ambulance, dial 999 from any telephone. No coins are needed for emergency calls from telephone booths.

Doctors and Dentists Local practitioners will usually treat visiting patients. Information is available from tourist-information centers, and names of doctors can also be found in the yellow pages of the telephone directory. The main hospital emergency rooms in the region are **Perth Royal Infirmary** (Tullylumb, Perth, tel. 01738/23311), **Stirling Royal Infirmary** (Livilands Gate, Stirling, tel. 01786/473151), and **Vale of Leven Hospital** (Main St., Alexandria, tel. 01389/54121).

Late-Night Pharmacies Late-night pharmacies are found only in the larger towns and cities. In an emergency, the police will provide assistance in locating a pharmacist. In rural areas, general practitioners may also dispense medicines.

Arriving and Departing by Plane

Airports and Airlines Perth and Stirling can be reached easily from **Edinburgh** and **Glasgow** airports (*see* Chapters 4 and 5) by train, car, or bus.

Arriving and Departing by Car, Train, and Bus

By Car Visitors will find an easy access to the area from the central belt of Scotland via the motorway network. The M9 runs within sight of the walls of Stirling Castle, and Perth can be reached via the M90 over the Forth Bridge.

By Train The Central Highlands are linked to Edinburgh and Glasgow by rail, with through routes to England (some direct-service routes from London take fewer than five hours). A variety of Saver ticket options are available, although in some cases on the Scotrail system, the discount fares must be purchased before your arrival in the United Kingdom.

By Bus There is a good network of buses connecting with the central belt via Edinburgh and Glasgow. Express services also link the larger towns in the Central Highlands with all main towns and cities in England.

Getting Around

By Car There is an adequate network of roads, and the area's proximity to the central belt speeds road communications. The Scottish Tourist Board's touring map is useful.

By Train The **West Highland Line** runs through the western portion of the area. Services also run to Stirling, Dunblane, Perth, and Gleneagles; destinations on the Inverness–Perth line include Dunkeld, Pitlochry, and Blair Athol.

By Bus The following companies offer reliable service on a number of convenient routes.
Allander Coaches Ltd. (Unit 19, Cloverfield Estate, Milngavie, Glasgow, tel. 0141/956–3636).
Citylink (Leonard St., bus station, Perth, tel. 01738/26848).
Midland Bluebird Bus Services (Goosecroft Rd. bus station, Stirling, tel. 01786/473763).
National Express (Walnut Grove, Perth, tel. 01738/33481), which operates locally under the name **Stagecoach.**

Guided Tours

Orientation The bus companies listed in Getting Around By Bus, *above,* offer a number of general orientation tours. Inquire at the nearest tourist information center, where tour reservations can usually be booked.

Special-Interest There are many taxi and chauffeur companies offering tailor-made tours by the day or week; the nearest tourist-information center is your best source for detailed, up-to-date information. In the eastern portion of the Central Highlands, try **Turpie's Tours** (3 Bridge Rd., Caputh, by Perth, tel. 01738/71607). Possibilities in the south and west include **Goosecroft Station Taxis** (Cunningham Rd., Springkerse Industrial Estate, Stirling, tel. 01786/472220), **Ians Taxi and Minibus** (Gargunnock filling station, Gargunnock by Stirling, tel. 01786/860207), and **Dumbarton and Alexandria T.O.A.** (Main St., Alexandria, tel. 01389/57171).

Do not miss the opportunity to take a boat trip on a Scottish loch. The S.S. *Sir Walter Scott* sails on Loch Katrine in the summer season; you can book it through the tourist-information center at Callander. On Loch Lomond there are a number of cruise possibilities: from Tarbet, **Cruise Loch Lomond** (Shore Cottage, Tarbet, tel. 013012/356); from Balloch, the *Lomond Duchess* and *Lomond Maid* (Balloch Marina, Riverside, tel. 01389/51481); and from Balmaha, **Macfarlane and Son** operates the **Royal Mail boat** to the islands on the loch and takes passengers (Balmaha Boatyard, tel. 0136087/214).

Exploring the Central Highlands

The main towns of Stirling and Perth are located at the junction of many routes, making both places natural starting points for Highland tours. Stirling itself is worth covering in some detail on foot. The successive waves of development of this important town—from castles and Old Town architecture to Victorian developments and urban and industrial sprawl—can be traced quite easily. There are also peripheral points of interest worth visiting, including the **Bannockburn Heritage Centre,** which recounts how Scotland secured its independence for 400 years in one of its few victories over the English, and the **Wallace Monument,** commemorating Scotland's earliest freedom fighter, William Wallace.

The Trossachs are a short distance from Stirling, and visitors usually cover them in a loop. Those visiting **Loch Lomond** can get there from either Glasgow or Stirling, and there are two other routes available as well. The main road up the west bank (A82) is not recommended for leisurely touring. Do use this road, however, if your are on your way to Oban, Kintyre, or Argyll. Loch Lomond is best seen from one of two cul-de-sac roads: by way of Drymen at the south end, up to Rowardennan or, if you are pressed for time, west from Aberfoyle to reach Loch Lomond near its north end, at Inversnaid. Visitors should note that in the Trossachs, the road that some maps show going all the way around Loch Katrine is a private road belonging to the Strathclyde Water Board and is open only to walkers and cyclists.

Getting around Perthshire is made interesting by the series of looped tours accessible from the A9, a fast main artery. Exercise caution while driving the A9 itself, however. There have been many auto accidents in this area. Although the entire route can be completed in a single day, travelers with some time on their hands who seek a little spontaneity can take their chances on a variety of accommodations in villages along the way.

Highlights for First-Time Visitors

Bannockburn Heritage Centre (*see* Tour 1)
Blair Castle (*see* Tour 3)
Doune Castle (*see* Tour 2)
Dunblane Cathedral (*see* Tour 2)
Loch Lomond Cruises (*see* Special-Interest Tours *above*)
Pass of Killiecrankie (*see* Tour 3)
Scone Palace (*see* Tour 3)
S.S. *Sir Walter Scott* on Loch Katrine (*see* Tour 2)
Stirling Castle (*see* Tour 1)
The Trossachs (*see* Tour 2)

Tour 1: Around Stirling

Numbers in the margin correspond to points of interest on the Stirling and Central Highlands maps.

❶ In some ways, **Stirling** is like a smaller version of Edinburgh. Its castle, built on a steep-sided plug of rock, dominates the landscape, and its Esplanade offers views of the surrounding valley-plain of the River Forth. To take advantage of its historical heritage (the Stuart

Argyll's
Ludging, **9**

Back Walk, **3**

Bothwell Ha, **5**

Church of the
Holy Rude, **6**

Darrow
House/Spittal
House, **4**

Mar's Wark, **10**

Old Stirling
Bridge, **12**

Smith Art
Gallery and
Museum, **2**

Star
Pyramid/Martyrs
Monument/
Ladies' Rock, **7**

Stirling Castle, **8**

Tolbooth, **11**

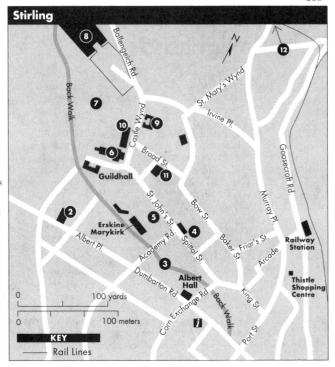

monarchs held court here from time to time, as they did in Edinburgh), Stirling maintains a busy tourism calender that includes a
summer program of open-air historical tableaux.

Opposite the tourist center on Dumbarton Road, where this tour
begins, visitors can see that an impressive proportion of Stirling's
town walls remain. Diagonally to the left is Corn Exchange Road,
with a modern statue of Rob Roy MacGregor, notorious cattle dealer
and drover, part-time thief and outlaw, and Jacobite (most of the
2 time). Farther along Dumbarton Road to the west is the **Smith Art
Gallery and Museum,** founded in 1874 with the bequest of a local
collector and now a good example of a community art gallery offering a varied exhibit program. *Tel. 01786/471917. Admission free.
Open Apr.–Sept., Tues.–Sat. 10:30–5, Sun. 2–5; Oct.–Mar., Tues.–Fri.
noon–5, Sat. 11:30–5, Sun. 2–5.*

Near Rob Roy's statue, a gentle but relentless uphill path known as
3 the **Back Walk** eventually leads to the city's most famous and worthwhile sight—**Stirling Castle.** The Back Walk will take you along the
outside of the city's walls, past a watchtower and the grimly named
Hangman's entry, cut out of the great whinstone boulders that once
marked the outer defenses of the town.

Walk east, keeping to the outside of the walls, until you reach Academy Road and the Old High School, built in 1854 on the site of the
former Greyfriars Monastery and now the Stirling Highland Hotel.
At the far end of the street, note two fine examples of Scottish do-
4 mestic architecture. Now used for private housing, **Darrow House**
dates from the 17th century. Look for the characteristically crow-
stepped gables, dormer windows, and a projecting turn-pike stair.

The adjacent **Spittal House** on the right has been restored to match its handsome partner. Turn left and uphill onto St. John's Street. There is another typical town house farther up the street, on the left, sometimes known as **Bothwell Ha** (Hall), that is said to have been owned by the Earl of Bothwell, Mary, Queen of Scots' third husband. Behind it, also on the left, is the former military detention barracks soon to be restored partly as offices and partly as a visitor center on the theme of crime and punishment. Adjacent is the **Erskine Marykirk,** a neoclassical church built in 1824 that now houses a youth hostel (*see* Dining and Lodging, *below*).

There are a number of points of interest at the top of St. John's Street. Most notable among them is the **Church of the Holy Rude,** with part of the nave surviving from the 15th century. A portion of the original medieval timber roof can also be seen. The church has the distinction of being the only church in Scotland still in use that witnessed the coronation of a Scottish monarch: James VI in 1567. Adjacent to the church is the **Guildhall,** built as Cowane's Hospital in 1639 for *decayed breithers* (unsuccessful merchants). The ancient facility is now the setting for summer concerts and evenings of participatory song, music, and dance, called ceilidhs. Above the entrance is a small, cheery statue of the founder himself, John Cowane, that is said to come alive on Hogmanay Night (December 31) to walk the streets with the locals and join in their New Year's revelry. *St. John St., tel. 01786/462373. Admission free. Open weekdays 9–5 (except when functions are being held).*

You'll encounter some unusual monuments at this point on the Back Walk. The most notable are the **Star Pyramid** of 1858 and the curious macabre glass-walled **Martyrs Monument,** erected in memory of two Wigtownshire girls who were drowned in 1685 for their Covenanting faith. At this point, you can't help but see the castle, which dominates the foreground. From **Ladies' Rock,** a high perch cosseted within the churchyard, there are excellent views of the looming fortress.

Stirling Castle's strategic position made it the grandest prize in the Scots Wars of Independence in the late-13th and early 14th centuries. The Battle of Bannockburn in 1314 was fought within sight of its walls, and the victory by Robert the Bruce (King Robert I) yielded both the castle and freedom from English subjugation for the Scots for almost four centuries.

King Robert's daughter Marjory married Walter, the High Steward of Scotland, and their descendants included the Stewart dynasty of Scottish monarchs (Mary, Queen of Scots, was a Stewart, though she preferred the French spelling, *Stuart*). The Stewarts were mainly responsible for many of the works that survive within the castle walls today. They made Stirling Castle their court and power base, creating fine Renaissance-style buildings that were not completely obliterated, despite subsequent reconstruction for military purposes.

Start your tour of the castle in the **Royal Burgh of Stirling Visitor Centre,** conspicuous on the Esplanade. After an audiovisual briefing, you will enter the castle from its outer defenses, which consist of a great curtain wall and batteries dating from 1708, built to bulwark earlier defenses by the main gatehouse. From this lower square the most conspicuous feature is the **palace,** built by King James V between 1538 and 1542. This edifice shows the influence of French masons in the decorative figures festooning the ornately worked outer walls. Overlooking the upper courtyard is the **Great**

Hall, built by King James IV in 1503. Before the Union of Parliaments in 1707, when the Scottish aristocracy sold out to England, this building had been used as one of the seats of the Scottish Parliament. After 1707 it sank into decline, becoming a riding school, then a barracks. Today, a slow restoration is under way.

Among the later works built for regiments stationed here, the **King's Old Building** stands out; it is a 19th-century baronial revival on the site of an earlier building. The oldest building on the site is the **Mint,** or **Coonzie Hoose,** perhaps dating as far back as the 14th century. Below is an arched passageway leading to the westernmost section of the ramparts, the **Nether Bailey.** You'll have the distinct feeling here that you are in the bow of a warship sailing up the *carselands* (valley-plain) of the Forth Valley, which fans out before the great superstructure of the castle.

This is the place, among the gun platforms and the crenellations of the ramparts, to ponder the strategic significance of Stirling. To the south lies the hump of the Touch and the Gargunnock Hills (part of the Campsie Hills), diverting would-be direct routes from Glasgow and the south. For centuries all roads into the Highlands across the narrow waist of Scotland led to Stirling, formerly the lowest bridging point of the River Forth. If you look carefully northward, you can still see the Old Stirling Bridge, for centuries the lowest and most convenient place to cross the river. For all these geographic reasons, the castle here was perhaps the single most important fortress in Scotland. *Central Stirling, tel. 0131/244–3101. Admission: £3.50 adults, £2 senior citizens, £1 children. Open Apr.–Sept., daily 9:30–5:15; Oct.–Mar., daily 9:30–4:15.*

Below the castle's Esplanade is the heart of the old town of Stirling, which you passed on the way up. As you walk down from the Esplanade along **Castle Wynd,** the path leads to a series of interesting buildings. In fact, below the Portcullis Hotel is one of the most important buildings surviving from the 16th century. This is **Argyll's Ludging,** now a youth hostel. Step into the courtyard and read the notice board that explains the three phases of its construction, from the 16th century onward. Notice that the building is actually older than the name it bears—that of Archibald, ninth Earl of Argyll, who bought it in 1666.

Farther down, you will encounter a long and ornate facade, windowless and roofless and constructed in a distinctive Renaissance style. Look for the armorial carved panels, the gargoyles, and the turrets flanking a railed-off *pend* (archway). This is **Mar's Wark** (Work or Building), the stark remains of a palace built in 1570 by Lord Erskine, Earl of Mar, as well as Stirling Castle governor. Mar's Wark was sieged and severely damaged during the 1745 Jacobite rebellion, but its admirably worn shell survives. *At top of Castle Wynd, tel. 0131/244–3101. View from outside only.*

When you stand in front of Mar's Wark and look downhill, you are gazing into the heart of the Old Town. One of the Old Town's most notable structures is the **Tolbooth** of 1705 (on the right), which has a traditional Scottish steeple and gilded weathercock. For centuries the Burgh Court handed down sentences here; the jail was next door. The Tolbooth is soon to house a new exhibition on the history of the Royal Burgh of Stirling. Opposite is a row of Scottish tenement-style housing, renovated and full of tenants.

Time Out   **Darnley's Coffee House** faces you at the foot of Dumbarton Road and serves reasonable coffee and fresh carrot cake, among other sweet treats. The building housing Darnley's is from the late-16th century and derives its name from a popular tale that maintains Lord Darnley generally preferred to stay here rather than at his wife's (Mary, Queen of Scots') residence in the castle.

⓬ Farther out is the **Old Stirling Bridge,** by the A9, off the center of town. Dating from the 15th century, the bridge can still be crossed on foot. It was near this site that the Scottish freedom fighter William Wallace and a ragged army of Scots won a major victory in 1297. Their story is told in an exhibition and audiovisual presentation at the **Wallace Monument** (*see* Tour 2, *below*).

The next year, rising from the uncertainties and timidity of the great lords of Scotland (ever unsure of which way to jump and whether or not to bow to England's demands), Robert the Bruce materialized as the nation's champion, and the last bloody phase of the Wars of
⓭ Independence began. This tale is recounted at the **Bannockburn Heritage Centre,** hidden among the sprawl of housing and commercial developments on the southern edge of Stirling. This was the site of the famed Battle of Bannockburn in 1314. In Bruce's day, the Forth had a shelved and partly wooded floodplain. He chose the site cunningly, noting the boggy ground on the lower reaches, in which the heavy horses of the English would founder. The atmosphere has been re-created within the center by means of an audiovisual presentation and an arresting mural depicting the battle in detail (look closely for some very unsavory goings-on), as well as models and costumed figures. *Off M80, tel. 01786/812664. Admission: £1.80 adults, 90p senior citizens and children. Open Apr.–Oct., daily 10– 5:30.*

Tour 2: The Trossachs and Loch Lomond

Numbers in the margin correspond to points of interest on the Central Highlands map.

Inspired by the views of mountainous terrain seen from the ramparts of Stirling Castle, you can now make your way out to the Highland line. Start by navigating out of Stirling on the A9 past the
⓮ pencil-thin **Wallace Monument** on the Abbey Craig, from which you can see the Ochil Hills as a rocky moorland beyond. Follow Bridge of Allan signs northward, crossing the River Forth by Robert Stephenson's New Bridge of 1832, next to the historic old one. The Wallace Monument is signposted at the next traffic circle. Up close, this Victorian shrine to William Wallace, built between 1856 and 1869, becomes less slim and soaring, revealing itself to be a substantial square tower with a creepy spiral stairway. An exhibition and audiovisual presentation tell Wallace's story. *Abbey Craig, tel. 01786/472140. Admission: £2.35 adults, £1.20 senior citizens and children. Open Apr.–Oct., daily 10–5; Nov.–Mar., weekends 11–3.*

You may wish to detour east for a minute or two on the A91, along the south side of the Abbey Craig, to visit **Cambuskenneth Abbey.** The scanty remains of this 13th-century religious seat lie in a sweeping bend of the River Forth, with the dramatic outline of Stirling Castle as a backdrop. Important meetings of the Scottish Parliament were once held here, and King Edward I of England visited in 1304. The abbey was looted and damaged during the Scots Wars of Independence (1307–14). The reconstructed tomb of King James III (who died in 1488) can be seen near the outline of the high altar.

The road west to **Bridge of Allan** lies along the edge of the Ochil Hills and runs past the campus of Stirling University. Bridge of

The Central Highlands

KEY

— Rail Lines

✈ Airport

0   10 miles

0   15 km

N

Fort Augustus

Loch Ness

Invergarry

Laggan

Loch Lochy

A82

Loch Oich

A86

Roughburn

Cromra

Loch Laggan

Catlodge

Laggan

Newtonmore

Kingussie

Dalwhinnie

Dalnaspidal Lodge

Loch Ericht

A9

Calvine

Blair Atholl

Blair Castle 33

Pass of **Killiecrankie**

32

30 **Pitlochry**

Queen's View

B8019

31 **Linn of Tummel**

Loch Tummel

Tummel Bridge

B846

B846

Castle Menzies 35

Aberfeldy 36

R. Tay

R. Tummel

Dowally

Spittal of Glenshee

A93

Kirkmichael

Dykendo

Bridge-of-Cally

Blairgowrie

Alyth

Rattray

R. Tay

Kenmore

37

Fearnan

Loch Rannoch 34

Rannoch

Blackwater Reservoir

Loch Treig

Allan was formerly a spa town and has substantial Victorian properties. Rejoin the A9 for a few moments' journey north to **Dunblane.**
Its 13th-century cathedral has been partly restored, and the oldest
part of the community—with its twisting streets and mellow town
houses—huddles around the square and churchyard where the cathedral stands.

Turn west onto the A820 and continue west for a few minutes to
another Highland-edge community, **Doune.** This was once a center
for pistol making. No Highland chief's attire was complete without
a prestigious and ornate pair of pistols. Today, Doune is more widely
known as the site of one of the best-preserved medieval castles in
Scotland. (It is signposted left as you enter the town from the Dunblane road.) It looks like an early castle is supposed to look: grim
windowed and high walled, with echoing stone vaults and numerous
drafts. Construction of the fortress began in the early 15th century
on a now-peaceful riparian tract. The best place to photograph this
squat, great-walled fort is from the bridge, a little way upstream,
which carries the A9 west from Stirling. *Off A84, tel. 0131/244–3101.
Admission: £2 adults, £1.25 senior citizens, 75p children, £4.50 family
ticket. Open Apr.–Sept., Mon.–Sat. 9:30–6, Sun. 2–6; Oct.–Mar., Mon.–
Wed. and Sat. 9:30–4, Thurs. 9:30–1, Sun. 2–4.*

Rejoin another main road, the A84, which continues to **Callander,** a
traditional Highland-edge resort. Callander bustles throughout the
year—even on Sunday during off-peak times—simply because it is
a gateway to Highland scenery within easy reach of Edinburgh and
Glasgow. As a result there is plenty of window-shopping here, plus
nightlife in pubs and a good choice of accommodations, from simple
bed-and-breakfasts to lavish, sophisticated hotels (*see* Dining and
Lodging, *below*).

Callander's **Rob Roy and Trossachs Visitor Centre,** housed in the
former St. Kessog's Church, provides visitors yet another encounter with the famed Rob Roy MacGregor. As defender of the down-
trodden and scourge of the authorities, MacGregor is known as a
tartan Robin Hood. An old-style and much revered Highland hero,
Rob Roy died peacefully at his home in 1734. You can learn more
about his high jinks in a high-tech account—replete with displays
and tableaux—in the modern visitor center. *Ancaster Sq., tel.
01877/330342. Admission: £2 adults, £1.50 senior citizens and children. Open Jan., Feb., Sat. and Sun. 10–4; Mar.–May and Oct.–Dec.,
daily 10–5; June and Sept., daily 9:30–7; July–Aug., daily 9 AM–10:30
PM.*

Time Out   **Pip's Coffee House,** just off the main street in the center, is bright
and cheerful and has an interesting picture gallery.

Callander's other attractions away from the bustle of the main
street are mainly rural in nature: a walk signposted from the east
end of the main street to the **Bracklinn Falls,** over whose lip Sir
Walter Scott once rode a pony to win a bet, or another walk through
the woods up to the **Callander Crags,** with views of the Lowlands as
far as the Pentland Hills behind Edinburgh. (This walk is for the fit
and well-shod only.)

Callander is the gateway to the Trossachs, but since it is on the main
road, the A84, it also attracts overnight visitors on their way to
Oban, Fort William, and beyond. All this traffic enters the proper
Highlands just north of Callander, where the thickly clad slopes
squeeze both the road and rocky river into the narrow **Pass of Leny.**

An abandoned railway—now a pleasant walking or bicycling path—also goes through the pass. If time permits, go part of the way along this path out of Callander past **Ben Ledi** mountain and Loch Lubnaig.

Beyond Strathyre and its extensive forestry-commission plantings, within a 20-minute drive of Callander, is a road that will take you
🔞 west to **Balquhidder** (pronounced *bal*-whidd-*er*). In this northern extension of the excursion, the first Highland glen that many visitors will see runs westward. Note its characteristics, seen throughout the north: a flat-bottomed, U-shape profile formed by prehistoric glaciers; extensive forestry plantings replacing much of the natural woodlands above; a sprinkling of farms; and farther up the glen, new hill roads bulldozed into the slopes to provide access for shepherds and foresters. Note also the shut-up look of some of the houses, many of which are second homes for affluent residents of the south. The glen is also where **Lochs Voil and Doune** spread out, adding to the stunning vistas. This area is often known as the Braes (Slopes) of Balquhidder and was once the home of the MacLarens and the MacGregors. Rob Roy MacGregor's grave is signposted beside Balquhidder itself. The site of his house, now a private farm, is beyond the car park at the end of the road.

The glen has no through road, although in earlier times local residents were familiar with hill passes to the north and south. There still exists, for example, a right-of-way from the churchyard where Rob Roy is buried, via the plantings in Kirkton Glen and then on to open windy grasslands and a blue *lochan* (little lake). This path eventually drops into the next valley, Glen Dochart, and rejoins the A84.

The A821 runs west along with the first and gentlest of the Trossachs lochs: **Loch Venachar.** The sturdy gray-stone buildings with a
🔞 small dam at the Callander end control the water fed into the River Teith (and, hence, into the Forth) to compensate for the Victorian tinkerings with the water supply. Within a few minutes the A821 becomes muffled in woodlands and twists gradually down to **Brig o' Turk.** (*Turk* here is Gaelic for *tuirc,* meaning wild boar, a species that sadly has been extinct in this region since about the 16th century.)

Time Out **Dundarroch and the Byre** (tel. 01877/376200) is a well-run pub and restaurant just beyond Brig o' Turk, with dark beams and loosely defined Victorian decor, as well as attentive, friendly service. It's a lunchtime haven (limited opening time in winter, so ring in advance), particularly on a wet day in the woodlands, but also offers a full evening menu. A number of signposted walks also start from here.

West of Brig o' Turk stretches **Loch Achray,** dutifully fulfilling expectations of what a verdant Trossachs loch should be: small, green, reedy meadows backed by dark plantations, rhododendron thickets, and lumpy, thickly covered hills. Note the car park on the left, where walkers begin their ascent of the steep, heathery **Ben An.** To enjoy the best Trossachs' views, you will need a couple of hours and your wind. If you don't have much time, continue driving to the end of Loch Achray, following the road (turn right) into a narrow pass. This is the heart of the Trossachs. During the time of Sir Walter Scott, the path was narrow and almost hidden by the overhanging crags and mossy oaks and birches. Today it leads to a slightly anticlimactic car park with a shop, a café, and a visitor center. Not readily visible from the park, the 90-year-old steamer, the S.S. *Sir Walter Scott,*

㉑ embarks on cruises of **Loch Katrine** every summer. To see the finest of the Trossachs lochs or to locate some of the landmarks cited in Scott's *Lady of the Lake*, you must—even for just a few minutes—go westward on foot. The road beyond the car park is open only to Strathclyde Water Board vehicles and is well paved and level.

After going back through the pass on the main A821, turn right and head south, to higher moorland blanketed with conifer plantations (some of which have near-mature timber planted about 60 years ago by the Forestry Commission). The conifers hem in the views of Ben Ledi and Ben Venue, which can be seen over the spiky green waves of trees as the road snakes around heathery knolls and hummocks. There is another viewpoint at the highest point here, indicated by a small car park on the right.

Soon the road swoops off the Highland edge and leads downhill.
㉒ Near the start of the descent, the **Queen Elizabeth Forest Park Visitor Centre** can be seen on the left. The center features displays on the life of the forest, a summer-only café, some fine views over the Lowlands to the south, and a network of footpaths. *Off A821. Open Easter–Oct., daily 10–6.*

The Trossachs end here. The route back east to Stirling gradually
㉓ leaves the hills behind and is noted mainly for the **Lake of Menteith,** a few minutes east of Aberfoyle. Mary, Queen of Scots, was stowed away at the lake for her own safety as a child in 1547. On a wooded islet the ruined **Inchmahome Priory,** where Mary was supposedly cosseted, can be reached by boat from the Port of Menteith.

Instead of returning to Stirling (barely half an hour), those visitors
㉔ who want to cover **Loch Lomond** in one day have a couple of options. To reach Loch Lomond quickly from Aberfoyle, you can choose to see either the southern, wider end of the loch—studded with islands—near the Highland line, or the more enclosed northern portion. The distances to Balmaha, toward the south end, and to Inversnaid farther north, are about the same: approximately 14 miles, though there is an optional extension of about 7 miles to Rowardennan north of Balmaha. These distances will be easier to follow by consulting your map. Both routes are recommended and are briefly described here. Which one you choose depends on your taste. The **Aberfoyle–Inversnaid** trip is bereft of tea shops. In fact, during the off-season, the route has, in certain places, a wild and windswept air when it extends beyond the shelter of trees. The **Aberfoyle–Balmaha** section (via Drymen) offers a wider choice of pubs and hotels—and even a good-quality dress shop in Drymen.

For the Aberfoyle–Inversnaid trip, take the B829 (signposted Inversnaid and Stronachlachar), which runs west from Aberfoyle and offers outstanding views of **Ben Lomond,** especially in the vicinity of **Loch Ard.** The next loch, where the road narrows and bends, is **Loch Chon,** dark and forbidding. Its ominous reputation is further enhanced by the local legend, the presence of a dog-headed monster prone to swallowing passersby. Beyond Loch Chon, the road climbs gently from the plantings to open moor with a breathtaking vista over **Loch Arklet** to the **Arrochar Alps,** the name given to the high hills west of Loch Lomond. Hidden from sight in a deep trench, Loch Arklet is dammed to feed Loch Katrine.

Go left at a road junction (a right will take you to Stronachlachar) and take the open road along Loch Arklet. These deserted green hills were once the rallying grounds of the Clan Gregor. Near the dam on Loch Arklet, on your right, **Garrison Cottage** recalls the days when the government had to billet troops here to keep the MacGregors in order.

From Loch Arklet, the road zigzags down to **Inversnaid,** where you will see a hotel, a house, and a car park, with Loch Lomond stretching out of sight above and below. The long-distance walkers' route, the **West Highland Way,** which runs 95 miles from Glasgow to Fort William, follows the bank here. Take a brief stroll up the path, particularly if you are visiting during the spring, when the oak-tree canopy is filled with birdsong. You may get an inkling why Scots get so romantic about their bonny, bonny banks.

The only return to Aberfoyle is by retracing the same route—except that you may wish to go down to **Stronachlachar** on Loch Katrine. This is where the steamer calls; the town is no more than a pier with neatly clipped hedges and a cluster of houses belonging to Strathclyde Water Board workers. Loch Katrine's water is taken by aqueduct and tunnel to Glasgow—a Victorian feat of engineering that has ensured the purity of the supply to Scotland's largest city for more than a hundred years.

The second way of getting to Loch Lomond from Aberfoyle involves a faster trip on the main road to **Drymen,** a respectable and cozy town in the Lowland fields, with shops and pubs catering to the well-to-do Scots who have moved here from Glasgow.

Time Out   Drymen has a solid handful of pubs and tea shops, but try the **Clachan Inn** (tel. 01360/60824), which offers appetizing bar meals.

The B837 from Drymen, signposted Rowardennan and Balmaha, heads northwest, and in a few minutes Loch Lomond comes into view. At the little settlement of **Balmaha,** the versatile recreational role filled by Loch Lomond becomes clearer: Cruising craft are at the ready, hikers appear out of woodlands on the West Highland Way, and day-trippers stroll at the loch's edge. The heavily wooded offshore islands look alluringly near. One of the best ways to explore them is to take a cruise with the boat-hire company **MacFarlane and Son** (Boatyard, Balmaha, Loch Lomond G63 0JG, tel. 0136087/214). (You can even rent a rowboat from MacFarlane's if you prefer doing your own exploration.) The island of **Inchcailloch** (*Inch-* is really *Innis,* Gaelic for *island*), just offshore, can be explored in an hour or two. There are pleasant pathways through oak woods planted in the 18th century, when the bark was used in the tanning industry.

Behind Balmaha is **Conic Hill,** a wavy ridge of bald heathery domes above the pine trees, and you can note from your map how Inchcailloch and the other islands line up with it. This geographic line is indicative of the Highland Boundary Fault, which runs through the loch and the hill.

If you want to take in even more of Loch Lomond, the cul-de-sac road continues northwest to **Rowardennan,** with the loch seldom more than a field's length away. Where the drivable road ends, in a car park crunchy with pinecones, you can ramble along one of the marked loch-side footpaths, or make your way towards not-so-nearby Ben Lomond.

Tour 3: Around Perthshire

㉕ Some say **Perth** took its name from a Roman camp, Bertha, on the shores of the Tay. Whatever the truth, this strategic site has been occupied continuously for centuries, even prior to its becoming a

Royal Burgh in 1210. Perth has long been a focal point in Scottish history, and several critical events took place here, including the assassination of King James I in 1437 and John Knox's preaching in St. John's Kirk in 1559. (Knox's sermon undoubtedly stirred his congregation: Afterward, they went rampaging through the town, igniting the Reformation in Scotland.) Later, the 17th-century religious wars in Scotland saw the town occupied first by the marquis of Montrose, then later by Oliver Cromwell's forces. Perth was also occupied by the Jacobites in the 1715 and 1745 rebellions.

Perth has been rebuilt and recast innumerable times, and, sadly, no trace remains of the pre-Reformation monasteries that once dominated the city skyline. In fact, modern Perth has swept much of its colorful history under a grid of bustling shopping streets. The town serves a wide rural hinterland and has a well-to-do air, making it one of the most interesting shopping towns aside from Edinburgh and Glasgow. Yet unlike Stirling, Perth's attractions—with the exception of the shops—are more scattered and take more time to reach on foot. Some, in fact, are far enough away to necessitate the use of a car, bus, or taxi. The following places are near the town center: **St. John's Kirk** (St. John St., tel. 01738/26159) dating from the 15th century, escaped the worst excesses of the mob and is now restored; **Perth Art Gallery and Museum** (George St., tel. 01738/32488), which has a wide-ranging collection of local history and archaeology, plus a rotating exhibit program; and the nearby **Fair Maid's House** (North Port, tel. 01738/25976), which features a Scottish crafts shop.

On the North Inch of Perth look for **Balhousie Castle** and the **Regimental Museum of the Black Watch.** Some will tell you the Black Watch was a Scottish regiment whose name is a reference to the color of their tartan. An equally plausible explanation, however, is that the regiment was established to keep an undercover watch on rebellious Jacobites. The *Black* is the Gaelic word *dubh*, meaning hidden or covert, used in the same way as the English word, *blackmail. Facing North Inch Park (entrance from Hay St.), tel. 01738/21281, ext. 8530. Admission free. Open weekdays 10–4:30 (3:30 in winter). Closed Dec. 23–Jan 3.*

The nearby Round House is home to the **Fergusson Gallery,** displaying a selection of 6,000 works—paintings, drawings, prints—by the Scottish artist, J.D. Fergusson. *Marshall Pl., tel. 01738/441944. Admission free. Open Mon.–Sat. 10–5.*

Off the A9, west of town, you can visit **Caithness Glass,** where from the viewing gallery you can watch glassworkers creating smoky-smooth bowls, vases, and other glassware. There is also a small museum, restaurant, and shop. *Inveralmond, Perth, tel. 01738/37373. Admission free. Factory open weekdays 9–4:30. Shop open Easter–Oct., Mon.–Sat. 9–5, Sun. 11–5; Oct.–Easter, Mon.–Sat. 9–5, Sun. 1–5.*

㉖ A modest selection of castles is also within easy reach. **Huntingtower Castle,** a curious double tower dating from the 15th century, is associated with a political attempt to wrest power from the young James VI in 1582. Some early painted ceilings survive, the vaguest hint of the sumptuous decor once found in many such ancient castles that are now reduced to bare and drafty rooms. *Off A85, tel. 0131/244–3101. Admission: £1.50 adults, £1 senior citizens, 75p children. Open Apr.–Sept., Mon.–Sat. 9:30–6, Sun. 2–6; Oct.–Mar., Mon.–Wed. and Sat. 9:30–4, Thurs. 9–1, Sun. 2–4.*

㉗ Much the same description applies to **Elcho Castle,** a fortified mansion on the east side of Perth. Some fabric and plasterwork still cling to the cold stone in this abandoned 15th-century seat of the earls of Wemyss. The effect is slightly eerie: Instead of a long-dead shell, there are hints of a building barely alive. *On River Tay, tel. 0131/244–3101. Admission: £1.20 adults, 75p children. Open Apr.–Sept., Mon.–Sat. 9:30–6, Sun. 2–6.*

㉘ Scone Palace is another story altogether: More cheerful and vibrant, the palace is the present home of the Earl of Mansfield and is open to visitors. Although it incorporates various earlier works, the palace today consists mainly of a 19th-century theme, featuring mock castellations that were fashionable at the time. There is plenty to see for the visitor with an interest in the acquisitions of an aristocratic Scottish family: magnificent porcelain, furniture, ivory, clocks, and 16th-century needlework. Visitor facilities also include a coffee shop, restaurant, gift shop, and play area, as well as extensive grounds that include a pinetum. The palace has its own chapel nearby, on the site of a long-gone abbey. The chapel stands by Moot Hill, the ancient meeting and crowning place of the Scottish kings. *Braemar Rd., tel. 01738/52300. Admission: £4.20 adults, £3.40 senior citizens, £2.30 children, £12.50 family ticket. Open Easter–Oct., Mon–Sat. 9:30–5, Sun. 1:30–5 (July–Aug., Sun 10–5).*

To take in the rest of Perthshire, go north on the A9 into the Highlands at **㉙ Dunkeld,** where the hills and woodlands converge. Exit from the A9 and cross Thomas Telford's handsome river bridge of 1809 to enter the town. Note the antiques shop on the right, facing the river across the bridge; it is well worth a browse. In Dunkeld you will find that the National Trust for Scotland not only cares for grand mansions and wildlands but also actively restores smaller properties. The work it completed under its "Little Houses" scheme can be seen in the square off the main street, just opposite the fish-and-chips shop. All the houses in the square were rebuilt after the 1689 Battle of Killiecrankie (*see below*), when, after its victory, the Jacobite army marched south and was defeated here.

㉚ The A9 continues north to **Pitlochry,** perhaps the typical central-Highland resort. Always full of leisurely hustle and bustle, Pitlochry has wall-to-wall souvenir and gift shops, large hotels recalling even more laid-back days, and a mountainous golf course. One popular attraction is the **Pitlochry Dam and Fish Ladder,** just behind the main street. So that generating needs do not clash with sports interests, most Scottish dams have salmon passes or ladders of some kind, enabling the fish to swim upstream to their spawning grounds. In Pitlochry, the fish ladder leads into a glass-paneled pipe so that they can observe the visitors.

For those with a whisky-tasting bent, Pitlochry also is home to **Edradour Distillery,** which claims to be the smallest single-malt distillery in Scotland (but then, so do others). *2¹/₂ mi east of Pitlochry, tel. 01796/472095. Admission free. Open for tours and tastings Mar.–Oct., Mon.–Sat. 9:30–5; shop also open Nov.–Feb., Mon.–Sat. 10–4.*

㉛ The **Linn of Tummel,** a series of marked walks along the river and through tall, mature woodlands, is a little way north of the town. Above the Linn, the new A9 is raised on stilts and gives an exciting view of the valley. Visitors can pick up a walks booklet at the **Killiecrankie Visitor Centre,** a short distance farther on. To reach the Linn and Killiecrankie from Pitlochry, stay on the old A9, heading north. From the old A9, note the B8019 road heading west. (The tour returns to this point later.) *Off A9, tel. 01796/473233. Admission: £1 adults, children free. Site open all year; Visitor Centre open Easter–mid-Oct., daily 10–5:30.*

㉜ The **Pass of Killiecrankie,** set among the oak woods and rocky river, was a key strategic point in the Central Highlands: A famous battle was won there in the Jacobite rebellion of 1689. The National Trust for Scotland's visitor center at Killiecrankie explains the significance of this, the first attempt to restore the Stuart monarchy. The battle was noted for the death of the Jacobite leader, James Graham of Claverhouse, also known as Bonnie Dundee, hit by a stray bullet; the rebellion fizzled out after that.

Only a few minutes farther north from the Pass of Killiecrankie sits ㉝ **Blair Castle.** Take the A9 to Blair Atholl, where the castle is clearly signposted. Because of its historic contents and its war-torn past, this is one of Scotland's most highly rated castle visits. White painted and turreted, Blair Castle has been home to successive dukes of Atholl and their family, the Murrays. One of the many fascinating details in the interior is a preserved piece of flooring that still bares marks of the red-hot shot fired through the roof during the 1745 Jacobite rebellion—the last occasion in Scottish history that a castle was besieged. The castle holds not only military artifacts—the duke is allowed to keep a private army, the Atholl Highlanders—but also a fine collection of furniture and paintings. Outside, extensive parklands are backed by high rounded hills. *Tel. 01796/481207. Admission: £4.50 adults, £3.50 senior citizens and children. Open Apr.–late Oct., daily 10–6 (last entry 5).*

From Blair the main A9 heads north over the watershed (by way of the Pass of Drumochter) to Speyside. To stay in Perthshire, return south to the B8019, noted earlier, below Killiecrankie. The B8019 turns into the B846 at Tummel Bridge and continues to Loch Rannoch. Take this section if you have plenty of time and are following ㉞ this tour over a few days. **Loch Rannoch,** with its shoreline birch trees and dark pines behind, is the quintessential Highland loch. Continuing westward the road ends at Rannoch, where you meet the West Highland railroad line on its way across Rannoch Moor to Fort William. Fans of Robert Louis Stevenson, especially of *Kidnapped,* will not want to miss the last, lonely section of road. Stevenson describes the setting:

The mist rose and died away, and showed us that country lying as waste as the sea; only the moorfowl and the peewees crying upon it, and far over to the east a herd of deer, moving like dots. Much of it was red with heather; much of the rest broken up with bogs and hags and peaty pools. . . .

Apart from the blocks of alien conifer plantings in certain places, little here has changed.

If you stay on the B846, heading south and then east, you will pass ㉟ **Castle Menzies.** This Z-plan 16th-century fortified tower/house is now the setting for the **Clan Menzies' Museum.** *Tel. 01887/820982. Admission: £2.50 adults, £1.50 senior citizens, 75p children. Open Apr.–mid-Oct., Mon.–Sat. 10:30–5, Sun. 2–5 (last entry 4:30).*

㊱ A little farther on, travelers will reach **Aberfeldy** by way of General Wade's Aberfeldy Bridge (1733). This is the most impressive example of an English-built military road, a five-arch, humpback bridge designed by William Adam. Aberfeldy itself is a sleepy town that is popular as a tourist base. If you wish to return to Perth, the A9 is only about a 10-mile drive east on the A827.

㊲ The next loop returns west to **Kenmore,** at the eastern end of Loch Tay. **Taymouth Castle** nearby has a famous parkland golf course. However, before continuing west, you should explore an interesting route running southeast from Kenmore. An unclassified road hair-pins spectacularly out of the valley, giving superb views over the Ben Lawers mountain range to the north of Loch Tay and back to Schiehallion. After taking that slight detour, take the north-bank road by Loch Tay, the A827. At Fearnan you can divert a few minutes northward to Fortingall to view the **Fortingall yew,** near the Fort-ingall Hotel, in the churchyard. Wearily resting its great limbs on the ground, this tree is thought to be more than 3,000 years old. Legend has it that Pontius Pilate was born beside it, while his father served as a Roman legionnaire in Scotland.

The A827 offers fine views west along Loch Tay toward Ben More ❸❽ and Stobinian. The sign to Ben Lawers also points toward **Killin,** a village with an almost-alpine flavor. Known for its modest but sur-prisingly diverse selection of crafts and woolen wares, Killin is also noted for its scenery. The **Falls of Dochart,** white-water rapids over-looked by a pine-clad islet, are located at the west end of the village. Across the River Dochart and near the golf course sit the ruins of **Finlarig Castle,** built by Black Duncan of the Cowl, a notorious Campbell laird. The castle's beheading pit is certainly the most hair-raising of its surviving features. The castle can be visited at any time.

Time Out   **Shutters Restaurant** (Main St., Killin, tel. 01567/820314) serves rea-sonably priced meals all day (11–3:30 only in winter). Also of interest is the display of old photographs.

Southwest of Killin the A827 joins the main A85. By turning south over the watershed, you will see fine views of the hill ridges behind Killin. The road leads into Glen Ogle, "amid the wildest and finest scenery we had yet seen . . . putting one in mind of prints of the Khyber Pass," as Queen Victoria recorded in her diary when she passed this way in 1842.

❸❾ The glen drops into the settlement of **Lochearnhead.** Make a left at the intersection, and you will see the **Lochearnhead Watersports Centre** by the shore of Loch Earn; the center offers instruction and equipment rentals for water-sports enthusiasts, from novices to ex-perts. **Loch Earn** is the last of the lochs on this Perthshire loop. Still on the A85 going east you will have good views of the long, gray screes of Ben Vorlich southward across the loch.

You will then drive by the village of **St. Fillans,** through lush Perth-shire estates and farmlands, and on to **Comrie.** The countryside east of Comrie looks more lush and is reminiscent of the Lowlands; the ❹⓪ higher hills can be seen to the north. **Crieff,** the hilly town you will encounter next, offers walks with Highland views from **Knock Hill** above the town, as well as tours of the **Glenturret Distillery,** sign-posted on the west side of the town. *Tel. 01764/652424. Admission: £2.70 adults, £1.90 senior citizens, £1.50 children 12–17, children under 12 free. Open Mar.–Dec., Mon.–Sat. 9:30–4:30, Sun. 11:30–4:30; Jan.–Feb., weekdays 11:30–2:30.*

Just south of Crieff is a paperweight manufacturer, part of a com-plex called the **Crieff Visitors Centre.** Adjacent to the complex is a small pottery factory and a restaurant. During the week there are surprisingly interesting tours of the factory grounds, where you can see Thistle hand-painted pottery, intricate millefiori glass, and lamp-work Perthshire paperweights being made. *A822, just south of Crieff, tel. 01764/654014. Admission free (small charge for pottery factory tour). Open daily 9–6 (until 5 in winter).*

Perth is less than half an hour away via the A85, but an equally interesting return can be made by diverting through Auchterarder.
41 On the way, the A822 passes **Drummond Castle,** with its unusual formal Italian garden. *Off Crieff/Muthill Rd., tel. 01764/681257. Admission to garden: £2 adults, £1 senior citizens and children. Gardens open May–Sept., daily 2–6 (last entry 5 PM).*

42 The A823 leads to **Auchterarder,** famous for the **Gleneagles Hotel** and its recreational facilities (*see* Dining and Lodging, *below*). A number of antiques shops have also made a name for themselves at Auchterarder. The nearby **Glenruthven Weaving Mill** has been converted into a heritage center with a Scottish theme. The steam engine that once powered the mill can also be viewed. From Auchterarder, the fast-moving A9 stretches northeast to Perth.

Central Highlands for Free

Bells Cherrybank Gardens (Cherrybank, off Glasgow Rd., Perth, tel. 01738/27330) has 18 acres of landscaped gardens and the Bells national heather collection. *Open May–mid-Oct., daily 9–5.*
Bracklinn Falls (*see* Tour 2)
The **Pitlochry Dam and Fish Ladder** (*see* Tour 3)
The **Trossachs** (*see* Tour 2)

What to See and Do with Children

Other than the sports-and-leisure facilities listed under Sports and Fitness, *below,* attractions for children are limited. There are several bicycle routes suitable for older children, however. And pony trekking is an option throughout the area (check with your local tourist information center for details). Near Perth, **Fairways Heavy Horse Centre** (Walnut Grove, tel. 01738/32561) offers Clydesdale horses for day rides. For £1.50 (£1 children) you can tour the center's stables and exercise fields.

Most children will enjoy both the **Rob Roy and Trossachs Visitor Centre** (*see* Tour 2), and the **Vane Farm Nature Centre** (near Loch Leven, Kinross, tel. 01577/862355). The latter is operated under the auspices of the Royal Society for the Protection of Birds and has a visitor center with a screened viewing area, nature trail, shop, picnic area, and two camouflaged shelters for observing wildlife, known as hides.

Off the Beaten Track

If Stirling is your base and you feel like taking a brisk evening walk and have your own transportation, seek out the little road that starts by the campus of Stirling University and climbs toward Sheriffmuir. On the way it passes close to the hill called **Dumyat,** on the breezy moors of the Ochils. A short walk is rewarded by superb views across the midland valley of Scotland, to Stirling and far beyond. The road is signposted Sheriffmuir from the old A9.

The ospreys that frequent Speyside's Loch Garten in summer get so much attention from conservation societies that they sometimes overshadow **Loch of the Lowes,** a Scottish Wildlife Trust reserve behind Dunkeld. Here the domestic routines of the osprey, one of Scotland's conservation success stories, can be observed in relative comfort. The reserve is off the A923 northeast of Dunkeld. *Tel. 01350/727337. Visitor center open Apr.–Sept., 10–5. Observation blind open at all times.*

Duncryne Hill has possibly the most outstanding Loch Lomond view from the south end. It takes only a few minutes' clambering up a bracken-covered hill to get there. You may be rewarded by a spectacular sunset. You can't miss this unmistakable dumpling-shaped hill, behind Gartocharn on the Balloch–Drymen road, the A811.

Glen Lyon is worth exploring if you are in the Killin area. Lyon is one of central Scotland's most attractive glens. All the elements of Scottish glens can be found here: a rushing river, forests, high hills on both sides, prehistoric sites complete with legendary tales, and the typical *big hoose* hidden on private grounds. There is even a dam at the head of the loch, as a reminder that little of Scotland's scenic beauty is unadulterated. You can reach the glen either by way of Fortingall (*see* Tour 3) or by a high road from Loch Tay.

Shopping

The Central Highlands presents an interesting assortment of shopping choices, ranging from the larger population centers of Perth and Stirling, where High Street stores compete with long-established local firms, to the smaller towns and villages, where the selection is more limited but the relaxed pace makes for a pleasant shopping environment.

Callander   Northwest of Stirling are the bustling shops of **Callander.** A vast selection of woolens is on display at **Kilmahog Woollen Mill** and **Trossachs Woollen Mill** (to the north of town at the Trossachs turning) and at the **Callander Woollen Mill** on Main Street. All the stores offer overseas mailing and tax-free shopping. **Presentations** (86 Main St.) stocks Scottish gifts and crafts and specializes in producing clan crests and badges that can be mailed anywhere in the world. Also uniquely Scottish is the stoneware of **Mounter Pottery** (Ancaster Square La.), which you can see being made.

Crieff   Like Perth, **Crieff** is a center for china and glassware. The **Crieff Visitors Centre** (A822, south of Crieff) has a gift shop that sells small and large lamp-work paperweights, millefiori glass, and hand-painted pottery. Nearby, at **Stuart Strathearn's** (Muthill Rd., tel. 01764/654004), Stuart crystal is produced and engraved; factory tours and a factory shop are also available here. If you want something to put in your new set of crystal glasses, visit **Glenturret Distillery** (tel. 01764/652424), just outside Crieff on the road to Comrie. The distillery offers guided tours and a free sampling of its product, Glenturret Pure Single Highland Malt.

Dunkeld   The small town of Dunkeld is home to the **Highland Horn and Deerskin Centre** (City Hall, Atholl St., tel. 01350/727569). Here stag antlers and cow horns are shaped into horn-handled walking sticks, cutlery, and tableware. Deerskin is made into shoes, handbags, wallets, and purses. The center offers a worldwide postal service and a tax-free shop.

Loch Lomond   If you are traveling west to Loch Lomond, visit **Mr. Macpherson,** who has a weaving shed at **Tarbet** (Inverhoulin, tel. 013012/269), where you can see tartans weaved in a traditional handloom manner. Also in Tarbet, housed in a converted church at Station Road, is **The Black Sheep,** which specializes in crafts and offers a good cup of coffee and a meal. South of Loch Lomond are some of the larger shopping centers: **Alexandria, Dumbarton,** and **Helensburgh.** Try **R & A Urie** (45 W. Clyde St., Helensburgh) for fine china and crystal (it has an export service) and nearby **MacGillivrays** (89 W. Clyde

St.) for Scottish gifts. Scottish silver jewelry, including the Charles Rennie Mackintosh Collection, is featured at **Hudsons Jewellers** (101 Main St., Alexandria). This part of the Central Highlands also offers an exceptional selection of paintings by contemporary Scottish artists: try **Helensburgh Fine Arts** (78 W. Clyde St., Helensburgh) or **The Rowan Gallery** (36 Main St., Drymen).

Perth **Perth** proffers an unusual buy: Scottish freshwater pearls from the River Tay, in delicate settings that take their theme from Scottish flowers. The Romans coveted these pearls. If you do, too, then you can make your choice at **Cairncross Jewellers and Goldsmiths** (18 St. John St.), where you can also admire a display of some of the more unusual shapes and colors of pearls found. Antique Scottish jewelry and silver can be found at **Timothy Hardie** (25 St. John St.), and **Whispers of the Past** (George St.) has a collection of linens and jewelry. A comprehensive selection of sheepskins, leather jackets, and hand-knit Aran sweaters are on sale at **L & C Proudfoot** (104 South St.). Perth is an especially popular hunting ground for china and glass: **Watson of Perth** (163–167 High St.) has sold exquisite bone china and cut crystal since 1900 and can pack your purchase safely for shipment overseas. Just outside Perth, at **Caithness Glass** (Inveralmond, off the A9 at the northern town boundary), you can see glassware being made and then buy the product in the factory shop.

Stirling In **Stirling, Murray Place** and the **Thistle Centre** provide all the standard High Street names. Lovers of antiquarian books should trek to the older part of town, where, at 55 King Street, the **Corn Exchange Bookshop** will keep them happy for an hour or two with its extensive number of titles, including books on every aspect of Scotland. Not far away, on Friars Street, is **Ezhe Hirsh,** a jeweler designing his own restrained and distinctive gold and silver items set with diamonds, pearls, opals, and other precious stones. At Nos. 6–8 is **R. R. Henderson Ltd.,** a kilt maker established in 1923 (knitwear and tweeds can be sent worldwide). Farther along, at Nos. 29–31, is **John M. Hay,** where you can buy a set of bagpipes or a record or cassette of Scottish music (it also offers an overseas-shipment service). Finally, do not miss the **medieval fairs** held on Broad Street from time to time during the summer season.

South of Stirling, at **Larbert,** don't miss **Barbara Davidson's pottery studio** (tel. 01324/554430) in a picturesque 18th-century farm setting. Here's a unique opportunity to buy a souvenir from one of the best-known potters in Scotland.

East of Stirling is **Mill Trail** country, along the foot of the Ochil Hills. A leaflet from a tourist-information center will lead you to the delights of a real mill shop and low mill prices—even on cashmere—at **Tillicoultry, Alva,** and **Alloa.**

Sports and Fitness

Bicycling The big attraction for cyclists is the dedicated Glasgow–Killin cycleway. This takes advantage of former railroad track-beds, as well as otherwise private roads plus some quiet minor roads, to get well into the Central Highlands by way of the Trossachs and Callander. Details (maps, leaflets, etc.) from Loch Lomond, Stirling, and Trossachs Tourist Board (*see* Essential Information, *above*). Away from the cycleway, the main roads can be quite busy with holiday traffic. You can rent bikes from:

Lochside Mountain Bike Hire (Lochside Guest House, Arrochar, tel. 013012/467), **Loch Tay Mountain Bike Hire** (Pedlars, Main St., Killin, tel. 01567/820652), **New Heights Mountain Bike Hire** (26 Barnton St., Stirling, tel. 01786/450809), **Trossachs Cycle Hire** (Trossachs Holiday Park, Aberfoyle, tel. 01877/382614), **Wheels** (Manse La., Callander, tel. 01877/331100).

Fishing There are several fishing options in the area, including course and game fishing, loch and river fishing, and sea angling. Tourist-information centers produce annually updated leaflets.

Golf **Blairgowrie** (Rosemount, tel. 01250/872622), 18 holes, 6,556 yards, par 72.

Callander (Aveland Rd., tel. 01877/330090), 18 holes, 5,125 yards, par 66.

Hiking Tourist-information centers carry information on a variety of local routes. The publications *Walk Loch Lomond and the Trossachs* or *Walk Perthshire* are invaluable for hikers and trekkers and are available at bookshops or tourist-information centers.

Horseback Riding **Coilessan Riding Centre** (Coilessan House, Ardgarten, Arrochar, tel. 013012/523) is an approved riding outfit for beginners and experienced riders alike, offering over 20 routes on hill and seashore tracts.

Water Sports **Lochearnhead Water Sports Centre** (Loch Earn, tel. 01567/830330) has sailboats, canoes, and sailboards for wind surfing.

Loch Tay Boating Centre (Carlin and Brett, Pier Rd., Kenmore, tel. 01887/830291) has cabin cruisers and canoes.

Dining and Lodging

Dining

The restaurants of this region have been continually improving over the past several years. Regional country delicacies, such as loch trout, river salmon, mutton, and venison, are now found regularly on modest menus; this was extremely rare just 20 years ago. The urban areas south and southwest of Stirling, in contrast, lack refinement in matters of eating and drinking. There you will find simple low-built pubs, often crowded and noisy but serving substantial food at lunchtime (eaten balanced on your knee, perhaps, or at a shared table). Three heavy courses at one of these pubs will cost you about £10.

Highly recommended restaurants are indicated by a star ★.

Category	Cost*
$$$$	over £40
$$$	£30–£40
$$	£15–£30
$	under £15

*per person for a three-course meal, including VAT

Lodging

In Stirling and Callander, as well as in the small towns and villages throughout the region, you will find a selection of tourist accommodations out of all proportion to the size of the communities. (The industrial towns are the exceptions.) Standards of less-expensive establishments have improved in recent years and are still improving. The grand hotels, though few, were brought into existence by the rich carriage trade of the 19th century, when travel in Scotland was the fashion, and the level of service at these places has, by and large, not slipped. You will also find many country hotels, however, that match the grand hotels in comfort.

Highly recommended hotels are indicated by a star ★.

Category	Cost*
$$$$	over £120
$$$	£100–£120
$$	£80–£100
$	under £80

*All prices are for a standard double room, including breakfast and tax.

Auchterarder
Lodging
★

Auchterarder House. This wood-paneled, richly furnished Victorian country mansion is secluded and superbly atmospheric. Once owned by the steam locomotive magnate James Reid, the Auchterarder House still shows all the ebullience of the Victorian railway age. Many of the bedrooms have their original furniture, and all share views of private parkland and the Perthshire countryside. All meals are served at a time suitable to the guest, and breakfast at noon is not unheard of. The plush, exuberantly styled dining room, filled with glittering glassware, is an appropriate setting for the hotel's excellent cuisine. *B8062, Perthshire PH3 1DZ, tel. 01764/663646. Restaurant reservations required. Jacket and tie required. 15 rooms with bath. Facilities: croquet. AE, DC, MC, V. $$$$*

Gleneagles Hotel. One of Britain's most famous hotels, Gleneagles is the very image of modern grandeur. Like a vast, secret palace, it stands hidden in breathtaking countryside amid three world-famous golf courses. Recreation facilities are seemingly endless, and there are also three restaurants: the elegant **Strathearn,** the **Dormy Grill** (at the 18th hole of the King's Course), and the **Country Club** (by the swimming pool). All this plus a shopping arcade, Champneys Health Spa, Gleneagles Mark Phillips Equestrian Centre, the British School of Falconry, and Gleneagles Jackie Stewart Shooting School make a stay here a luxurious and unforgettable experience. *PH3 1NF, tel. 01764/662231, fax 01764/662134. Reservations advised. Jacket and tie required in formal areas of the hotel after 7 PM; otherwise dress casual. 236 rooms with bath. Facilities: tennis, swimming pool, saunas, golf. AE, DC, MC, V. $$$$*

Balloch
Lodging
★

Cameron House. This luxury hotel offers a mix of top-quality hotel and country-club facilities (including swimming pools, a gymnasium, and squash courts) on the shores of Loch Lomond. Award-winning chef Jef Bland (formerly of the Caledonian Hotel in Edinburgh) oversees Scottish-French cuisine of the highest order, served in rich Victorian surroundings. Bedrooms are decorated in modern pastel shades with high-quality reproductions of antique furniture. *Loch Lomond, Alexandria, Dumbartonshire G83 8QZ, tel. 01389/55565, fax 01389/59522. Reservations advised. Dress: casual but neat. 68 rooms with bath. Facilities: lounge, bar, health club, 2 pools. AE, DC, MC, V. $$$–$$$$*

Brig o' Turk
Dining and
Lodging

Dundarroch and The Byre. This Victorian, antiques-furnished country house, set on 14 acres of grounds, offers first-class guest-house accommodations. The adjoining **Byre Restaurant** serves savory Scottish meals in a Victorian setting. Try the poached Tay salmon with hollandaise sauce. *Trossachs, Perthshire FK17 8HT, tel. 01877/376200, fax 01877/376202. Reservations advised. Dress: casual but neat. 3 rooms; 2 with bath, 1 with shower. MC, V. $*

Callander
Dining and
Lodging
★

Roman Camp. This former hunting lodge, dating from 1625, has 20 acres of gardens with river frontage, yet is within easy walking distance of Callander's town center. Private fishing on the River Teith is another attraction, as are the sitting rooms and the library, which, with their numerous antiques, are more reminiscent of a stately family home than a hotel. The restaurant has high standards, with a good reputation for its salmon, trout, and other seafood cooked in an imaginative, modern Scottish style, and a chef who won't serve the same main course twice. *Perthshire FK17 8BG, tel. 01877/330003. Reservations advised. Jacket and tie preferred. 14 rooms with bath or shower. AE, DC, MC, V. $$–$$$*

Denny
Lodging

Lochend Farm. Extensive views, wholesome farm cooking, and a pleasantly languid pace are the hallmarks of this peaceful working farm. It's only 5 miles from the M9/M80, so it also makes a good touring base. The traditionally furnished (and very comfortable) bedrooms have washbasins and share a private bathroom. *Carronbridge, Denny, Stirlingshire FK6 5JJ, tel. 01324/822778. 2 rooms. No credit cards. $*

Glenfarg
Dining and
Lodging

Bein Inn. Once a prosperous drovers' inn, this hotel has an air of leafy, languid seclusion, bordered as it is by a rippling river and a quiet rural road. The busy M90 is only 2 miles away, so you're also within easy reach by car of Edinburgh and Perth. The hotel itself retains the feel of an old inn with its friendly bar and traditionally furnished lounge and dining room. The latter features a Taste of Scotland menu and is popular with both guests and nonguests. All the bedrooms are spacious, with modern furnishings. *Perthshire PH2 9PY, tel. 01577/830216. Reservations advised. Dress: casual. 13 rooms with bath. MC, V. Restaurant reservations advised. $–$$*

Kinclaven
Dining and
Lodging

Ballathie House. This country-house hotel, located beside the River Tay, offers individually decorated bedrooms and comfortable, relaxed public rooms. Considering the region, it's not surprising that the restaurant menu emphasizes salmon, game, and fresh fruit. Breast of pheasant with blackberry sauce is a typical entrée. *Near Stanley, Perthshire PH1 4QN, tel. 01250/883268, fax 01250/883396. Reservations advised. Jacket and tie required. 28 rooms with bath. AE, DC, MC, V. $$$$*

Kinloch
Rannoch
Lodging

Cuilmore Lodge. This 18th-century croft has been carefully modernized to a very high standard, but it is the superb food which is most memorable: The hostess, Mrs. Steffan, has been awarded a special prize by the Taste of Scotland organization for her home-grown fruit and vegetables, and for her home baking. *Perthshire PH16 5QB, tel. 01882/632218. 2 rooms with bath. (Rate includes dinner). No credit cards. $*

Perth **Parklands.** A smart Georgian town house overlooking lush wood-
Dining and land—an ideal setting for this top-quality bed-and-breakfast—the
Lodging Parklands is perhaps best known for its cuisine, featuring Scottish
fish, game, and beef. The restrained decor and period furniture is
in keeping with the subdued but elegant ambience. *St. Leonards
Bank, PH2 8ER, tel. 01738/22451, fax 01738/22046. 14 rooms with
bath. Facilities: restaurant. AE, MC, V. $$*
Sunbank House. This early Victorian house, set on its own mani-
cured grounds on the outskirts of Perth, has superb views over the
city. Exceptionally high standards of decor, cuisine, and cleanliness
are vigilantly maintained. *50 Dundee Rd., PH2 7BA, tel. and fax
01738/24882. 10 rooms, 5 with bath, 5 with shower. MC, V. $*

Stirling **Heritage.** This elegant 18th-century establishment is run by a
Dining French family. The decor is all fanlights and candles; the menu fea-
tures such French and Scottish classics as coq au vin and beef esca-
lopes with wild mushrooms. *16 Allan Park, tel. 01786/473660, fax
01786/451291. Reservations advised. Dress: casual. MC, V. Closed
Christmas, Jan. 1. $$*
Cross Keys Inn. A quaint, stone-walled dining room adds atmos-
phere to this restaurant's varied traditional Scottish menu, which
includes roast beef, poached salmon, and game pie. If you have enjoyed your meal so much that you don't want to leave, there are
three cozy cottage-style bedrooms upstairs. *Main St., Kippen
(A811, west of Stirling), tel. 01786/870293. 3 rooms, no private facilities. Reservations advised. Jacket and tie preferred. MC, V. $*

Dining and **Stirling Highland Hotel.** This recently opened hotel occupies a hand-
Lodging some building that was once the Old High School. Many original
architectural features, retained during the conversion, add to the
historic atmosphere. The decor is old-fashioned in style, with solid
wood furnishings in tartan or florals and other low-key, neutral color
schemes. *Spittal St., FK8 IDU, tel. 01786/475444, fax 01786/462929.
76 rooms with bath, 4 suites. Facilities: 2 restaurants, piano bar,
sports and leisure club. AE, DC, MC, V. $$$*
Terraces Hotel. This is a centrally located hotel, useful for exploring
Stirling; since there is plenty of parking space, it makes a good base
for touring the region, too. It's a Georgian town house that has been
comfortably converted, and the service is attentive. The **Melville
Restaurant,** part of the hotel, serves something for all tastes: pasta,
steak, chicken, salmon, and seafood, all competently prepared and
served in relaxing brown- and bronze-tone surroundings. *4 Melville
Terr., FK8 2ND, tel. 01786/472268, fax 01786/450314. 18 rooms with
bath or shower. Facilities: restaurant (reservations preferred; jacket
and tie preferred). AE, DC, MC, V. $*

Lodging **Stirling Youth Hostel.** Purpose-built within the shell of a former
church, the hostel offers high-grade four- and six-bed rooms (and a
few doubles) with en suite facilities. Use of two common rooms, the
dining room, and the self-catering, fully equipped kitchen is in-
cluded in the bargain price of £9.95 per person, including breakfast.
*Erskine Marykirk, St. John's St., FK8 IDU, tel. 01786/473442. 128
beds. MC, V. $*
West Plean. This handsome house is part of a working farm. It also
has a walled garden and woodland walks. Well-cooked food and spa-
cious rooms make this bed-and-breakfast an excellent bargain.
*Denny Rd., FK7 8HA, tel. 01786/812208. 3 rooms with bath or shower.
No credit cards. $*

The Arts and Nightlife

The Arts

Outside the main cities, opportunities for cultural activities are limited, except when communities hold arts festivals—a growing phenomenon in Scotland—or if the community is on the itinerary of one of Scotland's major artistic companies; for example, the Scottish Opera. The following venues have a rotating program of cultural events, but check with local tourist-information centers for schedules of other events at such places as **Alloa Town Hall,** the **Guildhall** in **Stirling,** and **Denny Civic Theatre** in **Dumbarton.**

Theater The **Macrobert Arts Centre** (Stirling University, tel. 01786/461081) has a theater, art gallery, and studio with a program that ranges from films to pantomime. The **Perth Repertory Theatre** (High St., Perth, tel. 01738/21031) is a Victorian theater offering a variety of plays and musicals.

Pitlochry Festival Theatre (Pitlochry, tel. 01796/472680) presents six plays each season and features concerts on most Sundays. The theater is open from May to October.

Nightlife

The nightlife in the area tends toward ceilidhs and Scottish concerts. Folk evenings in a number of hotels are also popular. Consult local tourist-information centers for entertainment options. In general, local pubs are friendly and down-to-earth, with patrons who don't mind talking to visitors about what to see and do.

Nightclubs **Electric Whispers Nightclub** (40 Canal St., Perth, tel. 01738/30503).

Scorpios (35 James Sq., Crieff, tel. 01764/654772).

10 Argyll and the Isles

By Gilbert Summers

This popular and alluring region in western Scotland, divided in two by the long peninsula of Kintyre, is characterized by a splintered, complex seaboard. The west is an aesthetic delight, though it's regularly drenched by rain. The same soggy saga also holds true in the Great Glen area, but an occasionally wet foray is the price visitors pay for the glittering freshness of oakwoods and bracken-covered hillsides, and for the bright interplay of sea, loch, and rugged green peninsula.

Kintyre also separates the islands of the Firth of Clyde (including Arran), from the islands of the Inner Hebrides, the largest of which are Mull, Islay, and Jura. You could spend all your time touring these larger islands, but keep in mind that there are plenty of small islands that can also be explored—Bute in the Clyde estuary or the captivating gem of Colonsay between Islay and Mull, for example. Those visiting the mainland cannot avoid the touring center of Oban, an important ferry port with a main road leading south into Kintyre.

Essential Information

Important Addresses and Numbers

Tourist Information
Local tourist-information centers include **Bute and Cowal Tourist Board** (7 Alexandra Parade, Dunoon, Argyll, tel. 01369/3785, fax 01369/6085), **Isle of Arran Tourist Board** (Tourist Information Centre, The Pier, Brodick, Arran, tel. 01770/302140, fax 01770/302395), and **West Highlands and Islands of Argyll Tourist Board** (Albany St., Oban, tel. 01631/63122, fax 01631/64273). There are also seasonal information centers at Bowmore (Islay), Craignure (Mull), Inveraray, Lochgilphead, Lochranza (Arran), Tarbert, and Tobermory (Mull).

Emergencies
For police, fire, or ambulance, dial 999 from any telephone. No coins are needed for emergency calls from public telephone booths.

Doctors and Dentists
Information is available from your hotel, the local tourist-information center, and the police, or look under "Doctors" or "Dentists" in the Yellow Pages telephone directory. There is an emergency room at **West Highland Hospital** (Glencruitten Rd., Oban, tel. 01631/63727).

Late-Night Pharmacies
Pharmacies are not found in rural areas. In an emergency the police will provide assistance in locating a pharmacist. In rural areas general practitioners may also dispense medicines.

Arriving and Departing by Plane

Airports and Airlines
Although the nearest full-service airport for the entire area is in Glasgow (*see* Chapter 5), there are two airports within Argyll and the Isles. Both **Campbeltown** (on the mainland Kintyre peninsula) and the island of **Islay** are served daily by **Loganair** (tel. 0141/889–3181) from Glasgow.

Arriving and Departing by Car, Train, and Bus

By Car
The A85 reaches Oban, the main ferry terminal for Mull, and the A83 rounds Loch Fyne and heads down Kintyre to reach Kennacraig, the main ferry terminal for Islay. Farther down the A83 is Tayinloan, the ferry departure point for Gigha. Brodick (Arran) is reached from Ardrossan on the Clyde coast (A8/A78 from Glasgow), and Rothesay (Bute) from Wemyss Bay (same roads from Glasgow).

For information on ferry times contact **Caledonian MacBrayne** (*see* Getting Around by Car and Ferry, *below*).

By Train Oban (tel. 01631/63083) and Ardrossan (tel. 0141/204–2844) are the main rail stations. All trains connect with ferries.

By Bus Daily bus service from Glasgow Buchanan Street Station to Mid-Argyll and Kintyre is available through **Scottish Citylink** (tel. 0141/332–9191) and **National Express** (tel. 0141/332–4100).

Getting Around

By Car and Ferry Negotiating this area can be quite easy, except in peak season, when the roads around Oban may be congested. There are some single-lane roads, especially on the east side of the Kintyre peninsula and on the islands. Car-ferry services to and from the main islands are operated by **Caledonian MacBrayne** (CalMac, main office is at the Ferry Terminal, Gourock, tel. 01475/650100, fax 01475/637607; for reservations, tel. 01475/650000, fax 01475/637607). A *CalMac Hopscotch* ticket reduces the cost of island-hopping excursions. **Western Ferries** (tel. 0141/332–9766) operates the Islay–Jura ferry service.

By Train Aside from the main line to Oban, with stations at Dalmally, Loch Awe, Falls of Cruachan, Taynuilt, and Connel Ferry, there is no train service. You can travel from the pier head at **Craignure** on **Mull** to **Torosay** by narrow-gauge railway, a distance of about 1 mile.

By Bus The following companies operate in the area: **Arran Coaches** (Arran, tel. 01770/302121), **B. Mundell Ltd.** (Islay, tel. 01496/840273), **Bowman's Coaches** (Mull, tel. 016802/313), **C. MacLean** (Jura, tel. 0149/682–221), **Cowal Motor Service** (Dunoon, tel. 01369/3642), **Oban & District Buses** (Oban and Lorne, tel. 01631/62856), and **West Coast Motor Service** (Mid-Argyll and Kintyre, tel. 01586/552319).

Guided Tours

Orientation The bus companies listed above offer orientation tours.

Special-Interest Bowman's Coaches (*see above*) offers trips to Mull and Iona. **Gordon Grant Marine** (Staffa Ferries, Isle of Iona, tel. 016817/338) offers a "Three Isle" excursion to Mull, Iona, and Staffa, and also trips to the Treshnish Isles and to Staffa, from Mull. Other boat cruises are available on **Loch Etive Cruises** (from Taynuilt near Oban, tel. 018662/430, or call the tourist-information center at Oban). **Sea Life Cruises** on the MV *Alpha Beta* (from Dervaig on Mull, tel. 016884/223) offers three-, five-, and seven-day packages where you can assist with an ongoing whale and dolphin survey. **MacDougall's Tours** (Oban, tel. 01631/62133) runs half- and full-day touring and sailing expeditions to Mull and Iona. Boats leave daily mid-March through October.

Exploring Argyll and the Isles

Orientation

On mainland-based tours Loch Fyne tends to get in the way. It is a long haul around the end of this fjord-like sea loch to reach Inveraray, a popular destination. Ferry services provided by Caledonian MacBrayne (*see* Getting Around by Car, *above*) make all kinds of inter-island tours possible. From Ardrossan, southwest of Glasgow, you can reach the island of Arran, then exit westward to Kintyre by a short ferry crossing. You can continue to the islands of Islay and Jura, and from there a ferry can take you northeast to Oban. (All the ferries transport cars and pedestrians.) The tours described below begin on the mainland but also highlight the main islands.

Highlights for First-Time Visitors

Auchindrain Museum (*see* Tour 1)
Brodick Castle and Country Park (*see* Tour 2)
Crarae Gardens (*see* Tour 1)
Cruachan Dam Visitor Centre (*see* Tour 1)
Inveraray (*see* Tour 1)
Iona (*see* Tour 4)
Islay Woollen Mill (*see* Tour 3)
Kilchurn Castle (*see* Tour 1)
Kildalton Cross (*see* Tour 3)
Torosay Castle (*see* Tour 4)

Tour 1: Around Argyll

Numbers in the margin correspond to points of interest on the Argyll and the Isles map.

Just as it is impossible to avoid Fort William when touring the north, **❶** it is almost impossible to avoid **Oban** when touring this part of Scotland. Unlike Fort William, however, Oban has a legitimate waterfront and several ferry excursions from which to choose. It also has a more pleasant environment, though it does get busy during the peak season. Oban is a traditional Scottish resort where you can find ceilidhs and tartan kitsch, as well as late-night revelry in pubs and hotel bars. There is an inescapable sense, however, that just over the horizon, on the islands or down Kintyre, loom more peaceful and authentic environs. In short, though Oban makes a good starting point for your west-coast Scotland swing, it probably will not be the highlight.

Take the main A85 east out of town. After about 2 miles a sign points **❷** north (left) to **Dunstaffnage Castle,** once an important stronghold of the MacDougalls. There are outstanding views from the ramparts across the **Sound of Mull** and the **Firth of Lorne,** a nautical crossroads of sorts once watched over by Dunstaffnage Castle and commanded by the galleys (in Gaelic, *birlinn*) of the Lords of the Isles. *Tel. 0131/244–3101. Admission: £1.50 adults, £1 senior citizens, 75p children. Open Apr.–Sept., weekdays 9:30–6, Sun. 2–6.*

From the castle keep you should also be able to see **Connel Bridge,** 2 miles farther east. This elegant structure once carried a branch railway along the coast but has since surrendered to the all-conquering automobile. When you reach the bridge, look below the narrows in the shadow of the girders to see if the **Falls of Lora** are running. Upstream is fjord-like **Loch Etive** (with cruises from Oban); the water leaving this deep, narrow loch foams and fights with the sea tides, creating turbulence and curious cascades.

❸ Continue 6 miles on the A85 to Taynuilt. The **Bonawe Iron Furnace** is signposted to the left. No industrial activity takes place there now, but once the peaceful wooded slopes overlooked the smoky glow of furnaces burning local timber to make charcoal. The furnaces played a central role in the iron-smelting industry, which flourished

264

Argyll and the Isles

here between 1753 and 1876. Today, Historic Scotland cares for the well-preserved buildings. Also note that **Ardanaiseig House** (*see* Dining and Lodging, *below*) sits nearby, down the B845 side road on the right. *Bonawe, 12 mi east of Oban, off A85, tel. 0131/244–3101. Admission: £2 adults, £1.25 senior citizens, 75p children. Open Apr.– Sept., Mon.–Sat. 9:30–6, Sun. 2–6.*

❹ Continue through the narrow Pass of Brander to the **Cruachan Dam Power Station Visitor Centre.** The frequent railway-signal posts on the track above are actually avalanche warnings. **Ben Cruachan** is the mountain that gave you the view from Dunstaffnage Castle; now you have no view at all, since you are almost underneath it. If you want to go farther underneath the mountain, stop at the visitor center for instructions. Actually a horseshoe-shape series of peaks, Ben Cruachan has a dam built within its confines. Water flows down from the dam to Loch Awe, the loch on your right, turning turbines along the way. You can learn about this at the visitor center and on a half-mile minibus trip down a tunnel into a huge cavern-cum-turbine hall. Be sure to take this trip, which will bring you under several cubic miles of mountain. *Off A85, 18 mi east of Oban, tel. 0186/62–673. Admission: £1.80 adults, 50p children over 8 (under 8 free). Open Apr.–Oct., daily 9–4:30.*

By continuing east, you will reach Lochawe Station, where cruises (try the *Lady Rowena*) run from the pier. As an alternative you can ❺ visit **Kilchurn Castle,** a ruined fortress at the eastern end of Loch Awe. The castle was built by Sir Colin Campbell of Glenorchy in the 15th century and rebuilt in the 17th century. The Campbells had their original power base in this area. Park and cross the railway line, then walk across the grassy flats to the airy vantage points, complete with informative signs, amid the towers; from there you'll see more fine panoramas. *Northern tip of Loch Awe, 21 mi east of Oban, tel. 0131/244–3101.*

There is also a superb view from the **Duncan Ban Macintyre Monument** near Dalmally (*see* Off the Beaten Track, *below*). After the monument turn right on the A819, signposted Inveraray (possibly the most misspelled place in the Highlands). **Loch Awe** is the longest loch in Scotland; the road soon leaves its pleasant banks, turning south to join the A83. This road is usually busy carrying traffic from Glasgow and Loch Lomond by way of the high pass of the **Rest and Be Thankful.** (Though not covered in this tour, many visitors come up Loch Lomond and head west by the A83. The Rest and Be Thankful is perhaps its most scenic point—an aptly named, almost Alpine pass among high green slopes and gray rocks.)

Time Out   The simple decor—wood-top tables and fittings—lets you concentrate on the seafood at the **Loch Fyne Oyster Bar** (A83, on the approach to Loch Fyne). Local oysters and crisp white wine certainly are a far cry from roadside hamburgers and french fries.

Ardkinglas Woodland Garden, around the head of Loch Fyne (go left at the junction), is home to Scotland's tallest tree, a grand fir standing 200 feet high. *A83, 12 mi east of Inveraray, tel. 014996/261. Admission: £1 adults, children free. Open daily year-round.*

If neither the oysters nor the tall trees have diverted you, make a ❻ right at the A819/A83 junction for **Inveraray.** Note on the approaches to this little town the ornate 18th-century bridgework that carries the road along the lochside. This is the first sign that Inveraray is not just a higgledy-piggledy assembly of houses. In fact much of

Inveraray was designed as a planned town for the third Duke of Argyll. The present Campbell duke's seat is **Inveraray Castle,** a grayish-green, turreted stone castle that can be seen through the trees on the right. Like Inveraray, the castle was built around 1743. Plenty of this powerful family's history can be seen on a tour. *1/2 mi north of Inveraray, tel. 01499/2203. Admission: £3.50 adults, £2.50 senior citizens, £1.75 children, £9 family ticket. Open Apr.–June and Sept.–mid-Oct., Mon.–Thurs. and Sat. 10–1 and 2–5:30, Sun. 1–5:30; July and Aug., Mon.–Sat. 10–5:30, Sun. 1–5:30.*

The **Combined Operations Museum** sits nearby, a reminder that this sleepy place among the hills was an important wartime training area. *Cherry Park, tel. 01499/5218, fax 01499/2421. Admission: £1 adults, 80p senior citizens and children. Open Apr.–June and Sept.–mid-Oct., Mon.–Thurs., Sat. 10–6, Sun. 1–6; July and Aug., Mon.–Sat. 10–6, Sun. 1–6 (last admission 5:30).*

Other attractions include the **Inveraray Jail,** one of the latest generation of visitor centers. The old town jail and courtroom now house realistic courtroom scenes, period cells, and all the other paraphernalia that enable the visitor to glimpse life behind bars in Victorian times. The Inveraray Bell Tower has also made its mark with visitors: From this 126-foot granite tower rings Scotland's finest peal. *Inveraray, tel. 01499/2381. Admission: £3.85 adults, £2.50 senior citizens, £2 children, £10.70 family ticket. Open daily in summer 9:30–6 (last admission 5), daily in winter 10–5 (last admission 4).*

Continue along the loch southward beyond Inveraray to reach the ❼ **Auchindrain Museum.** Formally a communal tenancy farm, this 18th-century cooperative venture has been restored. The old thatched buildings provide information about early farming life in the Highlands. There is also an interpretation center and shop. *A83, 5 1/2 mi south of Inveraray, tel. 0149/95–235. Admission: £2.20 adults, £1.90 senior citizens, £1.60 children, £7.40 family ticket. Open Apr.–Sept., daily 10–5 (closed Sat. in Apr.).*

❽ Your next stop may be **Crarae Gardens,** farther south, which are occasionally likened to a wild valley in the Himalayas. Magnolias and azaleas give the area a moist and lush atmosphere, undoubtedly aided by the local rainfall. There are paths through the plantings to suit trekkers of every fitness level. *A83, 10 mi southwest of Inveraray, tel. 01546/86614 or 01546/86607. Admission: £2.50 adults, £1.50 children, £7 family ticket. Open daily 9–6 (or sunset if earlier); Visitor Centre open Easter–Oct.*

❾ **Lochgilphead,** the area's main town, is at its aesthetic best when the tide is in: **Loch Gilp,** really a bite out of Loch Fyne, reveals acres of mud at low tide. Where you go from here will depend on how much time you have. If, for example, you're spending only a day in the area, then follow the suggestion for a short looping tour, given here. If you have more time, you can go down Kintyre to take in the little island of Gigha (*see* Off the Beaten Track, *below*) or cross to Islay and Jura from Kennacraig, a short drive to the south.

Take the A816 Oban road north for 2 miles and turn left for the ❿ **Crinan Canal.** This waterway was opened in 1801 to enable fishing vessels to avoid the long haul around the south-stretching peninsula Kintyre and reach the Hebridean fishing grounds more easily. Shortly you will find yourself at the western end of the canal, where it drops to the sea in a series of lochs. This area can be a busy spot, with yachting enthusiasts strolling around and frequenting the coffee shop beside the Crinan Hotel.

⑪ To capture a glimpse of early Scottish history, return to the main road (A816), turn north, and look for a sign to **Dunadd** (4 mi north of Lochgilphead). If you follow the track to a rocky hump that rises out of the levels that lie around Crinan, you will find—by clambering up the rock—a basin, a footprint, and an outline of a boar carved on the smooth upper face of the knoll. This breezy refuge was once the capital of the early kingdom of Dalriada, founded by the first wave of Scots who migrated from Ireland. *West of A816, 4 mi northwest of Lochgilphead, tel. 0131/244–3101. Admission free.*

⑫ A little farther north sits **Carnasserie Castle,** a tower house with the peculiar distinction of having belonged to the writer of the first book printed in Gaelic. The writer was John Carswell, bishop of the Isles, who translated a text by the dour Scottish reformer John Knox into Gaelic and published it in 1567. *Off A816, 9 mi north of Lochgilphead, tel. 0131/244–3101. Admission free.*

Time Out | The **Cuilfail Hotel** (tel. 018522/274) at Kilmelford (A816), formerly a coaching inn, offers pleasant bar meals.

⑬ Before you reach Oban, one more side road may divert you. The B844 leads to the island of **Seil** via the Bridge over the Atlantic. This crossing is less spectacular than it sounds—the island is so close to the mainland that a single-span bridge, built in 1791, carries the
⑭ road across. From Seil, visitors are ferried to neighboring **Easdale Island.** Once Easdale and Seil were known as the slate islands: Extensive quarrying for roofing materials was undertaken on both isles.

Tour 2: Arran

Many Scots, especially those from Glasgow and the west, are well disposed toward **Arran,** which reminds them of unhurried childhood holidays. In fact, its cafés and boarding houses exude a 1950s mood, suggesting that this small isle has been caught in a time warp. Only a few decades ago the Clyde estuary was the coastal playground for the majority of the populace living in Glasgow and the Clydeside conurbation. Their annual holiday comprised a trip by steamer to any one of a number of Clyde coast resorts, known as going *doon the watter* (down the water, the estuary of the Clyde). Today the masses go to Spain, but, like other parts of the Clyde, the island of Arran has for a long time been associated with the healthy outdoor life.

To get to Arran, take the ferry from Androssan. During the ride, take a walk on deck and note the number of fellow travelers wearing walking boots. They're ready for the delights of **Goat Fell,** an impressive peak (2,868 ft) that gives the island one of the most distinctive profiles of any in Scotland.

⑮ In less than an hour from Ardrossan, the ferry arives in **Brodick** with the cone of Goat Fell and its satellites serving as an eye-catching backdrop to the northwest. As you will have seen while crossing, the southern half of the island is less mountainous: The Highland Boundary Fault crosses just to the north of Brodick Bay.

Brodick, the largest township on the island, is really just a village, with a frontage spaciously set back from a promenade and beach. Head south (left) from the pier by the A841, a road that encircles the island and makes it difficult to get lost. A sign to Corriegills moments later indicates the first of many short walks, which you may take if you have time. A walk to Corriegills offers fine views over Brodick Bay.

Beyond dense conifer woods the A841 drops suddenly into **Lamlash,** with views offshore to steep-flanked Holy Island. This entire area has a breezy seaside holiday atmosphere. To reach the highest point accessible by car on the island, go through the village and turn right beside the bridge. This is known as the **Ross Road.** It climbs steeply up a thickly planted valley, yielding fine views of Lamlash Bay.

The narrow road ends east of Sliddery with a return to the A841. Make a left by the church to reach nearby **Lagg.** This little community in a hollow beneath the sheltering trees sits peacefully by the banks of the Kilmory Water.

Time Out The **Lagg Hotel** (tel. 01770/870255), an inn since 1791, is a warm place offering appetizing buffet lunches on Sunday, and excellent bar lunches and evening meals the rest of the week.

Continue east on the A841 along the bottom end of the island past white-painted farmhouses and cottages. There are views across gently tilting fields to the steep hump of **Ailsa Craig,** offshore in the Firth of Clyde. Cheese connoisseurs will be pleased to know the creamery at Torrylinn makes Arran Cheddar from local milk. Beyond Kildonan the road twists north; the trees extend to the sea edge, where gannets seem to dive through the branches. The route soon reaches **Whiting Bay,** a string of hotels and well-kept property along the seafront. From there return to Brodick; on the way back you will enjoy scenic mountain views over the conifer spikes.

16 Brodick is the site of the **Isle of Arran Heritage Museum,** which documents the life of the island from ancient times to the present century. A number of buildings, including a cottage and *smiddy* (blacksmith's), have period furnishings and provide displays on prehistoric life, geology, farming, fishing, and many other aspects of the island's heritage. *Rosaburn, Brodick, tel. 01770/302636. Admission: £1.50 adults, £1 senior citizens, 75p children. Open Apr.–Oct., Mon.–Sat. 10–5.*

Just beyond the museum is a junction where the String Road cuts across the island. Drive up the String Road a short way to find a signpost to the right, for Glen Rosa. The road soon becomes undrivable, but visitors can walk through a long glen that offers a glimpse of the wild ridges that call so many outdoor enthusiasts to the island.

To find the island's most important draw for those other than the **17** outdoor enthusiasts, return to the A841. **Brodick Castle and Country Park** is on the north side of Brodick Bay, its red sandstone corseted by trees and parkland. Now under the auspices of the National Trust for Scotland, this former seat of the dukes of Hamilton has a number of rooms open to the public. The furniture, paintings, silver, and sporting trophies are opulent in their own right, but the real attraction is the brilliantly colored rhododendrons, particularly in late spring and early summer. Though there are many unusual species, you will find the ordinary deciduous yellow variety unmatched for its scent: Your initial encounter with them is comparable to hitting a wall of perfume. *1¹/₂ mi north of Brodick pier, tel. 01770/302202. Admission to castle, gardens, and park: £4 adults, £2 senior citizens and children; admission to gardens and park: £2 adults, £1 children. Castle open Easter and May–Sept., daily 1–5; late Apr. and early Oct.,*

Sat., Sun. 1–5 (last admission 4:30). Park and gardens open daily all year, 9:30–sunset.

Time Out An important feature of **Brodick Castle** is the tearoom, offering visitors, who may have walked many acres plunging their noses into every blossom, a chance to quench their thirst. The menu includes an assortment of sandwiches and cakes.

Northward from Brodick the road is built along a raised beach platform, a phenomenon quite common in Scotland and caused by the lifting of the land after its burden of ice melted at the end of the Ice Age. Large, round boulders rest on softer sandstones in certain places on the shore. These stones, called *erratics,* were once carried by glaciers off the granite mountains that loom in the distance to your left as you approach **Corrie.** This brief string of settlements has stores that sell pottery and crafts items, another common find on the island.

Farther along, at **Sannox,** a locale consisting of another cluster of houses, there is a sandy bay of ground granite, washed down from the mountainous interior. There are also outstanding views of the rugged hills of the interior, particularly the steep pyramid of **Cir Mhor.** The road then climbs away from the coast, although there is a good coastal walk from North Sannox. Look for red deer grazing above on the slopes of the green glen where the road runs.

⑱ The road rejoins the coast at **Lochranza.** This attractively situated settlement is yet one more community that focuses on crafts. The sheltered bay of Loch Ranza, spilling in shallows up the flat-bottomed glacial glen, is set off by a picturesque ruin. Situated on a low sand spit, **Lochranza Castle** is said to have been the landing place of Robert the Bruce, who returned from Rathlin Island in 1307 to start the campaign that won Scotland's independence. *Tel. 0131/244–3101. Admission free. Open Apr.–Sept., Mon.–Sat. 9:30–6, Sun. 2–6; Oct.–Mar., Mon.–Sat. 9:30–4, Sun. 2–4.*

⑲ Beyond Lochranza, the raised beach backed by a cliff continues to make a scenic platform for the road. There are fine views across the sound to the long rolling horizon of Kintyre. At **Catacol,** immediately after the Catacol Bay Hotel, sit the **Twelve Apostles,** a row of fishermen's houses identical except for differences in the window shapes (so they can be recognized from offshore). Farther south you can see the stranded former sea caves by Dougarie Lodge and the notched hills up Glen Iorsa, on the left.

⑳ Near the scattered homesteads of **Machrie**—which has a popular beach—look for a Historic Scotland sign to the **Machrie Moor Stone Circles.** The sign says the site is 1 mile farther, but on foot it feels a bit farther than that. A well-surfaced track will take you to a grassy moor by a ruined farm, where you will be able to see small rounded granite-boulder circles and much taller, eerie, red-sandstone monoliths. The Machrie area is littered with these sites: chambered cairns, hut circles, and standing stones dating from the Bronze Age.

Continuing to **Blackwaterfoot,** you can return to Brodick by the String Road, unless you want to drive the only part of the island not otherwise covered in the tour, the main road south as far as the Ross Road. If you decide to take the Ross Road, there are good views of Campbeltown Loch and the end of the Kintyre peninsula. Otherwise, to return to Brodick, turn left by the Kinloch Hotel, up the hill. There are more fine views of the granite complexities of Arran's hills: gray notched ridges beyond brown moor and, beyond the watershed, a vista of Brodick Bay. From this high point you roll down to Brodick, your starting point.

Tour 3: Islay and Jura

Islay   **Islay** has a personality distinct from that of the rest of the Hebrides. The western half, in particular, has large farms rather than crofts. A number of distilleries—the source of the island's delectable malt whiskies—provide jobs for the locals. Islay is also known for its wildlife, especially its birds, including the rare chough—a crow with red legs and beak—and, in winter, its barnacle geese.

㉑   The town of **Bowmore** is compact and about the same size (population 1,000) as the ferry port of Port Ellen, but is perhaps slightly better suited as a base for touring. Bowmore, which gives its name to the whisky made in the distillery (founded 1779) by the shore, is a tidy town. Its grid pattern was laid out in 1768 by the local landowner Daniel Campbell of Shawfield. Bowmore's Main Street stretches from pierhead to the dominating parish church of 1767, built in an unusual circular design—so the devil could not find a corner to hide in. The town has a modest selection of accommodations and restaurants despite its small size.

Time Out   Rub elbows with the locals at the **Harbour Inn** (Main St., tel. 01496/810330), with its cheerfully noisy and cramped public bar frequented by off-duty distillery workers who are happy to exchange island gossip. The excellent restaurant serves lunch 12–2, high tea 5–7:30, and dinner 7:30–9 (closed Sun.).

Many of Islay's best beaches—as well as wildlife and historical preserves—are in its western half, contrasting with the southeast area, which is mainly an extension of Jura's inhospitable quartzite hills. Take the A846 north out of Bowmore (signposted Bridgend) to the A847 in order to skirt the sand flats at the head of Loch Indaal. Follow the loch shores all the way to Bruichladdich, which, like Bowmore, is the name of a malt whisky, as well as a village with a distill-
㉒ ery. You will reach **Port Charlotte** a few minutes later. Above the road on the right, in a converted kirk, is the **Museum of Islay Life,** a haphazard but authentic and informative display of times past. *Tel. 0149/685–358. Admission: £1.20 adults, 60p children. Open Mar.–Oct., Mon.–Sat. 10–5, Sun. 2–5.*

For further exploration continue on the A847 into the wilder landscape of the **Rhinns of Islay.** At the southern end are the scattered cottages of **Portnahaven** and its twin, **Port Wemyss.** You can return to Port Charlotte by the bleak unclassified road that loops westward and passes by the recumbent stone circle at Coultoon and the chapel at Kilchiaran before reaching Port Charlotte.

To get a glimpse of Islay's peerless western seascapes, make a left onto the B8018, north of Bruichladdich. After 2 miles turn left again onto a little road that meanders past Loch Gorm and ends close to **Machir Bay** and its superb (and probably deserted) sandy beach. Soon after you turn around to go back, make a right, which will lead you to the derelict kirk of **Kilchoman.** In the kirkyard are some interesting grave slabs and two crosses of late-medieval date from the Iona school of carving, an excellent introduction to the island's wealth of stone carvings. (There was another Scottish "school" in Kintyre.) From Kilchoman turn right and then left to circle Loch Gorm, pausing as the road all but touches the coast at Saligo. It's worth a stroll beyond the former wartime camp to enjoy the view of some fine seascapes, especially if the westerlies are piling up high breakers on the rock ridges.

On the return journey east, turn right at the B8018, then left on the B8017. Take a left at Aoradh Farm onto a minor road that runs north along the west side of Loch Gruinart. The road soon brings you to **②③** **Kilnave** (Cill Naoimh on local maps). Kilnave's ruined chapel is associated with a dark tale in which a group of wounded Maclean clansmen were defeated in a nearby battle with the MacDonalds in 1598. The Macleans sought sanctuary in the chapel; their pursuers set its roof aflame, and the clansmen perished within. In the graveyard is a weathered, 8th-century carved cross.

Visitors are inevitably drawn to viewing the long reaches of **Loch Gruinart.** Dunes flank its sea outlet, and pale beaches rise out of the falling tides. For the best view return to the B8017, cross the flats at the head of the loch, and then go left and up its eastern shore. Park before a gate, where the road deteriorates. Those who appreciate wide skies, crashing waves, and lonely coast should continue on foot, possibly around the headland held together with marram grass. From the far dunes there are views of Colonsay and Oronsay across Hebridean waters, on which plumes and fans of white spray rise from hidden reefs. The priory on the island of Oronsay, with its famous carved cross, is barely distinguishable.

To discover what the south of the island has to offer, take the long straight of the A846 that passes the island airport just inland from the endless sandy curve of Laggan Bay. Before you reach Port Ellen, go straight ahead to a minor road to Imeraval, then make a right at a junction and then a left. This takes you to the southern peninsula **②④** of **The Oa,** a region of caves rich in tales of smuggling. Visitors to The Oa usually go as far as the Mull of Oa, the tip, where there is a monument recalling the 650 men who lost their lives when the troopships *Tuscania* and *Otranto* went down nearby in 1918.

Port Ellen is a sturdy community, founded in the 1820s, with much of its architecture still dating from the 19th century. It has a harbor, a few shops, and some inns, but not enough commercial development to mortgage its personality. The A846 continues eastward, passing more names known to the malt-whisky connoisseur: the whisky of the **Laphroaig distillery**—which offers tours—is perhaps one of the most distinctive of the local whiskies, with a tangy, peaty, seaweed/iodine flavor. *1¹/₂ mi along road to Ardbeg from Port Ellen, tel. 01496/302418 or 01496/302393. Tours by appointment.*

After Ardbeg the A846 becomes narrower and passes through a pleasantly rolling, partly wooded landscape. The reason for taking this route east is not to take a scenic tour of distillery premises, but to see the finest carved cross anywhere in Scotland: the 8th-century **②⑤** **Kildalton Cross.** Carved from a single slab of epidiorite rock, this ringed cross is encrusted on both sides with elaborate designs in the style of the Iona school. Interesting early grave slabs from the 12th and 13th centuries can also be seen in the yard around the chapel, which stands down a lonely side road, signposted from Ardbeg. From Kildalton retrace your route to Bowmore.

From Bowmore take the A846 north (following signs for Port Askaig) through Bridgend. Hardly a mile beyond, you will see a sign **②⑥** for the **Islay Woollen Mill.** Set in a wooded hollow by the river, the mill has a shop selling high-quality products that are woven on site. There is also a fascinating selection of working machinery to inspect.

If time permits, before reaching Port Askaig (a fairly frequent ferry service runs from here to Jura), you may wish to explore a side road **27** (to the left) a mile beyond Ballygrant. To get to **Loch Finlaggan,** make a left and then drive through a gate. At first sight, there is not a great deal to see. But the little island on the loch, with its scanty and overgrown traces of early buildings, was the council seat of the Lords of the Isles. This former western power base of the Clan Donald threatened the sovereignty of the Stuart monarchs of Scotland in its heyday: a reminder of how independent the Highlands were in those times. A cottage interpretative center is located nearby, with an exhibition relating to the ongoing excavations of the island ruins. *Small admission charge. Open Apr.–Sept., Sun., Tues., and Thurs. 2:30–5.*

Return to the main road (A846) and continue driving northeast. Note that just beyond Keills is another side road that will take you for a pleasant ride along the coast until you come to a turning space and parking lot at the **Bunnahabhain Distillery,** which sits on an attractive shore site (tel. 01496/840646, visits by appointment). There are impressive views of Jura on the way. Then retrace the route to the main road, going left then steeply downhill to the tiny ferry community by the pier.

Jura   Although it is possible to meet an Islay native in a local pub, such an event is statistically less likely on **Jura,** with its one road, one distillery, one hotel, and six sporting estates. In fact, visitors have a better chance of bumping into one of the island's 5,000 red deer, which outnumber the human population by at least 20 to one. The island has a much more rugged look than Islay, with its profiles of the Paps of Jura, a hill range at its most impressive when basking in the rays of a west-coast sunset.

Having crossed the Sound of Islay by ferry from Port Askaig (it takes just a few minutes), explorers will find it easy to choose which road to take—Jura only has one. Apart from the initial stretch it is all single-lane. The A846 starts off below one of the many raised beaches then climbs across poor moorland, providing scenic views across the Sound of Jura. Look for the standing stone, right, then note the ruined **Claig Castle** on an island just offshore. The Lords of the Isles built it to control the sound. Beyond the farm buildings of Ardfin, you reach **Jura House** in the woodlands, with its sheltered garden walks and fine views. *Tel. 0149/682–315. Admission to gardens: £2 adults, £1 students, children under 16 free. Open daily 9–5.*

28 Beyond Jura House the road turns northward for **Craighouse,** across open moorland with scattered forestry blocks and the faint evidence, in the shape of parallel ridges, of the original inhabitants' lazy beds or strip cultivation. The original settlements were cleared with the other parts of the Highlands when the island became more of a sheep pasture and deer forest. The road soon drops down to the community of Craighouse, home to the island's only distillery.

Time Out   The **Jura Hotel** (tel. 0149/682–243), in spite of its monopoly, genuinely welcomes its guests and can be relied on for high-quality accommodations and food.

29 The aptly named **Small Isles Bay** has a superb strip of beach to the north of Craighouse. As the road climbs away from the bay, the little cottage above the burn is a reminder of the history of this island: The cottage is the only survivor of a village with a population of 56 that was destroyed in 1841. Ironically, a sheep *fank* (fold) farther up the burn shows what happened to the stones of the demolished cottages. Although the landscapes of Jura seem devoid of life, they are in fact populated with many ghosts, most of which are missed by the casual visitor.

Beyond the River Corran the road climbs, offering austere views of the Paps, with their long quartzite screes and of the fine, though usually deserted, anchorage in the scoop of Lowlandman's Bay. The next section of road is more hemmed in and runs to **Lagg,** formerly a ferry-crossing point on the old cattle-driving road between here and Feolin. Beyond Lagg, the sea views are blocked by conifer plantings. Views of fjordlike **Loch Tarbert,** westward to the left, are at their best beside the forestry plantation a little farther on. At this point the road leads through a stretch of rough, uninhabited landscape. A gate and cattle grid by **Ardlussa** to the north mark the start of a Site of Special Scientific Interest in a shady oakwood. The coast here is rocky and unspoiled. Choose your own picnic site, but be sure to park sensibly. Yellow flag (a Scottish iris), bracken, strands of crisp seaweed on the salty grass, and background birdsong from the mossy woods make this an idyllic stretch when the sun shines. Try not to be too loud, so you won't distract the area's resident otter population.

The last house you will see is at **Lealt,** where you cross the river. Only a little way beyond this point the tarmac ends, rather abruptly, with a turning space paved into the hill. Ordinary cars should not attempt to go any farther on the remainder of this trail, though jeeps, rovers, and other high-clearance vehicles can make it through. The track beyond the surfaced road continues for another 5 miles to **Kinuachdrach,** a settlement that once served as a crossing point to Scarba and the mainland. The coastal footpath to Corryvreckan lies beyond, over the bare moors. This area has two enticements: The first, for fans of George Orwell, is the house of **Barnhill,** where the author wrote *1984;* the second, for wilderness enthusiasts, is the whirlpool of the **Corryvreckan** and the unspoiled coastal scenery.

To return to the ferry that will take you to Islay, you have no choice but to retrace your route. If time permits, however, the tearoom at Craighouse is worth a visit.

Tour 4: The Isle of Mull

It's possible to spend a long weekend on Mull and not meet a single resident who was born north of Manchester, England. Though Mull certainly has an indigenous population, the island is often referred to as the Officers' Mess because of its popularity with retired military men. It has a thriving tourist industry, with several thousand visitors per year making their way across the Ross of Mull to Iona, cradle of Scottish Christianity and ancient burial site of the kings of Scotland.

30 Most visitors arrive at **Craignure** by way of Oban, but you should also consider the short ferry crossing from Lochaline on a beautiful part of the mainland to **Fishnish,** a little west of Craignure. This summer-only service is first-come, first-served.

31 Either ferry will leave you close to Mull's two best-known castles, **Torosay** and **Duart. Torosay Castle** is probably more fun. It also has the novelty of a steam-and-diesel service on a narrow-gauge railway, which takes 20 minutes to run from the pier at Craignure to Torosay's grounds. Scottish baronial in style, Torosay has a friendly air.

Visitors have the run of much of the house, which is full of intrigue and humor by way of idiosyncratic information boards and informal family albums. The main feature of the castle's gardens—a gentle blend of formal and informal—is its Italian statue walk. *A849, 1¹/₂ mi southeast of Craignure, tel. 016802/421. Admission to castle and gardens: £3.50 adults, £1.50 children, £2.75 students and senior citizens; admission to gardens: £1.50 adults, £1 senior citizens, children, and students. Castle open Easter and mid-Apr.–mid-Oct., daily 10:30–5:30; gardens open summer, daily 9–7; winter, daily sunrise-sunset.*

㉜ The energetic can walk along the shore from Torosay to **Duart Castle;** if you're driving use the A849. This ancient Maclean seat was ruined by the Campbells in 1691 but bought and restored by Sir Fitzroy Maclean in 1911. *Off A849, tel. 016802/309. Admission: £3 adults, £2 senior citizens, £1.50 children, £7.50 family ticket. Open May–mid Oct., daily 10:30–6.*

Beyond Duart Castle the double-lane road narrows as it continues southwest, touched by sea inlets at Lochs Don and Spelve. Gray and green are the most prevalent colors of the interior, with vivid grass and high rock faces in Glen More. These stepped rock faces, the ㉝ by-product of ancient lava flows, reach their highest point in **Ben More,** the only island *munro* outside Skye. (A munro is a Scottish mountain over 3,000 ft high.) Its high, bald slopes are prominent by the time you reach the road junction at the head of Loch Scridain. Stay on the A849 for a pleasant drive the length of the **Ross of Mull,** a wide promontory with scattered settlements. Look to the right for good views of the dramatic cliff ramparts of Ardmeanach, the stubbier promontory to the north. The National Trust for Scotland cares ㉞ for the rugged stretch of coast known as the **Burg,** which is home to a 40 million-year-old fossil tree (at the end of a long walk from the B8035, signposted left off the A849).

The well-used A849 continues through the village of **Bunessan** and eventually ends in a long car-park opposite the houses of **Fionnphort.** The vast parking space is made necessary by the popu-㉟ larity of the nearby island of **Iona,** to which visitors cannot bring cars. Ferry service is frequent in summer months.

The fiery and argumentative Irish monk Columba chose Iona for the site of a monastery in AD 563 because it was the first place he landed from which he could not see Ireland. Christianity had been brought to Scotland (Galloway) by Saint Ninian in 397, but until Saint Columba's church was founded, the word had not spread widely among the ancient northerners, called Picts. Iona was the burial place of the kings of Scotland until the 11th century. It survived repeated Norse sackings and finally fell into disuse around the time of the Reformation. Restoration work began at the turn of this century, and later, in 1938, the **Iona Community** was founded. Today the restored buildings serve as a spiritual center under the jurisdiction of the Church of Scotland. The ambience of the complex is a curious amalgam of the ancient and the earnest. But beyond the restored cloisters the most mystifying aspect of all is the island's ability to absorb visitors and still feel peaceful—a phenomenon often remarked upon by tourists. Most folk only make the short walk from the ferry pier by way of the nunnery to the abbey. *Tel. 016817/404. Abbey gift and bookshop open Mon.–Sat. 10–5, Sun. noon–5; abbey coffeehouse open Mar.–Oct., Mon.–Sat. 11–4, Sun. noon–4.*

On your return to Mull retrace your route eastward and look for a sign on the right to Carsaig as you approach the head of Loch Scridain. This route takes you to the remote south coast. From the pierhead at the tiny settlement a rough path meanders west below **36** lava cliffs to the impressive **Carsaig Arches.** Taking on the arches is a separate excursion reserved for the agile.

After your foray to the arches take the B8035 at Loch Scridain. The road rises away from the loch to the conifer plantations and green slopes of **Gleann Seilisdeir.** Tiroran House (*see* Dining and Lodging, *below*), a coddling country house and perhaps the best hotel on Mull, is signposted left, which is also the way to the Burg. The main road through the glen breaches the stepped cliffs and drops to the shore, offering inspiring views of the island of Ulva guarding Loch na Keil. This stretch of the B8035, with splinters of rock from the heights strewn over it in places, feels remote. The high ledges eventually give way (not literally) to vistas of the screes of Ben More.

Continue to skirt the coast by way of the B8073, and you will enjoy a succession of fine coastal views with Ulva in the foreground. Beyond Calgary Bay the landscape is gentler, as the road leads to the **37** village of **Dervaig.** Just before Dervaig the **Old Byre** is signposted. An audiovisual presentation on the history of Mull plays here. *Every hr on the half-hr, £2 adults, £1.50 senior citizens and students, £1 children.*

Time Out The wholesome catering at the restaurant at the **Old Byre** heritage center (signposted just before Dervaig, tel. 016884/229), certainly will be appreciated by weary travelers, particularly those who enjoy thick and hearty homemade soups and real oatcakes. The restaurant is open Easter–mid-Oct., daily 10:30–6:30 (last admission 6).

In Dervaig the Mull Little Theatre (*see* The Arts and Nightlife, *below*) offers a varied program and claims the record as the smallest professional theater in the United Kingdom. After the small town **38** the road leads through woodlands to **Tobermory.** Founded as a fishing station, this community gradually declined, hastened by the arrival of the railroad station at Oban, which took away fishing traffic. However, the brightly painted crescent of 18th-century buildings gives Tobermory a Mediterranean look.

To return to the ferry, make your way southward on the A848, which yields pleasant, though unspectacular, views across to Morvern on the mainland. On the coast just beyond **Aros,** look back and across the river flats for a view of the ruined 13th-century **Aros Castle.** Continue through Salen to either Fishnish for Morven or Craignure for Oban.

Argyll and the Isles for Free

Crinan Canal (*see* Tour 1)
Dunadd Fort (*see* Tour 1)
Kilchurn Castle (*see* Tour 1)
Kildalton Cross (*see* Tour 3)
Loch Gruinart (*see* Tour 3)
Machrie Moor standing stones (*see* Tour 2)
Whisky distillery tours on Islay (*see* Tour 3)

What to See and Do with Children

The Argyll Wildlife Park has 60 acres with extensive collections of wildfowl and other Scottish wildlife. *Dalchenna, Inveraray on A83, tel. 01499/2284. Admission: £3.60 adults, £1.50 children, £3 senior citizens. Open daily 9:30–dusk. (Tearoom open Apr.–Oct.)*

Auchindrain Old Farming Township (*see* Tour 1)

Cruachan Dam Power Visitor Centre and Tour (*see* Tour 1)

Ganavan Sands Leisure Centre (tel. 01631/64100) has sandy beaches, an outdoor play area, a boating pool, and donkey rides. To get there, follow the road from the center of Oban, where the promenade starts.

Inveraray Jail (*see* Tour 1)

Lady Rowena Steam Launch runs an Edwardian peat-fired steamboat that cruises Loch Awe from BR station pier at Lochawe on A85. *Tel. 01838/200440 or 01838/200449. Reservations can be made on the spot or in advance.*

Mull and West Highland Narrow Gauge Railway (*see* Tour 4)

The Sea Life Centre displays native marine life in a spacious aquarium. One of the most entertaining places in Argyll, the center also has a shop and a café. *On the A828, Barcaldine, 11 mi north of Oban, tel. 01631/72386. Admission: £4.25 adults, £3.25 senior citizens, £2.95 children. Open Mar.–June and Sept.–Nov., daily 9–6; July and Aug., daily 9–7; Dec.–Feb., weekends 9–5. Call to check opening hours in winter season.*

A World in Miniature displays hand-crafted miniature rooms and furniture made to a ¹/₁₂th scale. *North pier, Oban, tel. 0185/26–272 or 01631/66300. Admission: £1.50 adults, £1 children, £4 family ticket. Open Easter–Oct., Mon.–Sat. 10–5, Sun. 2–5.*

Off the Beaten Track

Castle Sween, the oldest stone castle on the Scottish mainland (12th century), sits in a rocky sea-edge setting 15 miles southwest of Lochgilphead. The castle is reached by an unclassified road from Crinan yielding outstanding views of the Paps of Jura across the sound. There are also some attractive white sand beaches here.

Duncan Ban Macintyre Monument (Monument Hill) was erected in honor of the Gaelic poet Duncan Ban Macintyre (1724–1812), sometimes referred to as the Robert Burns of the Highlands. The monument is not far from the village of Dalmally, just east of the top end of Loch Awe in Argyll. From there, follow an old road running southwest toward the banks of Loch Awe. At the road's highest point, often called Monument Hill, the round, granite monument can be seen. The view from here is one of the finest in Argyll, taking in Ben Cruachan and the other peaks nearby, as well as Loch Awe and its scattering of islands.

Island of Gigha is a delectable Hebridean island, barely 5 miles long, sheltered in a frost-free, sea-warmed climate between Kintyre and Islay. The isle is noted for the **Achamore House Gardens.** It is possible to take the ferry (a 20-minute trip), walk to the gardens, and return to the mainland, all on a short day-trip, but there are good accommodations on the island. *Tel. 0158/35–254. Admission to gardens: £2 adults, £1 children. Open daily 10–dusk.*

Famous in song, the **Mull of Kintyre** is, in reality, a road to the light-house beyond Campbeltown at the tip of Kintyre. The narrow road crosses moors and sheep pastures. There is a parking place before the road suddenly dips to reach the lighthouse tower, placed well down the steep slope that tilts toward the sea. There is one caveat, however. Do not go down the hill. The best sunset views are from the adjacent moors, from which you can see Ireland quite clearly.

Shopping

The lure of great shopping is not what attracts visitors to this pre-dominantly rural area, although the day-to-day needs of the local population are well cared for. Nonetheless, there are several inter-esting crafts outlets; the islands, in particular, offer many opportu-nities to sample and purchase fine island whiskies. Starting in **Oban,** the **Oban Glass Studio** (part of Caithness Glass, Heritage Wharf, tel. 01631/63386) offers self-guided factory tours (weekdays) and a well-stocked factory shop.

Also worth a visit is the **Highbank Porcelain Pottery** (Highbank In-dustrial Estate, Lochgilphead, tel. 01546/602044), where visitors can watch slip casting, hand painting, and firing. Highbank also has a shop that sells pottery animals (including reasonably priced sec-onds).

East of Oban, in **Taynuilt,** stop at **Inverawe Fisheries and Smokery** (tel. 018662/446, open mid-Mar.–Dec., daily 9–5. The smoked salmon and other fish produced and served on the premises are impractical to take home (at least abroad), but they make a delicious picnic.

Also recommended are the products of **Loch Fyne Oysters** (Clachan Farm, on the A83, tel. 014996/264). You can sample them in the oys-ter bar, which serves all types of seafood and game products, before buying them in the adjacent Seafood Shop.

Farther down the A83, at **Inveraray,** you can buy Scottish crafts at the shop within **Inveraray Jail** (*see* Tour 1 in Exploring Argyll and the Isles, *above*). **Campbeltown** is the center for local shopping re-quirements on the Kintyre peninsula. Here you will also find **Oys-tercatcher Crafts and Gallery** (10 Hall St. and 2–4 Main St., tel. 01586/553070), with original paintings, woodcarvings, and knitwear.

A few miles north, at **Carradale,** is **Wallis Hunter Design** (The Stead-ing, tel. 015833/683), which makes gold and silver jewelry. Clachan is the home of **Ronachan Silks** (Ronachan Farmhouse, tel. 018804/242), which produces distinctive jewel-color scarves, cushion covers, and clothing.

On **Islay** you'll be spoiled by the sheer number of distilleries from which to choose. Most of them welcome visitors by appointment: **Bruichladdich** (Port Charlotte, tel. 01496/850221), **Caol Ila** (Port Askaig, tel. 01496/840207), **Bunnahabhain** (Port Askaig, tel. 01496/840646), **Isle of Jura** (Craighouse, Jura, tel. 0149/682–240), **Laphroaig** (Port Ellen, tel. 01496/302418), **Bowmore** (School St., Bowmore, tel. 01496/810441), and **Lagavoulin** (Port Ellen, tel. 01496/302250). Their delicious products, characterized by a peaty taste, can be purchased at off-license shops on the island, at local pubs, or at those distilleries that have shops. **The Islay Woollen Mill** (Bridgend, tel. 01496/810563) is also worth a visit, not only for its shop, but for its mill tour. Beside the usual tweed lengths, the mill has a distinctive range of hats, caps, and clothing made from its own cloth.

Arran's shops are particularly well stocked with island-produced goods: **Something Special** (The Pier, Brodick, tel. 01770/302831), stocks soaps, creams, and other beauty products made by **Arran Aromatics** from natural ingredients, and **Arran Provisions** (The Old Mill, Lamlash, tel. 01770/600606) is famous for its mustards, preserves, and marmalades. **Crafts of Arran** (Whiting Bay, tel. 01770/700251) prides itself on stocking craftwork produced in Arran. **Corriecraft and Antiques** (Corrie, tel. 01770/810661) also sells craftwork (though it may come from different parts of Scotland), together with a carefully chosen mix of small antiques and curios. At **Machrie** (near the stone circles at Machrie Moor) shoppers frequent the **Old Byre Showroom** (Auchencar Farm, tel. 01770/840227), which sells sheepskin goods, locally hand-knit "jumpers" (sweaters), leather goods, and tweeds.

The tiny island of **Iona** has one or two pleasant surprises for shoppers, the biggest being The Old Printing Press Bookshop (St. Columba Hotel, tel. 016817/304), an excellent antiquarian and secondhand bookshop. The shop at the **Abbey** is also worth a visit for its selection of Celtic-inspired gift items.

Near **Dervaig,** on the island of **Mull,** do not miss the **Old Byre Heritage Centre's craft shop** (nor the restaurant with delicious home baking). The shop's inventory is definitely more extensive than most and includes locally made, as well as other Scottish-produced items.

Sports and Fitness

Bicycling As a popular holiday destination and a ferry gateway, Oban gets a lot of traffic. Main routes to and from town are busy, and there are few side roads. Island roads may be single-track, so wear high-visibility clothing, especially in the busy summer months, and be *sure* to bring rain gear. Bicycles can be rented from **Argyll Hotel** (Argyll St., Dunoon, tel. 01369/2059), **Pedal Power** (Tobermory, tel. 01688/2226), and **On Yer Bike** (Salen, tel. 01680/300501), both on Mull, and **Oban Cycle Hire** (D. Grahams, 9–15 Combie St., Oban, tel. 01631/62069). Arran is a popular island for cycling, with a large number of bicycle-rental shops, including **Brodick Boat and Cycle Hire** (The Beach, Brodick, tel. 01770/302388), **Spinning Wheels** (The Trossachs, Corrie, tel. 01770/810640), **Whiting Bay Cycle Hire** (tel. 01770/700382), **Brodick Cycles** (Roselynn, Brodick, tel. 01770/302460), and **Mr. Bilsland** (The Gift Shop, Brodick, Isle of Arran, tel. 01770/302272). In Tarbert try **Tarbert Leisure Sports Ltd.** (The Columba Hotel, Tarbert, Argyll, tel. 01880/820802).

Fishing Local tourist-information centers (*see* Important Addresses and Numbers in Essential Information, *above*) provide information. Local fishing literature identifies at least 50 fishing sites on lochs and rivers for game fishing and at least 20 coastal settlements suited for sea angling.

Golf The area has about two dozen golf courses; notably scenic examples are the outstanding courses on Bute, as well as the fine coastal links, of which **Machrihanish** near Campbeltown is the most famous (tel. 0158/681–213; 18 holes, 6,228 yards, SSS 70). The local tourist-information centers can provide detailed leaflets.

Pony Trekking Explorers can take off from riding outlets on the mainland and on the islands: **Ballivicar Pony Trekking** (Ballivicar Farm, Port Ellen, Islay, tel. 01496/302251), **Castle Riding Centre and Argyll Trail Riding** (Brenfield, Ardrishaig, Argyll, tel. 01546/603274), **Cairnhouse**

Riding Centre (Blackwaterfoot, Arran, tel. 01770/860466), **Cloyburn Trekking Centre** (Brodick, Arran, tel. 01770/302108), **Lettershuna Riding Centre** (Appin, Argyll, tel. 01631/73227), and **Rothesay Riding Centre** (Canada Hill, Rothesay, Isle of Bute, tel. 01700/504971).

Water Sports The assortment of sea, island, and sea-loch make this a popular area for a variety of water sports. Local operators include **Linnhe Marine Watersports Centre** (Lettershuna, Appin, Argyll, tel. 01631/73227), though generally people bring their own equipment.

Dining and Lodging

Dining

This part of Scotland is not usually considered a great gastronomic center; it has only a few restaurants of distinction. Still, the ingredients used in dishes are of good quality and are locally produced: Fish, fresh from the sparkling lochs and sea, could hardly be better. Beef, lamb, and game are also common. In the rural districts, your best bet is to choose a hotel or guest house that can provide a decent evening meal as well as breakfast.

Highly recommended restaurants are indicated by a star ★.

Category	Cost*
$$$$	over £40
$$$	£30–£40
$$	£15–£30
$	under £15

per person for a three-course meal, including VAT; excluding drinks

Lodging

Accommodations in Argyll and the Isles range from châteaulike hotels to modest inns. The traditional provincial hotels and small coastal resorts have been modernized and equipped with all the necessary comforts, yet they retain their sense of personalized service and the charm that comes with older buildings. Away from these areas, however, your choices are more restricted, and your best overnight option, with some exceptions, is usually a modest guest house offering bed, breakfast, and an evening meal.

Highly recommended hotels are indicated by a star ★.

Category	Cost*
$$$$	over £120
$$$	£100–£120
$$	£80–£100
$	under £80

All prices are for a standard double room, including service, breakfast, and VAT.

Aros
Lodging

Kentallen Farm. This traditional stone farmhouse on a working farm serves as a high-standard bed-and-breakfast. Its unelaborate rooms with en suite facilities are a good value. Wonderful views across the Sound of Mull toward Ardnamurchan are a bonus. *Aros, Isle of Mull, tel. 01680/300427. 3 rooms with bath. No credit cards. $*

Ballygrant
Lodging

Kilmeny Farmhouse. There are fine views over the surrounding countryside from this white-painted traditional farmhouse, also on a working farm. It offers bed-and-breakfast accommodations with evening meal if desired. Home baking and homemade preserves make breakfast special. *Ballygrant, Isle of Islay PA45 7QW, tel. 01496/840668. 2 rooms, 1 with bath. No credit cards. $*

Brodick
Dining and
Lodging
★

Auchrannie Country House Hotel. Determined to leave behind the chips-and-crusted-ketchup school of cookery still found in a few establishments, the Auchrannie offers interesting, varied cuisine. When at its best, the Taste of Scotland menu is inventive in incorporating local produce, particularly seafood (try the marinaded scallops), into its dishes. The bedrooms are spacious and comfortable, done with distinctive colors and fabrics. There are plenty of public areas, including a delightful dining room housed in a conservatory projecting into the garden, and sophisticated leisure facilities. *Auchrannie Rd., Isle of Arran, tel. 01770/302234, fax 01770/302812. 28 rooms with bath. Facilities: 2 restaurants, fitness center, sauna, Jacuzzi, pool, beauty salon, boutique. MC, V. $$–$$$*
Kilmichael Country House Hotel. At the head of Glen Cloy, just outside of Brodick, is this 300-year-old mansion, built by the Fullerton family on land granted to them by Robert the Bruce and now an outstanding small hotel. It is furnished in Georgian oak antiques, Sanderson fabrics, and light, sunny colors. At one end of the blue-and-yellow sitting room, in what was once a private chapel, is a stained-glass window showing the Fullerton family crest. Cuisine in the hotel's restaurant is also exceptional: Salmon en croute with dill sauce, duck with kumquats, and salad of pigeon with walnuts and smoked bacon are examples of the marriage of fresh Scottish produce and international flair. *Brodick, Isle of Arran, KA27 8BY, tel. 01770/302219. 10 rooms with bath. Restaurant reservations required. Jacket and tie preferred. V. $–$$*

Connel
Lodging
★

Ronebhal Guest House. Loch Etive and the mountains beyond can be seen from this stone house near the busy town of Oban. Although Connel is on the main road, Ronebhal is set back within its own grounds. It offers bed-and-breakfast accommodation in spacious surroundings. *Connel, Argyll PA37 1PJ, tel. 01631/71310. 6 rooms, 3 with bath. MC, V. $*

Dervaig
Dining and
Lodging

Druimard Country House. From this attractive Victorian house on the outskirts of the village, there are loch and glen views over the River Bellart. The restaurant is elegantly furnished and offers an original menu with several vegetarian options. Local prawns sautéed with mushrooms in a wine-and-cream sauce and Argyll lamb with red-wine-and-rosemary sauce and apricot chutney tartlets are two popular dishes, and all vegetables are carefully prepared. Bed-and-breakfast accommodations are also available. *Dervaig, Isle of Mull, Argyll, tel. 016884/345. 6 rooms, 4 with bath. Restaurant reservations advised. MC, V. Closed Nov.–Feb. Hotel $$; Restaurant $–$$*

Dunoon
Lodging

Abbot's Brae. This sizeable Victorian bed-and-breakfast is set in woodland but has sea and hill views. Its bedrooms are furnished to luxury-hotel standard, but its rates are still low. You can choose to eat dinner here; meals are prepared using fresh local ingredients in a straightforward style, and there's a carefully chosen wine list. *West Bay, Dunoon, Argyll PA23 7QJ, tel. and fax 01369/5021. 7 rooms with bath. MC, V. $*

Kentallen
Dining and
Lodging
★

Holly Tree. Railway buffs should enjoy this converted Edwardian railway station, complete with some of its original fixtures and fittings, which have been carefully extended over the onetime platform to create a spacious restaurant. You may see seals in Loch Linnhe from your dinner table, along with memorable sunsets over the Ardgour mountains. The hotel's bedrooms are elegantly yet comfortably furnished—thick carpets, easy chairs, and good mattresses. The food is generally of a high standard, though appetizers and puddings may hit the mark more often than the main courses. *Kentallen, Appin, Argyll, tel. 0163174/292, fax 0631/74345. 12 rooms with bath or shower. Restaurant reservations required. Jacket and tie advised. MC, V. $$*

Kilchrenan
Dining and
Lodging
★

Ardanaiseig House. Set on the shores of Loch Awe and framed by rhododendron blossoms in May and June (the gardens are famous), this excellent, privately run hotel is worth the extra cost, especially when the rhododendrons are blooming. All the bedrooms, which vary in size, have been decorated individually in traditional style, and the public rooms, with an abundance of chintz and polished wood, are just as comfortable. The food more than matches the decor, featuring five imaginative courses prepared with local ingredients; home-smoked scallops, fresh fruit from the garden, pickled salmon, and wood pigeon are among the choices. *Kilchrenan, near Taynuilt, Argyll, tel. 018663/333, fax 018663/222. 14 rooms with bath. AE, DC, MC, V. Closed Nov.–mid-Apr. $$–$$$$*

Knipoch
Dining and
Lodging

The Knipoch Hotel. With a history dating to the 16th century, this sprawling Georgian-style house on the banks of Loch Feochan now has modern niceties—indoor plumbing and electric blankets, for example. Although the hotel offers views of the countryside, the food will undoubtedly command your attention first. The owners smoke their own fish, which is caught locally, and prepare their own pickles and marinades. The menu, though limited in choice, reflects the quality of local Scottish produce and is complemented by a long wine list. *Near Oban, Argyll, tel. 018526/251, fax 018526/249. 17 rooms with bath. AE, DC, MC, V. Closed mid-Nov.–mid-Feb. $$$–$$$$*

Oban
Dining and
Lodging

Manor House Hotel. Once the home of the Duke of Argyll, this 1780 stone house on the shore just outside Oban is now a hotel with great views of the sea. It's within easy walking distance of downtown Oban and the bus, train, and ferry terminals. The reception and public areas are furnished with many genuine antiques, and the bedrooms, with reproductions. Bed coverings and curtains are made of textured fabrics in warm colors such as gold, pink, and yellow. The restaurant serves both Scottish and French dishes, including lots of local seafood and game in season, complemented by a carefully chosen wine list. *Gallanach Rd., Oban, Argyll PA34 4LS, tel. 01631/62087, fax 01631/63053. 11 rooms with bath. Restaurant reservations advised. Jacket and tie preferred. MC, V. Open Feb.–Dec. $–$$*

Lodging

Dungrianach. This aptly named bed-and-breakfast ("the sunny house on the hill") is set in woodland with superb views of the ocean and islands, yet it is only a few minutes walk from Oban's ferry piers and town center. All rooms in this late Victorian house have private facilities and are decorated with handsome period furniture. *Pulpit Hill, Oban, Argyll PA34 4LX, tel. 01631/62840. 3 rooms with bath or shower. No credit cards. Closed Nov.–Mar. $*

✗

Kilchrenan House. A fully refurbished Victorian house only a few minutes' walk from the town center, Kilchrenan offers high-grade bed-and-breakfast in rooms with views out to sea and to the islands. *Corran Esplanade, Oban, Argyll PA34 5AQ, tel. 01631/62663. 10 rooms with bath. MC, V. Closed Nov.–Mar. $*

Port Appin
Dining and
Lodging

Airds Hotel. This former ferry inn dating from the 17th century has some of the finest views in all of Scotland. Located in a peaceful village 24 miles north of Oban, the long white building, backed by trees, has a friendly feel to it. Quilted bedspreads and family mementos make guests feel right at home. Shooting and fishing trips can be arranged. The restaurant serves Scottish cuisine, including deer and grouse dishes. *Port Appin, Argyll PA38 4DF, tel. 0163173/236, fax 0163173/535. 12 rooms with bath. Restaurant reservations advised. Jacket and tie preferred. AE, MC, V. Closed Jan. and Feb. $$$$*

Port Askaig
Dining and
Lodging

Port Askaig Hotel. This modernized drovers' inn by the roadside, with grounds extending to the shore, overlooks the Sound of Islay and the island of Jura and is conveniently located near the ferry terminal. Accommodations are comfortable without being luxurious, and the food is well prepared, using home-grown produce, but not very imaginative. *Port Askaig, Isle of Islay, Argyll, tel. 01496/840245, fax 01496/840295. 9 rooms, 5 with bath. No credit cards. $*

Strachur
Dining and
Lodging

Creggans Inn. This traditional inn overlooking Loch Fyne dates to the 17th century. Visitors can enjoy an appetizing lunch in the bar or a more formal dinner in the inn's attractive dining room, replete with views of the water. Once again, local produce and seafood, including Loch Fyne oysters, are staples on the menu. Accommodations are available: The bedrooms vary in size from large to rather small, but all are newly decorated in pastel shades. The staff is friendly and hospitable. *Strachur, Argyll, tel. 01369/86279, fax 01369/86637. 21 rooms, 17 with bath. Dinner reservations advised. AE, DC, MC, V. $*

Tiroran
Dining and
Lodging
★

Tiroran House. This secluded country-house hotel overlooks Loch Scridain and is surrounded by more than 50 acres of grounds and woodlands. Tiroran has the atmosphere of a privately run sporting lodge: Everyone eats at the same time under candlelight, with a fixed main course of lamb, beef, venison, or salmon and perhaps a choice of appetizer and traditional British puddings. The bedrooms are individually decorated, and the public rooms, including the conservatory dining room, are furnished in accordance with the price level. Note that the packed lunches have won awards for their excellence. *Tiroran, Isle of Mull, Argyll, tel. and fax 016815/232. 9 rooms with bath. No credit cards. Closed Nov.–Apr. $$$$*

Tobermory
Lodging

Tobermory Hotel. This 18th-century building by the quay on the northeastern tip of the island of Mull commands superb views. The ambience is crisp and bright, fresh flowers dot every windowsill, and the rooms are spacious and sunny (weather permitting, of course). *Tobermory, Isle of Mull, Argyll PA75 6NT, tel. 01688/2091. 17 rooms, 9 with bath or shower. MC, V. $–$$*

The Arts and Nightlife

The Arts

This predominantly rural area with a small population relies to a great extent on touring companies and small local exhibitions and events for its cultural fulfillment. Tourist-information centers (*see* Important Addresses and Numbers in Essential Information, *above*) can supply an up-to-date events list.

Theater **Mull Little Theatre** (Dervaig, Isle of Mull, tel. 016884/267) is Britain's smallest professional playhouse (43 seats) and presents a number of productions throughout the season. There is a restaurant nearby (*see* Druimard Country House in Dining and Lodging, *above*).

Film The **Highland Discovery Centre** (George St., Oban, tel. 01631/ 62444) shows feature films and also has a theater for plays.

Nightlife

Cabaret The **Highland Discovery Centre** (*see above*) features a summer cabaret, *This Is Scotland.*

11 Around the Great Glen

Loch Ness, Speyside

By Gilbert Summers

The ancient rift valley of the Great Glen is a dramatic feature on the map of Scotland, giving the impression that the top half of the country has slid southwest. Geologists confirm that this actually occurred, having matched granite from Strontian in Morvern, west of Fort William, with the same rocks found at Foyers, on the east side of Loch Ness, some 65 miles away. The Great Glen, with its sense of openness, lacks the grandeur of Glen Coe or the Torridons, but the highest mountain in the United Kingdom, Ben Nevis (4,406 ft), looms over its southern portals, and spectacular scenery lies within a short distance of the main glen.

Though it's the capital of the Highlands, Inverness has the flavor of a Lowland town, its winds blowing in a sea-salt air from the Moray Firth. Inverness is also home to one of the world's most famous monster myths: In 1933, during a quiet news week for the local paper, the editor decided to run a story about a strange sighting of something splashing about in Loch Ness. More than 60 years later the story lives on, and the dubious Loch Ness phenomenon continues to keep cameras trained on the deep waters, which have an ominous tendency to create mirages in still conditions. The loch also has the distinction of being Scotland's largest body of water.

Fort William, without a monster on its doorstep, makes do with Ben Nevis and the Road to the Isles, a title sometimes applied to the breathtakingly scenic route to Mallaig, which is best seen by rail. On the way, road and rail routes pass Loch Morar, the country's deepest body of water, which laid claim to its own monster, Morag. Morag threatened Loch Ness's publicity for a while, but she has kept a low profile in recent years.

Away from the Great Glen to the north lie the heartlands of Scotland, a bare backbone of remote mountains. The great hills that loom to the south can be seen clearly on either side of Strathspey, the broad valley of the River Spey. The area is also commonly known as Speyside. The Speyside/Strathspey area has scenic qualities and points of interest rivaling anything in the Great Glen.

Essential Information

Important Addresses and Numbers

Tourist Information
The principal centers in the area are the **Aviemore and Spey Valley Tourist Board** (Grampian Rd., tel. 01479/810363, fax 01479/811063), **Fort William and Lochaber Tourism** (Cameron Centre, Cameron Sq., tel. 01397/703781, fax 01397/705184), and **Inverness, Loch Ness, and Nairn Tourist Board** (23 Church St., tel. 01463/234353, fax 01463/710609).

Emergencies
For police, fire, or ambulance, dial 999 from any telephone. No coins are needed for emergency calls from phone booths.

Hospitals
Emergency rooms are located at the following hospitals: **Belford Hospital** (Belford Rd., Fort William, tel. 01397/702481), **Raigmore Hospital** (Perth Rd., Inverness, tel. 01463/704000), and **Town and County Hospital** (Cawdor Rd., Nairn, tel. 01667/452101).

Late-Night Pharmacies
Pharmacies are not common away from the larger towns. In an emergency, the police will assist you in locating a pharmacist. In Inverness, **Kinmylies Pharmacy** (1 Charleston Court, Kinmylies, tel. 01463/221094) is open weekdays until 6 and Saturday until 5:30. The pharmacy at the co-op superstore **Milton of Inshes** (Perth Rd., outside Inverness, tel. 01463/242525), is open Monday to Wednesday

9–8, Thursday and Friday 9–9, and Saturday 8–6. In Fort William, **Boots the Chemist** (High St., tel. 01397/705143) is open Monday to Saturday 8:45–5:30. A rotation system provides limited Sunday service— consult the list on any pharmacy door.

Arriving and Departing by Plane

Airports and Airlines   **Inverness Airport** (Dalcross, tel. 01463/232471) has flights from Glasgow operated by **Loganair** (tel. 0141/889–3181) and **British Airways** (tel. 0181/897–4000). Alternatively, Fort William has bus and train connections with Glasgow, so **Glasgow Airport** can be an appropriate access point. *See* Chapter 5, Glasgow, for further information.

Arriving and Departing by Car, Train, and Bus

By Car   As in all areas of rural Scotland, a car is a great asset for exploring the Great Glen and Speyside, especially since the best of the area is away from the main roads. The fast A9 brings you to Inverness in roughly three hours from Glasgow or Edinburgh, even if you take your time.

By Train   The area is surprisingly well served by train. There are sleeper connections from London to Inverness and Fort William, as well as reliable links from Glasgow and Edinburgh. For information call **Scotrail** (Fort William, tel. 01397/703791; Inverness, tel. 01463/238924) or contact any main-line station in Scotland.

By Bus   There is a long-distance **Citylink** service from Fort William to Glasgow (Glasgow coach station, tel. 0141/332–9191). Inverness is also well served from the central belt of Scotland (Inverness coach station, tel. 01463/233371).

Getting Around

By Car   You can use the main A9 Perth–Inverness road (via Aviemore) to explore this area or use one of the many other smaller roads (some of them old military roads) to explore the much quieter east side of Loch Ness. The same applies to Speyside, where a variety of options open up away from the A9, especially through the pinewoods by Coylumbridge and Feshiebridge, east of the main road. Mallaig, west of Fort William, also has improving road connections, but rail still remains the most enjoyable way to experience the rugged hills and loch scenery between these two places. In Morvern, the area across Loch Linnhe southwest of Fort William, you may encounter single-lane roads, which require slower speeds and concentration.

By Train   Though the Great Glen has no rail connection (in Victorian times Fort William and Inverness had different lines built by companies that could not agree), this area has the **West Highland line,** which links Fort William to Mallaig, a small fishing and ferry port on the west coast.

By Bus   There is limited service available in the Great Glen area and some local service running from Fort William (Highland Bus and Coach Company, tel. 01397/702373). A number of post-bus services will help get you to the more remote corners of the area. The timetable is available from the **Head Post Office** (Edinburgh, tel. 0131/550–8232) or the **District Head Post Office** (14–16 Queen's Gate, Inverness, tel. 01463/234111, ext. 248).

Guided Tours

Orientation From Fort William, **Highland Bus and Coach Company** (Travel Centre, Fort William, tel. 01397/702373) operates coach tours in the summer season. **Scotrail** (tel. 01397/703791) runs a not-to-be-missed steam-hauled service to Mallaig in the summer season (other non-steam connections run to Mallaig). Advance booking is recommended for Scotrail's steam service. **Caledonian MacBrayne** runs scheduled service and cruises to Skye, the Small Isles, and Mull from Mallaig (tel. 01475/650100, fax 01475/637607). **Arisaig Marine** (tel. 0168/75224) operates highly recommended Hebridean day cruises on the MV (motor vessel) *Shearwater* to the Small Isles and Skye from May to September.

From Inverness, **Highland Bus and Coach Company** (Inverness bus station, tel. 01463/233371) offers coach tours during the summer season, as do **Macdonald's Tours** (tel. 01463/240673), and **Spa Coaches** (tel. 01997/421311).

Special-Interest From Inverness, **Highland Insight Tours and Travel** (tel. 01463/831403), offers personalized touring holidays and full-day or half-day tours that cater to any interest, with **James Johnson Chauffeur Drive** (tel. 01463/790179) offering a similar service. **Linnmhor Limousines** (Linnmhor, Strathpeffer, tel. 01997/421528), has chauffeur-driven Rolls Royce limousines for daily hire. **Jacobite Cruises Ltd.** (Tomnahurich Bridge, Glenurquhart Rd., Inverness, tel. 01463/233999 or 01463/241730) runs morning and afternoon cruises to Loch Ness; morning and afternoon excursions to Urquhart Castle; and boat and coach excursions to the Monster Exhibition. **Macaulay Charters** (12 Pict Ave., Inverness, tel. 01463/225398) provides trips by boat to Nairn and the surrounding coastline, offering visitors the chance to see dolphins in their breeding area.

Exploring the Great Glen

Orientation

Of the two tours decribed below, the first takes in some of the byways of both the Great Glen and Speyside, demonstrating that the best sights are hidden from the main road. However, the tour initially highlights some of the attractions within easy reach of Inverness along the inner Moray Firth. The second tour, originating in Fort William, takes in the special qualities of birch-knoll and blue island West Highland views. The tours also point out the romantic and historic associations of this area, where the rash adventurer Prince Charles Edward Stuart both arrived for and departed after the final Jacobite rebellion of 1745–46.

Highlights for First-Time Visitors

Arisaig to the Small Isles by boat (*see* Guided Tours)
Cawdor Castle (*see* Tour 1)
Culloden Moor (*see* Tour 1)
Fort George (*see* Tour 1)
Fort William to Mallaig by steam-powered train (*see* Guided Tours)
Glen Nevis (*see* Off the Beaten Track)
Loch an Eilean (*see* Tour 1)
View down Loch Shiel (*see* Tour 2)

Tour 1: Speyside and Loch Ness

Numbers in the margin correspond to points of inter ‍
Glen Area map.

❶ **Inverness** seems designed for the tourist, with its banks, ‍
high-quality woolens, and well-equipped tourist information ‍
Compared with other Scottish towns, however, Inverness has ‍
to offer visitors with a keen interest in Scottish history. Frequent ‍
throughout its history Inverness was burned and ravaged by one or ‍
another of the restive Highland clans competing for dominance in ‍
the region. Thus a decorative wall panel here and a fragment of ‍
tower there are all that remain amid the modern shopping facilities ‍
and 19th-century downtown developments. One of the town's few ‍
historical landmarks is the **castle** (the local Sheriff Court), nestled ‍
above the river. The present structure is Victorian, built after a ‍
former fort was blown up by the Jacobites in the 1745 campaign. ‍
Because Jacobite tales are interwoven with landmarks throughout ‍
this entire area, you may enjoy your touring a little more if you first ‍
learn something about this thorny but colorful period of Scottish ‍
history. One of the best places to do this is at **Culloden,** just 5 miles ‍
east of Inverness on the B9006.

❷ At **Culloden Moor,** on a sleety April day in 1746, an army of 5,000 ‍
Jacobites under Prince Charles Edward Stuart faced 9,000 well-‍
armed British army troops at the command of the prince's distant ‍
cousin, General Cumberland. The latter became known in Scotland ‍
after the war as Butcher Cumberland because of the atrocities com-‍
mitted by his men after the battle ended. The story of the encounter, ‍
of how the ill-advised, poorly organized, and exhausted rebel army ‍
was swept aside by superior British firepower, is illustrated in the ‍
visitor center by a moving audiovisual presentation. *B9006, tel.* ‍
01463/790607. Admission to visitor center £1.80 adults, 90p senior ‍
citizens, children, and students. Site open all year. Visitor center open ‍
Apr.–Oct., daily 9–6; Nov., Dec., Feb., and Mar., daily 10–4.

Not far from Culloden, on a narrow road southeast of the battlefield, ‍
❸ are the **Clava Cairns,** dating from the Bronze Age. In a cluster ‍
among the trees, these stones and monuments constitute a large ‍
ring with passage graves, which consist of a central chamber below ‍
a cairn of stone reached via a passage. On-site information placards ‍
explain the graves' significance.

To get to the next chapter of the Highlands' history, drive northeast ‍
❹ from Culloden. Use either the B9039 or B9006 to get to **Fort George,** ‍
a fortress that was started in 1748 and completed some 20 years ‍
later. As a direct result of the battle at Culloden, the nervous gov-‍
ernment in London ordered the construction of a large fort on this ‍
promontory reaching into the Moray Firth. It survives today as per-‍
haps the best-preserved 18th-century military fortification in ‍
Europe. Because it is low lying, its immense scale can be seen only ‍
from within. The huge walls, as broad and high as harbor quays, are ‍
large enough to contain a complete military town. A walk along the ‍
wall-tops affords fine views of the Highland hills in the distance and ‍
of the firth immediately below. Even though no one has sighted a ‍
Jacobite here for more than 200 years, the army still uses the bar-‍
racks. And if you happen to meet any of the fort's current military ‍
residents, you will find them unfailingly polite. A visitor center and ‍
a number of tableaux at the fort portray the 18th-century Scottish ‍
soldier's way of life, as does the **Regimental Museum of the Queen's** ‍
Own Highlanders. *B9039, off A96 west of Nairn, tel. 0131/244–3101.*

A832
Garve
A835
Maryburgh
Cromarty
Cromarty Firth
Cromarty Firth
Moray Firth
Forres
Marybank
A832
Tore
Fort George **4**
A96
B9039
Nairn **5**
A939
A940
Beauly
Inverness **1**
B862
2 Culloden Moor
B9006
Cawdor **6** Castle
Dulsie Bridge
3 Clava Cairns
7
Official Loch Ness Monster Exhibition **25**
B852
A9
Lochindorb Castle **8**
A939
Cannich
A831
Drumnadrochit
Urquhart **26** Castle
Inverfarigaig **29** Forest Centre
Grantown-on-Spey **9**
B9007
Carrbridge **12**
Loch Ness **24** **28**
A82
A95
Boat of **11** Garten
10 Loch Garten Nature Reserve
Invermoriston
27 Whitebridge
Falls of Foyers
Aviemore **13**
B970
Loch Morlich
Glen More Forest Park **14**
A887
B862
MONADHLIATH MTS.
A9
Spey
Feshiebridge
Caledonian Canal **22**
23 Fort Augustus
Highland Folk Museum **17**
Loch Insh **15**
Invergarry
Loch Oich
Kingussie
Newtonmore
18 **16** Ruthven Barracks
CAIRNGORM MTS.
Loch Lochy
A82
Garvamore Bridge
Laggan
Clan Macpherson Museum
19
Parallel Roads of Glen Roy **20**
Loch Laggan
A86
Dalwhinnie
Spean Bridge
River Spean
Loch Ericht
G R A M P I A N
M O U N T A I N S
N
Blair Atholl
Loch Rannoch
A82
Kingshouse
Pitlochry
A9
Aberfeldy
KEY
Bridge of Orchy
A827
Kenmore
Loch Tay
Rail Lines
Airport
Ferry
Nessie
0   20 miles
0   30 km

Admission to fort: £2.50 adults, £1.50 senior citizens, £1 children; free admission to museum. Fort and museum open Apr.–Sept., Mon.–Sat. 9:30–6, Sun. 2–6; Oct.–Mar., Mon.–Sat. 9:30–4, Sun. 2–4. Last tickets sold 45 min before closing.

⑤ To the east is **Nairn,** which has the air of a Lowland town yet looks, administratively speaking, to Inverness as part of the Highlands. A once-prosperous fishing village, Nairn does in fact have something of a split personality. King James VI once boasted that there was a town in his kingdom so large that the residents at either end of town spoke different languages. He was referring to the fact that Nairn's fisherfolk spoke Lowland Scots by the sea, while the uptown farmers and crofters spoke Gaelic. The fishing boats have since moved to larger ports, but the town's historic flavor has been preserved in the **Nairn Fishertown Museum,** a hall crammed with artifacts, photographs, and model boats. This is an informal museum in the best sense, where the volunteer staff are full of information and eager to talk. *Laing Hall, King St., tel. 01667/453331. Admission: 30p adults, 15p children. Open June–Sept., Mon.–Sat. 2:30–4:30, also Mon., Wed., and Fri. evenings 6:30–8:30.*

⑥ Next head southwest to **Cawdor Castle.** Shakespeare's Macbeth was Thane of Cawdor, but the sense of history that exists within these turreted walls is more than fictional. Cawdor is a lived-in castle, not an abandoned, decadent structure to be preserved in aspic. The earliest part of the castle is the 14th-century central tower; the rooms contain family portraits, tapestries, fine furniture, and paraphernalia reflecting 600 years of history. Outside the castle walls there are sheltered gardens and walks. *B9090, 5 mi southwest of Nairn, tel. 01667/404615. Admission: £4 adults, £3.10 senior citizens, £2.20 children, £12 family ticket; garden and grounds only: £2. Open May–Sept., daily 10–5:30.*

If Cawdor has inspired you to seek the wild Highlands, make your way to the southeastern portion of the region, using either the unclassified roads southeast of Cawdor or heading northeast along the B9101 to pick up the A939 south. If you use the unclassified roads, you will find yourself in a classic Highland "edge" landscape, where the open moor contrasts with the improved upland pasture and thickets of birch and fir. (Clunas may be the first road sign you see, but reaching Dulsie is your first objective.) As you take to the higher ground, look for the longest views back over the Firth—you should still just barely be able to see Fort George in the distance. Follow what was the former military road built in the 1750s to service the garrison. Look for the point where the road crosses the River Find-
⑦ horn by a narrow span, the **Dulsie Bridge.** Just beyond the bridge, on the right, is a parking place and kissing gate. If you park and go through the gate, a walk of a few yards brings you to a viewpoint over the birch-scattered rocky confines of the river.

Shortly after Dulsie Bridge, turn right off the unclassified road onto the B9007. Shakespeare's Thane of Cawdor met the three prophesying witches on a bare moor very much like this one. Rolling folds of marbled purple and brown are broken here and there by a roofless cottage. You can either switch to the A938 and Carrbridge on Speyside heading south (*see below*), or if you have more time, you can take a short diversion to the east for a view of the lonely ruin of
⑧ **Lochindorb Castle.** What appears to be a walled enclosure fills and surrounds an entire island on Lochindorb loch. This 13th-century stronghold was the former power base of the Wolf of Badenoch (the marauding Earl of Buchan who damaged Elgin Cathedral). The castle was eventually dismantled by a 15th-century Thane of Cawdor,

on the order of the king. (Lochindorb's iron *yett* [gate] is now on view at Cawdor.)

❾ After you have viewed Lochindorb, drive farther south along the A939 to **Grantown-on-Spey.** This sturdy settlement, set amid tall pines which flank the River Spey, gives visitors access to many points of interest, including a heavily stocked heather nursery at nearby **Skye of Curr.** The A95, which runs southwest along the river, is an attractive road, but you may wish to follow the more tranquil

❿ B970 via **Nethy Bridge.** Then look for signs to the **Loch Garten Nature Reserve,** administered by the Royal Society for the Protection of Birds (RSPB). This sanctuary achieved fame when the osprey, a bird that was facing extinction in the early part of this century, returned to breed here. Instead of cordoning off the nest site, the RSPB encouraged visitors by constructing a blind from which to watch the birds. Now thousands of bird lovers visit annually to get a glimpse of the domestic arrangements of this fish-eating bird, which has since bred in many other parts of the Highlands. *Off B970, 8 mi northeast of Aviemore, tel. 01479/821409 or 0131/557–3136. Admission: £2 adults, £1 senior citizens, 50p children. Osprey observation post open May–Aug. 10–6:30; other areas of reserve open daily year-round.*

⓫ Near Loch Garten is **Boat of Garten,** a peaceful village where the scent of pine trees is interrupted by an equally evocative smell. This is the terminus of the **Speyside Railway,** and the acrid scent of smoke and steam hang faintly in the air near the authentically preserved station next to the **Boat Hotel.** The 5-mile train trip to Aviemore not only offers a chance to wallow in nostalgia, but also yields superb views southward to the high and often white domes of the Cairngorms.

Time Out   At the **Boat Hotel,** in Boat of Garten, you can have a friendly pub lunch while you wait for the train. The malt-whisky selection behind the bar also may be of interest.

⓬ In **Carrbridge,** just about 5 miles northwest of Boat of Garten (use A95 and then B9153), you'll find the **Landmark Visitor Centre,** an early pioneer in the move toward more sophisticated visitor attractions. It has an audiovisual presentation on the history of the Scottish Highlands, a permanent exhibition, a display on forestry with working steam-powered sawmill and a Clydesdale horse to haul the logs, a forestry workshop where you can try out forest skills such as bark peeling, plus a bookshop and restaurant. Outdoors are nature trails, a treetop trail, and a viewing platform, as well as plenty of diversions for children, such as a Wild Forest maze and an adventure playground. *Old A9, 6 mi north of Aviemore, tel. 01479/841613. Admission: £4.75 adults, £3.10 senior citizens and children, £14.50–£20.20 family ticket. Open Apr.–June, daily 9:30–6; July and Aug., daily 9:30–8; Sept. and Oct., daily 9:30–5:30; Nov.–Mar., daily 9:30–5.*

No matter which side of the Spey you choose to travel (the quiet B970 on the southeast side is recommended), signs will point you to

⓭ **Aviemore.** Once a quiet junction on the Highland Railway, Aviemore now possesses all the brashness and concrete boxiness of a year-round holiday resort. A resort environment certainly translates into a lot of things to do, however, and here you can swim, curl, skate, see a movie, dance, and shop. Signs will direct you to other sights, such as the **Cairngorm Whisky Centre,** which has one of the largest selections of malt whiskies in the world. *On the road to the Cairn-*

gorms, tel. 01479/810574. Open daily 9:30–4:30 (longer hrs in summer season).

The Aviemore area is a versatile walking base, but walkers must be properly dressed for high-level excursions onto the near-Arctic plateau. Visitors interested in skiing and rugged hiking can follow the **(14)** B970 from Aviemore past Loch Morlich in the **Glen More Forest Park** to the high car parks on the exposed shoulders of the **Cairngorm Mountains.** The chair lifts take you even higher, during and after the ski season, for extensive views of the broad valley of the Spey. But be warned: It can get very cold at over 3,000 feet, and weather conditions can change rapidly even in the middle of summer. *Off B9152, tel. 01540/651223 or 01479/861271. Open all year.*

While you are on the high slopes, you may sight the reindeer herd that was introduced here in the 1950s. In fact, by inquiring at the **Cairngorm Reindeer Centre,** by Loch Morlich, you can go along with the keeper on his daily check. *Loch Morlich, Glen More Forest Park, tel. 01479/861228. Admission: £3 adults, £2 children. Departures daily at 11 AM (subject to weather conditions). Centre open daily 10–6.*

The place that best sums up Speyside's piny ambience is probably **Loch an Eilean,** a mile or so south of Aviemore, signposted off the B970 (parallel with the main A9). A converted cottage on the **Rothiemurchus Estate** houses a visitor center (the area is a National Nature Reserve). Visitors should exercise care upon entering the cottage: It has an extremely low door and a very hard lintel! All around the loch you can still see some stands of old Scots pines; look for the characteristic red limbs high up. These are the descendants of the Caledonian Forest that once covered much of Scotland and now survives only in remnants. *Rothiemurchus Estate Visitor Centre, tel. 01479/810858. Free admission. Open daily 9–5.*

(15) About a mile west of **Feshiebridge** is **Loch Insh.** Other lochs in the vicinity, notably Loch an Eilean and Loch Garten, are what geologists call kettle holes—round depressions that remained after huge blocks of ice melted at the end of the Ice Age. Loch Insh is thought to be the remains of a much larger loch, which, until recent geological times, filled the valley's floor. Loch Insh is known for its recreational diversions; it has sailboats and canoes and is a popular water-sports center. Beyond the loch the valley floor broadens into marshland, the haunt of watery tribes of birds and hence birdwatchers. Look for ospreys here.

Gaunt against the rounded **Monadhliath Mountains** (*monadhliath* is Gaelic for gray moors) to the north is what appears, at first glance, to be a ruined castle on a mound. The remains are not of a castle, **(16)** however, but of **Ruthven Barracks,** roofless and redolent with tales of the '45 (as the last Jacobite rebellion is often called). The defeated Jacobite forces rallied here after Culloden, but then abandoned and blew up the government outpost they had earlier captured. *B970, ¹⁄₂ mi south of Kingussie, tel. 0131/244–3101. Admission free.*

The barracks lie within a few minutes of the village of **Kingussie** (pronounced Kin-*yoo*-see) and can be seen clearly from the main A9. **(17)** The village is of interest primarily because of the **Highland Folk Museum.** The interior exhibits are housed in what was an 18th-century shooting lodge, its paneled and varnished ambience still apparent. Displays include 18th-century furniture, clothing, and implements, and, outside, various types of Highland buildings have been reconstructed. In summer, local weavers and other artisans demonstrate Highland crafts. Visitors can wander around the grounds freely or see the highlights of the museum on a guided tour.

A9 at Kingussie, tel. 01540/661307. Admission: £2.50 adults, £1.50 senior citizens and children. Open Apr.–Oct., Mon.–Sat. 10–6, Sun. 2–6; Nov.–Mar., Mon.–Fri. 10–3.

Down the road from Kingussie is neighborly **Newtonmore,** home
⑱ of the **Clan Macpherson Museum.** One of many clan museums scattered throughout the old homelands, the Macpherson Museum displays a number of interesting artifacts associated with the '45 rebellion, as well as of clan chiefs of the even more distant past. *A9/A86, Newtonmore, tel. 01540/673332. Admission free (donation box). Open May–Sept., Mon.–Sat. 10–5:30, Sun. 2:30–5:30 (open at other times by appointment).*

At Newtonmore you will leave the great artery of the A9 behind. It veers off to the southeast for the Pass of Drumochter at this point. This tour continues westward on the A86 around the edge of the Monadhliath range, which separates Speyside from the Great Glen. The Monadhliath are less often explored by hill walkers than the Cairngorms, which form Speyside's southern side. At **Laggan,** where the main road crosses the young River Spey, an unclassified road runs west up the glen to **Garvamore.** If you are staying in the area and you are not pressed for time, it's worth making this detour
⑲ to view the **Garvamore Bridge** (about 6 mi from the junction, at the south side of the Corrieyarick Pass). This dual-arched bridge was built in 1735 by English General Wade, who had been charged with the task of improving Scotland's roads by a British government concerned that its troops would not be able to travel the Highlands quickly enough to quell an uprising.

If you opt not to take the Garvamore Bridge detour, you may continue south on the A86, which hugs the western shore of **Loch Laggan.** This was the route chosen by later road builders to avoid the high Corrieyarick Pass. Still quite narrow in a few places, this stretch of the A86 is a road to be enjoyed, offering superb views of the mountainous heartlands to the north, where high shoulders loom, and to the south, over the silvery spine of hills known as the **Grey Corries** and culminating with **Ben Nevis.**

In **Roybridge** you'll find the first of the Great Glen cul-de-sac diver-
⑳ sions. The so-called **Parallel Roads of Glen Roy** are three curious terraces, parallel and level, cut across the hillsides on both sides of the glen. Their levelness lends a clue to their origins as former shorelines of lochs dammed by ice that melted in stages at the end of the last Ice Age. *Unclassified road off A86 at Roybridge.*

Turn right and north at the junction with the main Great Glen road, the A82, to reach **Spean Bridge.** Uphill and beyond this little village,
㉑ easily visible from the road, is the arresting and dignified **Commando Memorial.** The rugged glens and hills of this area were a training ground for elite forces during World War II. Today, three battle-equipped figures on a high stone plinth overlook the panorama, while the veterans and younger generations who visit follow their gaze.

Time Out If you're passing Invergarry (just east of Loch Lochy) around lunchtime, consider a stop at the rambling **Glengarry Castle Hotel** (tel. 01809/501254), an interesting building with a pleasingly old-fashioned ambience. The hotel serves hearty soup-and-sandwich meals, though more substantial fare is also available. The ruined **Glengarry Castle,** a seat of the MacDonnell Clan, can be seen on the grounds. The hotel entrance is south of the A82–A87 road junction.

㉒ Traveling north up the Great Glen by the A82 takes you parallel to Loch Lochy (on the eastern shore) and over the **Caledonian Canal** at Laggan Locks. From this beautiful spot, which offers stunning vistas of lochs, mountains, and glens in all directions, you can look back on the impressive profile of Ben Nevis. The canal, which links the lochs of the Great Glen—Loch Lochy, Loch Oich, and Loch Ness—owes its origins to a combination of military as well as political pressures that emerged at the time of the Napoleonic Wars with France. (Mostly, the British needed a better and faster way to get naval vessels from one side of Scotland to the other.) The great Scottish engineer Thomas Telford surveyed the route in 1803. The canal, which took 19 years to complete, has 29 locks and 42 gates. Telford took advantage of the three lochs that lie in the Great Glen (which have a combined length of 45 miles), and only 22 miles of canal were constructed to connect the lochs and complete the waterway from coast to coast.

㉓ The best place to see the locks in action is at **Fort Augustus,** at the southern tip of Loch Ness. (Fort Augustus itself was captured by the Jacobite clans during the 1745 rebellion. Later the fort was rebuilt as a Benedictine abbey and boys' school.) The canal activity at a series of locks that rise from Loch Ness takes place in the village center.

㉔ From the B862 just east of Fort Augustus you'll get your first good long view of the formidable and famous **Loch Ness,** which has a greater volume of water than any other Scottish loch and a maximum depth of more than 800 feet. Early travelers who passed this way included English lexicographer Dr. Samuel Johnson and his guide and biographer James Boswell, who were on their way to the Hebrides in 1783. They remarked at the time about the condition of the population and the squalor of their homes. Another early travel writer, Thomas Pennant, noted that the loch kept the locality frost-free in winter. Even General Wade came here, his troops blasting and digging a road up much of the eastern shore. None of these observant early travelers ever made mention of a monster. Clearly, they had not read the local guidebooks.

㉕ If you're in search of the infamous beast Nessie, it's best to continue northward along the coast on the A82. At **Drumnadrochit** you will find the **Official Loch Ness Monster Exhibition,** which presents the facts and the fakes, the photographs, the unexplained sonar contacts, and the sincere testimony of eyewitnesses. It's then up to you to make up your own mind. *A831, tel. 01456/450573 and 01456/450218. Admission: £4 adults, £3 senior citizens and students, £2.50 children, £10.50 family ticket. Open July–mid-Sept., daily 9 AM–9:30 PM. Off-season opening times vary; please phone to check.*

㉖ **Urquhart Castle,** near Drumnadrochit, is another favorite monster-watching spot. This plundered fortress stands on a promontory overlooking the loch, as it has since the Middle Ages. Because of its central and strategic position in the Great Glen line of communication, the castle has a complex history involving military offense and defense, as well as its own destruction and renovation. The castle was begun in the 13th century and was destroyed before the end of the 17th century to prevent its use by the Jacobites. The ruins of what was one of the largest castles in Scotland were plundered for building material. Today swarms of bus tours pass through after investigating the Loch Ness phenomenon. *West shore of Loch Ness, 2 mi southeast of Drumnadrochit, tel. 0131/244–3101. Admission: £3 adults, £2 senior citizens, £1 children. Open Apr.–Sept., daily 9:30–6, Sun. 2–6; Oct.–Mar., Mon.–Sat. 9:30–6, Sun. 11:30–4.*

The west-bank road, the A82, offers intermittent views of the loch, often glittering hypnotically in the sun. You can be caught up in the fast-moving traffic on this busy road and find yourself in Inverness before you know it. Or you can choose a more leisurely alternative—combining monster watching with peaceful road touring—by taking the B862 from Fort Augustus and following the east-bank route to Inverness.

The B862 runs around the end of Loch Ness then climbs into moorland and forestry plantation. Fine views of Fort Augustus can be seen by climbing a few yards up and to the right, onto the moor; here you'll be able to see above the conifer spikes. The half-hidden track beside the road is a remnant of the military road built by General Wade. Loch Ness quickly drops out of sight, but is soon replaced by the peaceful, reedy **Loch Tarff.**

The B862 continues along the line of the former military route and **㉗** shows appropriate military precision nearly all the way to **White-bridge,** where a handsome single-arch Wade bridge (look for it on your right) has been restored. Just before the bridge is the **White-bridge Hotel,** a former Kingshouse, one of a chain of inns built by authorities in the 18th century to service the military roads. The Kingshouse name is still used by a few of Scotland's hotels. Beyond Whitebridge the small banks on either side of the road are thought to have survived from the military's original work in 1726; thus you find yourself traveling one of the earliest roads in the Highlands. Take the B852, left at the junction beyond Whitebridge, to regain the shores of Loch Ness by some fine woodlands.

Just before you reach the level of the loch at **Foyers,** a sign outside **㉘** the general store will direct you to the **Falls of Foyers.** Steep, pine-cone-strewn paths lead to a viewpoint where a thin waterfall streams into a dark pot and then down a ravine. The original volume of the falls was much reduced shortly before the turn of the century when the power generated here was harnessed for the first commercial application of hydroelectricity (1896), in an aluminum-smelting plant on a site by the loch.

The B852 meanders pleasantly from Foyers, offering some views of the loch on the way to **Inverfarigaig.** Just before the main road **㉙** bridge is the **Inverfarigaig Forest Centre,** on the right. The center has several displays on forestry activities, and a number of trails lead from the center into the woodlands. *Off of B862, Inverfarigaig, 17 mi southwest of Inverness, tel. 01320/6322. Admission free. Open Easter–mid-Oct., daily 9:30–7.*

Tour 2: Toward the Small Isles

㉚ **Fort William** probably has enough points of interest for visitors—a museum, exhibits, and shopping—to compensate for its less-than-picturesque milieu. The town's primary purpose is to serve the west Highland hinterland; its role as a tourist stop is secondary. Since this is a relatively wet part of Scotland, and since Fort William itself can always be explored if it rains, strike west toward the coast if the weather looks settled: On a sunny day, the Small Isles—Rhum, Eigg, Canna, and Muck—look as blue as the sea and sky together. From here you could also visit Skye via the ferry at Mallaig, or take a day cruise (*see* Off the Beaten Track, *below*) from Arisaig to the Small Isles for a glimpse of traffic-free island life.

Begin your visit to Fort William by stopping by the helpful tourist-information center in **Cameron Square.** Just a few doors down is the

West Highland Museum, which explores the theme of Prince Charles Edward Stuart and the 1745 rebellion. Included in the museum's folk exhibits is a section on tartans. *Cameron Sq., tel. 01397/702169. Admission: £1 adults, 60p senior citizens, 40p children. Open July and Aug., Mon.–Sat. 9:30–5:30, Sun. 2–5; Sept.–June, Mon.–Sat. 10–1 and 2–5 (closed Mon. Nov.–Mar.).*

The sound of a steam-train whistle may remind you that this is the terminus of Scotrail's spectacularly successful Fort William–Mallaig steam-hauled line. British Rail dispensed with steam traction about 30 years ago and ironically has had to hire locomotives from various steam-preservation societies to run its extra trains. However, not all the services to Mallaig are run by steam. If you visit Fort William by car, leave the car behind to take this trip. *Tel. 01397/703791.*

If you're not reliant on public transportation, you can make an interesting West Highlands circuit by traveling down the eastern side of **Loch Linnhe** to **Corran,** where a frequent ferry shuttles autos and foot passengers across the loch to **Ardgour.** (From the map you will see you can avoid the ferry by driving around the head of Loch Eil, but it's not a very scenic route.) From Ardgour, a reliable two-lane road runs along Loch Linnhe before turning into Glen Sanda, crossing the watershed, and running down to the long shores of **Loch Sunart.** This is a typical West Highlands sea loch: Orange wrack marks the tide lines, and herons stand muffled and miserable, wondering if it is worth risking a free meal at the local fish farm. As for the fish farms themselves, visitors will become accustomed to their floats and cages turning up in the foreground of every sea-loch view. The farms were originally hailed as the savior of the Highland economy because of the number of jobs they created, but questions are now being raised about their environmental effects, and the market for their product is being threatened by Scandinavian imports.

At **Salen** you have a choice. The B8007 runs west, blind-bending partly through thickets of rhododendrons to **Ardnamurchan,** the most western point of mainland Scotland and a must-see for those who love unspoiled coastal scenery. Here you'll find crofting communities and holiday homes.

If you are short on time, swing north instead from Salen along the B8044 and head for **Acharacle** (pronounced ak-*ar*-ra-kle). You'll pass through deep-green plantations and moorland lily ponds to reach this strung-out settlement backed by the hills of Moidart and **Loch Shiel.** The south end of Loch Shiel is shallow and reedy. The north end is more dramatic and sits deep within the rugged hills. A few minutes beyond Acharacle—where the main road turns sharply right—take the narrow road to the left, overhung in places by mossy trees, to emerge at **Castle Tioram.** This ruined keep dominates a bracken-green islet, barely anchored to the mainland by a sand spit. The castle was once the home of the chief of the MacDonalds of Clan Ranald, but the last chief burned the castle to prevent its falling into the hands of his enemies, the Campbells, during the 1715 Jacobite rebellion. Conservation agencies do not yet require an admission charge to this fragment of Highlands history guarding the south channel of Loch Moidart. *Reached by an unclassified road north of A861. Always accessible.*

The upper sandy reaches of **Loch Moidart** are reached by returning to the main road, climbing a high moorland pass and then dropping down to a two-lane road again. On the next ascent from the shores of Loch Moidart you'll be rewarded with stunning sea views. The

㉟ coast is reached by the mouth of **Loch Ailort** (pronounced *eye*-ort), and there are plenty of places to pull off among the boulders and birch scrub and sort out the view of the islands. Offshore in the ㊱ distance you'll be able to spot **Eigg,** a low island marked by the ㊲ dramatic black peak of An Sgurr. Beyond Eigg is the larger **Rhum,** with its range of hills, the Norse-named Rhum Coullin, looming cloud-capped over the island.

Loch Ailort itself is another picturesque inlet, now cluttered with the garish floats of fish cages. You meet the bustle of the main road again at its head, at the junction with the A830, the main road from Fort William to Mallaig. Turn left here to reach Mallaig. This road is sometimes called the Road to the Isles, a name borrowed from an old cattle-driving trail that once ran through the hills to the north until the railways put an end to the trade.

The breathtaking seaward views continue to distract you from the road (hence the earlier recommendation to take the train) as you ㊳ travel by **Loch nan Uamh** (from the Gaelic meaning cave, and pronouced *oo*-am). This loch is associated with Prince Charles Edward Stuart's nine-month stay on the mainland, during which he gathered a small army, marched as far south as Derby in England, alarmed the king, retreated to unavoidable defeat at Culloden in the spring, and then spent a few months as a fugitive in the Highlands. A cairn by the shore marks the spot where the prince was picked up by a French ship. Prince Charles never returned to Scotland, and many say it would have been better if he had not arrived in the first place. (Following Prince Charles' defeat, the Hanoverian government was more than a little vengeful, banning tartan, kilts, and other symbols of the Gael in a successful effort to dismantle the clan system.)

㊴ **Arisaig,** signposted off the A830, offers many options for dining and lodging (*see* Dining and Lodging, *below*). Beyond this point the road cuts across a headland to reach a stretch of coastline where the silver sands around Loch Morar are made glittering by the presence of mica in the local rock; clear water, blue sky, and white sand lend a tropical flavor to the beaches—when the sun shines. Sapphire seas and tiny bays backed by sandy wildflower meadows, called *machair,* conjure images of the Hebrides, Scotland's scatter of islands in the western seas. The nearest of these isles should be in plain view: not only Muck, Eigg, and Rhum, but also the magical Cuillin Hills of Skye, a little to the north.

A small, unclassified side road off to the right leads to an even ㊵ smaller road that will bring you to **Loch Morar,** the deepest of all the Scottish lochs (over 1,000 ft); the next deepest point is miles out into the Atlantic, beyond the Continental Shelf. Apart from this short public road, the area around the loch is all but roadless; the area to the immediate north and west, beyond Loch Nevis, one of the most remote in Scotland, is often referred to as the Rough Bounds of Knoydart.

㊶ After the approach along the coast, the town of **Mallaig** itself is anticlimactic. It has a few shops, and there is some bustle by the quayside when fishing boats unload or the Skye ferry departs. Mallaig is also the starting point for day cruises up the Sound of Sleat, which separates Skye from the mainland and offers views into rugged Knoydart and its sea lochs (*see* Off the Beaten Track, *below*).

You can get back to Fort William by retracing your route along the A830 to the **Lochailort** junction. From here, the road eastward to ㊷ Fort William has many points of interest. **Glenfinnan,** perhaps the most visitor-oriented stop on the way, has the most to offer visitors interested in Scottish history. Here the National Trust for Scotland has capitalized on the romance surrounding the story of the Jacobites and their intention of returning a Stuart monarch and the Catholic religion to a country that had become staunchly Protestant. In Glenfinnan in 1745 the sometimes-reluctant clans joined forces and rallied to Prince Charles Edward Stuart's cause. The raising of the prince's standard is commemorated by the Glenfinnan Monument (an unusual tower on the banks of Loch Shiel), and the story of his campaign is told in the nearby visitor center. Note that the figure at the top of the monument is of a Highlander, not the prince. *A830, tel. 01397/722250. Admission: £1 adults, 50p children. Open Apr.–May and early Sept.–late Oct., Mon.–Sat. 10–1 and 2–5, Sun. 10:30–1 and 2–5; June–early Sept., Mon.–Sat. 9:30–6, Sun. 10:30–6.*

The view down Loch Shiel from this point, with the monument in the foreground and the silver-gray hills tilting steeply into the water, is, along with Eilean Donan Castle in Wester Ross, one of the two most-photographed views in Scotland. Equally impressive (for visitors who have tired of the Jacobite "Will He No Come Back Again" sentiment) is the curving railway viaduct that stretches across the green slopes behind. The **Glenfinnan Viaduct,** 21 spans and 1,248 feet long, was in its time the wonder of the Highlands. The railway's contractor, Robert Mac Alpine, known as Concrete Bob by the locals, pioneered the use of mass concrete for viaducts and bridges when his company built the Mallaig extension, which was opened in 1901.

The Great Glen for Free

Castle Tioram (*see* Tour 2)
Clava Cairns (*see* Tour 1)
Inverfarigaig Forest Centre (*see* Tour 1)
Inverness Museum and Art Gallery is devoted to the history of the Highlands. Exhibits include fine collections of silver and bagpipes, while the gallery has art exhibitions changing monthly. *Castle Wynd, Inverness, tel. 0463/237114. Open Mon.–Sat. 9–5; July and Aug., also Sun. 2–5.*
Loch an Eilean (*see* Tour 1)
Rothiemurchus Estate Visitor Centre (*see* Tour 1)

What to See and Do with Children

Aigas Dam Fish Lift has a viewing chamber, from which migrating salmon can be seen swimming up the River Beauly. *Near Beauly. Open June–Oct., weekdays 10–11 and 2:45–3:45.*

Darnaway Farm Visitor Centre, of the Moray Estates, has farm animals, a woodland walk, and a place where children can watch the cattle being milked. *Off A96, 3 mi west of Forres, tel. 013094/469. Admission: £1.50 adults, £1 children. Open May–mid-Sept., daily 10–5.*

Fort George (*see* Tour 1)

Landmark Visitor Centre (*see* Tour 1)

The **Official Loch Ness Monster Exhibition** (*see* Tour 1)

Off the Beaten Track

Remote **Lochs Nevis and Hourn** are long, fjordlike sea lochs that can be seen from the Sound of Sleat between the mainland and Skye. Visitors can also reach the lochs by sea from Mallaig. Check the range of rail/cruise options promoted from Fort William by contacting the **Transport Centre** (tel. 01397/703791) at the Fort William Station or by calling **Bruce Watt Sea Cruises** (Western Isles Guest House, Mallaig, tel. 01687/2320).

Anyone with a day to spend in Fort William can visit at least a couple of the **Small Isles: Rhum, Eigg, Muck,** and **Canna.** Caledonian MacBrayne ferries (*see* Guided Tours, *above*) connect from Mallaig, but a better option is to contact **Murdo Grant** (Arisaig Marine, Arisaig, Inverness-shire, tel. 06875/224), who runs a service from the harbor at Arisaig. The MV *Shearwater,* a former naval inshore minesweeper, delivers supplies and mail as well as visitors to the diminutive island communities. What sets Grant's operation apart from the tourism-oriented excursions is that it offers visitors a glimpse of island life from a working vessel going about its summer routine. Also available for charter from Arisaig Marine is a fast twin-engine motor yacht, which can take up to 12 passengers for go-where-you-please cruises around the Small Isles and farther afield.

Two outstanding mountain landscapes, those of **Glens Affric and Cannich,** located toward the northern end and to the west of the Great Glen, can be viewed in one easy day from Inverness. For visitors who have limited time but wish to see the Scottish heartland, these two glens offer a cross section of landscape. Accessible by way of Beauly and Strathglass (A831), Glen Cannich is constricted by crags and birch-clad slopes before opening into a broad valley with a hydroelectric dam at its far end. Glen Affric is, if anything, even more aesthetically appealing, with oak woodlands and hayfields in the lower reaches and wild lochs (also dammed) and pine forests, similar to the Trossachs, but on a grander scale.

If you're touring the West Highlands, you can take the backdoor ferry route to the **island of Mull** (*see* Chapter 10) from the Lochaline in Morven, southwest of Fort William. This route affords views of moorland and woodland scenery and has little traffic. (No need to book car space on this ferry—just show up.)

At Corpach, do not miss **Treasures of the Earth,** an exhibition of gemstones, crystals, and fossils that include a 26-pound uncut emerald. *Tel. 01397/772283. Admission: £2.50 adults, £1.50 children. Open July, Aug., Sept., daily 9:30–7; Oct.–Dec., Feb.–June, daily 10–5 (open in Jan. by appointment only).*

Shopping

Aviemore   In Aviemore **Jigsaw Designs** (1 Grampian Rd.) manufactures unusual and distinctive three-dimensional jigsaw puzzles and models, as well as mobiles and wood-painted pictures. The **Cairngorm Whisky Centre** (tel. 01479/810574) at Rothiemurchus has one of the largest selections of malt whiskies in the world, more than 500. There is a tasting room to help you make your choice.

Fort William   The majority of the shops here are located along High Street, which in summer attracts ever-present, bustling crowds intent on stocking up for excursions to the west. **Ben Nevis Woollen Mill,** at the north end of town, is a major supplier of tartans, woolens, and tweeds and has a restaurant. On High Street try **J & K Ness** at **The Granite House** for Scottish jewelry (including some by local designer Pat Cheney), china and crystal giftware, wildlife sculptures, and other collectibles. Opposite J & K Ness, at 49 High Street, is the **Nevis Bakery,** which sells plain and chocolate-chip shortbread and can supply packed lunches if visitors find the weather too pleasant to eat indoors. (The same proprietors also run the **Harvester Restaurant,** farther along High Street.)

Grantown on Spey and Environs
Speyside Heather Centre, at Skye of Curr (tel. 0147985/359), not only has 200 varieties of heather for sale (some in sterile planting media), but also a crafts shop and floral-art sundries. **The Kist** (74 High St., Grantown on Spey), is a well-stocked high-quality gift shop specializing in local and Scottish crafts.

Inverness
Although Inverness has the usual High Street chain stores and department stores—including **Arnott's** and **Marks and Spencer**—the most interesting goods are to be found in the various specialty outlets in and around town.

For antiquarian books try the **Inverness Secondhand Bookshop** (in the Old High Church, Church St.), which also specializes in antique prints. **The Riverside Gallery** (11 Bank St.) sells paintings and prints of Scottish natural history and sporting themes. For contemporary art there's the **Highland Printmakers Workshop and Gallery** (20 Bank St.). **Duncan Chisholm and Sons** (47–51 Castle St.) manufactures Highlands dress, tartans, and Scottish crafts, and the **Scottish Sweater Store** (Drummond St.) stocks the famous Pringle and Lyle & Scott brand names. **James Pringle Ltd.** (Holm Woollen Mills, Dores Rd.) has a shop stocked with a vast selection of cashmere; lambswool; and Shetland knitwear, tartans, and tweeds.

In a different vein entirely is **Highland Aromatics** (Drumchardine, Kirkhill), where, in a converted church, sweet-smelling soaps with the scents of the Highlands are manufactured. **Highland Wineries** (Moniack Castle, Kirkhill) makes wines from Scottish ingredients such as birch sap.

Nairn and Environs
In Nairn do not miss **Nairn Antiques** (St. Ninian Pl., near the traffic circle) for a wide inventory of antique jewelry, glassware, furniture, pottery, and prints. At Gollanfield, midway between Nairn and Inverness, **Culloden Pottery** offers you the chance to throw your own pot (which is then fired, glazed, and mailed to your home) or to choose from an original and extensive selection of hand-thrown domestic stoneware. There is also a gift-and-crafts shop and a restaurant that prides itself on serving only fresh—never frozen—food; there are fine views from the restaurant as well. East of Nairn is the **Brodie Country Fare,** guaranteed to affect your wallet in a pleasant way. Unusual knitwear, quality clothing, gifts, toys, and a restaurant beckon from beyond the fare's foodstore and delicatessen. The fare is well worth a visit, which could be combined with a trip to nearby Brodie Castle.

Sports and Fitness

Beaches
The most extensive beaches are at **Nairn,** with miles of clean, golden sand. The best known are at **Morar,** home of the famous white-and-silver sands.

Bicycling
The Great Glen is a fairly rugged area, and there are only two routes that go through it. The B862/B852, which runs by the east side of

Loch Ness, is the less-trafficked and therefore a better bet for cyclists.

Bicycles can be rented from **Lee's Cycle Hire** (Fort William, tel. 01397/704204), **Nevis Outdoor Hire Centre** (Glen Nevis, tel. 01397/703601), and **Off Beat Bikes** (Fort William, tel. 01397/702663). Near Arisaig, **Bespoke Highland Tours** (The Bothy, Camusdarach, Inverness-shire, tel. 016875/272) rents bicycles and arranges tours of the Great Glen and the Highlands. At Spean Bridge is **Highland Wheelers** (Service Station, Spean Bridge, tel. 01397/712408). Aviemore has a wide choice of bicycle rental outlets, among them **Inverdruie Mountain Bikes** (at Inverdruie, on the Cairngorms road out of Aviemore, tel. 01479/810787), **Speyside Sports** (Main St., Aviemore, tel. 01479/810656), **Ellis Brighams** (Main St., tel. 01479/810175), and **Sporthaus** (Main St., tel. 01479/810655). Drumnadrochit, beside Loch Ness, has **Glen Cycles** (The Green, tel. 01456/450554), while Inverness outlets include **Pedalway** (7 Lovat Rd., tel. 01463/233456), **Sharps Cycle Hire** (Station Sq., tel. 01463/236684), and **Thorntons Cycles** (23 Castle St., tel. 01463/235078).

Fishing The Great Glen offers many rivers and lochs where you can fly-fish for salmon and trout. Tourist-information centers (*see* Important Addresses and Numbers in Essential Information, *above*) can provide information on locations, permits, and fishing rights (which differ from those in England and Wales). The fishing seasons are as follows: salmon, depending on the area, early February through September or early October; brown trout, March 15 to September 30; sea trout, May through September or early October; rainbow trout, no statutory-close season. Sea angling from shore or boat is also possible; information is available from tourist-information centers.

Golf As is the case with most of Scotland, there is a broad selection of courses, especially toward the eastern end of this area. Nairn, with two courses, is highly regarded among Scottish players. The following courses welcome visitors: **Inverness Golf Club** (tel. 01463/239882), **Nairn Dunbar Golf Club** (tel. 01667/452741), **Nairn Golf Club** (tel. 01667/453208), **Torvean Golf Course** (Inverness, tel. 01463/237543).

Skiing Aviemore is perhaps the most advanced ski resort in the area, though the word "resort" is only loosely applicable to skiing in Scotland. Sometimes lifts can't operate due to winds, for example. **Nevis Range on Aonach Mor** (tel. 01397/705825 or 01397/705826; ski hotline, tel. 01898/654660), near Fort William, offers some long runs.

Walking The Great Glen area is renowned for its hill-walking opportunities, but walkers should be fit and properly outfitted. Tourist-information centers (*see* Important Addresses and Numbers in Essential Information, *above*) can offer guidance on low-level routes, and several excellent hill-walking guides available locally can and should be consulted for high-level routes. Remember that on **Ben Nevis**, a popular route even for inexperienced hill-walkers, it can snow on the summit plateau at any time of the year. Ben Nevis is a large and dangerous hill.

Dining and Lodging

Dining

Highly recommended restaurants are indicated by a star ★.

Category	Cost*
$$$$	over £40
$$$	£30–£40
$$	£15–£30
$	under £15

per person for a three-course meal, including VAT; excluding drinks

Lodging

Highly recommended hotels are indicated by a star ★.

Category	Cost*
$$$$	over £120
$$$	£100–£120
$$	£80–£100
$	under £80

All prices are for a standard double room, including service, breakfast, and VAT.

Arisaig
Dining and Lodging

Arisaig House. This secluded and grand Victorian mansion offers tranquility and some marvelous scenery, including views of the Inner Hebrides. The bedrooms are plush and restful, with soft-pastel colors, original moldings, and antique furniture. The cuisine at the restaurant is quietly celebrated, with an emphasis on fresh local produce. *Beasdale (6 mi south of Mallaig on A830), Arisaig PH39 4NR, tel. 016875/622, fax 06875/626. 2 suites, 12 rooms with bath. Facilities: croquet, sailing, fishing, island trips, library, billiards, golfing at Trigh. MC, V. Closed Nov.–Easter. $$$–$$$$*

Arisaig Hotel. An old coaching inn close to the water, with magnificent views of the Small Isles, this hotel offers a slightly more modest environment than Arisaig House. The inn has retained its provinciality with simple decor and home cooking. High-quality local ingredients are used here to good advantage; locally smoked fish and king prawns are specialties, as are proper puddings, such as fruit crumbles and upside-down cakes. *PH39 4NH, tel. 016875/210, fax 016875/310. Dress: casual. 15 rooms, 6 with bath. MC, V. $*

Old Library Lodge and Restaurant. This guest house with a restaurant gives visitors another reason to believe that the village of Arisaig is unusually well endowed with good places to eat at all price levels. Situated on the waterfront, it offers traditional Scottish cooking, served in a beamed, pine-furnished dining room. The bedrooms are very comfortable, from flowery duvets to cozy armchairs. *PH39 4NH, tel. 016875/651. Dress: casual. 6 rooms with bath or shower. MC, V. Closed Nov.–Mar. $*

Aviemore
Dining

The Winking Owl. This lively restaurant, freshly decorated, popular with locals as well as visitors, is always busy serving English and Scottish dishes to crowds of families and 20-somethings on weekend holiday from the city. *Grampian Rd., tel. 01479/810646. Reservations advised. Dress: informal. MC, V. $–$$*

Dalcross
Lodging

Easter Dalziel Farm. This working 210-acre livestock and arable farm offers plenty of interest for guests staying one night or longer. The Victorian farmhouse, with log fire, home baking, and pretty gardens, is a welcome change from an impersonal hotel. *Dalcross, Inverness, tel. 01667/462213. 3 rooms. MC, V. Closed Dec.–Feb. $*

Drumnad-
rochit
Dining and
Lodging

Polmaily House. This country house is located on the northern edge of Loch Ness amid lovely parkland. Books, log fires, and a helpful staff contribute to an atmosphere that is warmer and more personal than that found at grander, more expensive hotels. The restaurant is noted for its traditional British cuisine, which takes advantage of fresh Highland produce. Tay salmon in pastry with dill sauce, roast rack of lamb with rosemary, and cold smoked venison with melon are examples of some flavorful dishes. *Milton, near A82, 12 mi southwest of Inverness, IV3 6XT, tel. 01456/450343, fax 01456/450813. Reservations advised. Dress: casual. 11 rooms with bath. Facilities: outdoor pool, croquet, tennis. MC, V. $$*

Lodging

Borlum Farmhouse. Spectacular views over Loch Ness are the outstanding feature of this guest house on a working farm. The rooms are individually decorated, most with light colors and antique furniture, and the food is well cooked. *Drumnadrochit, Inverness IV3 6XN, tel. 01456/450358. 6 rooms, 3 with bath. Facilities: riding center. MC, V. No smoking throughout. $*

Fort William
Dining and
Lodging
★

Inverlochy Castle. A red-granite Victorian castle, Inverlochy stands in 50 acres of woodland in the shadow of Ben Nevis, with striking Highland landscape on every side. Queen Victoria stayed here and wrote, "I never saw a lovelier or more romantic spot." Dating from 1863, the hotel retains the splendor of its period, with a fine frescoed ceiling, crystal chandeliers, and a handsome staircase in the Great Hall; paintings and hunting trophies everywhere; and plush, comfortable bedrooms. The restaurant is exceptional. Many of the specialties are made from local produce, as are roast saddle of roe deer and wood-pigeon consommé. Orange soufflé is the final touch. For those in search of some pampering, this is the place to stay—Inverlochy Castle spares no expense to ensure the comfort of its guests. *Torlundy (3 mi northeast of Fort William on A82), Inverness-shire PH33 6BN, tel. 01397/702177, fax 01397/702953. 16 rooms with bath. Restaurant reservations essential. Jacket and tie preferred. AE, MC, V. Closed Dec.–mid-Mar. $$$$*

The Factor's House. Next to the gates of Inverlochy Castle sits a guest house and restaurant with a reputation for preparing a good meal for your money. The restaurant aims to present traditional Scottish cooking at its best, offering such favorites as trout in oatmeal, venison pie, and Atholl brose (whipped cream with toasted oatmeal and whisky folded into it), all of which is prepared in a straightforward, appetizing manner. There are only seven bedrooms, with several comfortable sitting rooms. A stay here is a pleasant, friendly experience. *Torlundy, near Fort William, PH33 6SN, tel. 01397/705767, fax 01397/702953. Reservations advised. Dress: smart casual. 7 rooms; 5 with bath, 2 with shower. AE, DC, MC, V. Closed Dec.–Mar. No lunch. $$*

Glengarry Castle Hotel. This rambling, pleasantly old-fashioned mansion makes a good touring base; Invergarry is just south of Loch Ness and within easy reach of the Great Glen's best sights. Many rooms have superb views over Loch Oich. The food is reliably well-cooked in traditional Scottish style, with game, fish, and beef figuring most predominantly. *Inverness-shire, PH35 4HW, tel. 01809/501254, fax 01809/501207. 26 rooms with bath. Facilities: tennis, trout and pike fishing. AE, MC, V. $*

Inverness
Dining and
Lodging

Dunain Park Hotel. Guests receive individual attention in a private-house atmosphere in this 18th-century mansion 2½ miles southwest of Inverness on the A82. A log fire awaits you in the living room, where you can sip a drink and browse through books and magazines. Antiques and traditional decor make the bedrooms equally cozy and attractive. You can enjoy French-influenced Scottish dishes in the restaurant, where candlelight is reflected in bone china and crystal. Saddle of venison in port sauce and boned quail stuffed with pistachios are two of the specialties. *Dunain IV3 6JN, tel. 01463/230512, fax 01463/224532. Reservations advised. Jacket and tie required. 14 rooms with bath. Facilities: indoor heated pool, sauna, 14 acres of wooded gardens. AE, DC, MC, V. Closed 2 weeks in Feb. Hotel $$$$; Restaurant $$*

Bunchrew House. This turreted mansion set on the banks of the Beauly Firth abounds with handsome wood paneling. The dining room is particularly attractive, with fine antique furniture, and the lounge and comfortable bedrooms are decorated with velvet and chintz. The restaurant features Scottish cuisine with an unusual Portuguese/South African influence, using the best Aberdeen Angus beef, local salmon, and game. The grounds are extensive and are delightful for a predinner stroll, and the views of the Firth are superb. *Bunchrew, Inverness-shire IV3 6TA, tel. 01463/234917, fax 01463/710620. 11 rooms with bath. AE, MC, V. $$$*

Culloden House. This imposing Georgian mansion was Bonnie Prince Charlie's headquarters during the Battle of Culloden. Handsome public rooms with beautifully crafted plasterwork provide the ambience in a restaurant renowned for its fine cuisine (though occasionally the chef's wilder flights of fancy do not come off). The menu includes many adventurous entrées, a number of which feature the use of fruit to cut the richness of game, salmon, duck, or beef. Try the wild salmon in lobster sauce or venison in Madeira. *Culloden, 6 mi east of Inverness by A9 and B9006, IV1 2NZ, tel. 01463/790461, fax 01463/792181. 20 rooms with bath. Reservations advised. Jacket and tie required. AE, DC, MC, V. $$$*

★ **Daviot Mains Farm.** A 19th-century farmhouse, 5 miles south of Inverness on the A9, provides the perfect setting for home comforts and traditional Scottish cooking for guests only; lucky ones may find wild salmon on the menu. *Daviot Mains, tel. 01463/772215. 3 rooms; 1 with bath, 1 with shower. MC, V. $*

Lodging

Ballifeary House Hotel. A Victorian property that was redecorated in 1993 and is well maintained. Offering high standards of comfort and service, the Ballifeary is within easy reach of downtown Inverness. *10 Ballifeary Rd., IV3 5PJ, tel. and fax 01463/235572. 8 rooms with bath. No smoking in hotel. MC, V. Closed Nov.–Feb. $$*

Atholdene House. This family-run, 19th-century stone villa offers a friendly welcome and modernized accommodations. Evening meals can be provided for guests on request. The bus and railway stations are a short walk away. *20 Southside Rd., IV2 3BG, tel. 01463/233565. 9 rooms, 7 with bath. No credit cards. $*

Clach Mhuilinn. This modern residential family home is set in a pretty garden and has good parking facilities. It offers bed-and-breakfast of very high standard in an entirely nonsmoking environment. *7 Harris Rd., IV2 3LS, tel. 01463/237059. 3 rooms, 1 with shower. No credit cards. Closed Dec.–Feb. $*

Kingussie
Dining and
Lodging

The Cross. Meals are superb, and the wine list is even more extensive than Osprey's (*see below*). This is a "restaurant with rooms" in the French style, though it has recently moved to more spacious premises. Dinner, which could be breast of wood pigeon with onion confit or mousseline of pike with prawn sauce, is included in the price of your room. *Tweed Mill Brae, Kingussie, Inverness-shire PH21 1TC, tel. 01540/661166, fax 01540/661080. 9 rooms with bath. MC, V. Closed Dec.–Feb. and Tues. dinner. $$$$*

Osprey Hotel. This friendly hotel in the village of Kingussie has no special frills, just good basic home comforts and cooking. It is ideally located for skiing and hill walking. An impressive wine list complements such dishes as salmon with tarragon-and-leek sauce and venison steak with blackcurrants and lemon. *Kingussie, Inverness-shire PH21 1HX, tel. and fax 01540/661510. 7 rooms with bath. AE, MC, V. $*

Whitebridge
Dining and
Lodging
★

Knockie Lodge. Set on rising ground not far from Loch Ness, this former shooting lodge has superb views and is especially popular with fishermen and other outdoor-sports enthusiasts. Decorated with traditional and antique furniture, this hotel provides very peaceful surroundings, though with easy access to Inverness. The restaurant offers enticing fixed menus with a choice of desserts. The chef uses top-quality produce and prepares everything with great care. Bar lunches are also wholesome. The dining room is quite small, so advance reservations are needed if you are not a guest of the hotel. Dinner is included in the price of rooms. *Whitebridge IV1 2UP, tel. 01456/486276, fax 01456/486389. Reservations required. 10 rooms with bath. AE, DC, MC, V. Closed Nov.–Apr. $$$$*

The Arts and Nightlife

Do not visit this area expecting to have a big-city choice of late-night activities. With the exception of Inverness, evening entertainment revolves around pubs and hotels, with the ceilidh, a small, informal, musical get-together, and Scottish evening, a staged performance of tartan-clad Highland dancers—the most popular form of entertainment offered to visitors.

The Arts

Theater **Eden Court Theatre** (Bishops Rd., Inverness, tel. 01463/221718) offers not only drama, but also a program of music, film, and light entertainment.

Nightlife

Bars and
Lounges

Inverness has an array of bars and lounges. Among the most popular are **Gunsmith's** (Union St.), a traditional pub offering bar meals, and **DJ's Café Bar** (High St.), which serves everything from breakfast to late-night cocktails. **Fort William** offers a similarly wide range, and the pubs of **Aviemore** offer an après-ski ambience.

Cabaret

Scottish Showtime (Cummings Hotel, Church St., Inverness, tel. 01463/232531) and **McTavish's Kitchens** (High St., Fort William, tel. 01397/702406) are the two most popular choices in the region. They both offer Scottish cabaret of the tartan-clad dancer and bag-pipe/accordian variety.

Discos There are a number of places to go dancing, particularly in Inverness, some in local hotels. For example, the **Caledonian Hotel** (Church St., Inverness) holds regular ceilidhs in the summer season. To obtain a complete list, it is best to consult the local tourist-information center (*see* Important Addresses and Numbers in Essential Information, *above*).

In Aviemore, **Crofters** (tel. 01479/810624) at the Aviemore Mountain Resort has a bar open all day, with disco nightly until 1 AM.

12 The Northern Highlands

Sutherland and Wester Ross, Isle of Skye, the Outer Hebrides

By Gilbert Summers

The old counties of Ross and Cromarty (sometimes called Easter and Wester Ross), Sutherland, and Caithness constitute the most northern portion of mainland Scotland. The population is sparse; mountains and moorland limit the choice of touring routes; and distances are less important than whether the winding, hilly roads you travel are two lanes or one. On a map, this area seems far from major urban centers, but it is easy to get to. Inverness has an airport with direct links to Glasgow, and you can reach such destinations as the fishing town of Ullapool in about an hour by car from Inverness. In fact, much of the western seaboard is easy to get to from the Northern Highlands.

The area contains some of Scotland's most fascinating scenery. Much of Sutherland and Wester Ross, for example, is comprised of a rocky platform of Lewisian gneiss, certainly the oldest rocks in Britain, scoured and hollowed by glacial action into numerous lochs. On top of this rolling wet moorland landscape sit strangely shaped quartzite-capped sandstone mountains, eroded and pinnacled.

Many of the place-names in this region reflect its early links with Scandinavia. Sutherland, the most northern portion of mainland Scotland, was once the "southern land" of the Vikings. Scotland's most northern point, Cape Wrath, got its name from the Viking's word *hvarth,* meaning a "turning point," and Laxford, Suilven, and dozens of other names in the area have Norse rather than Gaelic derivations.

The islands of Skye and especially the Outer Hebrides, which are now often referred to as the Western Isles, are the stronghold of the Gaelic language. Skye, famous for the misty mountains called the Cuillins, has the scenic excitement, and the Outer Hebrides, some of Scotland's finest beaches.

Essential Information

Important Addresses and Numbers

Tourist Information

Caithness Tourist Board (Whitechapel Rd., off High St., Wick, tel. 01955/2596, fax 01955/4940), **Western Isles (Outer Hebrides) Tourist Board** (26 Cromwell St., Stornoway, tel. 01851/703088, fax 01851/705244), **Isle of Skye and South West Ross Tourist Board** (Tourist Information Centre, Portree, Isle of Skye, tel. 01478/612137, fax 01478/612141), **Ross and Cromarty Tourist Board** (Tourist Information Centre, North Kessock, tel. 0146/373–505, fax 01463/73701), **Sutherland Tourist Board** (The Square, Dornoch, tel. 01862/810400, fax 01862/810644). Seasonal tourist information centers can be found at Bettyhill, Bonar Bridge, Broadford (Skye), Castlebay (Outer Hebrides), Durness, Gairloch, Glen Shiel, Helmsdale, John o' Groats, Kyle of Lochalsh, Lochboisdale (Outer Hebrides), Lochcarron, Lochinver, Lochmaddy (Outer Hebrides), Strathpeffer, Tarbert (Outer Hebrides), Thurso, and Ullapool.

Emergencies

For police, fire, or ambulance, dial 999 from any telephone. No coins are needed for emergency calls from public telephone booths.

Late-Night Pharmacies

These are not found in rural areas. In an emergency the police will provide assistance in locating a pharmacist. In rural areas general practitioners may also dispense medicines.

Arriving and Departing by Plane

Airports and Airlines
The main airports for the Northern Highlands are **Inverness** and **Wick** (both on the mainland). There is direct air service from Glasgow to Inverness. Contact **Loganair** (tel. 0141/889–3181) and **British Airways** (tel. 0181/897–4000). Loganair also flies to Wick from Glasgow, while **Gill Air** (tel. 0191/286–2222) operates the Aberdeen–Wick service. There are island flight connections to the Outer Hebrides via Glasgow or Inverness. For Stornoway, the largest town in Lewis (Outer Hebrides) contact British Airways or Loganair. To fly to the Hebridean island of Barra contact Loganair; for Benbecula contact Loganair or British Airways.

Arriving and Departing by Car, Train, and Bus

By Car and Ferry
The fastest route to this area is the A9 to the gateway town of Inverness. The ferry services run by **Caledonian MacBrayne**, called CalMac, link the Outer Hebrides: Ferries run from Ullapool to Stornoway (tel. 01854/612358), from Oban to Castlebay and Lochboisdale (tel. 01631/62285), and from Uig on the island of Skye to Tarbert and Lochmaddy (tel. 01470/542219). Causeways link North Uist, Benbecula, and South Uist.

By Train
Main railway stations in the area include Oban (for Barra and the Uists) and Kyle of Lochalsh (for Skye) on the west coast or Inverness (for points north to Thurso and Wick). There is direct service from London to Inverness and connecting service from Edinburgh and Glasgow.

By Bus
National Express (tel. 01738/33481) runs buses to Inverness and beyond to Ullapool. **Scottish Citylink** (tel. 0141/332–9191) connects with Ullapool and Dingwall. There are also coach connections between the ferry ports of Tarbert and Stornoway.

Getting Around

You can use an 8- or 15-day **Freedom of Scotland Travelpass** in the Highlands and Islands area. The pass, which will save you money on **Scotrail, CalMac** ferries, and **Orkney** ferries, as well as on some bus lines, is available at main-line British Rail stations in London, the **Scottish Tourist Board** (19 Cockspur St., London, tel. 0171/9308661), and **British Travel** (4–12 Regent St., London, tel. 0171/730–3400). The pass is also widely available in Scotland at most large British Rail stations, at bus stations, at the CalMac Ferries at the Ferry Terminal, and at Gourock and the larger tourist-information centers in the Highlands of Scotland, including Aviemore, Inverness, Fort William, Oban, Thurso, Wick, John o' Groats, Dornoch, Lochinver, Durness, Arran (Brodick), and Bute (Rothesay).

By Car
Note that in this sparsely populated area, distances between gas stations can be considerable. Although getting around is easy, even on single-lane roads, the choice of routes is restricted by the rugged terrain.

An important caveat for visitors driving in this area: There are still some single-lane roads in this part of Scotland. These twisting, winding thoroughfares demand a degree of driving dexterity. Local rules of the road require that when two cars meet, whichever driver reaches a passing place first must stop in it or opposite it and allow the oncoming car to continue. Small cars tend to yield to large com-

mercial vehicles. Never park in passing places and never forget that
these sections of the road can also allow traffic behind you to pass.
Don't hold up a vehicle trying to pass you. In the northwest, tempers
flare over such discourtesies.

By Train Stations on the northern lines (Inverness to Thurso/Wick and In-
verness to Kyle of Lochalsh) include Muir of Ord, Dingwall; on the
Thurso/Wick line, Alness, Invergordon, Fearn, Tain, Ardgay, Cul-
rain, Invershin, Lairg, Rogart, Golspie, Brora, Helmsdale, Kildo-
nan, Kinbrace, Forsinard, Altnabreac, Scotscalder, and Georgemas
Junction; and on the Kyle line, Garve, Lochluichart, Achanalt,
Achnasheen, Achnashellach, Strathcarron, Attadale, Strome Ferry,
Duncraig, Plockton, and Duirinish.

By Bus **Highland Bus and Coach Company** provides bus service in the Highlands area (mainland and Skye, tel. 01463/233371). On the Outer
Hebrides a number of small operators and post buses—which also
deliver mail—run regular routes to most towns and villages. However the post-bus service becomes increasingly important in remote
areas. It supplements the regular bus service, which runs only a few
times per week because of the small population on the islands. A full
timetable of services for the Northern Highlands (and the rest of
Scotland) is available from the **District Head Post Office** (14–16
Queensgate, Inverness, tel. 01463/234111, ext. 248) or from the **Head
Post Office** (2–4 Waterloo Pl., Edinburgh, tel. 0131/550–8232).

By Air **Loganair** (tel. 0141/889–3181) operates flights between the islands
of Barra, Benbecula, and Stornoway in the Outer Hebrides.

Guided Tours

Orientation The bus companies named above also operate orientation tours in
summer, as does **Spa Coach Tours** (Strathpeffer, tel. 01997/421311),
which covers a large portion of the Northern Highlands and Skye.

Special- **North-West Frontiers** (19 West Terr., Ullapool, Wester Ross, tel.
Interest 01854/612571, fax 01854/612025) offers walking itineraries in some
of Scotland's most vivid scenery, in Skye, Wester Ross, and Sutherland. **Dunvegan Sea Cruises,** at Dunvegan Castle (tel. 01470/521206;
see Tour 2: Skye, *below*) offers a boat trip to the nearby seal colony
(£3.40 adults, £2.40 children) and also a spectacular trip up Loch
Dunvegan to see seals and many different kinds of birds (£6.50
adults, £4.50 children). A number of small firms run boat cruises
along the spectacular west-coast seaboard. Contact the local tourist
information center for details of local operators. On Skye there is
also a broad selection of mountain guides. A list can be obtained from
Skye's tourist-information center (*see* Important Addresses and
Numbers, *above*).

Exploring the Northern Highlands

Orientation

From Inverness, gateway to the Northern Highlands, roads fan out
like the spokes of a wheel to join the coastal route around the rim
of mainland Scotland. Most visitors tour from east to west, saving
the best scenery for last. The tour described below takes the visitor
quickly to the west. The main points of interest in the east are mentioned in the Off the Beaten Track section that follows the tour.

Highlights for First-Time Visitors

Corrieshalloch Gorge (*see* Tour 1)
Glen Brittle (*see* Tour 2)
Glen Torridon (*see* Tour 1)
Inverewe Gardens (*see* Tour 1)
Quiraing (*see* Tour 2)
View of the Cuillins from Elgol (*see* Tour 2)
View of Slioch from Loch Maree (*see* Tour 1)
View of Suilven from Lochinver (*see* Tour 1)

Tour 1: The Northern Landscapes— Wester Ross and Sutherland

Numbers in the margin correspond to points of interest on the Northern Highlands and Skye map.

It takes roughly one hour to travel from Inverness to Ullapool (on A9 and then A835), where you can catch a ferry to Stornoway on the isle of Lewis, part of the Outer Hebrides. If you're not rushing to catch a ferry, however, stop along the way in the former Victorian
❶ spa town of **Strathpeffer** on A834—where you can even taste the waters. Not far from Strathpeffer are the tumbling **Falls of Rogie,** where an alarmingly sagging suspension bridge leaves visitors with a fine view of the splashing waters below and an uneasy stomach.

If you really want to give yourself a touch of vertigo, however, the
❷ **Corrieshalloch Gorge** should be next on your sightseeing agenda. You can reach the gorge by following the A835 (to Ullapool) west of **Garve,** across the bare backbone of Scotland. As the road begins to drop down from the bleak lands of the interior, look for Braemore junction and continue on the A835. Shortly after, as you draw closer to the woods, you'll see the Corrieshalloch Gorge parking lot on the left. A burn draining the high moors plunges 150 feet into a 200-foot-deep, thickly wooded gorge. There is a suspension-bridge viewpoint and an atmosphere of romantic grandeur, like an old Scottish print come to life.

❸ The road then rolls down to **Ullapool** by the shores of salty **Loch Broom.** This community was founded in 1788 as a fishing station, to exploit the local herring stocks. In recent years the fishing activity here has included "klondyking," the direct purchase of fish from local boats by large, Eastern European factory ships. Ullapool has a cosmopolitan air and comes alive when the Lewis ferry docks and departs. There is a local potter and a modest selection of shops selling books, souvenirs, waterproof jackets and trousers, insect repellent, and other northwest touring aids.

Time Out Several years ago, the actor and his wife who now own **Ceilidh Place** (W. Argyle St., tel. 01854/612103) spotted a gap in the market for an enlightened eatery. Since then, this warm, friendly coffeehouse and restaurant has filled that niche in its own nonconformist way. The prices are sensible, and musicians perform here from time to time. The Ceilidh Place also offers excellent, reasonably priced accommodation (*see* Dining and Lodging, *below*).

If you travel northward, you will take a two-lane road, the A835/A837, which takes you past the strange landscape of **Wester Ross.** Look westward for the little mountain **Stac Polly**—which resembles a ruined fortress—and the humps of **Suilven.** At **Knockan,** about 15 miles north of Ullapool, a nature trail along a cliff illumi-

Isle of Lewis

Stornoway

Broad Bay

Laxay

Eye Peninsula

The Minch

Eddrachillis Bay

Stoer

Lochinver 6

Enard Bay

Sio

Summer Isles 7

Achiltibu

Shiaut Island

Gruinard Bay

An Teallach

Inverewe Gardens 8

Gairloch 9 A832

A832

Loch Maree 10

Kilmuir Croft Museum 19

Quiraing 18
Brogaig

Kilt Rock 17

Uig Bay

Uig

A856

A855

Loch Snizort

Trotternish

Old Man of Storr 16

Island of Rona

Loch Torridon

Inveralligin

Upper Loch Torridon

Kinlochewe

Achna

A896

Glen Torridon 11

12

Shieldaig

A890

Kensaleyre

Dunvegan Castle 20

A863

B885

Portree 15

Isle of Skye

Inner Sound

Isle of Raasay

Lochcarron 13

Strathcarron

Loch Kishorn
Loch Carron

Drynoch A863 Sconser

Scalpay

Kyle of Lochalsh

Auchtertyre

Glen Brittle 21

Luib 14

Broadford

Ferry

A850 Kyleakin

Dornie

Glenbrittle House

The Cuillins

Torrin

A851

Shiel Bridge

Strathaird

Isleornsay

Sound of Sleat

A87

Elgol 22

Sleat

Arnisdale

Cuillin Sound

Ardvasar 23

Clan Donald Centre/ Armadale Gardens

nates some of the interesting local geology, as well as the area's flora and fauna. If this jaunt sounds too energetic, a more restful alternative may be to enjoy the good views of the mountains from the
❹ **Inverpolly National Nature Reserve.**

Following the signs for Lochinver along Loch Assynt will bring you
❺ to the unattended ruins of **Ardvreck Castle,** on the edge of Loch Assynt. This was a clan MacLeod stronghold, built in the 15th century. From Ardvreck Castle it's only a 20-minute drive on a two-lane
❻ road to **Lochinver,** a charming community with a few choices of accommodations and places to eat. Behind the town the mountain Suilven rises abruptly. This unusual monolith is best seen from across the water, however: Take the cul-de-sac, **Baddidarach Road,** for the finest photo opportunity.

A single-lane unclassified road winds south from Lochinver, providing outstanding sea views within the first 5 miles. Do not fall victim to the breathtaking landscape, however: The road has several blind bends that demand special care. You will then be near what is perhaps Scotland's most remote bookshop. The road will swing left and inland immediately after **Loch Kirkaig;** nearby is a car park beside the River Kirkaig, and a short stroll away is **Achins Book and Craft Shop** (tel. 015714/262, look for signs by the river bridge). Its pleasant coffee shop is open Easter through October, daily (except Sunday) 10–5.

This wild though harmonious landscape of bracken and birch tree, heather and humped hill horizons, prevails until you see signs for
❼ **Achiltibuie:** You'll then encounter a strung-out line of crofts, many now owned by incomers. Offshore are the **Summer Isles,** romantic enough in thought, but in reality bleak and austere. In Achiltibuie there's a smokehouse that serves succulent smoked cuts of venison and other delicacies, and the Hydroponicum, a huge glass house that certainly looks out of place but is effective in producing giant strawberries.

Return to Ullapool, then retrace your route as far as the Braemore Road junction, noted earlier, which juts above the Corrieshalloch Gorge. Take the A832 toward **Gairloch.** Soon you will be traversing wild country once more. The toothed ramparts of the mountain **An Teallach** (pronounced *tyel*-lach, with Scots *ch*, of course) can be seen on the horizon ahead. The moorland route you travel is known chillingly as **Destitution Road.** It was commissioned in 1851 to give the local folk (long vanished from the area) some way of earning a living following the failure of the potato crop; it is said the workers were paid only in food.

The road descends to the woodlands of **Dundonnell** and to Loch Broom (*see* Dundonnell Hotel in Dining and Lodging, *below*). The coastal scenery hereabouts improves with views of **Gruinard Bay**
❽ and its white beaches, but the highlight for most travelers is **Inverewe Gardens,** another half hour to the south. The reputation of the gardens at Inverewe, in spite of their comparatively remote location, has grown steadily through the years. The main attraction lies in the contrast between the bleak coastal headlands and thin-soiled moors and the lush plantings of the garden behind the dense shelterbelts. These are proof of the efficiency of the warm North Atlantic Drift, part of the Gulf Stream, which takes the edge off winter frosts. (Inverewe is sometimes described as subtropical, but this is an inaccuracy which truly irritates the head gardener; do not expect coconuts and palm trees here.) *A832, 6 mi northeast of Gairloch, tel. 0144586/200. Admission: £3 adults, £1.50 children. Gardens*

open all year, daily 9:30–sunset. Visitor center open Apr.–mid-Oct.,
daily 9:30–5:30. Guided walks with the head gardener Apr.–mid-Oct.,
weekdays at 1:30.

Time Out   The National Trust for Scotland, which looks after the gardens, also
runs an adequate **tearoom** (tel. 0144586/200) with a selection of
cakes and biscuits.

❾ Gairloch, the region's main center, lies to the south of the gardens
and has some shops and accommodations. The **Myrtle Bank Hotel**
(tel. 01445/2004), for instance, serves cream-scone teas as well as
bar meals. Also in the village is the **Gairloch Heritage Museum,** with
exhibitions covering the area from prehistoric times to the present.
Gairloch has one further advantage: Lying just a short way from
the mountains of the interior, this small oasis often escapes the rain
clouds that sometimes cling to the high summits. Guests can enjoy
a game of golf here and perhaps stay dry, even when the nearby
Torridon hills are deluged.

From Gairloch the road goes inland to one of Scotland's most scenic
❿ lochs, **Loch Maree.** Look for the sign, soon after the road reaches
the loch side, for **Victoria Falls,** an attractive waterfall named after
the queen who visited them. The harmonious environs of the loch,
with its tall Scots pines and the mountain Slioch looming as a backdrop, witnessed the destruction of much of its tree cover in the 18th
century. Iron ore was shipped in and smelted using local oak to feed
the furnaces. Oak now grows here only on the northern limits of the
range.

The Nature Conservancy Council has an information center and nature trails by the loch side. Red deer sightings are virtually guaranteed; locals say the best place to spot another local denizen, the
pine marten, is around the trash containers in the parking turnoffs.

The tall pines of Loch Maree prepare the visitor for the contrasting
⓫ scenic spectacle of **Glen Torridon,** which you can reach by turning
right at Kinlochewe. Some say that Glen Torridon has the finest
mountain scenery in Scotland. It consists mainly of the long gray
quartzite flanks of **Ben Eighe** (rhymes with *say*), which make up
Scotland's oldest national nature reserve, and **Liathach** (pronounced *leea*-gach), with its distinct ridge profile that looks like the
keel of an upturned boat. At the far end of the glen the National
Trust for Scotland operates a visitor center that explains the ecology
and geology of the area.

Not too far from the southern coast of Upper Loch Torridon is
⓬ **Shieldaig,** a village that sits in an attractive crescent over a loch of
its own, **Loch Shieldaig.** For an atmospheric evening foray, walk
north toward Loch Torridon at the northern end of the village, by
the church. The path is fairly well made, though hiking shoes are
recommended. You will find exquisite views and tiny rocky beaches.

You can then continue driving south by the A896, passing **Rassal Ash
Wood** on your left. The lushness of the fenced-in area within this
small nature reserve is a reminder of what Scotland might have
been had sheep and deer not been kept here in such high numbers.
The combined nibbling of these animals ensures that Scotland's
natural tree cover does not regenerate without human intervention.

⓭ The road continues past **Kishorn** to **Lochcarron,** a village strung
along the shore. The community has an ample number of bed-and-
breakfast accommodations. Return toward Inverness by the A890,

a single-lane road in some stretches, with plenty of open vistas across the deserted heart of northern Scotland.

Tour 2: Skye, the Misty Island

Skye ranks near the top of most visitors' priority lists: The romance of Bonnie Prince Charlie, the misty **Cuillin Mountains,** and the ease of the five-minute crossing from the mainland all contribute to its popularity. The following tour takes you around the island in two or three days. Orientation is easy: Follow the only roads around the loops on the northern part of the island. There are some stretches of single-lane road, but none is a problem.

⑭ After making the crossing from Kyle of Lochalsh, follow the A850 along the coast. At **Luib,** note the **Old Skye Crofter's House,** with its traditional thatch and 19th-century furnishings. The hills ahead have a reddish hue—they comprise the **Red Cuillin,** the gentler companions of the Black Cuillins, which swing spectacularly into view on the approaches to **Sligachan,** which consists of a hotel and a bridge.

⑮ Turning away from the hills, the road goes north through tranquil scenery to **Portree,** the population center of the island. Not overburdened by historical features, Portree is a pleasant center clustered around a small and sheltered bay. If you're looking for a convenient, friendly place to pass the night, try the nearby Cuillin Hills Hotel (*see* Dining and Lodging, *below*).

To see the northern peninsula of **Trotternish,** head out on the A855, noting the cliffs rising to your left. The cliffs are actually the edge of an ancient lava-flow that runs for miles as your rugged companion, set back from the road. In some places the hardened lava has created spectacular features. Soon you will see one of them on the **⑯** horizon: a curious pinnacle called the **Old Man of Storr.** Continue **⑰** past neat white crofts and forestry plantings until you reach **Kilt Rock.** Everyone on the Skye-tour circuit stops here to peep gingerly over the cliffs for a look at the curious geology of the cliff edge. Here, bands of two different types of rock give a folded, pleated effect just like the material of a kilt.

⑱ Even more spectacular is the **Quiraing,** 5 miles farther. For a closer view of the strange pinnacles and rock forms, make a left onto a small road at **Brogaig** by **Staffin Bay.** There is a car park near the point where this road breaches the ever-present cliff line, though you will have to be physically fit to walk back toward the Quiraing itself, where the rock formations and cliffs are most dramatic. The trail is on uneven, stony ground, and it's a steep scramble up to the rock formations. In ages past, stolen cattle were hidden deep within the Quiraing's rocky jaws.

⑲ Return to the main A855, continuing around the top end of Trotternish, to the **Kilmuir Croft Museum,** where you can see the old farming ways brought to life. Included in the displays and exhibits are documents and photographs, reconstructed interiors, and implements. Flora Macdonald, helpmate of Prince Charles Edward Stuart, is buried nearby.

The west coast of Trotternish is pleasant, but this is probably all you could easily manage in one day. You may want to return to Portree **⑳** and spend the night before making a separate expedition to **Dunvegan Castle.** In a commanding position above a sea loch, Dunvegan has been the seat of the chiefs of Clan Macleod for more than 700 years. Though greatly changed over the centuries, a gloomy ambience prevails, and there is plenty of family history on display, notably the fascinating "Fairy Flag"—a silk banner, thought to be originally from Rhodes or Syria and believed to have magically saved the clan from danger. The banner's powers are said to suffice for only one more use. *Tel. 01470/521206. Admission: £4 adults, £3.60 senior citizens and students, £2.20 children; garden only, £2.40 adults, £1.50 children. Open mid-Mar.–Oct., Mon.–Sat. 10–5:30, Sun. 1–5:30 (last entry 5).*

There are two other excursions to consider, both taking in spectacular mountain scenery. The first is to **Glen Brittle,** off the A863 on the west side of the island. This jaunt provides some fine views of the Cuillin ridges—not a place for the ordinary walker (there are many dangerous ridges and steep faces). The second suggestion follows a small road, a cul-de-sac resembling Glen Brittle, which leads you to one of the finest views in Scotland. At **Broadford,** take the A881 for Elgol. This road passes through **Strath Suardal** and little **Loch Cill Chriosd (Kilchrist)** by a ruined church. If there are cattle wading in the loch and the light is soft—typical of Skye—then this place takes on the air of a romantic Victorian oil painting. Mindful of the marble quarry at **Torrin** and the breathtaking views of the mountain **Blaven,** simply follow the road to Elgol. This is just a gathering of crofts along the suddenly descending road, which ends at a pier. You can admire the heart-stopping profile of the Cuillin peaks from the shore or, at a point about halfway down the hill, find the path that goes toward them across the rough grasslands. Either way, you may want to stop for a cup of tea at the local tea shop, right by the road.

To leave the island you can take the alternative ferry running from **Armadale** to **Mallaig.** If you go this way, you can visit the popular **Clan Donald Centre** and **Armadale Gardens** on the A851. The center tells the story of the Macdonalds and their proud title: the Lords of the Isles. In the 15th century they were powerful enough to threaten the authority of the Stuart monarchs of Scotland. There is also a major exhibition in a restored part of the castle, as well as extensive gardens and nature trails. *A851 at Armadale, ½ mi north of Armadale Pier; tel. 014714/305 or 014714/227. Admission to center: £3.20 adults, £2.20 senior citizens and children, £9 family ticket. Center open Apr.–Oct., daily 9:30–6. Gardens open at all times.*

Tour 3: The Outer Hebrides (Western Isles)

Numbers in the margin correspond to the points of interest on the Outer Hebrides map.

The Outer Hebrides—in common parlance also known as the Western Isles—stretch about 130 miles from end to end and lie about 50 miles from the Scottish mainland. This splintered archipelago extends from the pugnacious Butt of Lewis in the north to the 600-foot Barra Head on Berneray in the south, whose lighthouse has the greatest arc of visibility in the world. The **Isle of Lewis and Harris** is the northernmost and largest of the group. The island's only major town, **Stornoway,** is situated on a big, nearly landlocked harbor on the east coast of Lewis.

Just south of the Sound of Harris is **North Uist,** rich in monoliths and chambered cairns and other reminders of a prehistoric past. Though it is one of the smaller islands in the chain, **Benbecula,** sandwiched between North and South Uist and sometimes referred to as the Hill of the Fords, is in fact less bare and neglected looking than its bigger neighbors to the north. **South Uist,** once a refuge of the old Catholic faith, is dotted with ruined forts and chapels; in summer its wild gardens burst with riots of Alpine and rock plants. **Eriskay** and a scattering of islets almost block the 6-mile strait between South Uist and **Barra**, the southernmost major formation in the Outer Hebrides, an isle you can walk across in an hour.

Lewis and Harris **㉔** The port capital for the Outer Hebrides is **Stornoway** on Lewis, which can be reached by car ferry from Ullapool on the mainland. This is probably the most convenient starting point for a driving tour of the islands if you're approaching the Western Isles from the Northern Highlands. In Stornoway itself are two museums that vividly illustrate Lewis's past. The **An Lanntair Gallery** offers a varied program of contemporary and traditional exhibitions that change monthly, as well as frequent musical and theatrical events emphasizing traditional Gaelic culture. *Town Hall, S. Beach St., Stornoway, tel. 01851/703307. Admission free. Open Mon.–Sat. 9–5:30.*

Displays at the **Museum nan Eilean (Museum of the Isles)** focus on key aspects of the island's history, as well as the daily life and work of its people. There are exhibits on archaeology, agriculture, fishing, and the sea. *Francis St. Contact the tourist information center for details of opening times.*

The best road to use to explore the territory north of Stornoway is the A857, which runs first across the island to the northwest and then to the northeast all the way to Port of Ness (about 30 miles). At the northernmost point of the island—just a few minutes north-**㉕** west of **Port of Ness** along the B8014—stands the **Butt of Lewis lighthouse,** designed by David and Thomas Stevenson (of the prominent engineering family, whose best-known member was, ironically, the novelist Robert Louis Stevenson). The lighthouse was first lit in 1862. The adjacent cliffs provide a good vantage point for viewing seabirds, whales, and porpoises.

Time Out The **Harbour View Tearoom** in Port of Ness is the perfect place to recharge your batteries before heading back south. Delicate fish pâtés, a choice of real (not bagged) teas, and scrumptious cakes are served in a cozy room in what used to be a boatbuilder's house. Accommodations are also available here.

Go back south on the A857 and pick up the A858 at Barvas. From there it's about a 10-minute drive to the small community of **Arnol.** **㉖** Look for signs off the A858 for the **Arnol Black House,** a well-preserved example of an increasingly rare type of traditional Hebridean home. Once in common use throughout the islands (as recently as 50 years ago), these dwellings were built without mortar and thatched on a timber framework without eaves. Other characteristic features include an open central peat hearth and the absence of a chimney—hence the sooty atmosphere and the designation "black." On display inside are many of the house's original furnishings. *Off A858, Arnol, tel. 0131/244–3101. Admission: £1.50 adults, £1 senior citizens, 75p children. Open Apr.–Sept., Mon.–Sat. 9:30–6; Oct.–Mar., Mon.–Sat. 9:30–4.*

Continue south on A858 another 5 miles or so to reach **Shawbost,** **㉗** home of the **Shawbost School Museum.** This museum came to life as a result of the so-called Highland Village Competition in 1970, during which school pupils gathered artifacts and contributed to displays aimed at illustrating a past way of life in Lewis. Though it has, sadly, become a bit dog-eared and dusty, the museum does provide a glimpse at the old life and customs of the island. *A858, tel.*

The Outer Hebrides

ATLANTIC OCEAN

Isle of Lewis and Harris

Butt of Lewis lighthouse 25
Butt of Lewis

Port of Ness

A857

Arnol Black House 26
Barvas
Tolsta

Shawbost
27 **Shawbost School Museum**
Arnol

B895

East Loch Roag
Loch Roag

28 **Dun Carloway**

Callanish

Valtos

Stornoway
Tiumpan Head

24 **Stornoway**
Eye Peninsula

29 **Callanish Standing Stones**

Brenish

MORSGAIL FOREST

Lewis

A859

Seaforth Island

TO ULLAPOOL

Amhuinnsuidhe
FOREST OF HARRIS

Amhuinnsuidhe Castle 32

B887

31 **Rhenigidale**

Traigh Luskentyre 33

Tarbert

The Minch

Luskentyre

30

South Harris

A859

Tarbert

Loch Seaforth

Harris

Sound of Harris

34 **St. Clement's Church**

Rodel

North Uist

Newtonferry 35

Balranald Nature Reserve 38

Trinity Temple 36
37

Bayhead

A865

A867
Lochmaddy

Barpa Langass Chambered Cairn

Clachan-a-Luib

Uig
Trotternish

Grimsay

Benbecula

39 **Our Lady of the Isles**

Loch Druidibeg National Nature Reserve 40

A865

Sandwick

Isle of Skye

Ormaclete Castle 41

Howmore

Sea of Hebrides

Flora Macdonald's birthplace 42

Lochboisdale

South Uist

N

Barra

Eoligarry

Cille Bharra 44

Castlebay

Kisimul Castle 43

KEY

Ferry Lines

0 — 10 miles
0 — 15 km

Berneray
Barra Head

TO OBAN

01851/71213. Admission: voluntary donation. Open Apr.–Nov., Mon.–Sat. 10–6.

㉘ Approximately 8 miles farther south on A858, at **Dun Carloway,** you can see one of the best preserved Iron Age brochs in Scotland. The mysterious circular defensive towers of the Dun Carloway broch, built about 2,000 years ago possibly as protection against seaborne raiders, provide fine views of a typical Lewis landscape. Parts of the storied walls still stand as high as 30 feet. *A858, tel. 0131/244-3101. Admission free. Open 24 hrs.*

Follow A858 about 10 miles to the southeast, along the inlet called East Loch Roag, to reach **Callanish.** A few miles west of the village

㉙ (along B8012) are the **Callanish Standing Stones,** a setting of megaliths rated second only to Stonehenge in England. Probably positioned in several stages between 3,000 and 1,500 BC, this grouping is made up of an avenue of 19 monoliths extending northward from a circle of 13 stones, with other rows leading south, east, and west. It's believed they may have been used for astronomical observations. The site is accessible at any time. There is a tearoom and an interesting craft shop with locally woven tweeds in the restored black house beside the gate leading to the stones.

㉚ To reach **Tarbert,** the main port of Harris, head back east toward Stornoway on the A858 and pick up the A859 south (a distance of some 50 miles). If you want to break up the ride south, you could make a slight detour about two-thirds of the way down A859 to ex-

㉛ plore the area around **Rhenigidale.** Considered to be the most isolated inhabited village in Harris, Rhenigidale was for a long time accessible only by sea or via a rough hill path. A road completed in the early 1990s, which offers fine views high above Loch Seaforth, has now linked the village with the rest of Scotland.

㉜ About 10 miles northwest of Tarbert on the B887 stands **Amhuinn-suidhe Castle** (the name is almost impossible to pronounce—try *avun-shooee*), a turreted structure built in the 1860s by the earls of Dunmore as a base for fishing and hunting in the North Harris deer forest. The castle overlooks the sea and is close to the Amhuinn-suidhe River, where you can see salmon leaping the nearby falls. These falls, which are on the castle grounds, can be seen only from the road.

㉝ **Traigh Luskentyre,** roughly 5 miles southwest of Tarbert, is a spectacular example of Harris's tidy selection of beaches—2 miles of yellow sands adjacent to **Traigh Seilebost** beach, where there are superb views northward to the hills of the Forest of Harris.

㉞ At the southernmost point of the island, about a 20-mile drive from Tarbert, is the community of **Rodel.** Here you'll find **St. Clement's Church,** a cruciform church standing on a prominent site right on route A859. It was built around 1500 and contains the magnificently sculptured tomb of the church's builder, Alasdair Crotach, eighth chief of Dunvegan Castle.

North Uist At **Newtonferry (Port nan Long),** the port of entry for ferries coming

㉟ from Harris (via Berneray), stand the remains of what was reputed to be the last inhabited broch in North Uist, **Dun an Sticar.** This defensive tower, approached by a causeway over the loch, was occupied by Hugh MacDonald, a descendant of MacDonald of Sleat, until 1602.

Eight miles southwest of Lochmaddy, off the A865, are the ruins of

㊱ **Trinity Temple (Teampull na Trionaid),** a medieval college and monastery said to have been founded by Beathag, daughter of Somerled, progenitor of the Clan Donald, in the 13th century. *Admission free.*

㊲ Sitting very close to the A867 on the stretch between Lochmaddy and Clachan is the **Barpa Langass Chambered Cairn.** Dating from the third millennium BC, this is the only chambered cairn in the Western Isles known to have retained its inner chamber fully intact.

㊳ On the western side of North Uist, about 3 miles northwest of Bayhead, which you can reach via A865, is the **Balranald Nature Reserve,** administered by the Balranald branch of the Royal Society for the Protection of Birds. Large numbers of waders and seabirds, including red-necked phalarope, can be seen here in a varied habitat of loch, marsh, machair (grasslands just behind the beach), and sandy and rocky shore. The reserve can be viewed anytime, but visitors are asked to keep to the paths during breeding season (March to July) so as not to disturb the birds. *Reception cottage at Goular, tel. 01463/715000 or 0131/557–3136. Admission free. Open daily all year.*

South Uist South Uist is connected to North Uist via Grimsay, Benbecula, and three causeways. You can travel the length of South Uist along route A865, making short treks off this main road on your way to Lochboisdale on the southeastern coast of the island; at Lochboisdale you can get ferries to Barra, the southernmost principal island of the Outer Hebrides, or to Oban on the mainland.

㊴ About 5 miles south of the causeway from Benbecula, atop Reuval Hill, stands the 125-foot-high statue of the Madonna and Child known as **Our Lady of the Isles.** The work of sculptor Hew Lorimer, the statue was erected in 1957 by the local Catholic community. A few miles farther south, to the west of A865, you will come to the **㊵** **Loch Druidibeg National Nature Reserve** (tel. 01870/620206). One of only two remaining British native—nonmigrating—populations of greylag geese make their home here in a fresh and brackish loch environment. (Stop at the warden's office for full information about access.)

㊶ A few miles south of Howmore, just west of A865, stand the ruins of **Ormaclete Castle,** which was built in 1708 for the chief of the Clan Ranald, but was accidentally destroyed by fire in 1715 on the eve of the Battle of Sheriffmuir, during which the chief was killed. At Gearraidh Bhailteas (just west of A865 near Milton), you can see the ruins **㊷** of **Flora Macdonald's birthplace.** South Uist's most famous daughter, Flora helped the Young Pretender Prince Charles Edward Stuart avoid capture and was feted as a heroine afterward.

Barra Barra is an island with a rocky east coast and a west coast of sandy **㊸** beaches. **Kisimul Castle,** the largest ancient monument in the Western Isles, is situated on an islet in Castlebay, Barra's principal harbor. Kisimul was the stronghold of the Macneils of Barra, noted for their lawlessness and piracy. The main tower dates from about AD 1120. A restoration that was completed in 1970 was started by the 45th clan chief, an American architect. *Tel. 01871/810336. Admission: £2.50 (includes short boat ride to the castle). Open May–Sept., Wed. and Sat. afternoons.*

Craigston Museum, in a thatched cottage at Baile ne Creige (Craigston), displays artifacts of local crofting life. (It's open only during the main summer season.) At Eolaigearraidh (Eoligarry), the departure point for the passenger ferry to South Uist, you can view **㊹** **Cille Bharra,** the ruins of the church dedicated to the saint who gave his name to the island. Also nearby is the restored **chapel of St. Mary** and part of a medieval monastery and cemetery.

Barra's airport is at the north end of the island on a simple stretch of sand known as **Traigh Moor** (the Cockle Strand)—which is washed twice daily by the tides. The departure and arrival times for the daily flights to and from Glasgow, Benbecula, and Stornoway are scheduled to coincide with low tide.

What to See and Do with Children

Baile an Or. On the site of an 1869 gold rush (*baile an or* means *gold town*), panning is still possible, using pans supplied by Strathullie Local and Scottish Crafts. *Helmsdale, tel. 014312/343.*

Timespan. The dramatic story of the Highlands's history and geography is told through life-size displays, sound effects, and an audiovisual program. Exhibits here contain artifacts preserved by the local heritage society. This living statement of Highland life is well worth seeing. *Helmsdale, Sutherland, tel. 014312/327. Admission: £2.75 adults, £2.20 students and senior citizens, £1.65 children, £7.20 family ticket. Open Apr.–Oct., Mon.–Sat. 10–5, Sun. 2–5. 6 PM closing time in July and Aug.*

Off the Beaten Track

It can be argued that all of the Northern Highlands are off the beaten track. Below are some examples of the peerless views and open countryside for which the area is renowned.

Applecross. The tame way to reach this little community facing Skye is by a coastal road from near Shieldaig; the exciting way is by a series of hairpin turns up the steep wall at the head of a corrie (a glacier-cut mountain valley), approached from the A896 a few miles farther south. There are spectacular views of Skye from the bare plateau on top, and you can boast afterward that you have been on what is probably Scotland's highest motorable road. The town of Applecross itself is pleasant but not riveting.

Cape Wrath. Those that tour far to the north will want to go all the way to the northwest tip of Scotland. You can't drive the entire way in your own car; a ferry carries you across the Kyle of Durness, a sea inlet, then a minibus takes you to the lighthouse. The highest mainland cliffs in Scotland lie between the Kyle and Cape Wrath. These are the 800-foot **Cleit Dubh** (the name means "black cleft" in Gaelic and comes from the Old Norse *klettr,* or crag).

Drumbeg loop from Lochinver. Bold souls spending time at Lochinver may enjoy the interesting single-lane B869 Drumbeg loop to the north of Lochinver—it has several challenging hairpin turns along with breathtaking views. (The junction is just north of the River Inver bridge on the outskirts of the village, signed Stoer and Clashnessie.) Just beyond the scattered community of Stoer, a road leads west to **Stoer Point Lighthouse.** Energetic walkers can hike across the short turf and heather along the cliff top for fine views east toward the profiles of the northwest mountains. There is also a red-sandstone sea-stack to view: the **Old Man of Stoer.** This makes a pleasant excursion on a long summer evening. If you stay on the Drumbeg section, there is a particularly tricky hairpin turn in a steep dip that may force you to take your eyes off the fine view of Quinag, yet another of Sutherland's shapely mountains.

Eas Coul Aulin waterfall. This is the longest waterfall in the United Kingdom. Located east of the Kylesku Bridge on the A894, these falls have a 685-foot drop. A rugged walk that leads to the falls is popular with hikers; in summer, cruises offer a less taxing way to view the falls. *At the head of Loch Glencoul, 3 mi west of A894; contact the tourist information center in Ullapool or Lochinver for more information.*

Shopping

Northern Highlands

As in Argyll and the Western Isles, shopping in the Northern Highlands tends to be more interesting for the variety of crafts available rather than for the number and types of shops. After all, the population of the area is scattered, and if the locals have any special needs, they can travel to the larger population centers, as well as to Inverness. Perhaps the best-known purveyor of crafts in the northeastern corner of the area is **Caithness Glass** (Wick Industrial Site, Wick Airport, tel. 01955/2286), also with branches at Oban and Perth. Producing a distinctive style of glassware and paperweights familiar to those traveling around Scotland (most of the better gift shops stock Caithness Glass), the factory has tours of the glassblowing workshops and a shop stocking the full product range.

There are two other interesting crafts outlets farther south: At **Golspie** the **Orcadian Stone Company** (Main St., Golspie, tel. 01408/633483) makes stone products (including items made from local Caithness slate and modern versions of the carpet bowls, beloved of the Victorians and of today's interior designers), jewelry, incised plaques, and prepared mineral specimens. There is also a geological exhibition on site.

The former **town jail of Dornoch** (Castle St., Dornoch, tel. 01862/810555) is now a textile-and-crafts center where tartans are woven. There's also an exhibition of prison life in past times just to remind you of the building's origins.

At **Lochinver,** on the west coast, **Highland Stoneware** (Baddidarroch, Lochinver, tel. 01571/844376) manufactures tableware and decorative items with hand-painted designs of Highland wildflowers, animals, and landscapes. There is a showroom where you can browse and purchase wares.

At **Inverkirkaig,** just south of Lochinver, do not miss **Achins Book and Craft Shop** (Inverkirkaig, tel. 015714/262): Anyone with enough courage to run a bookshop with an ample inventory this far from a main population center deserves all the customers he or she can get. The range of stock—especially Scottish books on natural history, hill walking, fishing, and crafts—is worth a browse. Also available is a well-chosen variety of craftware: knitwear, tweeds, and pottery.

There are also several well-stocked gift shops south of Lochinver, at **Ullapool.** In **Lochcarron,** the premises of **Lochcarron Weavers** (North Strone, Lochcarron, tel. 015202/212) are open to the public: Weavers can be seen at work, producing pure-wool worsted tartans that can be bought on site or at the firm's other outlets in the area.

East of Lochcarron, at **Achnasheen,** is the **Highland Line Craft Centre** (center of Achnasheen, tel. 0144/588227), where silver and gold jewelry is made, and you can watch the silversmiths; products are available in the shop on the premises.

Skye

Shopping is limited on Skye, although there are quite a few gift outlets—as well as more crafts businesses—that cater to visitors. Among those worth a visit: **Ragamuffin** (Armadale Pier, tel. 014714/217), which specializes in designer knitwear and clothing, and **Skye**

Batiks (Armadale, tel. 014714/396), where designs are influenced by Celtic motifs, and wall hangings and cotton, silk, and linen clothing are for sale at reasonable prices. **Harlequin Knitwear** (Duisdale, Sleat, tel. 014713/321) sells colorful wool sweaters designed by local designers. **Skye Silver** (The Old School, Colbost, tel. 0147081/263) makes gold and silver jewelry with a Celtic theme. **Craft Encounters** (Broadford, tel. 01471/822201) stocks an array of Scottish crafts, including marquetry and jewelry. For wood-fired stoneware, try **Edinbane Pottery** (Edinbane, tel. 0147/082234). There are also several art galleries and studios of interest on Skye, among them **Skye Original Prints** (Portree, tel. 01478/2388).

Outer Hebrides
At the **Callanish Stones Craft Shop,** Beatrice Schulz sells craft items, knitwear, and tweed lengths in a kaleidoscopic range of colors. She also has a shop in Stornoway (9 Braehead St., tel. 01851/703337) with a similar range of stock. At **Stornoway Pottery** (confusingly not at Stornoway, but at **Borve,** on the road to Ness, tel. 01851/85345), you can buy squat pottery glazed in a wash of red and blue. Harris tweed is available at many outlets on the islands, including some of the weavers' homes. Try **Norman MacDonald** (35 Arnol, Isle of Lewis, tel. 01851/71531) or **Alistair Campbell** (4 Plocrabol, Isle of Harris, tel. 01859/81217). On South Uist, **Hebridean Jewelry** (Garrieganichy, Lochdar, tel. 01870/4288) makes decorative jewelry and framed pictures; the owners also run a crafts shop.

Sports and Fitness

Bicycling
Be prepared to meet holiday traffic at peak season. Some side roads (and even, in the far northwest, some main roads) are single track and narrow, meaning there will be traffic coming the other way between passing places. High-visibility clothing is advised.

Bicycles may be rented from **The Bike Shop** (35 High St., Thurso, tel. 01847/66124 or 01847/64223), **Island Cycles** (The Green, Portree, tel. 01478/613121), **Alex Dan Cycle Centre** (67 Kenneth St., Stornoway, tel. 01851/704025), **Barra Cycle Hire** (Brendan Rd., Castlebay, tel. 018714/284), **Skye Bike** (The Pier, Clanachan, tel. 01599/4795), **The Ferry Filling Station** (Ardvasar, Skye, tel. 014714/249), and **Broadford Bicycle Hire** (Fairwinds, Elgol Rd., Broadford, tel. 01471/822270), **Kintail Crafts** (Glenshiel, tel. 0159–981/345), **Raasay Outdoor Centre** (Raasay House, Isle of Raasay, tel. 01478/660266).

Fishing
The possibilities for fishing are endless here, as a glance at the loch-littered map of Sutherland suggests. As in other parts of Scotland, post offices, local shops, and hotels usually sell permits to fish in local waters, and tourist-information centers carry lists of the best locales for fishing.

Golf
There are only about 15 courses in the area—a low number compared with other regions of Scotland—with almost no courses on the west coast, though **Gairloch Golf Club** has its enthusiasts. *60 mi west of Dingwall, tel. 01445/2407. 9 holes, 1,942 yards, SSS 71.*

The best-known club in the area is **Royal Dornoch.** Were it not for its northern location, the club would undoubtedly be a candidate for the Open Championship. *40 mi north of Inverness, tel. 01862/810219. 18 holes, 6,581 yards, SSS 72.*

Pony Trekking
Pony trekking was invented to give the sturdy highland ponies a job to do when they weren't carrying dead deer off the hills during the "stalking" (deer-hunting) season. Treks last from two hours to a

whole day, and ponies can be found to suit all ages and levels of experience.

Contact one of the following centers for information about specific opportunities and costs: **The Black Isle Riding Centre** (tel. 0146373/707), **Uig Pony Trekking** (Skye, tel. 0147/042205), **Sandford Trekking and Riding** (Struan, Skye, tel. 0147072/225), and **Latheron Pony Centre** (tel. 015934/224).

Water Sports   **Raasay Outdoor Centre** (Raasay House, Isle of Raasay, near Kyle, Wester Ross, tel. 01478/660266) offers a variety of courses in canoeing, sailing, windsurfing, and navigation skills.

Dining and Lodging

Dining

In an area with such a low population, the choice of restaurants is inevitably restricted. The places selected below can be relied upon for both accommodations and acceptable standards in the dining room.

Highly recommended restaurants are indicated by a star ★.

Category	Cost*
$$$$	over £40
$$$	£30–£40
$$	£15–£30
$	under £15

per person for a three-course meal, including VAT; excluding drinks

Lodging

This region of Scotland has some good modern hotels and some charming inns but not many establishments in the more expensive categories. Travelers often find that the most enjoyable accommodations are low-cost guest houses (often family run), offering bed-and-breakfast. Dining rooms of country-house lodgings frequently reach the standard of top-quality restaurants.

Highly recommended hotels are indicated by a star ★.

Category	Cost*
$$$$	over £120
$$$	£100–£120
$$	£80–£100
$	under £80

All prices are for a standard double room, including breakfast and tax.

Dundonnell
Dining and
Lodging

Dundonnell Hotel. Set on the roadside by Little Loch Broom, just south of Ullapool, this hotel has been a family-run enterprise since 1962 and has cultivated a solid reputation for hospitality and cuisine. The bedrooms are decorated in a fresh, modern style, with light, floral curtains and bedspreads, contemporary furnishings, and modern comforts including tea- and coffee-making equipment, and many have stunning views over pristine hills and lochs, as do the public rooms. The Taste of Scotland menu features homemade soups, fresh seafood, and desserts well worth leaving room for. *Dundonnell, near Garve, Ross-shire, tel. 01854/633204, fax 01854/633366. 30 rooms with bath. Facilities: restaurant (reservations advised, dress casual), bar. MC, V. $–$$*

Harris
Dining and
Lodging
★

Ardvourlie Castle. A former Victorian hunting lodge that still retains its character, Ardvourlie is set in splendid isolation amid the dramatic mountain scenery of Harris, an ideal habitat for hill walking. The bathrooms are magnificent, with mahogany paneling and Victorian-style fixtures, and the decor of the bedrooms and public rooms is bold, idiosyncratic, and entirely in keeping with the High Victorian atmosphere of the castle. The country-house hospitality is perpetuated by the well-stocked library and roaring fires. The cooking is along traditional lines and is of a high standard, favoring fresh local produce and, often, wild game. The portions are generous. *Isle of Harris, tel. 01859/502307. Facilities: restaurant (reservations essential; dress casual). 5 rooms, 3 with private bath. No credit cards. $–$$*

Kylesku
Dining and
Lodging

Linne Mhuirich. A modern croft house offering Taste of Scotland bed, breakfast, and evening meal. It is set in the middle of open country with superb mountain scenery all around. Local fish and home baking are high points. *Unapool Croft Rd., Kylesku, via Lairg, Sutherland IV27 4HW, tel. 01971/502227. 3 rooms, 1 with bath. No credit cards. Open May–Oct. No smoking. $*

Scourie
Dining and
Lodging

Eddrachilles Hotel. This old, established traditional inn has one of the best views of any hotel in Scotland—across the islands of Eddrachillis Bay (which can be explored by boat from the hotel). The hotel sits on 320 acres of private moorland and is just south of the Handa Island bird sanctuary. Inside and outside, the hotel is well preserved. The bedrooms are modern and comfortable, and each is outfitted with tea- and coffee-making facilities. The chef uses local produce to prepare meals cooked in straightforward Scottish style, with the emphasis on fish and game. *Badcall Bay, Scourie, tel. 01971/502080, fax 01971/502477. 11 rooms with bath or shower. Facilities: restaurant (reservations essential, dress casual), bar. MC, V. Closed Nov.–Feb. $*

Skye
Dining and
Lodging

Kinloch Lodge. This hotel offers elegant comfort on the edge of the world. Run by Lord and Lady MacDonald with flair and considerable professionalism, Kinloch Lodge is a supremely comfortable country house, with warm, restful lounges, snug bedrooms, and a handsome dining room that serves imaginative cuisine. *Sleat IV43 8QY, tel. 014713/333, fax 014713/277. 10 rooms with bath. Facilities: restaurant (reservations advised, dress casual but neat), fishing. MC, V. Closed Dec.–early May. $$$–$$$$*

Cuillin Hills Hotel. Situated on lovely grounds just outside Portree, this gabled hotel is within easy walking distance of the town center. Many of the rooms have outstanding views over Portree Bay toward the Cuillin Hills. Bedrooms are reasonably spacious and well equipped, decorated in a pleasant, fairly neutral style. The public rooms give you a choice of sitting areas and a friendly bar. The meals, especially seafood dishes, are prepared in straightforward fashion, with few gimmicks and a lot of flavor. *Portree, Isle of Skye, tel. 01478/612003, fax 01478/613092. 26 rooms with bath. Facilities: restaurant (reservations advised, jacket and tie preferred), bar. AE, MC, V. $*

Torridon
Dining and Lodging

Loch Torridon Hotel. Once a shooting lodge, and still right on the shore of Loch Torridon with forest and mountains rising behind, the hotel provides a real Highland welcome. Log fires, handsome plasterwork ceilings, mounted stag heads, and traditional furnishings set the mood downstairs, while bedrooms are decorated in restrained pastel shades with antique mahogany furniture. The restaurant makes elaborate use of local seafood, salmon, beef, lamb, and game, and the cellar includes many fine wines. *By Achnasheen, Wester Ross IV27 2EY, tel. 01445/791242, fax 01445/791296. 19 rooms, 18 with bath, 1 with shower. Facilities: restaurant (reservations essential, jacket and tie preferred). MC, V. $-$$*

Ullapool
Dining and Lodging
★

Altnaharrie Inn. Be prepared for a real treat. Follow the A9/A832 to the A835 for 60 miles from Inverness, to Ullapool, where a private launch takes you to this inn in Dundonnell, some 5 miles south, on the banks of Loch Broom. The restaurant is superb: A set menu of local specialties is skillfully prepared, including scallops in white-burgundy-and-bitter-cress sauce and medallions of roe deer with leek, grape juniper, and dill sauce, with wild-raspberry ice cream and a selection of cheeses to finish. Bedrooms are comfortable and have quality furnishings; you will need to book far in advance for this popular inn. *Ullapool, Highland IV26 2SS, tel. 01854/633230. 8 rooms; 7 with bath, 1 with shower. Facilities: restaurant, 2 lounges. No credit cards. Closed Nov.–Easter. $$$$ (rates include dinner)*

Ceilidh Place. This hostelry is extremely comfortable; guests can while away the hours on deep luxurious sofas in the first-floor sitting room—which overlooks the bay—or borrow one of the many books scattered throughout the inn to read back in the room or over breakfast. About as far away in style as you can get from a major chain hotel, the Ceilidh Place must be taken strictly on its own terms—relax and fit in and you will thoroughly enjoy a stay here. The inn's restaurant specializes in seafood and vegetarian cooking, and ceilidhs and other musical events are held here frequently. *W. Argyle St., Ullapool IV26 2TY, tel. 01854/612103, fax 01854/612886. 24 rooms, 10 with bath. Facilities: restaurant (reservations essential, dress casual). AE, DC, MC, V. $-$$*

The Arts and Nightlife

The Arts

The **Lyth Arts Centre,** between Wick and John o' Groats on the A9, is set in an old country school. From April to September each year, it hosts frequent performances by quality touring music and theater companies (admission: £7 adult, £4 concessions; part of the circuit of British Arts Centres). In July and August there are also local and touring exhibitions of contemporary fine art (small admission charge). *4 mi off A9, tel. 01955–84/270 or 0131/226–6424. Open Apr.–Sept. daily 10–6.*

The **Ceilidh Place** in Ullapool (*see* Dining and Lodging, *above*) frequently presents ceilidhs and entertainment featuring typical Northern Highland music. **An Lanntair,** in the Stornoway town hall (Isle of Lewis and Harris), also conducts an eclectic program of monthly exhibitions and evening events. Various Scottish ballet- and opera-touring companies perform in local halls. Consult tourist-information centers' event lists for details.

Nightlife   The nightlife here is confined mainly to hotels and pubs. Ceilidhs, dances, and concerts are performed on a sporadic basis and advertised locally.

13 The Northern Isles

Orkney and Shetland

By Gilbert Summers

Both Orkney and Shetland possess a Scandinavian heritage that gives them an ambience different from any other region of Scotland. For mainland Scots, visiting this archipelago is a little like traveling abroad without having to worry about a different language or currency. Both of these isles are bound by the sea, and both are essentially bleak and austere, with awesome seascapes and genuinely warm, friendly people. Neither island has yet been overrun by tourists. Orkney is the greener of the two island groupings, which number 200 islets between them.

There are more prehistoric sites in Orkney than anywhere else in the United Kingdom, although Shetland also has a few historic sites of great interest. Orkney's wealth of sites includes stone circles, burial chambers, ancient settlements, and fortifications that emphasize many centuries of continuous settlement. Most of the sites are open to view, offering an insight into the life of bygone eras. At Maes Howe, for example, visitors will discover that graffiti is not solely a problem borne by today's troubled youths: The Vikings left their marks here in the 8th century.

The differences between Orkney and Shetland can be summed up with the description that an Orcadian is a farmer with a boat, while a Shetlander is a fisherman with a croft (small farm). Shetland, rich in ocean views and sparse landscapes, is endowed with a more remote atmosphere than its neighbor Orkney. However, don't let Shetland's bleak countryside fool you; this island is far from being a backwater island. Oil money from the mineral resources around its shores and the fact that it has been a crossroads in the northern seas for centuries have helped make it a cosmopolitan place.

Essential Information

Important Addresses and Numbers

Tourist Information
The two main sources of tourist information in the area are the **Orkney Tourist Board** (Broad St., Kirkwall, Orkney, tel. 01856/872856, fax 01856/875056) and **Shetland Isles Tourism** (Information Centre, Market Cross, Lerwick, Shetland, tel. 01595/3434, fax 01595/5807).

Discount Pass
A joint entry ticket to all of Historic Scotland's Orkney sights is available from the sights themselves. The ticket lasts until you've seen all the sights and costs £6 adults, £3 senior citizens, £2 children.

Emergencies
For police, fire, or ambulance, dial 999 from any telephone. No coins are needed for emergency calls from public telephone booths.

Doctors and Dentists
Most general practitioners will see visitor patients by appointment or immediately in case of emergency. Your hotel or local tourist-information center can advise you accordingly. You can also consult the Yellow Pages of the telephone directory, under "Doctor" or "Dentist." Hospitals with emergency rooms are **Gilbert Bain Hospital** (South Rd., Lerwick, Shetland, tel. 01595/5678) and **Balfour Hospital** (New Staffa Rd., Kirkwall, Orkney, tel. 01856/872763).

Late-Night Pharmacies
There are no late-night pharmacies on the islands. In case of emergency, police can provide assistance in locating pharmacists. Doctors in rural areas also dispense medication.

Arriving and Departing by Plane

Airports and Airlines
British Airways (Aberdeen Airport, tel. 01224/722331, ext. 5122) provides regular service to **Sumburgh Airport,** in Shetland, 25 miles

from Lerwick. You can also reach Sumburgh from Inverness via **Kirkwall** in Orkney, or directly from Edinburgh on **Loganair** (tel. 0141/889–3181 or 01595/84–246). Loganair also has direct flights to Lerwick (Tingwall) and Sumburgh airports and to **Unst.** You can get to Kirkwall on British Airways' direct flights from Aberdeen.

Arriving and Departing by Car, Train, and Bus

By Car To get to Lerwick, Shetland, take the ferry from the port in Aberdeen. To reach Stromness, Orkney, take the ferry from the port in Scrabster. Contact **P & O Ferries** (Orkney and Shetland Services, Jamieson's Quay, Aberdeen, tel. 01224/572615, fax 01224/574411) for reservations.

By Train There are no trains on Orkney or Shetland, although Aberdeen (for the Shetland ferry) is well served by train (for information contact the Aberdeen Travel Centre, tel. 01224/594222), and Thurso is the terminus of the far-north line. From Thurso a bus connects to Scrabster for Orkney. Contact the Inverness Travel Centre (tel. 01463/238924) for information on Inverness and Thurso-to-Scrabster service.

By Bus Aberdeen and Thurso have reliable bus links to and from all over Scotland: **Scottish City Link** (Guild St., Aberdeen, tel. 01224/212307) and **National Express** (Friarton Rd., Perth, tel. 01738/33481).

Getting Around

By Car Because of the oil wealth, the roads on Shetland are in very good shape. Both Orkney and Shetland are part of a network of islands with interconnecting ferries that are heavily subsidized. It's a good idea to book ferry tickets in advance. For information, contact Shetland Isles Tourism (*see* Important Addresses and Numbers, *above*) or tel. 01957/82259 or 01957/82268 if you are visiting during peak season. Shetland visitors who want to get to Orkney can do so by way of ferry from Scalloway on Shetland to Kirkwall, Orkney's largest town.

Orkney also has causeways connecting some of the islands, but using these roads will, in some cases, take you on fairly roundabout routes, thus making for a longer journey than you might have if you took a ferry.

Car Rental Although Shetland has a number of car-rental firms, you have the option of taking your car from Aberdeen by sea. The rule of thumb is that for any visit under five days it is cheaper to rent a car in Shetland. Most of the rental companies are based in Lerwick; they include **Star Rent-a-Car** (22 Commercial St., Lerwick, tel. 01595/2075) and **Bolts Car and Minibus Hire** (tel. 01595/2855, 26 North Rd., Lerwick). On Orkney try **J & W Tait** (Sparrowhawk Rd., Hatston Industrial Estate, Kirkwall, tel. 01856/872490) or **James D. Peace & Co.** (Junction Rd., Kirkwall, tel. 01856/872866).

By Train There are no trains on Shetland or Orkney.

By Bus The main bus services on Orkney are operated by **James D. Peace & Co.** (tel. 01856/872866), **Causeway Coaches** (tel. 01856/83444), and **Shalder Coaches** (tel. 01856/850809); on Shetland by **Shalder Coaches** (tel. 0159588/217) and **J. Leask** (tel. 01595/3162).

By Air Note that because of the isolation of Orkney and Shetland there is a network of inter-island flights. Tourist-information centers (*see*

Important Addresses and Numbers, *above*) will provide details, or call Loganair (*see* Arriving and Departing by Plane, *above*).

Guided Tours

Orientation In addition to the bus companies mentioned above, well-run personally guided tours are offered in Orkney by **Go-Orkney** (tel. 01856/874260). Other companies that schedule general orientation tours include **Causeway Coaches** (tel. 01856/83444), **Rosie Coaches** (tel. 01856/75227), and **Shalder Coaches** (tel. 01856/850809). The tour companies that service Shetland are **J. Leask** (tel. 01595/3162) and **Shalder Coaches** (tel. 0159588/217).

Special- All the above companies run special-interest tours to specific places
Interest of interest on the islands, and most can also tailor tours to your interests. Guided walks are available on Orkney: Contact **Wildabout** (through Orkney Tourist Board) for details of early morning, late evening, and all-day walks with an environmental theme.

Exploring the Northern Isles

Highlights for First-Time Visitors

Esha Ness Cliffs (*see* Tour 1)
Italian Chapel (*see* Tour 2)
Jarlshof (*see* Tour 1)
Maes Howe (*see* Tour 2)
Mousa Broch (*see* Tour 1)
Ring of Brogar (*see* Tour 2)
St. Magnus Cathedral, Kirkwall (*see* Tour 2)
Shetland Croft Museum (*see* Tour 1)
Skara Brae (*see* Tour 2)

Tour 1: Around Shetland

Numbers in the margin correspond to points of interest on the Shetland Islands map.

The Shetland coastline is an incredible 900 miles due to all the indentations, yet there isn't a point on the island farther than 3 miles from the sea. Settlements away from Lerwick, the primary town, are small and scattered. By asking for directions, you may find yourself having tea with a resident.

❶ Visitors would be remiss if they failed to explore some of **Lerwick**'s nearby diversions before venturing beyond it. **Fort Charlotte** is a 17th-century Cromwellian stronghold, built to protect the Sound of Bressay. *Tel. 0131/244–3101. Admission free. Open Apr.–Sept., Mon.–Sat. 9:30–6, Sun. 2–6; Oct.–Mar., Mon.–Sat. 9:30–4, Sun. 2–4.*

The **Shetland Museum** in Lerwick gives an interesting account of the development of the town and includes displays on archaeology, art and textiles, shipping, and folk life. *Lower Hillhead, tel. 01595/5057. Admission free. Open Mon., Wed., Fri. 10–7, Tues., Thurs., Sat. 10–5.*

Shetland Islands

Muckle Flugga

Herma Ness

Unst

Burrafirth

15 **Haroldswick**

Baltasound

Bluemull Sound

A968

Gloup

B9082

Uyeasound

Yell

14

Gutcher **13**

Muness Castle

Mid Yell

A968

Fetlar

Isbister

Yell Sound

Funzie

Ronas Hill **11**

A970

B9081

Colgrave Sound

Esha Ness **10**

B9078

Ulsta

Out
Skerries

Hillswick

Ura Firth

Toft

12 **Burravoe**

St. Magnus
Bay

Brae **9**

B9076

Hamnavoe

Whalsay

Papa Stour

Muckle
Roe

B9071

Voe

Laxo

Brough

Sandness

Mainland

A971

Bixter

B9075

Kergord

B9075

8

Walls

Culswick

Island of
Bressay

Lerwick **1**

Scalloway **7**

Isle of
Noss

TO KIRKWALL

Quarff

2 **Clickhimin
Broch**

Sandwick

A970

3

**St. Ninian's
Isle** **6**

**Broch
of Mousa**

Levenwick

N

Loch of
Spiggie

B9122

4 **Shetland
Croft
House
Museum**

Fitful
Head

Jarlshof

5 Sumburgh

0 _____ 10 miles

Sumburgh Head

0 _____ 15 km

Sumburgh Roost

TO FAIR ISLE

TO
ABERDEEN

Time Out Near the harbor in Lerwick, the **Kvelsdro House Hotel** (tel. 01595/ 2195) serves hearty pub grub meals; try the breaded haddock or steak pie.

② **Clickhimin Broch,** on the site of what was originally an Iron-Age fortification, can be your introduction to the mysterious Pictish monuments, whose meaning is still largely obscure. *1 mi south of Lerwick, tel. 0131/244–3101. Admission free. Open Apr.–Sept., Mon.– Sat. 9:30–6, Sun. 2–6; Oct.–Mar., Mon.–Sat. 9:30–4, Sun. 2–4.*

From the broch go south on the A970, and you will find vivid views of the cliffs at the south end of the island of Bressay, which shelters **③** Lerwick harbor. The **Broch of Mousa,** the most complete of all the broch towers remaining in Scotland, can be reached by boat from Sandwick, just off the main road. *Mousa, tel. 0131/244–3101. Admission free. Open Apr.–Sept., Mon.–Sat. 9:30–6, Sun. 2–6; Oct.–Mar., Mon.–Sat. 9:30–4, Sun. 2–4. Boat for hire May–Sept. afternoons, Sat., Sun. mornings, some evenings.*

④ Continue south on A970 until you see a sign for the **Shetland Croft House Museum.** This traditionally constructed 19th-century thatched house contains a broad range of artifacts that depict the former way of life of the rural Shetlander, which the museum attendant will be delighted to discuss with you. *Voe, Dunrossness, unclassified road east of A970, tel. 01595/5057. Admission: £1 adults, 50p children. Open May–Sept., daily 10–1 and 2–5.*

The A970 then continues south to **Sumburgh.** The big attraction **⑤** here is **Jarlshof,** a centuries-old site that includes the extensive remains of Norse buildings, as well as prehistoric wheel houses and earth houses representing thousands of years of continuous settlement. The site also includes a 17th-century laird's (landowner's) house built on the ruins of a medieval farmstead. *Sumburgh Head, tel. 0131/244–3101. Admission: £2 adults, £1.25 senior citizens, 75p children. Open Apr.–Sept., Mon.–Sat. 9:30–6, Sun. 2–6. Closed Oct.– Mar.*

⑥ Retrace your route to **Skelberry,** making a left on the B9122. It was on nearby **St. Ninian's Isle**—actually a "tombolo," a term for a spit of sand that moors an island to the mainland—where archaeologists in the 1950s uncovered the St. Ninian treasure, a collection of 28 silver objects from the 8th century. This Celtic silver is now in the Royal Museum of Scotland in Edinburgh (*see* Chapter 4), though good replicas are on view in the Shetland Museum in Lerwick (*see above*).

⑦ West of Lerwick, on the western coast of Mainland Island, is **Scalloway.** Look for the information board just off the main road (A970), which overlooks the settlement and its castle. **Scalloway Castle** was built in 1600 by Earl Patrick, who coerced the locals to build it for him. He was executed in 1615 for his cruelty and misdeeds, and the castle was never used again. *6 mi west of Lerwick, tel. 0131/244–3101. Admission free. Open Apr.–Sept., Mon.–Sat. 9:30–6, Sun. 2–6; Oct.– Mar., Mon.–Sat. 9:30–4, Sun. 2–4.*

⑧ Take the B9075 east off the A970, at the head of a narrow sea inlet. This leads into the unexpectedly green valley of **Kergord,** noted for its thick carpet of trees. This would be unremarkable farther south, but here it is a novelty.

⑨ Rejoin the A970 by making a left off the B9075 at Laxo, then drive through Voe to **Brae,** home of the Busta House Hotel (*see* Lodging, *below*), probably the best hotel on the island. Beyond Brae the main road meanders past **Mavis Grind,** a strip of land so narrow you can throw a stone—if you are strong—from the Atlantic, in one inlet, to the North Sea, in another.

Time Out   Follow the A970 left for Hillswick to reach the **St. Magnus Bay Hotel** (tel. 0180623/372), which serves fresh fish in a wood-panel bar and dining room.

⑩ For outstanding views of the rugged, forbidding cliffs around **Esha Ness,** return to the A970 and drive a few miles to the northeast, then turn left onto the B9078. On the way, look for the sandstone stacks in the bay that resemble a Viking galley under sail. After viewing the cliffs at Esha Ness, return to join the A970 at Hillswick and follow an ancillary road from the head of Ura Firth. This road **⑪** provides vistas of rounded, bare **Ronas Hill,** the highest hill in Shetland. Though only 1,468 feet high, it is noted for its arctic-alpine flora growing at low levels.

To visit Yell and Unst, the two main northern islands, go south as far as Brae and take the B9076. After crossing over from the Shetland port of Toft to Ulsta, on the island of **Yell,** take the B9081 east **⑫** to **Burravoe.** There's not a lot to say about the blanket bog that covers two-thirds of Yell, but the **Old Haa** (hall) of Burravoe, the oldest building on the island, is architecturally interesting and has a museum upstairs. One of the displays tells the story of the wrecking of the German sailship, the *Bohus,* in 1924. A copy of the ship's figurehead is displayed outside the Old Haa itself; the original is at the shipwreck site overlooking Otters Wick, along the coast on the B9081. *Tel. 0195782/339 or 01957/2127. Admission free. Open Apr.–Sept., Tues., Wed., Thurs., and Sat. 10–4, Sun. 2–5.*

Time Out   The **Old Haa,** formerly a merchant's house, serves light meals with home-baked buns, cakes, scones, and other goodies; has a craft shop; and acts as a kind of unofficial information point. The staff, like all native Shetland folk, are friendly and give advice to sightseers.

⑬ Rejoin the main A968 at Mid Yell to reach **Gutcher,** the ferry pier. If time permits, turn left on the B9082 for a pleasant drive to **Gloup,** a cluster of houses at the end of the road. Behind a croft, in a field overlooking a long voe (sea inlet) is the **Gloup Fisherman's Memorial,** which recalls an 1881 tragedy involving all hands of 10 six-oared local fishing boats.

Take the ferry to the other side of the Bluemull Sound to **Unst,** the northernmost inhabited island in Scotland. Because of its strategic location—it protrudes well into the northern seas—Unst is inhabited by the military. Follow the A968 until you reach the right turn **⑭** on the B9084 for **Muness Castle.** Scotland's northernmost castle, it was built just before the end of the 16th century. Those visiting the castle will be pleasantly surprised to find some photogenic Shetland ponies in the field nearby. *Southeast corner of Unst, tel. 0131/244–3101. Admission free. Ask for the key-keeper. Open Apr.–Sept., Mon.–Sat. 9:30–6, Sun. 2–6; Oct.–Mar., Mon.–Sat. 9:30–4, Sun. 2–4.*

Just to the north is the **Keen of Hamar** national nature reserve. **⑮** Farther north is **Haroldswick,** with its post office and heritage center. If you take the B9086 at Haroldswick you will go around the head of **Burra Firth** (a sea inlet) and eventually reach a parking lot. From there a path goes north across moorland and up a gentle hill. Bleak and open, this is bird-watchers' territory and is replete with diving skuas—single-minded sky pirates that attack anything that strays near their nest sites. Gannets, puffins, and other seabirds nest in spectacular profusion by the cliffs on the left as you look out to sea. Visitors should make sure they keep to the path; this is a national nature reserve.

At the top of the hills, amid the windy grasslands, you can see **Muckle Flugga** to the north, a series of tilting offshore rocks with a lighthouse on the largest of these sea-battered protrusions. This is the northernmost point in Scotland; the sea rolls out on three sides, no land lies beyond.

Tour 2: Around Orkney

Numbers in the margin correspond to points of interest on the Orkney Islands map.

Orkney has the greatest concentration of prehistoric sites in Scotland. Visitors traveling to Orkney from the mainland can take a ferry from Scrabster—located roughly 2 miles northwest of Thurso off the A836—to **Stromness** on Mainland. You will find two points of interest in Stromness as soon as you arrive. The **Pier Arts Centre** is a former Stromness merchant's house (circa 1800) and has adjoining buildings that now serve as a gallery with a permanent collection of 20th-century paintings and sculptures. *Victoria St., tel. 01856/850–209. Admission free. Open Tues.–Sat. 10:30–12:30 and 1:30–5; also Sun. in July and Aug. 2–5.*

Nearby, the **Stromness Museum** has a varied collection of natural-history material on view, including preserved birds and Orkney shells. The museum also displays exhibits on fishing, shipping, whaling, and the Hudson Bay Company, as well as ship models and a feature on the German fleet that was scuttled on Scapa Flow. *Stromness, tel. 01856/850025. Admission: £1 adults, 50p children. Open Mon.–Sat. 10:30–12:30 and 1:30–5.*

Located just off the A965, 5 miles northeast of Stromness, the **Ring of Brogar** is a magnificent circle of 36 stones (originally 60) surrounded by a deep ditch. When the fog descends over the stones—a frequent occurrence—their looming shapes seem to come alive. Though their original use is uncertain, it is not hard to imagine strange rituals taking place here in the misty past. *Between Loch of Harray and Loch of Stenness, 5 mi northeast of Stromness, tel. 0131/244–3101. Admission free. Open at all times.*

One mile farther on the A965 brings visitors to another ancient site, the huge burial mound of **Maes Howe** (circa 2,500 BC), which measures 115 feet in diameter and contains an enormous burial chamber. It was raided by Vikings in the 12th century, and Norse crusaders sheltered here, leaving a rich collection of runic inscriptions. *Off A965, 9 mi west of Kirkwall, tel. 0131/244–3101. Admission: £2 adults, £1.25 senior citizens, 75p children, or joint entry ticket to all Historic Scotland's Orkney sights. Open Apr.–Sept., Mon.–Sat. 9:30–6, Sun. 2–6; Oct.–Mar., Mon.–Sat. 9:30–4, Sun. 2–4.*

To reach the neolithic village of **Skara Brae,** take the A965 west to the B9056. There you will find houses joined by covered passages and stone beds, fireplaces, and cupboards that have survived since the village was first occupied around 3,000 BC. The site was preserved in sand until it was uncovered in 1850. *19 mi northwest of Kirkwall, tel. 0131/244–3101. Admission: £2.50 adults, £1.50 senior citizens, £1 children, or joint entry ticket to all Historic Scotland's Orkney sights. Open Apr.–Sept., Mon.–Sat. 9:30–6, Sun. 2–6; Oct.–Mar., Mon.–Sat. 9:30–4, Sun. 2–4.*

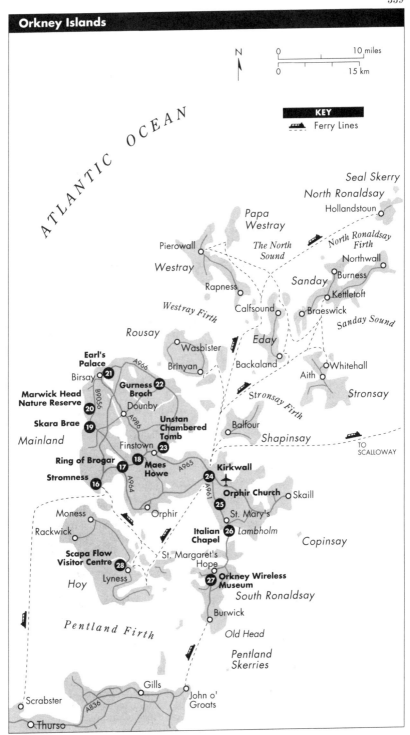

Orkney Islands

N

0 — 10 miles
0 — 15 km

KEY
Ferry Lines

ATLANTIC OCEAN

Seal Skerry
North Ronaldsay
Hollandstoun

Papa Westray

Pierowall

The North Sound

North Ronaldsay Firth

Westray

Rapness

Sanday
Northwall
Burness
Kettletoft
Braeswick

Calfsound

Westray Firth

Rousay
Wasbister
Eday

Brinyan

Backaland

Sanday Sound

Whitehall
Aith
Stronsay

Earl's Palace 21
Birsay

A966

Stronsay Firth

Gurness Broch 22

Marwick Head Nature Reserve 20

B9056

Dounby

Skara Brae 19

Unstan Chambered Tomb 23

Balfour

Shapinsay

Mainland

A986

Finstown

TO SCALLOWAY

Ring of Brogar 17 18
Maes Howe

A965

Kirkwall 24

Stromness 16

A964

Orphir

Orphir Church
25
St. Mary's

Skaill

Moness

Rackwick

St. Margaret's Hope

Italian Chapel 26 *Lambholm*

Copinsay

Scapa Flow Visitor Centre 28
Lyness

Hoy

Orkney Wireless Museum 27

South Ronaldsay

Burwick

Old Head

Pentland Firth

Pentland Skerries

Scrabster

Gills

John o' Groats

A836

Thurso

⑳ To the north of Skara Brae, up the B9056, sits the **Marwick Head Nature Reserve,** with its spectacular seabird cliffs, tended by Scotland's Royal Society for the Protection of Birds. The **Kitchener Memorial,** which recalls the sinking of the cruiser HMS *Hampshire* with Lord Kitchener aboard in 1916, can also be seen in the reserve, on a cliff-top site. *Access to reserve along path north from Marwick Bay, tel. 01856/850176. Admission free. Open at all times.*

Just beyond Marwick at Birsay (25 mi northwest of Kirkwall) is **㉑** **Earl's Palace,** the impressive remains of a 16th-century palace built by the earls of Orkney. *Birsay, tel. 0131/244–3101. Admission free. Open at all times.*

Nearby is the **Brough of Birsay,** the remains of a Romanesque church (and a Norse settlement) on an island accessible only at low tide. Lest you are swept away, check the tide tables before setting out. *Birsay, tel. 0131/244–3101. Admission free. Open all year, subject to tides.*

㉒ The **Gurness Broch,** an Iron-Age tower standing more than 10 feet high, is located off the A966, about 8 miles from Birsay along Orkney's northern coast. The broch is surrounded by stone huts. *Off A966 at Aikerness, 14 mi northwest of Kirkwall, tel. 0131/244–3101. Admission: £2 adults, £1.25 senior citizens, 75p children, or joint entry ticket to all Historic Scotland's Orkney sights. Open Apr.–Sept., Mon.–Sat. 9:30–6, Sun. 2–6.*

㉓ To reach the **Unstan Chambered Tomb** from the Gurness Broch, simply follow the A966 south for about 10 miles to Finstown. This 5,000-year-old cairn containing a chambered tomb is midway between Stromness and Kirkwall: roughly 3.5 miles from each. Pottery that has been found within the tomb is now known as Unstan ware. *Tel. 0131/244–3101. Admission free. Open Apr.–Sept., Mon.–Sat. 9:30–6, Sun. 2–6; Oct.–Mar., Mon.–Sat. 9:30–4, Sun. 2–4.*

㉔ Take the A965 east, straight into **Kirkwall,** to reach **Earl Patrick's Palace,** built in 1607 and perhaps the best surviving example of Renaissance architecture in Scotland. The **Bishop's Palace** nearby dates from the 13th century, though its round tower was added in the 16th century. *Kirkwall. Admission to both: £1.20 adults, 75p children, or joint entry ticket to all Historic Scotland's Orkney sights. Both open Apr.–Sept., Mon.–Sat. 9:30–6, Sun. 2–6.*

Founded by Jarl Rognvald in 1137 and dedicated to his uncle St. Magnus, **St. Magnus Cathedral** in Kirkwall was built between 1137 and 1200; however, additional work was carried out during the following 300 years. The cathedral is still in use and contains some of the best examples of Norman architecture in Scotland. The ornamentation on some of the tombstones is particularly striking. *Open May–Aug., Mon.–Sat. 9–5; Sept.–Apr., Mon.–Sat. 9–1 and 2–5, open Sun. for services only.*

㉕ The remains of the 12th-century **Orphir Church,** Scotland's only circular medieval church (12th century), lie near the A964, 8 miles southwest of Kirkwall. *Tel. 0131/244–3101. Admission free. Open at all times.*

Travelers can reach **South Ronaldsay** via the A961 causeway heading **㉖** south. The island's first distinctive point is the **Italian Chapel,** located below the small village of St. Mary's. It was here, by the shore at Lambholm, in 1943, that Italian prisoners of war, using a Nissen hut, created a beautiful chapel from scrap metal and concrete. *Lambholm. Admission free. Open at all times.*

㉗ The **Orkney Wireless Museum,** located about 10 miles south on the A961 at St. Margaret's Hope, is a museum of wartime communications at Scapa Flow. Thousands of service men and women were stationed here and used the equipment displayed to protect the Home Fleet. The museum also contains many handsome 1930s wireless radios. *St. Margaret's Hope, 11 mi south of Kirkwall, tel. 01856/874272. Small admission charge. Open Apr.–Sept., daily 10–7.*

㉘ The **Scapa Flow Visitor Centre,** off the B9047 at Lyness on Hoy, has a growing collection of material portraying the strategic role of the sheltered anchorage of Scapa Flow (said to be Britain's best diving site) in two world wars. *Lyness, tel. 01856/79300. Admission: £1 adults, 50p children. Open May–Sept., Mon.–Fri. 9–4, Sat. 9–3:30, Sun. 9–6; Oct.–Apr., Mon.–Fri. 9–4.*

Off the Beaten Track

Tended by the Royal Society for the Protection of Birds, the **North Hoy Nature Reserve,** home to vast numbers of land birds and seabirds, is comprised of high ground and moor. Huge cliffs nearby include the Old Man of Hoy, a 450-foot sea stack. Visitors can visit the reserve any time by boat from Stromness. *Tel. 0185679/298. Admission free. Open at all times.*

The **Knap of Howar** is one of the oldest inhabited sites in Europe. Its two 5,000-year-old dwellings—which have yielded some unusual artifacts, such as whalebone mallets, a spatula, and stone grinders—can be found on the west side of Papa Westray, off the island of Westray. *West of Holland House, tel. 0131/244–2903. Admission free.*

Shopping

Neither Orkney nor Shetland is visited expressly for shopping. However, both have attracted high-quality crafts workers, and, in the United Kingdom, Shetland is almost synonymous with distinctive knitwear.

On Shetland, **Hjaltasteyn** handcrafted gems and jewelry (161 Commercial St., Lerwick) and **Shetland Silvercraft** jewelery and other small goods (workshop: Sound Side, Weisdale, and at J. G. Rae, Lerwick) are manufactured close to each other on the West Mainland. In Scalloway the **Shetland Woollen Company** is one of many operators with a selection of Shetland knitwear. Other places for knitwear and woolen goods in Lerwick include **Anderson & Co.** (The Shetland Warehouse, Commercial St.) and **Millers** (108–110 Commercial St., Lerwick). In Sandwick you'll find **Lawrence J. Smith.** In Lerwick **J. G. Rae Limited** (92 Commercial St.) stocks Shetland Silvercraft and gold and silver jewelry with Norse and Celtic motifs, while **Shetland Workshop Gallery** (Burns La.) has a good selection of pottery, knitwear, and crafts.

On Orkney, Kirkwall is the main shopping hub. Do not miss **Ola Gorrie at the Longship** (7–9 Broad St.). The shop designs gold and silver jewelry with Celtic and Norse themes, including a delightful representation of a dragon, originally drawn on the wall of the burial chamber at Maes Howe. Also in Kirkwall is **Ortak Jewelry** (10 Albert St.), which stocks a potpourri of gifts. At **Judith Glue** (25 Broad St.) visitors can purchase designer knitwear with traditional patterns, as well as watercolors, prints, and Orkney-made crafts. **Fursbreck Pottery** on Harray offers an unusual range of ceramics. **Joker Jewelry,** at the East School in Holm, makes eye-catching and whimsical clocks, brooches, and other jewelry using animal motifs (especially puffins).

Sports and Fitness

Bicycling The islands do not have much traffic, but the ever-present wind is a factor to be considered when making cycling plans. Bicycles can be rented on Shetland from **Puffins Pedals** (Mounthooly St., Lerwick, tel. 01595/5065) or **Eric Brown** (68 Commercial St., Lerwick, tel. 01595/3733); on Orkney from **Wishart's Shop** (Pier Head, Stromness, tel. 01856/850275), **Patterson's Cycle Hire** (Kirkwall, tel. 01856/873097), or the **Baby Linen Shop** (Stromness, tel. 01856/850255).

Diving Orkney, especially the former wartime anchorage of Scapa Flow, claims to have the best dive sites in Britain. Part of the attraction is the remains of the German navy, scuttled here in 1919. Consult the Orkney Tourist Board (*see* Important Addresses and Numbers in Essential Information, *above*) for information on the many boat rental firms offering diving charters. Shetland also has exceptional underwater visibility, perfect for viewing the treasure wrecks and abundant marine life. The Shetland Isles Tourism (*see* Important Addresses and Numbers in Essential Information, *above*), as well as the **Skolla Diving Centre** (Gulberwick, tel. 01595/4175), can provide the necessary information.

Fishing Sea angling is such a popular sport in Orkney that the local tourist board advises fishermen to book early. There are at least seven companies offering sea-angling boat rentals, with fishing rods available in most cases. Loch angling in Orkney is also popular; Loch of Harray and Loch of Stenness are the best-known spots. Contact the Orkney Tourist Board (*see* Important Addresses and Numbers in Essential Information, *above*) for information. Shetland, also renowned for sea angling, holds several competitions throughout the year. Contact the **Shetland Association of Sea Anglers** via the tourist-information center (*see* Important Addresses and Numbers in Essential Information, *above*) for further information.

Pony Trekking There is only one riding center on Shetland: **Broothom Ponies** (Braeside, Dunrossness, tel. 01950/60556). There are no riding centers on Orkney.

Water Sports There are good anchorages among Orkney's many islands. Sailboat-rental companies include **Scapa Flow Yacht Charters** (Stromness, tel. 01856/850587). There are also sailboats available from Shetland. Details may be obtained from the **Lerwick Boating Club,** which can be contacted through the Shetland Isles Tourism (*see* Important Addresses and Numbers in Essential Information, *above*).

Dining and Lodging

Dining

Category	Cost*
$$$$	over £25
$$$	£15–£25

$$	£10–£15
$	under £10

per person for a three-course meal, including VAT

Lodging

Category	Cost*
$$$$	over £120
$$$	£100–£120
$$	£80–£100
$	under £80

All prices are for a standard double room, including service, breakfast, and VAT.

Highly recommended hotels and restaurants are indicated by a star ★.

Orkney
Dining and Lodging
★

The Creel Restaurant. This seafront restaurant with a cottage-style interior serves local seafood (including lobster) as its specialty, prepared personally by the owner/chef. The Creel also has some modest accommodations: Three rooms are offered in an inexpensive bed-and-breakfast style. *Front Rd., St. Margaret's Hope, tel. 01856/83311. Reservations required. Dress: casual but neat. 3 rooms with bath. MC, V. Closed Jan. Hotel $; Restaurant $$*

Foveran Hotel. Surrounded by 34 acres of grounds and overlooking Scapa Flow, this warm hotel has an attractive light-wood, Scandinavian-style dining room and an open fire in its sitting room. The menu features Taste of Scotland, and the homemade soups, pâtés, and seafood have helped secure the restaurant's reputation as a very dependable place to eat. *St. Ola, Orkney KW15 1SF, tel. 01856/872389, fax 01856/876430. 8 rooms with bath. Facilities: restaurant, 2 lounges. MC, V. Hotel $; Restaurant $$*

Lodging

Polrudden Guest House. Quietly situated yet close to the town center and public parks, this modern guest house offers a high standard of accommodation for the price. Different-colored, matching curtains and quilt covers complement the cream-color rooms and pine furnishings. *Pickaquoy Rd., Kirkwall, tel. and fax 01856/874761. 7 rooms with shower. No credit cards. $*

Shetland
Dining and Lodging
★

Busta House. Probably the best hotel in Shetland, the Busta House dates in part from the 16th century and is surrounded by terraced grounds. Bedrooms are well furnished in traditional style—floral chintzes and antique furniture—and the 16th-century Long Room is a delightful place to sample the hotel's selection of malt whiskies while sitting beside a peat fire. The dining room features a Taste of Scotland menu, with Shetland salmon and lamb usually available. *Brae, Shetland ZE2 9QN, tel. 0180622/506, fax 0180622/588. Facilities: restaurant (dress smart casual), bar. 20 rooms with bath or shower. AE, DC, MC, V. Hotel $$; Restaurant $$$*

Bremner's Guest House. Comfortable and relaxed, this modern house boasts stunning sunset views which rival those anywhere in the United Kingdom. The rooms are clean and functional, much like the rest of this family-run bed-and-breakfast inn. *Barns, Newgord, Westing, Uyeasound, Unst, tel. 0195785/249. 2 twin rooms share 1 bath. No credit cards. $*

The Old Manse. The oldest inhabited building in Lerwick is now a friendly guest house, located on a quiet side street in the town center. The house dates from 1685 and was built for Lerwick's first minister. Furnishings are traditional, in keeping with the pleasantly aged feel of the house. Dinners are also traditional Scottish, mostly fish, beef, and stews. *9 Commercial St., Lerwick, tel. 01595/6301. 3 rooms, 1 with shower, 2 with bath shared between them. No credit cards. $*

Shetland Hotel. Modern and well appointed (a result of the oil boom in the area and the needs of high-flying oil executives), this hotel is located directly opposite the ferry terminal in Lerwick. The hotel is decorated in an attractive blend of peach, burgundy, and blue color schemes. The food ranges from rich and filling to rich and much too filling, with sometimes wildly clashing flavors. One entrée consists of a folded fillet of beef with Stilton cheese inside, coated in oatmeal and served with a rich red-currant sauce: enough of a meal to sink the Shetland ferry! *Holmsgarth Rd., Lerwick ZE1 0RB, tel. 01595/5515, fax 01595/5828. 66 rooms with bath. Facilities: 2 restaurants, 2 bars. AE, DC, MC, V. $*

The Arts and Nightlife

The Arts

Shetland has quite a strong cultural identity, thanks to its Scandinavian heritage. There are books of local dialect verse, a whole folklore contained in knitting patterns, and a strong tradition of fiddle-playing, for example. In the middle of the long winter, at the end of January, the Shetlanders celebrate their Viking culture with the **Up-Helly-Aa festival,** which involves much merrymaking, dressing up, and the burning of a replica of a Viking longship. The end of January, however, is hardly a peak time for tourists. The **Shetland Folk Festival,** held in late April/early May, and the **Shetland Accordian and Fiddle Festival,** in October, both attract large numbers of visitors. Shetland Isles Tourism (*see* Important Addresses and Numbers in Essential Information, *above*) can provide information on both festivals.

Orkney's cultural highlight is the **St. Magnus Festival,** a festival of music based in Kirkwall and usually held the third week in June (tel. 01856/872669 for details). Orkney also has an annual folk festival at the end of May. The Orkney Tourist Board (*see* Important Addresses and Numbers in Essential Information, *above*) carries a full events list. **The Pier Arts Centre** (Victoria St., tel. 01856/850209) focuses on artistic life in Stromness, with an eclectic display of paintings and sculptures and changing exhibitions, often by local artists.

Nightlife

No one goes to Orkney or Shetland for the nightlife, although bars and lounges with live entertainment are common in Lerwick on Shetland, thanks to the fluctuating population of oil workers and boat crews. The same is true in Kirkwall. Tourist-information centers (*see* Important Addresses and Numbers in Essential Information, *above*) will provide information on local concerts and summer programs for visitors.

Index

Abbey of Paisley, *136*
Abbeys
the Borders and the
Southwest, *160, 162,
163–164, 167–168*
Central Highlands, *241*
Fife and Angus,
191–192
Glasgow, *136*
the Northeast, *224*
Abbotsford House, *164*
Aberdeen, *202*
the arts, *231*
car rentals, *204*
children, attractions
for, *222–223*
climate, *5*
doctors, *203*
emergencies, *203*
free attractions, *221–222*
guided tours, *205*
hotels, *227–228*
nightlife, *231–232*
pharmacies, *203*
restaurants, *227–228*
Seaton Park, *211*
shopping, *224–225*
sightseeing, *205–211,
221–224*
sports, *226–227*
tourist information,
202–203
transportation, *203–205*
Aberdeen Art Gallery,
208
Aberdeen Maritime
Museum, *210, 222*
Aberdeen University,
206, 208
Aberdour, *197–198*
Aberfeldy, *250*
Aberlour, *221*
Achamore House
Gardens, *277*
Acharacle, *298*
Acheson House, *79*
Achiltibuie, *316*
Achnasheen, *325*
Aden Country Park,
223
Adventure
Playground, *222*
Aigas Dam Fish Lift,
300

Ailsa Craig, *269*
Alloway, *151*
Alva, *112*
American Express, *9*
Amhuinnsuidhe
Castle, *322*
Amusement parks, *222*
Andrew Carnegie
Birthplace Museum,
113
Angus. *See* Fife and
Angus
Angus Folk Museum,
193
An Lanntair Gallery,
320
Anstruther, *187–188,
198*
An Teallach, *316*
Applecross, *324*
Aquariums
Argyll and the Isles,
277
Fife and Angus, *194*
Arbigland Gardens,
168
Arbroath, *191–192, 200*
Arbroath Abbey,
191–192
Arbroath Cliffs
Nature Trail, *193*
Ardanaiseig House,
266
Ardgour, *298*
Ardkinglas Woodland
Garden, *266*
Ardlussa, *274*
Ardnamurchan, *298*
Ardvreck Castle, *316*
Ardwell House
Gardens, *170*
Argyll and the Isles,
261
the arts, *284*
children, attractions
for, *277*
doctors, *261*
emergencies, *261*
free attractions, *276*
guided tours, *262*
hotels, *280–283*
nightlife, *284*
pharmacies, *261*

restaurants, *266, 268,
269, 270, 271, 273, 276,
280–283*
shopping, *278–279*
sightseeing, *262–278*
sports, *279–280*
tourist information, *261*
transportation, *261–262*
Argyll's Ludging, *240*
Argyll Wildlife Park,
277
Arisaig, *299, 304*
Armadale Gardens, *319*
Arnol, *320*
Aros, *276, 281*
Aros Castle, *276*
Arran Island, *268–271,
279*
Arrochar Alps, *246*
Art galleries and
museums
Aberdeen, *208*
the Borders and the
Southwest, *165, 170*
Central Highlands, *238,
248*
Edinburgh, *81, 84*
Fife and Angus, *189,
191*
Glasgow, *131–132, 135,
136*
Great Glen, *300*
the Northeast, *219*
Northern Highlands,
320
Northern Isles, *338*
Arthur's Seat
(mountain), *80*
ATMs (automated
teller machines), *9*
Auchindrain Museum,
267
Auchterarder, *252, 256*
Auchterless, *228*
Aviemore, *293–294,
301, 305, 308*
Ayr, *140, 151*
Ayrshire and the
Clyde Coast, *150–154*

Baby-sitting services,
19
Bachelors' Club, *151,
154*
Baile an Or

(gold rush site), *324*
Balhousie Castle, *248*
Ballater, *213, 228*
Balloch, *256–257*
Ballygrant, *281*
Balmaha, *247*
Balmoral Castle, *214*
Balquhidder, *245*
Balranald Nature
Reserve, *323*
Balvenie (castle), *221*
Banchory, *213, 229*
Banff, *229*
Bannockburn
Heritage Centre, *237,
241*
Barnhill (Orwell
house), *274*
Barpa Langass
Chambered Cairn,
323
Barrack Street
Museum, *191*
Barra Island, *320, 323*
Barrie, Sir James, *193*
Baxters Visitors
Centre, *218–219*
Beaches
Great Glen, *302*
Northern Highlands,
322
Belhaven Bay, *117*
Bells Cherrybank
Gardens, *252*
Ben An, *245*
Benbecula Island, *319*
Ben Cruachan, *266*
Ben Eighe, *317*
Ben Ledi (mountain),
245
Ben Lomond, *246*
Ben More, *275*
Ben Nevis, *295, 303*
Berwick-Upon-Tweed,
163
Bicycling, *28–29*
Aberdeen, *226*
Argyll and the Isles,
279
the Borders and the
Southwest, *175*
Central Highlands,
254–255
Edinburgh, *91*

Bicycling (*continued*)
Fife and Angus, *196*
Glasgow, *140*
Great Glen, *302–303*
the Northeast, *226*
Northern Highlands, *326*
Northern Isles, *342*
off-road, *28–29*
tours, *29*
transporting, *29*
Biggar, *155, 171*
Biggar Puppet Theatre, *171*
Bishop's Palace, *340*
Blackness, *111*
Blackwaterfoot, *270–271*
Blair Castle, *250*
Blaven, *319*
Blowplain Open Farm, *171*
Boating and sailing
Argyll and the Isles, *280*
the Borders and the Southwest, *176*
Central Highlands, *255*
Glasgow, *141*
Northern Highlands, *327*
Northern Isles, *342*
Boat of Garten, *293*
Boat tours
Argyll and the Isles, *277*
Central Highlands, *236*
Glasgow, *125*
Bon-Accord Centre, *208*
Bonawe Iron Furnace, *263, 266*
the Borders and the Southwest, *157*
the arts, *179*
children, attractions for, *171*
emergencies, *158*
guided tours, *159*
hotels, *176–179*
nightlife, *179*
pharmacies, *158*
restaurants, *164, 170, 176–179*
shopping, *173–175*
sightseeing, *159–173*
sports, *175–176*
tourist information, *158*
transportation, *158–159*
Boreland, *176*

Borthwick Castle, *116*
Boswell, James, *80–81, 223, 296*
Botanic Gardens (Fife), *191*
Botanic Garden (Edinburgh), *84*
Botanic Gardens (Glasgow), *133*
Botanic Gardens (Logan), *170–171*
Bothwell Castle, *154*
Bothwell Ha, *239*
Bowhill, *165*
Bowhill Adventure Playground, *171*
Bowmore, *271*
Bracklinn Falls, *244*
Brae, *336*
Braeloine Interpretive Centre, *213*
Braemar, *7, 214, 229*
Braemar Castle, *214*
Braemar Royal Highland Gathering, *7, 214*
Brass Rubbing Centre, *85*
Brechin, *192, 200*
Bridge of Allan, *241, 244*
Brig o'Feuch, *213*
Brig o'Turk, *245, 257*
British Golf Museum, *187*
British Open Championship, *6*
Broadford, *319*
Broch of Mousa, *336*
Brochs (circular defensive towers), *322, 336, 340*
Brodick, *268–269, 281*
Brodick Castle and Country Park, *269–270*
Brogaig, *318*
Brough of Birsay, *340*
Broughty Castle, *191*
Bruce's Stone, *170*
Buckie, *219*
Buckie Drifter (maritime museum), *219*
Bullers of Buchan, *223*
Bunessan, *275*
Bunnahabhain Distillery, *273, 278*

The Burg (coastal area), *275*
Burns, Robert, *79, 83, 150, 151, 154, 167, 209*
Burns Memorial and Gardens, *151*
Burns Night dinners, *6*
Burra Firth, *337*
Burravoe, *337*
Burrell Collection, *135*
Business hours, *30–31*
Bus travel
Aberdeen, *204, 205*
Argyll and the Isles, *262*
the Borders and the Southwest, *158, 159*
Central Highlands, *236*
Edinburgh, *69, 70*
from England, *25*
Fife and Angus, *183–184*
Glasgow, *123–124, 125*
Great Glen, *287*
the Northeast, *204, 205*
Northern Highlands, *311, 312*
Northern Isles, *333*
passes, *15–16*
within Scotland, *26*
Butt of Lewis lighthouse, *320*

Cabaret, *284, 308–309*
Caerlaverock Castle, *167*
Caerlaverock National Nature Reserve, *167*
Cairngorm Mountains, *294*
Cairngorm Reindeer Centre, *294*
Cairngorm Whiskey Centre, *293–294*
Cairns. *See* Stone circles and cairns
Caithness Glass, *248, 254, 325*
Caledonian Canal, *296*
Callander, *244, 253, 257*
Callanish Standing Stones, *322*
Calton Burial Ground, *82*
Cambuskenneth Abbey, *241*
Camcorders, travel with, *12*
Camera Obscura, *73*

Cameras, travel with, *12*
Campbeltown, *278*
Camping, *17, 226*
Campus accommodations, *17*
Canna Island, *301*
Cannonball House, *73*
Canoeing, *226, 255*
Canongate Kirk, *79*
Canongate Tolbooth, *78*
Cape Wrath, *324*
Cardoness Castle, *169*
Car leasing, *14–15*
Carnasserie Castle, *268*
Carnegie, Andrew, *113*
Carradale, *278*
Carrbridge, *293*
Car rentals, *14–15. See also under cities and areas*
Carsaig Arches, *276*
Car travel, *27–28*
Aberdeen, *204, 205*
Argyll and the Isles, *261–262*
the Borders and the Southwest, *158, 159*
Central Highlands, *235, 236*
disabilities, travelers with, *19*
Edinburgh, *69–70*
Fife and Angus, *183*
gasoline, *27–28*
Glasgow, *123, 124*
Great Glen, *287*
leasing, *14–15*
the Northeast, *204, 205*
Northern Highlands, *311–312*
Northern Isles, *333*
rental, *14–15*
roadways, *27*
rules of the road, *27*
Cash machines, *9*
Casinos
Aberdeen, *232*
Edinburgh, *107*
Castle Campbell, *112*
Castle Douglas, *168*
Castle Fraser, *216*
Castle Kennedy Gardens, *170*
Castle Menzies, *250*
Castles

Argyll and the Isles, *263, 266, 267, 268, 269–270, 273, 274–275, 276, 277*
Ayrshire, *150–151, 154*
the Borders and the Southwest, *162, 167, 168–169, 170, 172*
Central Highlands, *238, 239–240, 244, 248–249, 250–251, 252*
Edinburgh, *72–73*
Fife and Angus, *184, 187, 188, 191, 192, 193, 194*
Great Glen, *289, 292–293, 295, 296, 298*
the Lothians, *112, 116, 117–118*
the Northeast, *211, 213, 214–215, 216, 221, 223–224*
Northern Highlands, *316, 318–319, 322, 323*
Northern Isles, *336, 337*
Castle Sween, *277*
Castle Tioram, *298*
Catacol, *270*
Cawdor Castle, *292*
Celtic Christian artifacts, *193*
Cemeteries
Edinburgh, *79, 82*
Glasgow, *127*
Islay, *272*
Central Highlands, 234–235
the arts, *259*
children, attractions for, *252*
doctors, *235*
emergencies, *235*
free attractions, *252*
guided tours, *236*
hotels, *256–258*
nightlife, *259*
pharmacies, *235*
restaurants, *240–241, 244, 245, 247, 251, 255–258*
shopping, *253–254*
sightseeing, *237–253*
sports, *254–255*
tourist information, *235*
transportation, *235–236*
Ceres, *198*
Chapel of St. Mary, *323*
Chapel of the Order of the Thistle, *77*

Chatelherault, *154*
Children, traveling with, *18–19. See also under cities and areas*
Chronology of Scotland, *40–43*
Churches
Aberdeen, *208, 209, 210–211*
the Borders and the Southwest, *167*
Central Highlands, *239, 248*
Clyde Valley, *154*
Edinburgh, *72, 73, 77*
Fife and Angus, *184, 194*
Glasgow, *127*
the Lothians, *113, 114, 117*
the Northeast, *218, 220*
Northern Highlands, *322, 323*
Northern Isles, *340*
Church of the Holy Rude, *239*
Cille Bharra, *323*
Cir Mhor, *270*
City Chambers (Edinburgh), *78*
City Chambers (Glasgow), *127*
Claig Castle, *273*
Clan Donald Centre *319*
Clan Macpherson Museum, *295*
Clan Menzies' Museum, *250*
Clatt, *215*
Clava Cairns, *289*
Claypotts Castle, *191*
Cleit Dubh, *324*
Clickhimin Broch, *336*
Climate, *5–6*
Clothing for the trip, *7*
Clyde Valley, *154–155*
Cockburnspath, *170*
Codona's Amusement Park, *222*
Coldstream, *159, 162*
Coldstream Museum, *162*
Colinton, *86*
Colleges and universities
Aberdeen, *206, 208, 210*
Glasgow, *132*
St. Andrews, *187*
Columba, St., *275*

Combined Operations Museum, *267*
Comlongon Castle, *167*
Commando Memorial, *295*
Commercial Union Insurance building, *209*
Comrie, *251*
Conic Hill, *247*
Connel, *281*
Connel Bridge, *263*
Consulates
Edinburgh, *67*
Coonzie Hoose *240*
Corgarff Castle, *214–215*
Corran, *298*
Corrie, *270*
Corrieshalloch Gorge, *313*
Corryvreckan, *274*
Costs of the trip, *10*
Craig, James, *81*
Craigellachie, *221*
Craighouse, *273*
Craigievar Castle, *216*
Craignure, *274*
Craigston Museum, *323*
Craigtoun Country Park, *194*
Crail, *187*
Crail Museum and Heritage Center, *187*
Cramond, *86*
Crarae Gardens, *267*
Crathes Castle, *211, 213*
Creetown, *169*
Crichton Castle, *116*
Crieff, *251, 253*
Crinan Canal, *267*
Crombie Country Park, *191*
Crombie Woollen Mill, *221*
Crosses, carved, *272*
Cruachan Dam Power Station, *266*
Cuillin Mountains, *318*
Cullen, *219–220*
Culloden Moor, *289*
Culross, *112–113*
Culzean Castle and Country Park, *151*
Cupar, *189*
Currency of Scotland, *9*
Customs, *10–11*

Dairsie, *194*
Dalbeattie, *168, 176*
Dalcross, *305*
Dalkeith Park, *85*
Dalmeny House, *109*
Dance
Aberdeen, *231*
Edinburgh, *107*
Glasgow, *149*
Darnaway Farm Visitor Centre, *300*
Darrow House, *238*
David Livingstone Centre, *154*
Dean Castle and Country Park, *154*
Deep Sea World, *85*
Denny, *257*
Dervaig, *276, 279, 281, 284*
Destitution Road, *316*
Dick Institute, *154*
Dirleton Castle, *118*
Disabilities, hints for travelers with, *19–20*
Discos
in Aberdeen, *232*
in Arbroath, *200*
in Brechin, *200*
in Dundee, *200*
in Edinburgh, *108*
in the Great Glen, *308*
Distilleries
Argyll and the Isles, *272, 273, 278*
Central Highlands, *249, 251, 253*
Edinburgh, *73*
the Northeast, *216, 220–221*
Dollar, *112*
Doonies Farm, *222*
Dornoch, *325*
Doune, *244*
Drumbeg loop, *324*
Drum Castle, *211*
Drumlanrig Castle, *172*
Drummond Castle, *252*
Drumnadrochit, *296, 305*
Drybridge, *229–230*
Dryburgh Abbey, *163*
Drymen, *247*
Duart Castle, *274, 275*
Duddingston, *86*
Dufftown, *220–221*
Dulsie Bridge, *292*
Dumbarton, *150*
Dumfries, *167, 174, 180*
Dumyat, *252*

Dunadd, *267*

Dun an Sticar, *322*

Dunbar, *117*

Dunblane, *244*

Duncan Ban
Macintyre
Monument, *266, 277*

Dun Carloway, *322*

Duncryne Hill, *253*

Dundee, *182*
the arts, *199–200*
hotels, *198*
nightlife, *200*
restaurants, *198*
shopping, *195–196*
sightseeing, *189, 191*
sports, *197*
tourist information, *182*

Dundonnell, *316–317, 328*

Dunfermline, *113*

Dunfermline Abbey
and Palace, *113*

Dumferline District
Museum, *113*

Dunkeld, *249, 253*

Dunoon, *281–282*

Dunskey Castle, *170*

Dunstaffnage Castle, *263*

Dunvegan Castle, *318–319*

Duthie Park and
Winter Gardens, *222*

Duties, *10–11*

Earl Patrick's Palace, *340*

Earl's Palace, *340*

Earth Pillars, *219*

Eas Coul Aulin
waterfall, *324–325*

Easdale Island, *268*

Eastwood Butterfly
Kingdom, *134–135*

Edinburgh, *65–66*
the arts, *105–107*
Calton Hill, *82–83*
Canongate, *78*
Charlotte Square, *83*
children, attractions
for, *85–86*
climate, *6*
Colinton, *86*
consulates, *67*
Cramond, *86*
Dalkeith Park, *86*
Duddingston, *85*
emergencies, *67*
excursions, *109–118*

festivals, *7, 105–106*
free attractions, *84*
George Street, *88*
Grassmarket, *76, 89*
guided tours, *70–71*
Holyrood Park, *80*
hospital, *67*
hotels, *100–105*
Leith, *86*
lost and found, *67*
map sellers, *70*
money-changing
services, *67*
Moray Place, *84*
The Mound (street), *81*
New Town, *80–84*
nightlife, *107–108*
Old Town, *72–73, 76–80*
Pentlands, the, *86*
pharmacies, *67*
post offices, *67*
Princes Street, *81–82, 87–88*
restaurants, *73, 76, 78, 79, 82, 83, 84, 92–99*
Royal Mile, *73, 88–89*
St. Andrew Square, *83*
shopping, *82, 87–90*
sightseeing, *71–86*
sports, *91–92*
Stafford Street, *89*
Stockbridge, *89*
Swanston, *86*
tourist information, *66–67*
transportation in, *69–70*
transportation to, *67–69*
travel agencies, *67*
Upper Bow, *73, 76*
The Vennel (street), *76*
Victoria Street, *76, 89*
West Bow, *89*
William Street, *89*

Edinburgh Butterfly
and Insect World, *85*

Edinburgh Castle, *72–73*

Edinburgh Crystal
Visitor Centre, *114*

Edinburgh Festival
Fringe, *106*

Edinburgh Film
Festival, *106*

Edinburgh Folk
Festival, *106*

Edinburgh
International
Festival, *7, 105–106*

Edinburgh Military
Tattoo, *7, 106*

Edinburgh Zoo, *86*

Edradour Distillery, *249*

Edzell Castle, *192*

Egyptian Halls, *131*

Eigg Island, *299, 301*

Elcho Castle, *248–249*

Elderhostel program, *20–21*

Elgin, *218, 225*

Elgol, *319*

Emergencies
Aberdeen and the
Northeast, *203*
Argyll and the Isles, *261*
Around the Glen, *286*
Borders and the
Southwest, *158*
Central Highlands, *235*
Edinburgh and the
Lothians, *67*
Fife and Angus, *182*
Glasgow, *121*
Great Glen, *286*
Northern Highlands, *310*
Northern Isles, *332*

Eriskay Island, *320*

Erskine Marykirk, *239*

Esha Ness, *337*

Fair Maid's House, *248*

Fairways Heavy
Horse Centre, *252*

Falkland, *188*

Falkland Palace, *188*

Falls of Dochart, *251*

Falls of Foyers, *297*

Falls of Lora, *263*

Falls of Rogie, *313*

Farmhouse and
crofting holidays, *33*

Farms
Aberdeen, *222*
the Borders and the
Southwest, *171*
Great Glen, *300*

Fergusson Gallery, *248*

Ferry service, *26–27*
Aberdeen, *204*
Argyll and the Isles, *262*
Borders and the
Southwest, *158*
Great Glen, *301*

Northern Highlands, *311*

Northern Isles, *324*

Feshiebridge, *294*

Festivals and
seasonal events, *6–7, 105–106*

Fife and Angus, *182*
the arts, *199–200*
children, attractions
for, *194*
doctors, *183*
emergencies, *182*
free attractions, *193–194*
guided tours, *184*
hotels, *197–199*
nightlife, *200*
pharmacies, *183*
restaurants, *189, 197–199*
shopping, *195–196*
sightseeing, *184–195*
sports, *196–197*
tourist information, *182*
transportation, *183–184*

Fife Folk Museum, *189*

Film
Aberdeen, *231*
Dundee, *200*
Edinburgh, *107*
Glasgow, *149*
Oban, *284*

Findochty, *219*

Finlarig Castle, *251*

Fionnphort, *275*

Firth of Lorne, *263*

Fishing
Argyll and the Isles, *279*
the Borders and the
Southwest, *175*
Central Highlands, *255*
Fife and Angus, *196*
Glasgow, *140*
Great Glen, *303*
the Northeast, *226*
Northern Highlands, *326*
Northern Isles, *342*

Fishnish, *274*

Flight insurance, *13*

Flodden Wall, *76*

Floors Castle, *162*

Fochabers, *218–219, 225*

Fochabers Folk
Museum, *219*

Fordyce, *220, 230*

Forfar, *198–199*

Fort Augustus, *296*

Fort Charlotte, *334*

Fort George, *289, 292*

Forth bridges, *109*

Fortingall yew, *251*

Fort William, *286*

emergencies, *286*

guided tours, *288*

hotels, *305*

restaurants, *305*

shopping, *301–302*

sightseeing, *297–298*

sports, *303*

tourist information, *286*

transportation, *287*

Fossil tree, *275*

Foyers, *297*

Fyvie Castle, *223–224*

Gaelic language, *12–13*

Gairloch, *317*

Gairloch Heritage
Museum, *317*

Galashiels, *164, 177*

Galloway. *See* the
Borders and the
Southwest

Galloway Forest
Park, *169*

Ganavan Sands
Leisure Centre, *277*

Gardens

Aberdeen, *209*

Argyll and the Isles,
266, 267, 277

the Borders and the
Southwest, *164, 168,
170–171*

Central Highlands, *252*

Edinburgh, *84*

Fife and Angus, *191*

Glasgow, *130, 133*

the Northeast, *215, 223*

Northern Highlands,
316–317, 319, 320

Gardner's Warehouse,
131

Garrison Cottage,
246–247

Garvamore Bridge, *295*

Gatehouse-of-Fleet,
169, 174, 177

Gay and lesbian
travelers, hints for, *21*

Gem Rock Museum,
169

Georgian House, *83*

Gifford, *117*

Gilbert Scott
Building, *132*

Gladstone's Land
(tenement), *76*

Glamis, *193*

Glamis Castle, *193*

Glasgow, *120–121*

Argyle Street, *137*

the arts, *148–149*

The Barras (market),
130, 138

Blythswood Square,
138–139

Buchanan Street,
137–138

Byres Road, *139*

car rentals, *122*

children, attractions
for, *134–135*

climate, *6*

dentists, *122*

emergencies, *121*

excursions, *150–155*

festivals, *6*

free attractions, *134*

George Square, *126–127*

Glasgow Cross, *127*

Glasgow Green, *130*

guided tours, *125*

hospitals, *121*

hotels, *145–148*

Kelvingrove Park, *132*

Medieval Glasgow,
126–127, 130–131

Merchant City, *130, 138*

nightlife, *149*

Paisley, *136*

pharmacies, *122*

Pollok Country Park,
135–136

post office, *122*

restaurants, *134,
141–145*

Royal Exchange
Square, *131*

St. Enoch Square, *137*

shopping, *136–140*

sightseeing, *126–136*

sports, *140–141*

subway system, *124*

tourist information, *121*

transportation in,
124–125

transportation to,
122–124

Victoria Park, *135*

Virginia Court, *131*

West End, *131–134, 139*

West Regent Street,
138–139

Glasgow Cathedral,
127

Glasgow Mayfest, *6*

Glasgow School of
Art, *134*

Glasgow Zoo, *135*

Glass-making, *114,
248, 253, 254, 278, 325*

Gleann Seilisdeir, *276*

Glen Affric, *301*

Glen Brittle, *319*

Glenbuchat Castle, *215*

Glen Cannich, *301*

Glenfarg, *257*

Glenfiddich malt
whisky, *220–221*

Glenfinnan, *299–300*

Glengarry Castle, *295*

Glenlivet, *230*

Glen Lyon, *253*

Glen More Forest
Park, *294*

Glen Muick, *213*

Glenrothes, *188*

Glenruthven Weaving
Mill, *252*

Glens of Angus, *195*

Glen Torridon, *317*

Glen Trool, *169–170*

Glenturret Distillery,
251

Gloup, *337*

Gloup Fisherman's
Memorial, *337*

Goat Fell (peak), *268*

Gold-panning, *324*

Golf, *57–58*

Aberdeen, *59, 226*

Argyll and the Isles,
279

Ayrshire and the Clyde
Coast, *58–59*

the Borders and the
Southwest, *175*

British Open
Championship, *6*

Central Highlands, *255*

courses, *60–63, 91–92*

Dornoch Firth, *60*

East Lothian, *59*

Edinburgh, *91–92*

Fife and Angus, *59,
187, 196*

Glasgow, *140*

Great Glen, *303*

the Lothians, *118*

Moray Coast, *60*

the Northeast, *226*

Northern Highlands,
326

Perthshire, *59*

St. Andrews, *187, 196*

Speyside, *59–60*

Stewartry, *58*

Golspie, *325*

Gordon District's
Castle Trail, *215*

Government tourist
offices, *2*

Grampian Transport
Museum, *216*

Grangemouth
Refinery, *111*

Grantown-on-Spey,
293, 302

Great Glen, *286*

the arts, *307*

children, attractions
for, *300*

emergencies, *286*

free attractions, *300*

guided tours, *288*

hospitals, *286*

hotels, *304–307*

nightlife, *307–308*

pharmacies, *286–287*

restaurants, *293, 295,
304–307*

shopping, *301–302*

sightseeing, *288–301*

sports, *302–303*

tourist information, *286*

transportation, *287*

Gretna, *165, 167*

Grey Corries, *295*

Greyfriars Bobby
(sculpture), *77*

Grey Mare's Tail
(waterfall), *172*

Gruinard Bay, *316*

Guildhall (Stirling), *239*

Gullane (golf course),
118

Gurness Broch, *340*

Gutcher, *337*

Haddington, *118*

Haddo House, *223*

Haggs Castle, *135*

Halliwell's House, *165*

Hamilton
Mausoleum, *154*

Hamilton Old Parish
Church, *154*

Harestanes Visitor
Centre, *161*

Haroldswick, *337*

Harris, Isle of, *319, 328*

Hawick, *165*

Hawick Museum, *165*

Hazlehead Park and
Zoo, *222*

Health clubs
Aberdeen, *226*
the Borders and the
Southwest, *175*
Fife and Angus,
196–197
Glasgow, *140–141*
Health insurance, *13*
Helicopter tours, *125*
Hermitage Castle,
161, 172
**Highland Folk
Museum,** *294–295*
Hiking
Central Highlands, *255*
Great Glen, *303*
Hillend Ski Centre, *85*
Hill of Tarvit House,
189
Hirsel (estate), *162*
**His Majesty's
Theatre,** *208–209, 231*
Home exchanges, *32*
Hopetoun House, *109,
111*
Horseback riding. *See
also* Pony trekking
the Borders and the
Southwest, *175–176*
Central Highlands, *255*
Hotels, *32–33. See also
under cities and areas*
children,
accommodations for,
18–19
older travelers,
accommodations for, *21*
tipping, *30*
House of Dun, *192*
House of the Binns,
111
Houses, historic
Aberdeen, *208, 210*
Argyll and the Isles,
266
Ayrshire, *151, 154*
the Borders and the
Southwest, *161, 163,
164, 172*
Central Highlands, *238,
239*
Edinburgh *73, 76, 78,
79, 82, 83*
Fife and Angus, *189,
192*
Glasgow, *127, 131, 134,
135–136*
the Lothians, *109, 111,
118*
the Northeast, *223*

Northern Highlands,
318, 320
**Hunterian Art
Gallery,** *132*
Hunterian Museum,
132
Huntingtower Castle,
248
Huntly House, *78*
Hutcheson's Hall,
130

Inchcailloch, *247*
Inchmahome Priory,
246
**Industrial heritage
sites**
Clyde Valley, *154–155*
Paisley, *136*
Insurance, *13–14*
car, *15*
**International Jazz
Festival,** *107*
Inveraray, *266–267, 278*
Inveraray Castle, *267*
Inveraray Jail, *267, 278*
Inverewe Gardens,
316–317
**Inverfarigaig Forest
Centre,** *297*
Invergarry, *306*
Inverkirkaig, *325*
Inverness, *286*
the arts, *307*
emergencies, *286*
guided tours, *288*
hotels, *306–307*
nightlife, *307–308*
restaurants, *306*
shopping, *302*
sightseeing, *289, 301*
sports, *303*
tourist information, *286*
transportation, *287*
**Inverness Museum
and Art Gallery,** *300*
**Inverpolly National
Nature Reserve,** *316*
Inversnaid, *247*
Iona Community, *275*
Iona Island, *275, 279*
**Iron-smelting
industry,** *263, 266*
Island of Gigha, *277*
Islay Island, *271–273,
278*
Islay Woollen Mill,
272, 278
**Isle of Arran Heritage
Museum,** *269*

Isle of Whithorn, *173*
Italian Chapel, *340*
Itineraries, *34–37*

Jails, *267, 325*
Jarlshof, *336*
Jedburgh, *159,
160–161, 177*
Jedburgh Abbey, *160*
Jenners (department
store), *82*
Jogging, *140*
John Knox House, *78*
**John Muir Country
Park,** *117*
Johnson, Samuel,
80–81, 223, 296
Jones, John Paul, *168*
Jura House, *273*
Jura Island, *273–274*

Keen of Hamar, *337*
**Kelburn Castle and
Country Park,**
150–151
Kellie Castle, *188*
Kelso, *161–162, 177–178*
Kelso Abbey, *162*
Kelvingrove (art
museum), *131–132*
Kenmore, *250*
Kentallen, *282*
Kergord, *336*
**Kerr's Miniature
Railway** (Arbroath),
194
Kibble Palace, *133*
Kilchoman, *271*
Kilchrenan, *282*
Kilchurn Castle, *266*
Kildalton Cross, *272*
Kildrummy Castle, *215*
**Killiecrankie Visitor
Centre,** *249*
Killin, *251*
**Kilmuir Croft
Museum,** *318*
Kilnave, *272*
Kilt Rock, *318*
Kincardine O'Neill, *213*
Kinclaven, *257*
King James Tower, *80*
King's College, *210*
King's Old Building,
240
Kingussie, *294–295, 307*
Kinloch Rannoch, *257*
Kinuachdrach, *274*
Kirkcudbright, *169*

**Kirk of the
Greyfriars,** *77*
Kirkwall, *340*
Kirriemuir, *193*
Kishorn, *317*
Kisimul Castle, *323*
Kitchener Memorial,
340
Knap of Howar, *341*
Knipoch, *282*
Knockan, *313, 316*
Kylesku, *328*

Ladies' Rock, *239*
**Lady Rowena Steam
Launch,** *277*
Lady Stair's House, *76*
Lagg, *269, 274*
Laggan, *295*
Lake of Menteith, *246*
Lamlash, *269*
Lanark, *154*
**Landmark Visitor
Centre,** *293*
Land o'Burns Centre,
151
Language concerns,
12–13
Laphroaig distillery,
272, 278
Laptop computers,
travel with, *12*
Larbert, *254*
Lead mining, *172*
Lealt, *274*
Leith, *86*
Lennoxlove House, *118*
Lerwick, *333, 334*
Leuchars, *194*
**Lewis and Harris, Isle
of,** *319, 320, 322, 328*
Liathach, *317*
Libraries
the Borders and the
Southwest, *164*
Edinburgh, *76–77*
Glasgow, *131, 133*
Lighthouses, *320, 324*
Linlithgow Palace, *111*
Linn of Dee, *214*
Linn of Tummel, *249*
Little Cross (Elgin),
218
**Little Marco's
Leisure Centre,** *85*
**Little Wheels
Museum,** *170*
Livingston, David, *154*
Local Hero (film), *223*
Loch Achray, *245*

Loch Ailort, *299*
Loch an Eilean, *294*
Loch Ard, *246*
Loch Arklet, *246*
Loch Awe, *266*
Loch Broom, *313*
Lochcarron, *317, 325*
Loch Chon, *246*
Loch Cill Chriosd, *319*
Loch Doune, *245*
Loch Druidibeg
  National Nature
  Reserve, *323*
Loch Earn, *251*
Lochearnhead, *251*
Loch Etive, *263*
Loch Finlaggan, *273*
Loch Garten Nature
  Reserve, *293*
Loch Gilp, *267*
Lochgilphead, *267*
Loch Gruinart, *272*
Loch Hourn, *301*
Lochinch Castle, *170*
Lochindorb Castle,
  292–293
Loch Insh, *294*
Lochinver, *316, 324,*
  325
Loch Katrine, *246*
Loch Kirkaig, *316*
Loch Laggan, *295*
Loch Leven, *188–189*
Loch Linnhe, *298*
Loch Lomond, *237*
  cruises, *236, 247*
  shopping, *253–254*
  sightseeing, *246–247*
Loch Maree, *317*
Loch Moidart, *298*
Loch Morar, *299*
Loch nan Uamh, *299*
Loch Ness, *286,*
  296–297
Loch Nevis, *301*
Loch of the Lowes,
  252
Loch Rannoch, *250*
Lochranza, *270*
Lochranza Castle,
  270
Loch Shiel, *298*
Loch Shieldaig, *317*
Loch Sunart, *298*
Loch Tarbet, *274*
Loch Tarff, *297*
Loch Venachar, *245*
Loch Voil, *245*
Logan Botanic
  Gardens, *170–171*

the Lothians
  golf, *118*
  Midlothian and East
    Lothian, *113–118*
  restaurants, *111, 114,*
    117
  West Lothian and the
    Forth Valley, *109–113*
Lower Largo, *188*
Luggage
  airline rules on, *7–8*
  insurance for, *13*
Luib, *318*

Macdonald, Flora, *323*
MacGregor, Rob Roy,
  244
the Machars, *173*
Machir Bay, *271*
Machrie, *270*
Machrie Moor Stone
  Circles, *270*
Mackintosh, Charles
  Rennie, *134*
McLehose, Agnes, *79*
Maclellan's Castle, *169*
McManus Galleries,
  189, 191
Maes Howe (burial
  mound), *338*
Mail, *30*
Mallaig, *299, 319*
Manderston House,
  172
Marischal College,
  206, 208
Marischal Museum,
  222
Mar's Wark, *240*
Martyrs Monument,
  239
Marwick Head
  Nature Reserve, *340*
Mary, Queen of Scots,
  80, 111, 116, 118, 160,
  161, 188
Mary, Queen of Scots,
  House, *161*
Mauchline, *154*
Mavis Grind, *337*
Medical services. *See*
  emergencies *under*
  cities and areas
Meigle, *193*
Mellerstain House, *163*
Melrose, *163–164, 178*
Melrose Abbey,
  163–164
Melrose Station, *164*

Mercat Cross
  (Aberdeen), *209*
Mercat Cross
  (Edinburgh), *77*
Merchant's House, *131*
Mill Glen, *112*
Mill of Towie, *220*
Mills Observatory,
  193–194
Mint (Coonzie Hoose),
  240
Mitchell Library, *133*
Moffat, *174, 178*
Monadhliath
  Mountains, *294*
Money, *8–10*
Mons Meg (cannon),
  72–73
Montrose, *192*
Mortlach Church, *221*
Muck Island, *301*
Muckle Flugga, *338*
Muir, John, *117*
Muirfield (golf course),
  118
Mull, Isle of, *274–276,*
  279, 284, 301
Mull of Galloway, *171*
Mull of Kintyre, *278*
Muness Castle, *337*
Mungo, St., *127*
Museum nan Eilean,
  320
Museum of
  Antiquities, *84*
Museum of
  Childhood, *78, 85*
Museum of
  Education, *135*
Museum of Farming
  Life, *223*
Museum of Islay Life,
  271
Museum of Scottish
  Lead Mining, *172*
Museum of
  Transport, *132*
Museums. *See also*
  Art galleries and
  museums
  Aberdeen, *208, 210,*
    219, 222
  Argyll and the Isles,
    267, 269, 271
  Ayrshire, *151, 154*
  the Borders and the
    Southwest, *162, 164,*
    165, 167, 169, 170, 172,
    173

Central Highlands, *238,*
  248, 250
Clyde Valley, *155*
Edinburgh, *72, 76, 77,*
  78, 84, 85
Fife and Angus,
  187–188, 189, 191, 192,
  193
Glasgow, *127, 130,*
  131–132, 133, 135, 136
Great Glen, *289, 292,*
  294–295, 298
the Lothians, *113, 116*
the Northeast, *216,*
  219, 222
Northern Highlands,
  317, 318, 320, 322, 323
Northern Isles, *334,*
  336, 338, 341
Music, classical
  Aberdeen, *231*
  Dundee, *200*
  Edinburgh, *107*
  Glasgow, *148*
Music, popular
  Aberdeen, *232*
  Argyll and the Isles,
    284
  Central Highlands, *259*
  Edinburgh, *107, 108*
  Fife and Angus, *200*
  Great Glen, *307–308*

Nairn, *292, 302*
Nairn Fishertown
  Museum, *292*
National Gallery of
  Scotland, *81*
National Library of
  Scotland, *76–77*
National Monument,
  82–83
Nature Conservancy
  Council, *317*
Nature reserves
  Argyll and the Isles,
    277
  the Borders and the
    Southwest, *167*
  Central Highlands, *252*
  Great Glen, *293*
  Northern Highlands,
    316, 317, 323
  Northern Isles, *337,*
    340, 341
Necropolis (Glasgow),
  127
Nelson Monument, *83*
Netherbow Arts
  Centre, *78*

Netherbow Port, 78
Nethy Bridge, 293
New Lanark, 154–155
New Luce, 170
Newtonferry, 322
Newtongrange, 116
Newtonmore, 295
Newton Stewart, 169
New Town Conservation Centre, 84
Norse artifacts, 336
North Berwick, 118
Northeast, 202. See also Aberdeen
guided tours, 205
hotels, 227–230
restaurants, 213, 215, 220, 221, 227–230
Royal Deeside, 211–216, 225
shopping, 225
sightseeing, 211–224
sports, 226–227
tourist information, 203
transportation, 203–205
Northeast Scotland Agricultural Heritage Centre, 223
Northern Highlands, 310
the arts, 329
children, attractions for, 324
emergencies, 310
guided tours, 312
hotels, 327–329
nightlife, 330
pharmacies, 310
restaurants, 313, 317, 320, 327–329
shopping, 325
sightseeing, 312–325
sports, 326–327
tourist information, 310
transportation, 311–312
Northern Isles. See Orkney Islands; Shetland Islands
North Hoy Nature Reserve, 341
North Uist Island, 319, 322–323

Oa region, 272
Oban, 263, 276, 278, 279, 282–283, 284
Ochil Hills, 112
Ochil Hills Woodland Park, 112

Official Loch Ness Monster Exhibition, 296
Old Byre, 276
Old Deer, 230
Older travelers, hints for, 20–21
Old Haa, 337
Old Man of Storr (pinnacle), 318, 324
Old Skye Crofter's House, 318
Old Stirling Bridge, 241
Opera
Aberdeen, 231
Glasgow, 149
Orkney Islands, 332
the arts, 344
climate, 6
discount pass, 332
doctors, 332
emergencies, 332
ferry service, 27
guided tours, 334
hotels, 343
nightlife, 344
pharmacies, 332
restaurants, 342–343
shopping, 341–342
sightseeing, 338–341
sports, 342
tourist information, 332
transportation, 332–334
Orkney Wireless Museum, 341
Ormaclete Castle, 323
Ormiston Institute, 164
Orphir Church, 340
Orwell, George, 274
Our Lady of the Isles (statue), 323
Outer Hebrides
shopping, 326
sightseeing, 319–324
tourist information, 310
transportation, 311–313
Outlook Tower, 73

Package deals, 3–4
Paisley, 136
Paisley Museum and Art Gallery, 136
Palace of Holyroodhouse, 79–80
Palaces
Central Highlands, 239, 249
Edinburgh, 79–80
Fife and Angus, 188

Glasgow, 133
the Lothians, 111, 113
Northern Isles, 340
Parallel Roads of Glen Roy, 295
Parks, country and forest
Argyll and the Isles, 269–270
Ayrshire, 151
the Borders and the Southwest, 169
Central Highlands, 246
Fife and Angus, 191, 194
Glasgow, 135–136
Great Glen, 294
the Lothians, 117
the Northeast, 223
Parliament House, 77
Pass of Killiecrankie, 250
Pass of Leny, 244–245
Passports, 10
Peebles, 174, 178–179
Penicuik, 114
Pennan, 223
the Pentlands, 86
People's Palace, 130
Perth, 234
the arts, 259
festivals, 6
hotels, 258
nightlife, 259
restaurants, 258
shopping, 254
sightseeing, 247–249
Perth Art Gallery and Museum, 248
Perth Festival of the Arts, 6
Peter Anderson Woollen Mill, 164
Peter Anson Gallery, 219
Photographers, tips for, 12
Picture Gallery, 80
Pier Arts Centre, 338
Pitlochry, 249, 259
Pitlochry Dam and Fish Ladder, 249
Pitlochry Festival Theatre, 259
Pitmedden Garden, 223
Pittenweem, 188
Planetariums and observatories
Dundee, 193–194

Plane travel
Aberdeen, 203–204
Argyll and the Isles, 261
the Borders and the Southwest, 158
Central Highlands, 235
with children, 18
Edinburgh, 67–69
from England, 24
Fife and Angus, 183
Glasgow, 122–123
Great Glen, 287
insurance for, 13–14
luggage rules, 7–8
from North America, 22–24
Northern Highlands, 311, 312
Northern Isles, 332–333
within Scotland, 25
Pluscarden Abbey, 224
Pollok Country Park, 135–136
Pollok House, 135–136
Pony trekking,
Argyll and the Isles, 279–280
Northern Highlands, 326–327
Northern Isles, 342
Port Appin, 283
Port Askaig, 283
Port Charlotte, 271
Port Ellen, 272
Portnahaven, 271
Portpatrick, 170
Portree, 318
Portsoy, 220, 225
Port Wemyss, 271
Port William, 179
Potarch, 213
Pound sterling, 9
Priorwood Gardens, 164
Provand's Lordship (house), 127
Provost Ross's House, 210
Provost Skene's House, 208

Queen Elizabeth Forest Park Visitor Centre, 246
Queen Elizabeth 2 (ship), 24
Quiraing, 318
Quothquan, 179

Rail passes, *15–16, 26*
Railroads
  Arbroath, *194*
  Great Glen, *293*
Rassal Ash Wood, *317*
Red Castle, *194*
Regent Arch, *82*
Regimental Museum
  of the Black Watch,
  248
Regimental Museum
  of the Queen's Own
  Highlanders, *289, 292*
Regimental Museum
  of the Royal
  Highland Fusiliers,
  133
Register House, *82*
Reindeer Centre, *294*
Rest and Be Thankful
  (pass), *266*
Restaurants, *30, 31–32.*
  See also under cities
  and areas
Rhenigidale, *322*
Rhinns of Islay, *271*
Rhum Island, *299, 301*
Ring of Brogar, *338*
River Carron, *111*
Robert Burns Centre,
  167
Robert Burns
  Monument, *83*
Robert Gordon's
  University, *208*
Robert Smail's
  Printing Works, *171*
Robert the Bruce, *270*
Rob Roy and
  Trossachs Visitor
  Centre, *244*
Rockcliffe, *168*
Rodel, *322*
Ronas Hill, *337*
Rosemount
  Celebration Centre,
  222
Rosslyn Chapel, *114*
Ross of Mull, *275*
Round Tower
  (Brechin), *192*
Rowardennan, *247*
Roxburgh, *162*
Roxburghe Castle, *162*
Royal & Ancient Golf
  Club of St. Andrews,
  187
Royal Bank of
  Scotland
  headquarters, *83*

Royal Botanic
  Garden, *84, 170*
Royal Burgh of
  Stirling Visitor
  Centre, *239*
Royal Deeside,
  211–216, 225
Royal Exchange, *131*
Royal Museum of
  Scotland, *77*
Royal Scottish
  Academy, *81*
Roybridge, *295*
RRS *Discovery*, *189*
Rugby, *92*
Ruthven Barracks, *294*
Ruthwell Church and
  Cross, *167*

Sailing. *See* Boating
  and sailing
St. Andrews
  the arts, *199*
  golf, *187, 196*
  hotels, *199*
  nightlife, *200*
  restaurants, *199*
  shopping, *195*
  sightseeing, *184, 187*
  sports, *196*
  tourist information, *182*
St. Andrews Castle,
  184, 187
St. Andrew's
  University, *187*
St. Boswells, *179*
St. Clement's Church,
  322
St. Fillans, *251*
St. Giles Church, *218*
St. Giles's Cathedral,
  77
St. John's Kirk, *248*
St. Machar's
  Cathedral, *210–211*
St. Magnus
  Cathedral, *340*
St. Margaret's Chapel,
  72
St. Monans, *188*
St. Nicholas Centre,
  208
St. Nicholas Kirk, *209*
St. Ninian's Isle, *336*
St. Rule's Church, *184*
Salen, *298*
Salmon industry, *219*
Sandend, *230*
Sandyhills, *168*
Sannox, *270*

Satrosphere (museum),
  222
Savings Bank
  Museum, *167*
Scalloway Castle, *336*
Scapa Flow Visitor
  Centre, *341*
Scone Palace, *249*
Scotch Whisky
  Heritage Centre, *73*
Scots language, *12–13*
Scott, Sir Walter,
  81–82, 83, 163, 164, 234
Scottish Deer Centre,
  194
Scottish Fisheries
  Museum, *187–188*
Scottish Mining
  Museum, *116*
Scottish National
  Gallery of Modern
  Art, *84*
Scottish National
  Portrait Gallery, *84*
Scottish National
  War Memorial, *72*
Scottish Record
  Office, *84*
Scottish Stock
  Exchange, *131*
Scottish United
  Services Museum,
  72
Scott Monument,
  81–82
Scott's View, *163*
Scourie, *328*
Scuba diving, *342*
Sea Life Centre
  (Oban), *277*
Sea Life Centre (St.
  Andrews), *194*
Seil Island, *268*
Selkirk, *165, 179*
Shawbost School
  Museum, *320, 322*
Shetland Croft House
  Museum, *336*
Shetland Islands, *332*
  the arts, *344*
  doctors, *332*
  emergencies, *332*
  guided tours, *334*
  hotels, *343–344*
  nightlife, *344*
  pharmacies, *332*
  restaurants, *336, 337,*
  342–344
  shopping, *341*
  sightseeing, *334–338*

sports, *342*
tourist information, *332*
transportation, *332–334*
Shetland Museum, *334*
Shetland ponies, *337*
Shieldaig, *317*
Ships, historic, *189*
Ship travel, *24*
Shopping, *31. See also*
  under cities and areas
Signal Tower
  Museum, *192*
Skara Brae, *338*
Skelberry, *336*
Skiing
  Edinburgh, *85, 92*
  Great Glen, *303*
  the Northeast, *226–227*
Skye, Isle of, *310,*
  318–319, 325–326,
  328–329
Skye of Curr, *293*
Sligachan, *318*
Smailholm Tower, *163*
Small Isles, *301*
Small Isles Bay, *273*
Sma' Shot Cottages,
  136
Smith, Adam, *79*
Smith Art Gallery
  and Museum, *238*
Soccer
  Edinburgh, *92*
  Glasgow, *141*
Sound of Mull, *263*
Southerness, *168*
South Ronaldsay
  Island, *340*
South Uist Island,
  319–320, 323
Soutra Mains, *117*
Spean Bridge, *295*
Speyside Railway, *293*
Spittal House, *239*
Stac Polly, *313*
Staffin Bay, *318*
Star Pyramid, *239*
Stevenson, Robert
  Louis, *250*
Stewartry Museum,
  169
Stirling
  the arts, *259*
  hotels, *258*
  restaurants, *240–241,*
  258
  shopping, *254*
  sightseeing, *237–241*
  tourist information, *235*

Index

Stirling Castle, *238*, *239–240*
Stirling's Library, *131*
Stoer Point Lighthouse, *324*
Stoker, Bram, *223*
Stone carvings, *271*, *272*
Stone circles and cairns
Argyll and the Isles, *270*
Great Glen, *289*
Northern Highlands, *322*
Northern Isles, *338*
Stornoway, *319*, *320*
Storybook Glen, *222–223*
Strachur, *283*
Stranraer, *160*, *170*
Strathpeffer, *313*
Strath Suardal, *319*
Stromness, *338*
Stronachlachar, *247*
Student and youth travel, *16–17*
Subway (Glasgow), *124*
Suggested itineraries, *34–37*
Suilven, *313*
Sumburgh, *336*
Summer Isles, *316*
Swanston, *86*
Sweetheart Abbey, *167*
Swinton, *179*

Tam o'Shanter Museum, *151*
Tantallon Castle, *117–118*
Tarbert, *322*
Tarbolton, *151*, *154*
Taxes, *10*
Taxis
in Aberdeen, *205*
in Edinburgh, *70*
in Glasgow, *125*
Taymouth Castle, *250–251*
Taynuilt, *278*
Telephones, *30*
Tenement House, *134*
Teviotdale Leisure Centre, *171*
Theater
Aberdeen, *231*

Argyll and the Isles, *284*
Central Highlands, *259*
Edinburgh, *106–107*
Fife and Angus, *199–200*
Glasgow, *148*
Great Glen, *307*
Thirlestane Castle, *171*
Threave Castle, *168–169*
Threave Gardens, *168*
Timespan (audiovisual program), *324*
Tipping, *30*
Tiroran, *283*
Tobermory, *276*, *283*
Tolbooth Arts Centre, *169*
Tolbooth Kirk, *73*
Tolbooths
Aberdeen, *209*
Edinburgh, *77*
Stirling, *240*
Torosay Castle, *274–275*
Torridon, *329*
Torrin, *319*
Tour groups, *2–5*
Tourist information, *2. See also under cities and areas*
Town House (Aberdeen), *209*
Trades House, *130*
Traigh Luskentyre, *322*
Traigh Seilebost, *322*
Train travel. *See also Railroads*
Aberdeen, *204*
Argyll and the Isles, *262*
the Borders and the Southwest, *158*, *159*
Central Highlands, *235*, *236*
Edinburgh, *69*, *70*
from England, *24–25*
Fife and Angus, *183*
Glasgow, *123*, *124–125*
Great Glen, *287*
the Northeast, *204*
Northern Highlands, *311*, *312*
older travelers, *20*
rail passes, *15–16*, *26*

within Scotland, *25–26*
youth passes, *17*
Traquair House, *164*
Traveler's checks, *8*
Treasures of the Earth (gemstone exhibitions), *301*
Trimontium Exhibition, *164*
Trinity Temple, *322–323*
Tron Kirk, *78*
Troon, *140*
the Trossachs, *241–247*
Trotternish, *318*
Tugnet Ice House, *219*
Tweeddale. *See* the Borders and the Southwest
Tweedhope Sheepdogs, *172*
Twelve Apostles (fishermen's houses), *270*

Udny Station Village, *230*
Ullapool, *313*, *316*, *325*, *329*
Unicorn (ship), *189*
Union Bridge,
Union Terrace Gardens, *209*
University Botanic Gardens, *191*
University of Glasgow, *132*
Unstan Chambered Tomb, *340*
Unst Island, *337*
Upper Solway Firth, *167*
Urquhart Castle, *296*

Value added tax (VAT), *10*
Vane Farm Nature Centre, *252*
Vane Farm Nature Reserve, *188–189*
Victoria Falls, *317*
Villa rentals, *33*
Visas, *10*

Wallace Monument, *237*, *241*
Waterfalls

Argyll and the Isles, *263*
the Borders and the Southwest, *172*
Central Highlands, *244*, *251*
Great Glen, *297*
Northern Highlands, *313*, *317*, *324–325*
Waterloo Monument, *161*
Weather information, *6*
Weddings, joke, *165*
Wemyss Bay, *150*
Wester Ross, *313*
Western Union, *9*
West Highland Museum, *298*
West Highland Way, *247*
West Register House, *84*
White and Brown Caterthuns, *194–195*
Whitebridge, *297*, *307*
Whitekirk, *117*
Whithorn Dig and Visitor Centre, *173*
Whithorn Museum, *173*
Whiting Bay, *269*
Wigtown, *173*
Wildlife reserves. *See* Nature reserves
Wilton Lodge Park, *165*
Winter Gardens, *130*
Wiring money, *9*
Woolen industry, *164*, *221*, *272*
World in Miniature (exhibit), *277*
Wrights of Trowmill (workaday shop), *165*
The Writers' Museum, *76*

Yell, *337*
Youth hostels, *17*

Zoos
Aberdeen, *222*
Edinburgh, *86*
Glasgow, *135*

Escape to ancient cities and exotic

islands

with CNN Travel Guide, a

wealth of valuable advice. Host Valerie Voss will take you

to all of your favorite destinations,

including those off the beaten path.

Tune into your passport to the world.

CNN TRAVEL GUIDE

SATURDAY 10:00 PMᴘᴛ   SUNDAY 8:30 AMᴇᴛ

Personal Itinerary

Departure *Date*

Time

Transportation

Arrival *Date*   *Time*

Departure *Date*   *Time*

Transportation

Accommodations

Arrival *Date*   *Time*

Departure *Date*   *Time*

Transportation

Accommodations

Arrival *Date*   *Time*

Departure *Date*   *Time*

Transportation

Accommodations

Personal Itinerary

Arrival *Date*   *Time*

Departure *Date*   *Time*

Transportation

Accommodations

Arrival *Date*   *Time*

Departure *Date*   *Time*

Transportation

Accommodations

Arrival *Date*   *Time*

Departure *Date*   *Time*

Transportation

Accommodations

Arrival *Date*   *Time*

Departure *Date*   *Time*

Transportation

Accommodations

The only guide to explore a
Disney World® you've never seen before:

The one for grown-ups.

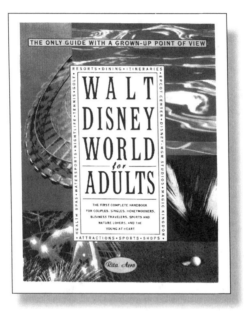

0-679-02490-5 $14.00 ($18.50 Can)

This is the only guide written specifically for the millions
of adults who visit Walt Disney World® each year <u>without</u>
kids. Upscale, sophisticated, packed full of facts and
maps, *Walt Disney World® for Adults* provides up-to-date
information on hotels, restaurants, sports facilities, and
health clubs, as well as unique itineraries for adults. With
Walt Disney World® for Adults in hand, you'll get the
most out of one of the world's most fascinating, most
complex playgrounds.

At bookstores everywhere, or call **1-800-533-6478.**

Fodor's Travel Guides

Available at bookstores everywhere, or call 1–800–533–6478, 24 hours a day.

U.S. Guides

Alaska

Arizona

Boston

California

Cape Cod, Martha's Vineyard, Nantucket

The Carolinas & the Georgia Coast

Chicago

Colorado

Florida

Hawaii

Las Vegas, Reno, Tahoe

Los Angeles

Maine, Vermont, New Hampshire

Maui

Miami & the Keys

New England

New Orleans

New York City

Pacific North Coast

Philadelphia & the Pennsylvania Dutch Country

The Rockies

San Diego

San Francisco

Santa Fe, Taos, Albuquerque

Seattle & Vancouver

The South

The U.S. & British Virgin Islands

USA

The Upper Great Lakes Region

Virginia & Maryland

Waikiki

Walt Disney World and the Orlando Area

Washington, D.C.

Foreign Guides

Acapulco, Ixtapa, Zihuatanejo

Australia & New Zealand

Austria

The Bahamas

Baja & Mexico's Pacific Coast Resorts

Barbados

Berlin

Bermuda

Brittany & Normandy

Budapest

Canada

Cancún, Cozumel, Yucatán Peninsula

Caribbean

China

Costa Rica, Belize, Guatemala

The Czech Republic & Slovakia

Eastern Europe

Egypt

Euro Disney

Europe

Florence, Tuscany & Umbria

France

Germany

Great Britain

Greece

Hong Kong

India

Ireland

Israel

Italy

Japan

Kenya & Tanzania

Korea

London

Madrid & Barcelona

Mexico

Montréal & Québec City

Morocco

Moscow & St. Petersburg

The Netherlands, Belgium & Luxembourg

New Zealand

Norway

Nova Scotia, Prince Edward Island & New Brunswick

Paris

Portugal

Provence & the Riviera

Rome

Russia & the Baltic Countries

Scandinavia

Scotland

Singapore

South America

Southeast Asia

Spain

Sweden

Switzerland

Thailand

Tokyo

Toronto

Turkey

Vienna & the Danube Valley

AT LAST

YOUR OWN PERSONALIZED LIST OF WHAT'S GOING ON IN THE CITIES YOU'RE VISITING.

KEYED TO THE DAYS WHEN YOU'LL BE THERE, CUSTOMIZED FOR YOUR INTERESTS, AND SENT TO YOU BEFORE YOU LEAVE HOME.

GET THE INSIDER'S PERSPECTIVE. . .

UP-TO-THE-MINUTE
ACCURATE
EASY TO ORDER
DELIVERED WHEN YOU NEED IT

Fodor's WORLDVIEW
TRAVEL UPDATE

Now there is a revolutionary way to get customized, time-sensitive travel information just before your trip.

Now you can obtain detailed information about what's going on in each city you'll be visiting <u>before</u> you leave home—up-to-the-minute, objective information about the events and activities that interest you most.

Travel Updates contain the kind of time-sensitive insider information you can get only from local contacts – or from city magazines and newspapers once you arrive. But now you can have the same information before you leave for your trip.

The choice is yours: current art exhibits, theater, music festivals and special concerts, sporting events, antiques and flower shows, shopping, fitness, and more.

The information comes from hundreds of correspondents and thousands of sources worldwide. Updated continuously, it's like having your own personal concierge or friend in the city.

You specify the cities and when you'll be there. We'll do the rest — personalizing the information for you the way no guidebook can.

It's the perfect extension to your Fodor's guide and the best way to make the most of your valuable travel time.

Use Order Form on back or call 1-800-799-9609

Your Itinerary:
Customized reports available for 160 destinations

a
air
tour
9902

Regent's
The annu
in this an
domain of
tion as Joe P
worthwhile. It
the perfomance
Tickets are usually
venue. Alternate
mances are cancelled
given. For more infor
Open-Air Theatre, Inner
NW1 4NP Open Air The
Tel: 935-5756. Ends: 9-11-9

International Air Tattoo
Held biennially, the
military air dis
d e m o s t
tions

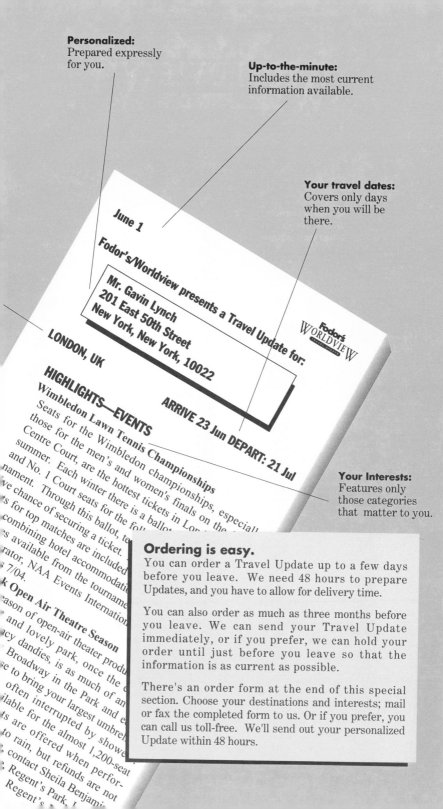

Personalized:
Prepared expressly for you.

Up-to-the-minute:
Includes the most current information available.

June 1

Fodor's/Worldview presents a Travel Update for:

Mr. Gavin Lynch
201 East 50th Street
New York, New York, 10022

Fodor's WORLDVIEW

Your travel dates:
Covers only days when you will be there.

LONDON, UK

ARRIVE 23 Jun DEPART: 21 Jul

HIGHLIGHTS—EVENTS

Wimbledon Lawn Tennis Championships

Seats for the Wimbledon championships, especiall those for the men's and women's finals on the Centre Court, are the hottest tickets in Lor summer. Each winter there is a ballot and No. 1 Court seats for the fol nament. Through this ballot, to ve chance of securing a ticket. s for top matches are included combining hotel accommodati s available from the tournam rator, NAA Events Internation s 7/04.

k Open Air Theatre Season
ason of open-air theater produ and lovely park, once the a cy dandies, is as much of an Broadway in the Park and e se to bring your largest umbrel often interrupted by showe ilable for the almost 1,200-seat ts are offered when perfor to rain, but refunds are not contact Sheila Benjami Regent's Park. I Regent's

Your Interests:
Features only those categories that matter to you.

Ordering is easy.

You can order a Travel Update up to a few days before you leave. We need 48 hours to prepare Updates, and you have to allow for delivery time.

You can also order as much as three months before you leave. We can send your Travel Update immediately, or if you prefer, we can hold your order until just before you leave so that the information is as current as possible.

There's an order form at the end of this special section. Choose your destinations and interests; mail or fax the completed form to us. Or if you prefer, you can call us toll-free. We'll send out your personalized Update within 48 hours.

**Special concerts—
who's performing
what and where**

**One-of-a-kind,
one-time-only events**

**Special interest,
in-depth listings**

Children — Events
Angel Canal Festival
The festivities include a children's funfair, entertainers, a boat rally and displays on the water. Regent's Canal. Islington. N1. Tube: Angel. Tel: 267 9100. 11:30am-5:30pm. 7/04.
Blackheath Summer Kite Festival
Stunt kite displays with parachuting teddy bears and trade stands. Free admission. SE3. BR: Blackheath. 10am. 6/27.
Megabugs
Children will delight in this infestation of giant robotic insects, including a praying mantis 60 times life size. Mon-Sat 10am-6pm; Sun 11am-6pm. Admission 4.50 pounds. Natural History Museum, Cromwell Road. SW7. Tube: South Kensington. Tel: 938 9123. Ends 10/01.
Childminders
This establishment employs only women, providing nurses and qualified nannies to

Music — Jazz & Blues
Tito Puente's Golden Men of Latin Jazz
The father of mambo and Cuban rumba king comes to town. Royal Festival Hall. South Bank. SE1. Tube: Waterloo. Tel: 928 8800. 8pm. 7/15.
Georgie Fame and The New York Band
Riding a popular tide with his latest album, the smoky-voiced Fame and his keyboard are on a tour yet again. The Grand. Clapham Junction. SW11. BR: Clapham Junction. Tel: 738 9000. 7:30pm. 7/07.
Jacques Loussier Play Bach Trio
The French jazz classicist and colleagues. Kenwood Lakeside. Hampstead Lane. Kenwood. NW3. Tube: Golders Green, then bus 210. Tel: 413 1443. 7pm. 7/10.
Tony Bennett and Ronnie Scott
Royal Festival Hall. South Bank. SE1. Tube: Waterloo. Tel: 928 8800. 8pm. 7/11.
Santana
Royal Festival Hall. South Bank. SE1. Tube: Waterloo. Tel: 928 8800. 8pm. 7/12.
Count Basie Orchestra and Nancy Wilson Trio
Royal Festival Hall. South Bank. SE1. Tube: Waterloo. Tel: 928 8800. 8pm. 7/14.
King Pleasure and the Biscuit Boys
Royal Festival Hall. South Bank. SE1. Tube: Waterloo. Tel: 928 8800. 6:30 and 9pm. 7/16.
Al Green and the London Community Gospel Choir
Royal Festival Hall. South Bank. SE1. Tube: Waterloo. Tel: 928 8800. 8pm. 7/13.
BB King and Linda Hopkins
Mother of the blues and successor to Bessie Smith, Hopkins meets up with "Blues Boy" King. Royal Festival Hall. South Bank. SE1. 6:30 and 9pm.

Music — Classical
Marylebone Sinfonia
Kenneth Gowen conducts music by Pucc and Rossini. Queen Elizabeth Hall. South Bank. SE1. Tube: Waterloo. Tel: 928 8800. 7:45pm. 7/16.
London Philharmonic
Franz Welser-Moest and George Benjamin conduct selections by Alexander Goe Messiaen, and some of Benjamin's own compositions. Queen Elizabeth Hall. South Bank. SE1. Tube: Waterloo. Tel: 928 8800. 8pm.
London Pro Arte Orchestra and Forest Choir
Murray Stewart conducts selection Rossini, Haydn and Jonathan Willcocks. Queen Elizabeth Hall. South Bank. Tube: Waterloo. Tel: 928 8800. 7:45pm.
Kensington Symphony Orchestra
Russell Keable conducts Dvorak's D Hall. South Bank.

Here's what you get . . .

Detailed information about what's going on — precisely when you'll be there.

Show openings during your visit

Handy pocket-size booklet

Reviews by local critics

Exhibitions & Shows—Antique & Flower
Westminster Antiques Fair
Over 50 stands with pre-1830 furniture and other Victorian and earlier items. Thu-Fri 11am-8pm; Sat-Sun 11am-6pm. Admission 4 pounds, children free. Old Royal Horticultural Hall. Vincent Square. SW1. Tel: 0444/48 25 14. 6-24 thru 6/27.

Royal Horticultural Society Flower Show
The show includes displays of carnations, summer fruit and vegetables. Tue 11am-7pm; Wed 10am-5pm. Admission Tue 4 pounds, Wed 2 pounds. Royal Horticultural Halls. Greycoat Street and Vincent Square. SW1. Tube: Victoria. 7/20 thru 7/21.

Hampton Court Palace International Flower Show
Major international garden and flower show taking place in conjunction with

Theater — Musical
Sunset Boulevard
In June, the four Andrew Lloyd Webber musicals which dominated London's stages in the 1980s (Cats, Starlight Express, Phantom of the Opera and Aspects of Love) are joined by the composer's latest work, a show rumored to have his best music to date. The 1950 Billy Wilder film about a helpless young writer who is drawn into the world of a possessive, aging silent screen star offers rich opportunities for Webber's evolving style. Soaring, aching melodies, lush technical effects and psychological thrills are all expected. Patti Lupone stars. Mon-Sat at 8pm; matinee Thu-Sat at 3pm. In-person sales only at the box office; credit card bookings, Tel: 344 0055. Admission 15-32.50 pounds. Adelphi Theatre. The Strand. WC2. Tube: Charing Cross. Tel: 836 7611. Starts: 6/21.

Leonardo A Portrait of Love
A new musical about the great Renaissance artist and inventor comes in for a London pre-... tested by a brief run at Oxford's Old ... The work explores ...

Spectator Sports — Other Sports
Greyhound Racing: Wembley Stadium
This dog track offers good views of greyhound racing held on Mon, Wed and Fri. No credit cards. Stadium Way. Wembley. HA9. Tube: Wembley Park. Tel: 902 8833.

Benson & Hedges Cricket Cup Final
Lord's Cricket Ground. St. John's Wood Road. NW8. Tube: St. John's Wood. Tel: 289 1611. 11am. 7/10.

Business-Fax & Overnight Mail
Post Office, Trafalgar Square Branch
Offers a network of fax services, the Intelpost system, throughout the country and abroad. Mon-Sat 8am-8pm, Sun 9am-5pm. William IV Street. WC2. Tube: Charing Cross. Tel: 930 9580.

Fodor's WORLDVIEW
TRAVEL UPDATE

London, England
Arriving: June 23
Departing: July 21

Interest Categories

For <u>your</u> personalized Travel Update, choose the categories you're most interested in from this list. Every Travel Update automatically provides you with *Event Highlights* - the best of what's happening during the dates of your trip.

1.	**Business Services**	Fax & Overnight Mail, Computer Rentals, Photocopying, Protocol, Secretarial, Messenger, Translation Services

Dining

2.	**All Day Dining**	Breakfast & Brunch, Cafes & Tea Rooms, Late-Night Dining
3.	**Local Cuisine**	In Every Price Range—from Budget Restaurants to the Special Splurge
4.	**European Cuisine**	Continental, French, Italian
5.	**Asian Cuisine**	Chinese, Far Eastern, Japanese, Other
6.	**Americas Cuisine**	American, Mexican & Latin
7.	**Nightlife**	Bars, Dance Clubs, Casinos, Comedy Clubs, Ethnic, Pubs & Beer Halls
8.	**Entertainment**	Theater—Comedy, Drama, English Language, Musicals, Dance, Ticket Agencies
9.	**Music**	Country/Western/Folk, Classical, Traditional & Ethnic, Opera, Jazz & Blues, Pop, Rock
10.	**Children's Activities**	Events, Attractions
11.	**Tours**	Local Tours, Day Trips, Overnight Excursions, Cruises
12.	**Exhibitions, Festivals & Shows**	Antiques & Flower, History & Cultural, Art Exhibitions, Fairs & Craft Shows, Music & Art Festivals
13.	**Shopping**	Districts & Malls, Markets, Regional Specialities
14.	**Fitness**	Bicycling, Health Clubs, Hiking, Jogging
15.	**Recreational Sports**	Boating/Sailing, Fishing, Golf, Ice Skating, Skiing, Snorkeling/Scuba, Swimming, Tennis & Racquet
16.	**Spectator Sports**	Auto Racing, Baseball, Basketball, Boating & Sailing, Football, Golf, Horse Racing, Ice Hockey, Rugby, Soccer, Tennis, Track & Field, Other Sports

Please note that interest category content will vary by season, destination, and length of stay.